GW01452625

Licensing Law Handbook

THIRD EDITION

Other titles available from Law Society Publishing:

Building Safety Act 2022
General editors: Andrew Butler KC and Ian Quayle

Client Care in Conveyancing
Priscilla Sinder

Conveyancing Checklists, 4th edition
Frances Silverman and Russell Hewitson

Conveyancing Handbook, 31st edition
General Editor: Frances Silverman

Conveyancing Quality Scheme Toolkit, 4th edition
The Law Society

Forfeiture of Leases
Peter Petts and Jamal Demachkie

Post-completion
Priscilla Sinder and Fiona du Feu

Property Development, 4th edition
Gavin Le Chat

Property Practitioner's Guide to the First-tier Tribunal
Andrea Nicholls and Julia Petrenko

Renewal of Business Tenancies, 3rd edition
Michael Haley

Stamp Duty Land Tax Handbook, 2nd edition
Sean Randall

Titles from Law Society Publishing can be ordered from all good bookshops or direct
(visit our online shop at **www.lawsociety.org.uk/bookshop**).

LICENSING LAW HANDBOOK

A Practical Guide to Alcohol and Entertainment Licensing

THIRD EDITION

Russell Hewitson

The Law Society

All rights reserved. No part of this publication may be reproduced in any
material form, whether by photocopying, scanning, downloading onto
computer or otherwise without the written permission of the Law Society
except in accordance with the provisions of the Copyright, Designs and
Patents Act 1988. Applications should be addressed in the first instance, in
writing, to Law Society Publishing. Any unauthorised or restricted act in
relation to this publication may result in civil proceedings and/or criminal
prosecution.

Whilst all reasonable care has been taken in the preparation of this
publication, neither the publisher nor the author can accept any
responsibility for any loss occasioned to any person acting or refraining
from action as a result of relying upon its contents.

The views expressed in this publication should be taken as those of the
author only unless it is specifically indicated that the Law Society has
given its endorsement.

© The Law Society 2024

Crown copyright material is reproduced with the permission of the
Controller of His Majesty's Stationery Office

ISBN-13: 978-1-78446-248-2

First published in 2006
Second edition published in 2013

This third edition published in 2024 by the Law Society
113 Chancery Lane, London WC2A 1PL

Typeset by Data Standards Ltd, Frome, Somerset
Printed by CPI Group (UK) Ltd, Croydon CR0 4YY

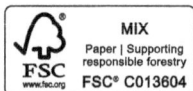

MIX
Paper | Supporting
responsible forestry
FSC
www.fsc.org   FSC® C013604

The paper used for the text pages of this book is FSC® certified. FSC (the
Forest Stewardship Council®) is an international network to promote
responsible management of the world's forests.

Contents

Preface		xiv
Table of cases		xvi
Table of statutes		xix
Table of statutory instruments		xxvii
Table of treaties and conventions		xxxii
Abbreviations		xxxiii

1   Introduction   **1**

   1.1   Introduction   1
   1.2   Background   1
   1.3   The Licensing Act 2003   2
   1.4   Overview of the Act   3
   1.5   Human rights and licensing   4

2   Licensing authorities   **12**

   2.1   Introduction   12
   2.2   Licensing authorities   12
   2.3   The general duties of licensing authorities   13
   2.4   Statement of licensing policy   13
   2.5   The contents of a statement of licensing policy   15
   2.6   Challenging a statement of licensing policy   30
   2.7   Licensing committees   30
   2.8   The licensing register   31
   2.9   Notification to persons with an interest in the premises   33
   2.10   Proceedings of the licensing committee   34
   2.11   Delegation of functions by a licensing committee   34
   2.12   Ministerial guidance   35
   2.13   Information   37
   2.14   Procedures for giving notices   37
   2.15   Late night levy   38

3   Licensable activities   **46**

   3.1   Introduction   46
   3.2   The sale by retail of alcohol   47

3.3   The supply of alcohol by or on behalf of a club to, or to the order
      of, a member of the club   50
3.4   The provision of regulated entertainment   50
3.5   The provision of late night refreshment   52
3.6   Authorisation for licensable activities and qualifying club
      activities   52

4   Regulated entertainment   54

4.1   Introduction   54
4.2   Types of entertainment   59
4.3   Exemptions   61
4.4   Particular premises and events   69

5   Late night refreshment   72

5.1   Introduction   72
5.2   What is late night refreshment?   72
5.3   Hot food or hot drink   73
5.4   Exempt supplies   73

6   Personal licences   79

6.1   Introduction   79
6.2   Definition of personal licence   80
6.3   Who can apply for a personal licence?   80
6.4   Application for a personal licence   81
6.5   Entitlement to work in the United Kingdom   82
6.6   The application form   83
6.7   Determination of an application   85
6.8   Notification of the grant or refusal of a personal licence   87
6.9   Issuing of a personal licence   87
6.10 Accredited licensing qualifications   88
6.11 Convictions for a relevant offence or foreign offence   91
6.12 Immigration penalty   99
6.13 Appeals   99
6.14 Duration of a personal licence   100
6.15 Convictions during the application process   100
6.16 Convictions during the currency of a personal licence   102
6.17 Surrender of a personal licence   106
6.18 Theft or loss of a personal licence   106
6.19 Duty to notify changes   106
6.20 Updating a personal licence   106
6.21 Duty to produce a personal licence   107

7   Premises licences   108

7.1   The meaning of premises licences   108
7.2   Applicants for premises licences   113

7.3	Making an application	117
7.4	The application form	118
7.5	The plan	123
7.6	Advertising the application by the applicant	124
7.7	Advertising the application by the licensing authority	126
7.8	Notice to responsible authorities	127
7.9	Inspection of premises	128
7.10	Determination of the application	129
7.11	Conditions	132
7.12	Notification of the grant or refusal of an application	145
7.13	Form of licence and summary	145
7.14	Theft or loss of a licence	146
7.15	Duration of a premises licence	146
7.16	Lapse of a licence	147
7.17	Surrender	147
7.18	Updating a premises licence	148
7.19	Duty to keep and produce a premises licence	148
7.20	Suspension of a premises licence	149

8	**The operating schedule**	**151**
8.1	Introduction	151
8.2	Contents of the operating schedule	151
8.3	Completing the standard form of operating schedule	153
8.4	Opening hours	156
8.5	Preparing an operating schedule	156
8.6	Risk assessment	158
8.7	Prevention of crime and disorder	158
8.8	Public safety	159
8.9	The prevention of public nuisance	161
8.10	The protection of children from harm	164
8.11	Best practice guidance publications	165

9	**Designated premises supervisor**	**167**
9.1	Introduction	167
9.2	Who is the designated premises supervisor?	167
9.3	Initial appointment of a designated premises supervisor	168
9.4	Change of designated premises supervisor	168
9.5	Police objections	172
9.6	Request to be removed as designated premises supervisor	173

10	**Relevant representations**	**174**
10.1	Introduction	174
10.2	Relevant representations – general	174
10.3	Relevant representations – specific applications under the Act	181
10.4	Making a representation	184

11 Conditions 188

11.1 Introduction 188
11.2 General requirements for conditions 188
11.3 Naming, packing and promotion in retail premises 190
11.4 Hours of trading 191
11.5 The performance of plays 192
11.6 Censorship 192
11.7 Major festivals and carnivals 192
11.8 Fixed prices 193
11.9 Large capacity venues used exclusively or primarily for the 'vertical' consumption of alcohol 194
11.10 Dancing in certain small premises 194
11.11 Licence review for live and recorded music 195

12 Interim authorities 196

12.1 Introduction 196
12.2 Giving an interim authority 196
12.3 Form of interim notice 198
12.4 The effect of an interim authority notice 200
12.5 Cancellation of an interim authority following objections 201
12.6 Reinstatement of a lapsed licence 202

13 Provisional statements 204

13.1 Introduction 204
13.2 Premises in respect of which an application can be made 205
13.3 Applicants for provisional statements 205
13.4 Applying for a provisional statement 206
13.5 The application form 206
13.6 Advertising 209
13.7 Notice to responsible authorities 210
13.8 Determination of the application 210
13.9 Subsequent action and restrictions on representations 212
13.10 Power to inspect the premises 213

14 Variation of a premises licence 215

14.1 Introduction 215
14.2 Applying for a minor variation 216
14.3 Applying for a full variation 224
14.4 Change of name or address 231

15 Review of a premises licence 232

15.1 Introduction 232
15.2 Who can apply for a review? 232
15.3 When can an application be made? 233

15.4   Making an application   233
15.5   The application form   233
15.6   Advertising the application   236
15.7   Rejection of the application   237
15.8   Determination of the application for review   238
15.9   Notification of the decision   242
15.10 Relevant representations   242
15.11 Inspection of premises   243
15.12 Summary reviews in serious cases of crime or disorder   243

16   Transfer of a premises licence   **251**

16.1   Introduction   251
16.2   Who can apply for a transfer?   251
16.3   Applying for a transfer   251
16.4   Interim effect   255
16.5   Determination of the application   256
16.6   Notification of the determination   257

17   Clubs   **258**

17.1   Introduction   258
17.2   Club premises certificate   259
17.3   Qualifying clubs   260
17.4   Associate members   261
17.5   The establishment and conduct of a club in good faith   262
17.6   Registered societies, friendly societies, etc.   262
17.7   Miners' welfare institutes   263
17.8   Application for a club premises certificate   264
17.9   Determination of the application   269
17.10 Action following the grant or rejection of an application   271
17.11 Mandatory and prohibited conditions   272
17.12 The form of the certificate and summary   273
17.13 Theft or loss   274
17.14 Period of validity of a club premises certificate   274
17.15 Surrender of a club premises certificate   274
17.16 Change of club name or alteration of club rules   275
17.17 Change of relevant registered address of a club   275
17.18 Withdrawal of a club premises certificate   276
17.19 Duties in relation to a club premises certificate   277
17.20 Police powers to enter and search club premises   278
17.21 Suspension of a club premises certificate   279

18   Variation of a club premises certificate   **280**

18.1   Introduction   280
18.2   Applying for a minor variation   280
18.3   Applying for a variation   285
18.4   The application form   285

18.5	Advertising	287
18.6	Notice to responsible authorities	289
18.7	Determination of the application	289
18.8	Notification of a decision	291
18.9	Inspection of premises	292

19   Review of a club premises certificate   **293**

19.1	Introduction	293
19.2	Who can apply for a review?	293
19.3	When can an application be made?	294
19.4	Making an application	294
19.5	The application form	294
19.6	Advertising the application	296
19.7	Rejection of the application	297
19.8	Determination of the application for review	298
19.9	Notification of the decision	299
19.10	Relevant representations	299
19.11	Inspection of premises	299

20   Permitted temporary activities   **301**

20.1	Introduction	301
20.2	Meaning of 'permitted temporary activity'	302
20.3	The relevant licensing authority	302
20.4	Relevant person	303
20.5	Persons entitled to give a temporary event notice	303
20.6	Form and content of a temporary event notice	303
20.7	Making an application – standard temporary event notice	307
20.8	Making an application – late temporary event notice	308
20.9	Minimum period between event periods	309
20.10	Acknowledgement of a temporary event notice by a licensing authority	310
20.11	Withdrawal of a temporary event notice	311
20.12	Objection to a temporary event notice	311
20.13	Modification of a standard temporary event notice following an objection	314
20.14	Limits on temporary event notices	315
20.15	Right of entry where a temporary event notice has been given	317
20.16	Duty to keep and produce a temporary event notice and statement of conditions	318
20.17	Theft, loss, etc. of a temporary event notice or statement of conditions	319

21   Offences   **320**

21.1	Introduction	320
21.2	Unauthorised licensable activities	321
21.3	Drunkenness and disorderly conduct	325

21.4 Smuggled goods 328
21.5 Offences on vehicles and trains 328
21.6 False statements 330
21.7 Prosecutions 330
21.8 Offences by bodies corporate, partnerships and unincorporated associations 330
21.9 Minimum pricing for alcohol in Wales 332
21.10 Exclusion orders 336

22 Offences involving children **337**

22.1 Introduction 337
22.2 Unaccompanied children prohibited from certain premises 337
22.3 Sale of alcohol to children 340
22.4 Allowing the sale of alcohol to children 341
22.5 Persistently selling alcohol to children 342
22.6 Purchase of alcohol by or on behalf of children 343
22.7 Consumption of alcohol by children 345
22.8 Delivering alcohol to children 346
22.9 Sending a child to obtain alcohol 347
22.10 Prohibition of unsupervised sales by children 347
22.11 Giving intoxicating liquor to children under five 348
22.12 Confiscation of alcohol 349

23 Early morning alcohol restriction orders **350**

23.1 Introduction 350
23.2 Power to make an early morning alcohol restriction order 351
23.3 Procedural requirements for early morning alcohol restriction orders 352
23.4 Making an early morning alcohol restriction order 354
23.5 Hearing 355
23.6 Variation and revocation of an early morning alcohol restriction order 355
23.7 Exceptions 356
23.8 Enforcement of an early morning alcohol restriction order 356

24 Closure of premises **357**

24.1 Introduction 357
24.2 Orders to close premises in an area experiencing disorder 357
24.3 Closure of premises associated with nuisance or disorder 359
24.4 Closure notices for persistently selling alcohol to children 371
24.5 Closure of unlicensed premises 373
24.6 Police immunity from liability for damages 378

25 Hearings **379**

25.1 Introduction 379

25.2   When must a hearing be held?   380
25.3   Notice of hearing   380
25.4   Action following receipt of a notice of a hearing   381
25.5   Dispensing with a hearing   382
25.6   Withdrawal of a representation   382
25.7   Power to extend time   382
25.8   The hearing   383
25.9   Procedure at the hearing   384
25.10 Failure of parties to attend the hearing   385
25.11 Determination of the application   385
25.12 Record of a hearing   386
25.13 Irregularities   386
25.14 Notices   386
25.15 The impact of the Human Rights Act 1998   387

26   Appeals   388

26.1   Introduction   388
26.2   Procedure for an appeal   393
26.3   Licensing policy statements and the Secretary of State's
       guidance   394
26.4   Premises licences   394
26.5   Club premises certificates   398
26.6   Temporary event notices   400
26.7   Personal licences   401
26.8   Closure orders   402
26.9   Giving reasons   403
26.10 Implementing the determination of the magistrates' courts   403
26.11 Appeals to the High Court   404

27   Pavement licences   406

27.1   Introduction   406
27.2   Pavement licences   406
27.3   Application for a pavement licence   407
27.4   Fee for a pavement licence   408
27.5   Conditions   408
27.6   Advertising an application   411
27.7   Determination of an application   411
27.8   Duration of a licence   413
27.9   Enforcement and revocation   413
27.10 Removal of furniture   414

APPENDICES

A   Operating schedule toolkit – risk assessment   415

B   Licensing Act 2003 representation form   423

C   Scale of fines   424

D   Useful websites   425

Index   426

Preface

When it was introduced, the Licensing Act 2003 ('the Act') radically overhauled the various laws and procedures relating to the sale of alcohol and the provision of entertainment to create a unified structure. Since the last edition of this book was published, a number of amendments have been made to the Act.

There are now provisions in the Act for pavement licences. These are licences which allow a licence-holder to place removable furniture over certain highways adjacent to the premises for certain purposes. The Levelling Up and Regeneration Act 2023 has made permanent the original provisions set out in the Business and Planning Act 2020.

The Business and Planning Act 2020 also provided temporary amendments to the Act which enabled on-sales premises licence holders to automatically additionally undertake off-sales, without any need to amend their licence. This meant that when pubs and restaurants were initially closed because of the pandemic, they were able to make take-away sales of alcohol. Once premises were able to re-open, this then enabled them to serve alcohol in the area covered by any pavement licence that they had. The Alcohol Licensing (Coronavirus) (Regulatory Easements) (Amendment) Regulations 2023, SI 2023/990, have extended the duration of these amendments (which had been due to expire on 30 September 2023) to 31 March 2025. As these are temporary measures, they have not been covered in the text.

Changes have been made to the late-night levy to:

- allow licensing authorities the power to apply the levy to late-night refreshment premises to assist with the cost of policing the night time economy;
- allow local authorities to target the levy in smaller geographical areas where the night time economy places demand on policing, rather than having to implement it across the entirety of their area;
- permit Police and Crime Commissioners the right to formally request that a licensing authority consult on implementing a levy; and
- require licensing authorities to publish information about how the revenue raised from the levy is spent.

It should be noted that the definitions in the Act of 'beer', 'cider', 'denatured alcohol', 'dutiable alcoholic liquor', 'strength' and 'wine' refer to meanings in the Alcoholic Liquor Duties Act 1979 and the Finance Act 1995 but these provisions in those two Acts have been repealed. The text therefore refers to the current meanings in the Finance (No.2) Act 2023 even though the Act has not been updated with these new definitions.

The Act has also been amended by the Immigration Act 2016, but it must be noted that no consequential amendments have been made to the Licensing Act 2003 (Hearings) Regulations 2005, SI 2005/44 so there is no provision for a hearing where an immigration objection notice has been given.

On 11 July 2024, Chamberlain J. in *Walk Safe Security Services Ltd* v. *London Borough of Lewisham* [2024] EWHC 1787 (Admin) determined that, under the Licensing Act 2003 and the Licensing Act 2003 (Hearings) Regulations 2005, SI 2005/44, it was lawful for licensing committees in England to hold licensing hearings remotely. Unfortunately, this decision came too late to be incorporated into the text.

My aim in writing this book has been to provide a practical guide to both the law and procedures. I hope that it will be useful for all those involved in licensing law and will become their first point of reference.

Copies of the Act, the Regulations which have been made under it and the Guidance issued by the Secretary of State under s.182 of the Act have not been included. This is partly because space does not permit it, but also because these are all easily accessible on the internet. Licensing authorities have made available on their websites copies of application forms, notices, etc. and so it is hoped that licensing practitioners will find that this book and the information available on the internet complement each other. I have included in the text, where relevant, extracts from the Guidance as at the date of publication. The current version of the Guidance should be checked to ensure that no changes have been made since publication. No offence is intended by reference in the text to 'he', for which please read 'he or she' as appropriate.

I am grateful to the staff of the Law Society, in particular Nia Cummings, for her encouragement and patience.

Finally, my love and thanks go to Andrea and Dominique without whose constant help, support and encouragement this new edition would not have been possible. This book is dedicated to them.

The law is stated as at 1 July 2024.

Russell Hewitson
Cleadon Village, Sunderland
July 2024

Table of cases

Adamson v. Waveney DC [1997] 2 All ER 898, QBD 6.11.3
Aldemir v. Cornwall Council [2019] EWHC 2407 (Admin) 26.1
Associated Provincial Picture Houses Ltd v. Wednesbury Corp [1948] 1 KB
   223, CA 25.15, 26.1
Barking and Dagenham LBC v. Bass Taverns [1993] COD 453, DC 21.2.1
Beauchamp Pizza Ltd v. Coventry City Council [2010] EWHC 926 (Ch); [2020]
   LLR 1 .... 7.16, 12.6
Blackpool Council Licensing Authority v. Howitt [2008] EWHC 3300 (Admin);
   [2009] 4 All ER 154 .... 2.3
Blustarling Ltd v. Westminster City Council (1996) The Times, 24 July, QBD 26.1
British Amusement Catering Trades Association (BACTA) v. Westminster City
   Council [1989] AC 147; [1988] 2 WLR 485, HL 4.2.2
British Beer & Pub Association v. Canterbury City Council [2005] EWHC
   1318 (Admin); (2005) 169 JP 521 .... 2.6, 7.10.2, 11.1
Cambridgeshire CC v. Kama [2006] EWHC 3148 (Admin); (2007) 171 JP 194 ...... 21.2.4
Carmarthenshire CC v. Llanelli Magistrates' Court [2009] EWHC 3016
   (Admin); [2010] All ER (D) 209 (Apr) 2.3, 15.8
Crawley BC v. Attenborough [2006] EWHC 1278 (Admin); (2006) 170 JP 593 .... 26.1
Croydon LBC v. Pinch a Pound (UK) Ltd [2010] EWHC 3283 (Admin); [2011]
   1 WLR 1189 .... 21.2.4
Davies v. Carmarthenshire CC [2005] EWHC 464 (Admin) 21.2.4
Dombo Beheer BV v. Netherlands (A/274-A) (1994) 18 EHRR 213 .... 1.5.3
Extreme Oyster and Star Oyster Ltd v. Guildford BC [2013] EWHC 2174
   (Admin); [2014] PTSR 325 .... 2.11, 7.2.4
Graff v. Evans (1882) 8 QBD 373 .... 17.1
Green v. Inner London Justices (1994) 19 LR 13 .... 7.1.2
Hall & Woodhouse Ltd v. Poole BC [2009] EWHC 1587 (Admin); [2010] 1 All
   ER 425 .... 21.2.1
Hussain v. Waltham Forest LBC [2020] EWCA Civ 1539; [2021] 1 WLR 922 .... 6.11.6
James v. United Kingdom (A/98) (1986) 8 EHRR 123 .... 1.5.3
Kavanagh v. Chief Constable of Devon and Cornwall [1974] QB 624; [1974]
   2 WLR 762, CA 26.2
Khan v. Coventry Magistrates' Court [2011] EWCA Civ 751; (2011) 175
   JP 429 .... 15.2, 15.8, 26.1
Leeds City Council v. Hussain [2002] EWHC 1145 (Admin) 26.1
Luminar Leisure Ltd v. Wakefield Magistrates' Court [2008] EWHC 1002
   (Admin); (2008) 172 JP 345 .... 7.10.3
Marathon Restaurant v. Camden LBC [2011] EWHC 1339 (QB); [2011] All ER
   (D) 261 (May) 26.1
McCarthy v. Jones [2023] EWCA Civ 589 .... 26.1

Moreno Gomez v. Spain (4143/02) (2005) 41 EHRR 40 .... 1.5.5
Neale v. RMJE (A Minor) (1985) 80 Cr App R 20, DC 21.3.2
Petherick v. Sargent (1862) 26 JP 135 .... 21.3.2
Porky Pint Ltd v. Stockton on Tees BC [2023] EWHC 128 (Admin); [2023] 1
    WLR 2735 .... 2.3
Porter v. Magill [2001] UKHL 67; [2002] 2 AC 357 .... 1.5.3
Portsmouth City Council v. 3D Entertainment Group (CRC) Ltd [2011] EWHC
    507 (Admin); [2011] ACD 52 .... 26.1
Prasannan v. Kensington and Chelsea RLBC [2010] EWHC 319 (Admin);
    [2011] 1 Costs LR 14 .... 26.1
R v. Bell (Jennifer) [2009] EWCA Crim 875 .... 6.16.2
R v. Bromley Licensing Justices, ex p. Bromley Licensed Victuallers [1984]
    1 WLR 585; [1984] 1 All ER 794 .... 20.6
R v. Dudley Crown Court, ex p. Pask (1983) 143 JP 417 .... 13.3
R v. G [2003] UKHL 50; [2004] 1 AC 1034 .... 21.6
R v. Hastings Justices, ex p. McSpirit (1998) 162 JP 44, QBD 6.11.3
R v. Howard (Licensing) [1902] 2 KB 363, CA 26.2
R v. Liverpool Crown Court, ex p. Goodwin [2002] LLR 698 .... 7.1.2
R (on the application of A3D2 Ltd (t/a Novus Leisure)) v. Westminster
    Magistrates' Court [2011] EWHC 1045 (Admin); [2011] LLR 303 .... 26.1, 26.2
R (on the application of Aggregate Industries UK Ltd) v. English Nature [2002]
    EWHC 908 (Admin); [2003] Env LR 3 .... 2.6
R (on the application of Albert Court Residents' Association) v. Westminster
    City Council [2011] EWCA Civ 430; [2012] PTSR 604 .... 7.10.3, 10.2.2, 14.3.8
R (on the application of Bassetlaw DC) v. Worksop Magistrates' Court [2008]
    EWHC 3530 (Admin); (2009) 173 JP 599 .... 15.8
R (on the application of Bednash) v. Westminster City Council [2014] EWHC 2160
    (Admin) 12.4
R (on the application of Bristol Council) v. Bristol Magistrates' Court [2009]
    EWHC 625 (Admin) 7.10.2
R (on the application of Cambridge City Council) v. Alex Nestling Ltd [2006]
    EWHC 1374 (Admin); (2006) 170 JP 539 .... 26.1
R (on the application of Chief Constable of Lancashire) v. Preston Crown Court
    [2001] EWHC Admin 928; [2002] 1 WLR 1332 .... 1.5.3
R (on the application of Chief Constable of Nottinghamshire Police) v. Nottingham
    Magistrates' Court [2009] EWHC 3182 (Admin); [2010] 2 All ER 342 .... 26.1
R (on the application of Daniel Thwaites Plc) v. Wirral Borough Magistrates'
    Court [2008] EWHC 838 (Admin); [2008] 1 All ER 239 .... 2.12, 26.1
R (on the application of Developing Retail Ltd) v. East Hampshire Magistrates'
    Court [2011] EWHC 618 (Admin) 26.1
R (on the application of Festiva Ltd) v. Highbury Corner Magistrates' Court
    [2011] EWHC 3043 (Admin); (2012) 109(17) LSG 18 .... 26.11.2
R (on the application of Hammersmith and Fulham LBC) v. Food City Express
    Ltd [2008] EWHC 3520 (Admin); [2008] All ER (D) 120 (Oct) 26.1
R (on the application of Harpers Leisure International Ltd) v. Chief Constable of
    Surrey [2009] EWHC 2160 (Admin); [2010] PTSR 231 .... 15.8
R (on the application of Holding & Barnes Plc) v. Secretary of State for the
    Environment, Transport and the Regions [2001] UKHL 23; [2003] 2 AC 295 ..... 1.5.3

R (on the application of Hope & Glory Public House Ltd) *v.* City of Westminster
  Magistrates' Court [2011] EWCA Civ 31; [2011] 3 All ER 579; [2009]
  EWHC 1996 (Admin); [2009] LLR 742 .... 1.5.3, 26.1
R (on the application of Murco Petroleum Ltd) *v.* Bristol City Council [2010]
  EWHC 1992 (Admin) 7.1.2
R (on the application of Port Regis School Ltd) *v.* North Dorset DC [2006] EWHC
  742 (Admin); [2007] 1 P & CR 29 .... 2.7
R (on the application of Raphael) *v.* Highbury Corner Magistrates' Court [2011]
  EWCA Civ 462; [2012] PTSR 427 .... 2.11
R (on the application of South Northamptonshire Council) *v.* Towcester Magistrates'
  Court [2008] EWHC 381 (Admin) 6.7.3
R (on the application of T) *v.* Chief Constable of Greater Manchester [2014]
  UKSC 35; [2015] AC 49 .... 6.11.6
R (on the application of Townlink Ltd) *v.* Thames Magistrates' Court [2011]
  EWHC 898 (Admin) 26.1
Sagnata Investments Ltd *v.* Norwich Corp [1971] 2 QB 614; [1971] 3 WLR 133,
  CA 26.1
Sameen *v.* Abeyewickrema [1963] AC 597; [1963] 2 WLR 1114, PC 2.9
Semple *v.* DPP [2009] EWHC 3241 (Admin); [2010] 2 All ER 353 .... 21.3.4
Solomon *v.* Green (1955) 119 JP 289, DC 22.6.3
Sporrong & Lonnroth *v.* Sweden (A/52) (1983) 5 EHRR 35 .... 1.5.4
Stepney BC *v.* Joffe [1949] 1 KB 599, DC 26.1
Streames *v.* Copping [1985] QB 920; [1985] 2 WLR 993, DC 26.11.1
Taylor *v.* Manchester City Council [2012] EWHC 3467 (Admin); [2013] 2 All
  ER 490 .... 14.3.8
Timmis *v.* Millman (1965) 109 Sol Jo 31, DC 22.6.3
Tre Traktorer AB *v.* Sweden (A/159) (1991) 13 EHRR 309 .... 1.5.3, 1.5.4
Vane *v.* Yiannopoulos [1965] AC 486; [1964] 3 WLR 1218, HL 21.3.1
Westminster City Council *v.* Croyalgrange Ltd [1986] 1 WLR 674, HL 21.2.1
Westminster City Council *v.* Zestfair (1989) 153 JP 613, DC 26.2

Table of statutes

Alcoholic Liquor Duties Act
1979 .... Preface, 3.2.2, 7.11.2
s.2 .... 3.2.2
Anti-Social Behaviour, Crime and Policing
Act 2014 .... 2.5.5, 5.4.1, 23.1, 24.1
Part 4 .... 15.12.1
s.76 .... 23.8
(1)–(5) 24.3.1
(6) 24.3.1, 24.3.4
(7), (8) 24.3.1
s.77(1)–(5) 24.3.2
(2)(b) 24.3.3
s.78 .... 24.3.5
(1)–(3), (6) 24.3.3
s.79 .... 24.3.4, 24.3.6, 24.3.7,
24.3.8, 24.3.10
s.80 .... 23.8, 24.3.1, 24.3.4,
24.3.11
(1)–(9) 24.3.5
s.81 ...... 24.3.8, 24.3.10, 24.3.11
(2)–(4) 24.3.5
s.82 .... 24.3.11
(1)–(8) 24.3.6
s.83(1)–(7) 24.3.7
s.84 .... 24.3.8, 24.3.11
s.85(1) 24.3.9, 24.3.10
(2)–(5) 24.3.9
s.86(1), (2), (3), (6) 24.3.10
s.87(1), (3), (4) 24.3.11
s.88(1)–(5) 24.3.12
s.89(1), (2) 24.3.13
s.90(1)–(5) 24.3.14
s.91 .... 24.3.15
s.92(1) 24.3.1, 24.3.5
Banking and Financial Dealings Act
1971 .... 20.7, 20.8
Broadcasting Act 1990 .... 4.3.5
Business and Planning
Act 2020 .... Preface, 27.5
Part 1 .... 27.1

Care Standards Act 2000
Part 1
s.2(2) 7.2
Part 2 .... 7.2
Charities Act 2011 .... 17.7
s.30(2) 5.4.4
Children and Young Persons Act 1933
s.5 .... 22.11
Cinemas Act 1985 .... 6.11.1
Civil Partnership Act 2004 .... 20.6.2
Civil Procedure Code (Ceylon) 2.9
Coal Industry Act 1994 .... 17.7
Companies Act 2006
s.1028 .... 7.16, 12.6
Confiscation of Alcohol
(Young Persons) Act 1997 .... 22.1
s.1 .... 22.12
Co-operative and Community Benefit
Societies Act 2014 .... 17.6
Copyright, Designs and Patents Act
1988
s.107(1)(d)(iii) 6.11.1
(3) 6.11.1
s.198(2) 6.11.1
s.297(1) 6.11.1
s.297A(1) 6.11.1
Corporation Tax Act 2010
s.658 .... 2.15.2
Counter-Terrorism Act 2008
s.41 .... 6.11.1
Criminal Attempts Act 1981
s.1 .... 6.11.1
Criminal Justice and Police Act
2001 .... 24.1
Part 1 .... 22.5
s.19 .... 24.5
Criminal Justice Act 1925
s.33 .... 21.8.5
Criminal Justice Act 2003 .... 7.9, 13.10,
15.11, 17.8.6, 18.9, 19.11, 20.15, 21.10

s.280(2), (3) 24.5.7
s.281(5) 24.3.10
Sched.15
  Part 1 .... 6.11.1
  Part 2
    para.95 .... 6.11.1
  Part 3 .... 6.11.1
Sched.26
  para.56(1) 24.5.7
    (2)(a), (b) 24.5.7
Criminal Law Act 1977
  s.1 .... 6.11.1
Customs and Excise Management Act 1979
  ss.20A, 22A 7.1.3
  s.170(1)(a) 6.11.1
  s.170B 6.11.1
Data Protection Act 2018 .... 6.11.7
  s.45 .... 6.4, 6.11.4
  (2) 6.11.7
Deregulation Act 2015 .... 6.14
Education Act 1996
  s.4 .... 7.2
  s.579(1) 7.2
Equality Act 2010 .... 2.5.10
  s.149 .... 27.5.1
Finance Act 1995 .... Preface
  s.5 .... 3.2.2
Finance (No.2) Act 2023 .... Preface
  ss.44, 45, 90 .... 3.2.2
Sched.6
  paras.3, 5, 6–10, 11 .... 3.2.2
Firearms Act 1968 .... 6.11.1
Firearms (Amendment) Act 1997 .... 6.11.1
Food Safety Act 1990
  ss.14, 15 .... 6.11.1
Forgery and Counterfeiting Act 1981
  ss.18, 19 .... 6.11.1
Fraud Act 2006 .... 6.11.1
Friendly Societies Act 1974 .... 17.6
Friendly Societies Act 1992 .... 17.6
Further and Higher Education Act 1992
  s.65 .... 7.2
  s.90(1) 7.2
  s.91(5) 7.2
Gambling Act 2005
  s.19(3) 4.3.7
  s.46 .... 6.11.1
  ss.74, 163 .... 2.15.2
  Sched.11, Part 1 .... 7.1.4

Gaming Act 1968
  s.7(2) 6.11.1
Greater London Council (General Powers) Act 1966
  s.21(1) 5.4.3
Health Act 2006 .... 27.5.2
Health and Safety at Work etc. Act 1974
  s.18 .... 7.8, 10.2.1, 23.3
  s.19 .... 7.9, 17.8.6
Health and Social Care Act 2008
  Part 1 .... 7.2
Higher Education and Research Act 2017
  ss.39, 97 .... 7.2
Highways Act 1980 .... 7.1.2
  Part 7A 27.2
Human Rights Act 1998 .... 1.5.3. 2.6, 25.15
  s.1(1) 1.5.2
  s.2(1) 1.5.1
  s.3(1) 1.5.1
  s.6(1) 1.5.1, 24.3.13, 24.6
  (2), (3) 1.5.1
  s.7(1) 1.5.1
  s.8 .... 1.5.1
  Sched.1, art.6 .... 15.2
Immigration Act 1971 ... 6.5, 6.11.1, 7.2.5, 21.2.5
  s.24b 7.4.1, 9.4.2, 12.3.1, 16.3.1
Immigration Act 2014 .... 6.11.1, 21.2.5
  s.23 .... 6.12
Immigration Act 2016 ...... Preface, 6.11.1, 7.8, 10.2.1, 21.2.5
  s.38 .... 15.12.1, 24.1
  Sched.6 .... 15.12.1, 24.1, 24.3.16
  Sched.10, Part 1 .... 6.5, 7.2.5
Immigration, Asylum and Nationality Act 2006
  s.15 .... 6.12, 7.4.1, 9.4.2, 12.3.1, 16.3.1
  s.21 .... 7.4.1, 9.4.2, 12.3.1, 16.3.1
Interpretation Act 1978 .... 22.3
  s.5 .... 12.4
  Sched.1 .... 12.4
Landlord and Tenant Act 1954
  Part II 3.2.1
Late Night Refreshment Houses Act 1969 .... 6.11.1
Law of Property Act 1925 .... 2.9

Legal Aid, Sentencing and Punishment of
  Offenders Act 2012
  s.85 .... 21.6
Legal Services Act 2007 .... 7.19, 17.19.2
Legislative and Regulatory
  Reform Act 2006 .... 2.5.2
Levelling Up and Regeneration Act
  2023 .... Preface
Licensed Premises (Exclusion of
  Certain Persons) Act 1980 .... 21.10
Licensing Act 1964 ..... 1.5.3, 6.11.1, 7.1.2
  s.6(1) 13.3
Licensing Act 2003 .... Preface, 1.1, 1.3,
  1.4.1, 1.4.5, 1.4.6, 1.4.7, 1.5.1. 1.5.4,
  2.1, 2.5, 2.5.2, 2.5.4, 2.5.6, 2.5.7,
  2.5.11, 3.3, 4.1, 4.1.1, 4.2.6, 4.2.7,
  4.2.9, 4.3.4, 4.4.2, 5.3, 6.10, 6.11.4,
  7.2.4, 7.6.3, 7.11.7, 8.5, 10.1, 10.2.2,
  11.2.1, 11.2.2, 11.5, 11.6, 11.7, 13.8.1,
  15.1, 17.1, 18.2.3, 18.7.1, 19.1, 22.11,
  24.3.18, 25.1, 25.8, 25.11, 26.3, 26.4.9,
  26.9, 26.10, 26.11.1, 27.1, App.B
  Part 1 .... 1.3
  s.1(1) 3.1, 3.2, 5.1
    (2) 3.1, 17.2
    (5) 3.5, 5.2
  s.2(3) 3.6
  Part 2 .... 1.3
  s.3(1), (2) 2.2
  s.4 .... 2.12, 10.2.1
    (1), (3) 2.3
  s.5 .... 2.3, 2.4, 5.4.1
    (3) 2.4, 2.5.4, 2.6
    (4), (6D) 2.5.4
    (8) 2.4
  s.5A 2.5.4
  s.7(1) 2.7
    (9) 2.7
  s.8 .... 2.8, 2.9
    (3)–(7) 2.8
  s.9(1) 2.10
  s.10(1), (4) 2.11
  Part 3 .... 1.3, 7.1
  s.11 .... 7.1
  s.12(3)(a), (b) 7.3
  s.13(2) 7.9, 17.8.6
    (4) 7.8, 10.2.1
  s.15(1), (2) 9.2
  s.16 .... 7.2, 13.1
  s.17 .... 7.10.1, 14.1

s.17(1) 7.3
  (3) 7.1.2, 8.1
  (4) 7.1.2, 8.2
  (5) 14.3.5
  (a) 7.6
  (aa) 7.7
  (6)(a), (b) 7.8
s.18 .... 2.5.4, 7.10.2
  (2)(a) 11.1
  (3)(a) 7.10.3
  (4)(a)(i) 11.1
  (6) 10.3.1
  (7) 10.3.1
  (b) 10.2.3
  (10) 7.10.2, 7.10.3
s.19 .... 7.11.2
  (2) 7.11.3
  (3) 6.1, 7.11.3
  (4) 7.19
s.19A 7.11.2, 7.19, 11.8
s.20(3) 7.11.4
s.21 .... 7.11.5, 11.10
s.22 .... 7.11.6
s.23 .... 7.12
s.24 .... 7.5, 7.13
s.25 .... 7.14
s.25A 14.1
  (6) 7.11.3
s.26 .... 7.15
s.27 .... 7.16, 12.1
s.28 .... 7.17
s.29(1) 13.2
  (2) 13.3
  (3) 13.8.2
  (7) 13.8.3
s.30 .... 13.6
s.31(2) 13.8.2
  (3)(c) 13.8.3
  (5), (6) 10.3.2, 13.8.3
  (7) 13.8.3
s.32 .... 10.3.1, 10.3.2, 13.6, 13.9
s.33 .... 7.18.1, 14.1, 14.4
s.34 .... 14.1, 14.3
s.35 .... 2.5.4
  (2) 14.3.8
  (3)(a) 14.3.8
  (b) 14.3.87
  (4) 14.3.8
  (5), (6) 10.3.3
  (7) 14.3.8

s.36(1), (3), (4), (5) 14.3.9
   (6) 14.3.8
   (7) 14.3.8
s.37 .... 9.4.1, 14.1
   (4), (4A), (4B) 9.4.5
   (5), (6) 9.5
s.38(1) 9.4.7
s.39 .... 9.4.8
s.40 .... 9.4.9
s.41 .... 9.6, 14.1
ss.41A–41C 14.1
s.41A 14.2
s.41B(2) 10.3.4, 14.2.7
s.41B(3)–(9) 14.2.7
   (10) 10.3.4, 14.2.7
s.41C(1)–(5) 14.2.8
s.41D 14.1
   (5), (6) 7.11.3
s.42 .... 14.1, 16.2
s.43 .... 12.6, 16.4
   (5) 16.4
s.44 .... 16.5
s.45(1) 16.6
s.46 .... 16.6
s.47(3A), (4) 12.2
   (5) 12.2
   (6) 12.4
   (7)(a), (aa) 12.2, 12.4
     (b) 12.4
   (7A) 12.3
   (9) 12.4
   (10) 12.4
s.48(1), (2), (2A), (2B) 12.5
   (3)(a) 25.3
s.49(1)–(3) 12.3.3
   (4)–(6), (8) 12.2
s.51 .... 14.3.8, 15.2
   (1) 15.3, 15.4
   (4)–(6) 15.7
s.52 .... 7.15, 15.8
   (7), (8) 10.3.5, 15.10
   (10) 15.9
   (11) 26.4.11
s.52A 7.11.3
s.53 .... 15.2
ss.53A–53D 15.12, 15.12.1
s.53A 15.12.4
   (2) 15.12.2
s.53B 15.12.4
   (2) 15.12.2

s.53D(1) 15.12.4
s.54 .... 9.6
s.55A 7.15, 7.20
s.56 .... 7.18.2
ss.57, 58 .... 7.19
s.59 .... 13.10
   (3) 7.9, 15.11
   (4) 15.11
   (5), (6) 7.9, 15.11
Part 4 .... 1.3, 17.2
s.61 .... 17.3
s.62 .... 7.2, 17.3, 17.3.1, 17.4,
                  17.6, 17.7
s.63(3) 17.5
s.64 .... 17.3, 17.3.2, 17.6, 17.7
s.65(2), (4) 17.6
s.66(1), (2) 17.7
s.67 .... 17.4
s.71 .... 17.9.1
   (1), (2) 17.8
   (4) 8.1, 17.8.4
   (5) 8.2, 17.8.4
   (6)(a) 17.8.5
   (7) 17.8.5
s.72 .... 2.5.4
   (2) 17.9.2
    (a) 11.1
   (3)(a) 17.9.3
   (4) 17.9.3
    (a)(i) 11.1
   (5), (6) 17.9.3
   (7), (8) 10.3.7, 17.9.4
   (9) 17.9.4
   (10) 17.9.3
s.73(1) 17.9.3
s.73A 17.11.1, 17.19.2
s.73B 11.8, 17.11.1, 17.19.2
s.74 .... 17.11.2
s.75(1), (2) 17.11.3
s.76 .... 17.11.4
s.77(1), (2) 17.10.1
   (3) 17.10.2
s.78 .... 17.12.1
   (1) 17.12.2
s.79 .... 17.13
s.80 .... 17.14
s.81 .... 17.15
s.82 .... 17.16
s.83(1), (2) 17.17
s.84 .... 18.1, 18.2, 18.3

s.84(4) 18.5.1
s.85 .... 2.5.4
　(2) 18.7.2
　(3)(a) 18.7.3
　(4) 18.7.3
　(5), (6) 10.3.8
　(7) 18.7.3
s.86(1), (4) 18.8
　(7) 18.7.3
s.86A 18.2
s.86B(2) 10.3.9, 18.2.5
　(3)–(9) 18.2.5
　(10) 10.3.9, 18.2.5
s.86C(1)–(5) 18.2.6
s.87(1) 19.2, 19.3, 19.4
　(4)–(7) 19.7
s.88 .... 17.18.1
　(3), (4) 19.8
　(7), (8) 10.3.10, 19.10
　(10) 19.9
　(11) 26.5.6
s.89 .... 19.2
s.90(2), (4) 17.18.2
　(5), (6) 17.18.3
s.92A 17.21
s.93(1), (2) 17.19.1
ss.94, 95 .... 17.19.2
s.96(1) 19.11
　(2)–(4) ... 17.8.6, 18.9, 19.11
　(5), (6) ... 17.8.6, 18.9, 19.11
　(7), (8) 17.8.6
s.97 .... 17.20
Part 5 .... 1.3, 20.1
s.98 .... 20.2
s.99 .... 20.3
s.99A 20.4
s.100(1)–(3) 20.5
　(4), (5) 20.6
　(6) 11.1, 20.6
　(7) 20.7, 20.8
　(8), (9) 20.6
s.100A(2)(a), (b) 20.7
　(3) 20.8
　(4) 20.7, 20.8
s.101 .... 20.14.4
　(2)(c), (d) 20.9
　(3), (4) 20.9
s.102 .... 20.10
s.103 .... 20.11
s.104A 20.10

s.104A(1), (3) 20.12.2
s.105(2)(a) 25.3
　(4), (5) 20.12.3
s.106(3), (4) 20.13
s.106A 20.13.1
s.107 .... 20.10, 20.12.1
　(1) 20.14.5
　(2) 20.14.1
　(3) 20.14.2
　(4), (5) 20.14.3
　(6) 20.14.4
　(9), (10) 20.14.4
　(13)(a) 20.14.3
s.108(2), (5) 20.15
s.109(5), (6) 20.16
s.110 .... 20.17
Part 6 .... 1.3, 6.1, 20.1
s.111 .... 6.2
s.113(1) 6.11.1
　(3) 6.11.2
s.115(1), (2A), (3), (4) 6.14
s.116(1)–(3) 6.17
s.117(2) 6.3, 6.4
s.118(1), (2) 6.3
s.120 .... 6.10
　(2) 6.3, 6.7.1, 6.7.3
　(3) 6.7.2
　(4) 6.7.3
　(5) 6.11.2
　(7)(b) 6.7.3
　(7A) 6.7.3
s.122(1). (2), (2A) 6.8
s.123(1)–(3) 6.15
s.124 .... 26.7.3
　(2), (3), (3A), (3B),
　(4), (5), (5A), (6), (7) 6.15
s.125 .... 6.9
s.126(1), (3), (5) 6.18
s.127(1), (3)–(5) 6.19
s.128(1), (3), (6), (7) 6.16.1
s.129(2)–(4) 6.16.2
s.130(7)–(9) 6.16.2
s.131(3), (4) 6.16.3
s.132(2), (2B), (3)–(5) 6.16.4
s.132A(3)–(8),
　(10)–(14) 6.16.5
s.134(1)–(6) 6.20
s.135(2), (3), (5), (6) 6.21
Part 7 .... 1.3, 21.1
s.136 .... 21.1.1, 23.8

s.136(1)(a) .. 12.1, 21.2.1, 21.2.4
   (b) 21.2.1
   (2), (4) 21.2.1
s.137 .... 21.1.1, 21.2.4
   (1) 21.2.2
s.138 .... 21.1.1, 21.2.4
   (1) 21.2.3
s.139 .... 12.1, 21.2.4
s.140 .... 21.1.2, 21.3.1
s.141 .... 21.1.2
   (3) 21.3.2
s.142 .... 21.1.2, 21.3.3
s.143 .... 21.1.2, 21.3.4
   (4) 21.3.4
s.144 .... 21.1.3, 21.4
ss.145–155 .... 22.1
s.145 .... 21.1.4, 22.2.3
   (5) 22.2.1, 22.2.2
   (6)–(8) 22.2.4
s.146 ..... 21.1.4, 21.7, 22.5, 24.4
   (1)–(7) 22.3
s.147 .... 21.1.4, 21.7, 22.4, 22.5,
                           24.4
s.147A 21.1.4, 21.7, 22.5,
                           24.4
s.147B 22.5
s.149 .... 21.1.4
   (1), (2) 22.6.1
   (3) 22.6.2
   (4), (5) 22.6.3
   (6) 22.6.2
s.150 .... 21.1.4
   (1) 22.7.1
   (2) 22.7.2
s.151 .... 21.1.4
   (1), (2), (4), (6) 22.8
s.152 .... 21.1.4
   (1), (2) 22.9
s.152 .... 21.1.4
s.153 .... 22.10
s.154 .... 22.3
s.156 .... 21.1.5, 21.5.1
   (3) 21.5.1
s.157 .... 21.1.5, 21.5.2
s.158 .... 7.4.1, 7.6.3, 9.4.2,
  12.3.1, 13.5.1, 13.6, 14.2.2,
  14.2.5, 14.3.2, 14.3.5, 15.5.1,
  16.3.1, 17.8.1, 17.8.5, 18.2.3,
  18.4.1, 18.6, 19.5.1, 21.1.6,
                           21.6

s.159 .... 22.6.3
Part 8 .... 1.3, 24.1, 24.2
s.160(4)–(7) 24.2
ss.161–166 .... 24.1
s.161 .... 23.1
s.167(1), (1A), (2)–(4) ... 24.3.16
   (5) 24.3.16
   (a) 25.3
   (6), (8) 24.3.16
   (9), (10) 10.3.6, 24.3.16
   (11) 24.3.16
s.168 .... 24.3.17
ss.169A, 169B 24.1, 24.4
s.170 .... 24.6
s.171(5) 24.2
Part 9 .... 1.3
s.172 .... 4.3.11, 4.3.12, 4.3.13,
               11.11, 23.1, 23.8
   (1), (4) 11.4.2
ss.172A–172E 23.1
s.172A 23.2
s.172B 23.4
   (1) 23.3
s.172C 23.4
s.172D 23.6
s.172E 23.7
s.173 .... 7.1.1
   (1) 7.1.3
s.174 .... 7.1.1, 7.1.3
s.175 .... 7.1.1, 7.1.5
s.176 .... 7.1.1, 7.1.2
s.177(8) 11.10
s.177A 11.11
   (3), (4) 4.3.13, 4.3.15
s.178 .... 2.9
s.179 .... 21.2.5
s.180 .... 21.2.6
s.181(2) 26.1
s.182 ..... Preface, 2.3, 2.12, 26.1
s.184 .... 2.14
   (7) 17.12.1
s.185 .... 2.13
s.186(3) 21.7
s.187(1), (2) 21.8.1
   (4) 21.8.2
   (6) 21.8.3
   (7) 21.8.4
s.188(1)–(5) 21.8.5
s.189 .... 5.4.4, 7.1.1
   (5) 7.1.1, 13.2

s.190 .... 7.1.1
s.191 .... 3.2.2
    (2) 3.2.2
s.192 .... 3.2.1
s.192A 6.5, 7.2.5
s.193 .... 3.2.2, 4.3.3, 7.1.1,
        7.11.3, 17.4, 20.7, 20.8,
        20.14.3, 21.2.1, 21.5.1
Sched.1 .... 3.4, 4.1.2, 4.4.4
  Part 1
    para.2(1)(g) 11.10
        (h) 21.2.1
  Part 2 .... 4.3
    para.5 .... 4.2.2, 4.4.3
    para.6 .... 4.2.2
    para.7 .... 4.4.3
    para.9 .... 1.5.6
    para.12ZA 5.4.1
    para.12A 11.11
    para.12B 4.4.1
    para.12C 11.11
  Part 3
    para.14 .... 4.2.1
    para.15 .... 4.2.2
    para.16 .... 4.2.3
    para.17 .... 4.2.4
    para.18 .... 4.2.5
    para.19 .... 4.3.11
        (3) 5.4.1
    paras.20, 21 ...... 4.3.11, 5.4.1
Sched.2 .... 3.5, 5.2, 5.4
  para.3 .... 3.1
Sched.4 .... 6.11.1
Sched.5 .... 26.1
  para.14 .... 17.18.2
  para.17(1), (2), (2A), (4), (5),
    (5A), (5B), (6)–(8) 6.13
Licensing (Occasional Permissions) Act
  1983 .... 6.11.1
Live Music Act 2012 .... 4.1.1
Local Government Act 2003
  s.46 .... 2.15.2
Local Government Finance Act 1988
  s.43(4A) 2.15.3
    (6A) 2.15.2
Local Government (Miscellaneous
  Provisions) Act 1982
  s.6 .... 6.11.1
  Sched.1 .... 6.11.1
  Sched.3 .... 4.3.10

para.2A 3.4, 4.1.1
    (2) 4.3.11
Localism Act 2011
  s.27(1) 1.5.3
London Government Act 1963
  Sched.12 .... 6.11.1
London Local Authorities Act
  1990 .... 6.11.1
London Local Authorities Act 1995
  ss.14, 16 .... 5.4.3
Magistrates' Courts Act 1980 .... 24.5.2,
                                        24.5.5
  s.53(3) 26.2
  s.111(1), (2), (5), (6) 26.11.1
  s.127(1) 21.7
  Sched.3 .... 21.8.5
Medicines Act 1968
  s.130 .... 3.2.2
Mental Capacity Act 2005 .... 7.16, 12.2
Merchant Shipping Act 1995
  s.256 .... 7.9, 17.8.6
Miners' Welfare Act 1952
  s.12(3) 17.7
Misuse of Drugs Act 1971 .... 15.8
  s.4(1)(a)–(c) 17.20
    (2) 6.11.1
    (3) 6.11.1
  s.5(3) 6.11.1
  s.8 .... 6.11.1
National Health Service Act 2006 .... 2.4,
                                7.8, 10.2.1, 23.3
  ss.25, 275 .... 7.2
National Health Service (Wales) Act
  2006
  ss.11, 18 .... 7.2
Police Act 1996
  s.89(2) 7.9, 13.10, 15.11, 17.8.6,
                18.9, 19.11, 20.15
Police Act 1997
  Part 5 .... 22.5
  s.112 .... 6.4, 6.11.4, 6.11.5
  s.113A 6.4, 6.11.4, 6.11.6
  s.113B 6.11.6
Police Reform Act 2002
  s.38 .... 24.6
Police Reform and Social Responsibility
  Act 2011
  Part 2 .... 2.15
  s.121 .... 2.11
  s.126 .... 2.15.1

Policing and Crime Act 2017 .... 2.5.4
Private Places of Entertainment
(Licensing) Act 1967 .... 6.11.1
Private Security Industry Act 2001
    s.3 .... 6.11.1
      (2) 7.11.5
    s.4(4) 7.11.5
    Sched.2
      para.2(1)(a) 7.11.5
      para.8(3)(a)–(d) 7.11.5
Psychoactive Substances Act 2016
    s.4 .... 6.11.1
    s.5 .... 6.11.1
      (1), (2) 17.20
    ss.7, 8 .... 6.11.1
Public Health (Minimum Price for
Alcohol) (Wales) Act 2018 .... 6.11.1,
                21.9, 21.9.4
Railways Act 1993
    ss.6, 8 .... 21.5.2
    s.83 .... 7.1.3, 21.5.2
Recreational Charities Act 1958
    s.2 .... 17.7
Regulation of Investigatory Powers Act
2000
    s.81(2), (3) 15.12.1
Rehabilitation of Offenders Act
1974 .... 6.11, 6.11.2, 6.11.7
    s.1 .... 6.11.3
    s.4(2)(a), (b) 6.11.6
      (4) 6.11.6
    s.5 .... 6.11.3
    s.7(3) 6.11.3
    s.114 .... 6.11.3
    Sched.2
      para.3(3), (4) 6.11.6
      para.4 .... 6.11.6
    Sched.18 .... 6.11.3
Road Traffic Act 1988
    ss.3A, 4, 5 .... 6.11.1

s.6(6) 6.11.1
Royal Charter of Richard II 1382 .... 6.10
Royal Charter 1611 (Vintners) 6.10
Senior Courts Act 1981
    s.28A(3) 26.11.1
    s.31 .... 26.11.2
Sexual Offences Act 1956
    ss.8, 18 .... 6.11.1
Sexual Offences Act 1967
    s.4 .... 6.11.1
Sexual Offences Act 2003
    Sched.3 .... 6.11.1
Theatres Act 1968
    s.13 .... 6.11.1
Theft Act 1968
    ss.1, 8–11 .... 6.11.1
    s.12(2)(b) 6.11.1
    ss.12A, 13, 15, 15A, 16, 17,
      19–22, 24A, 25 .... 6.11.1
Theft Act 1978
    ss.1, 2 .... 6.11.1
Tobacco Products Duty Act 1979
    ss.8G, 8H 6.11.1
Town and Country Planning
Act 1990 .... 7.8, 10.2.1, 23.3
Trade Descriptions Act 1968
    s.1 .... 6.11.1
Trade Marks Act 1994
    s.92(1), (2) 6.11.1
Value Added Tax Act 1994 .... 7.11.2
Video Recordings Act 1984
    s.4 .... 7.11.4
Violent Crime Reduction Act 2006 ... 15.1,
                  21.10
    ss.28, 36 .... 6.11.1
Water Resources Act 1991
    s.221(1) 7.8, 10.2.1, 23.3
Weights and Measures Act 1985
    s.69 .... 7.8, 10.2.1
    s.72(1) 22.6.1

Table of statutory instruments

Airports Licensing (Liquor) Order 2005, SI 2005/1733 .... 7.1.3
Alcohol Licensing (Coronavirus) (Regulatory Easements) (Amendment) Regulations
  2023, SI 2023/990 .... Preface
Business Protection from Misleading Marketing Regulations 2008, SI 2008/1276
  reg.6 .... 6.11.1
Consumer Protection from Unfair Trading Regulations 2008, SI 2008/1277
  regs.8–12 .... 6.11.1
Courts Act 2003 (Consequential Provisions) Order 2005, SI 2005/886 .... 26.1
Criminal Procedure Rules 2020, SI 2020/759 .... 24.5.8
Denatured Alcohol Regulations 2005, SI 2005/1524 .... 3.2.2
Human Medicines Regulations 2012, SI 2012/1916
  reg.2 .... 3.2.2
Late Night Levy (Application and Administration) Regulations 2012,
  SI 2012/2730 .... 2.15.1, 2.15.5
Late Night Levy (Expenses, Exemptions and Reductions) Regulations 2012,
  SI 2012/2550 .... 2.15.2, 2.15.3
Licensing Act 2003 (Early Morning Alcohol Restriction Orders) Regulations
  2012, SI 2012/2551
  reg.4 .... 23.3
  reg.14 .... 23.4
  reg.15 .... 23.7
  Sched.1 .... 23.2
  Sched.2 .... 23.3
Licensing Act 2003 (Hearings) Regulations 2005,
  SI 2005/44 .... Preface, 2.10, 10.4.3, 15.12.2, 25.1, 25.2,
                                                        25.3, 25.6, 25.9, 25.13, 25.14
  reg.5 .... 6.7.3. 6.15, 7.10.3, 9.4.8, 12.5, 13.8.3, 14.3.8, 15.8,
                                                        16.5, 17.9.3, 18.7.3, 19.8, 20.12.3, 23.5
    (2) 23.5
  reg.6(2) 12.5, 20.12.3
    (3) 15.12.3
    (4) 6.7.3, 6.15, 7.10.3, 9.4.8, 13.8.3, 14.3.8, 15.8,
                                                        16.5, 17.9.3, 18.7.3, 19.8, 23.5
  reg.7(2) 6.7.3, 6.15, 7.10.3, 9.4.8, 12.5, 13.8.3, 14.3.8, 15.8,
                                                        15.12.3, 16.5, 17.9.3, 18.7.3, 19.8, 23.5
  reg.8 .... 15.12.3
    (2) 1.5.3
  reg.10 .... 10.2.3
  reg.23 .... 1.5.3
  reg.26(1) 20.12.3

reg.26(3) 23.5
reg.28(1) 13.8.3
    (3) 23.5
Sched.1
    para.2 .... 13.8.3
    para.3 .... 14.3.8
    para.4 .... 9.4.8
    para.5 .... 16.5
    para.6 .... 12.5
    para.7 .... 15.8
    para.8 .... 17.9.3
    para.9 .... 18.7.3
    para.10 .... 19.8
    para.11 .... 20.12.3
    para.12 .... 6.7.3
    para.14 .... 6.15
    para.15A 23.5
Sched.2
    para.1 .... 7.10.3
    para.2 .... 13.8.3
    para.3 .... 14.3.8
    para.4 .... 9.4.8
    para.5 .... 16.5
    para.6 .... 12.5
    para.7 .... 15.8
    para.7A 15.12.3
    para.8 .... 17.9.3
    para.9 .... 18.7.3
    para.10 .... 19.8
    para.11 .... 20.12.3
    para.12 .... 6.7.3
    para.14 .... 6.15
    para.15A 23.5
Sched.3
    para.1 .... 7.10.3
    para.2 .... 13.8.3
    para.3 .... 14.3.8
    para.4 .... 9.4.8
    para.5 .... 16.5
    para.6 .... 12.5
    para.7 .... 15.8
    para.7A 15.12.3
    para.8 .... 17.9.3
    para.9 .... 18.7.3
    para.10 .... 19.8
    para.11 .... 6.7.3
    para.13 .... 6.15
    para.15 .... 23.5
Sched.5
    para.1 .... 7.10.3

Licensing Act 2003 (Late Night Refreshment) Regulations 2015, SI 2015/1781 .... 5.4.1
Licensing Act 2003 (Licensing Authority's Register) (Other Information) Regulations
    2005, SI 2005/43 .... 2.8
Licensing Act 2003 (Mandatory Licensing Conditions) Order 2010,
    SI 2010/860 .... 7.11.2, 17.11.1
Licensing Act 2003 (Mandatory Licensing Conditions) Order 2014,
    SI 2014/1252 .... 7.11.2, 17.11.1
Licensing Act 2003 (Miscellaneous Amendments) Regulations 2017,
    SI 2017/411
        reg.14(1), (14) 16.3, 16.4
        Sched.15 .... 16.3, 16.4
Licensing Act 2003 (Permitted Temporary Activities) (Notices)
    Regulations 2005, SI 2005/2918 .... 20.6.1, 20.6.2, 20.12.3
        regs.2, 7 .... 20.12.2, 20.13.1, 20.14.5
        Sched.1 .... 20.6
        Sched.2 .... 20.12.2
        Sched.3 .... 20.13.1
        Sched.4 .... 20.14.5
Licensing Act 2003 (Persistent Selling of Alcohol to Children) (Prescribed Form of
    Closure Notice) Regulations 2012, SI 2012/963 .... 24.4
Licensing Act 2003 (Personal Licences) Regulations 2005, SI 2005/41 .... 6.4, 6.10
        reg.5 .... 6.9
        reg.9 .... 6.6.3
        regs.10, 11 .... 6.6.1
        Sched.3 .... 6.11.2, 6.11.4, 6.12
Licensing Act 2003 (Premises Licences and Club Premises Certificates)
    Regulations 2005, SI 2005/42 .... 7.10.1, 13.8.1, 17.9.1, 18.7.1, 20.6.1
        reg.7 .... 7.8, 10.2.1
        reg.8 .... 12.2
        reg.21 .... 7.4.3, 9.4.4, 9.6, 10.4.2, 12.3.3, 13.5.3,
                                 14.2.4, 14.3.4, 15.5.3, 18.2.2, 18.4.3
        reg.21A 9.6
            (1) 7.4.3, 9.4.4, 12.3.3, 18.2.2, 18.4.3
            (3), (4) 7.4.3, 12.3.3
        reg.21B 15.5.3
        reg.22 .... 7.8, 10.2.2
            (1)(b) 15.5.4, 19.5.4
        reg.23 .... 7.5
        reg.24 .... 7.5
            (2) 16.3, 16.4
        reg.25 .... 7.6, 14.3.5, 18.5.1
        reg.26 .... 7.6, 14.3.5, 18.5.1
            (2) 13.6
        reg.26A 14.2.5, 18.2.3
        reg.26B 7.7, 14.3.6, 18.5.2
        reg.26C 7.7, 14.3.6, 18.5.2
            (2) 13.6
        reg.27 .... 7.8, 13.7, 14.2.6, 14.3.7, 18.2.4, 18.6
        reg.27A 7.8, 13.7, 14.2.6, 14.3.7, 15.5.4, 18.2.4, 18.6, 19.5.4
        reg.29 .... 15.5.4, 19.5.4

reg.31 .... 10.2.4
reg.32 .... 15.7
regs.33, 34 .... 7.13
reg.36A 15.12.1
regs.37–39 .... 24.3.16
reg.38 .... 15.6, 15.12.3, 19.6
    (2)(a) 15.12.1
reg.39 .... 15.6, 15.12.3, 19.6
Sched.1 .... 2.9
Sched.2 .... 7.4
Sched.3 .... 13.5
Sched.4 .... 14.3.1
Sched.4A 7.11.3
Sched.4B 14.2.1, 18.2.1
Sched.5 .... 9.4.1
Sched.6 .... 16.3
Sched.7 .... 12.3
Sched.8 .... 15.5
Sched.8 .... 19.5
Sched.8A 15.12.1
Sched.9
    Part A 17.8
    Part B 17.8.1
Sched.10 .... 18.4
Sched.11 .... 9.3, 9.4.1
    Part B 16.3, 16.4
Sched.12
    Parts A, B 7.13
Sched.13
    Part A 17.12.1
    Part B 17.12.2
Magistrates' Courts Rules 1981, SI 1981/552
    rules 14, 34 .... 26.2
    rules 76–78, 81 .... 26.11.1
Management of Health and Safety at Work Regulations 1999, SI 1999/3242 .... 7.11.7
Openness of Local Government Bodies Regulations 2014, SI 2014/2095 .... 25.8
Provision of Services Regulations 2009, SI 2009/2999 .... 7.4.2
Public Health (Minimum Price for Alcohol) (Minimum Unit Price) (Wales)
    Regulations 2019, SI 2019/1472 (W.260) 21.9.1
Regulation (EU) 2016/679 on the protection of natural persons with regard to the
    processing of personal data and on the free movement of such data
    art.15 .... 6.4, 6.11.4
Regulatory Reform (Fire Safety) Order 2005, SI 2005/1541 .... 8.8
    reg.31 .... 24.1
Rehabilitation of Offenders Act 1974 (Exceptions) Order 1975, SI 1975/1023 .... 6.11.6
Smoke-free (Premises and Enforcement) Regulations 2006, SI 2006/3368 .... 27.5.2
Smoke-free (Signs) Regulations 2012, SI 2012/1536 .... 27.5.2
Veterinary Medicines Regulations 2006, SI 2006/2407
    reg.2 .... 3.2.2
Veterinary Medicines Regulations 2013, SI 2013/2033 .... 3.2.2

Weights and Measures (Intoxicating Liquor) Order 1988, SI 1988/2039 .... 7.11.2
Welsh Language (Gambling and Licensing Forms) Regulations 2010,
    SI 2010/2440 .... 7.13
Workplace (Health, Safety and Welfare) Regulations 1992, SI 1992/3004
    reg.2(1) 4.3.14

Table of treaties and conventions

Agreement on the European Economic Area (Oporto, 2 May 1992) 6.10
   Protocol (Brussels, 17 March 1993) 6.10
European Convention on Human Rights 1.5.1, 24.6
   arts.2–12 .... 1.5.2
   art.6 .... 15.2, 25.15
      (1) 1.5.3, 2.6, 7.10.3
   art.8 .... 1.5.5
   art.9 .... 1.5.6
   art.10(2) 1.5.6
   art.14 .... 1.5.2, 1.5.6
   arts.16–18 .... 1.5.2
   art.26 .... 1.5.1
   art.27(2) 1.5.1
   arts.31, 46 .... 1.5.1
   First Protocol
      art.1 .... 1.5.4, 2.6
      arts.1–3 .... 1.5.2
   Sixth Protocol
      arts.1, 2 .... 1.5.2

Abbreviations

ACRO	ACRO Criminal Records Office
AWRS	Alcohol Wholesaler Registration Scheme
BBFC	British Board of Film Classification
BECTU	Broadcasting, Entertainment, Communications and Theatre Union
BID	business improvement district
CIA	cumulative impact assessment
CIEH	Chartered Institute of Environmental Health
DBS	Disclosure and Barring Service
ECHR	European Convention on Human Rights
EEA	European Economic Area
EMRO	early morning alcohol restriction order
HMRC	HM Revenue and Customs
HSE	Health and Safety Executive
HVVDs	high volume vertical drinking establishments
IOA	Institute of Acoustics
LACORS	Local Authorities Coordinators of Regulatory Services
NPCC	National Police Chiefs' Council
PASS	Proof of Age Standards Scheme
PCC	Police and Crime Commissioner
PND	penalty notice for disorder
PSPO	public spaces protection order
SIA	Security Industry Authority
URN	Unique Registration Number

CHAPTER 1

Introduction

1.1 INTRODUCTION

The Licensing Act 2003 was the culmination of a review of licensing law and procedure which was started in the late 1990s and introduced radical changes to licensing practices and procedures. The Act came fully into force on 24 November 2005.

The Act establishes a single integrated scheme for licensing premises which are used for the supply of alcohol, to provide regulated entertainment or to provide late night refreshment. Permission to carry on one or more of these activities is contained in a single authorisation, which will either be a 'premises licence', a 'club premises certificate' in the case of a qualifying club, or a 'temporary event notice' in the case of temporary licensable activities.

1.2 BACKGROUND

In April 2000, the Government published a White Paper entitled *Time for Reform: Proposals for the Modernisation of Our Licensing Laws* (Cm 4696, 2000). This set out the Government's proposals for modernising and integrating the alcohol, public entertainment, theatre, cinema, night café and late night refreshment house licensing schemes in England and Wales. The key aims of the Government's proposals were to reduce crime and disorder, to encourage tourism, to reduce alcohol misuse and to encourage the self-sufficiency of rural communities.

The Home Secretary in his foreword to the White Paper said:

> The current alcohol licensing system is an amalgam of 19th century legislation, intended to suppress drunkenness and disorder, and later additions. The law is complex, and involves a great deal of unnecessary red tape for business. We owe the magistrates and the police a large debt of gratitude for doing their best to make the system work; but it has been impossible to prevent inconsistencies and arbitrary decisions from arising. At the same time, there are too few effective sanctions against premises attract-

ing trouble. The rules governing the admission of children to licensed premises are obscure and deeply confusing. The controls on under-age 'off sales' are inadequate. It is also difficult to find in the present arrangements for licensing the sale of alcohol any real accountability to local residents whose lives are fundamentally affected by the decisions taken. The time has come to develop a better system.

There is a parallel and separate system of public entertainment licensing, under which local authorities issue licences for premises that may or may not also have a liquor licence. These laws too are complex and riddled with anomalies. The intersection of the two licensing systems imposes unnecessary costs and burdens on business.

To complete the picture we are proposing to reform the regulation of late night refreshment services (night cafes) which are subject to yet another separate licensing system, also complex and out of date. Licensing here is meant to prevent disorder and unreasonable disturbance to residents in the neighbourhood, and needs to be refocused on these key issues.

Our overall aim is to bring about reform which assures the safety of the public, better protects children and safeguards all against crime, disorder and disturbance; the decisions we make on these issues will in turn help to shape the future of our villages, towns and cities.

1.3 THE LICENSING ACT 2003

The Act introduced a unified system to regulate licensable activities. These are the sale and supply of alcohol, the provision of regulated entertainment and the provision of late night refreshment.

The Act is divided into the following nine parts:

- Part 1 – licensable activities;
- Part 2 – licensing authorities;
- Part 3 – premises licences;
- Part 4 – clubs;
- Part 5 – permitted temporary activities;
- Part 6 – personal licences;
- Part 7 – offences;
- Part 8 – closure of premises;
- Part 9 – miscellaneous and supplementary.

The policy behind the new system of licensing for licensable activities is to promote four licensing objectives:

- the prevention of crime and disorder;
- public safety;
- the prevention of public nuisance; and
- the protection of children from harm.

The system of licensing is achieved via the provision of authorisations through personal licences, premises licences, club premises certificates and temporary event notices.

1.4 OVERVIEW OF THE ACT

1.4.1 Licensing authorities

Authorisations to carry on licensable activities are granted by licensing authorities. With minor exceptions, these will be the local authority for the area in which the premises are situated or, in the case of personal licences, in which the applicant is normally resident.

The Act provides procedures for regulating the discharge by the licensing authority of its functions. Authorities are required to publish a licensing policy at least every five years following consultation.

1.4.2 Personal licences

A personal licence authorises an individual to sell or supply alcohol, or authorises the sale or supply of alcohol, for consumption on or off premises for which a premises licence is in force for the carrying on of that activity. In order to obtain a personal licence a person must be aged 18 or over, be entitled to work in the United Kingdom, possess a recognised licensing qualification, not had a personal licence forfeited within the previous five years and have not been convicted of a relevant offence or a foreign offence or required to pay an immigration penalty.

Where a person has been convicted of a relevant offence or foreign offence, following notification to the chief officer of police and consideration of any objections from the police the licensing authority must grant a personal licence unless it considers that doing so would undermine the crime prevention objective. Where a person has been given an immigration penalty notice, following notification to the Secretary of State (through Home Office Immigration Enforcement) and consideration of any objections from the Secretary of State, the licensing authority must grant a personal licence unless it considers that doing so would undermine the prevention of illegal working in licensed premises.

A personal licence lasts indefinitely.

1.4.3 Premises licences

A premises licence authorises the licence holder to use premises for licensable activities. The premises licence contains various information including the operating conditions which regulate the use of the premises for licensable activities in line with the licensing objectives.

A premises licence has effect until it is revoked or surrendered. It is otherwise not time limited unless the applicant has requested that it be granted only for a limited period.

Representations concerning the promotion of the licensing objectives may be made about an application for the grant of a premises licence, for example by local residents and businesses, the police, the fire and rescue authority and public bodies with responsibility for environmental health. Once a premises licence has been granted, these persons and bodies may seek a review of the licence and its attached conditions.

1.4.4 Club premises certificates

A club premises certificate authorises a qualifying club to use club premises for qualifying club activities. Qualifying club activities are the supply of alcohol by or on behalf of a club to a member of the club, the sale by retail of alcohol by or on behalf of a club to a guest of a member for consumption on the premises and the provision of regulated entertainment by or on behalf of a club for its members and guests.

As with premises licences the right to make representations on the application for a club premises certificate is given to a range of persons and bodies.

1.4.5 Temporary event notices

The Act also provides arrangements for the carrying on of licensable activities at temporary events with fewer than 500 people attending. These arrangements are based on the organiser of the event notifying the licensing authority about the event and an acknowledgement by that authority of the notification.

1.4.6 Enforcement

On a review of a premises licence or a club premises certificate a licensing authority may suspend or revoke the licence or certificate, exclude specific licensable activities from the licence or certificate or modify operating conditions attaching to the licence or certificate. These powers must be exercised with a view to promoting the licensing objectives.

The Act also gives the police powers to close licensed premises where there is disorderly behaviour and excessive noise.

1.4.7 Offences

The Act contains a range of offences, inspection powers and enforcement provisions.

1.5 HUMAN RIGHTS AND LICENSING

1.5.1 Introduction

The Human Rights Act 1998 came into force on 2 October 2000 and incorporated parts of the European Convention on Human Rights (ECHR) into English law. It gives further effect to the 'Convention rights'. This effect is twofold. First, existing and future legislation must be interpreted in a way which is compatible with the Convention rights (s.3(1)). Secondly, it is unlawful for any public authority to act in a way which is incompatible with a Convention right (s.6(1)).

A 'public authority' includes a court or tribunal, and any person certain of whose functions are of a public nature (s.6(3)). This will include local authorities acting as licensing authorities under the Licensing Act 2003 and they must therefore act compatibly with Convention rights when exercising their licensing functions. In addition, magistrates' courts hearing appeals under the Act and chief officers of police exercising their functions under the Act must also act compatibly with Convention rights.

It will not be unlawful if a public authority cannot act compatibly because of either primary legislation or provisions made under primary legislation that cannot be read or given effect in a way that is compatible (s.6(2)). A person who claims that a public authority has acted, or proposes to act, unlawfully may bring proceedings against the authority for breach of its statutory duty in s.6, or rely on the Convention right or rights concerned in any legal proceedings, provided he is, or would be, a victim of the unlawful act (s.7(1)). If the court decides that the act or proposed act is, or would be, unlawful it may grant such relief or remedy, or make such order, within its powers as it considers just and appropriate (s.8).

Section 2(1) indicates that a court or tribunal, when deciding a question which has arisen in connection with a Convention right, must take into account any:

- judgment, decision, declaration or advisory opinion of the European Court of Human Rights;
- opinion of the European Commission of Human Rights given in a report adopted under art.31 of the Convention as to whether there has been a violation of Convention rights;
- decision of the European Commission of Human Rights in connection with arts.26 or 27(2) of the Convention as to the admissibility of petitions claiming a violation of Convention rights; and
- decision of the Committee of Ministers taken under art.46 of the Convention, whenever made or given, so far as, in the opinion of the court or tribunal, it is relevant to the proceedings in which that question has arisen.

1.5.2 Convention rights

Section 1(1) provides that Convention rights are the rights and fundamental freedoms set out in:

- arts.2–12 and 14 of the Convention;
- arts.1–3 of the First Protocol; and
- arts.1 and 2 of the Sixth Protocol,

as read with arts.16–18 of the Convention. The Convention rights which have relevance to licensing law are:

- art.6 – the right to a fair trial;
- art.1 of the First Protocol – protection of property;
- art.8 – protection of private and family life; and
- art.14 – freedom from discrimination.

1.5.3 The right to a fair trial

Article 6(1) provides that:

> In the determination of his civil rights and obligations or of any criminal charge against him, everyone is entitled to a fair and public hearing within a reasonable time by an independent and impartial tribunal established by law. Judgment shall be pronounced publicly but the press and public may be excluded from all or part of the trial in the interest of morals, public order or national security in a democratic society, where the interests of juveniles or the protection of the private life of the parties so require, or to the extent strictly necessary in the opinion of the court in special circumstances where publicity would prejudice the interests of justice.

There will be a determination of a civil right where there is a dispute over a civil right (*James* v. *United Kingdom* (A/98) (1986) 8 EHRR 123).

The rights of a person involved in licensable activities under the Act will be 'civil rights' under art.6(1) (*Tre Traktorer AB* v. *Sweden* (A/159) (1991) 13 EHRR 309). This was confirmed by the Joint Committee on Human Rights in its Fourth Report on the Licensing Bill at para.7:

> As the rights of those in possession of property, and perhaps those entertainers whose freedom of expression would be limited, are civil rights within the meaning of ECHR Article 6.1, the licensing procedures would have to be compatible with the right to a fair hearing by an independent and impartial tribunal under that Article.

Applicants

Applicants for an authorisation under the Act have the right to have their applications determined in a manner compatible with art.6(1). This was confirmed in relation to an application for an on-licence under the Licensing Act 1964 in *R. (on the application of Chief Constable of Lancashire)* v. *Preston Crown Court* [2001] EWHC Admin 928; [2002] 1 WLR 1332. In this case, the right to apply for an on-licence was within 'civil rights and obligations' as it related to the applicant's right to make a living and pursue commercial activity. As authorisations under the Act also relate to commercial activity, they must be determined in a way which is compatible with art.6(1).

An applicant must have an opportunity to put his case, and there must be 'equality of arms'. In *Dombo Beheer BV* v. *Netherlands* (A/274-A) (1994) 18 EHRR 213, the European Court of Human Rights stated at para.33 that:

'equality of arms' implies that each party must be afforded a reasonable opportunity to present his case – including his evidence – under conditions that do not place him at a substantial disadvantage *vis-à-vis* his opponent.

The Licensing Act 2003 (Hearings) Regulations 2005, SI 2005/44 ('Hearings Regulations'), reg.8(2) provides that a party to a hearing must request permission for any other person, other than someone representing him, to appear and he must give an indication of how that person will assist the licensing authority. Regulation 23 requires that a hearing take the form of a discussion led by the licensing authority and permits cross-examination only if the licensing authority considers it necessary. A refusal of permission may well infringe art.6(1). In *R. (on the application of Hope & Glory Public House Ltd)* v. *City of Westminster Magistrates' Court* [2011] EWCA Civ 31; [2011] 3 All ER 579, the Court of Appeal agreed that the form of appeal provided for by the Act amply satisfies the requirements of art.6.

Independent and impartial tribunal

Under art.6(1) the tribunal must be 'independent and impartial'. A body carrying out administrative functions may be a tribunal for the purposes of art.6(1). A local authority exercising licensing functions will be exercising administrative functions together with a quasi-judicial function and will therefore be a tribunal for the purposes of art.6(1).

In order to be independent, the tribunal must be independent of the parties to the dispute and also independent of the executive. A local authority is part of the executive and therefore not independent. However, where the tribunal is not independent, art.6(1) will be satisfied if there is a right of appeal to a body which is an independent tribunal (*R. (on the application of Holding & Barnes Plc)* v. *Secretary of State for the Environment, Transport and the Regions* [2001] UKHL 23; [2003] 2 AC 295). The Act provides that there is a right of appeal to the magistrates' court and a further right of appeal to the High Court. This will be sufficient to comply with art.6(1).

The tribunal must also be 'impartial'. This means that there must not be any bias on the part of any member of the tribunal and that there must be no doubt as to the tribunal's impartiality. The first of these requirements is subjective while the other is objective. The approach which will be taken was laid down by the House of Lords in *Porter* v. *Magill* [2001] UKHL 67; [2002] 2 AC 357 at [102] as follows:

The court must first ascertain all the circumstances which have a bearing on the suggestion that the judge was biased. It must then ask whether those circumstances would lead a fair-minded and informed observer to conclude that there was a real possibility, or a real danger, the two being the same, that the tribunal was biased.

In relation to the Act, bias may arise where a member of the licensing committee is a councillor for the ward in which the particular premises are situated and he or she makes representations on behalf of a person living in the ward.

A local authority must promote and maintain high standards of conduct by members and co-opted members of the authority (Localism Act 2011, s.27(1)). In discharging its duty, a local authority must, in particular, adopt a code dealing with the conduct that is expected of members and co-opted members of the authority when they are acting in that capacity. Licensing committee members, representing others or acting in their own right, would need to consider carefully at a committee meeting whether they had a prejudicial interest in any matter affecting the licence or certificate of the premises in question which would require them to withdraw from the meeting when that matter is considered (e.g. where a councillor has made representations in his capacity as an elected member of the licensing authority). In addition, a member with a prejudicial interest in a matter should not seek to influence improperly a decision on the licence or certificate in any other way.

1.5.4   Protection of property

Article 1 of the First Protocol to the European Convention of Human Rights provides:

> Every natural or legal person is entitled to the peaceful enjoyment of his possessions. No one shall be deprived of his possessions except in the public interest and subject to the conditions provided for by law and by the general principles of international law.
>
> The preceding provisions shall not, however, in any way impair the right of a State to enforce such laws as it deems necessary to control the use of property in accordance with the general interest or to secure the payment of taxes or other contributions or penalties.

This is a qualified right and so the State may interfere with it in restricted circumstances. Before a State can interfere, the interference must be:

- prescribed by law;
- in pursuit of one or more specified legitimate aims; and
- no more than is necessary in a democratic society (the test for this is whether it is proportionate).

The right may be engaged where the State interferes with a person's possessions. In *Tre Traktorer AB* v. *Sweden* (A/159) (1991) 13 EHRR 309 the argument that a licence was not a possession was rejected. The European Court of Human Rights stated (at [53]):

> The Government argued that a licence to serve alcoholic beverages could not be considered to be a 'possession' within the meaning of Article 1 of the Protocol. This provision was therefore, in their opinion, not applicable to the case.
>
> Like the Commission, however, the Court takes the view that the economic interests connected with the running of *Le Cardinal* were 'possessions' for the purposes of Arti-

cle 1 of the Protocol. Indeed, the Court has already found that the maintenance of the licence was one of the principal conditions for the carrying on of the applicant company's business, and that its withdrawal had adverse effects on the goodwill and value of the restaurant.

Such withdrawal thus constitutes, in the circumstances of the case, an interference with TTA's right to the 'peaceful enjoyment of [its] possessions'.

While the court did not conclude that a licence was a possession, it did decide that economic interests in the property in respect of which a licence is held can amount to 'possessions'. Thus economic interests connected with the running of premises under a premises licence or under a club premises certificate should be regarded as 'possessions'. The State will therefore interfere with a property right if the licence or certificate is revoked or varied. In the case of an application for a new licence or certificate, a refusal will not be an interference with a property right as there is no economic interest in existence connected with the licence.

Article 1 distinguishes between a 'deprivation' of possessions and 'control' of them. In *Sporrong & Lonnroth* v. *Sweden* (A/52) (1983) 5 EHRR 35, the European Court of Human Rights stated (at [61]) that art.1:

comprises three distinct rules. The first rule, which is of a general nature, enounces the principle of peaceful enjoyment of property; it is set out in the first sentence of the first paragraph. The second rule covers deprivation of possessions and subjects it to certain conditions; it appears in the second sentence of the same paragraph. The third rule recognises that the States are entitled, amongst other things, to control the use of property in accordance with the general interest, by enforcing such laws as they deem necessary for the purpose; it is contained in the second paragraph.

The Court must determine, before considering whether the first rule was complied with, whether the last two are applicable.

When applying the first rule the court went on to say (at [69]):

the Court must determine whether a fair balance was struck between the demands of the general interest of the community and the requirements of the protection of the individual's fundamental rights. The search for this balance is inherent in the whole of the Convention and is also reflected in the structure of Article 1.

Once some form of interference has been established the court will apply the following three-part test in order to decide whether the interference is justified:

- it will first consider whether the interference is compatible with the rule of law and is sufficiently accessible and foreseeable;
- it will then consider whether the interference is in the public interest; and
- finally it will consider whether the interference strikes a fair balance between the general interests of the community and the protection of the individual's rights.

Controlling the use of property under the Act by granting premises licences and club premises certificates will advance the general interests of the community, and can be justified by the four licensing objectives contained in the Act (see **1.3**).

1.5.5 Right to respect for private and family life

Article 8 provides that:

1. Everyone has the right to respect for his private and family life, his home and his correspondence.
2. There shall be no interference by a public authority with the exercise of this right except such as is in accordance with the law and is necessary in a democratic society in the interests of national security, public safety or the economic well-being of the country, for the prevention of disorder or crime, for the protection of health or morals or for the protection of the rights and freedoms of others.

Article 8 protects private and family life from interference by the State. In relation to licensing, interference could arise in the exercise of the powers to inspect and search premises where the premises in question are also someone's home. In such a situation, art.8 will be engaged.

Article 8 also protects people's enjoyment of the amenities of their home, for example against intrusion from noise. In *Moreno Gomez* v. *Spain* (4143/02) (2005) 41 EHRR 40, the European Court of Human Rights held that there had been a violation of art.8 where the local authority had failed to take action to deal with night-time disturbances and noise pollution caused by night clubs near the applicant's home.

1.5.6 Prohibition of discrimination

Article 14 provides:

The enjoyment of the rights and freedoms set forth in this Convention shall be secured without discrimination on any ground such as sex, race, colour, language, religion, political or other opinion, national or social origin, association with a national minority, property, birth or other status.

Article 14 does not create an independent right and it operates only to prevent discrimination in respect of other Convention rights. Concern was raised by the Joint Committee on Human Rights when it was considering the Licensing Bill about the exemption in Sched.1, para.9 for the provision of entertainment or entertainment facilities for the purposes of, or for purposes incidental to, a religious meeting or service, or at a place of public worship. The Committee in its Fifteenth Report of Session 2002-03 at para.5.1 said that:

In our Twelfth Report, we drew the attention of each House to our view that the proposals for exempting places used for public worship from the requirements of the licensing regime, and allowing certain other places associated with places of public worship to obtain licenses without paying the usual fee, might be regarded as discriminating against the occupiers and users of purely secular premises. We were concerned that these exemptions might give rise to a significant risk of violating the right to be free of discrimination under ECHR Article 14, taken together with ECHR Articles 9 (right to freedom of religion, conscience and belief) and 10 (freedom of expression). We were also concerned that there was a risk that the exemptions might– '... leave a patchwork of different licensing requirements without a coherent rationale, calling in question the existence of a pressing social need for the restriction on freedom of expression through a licensing regime for public entertainment, and so undermining the Government's claim that such a licensing regime is a justifiable interference with the right to freedom of expression under ECHR Article 10.2'.

The Government's response was summarised in paras.5.3 and 5.4 as follows:

5.3 ... So far as is relevant to this issue, the Department pointed out that the exemption for places of public religious worship from the requirements of entertainment licensing law would benefit people who were using the premises for the enjoyment of secular entertainment there. Those people might be of any religious affiliation or of none. In addition, the exemption for religious venues is a recognition of the– '... distinct pastoral role in the community played by many of the faiths and the wider responsibility that, for example, the church has in bringing the community together'.

5.4 The Minister also drew attention to the central role of the churches to the development of music in this country, particularly because churches provide venues large enough for the performance of many pieces of music requiring large forces. For these reasons, the Government argued that Articles 9, 10 and 14 are not engaged, but that, if they were engaged, there is a rational and objective justification for the exemption which does not call into question the pressing social need to regulate public entertainment in general.

CHAPTER 2

Licensing authorities

2.1 INTRODUCTION

The Act has transferred responsibility for alcohol licensing from the magistrates' courts to local authorities. This has brought the licensing regimes for alcohol, public entertainment, cinemas, theatres, late night refreshment and night cafés under the responsibility of a single authority. The Government in its White Paper entitled *Time for Reform: Proposals for the Modernisation of Our Licensing Laws* (Cm 4696, 2000) set out in para.123 the following reasons for giving local authorities these responsibilities:

- accountability: we strongly believe that the licensing authority should be accountable to local residents whose lives are fundamentally affected by the decisions taken.
- accessibility: many local residents may be inhibited by court processes, and would be more willing to seek to influence decisions if in the hands of local councillors.
- crime and disorder: local authorities now have a leading statutory role in preventing local crime and disorder, and the link between alcohol and crime persuasively argues for them to have a similar lead on licensing.

2.2 LICENSING AUTHORITIES

Section 3(1) provides that the following are a 'licensing authority':

- the council of a district in England;
- the council of a county in England in which there are no district councils;
- the council of a county or county borough in Wales;
- the council of a London borough;
- the Common Council of the City of London;
- the Sub-Treasurer of the Inner Temple;
- the Under-Treasurer of the Middle Temple; and
- the Council of the Isles of Scilly.

For the purposes of the Act, a licensing authority's area is the area for which the authority acts (s.3(2)).

2.3 THE GENERAL DUTIES OF LICENSING AUTHORITIES

Section 4(1) provides that when carrying out its functions under the Act a licensing authority must do so with a view to promoting the four licensing objectives, which are:

- the prevention of crime and disorder;
- public safety;
- the prevention of public nuisance; and
- the protection of children from harm.

There is no requirement that a licensing authority must achieve the licensing objectives, but it must carry out its functions under the Act with a view to promoting them.

In carrying out its licensing functions a licensing authority must also have regard to its statement of licensing policy published under s.5 and any guidance issued by the Secretary of State under s.182 (s.4(3)) ('the Guidance') (see **2.12**).

In relation to the prevention of crime and disorder, the word 'and' is disjunctive so that the licensing objectives are the prevention of crime and/or the prevention of disorder (*Blackpool Council Licensing Authority* v. *Howitt* [2008] EWHC 3300 (Admin); [2009] 4 All ER 154).

The public safety objective was considered in *The Porky Pint Ltd* v. *Stockton on Tees BC* [2023] EWHC 128 (Admin); [2023] 1 WLR 2735 where the court held that the licensing objectives were not restricted to 'alcohol-related' matters, and the fact that 'public health' was not a licensing objective did not, on its ordinary and natural meaning, exclude it from consideration of whether the public safety objective was engaged and relevant.

In *Carmarthenshire CC* v. *Llanelli Magistrates' Court* [2009] EWHC 3016 (Admin); [2010] All ER (D) 209 (Apr), the court made a declaration that, on an appeal from a decision of a local authority relating to the review of a premises licence, magistrates should take such steps as they consider necessary for the promotion of the licensing objectives.

2.4 STATEMENT OF LICENSING POLICY

Section 5 provides that a licensing authority must determine its policy with respect to the exercise of its licensing functions at least every five years. Before the start of a five-year period it must publish a statement of licensing policy. This policy is referred to in the Act as a 'licensing statement'. 'Five-year period' means either the period of five years ending with 6 January 2016 and each subsequent period of five years, or, where a licensing authority has replaced its policy during a five-year period, the period of five years to which the most recently published statement relates, and each subsequent period of five years (s.5(8)). So where a licensing authority reviews its policy during the five-year period and publishes a revised policy, a new five-year period starts on the date it is published. A local authority will publish its licensing policy on its website.

Before determining its policy for a five-year period, a licensing authority must, under s.5(3), consult the following:

- the chief officer of police for the licensing authority's area;
- the fire and rescue authority for its area;
- each Local Health Board for an area any part of which is in the licensing authority's area; there are seven local health boards in Wales and each one is responsible for planning and delivering NHS services (such as dental, optical, pharmacy and mental health services) within its area as well as being responsible for improving physical and mental health outcomes, promoting well-being, reducing health inequalities across their population and commissioning services from other organisations to meet the needs of their residents;
- each local authority in England whose public health functions within the meaning of the National Health Service Act 2006 are exercisable in respect of an area any part of which is in the licensing authority's area;
- such persons as the licensing authority considers to be representative of holders of premises licences issued by that authority, for example the Federation of Licensed Victuallers Associations (for public houses), the UK Cinema Association (for film exhibitions), UK Theatre (for theatres);
- such persons as the licensing authority considers to be representative of holders of club premises certificates issued by that authority, for example the Working Men's Club and Institute Union;
- such persons as the licensing authority considers to be representative of holders of personal licences issued by that authority, for example a trade association or a professional body; and
- such other persons as the licensing authority considers to be representative of businesses and residents in its area, for example a local chamber of commerce or a residents' association.

The Guidance at para.14.5 provides:

> The views of all these persons or bodies should be given appropriate weight when the policy is determined. It is recognised that in some areas, it may be difficult to identify persons or bodies that represent all parts of industry affected by the provisions of the 2003 Act, but licensing authorities must make reasonable efforts to do so. Licensing authorities should note that the terms of the 2003 Act do not prevent them consulting other bodies or persons.

A licensing authority is not precluded from consulting with other persons or bodies in addition to those it is required to consult under s.5(3), so for example certain authorities may consider it essential to consult the local Community Safety Partnership, British Transport Police, local Accident and Emergency Departments, bodies representing consumers, local police consultative groups or those charged locally with the promotion of tourism. They may also consider it valuable to consult local performers, performers' unions (such as the Musicians' Union and Equity) and entertainers involved in the cultural life of the local community.

Subject to the statutory requirements, para.14.6 of the Guidance makes it clear that it is for each licensing authority to decide the extent of its consultation, and whether any particular person or body is representative. Paragraph 14.6 goes on to state that while it is clearly good practice to consult widely, this may not always be necessary or appropriate (for example, where a licensing authority has recently carried out a comprehensive consultation in relation to a revision to its policy made within five years of a full revision to it). As such, it may decide on a simple consultation with those persons listed. Paragraph 14.7 provides that licensing authorities should consider very carefully whether a full consultation is appropriate as a limited consultation may not allow all persons sufficient opportunity to comment on and influence local policy (for example, where an earlier consultation was limited to a particular part of the policy, such as a proposal to introduce a cumulative impact policy).

While a licensing authority is free to decide the full extent of its consultation beyond those it is required to consult, the Guidance at para.14.8 issues the following warning:

> Fee levels are intended to provide full cost recovery of all licensing functions including the preparation and publication of a statement of licensing policy, but this will be based on the statutory requirements. Where licensing authorities exceed these requirements, they will have to absorb those costs themselves.

During each five-year period a licensing authority must keep its licensing policy in respect of that period under review and make any revisions it considers appropriate. Before making a revision, the licensing authority must carry out a consultation exercise. If a revision is made, the licensing authority must publish a statement of the revision or the revised licensing statement.

2.5 THE CONTENTS OF A STATEMENT OF LICENSING POLICY

The Guidance recommends that a licensing policy should begin by stating the four licensing objectives which the licensing policy should promote (para.14.9). While a licensing policy may set out a general approach to making licensing decisions, it must not ignore or be inconsistent with provisions in the Act, for example, it must not undermine the right of any person to apply under the terms of the Act for a variety of permissions and to have any such application considered on its individual merits (para.14.10). Similarly, no policy should override the right of any person to make representations on an application or to seek a review of a licence or certificate where provision has been made for them to do so in the Act (para.14.11).

A licensing policy should make it clear that:

1. Licensing is about regulating licensable activities on licensed premises, by qualifying clubs and at temporary events within the terms of the Act, and that the conditions attached to various authorisations will be focused on matters which are within the control of individual licence holders and others with relevant authorisations, i.e. the premises and its vicinity (para.14.12).

2. Licensing law is not the primary mechanism for the general control of nuisance and antisocial behaviour by individuals once they are away from the licensed premises and, therefore, beyond the direct control of the individual, club or business holding the licence, certificate or authorisation concerned but nonetheless, it is a key aspect of such control and licensing law will always be part of a holistic approach to the management of the evening and night-time economy in town and city centres (para.14.13).

In addition, a licensing policy should consider:

- licence conditions;
- enforcement;
- entertainment provision;
- the cumulative impact of licensed premises;
- public spaces protection orders;
- licensing hours;
- children;
- integration with other strategies;
- planning and building control;
- promotion of equality; and
- administration, exercise and delegation of functions.

2.5.1 Licence conditions

A licensing policy should, according to paras.14.14 and 14.15 of the Guidance, reflect the general principles regarding licence conditions (see **Chapter 11**) and include a firm commitment to avoid attaching conditions that duplicate other regulatory regimes as far as possible.

2.5.2 Enforcement

A licensing policy should deal with enforcement issues, and paras.14.16 and 14.17 of the Guidance provide:

14.16 The Government recommends that licensing authorities should establish and set out joint enforcement protocols with the local police and the other authorities and describe them in their statement of policy. This will clarify the division of responsibilities for licence holders and applicants, and assists enforcement and other authorities to deploy resources more efficiently.

14.17 In particular, these protocols should also provide for the targeting of agreed problem and high-risk premises which require greater attention, while providing a lighter touch for low risk premises or those that are well run. In some local authority areas, the limited validity of public entertainment, theatre, cinema, night café and late night refreshment house licences has in the past led to a culture of annual inspections regardless of whether the assessed risks make such inspections necessary. The 2003 Act does not require inspections to take place save at the discretion of those charged with this role. Principles of risk assessment and targeted inspection (in line with the Regulators' Code) should prevail and, for example, inspections should not be undertaken routinely but when and if they are judged necessary. This should ensure that resources are used efficiently and for example, are more effectively concentrated on problem premises. Licensing authorities should also remind operators of licensed premises that it is incumbent on them to provide appropriate training for their staff to ensure the promotion of the licensing objectives.

The Regulators' Code came into statutory effect on 6 April 2014 under the Legislative and Regulatory Reform Act 2006 and provides a clear, flexible and principles-based framework for how regulators should engage with those they regulate (see further **www.gov.uk/government/publications/regulators-code**).

2.5.3 Entertainment provision

A licensing policy should deal with entertainment provision, and para.14.18 of the Guidance provides:

Statements of licensing policy should set out the extent to which the licensing authority intends to facilitate a broad range of entertainment provision for enjoyment by a wide cross-section of the public. Statements of licensing policy should address what balance is to be struck between promoting the provision of entertainment and addressing concerns relevant to the licensing objectives. Licensing authorities should be conscious that licensing policy may inadvertently deter live music by imposing indirect costs of a disproportionate nature, for example a blanket policy that any pub providing live music entertainment must have door supervisors.

2.5.4 The cumulative impact of licensed premises

Paragraph 14.19 of the Guidance provides:

There can be confusion about the difference between the 'need' for premises and the 'cumulative impact' of premises on the licensing objectives, for example, on crime and disorder. 'Need' concerns the commercial demand for another pub or restaurant or hotel and is a matter for the planning authority and for the market. This is not a matter for a licensing authority in discharging its licensing functions or for its statement of licensing policy.

What is cumulative impact?

The Guidance provides:

14.20 The concept of 'Cumulative impact' has been described within this guidance and used by licensing authorities within their statements of licensing policy since the commencement of the 2003 Act. 'Cumulative impact assessments' were introduced in the 2003 Act by the Policing and Crime Act 2017, with effect from 6 April 2018. Cumulative impact is the potential impact on the promotion of the licensing objectives of a number of licensed premises concentrated in one area.

14.21 In some areas where the number, type or density of licensed premises, such as those selling alcohol or providing late night refreshment, is high or exceptional, serious problems of nuisance and disorder may arise outside or some distance from those premises. Such problems generally occur as a result of large numbers of drinkers being concentrated in an area, for example when leaving premises at peak times or when queuing at fast food outlets or for public transport.

14.22 Queuing in itself may lead to conflict, disorder and anti-social behaviour. More-over, large concentrations of people may also attract criminal activities such as drug dealing, pick pocketing and street robbery. Local services such as public transport, public lavatory provision and street cleaning may not be able to meet the demand posed by such concentrations of drinkers leading to issues such as street fouling, littering, traffic and public nuisance caused by concentrations of people who cannot be effectively dispersed quickly.

14.23 Variable licensing hours may facilitate a more gradual dispersal of customers from premises. However, in some cases, the impact on surrounding areas of the behaviour of the customers of all premises taken together will be greater than the impact of customers of individual premises. These conditions are more likely to arise in town and city centres, but may also arise in other urban centres and the suburbs, for example on smaller high streets with high concentrations of licensed premises.

Cumulative impact assessments

The Guidance provides:

14.24 A cumulative impact assessment (CIA) may be published by a licensing author-ity to help it to limit the number or types of licence applications granted in areas where there is evidence to show that the number or density of licensed premises in the area is having a cumulative impact and leading to problems which are undermining the licensing objectives. CIAs relate to applications for new pre-mises licences and club premises certificates and applications to vary existing premises licences and club premises certificates in a specified area.

14.25 Section 5A of the 2003 Act sets out what a licensing authority needs to do in order to publish a CIA and review it, including the requirement to consult with the persons listed in section 5(3) of the 2003 Act. The 2003 Act does not stipu-late how the CIA should be used once published, because the requirements for determining applications for new licences or variations are the same in areas with a CIA as they are elsewhere, as set out in sections 18, 35, 72 and 85 of the Act. However, any CIA published by a licensing authority must be summarised in its statement of licensing policy. Under section 5(6D) a licensing authority must also have regard to any CIA it has published when determining or revising its statement of licensing policy.

14.26 The CIA must include a statement saying that the licensing authority considers that the number of premises licences and/or club premises certificates in one or more parts of the area described is such that it is likely that granting further licences would be inconsistent with the authority's duty to promote the licensing objectives. As part of the publication a licensing authority must set out the evidential basis for its opinion.

14.27 CIAs may relate to premises licensed to carry on any licensable activity, including the sale of alcohol for consumption on or off the premises, and the provision of late night refreshment. This includes late night refreshment providers which are not licensed to sell alcohol. A CIA may relate to all premises licences and club premises certificates in the area described in the assessment or parts thereof, or only to premises of a particular kind described in the assessment. For example, it may be appropriate for the licensing authority to only include off-licences or nightclubs within the scope of its assessment. The licensing authority must make clear, when publishing its CIA, which premises types it applies to. CIAs do not apply to TENs; however it is open to the police and environmental health authority (as relevant persons) to refer to evidence published within a CIA when objecting to a TEN.

14.28 While the evidence underpinning the publication of a CIA should generally be suitable as the basis for a decision to refuse an application or impose conditions, it does not change the fundamental way that decisions are made under the 2003 Act. Each decision in an area subject to a CIA therefore still needs to be made on a case-by-case basis and with a view to what is appropriate for the promotion of the licensing objectives. Importantly, the publication of a CIA would not remove a licensing authority's discretion to grant applications for new licences or applications to vary existing licences, where the authority considers this to be appropriate in the light of the individual circumstances of the case.

Evidence of cumulative impact

A licensing authority must have an evidential basis for deciding to publish a cumulative impact assessment (CIA) (Guidance, para.14.29):

Local Community Safety Partnerships and responsible authorities, such as the police and the environmental health authority, may hold relevant information which would inform licensing authorities when establishing the evidence base for publishing a CIA. Evidence of cumulative impact on the promotion of the licensing objectives needs to relate to the relevant problems identified in the specific area to be covered by the CIA. Information which licensing authorities may be able to draw on includes:

- local crime and disorder statistics, including statistics on specific types of crime and crime hotspots;
- statistics on local anti-social behaviour offences;
- health-related statistics such as alcohol-related emergency attendances and hospital admissions;
- environmental health complaints, particularly in relation to litter and noise;
- complaints recorded by the local authority, which may include complaints raised by local residents or residents' associations;
- residents' questionnaires;
- evidence from local and parish councillors; and
- evidence obtained through local consultation.

Paragraph 14.30 goes on to say:

The licensing authority may consider this evidence, alongside its own evidence as to the impact of licensable activities within its area, and consider in particular the times at which licensable activities are carried on. Information which may inform consideration of these issues includes:

- trends in licence applications, particularly trends in applications by types of premises and terminal hours;
- changes in terminal hours of premises;
- premises' capacities at different times of night and the expected concentrations of drinkers who will be expected to be leaving premises at different times.

Paragraphs 14.31, 14.32 and 14.33 of the Guidance provide:

14.31 Where existing information is insufficient or not readily available, but the licensing authority believes there are problems in its area resulting from the cumulative impact of licensed premises, it can consider conducting or commissioning a specific study to assess the position. This may involve conducting observations of the night-time economy to assess the extent of incidents relating to the promotion of the licensing objectives, such as incidences of criminal activity and anti-social behaviour, examples of public nuisance, specific issues such as underage drinking and the key times and locations at which these problems are occurring.

14.32 In order to identify the areas in which problems are occurring, information about specific incidents can be mapped and, where possible, a time analysis undertaken to identify the key areas and times at which there are specific issues.

14.33 After considering the available evidence and consulting those individuals and organisations listed in section 5(3) of the 2003 Act and any others, a licensing authority may be satisfied that it is appropriate to publish a CIA. The CIA should also be considered alongside local planning policy and other factors which may assist in mitigating the cumulative impact of licensed premises, as set out in paragraph 14.47.

Steps to publishing a cumulative impact assessment

The Guidance at para.14.34 sets out the following steps to be followed by a licensing authority when deciding whether to publish a CIA:

- Identify concern about crime and disorder; public safety; public nuisance; or protection of children from harm in a particular location.
- Consider whether there is good evidence that crime and disorder or nuisance are occurring, or whether there are activities which pose a threat to public safety or the protection of children from harm.
- If there is evidence that such problems are occurring, identify whether these problems are being caused by the customers of licensed premises, or that cumulative impact is imminent.
- Identify the boundaries of the area where problems are occurring (this can involve mapping where the problems occur and identifying specific streets or localities where such problems arise).
- Consult with those specified in section 5(3) of the 2003 Act. As with consultations in respect of the licensing policy statement as a whole, it is for each licensing

authority to determine the extent of the consultation it should undertake in respect of a CIA (subject to the statutory requirements).

- For the purposes of the consultation provide the persons specified in section 5(3) with the following information:

    – the reasons why it is considering publishing a CIA;
    – a general indication of the part or parts of its area which it is considering describing in the assessment;
    – whether it considers that the assessment will relate to all premises licence and club premises certificate applications and variation applications, or only to those of a particular kind described.

- Subject to the outcome of the consultation, include and publish details of the CIA, including the evidence in support of the assessment and the particular kinds of premises the assessment relates to. Licensing authorities are not restricted to using general terms such as on-trade, off-trade and refreshment providers, and can apply their own descriptions such as vertical-drinking bars and night clubs if appropriate.
- Summarise the licensing authority's opinion in light of the evidence of cumulative impact (or any revision to an existing opinion) in the licensing policy statement and explain within the policy statement how the authority has had regard to any CIAs it has published under section 5A. The summary within the licensing policy statement should include, but is not limited to: the nature of the problems identified and the evidence for such problems; the geographical extent of the area covered by the assessment; the types of premises described in the assessment; and the types of applications for which it would likely be inconsistent with the licensing authority's duty to promote the licensing objectives to grant.

Reviewing the cumulative impact assessment

Paragraphs 14.35–14.38 of the Guidance provide:

14.35 After publishing a CIA the licensing authority must, within three years, consider whether it remains of the opinion set out in the assessment. In order to decide whether it remains of this opinion it must again consult the persons listed in section 5(3). If having consulted with the statutory list of persons the licensing authority decides that it is no longer of the opinion set out in the CIA, it must publish a statement to that effect. The statement must make clear that any reference to the CIA in its licensing policy statement no longer applies. The licensing authority should remove any reference to the CIA within its licensing policy statement at the earliest opportunity.

14.36 If having consulted the licensing authority decides that it remains of the opinion set out in the assessment, it must revise the CIA to include a statement to that effect and set out the evidence as to why it remains of that opinion. It will be important for any evidence included in the revised CIA to be robust and relevant to the current problems described. This is likely to involve the collation of fresh or updated evidence of the kind described in the above section on evidence of cumulative impact. The licensing authority must also at this stage publish any other material change to the assessment. For example if the types of premises or area described in the assessment have changed due to a shift in the nature of the problems being experienced or where there is evidence of the emergence of a new type of problem.

14.37 In each case the three year period for reviewing a CIA begins with the original date of the publication of the CIA or the date that a CIA was last revised. Where a licensing policy statement as a whole is due for review, under the five year review period under section 5(4), and this occurs before the end of the three year CIA review period, licensing authorities may wish to use this as an opportunity to carry out a review of the evidence in support of the CIA. However, licensing authorities are free to carry out consultations and reviews of their CIAs (and/or licensing policy statements) at more regular intervals if they consider this to be appropriate.

14.38 As Cumulative Impact Policies were not part of the 2003 Act, there are no transitional provisions that apply to CIPs that were in place before 6 April 2018. However, any existing CIPs should be reviewed at the earliest practical opportunity to ensure they comply with the legislation. It is recommended that the review should take place within three years of the commencement of the legislation on CIAs or when the licensing policy statement is next due for review, whichever is sooner. This will ensure that any CIPs in place before the commencement of the provisions on CIAs adhere to the principles in the legislation (in particular concerning relevant evidence and consultation).

Effect of cumulative impact assessments

When publishing a CIA, a licensing authority is required to set out evidence of problems that are being caused or exacerbated by the cumulative impact of licensed premises in the area described. The evidence is used to justify the statement in the CIA that it is likely that granting further premises licences and/or club premises certificates in that area (limited to a kind described in the assessment), would be inconsistent with the authority's duty to promote the licensing objectives (Guidance, para.14.39).

The Guidance at paras.14.40–14.43 provides:

14.40 In publishing a CIA a licensing authority is setting down a strong statement of intent about its approach to considering applications for the grant or variation of premises licences or club premises certificates in the area described. Having published a CIA a licensing authority must have regard to the assessment when determining or revising its statement of licensing policy. It is therefore expected that, in respect of each relevant application in the area concerned, the licensing authority will be considering whether it is appropriate to make a representation to its committee as a responsible authority in its own right. The CIA does not, however, change the fundamental way that licensing decisions are made. It is therefore open to the licensing authority to grant an application where it considers it is appropriate and where the applicant can demonstrate in the operating schedule that they would not be adding to the cumulative impact. Applications in areas covered by a CIA should therefore give consideration to potential cumulative impact issues when setting out the steps that will be taken to promote the licensing objectives. Where relevant representations are received and a licensing authority decides to grant an application it will need to provide the applicant, the chief officer of police and all parties who made relevant representations with reasons for granting the application and this should include any reasons for departing from their own policy.

14.41 The CIA must also stress that it does not relieve responsible authorities (or any other persons) of the need to make relevant representations where they consider it appropriate to do so for the promotion of the licensing objectives. Anyone making a representation may base it on the evidence published in the CIA, or the fact that a CIA has been published. It remains incumbent on all responsible authorities and other persons to ensure that their representations can withstand the scrutiny to which they would be subject at a hearing. As with all licensing applications under the 2003 Act, if there are no representations, the licensing authority must grant the application in terms that are consistent with the operating schedule submitted.

14.42 The absence of a CIA does not prevent any responsible authority or other person making representations on an application for the grant or variation of a licence on the grounds that the premises will give rise to a negative cumulative impact on one or more of the licensing objectives, However, in each case it would be incumbent on the person making the representation to provide relevant evidence of cumulative impact.

14.43 As noted above, CIAs may apply to the impact of a concentration of any licensed premises, including those licensed for the sale of alcohol on or off the premises, and premises licensed to provide late night refreshment. When establishing its evidence base for publishing a CIA, licensing authorities should be considering the contribution to cumulative impact made by different types of premises within its area, in order to determine the appropriateness of including different types of licensed premises within the CIA.

Limitations on special policies relating to cumulative impact

A CIA should never be absolute and the Guidance at para.14.44 provides:

A CIA should never be absolute. Statements of licensing policy should always allow for the circumstances of each application to be considered properly and for applications that are unlikely to add to the cumulative impact on the licensing objectives to be granted. After receiving relevant representations in relation to a new application for or a variation of a licence or certificate, the licensing authority must consider whether it would be justified in departing from its CIA in the light of the individual circumstances of the case. The impact can be expected to be different for premises with different styles and characteristics. For example, while a large nightclub or high capacity public house might add to problems of cumulative impact, a small restaurant or a theatre may not. If the licensing authority decides that an application should be refused, it will still need to show that the grant of the application would undermine the promotion of one or more of the licensing objectives and that appropriate conditions would be ineffective in preventing the problems involved.

In addition, there are other limitations on the use of a CIA:

1. It should never be used as a ground for 'revoking an existing licence or certificate when representations are received about problems with those premises', and where the licensing authority has concerns about the effect of activities at premises between midnight and 6 am on the promotion of the licensing objectives in a specific area, it may introduce an early morning alcohol restriction order (EMRO) if there is sufficient evidence to do so (Guidance, para.14.45). The 'cumulative impact' on the promotion of the licensing objectives of a concentration of licensed premises should only

give rise to a relevant representation when an application for the grant or variation of a licence or certificate is being considered.

2.   It must not impose quotas based on either the number of premises or the capacity of those premises (Guidance, para.14.46). This is because quotas that indirectly have the effect of predetermining the outcome of any application would have no regard to the individual characteristics of the premises concerned.

Other mechanisms for controlling cumulative impact

A licensing policy should also indicate the other mechanisms both within and outside the licensing regime that are available for addressing problems caused by any customers behaving badly. The Guidance at para.14.47 suggests that these include:

- planning control;
- positive measures to create a safe and clean town centre environment in partnership with local businesses, transport operators and other departments of the local authority, including best practice schemes such as Best Bar None, Pubwatch or BIDs;
- Community Protection Notices;
- the provision of CCTV surveillance in town centres, taxi ranks, provision of public conveniences open late at night, street cleaning and litter patrols;
- powers of local authorities to designate parts of the local authority area as places where alcohol may not be consumed publicly;
- the confiscation of alcohol from adults and children in designated areas;
- police enforcement of the general law concerning disorder and antisocial behaviour, including the issuing of fixed penalty notices;
- prosecution for the offence of selling alcohol to a person who is drunk (or allowing such a sale);
- raising a contribution to policing the late night economy through the Late Night Levy; and
- Early Morning Alcohol Restriction Orders . . . .

Paragraph 4.48 of the Guidance goes on to state:

As part of its licensing policy statement, the licensing authority may also wish to consider the use of alternative approaches such as fixed closing times, staggered closing times and zoning. Such policy restrictions would need to be evidence-based and would be subject to the merits of each case in accordance with what is appropriate for the promotion of the licensing objectives. The licensing authority would be expected to justify the use of such measures as an appropriate means of managing problems in its area.

2.5.5   Public spaces protection order

A public spaces protection order (PSPO) is an order under the Anti-Social Behaviour, Crime and Policing Act 2014 which bans specific acts in a designated area. An order can be used to restrict the drinking of alcohol in a public place where this has or is likely to have a detrimental effect on the quality of life on those in the locality, be persistent or continuing in nature, and unreasonable.

The Guidance provides:

> 14.49 ... Where a local authority occupies or manages premises, or where premises are managed on its behalf, and it licenses that place for alcohol sales, the PSPO will not apply when the licence is being used for alcohol sales (or 30 minutes after), but the place will be subject to the PSPO at all other times. This allows local authorities to promote community events whilst still using a PSPO to tackle the problems of anti-social drinking.
>
> 14.50 It should be noted that when one part of a local authority seeks a premises licence of this kind from the licensing authority, the licensing committee and its officers must consider the matter from an entirely neutral standpoint. If relevant representations are made, for example, by local residents or the police, they must be considered fairly by the committee. Anyone making a representation that is genuinely aggrieved by a positive decision in favour of a local authority application by the licensing authority would be entitled to appeal to the magistrates' court and thereby receive an independent review of any decision.

2.5.6 Licensing hours

In relation to licensing hours, the Guidance at para.14.51 provides that:

> ... the Government acknowledges that different licensing approaches may be appropriate for the promotion of the licensing objectives in different areas. The 2003 Act gives the licensing authority power to make decisions regarding licensed opening hours as part of the implementation of its licensing policy statement and licensing authorities are best placed to make such decisions based on their local knowledge and in consultation with other responsible authorities. However, licensing authorities must always consider each application and must not impose predetermined licensed opening hours, without giving individual consideration to the merits of each application.

Paragraph 14.52 goes on to state:

> Statements of licensing policy should set out the licensing authority's approach regarding licensed opening hours and the strategy it considers appropriate for the promotion of the licensing objectives in its area. The statement of licensing policy should emphasise the consideration which will be given to the individual merits of an application. The Government recognises that licensed premises make an important contribution to our local communities, and has given councils a range of tools to effectively manage the different pressures that licensed premises can bring. In determining appropriate strategies around licensed opening hours, licensing authorities cannot seek to restrict the activities of licensed premises where it is not appropriate for the promotion of the licensing objectives to do so.

2.5.7 Children

The Guidance at para.14.56 provides that:

> The 2003 Act does not automatically permit unaccompanied children under the age of 18 to have free access to premises where the consumption of alcohol is not the exclusive or primary activity or to the same premises even if they are accompanied, or to

premises where the consumption of alcohol is not involved. Subject only to the provisions of the 2003 Act and any licence or certificate conditions, admission will always be at the discretion of those managing the premises. The 2003 Act includes no presumption of giving children access but equally, no presumption of preventing their access to licensed premises. Each application and the circumstances of individual premises must be considered on their own merits.

The Guidance at para.14.57 provides that a licensing policy should not:

seek to limit the access of children to any premises unless it is appropriate for the prevention of physical, moral or psychological harm to them ... It may not be possible for licensing policy statements to anticipate every issue of concern that could arise in respect of children in relation to individual premises and therefore the individual merits of each application should be considered in each case.

A licensing policy should make clear the range of alternatives which may be considered for limiting the access of children where that is appropriate for the prevention of harm to them (Guidance, para.14.58). The Guidance at para.2.33 provides that in addition to the mandatory condition regarding age verification, these can include:

- restrictions on the hours when children may be present;
- restrictions or exclusions on the presence of children under certain ages when particular specified activities are taking place;
- restrictions on the parts of premises to which children might be given access;
- age limitations (below 18);
- restrictions or exclusions when certain activities are taking place;
- requirements for an accompanying adult (including for example, a combination of requirements which provide that children under a particular age must be accompanied by an adult); and
- full exclusion of people under 18 from the premises when any licensable activities are taking place.

A statement of licensing policy should make it clear that conditions requiring the admission of children to any premises cannot be attached to a licence or a certificate and where no licensing restriction is appropriate, this should be a matter for the discretion of the licence holder, club or premises user (Guidance, para.14.59).

Representations may be made by a responsible authority in relation to the protection of children, and the Guidance at para.14.61 provides:

A statement of licensing policy should indicate which body the licensing authority judges to be competent to act as the responsible authority in relation to the protection of children from harm. This may be the local authority social services department, the Local Safeguarding Children Board or other competent body as agreed locally. It would be practical and useful for statements of licensing policy to include the descriptions of the responsible authorities in any area and appropriate contact details.

In relation to premises which give film exhibitions, the Guidance at para.14.62 provides that a licensing policy:

should make clear that in the case of premises giving film exhibitions, the licensing authority will expect licence holders or clubs to include in their operating schedules arrangements for restricting children from viewing age-restricted films classified according to the recommendations of the British Board of Film Classification or the licensing authority itself . . . .

2.5.8 Integration with other strategies

A licensing policy should provide clear indications of how the licensing authority will secure the proper integration of its licensing policy with local crime prevention, planning, transport, tourism, equality schemes, cultural strategies and any other plans introduced for the management of town centres and the night-time economy (Guidance, para.14.63). As many of these strategies will not be directly related to promoting the licensing objectives but will indirectly affect them, it is important that they are coordinated and integrated. A licensing policy should also consider the prevalence, prevention and reporting of sexual harassment and misconduct and broader violence against women and girls crimes (Guidance, para.14.64).

2.5.9 Planning and building control

The Guidance at paras.14.65, 14.66 and 14.67 provides:

14.65 The statement of licensing policy should indicate that planning permission, building control approval and licensing regimes will be properly separated to avoid duplication and inefficiency. The planning and licensing regimes involve consideration of different (albeit related) matters. Licensing committees are not bound by decisions made by a planning committee, and vice versa. However, . . ., licensing committees and officers should consider discussions with their planning counterparts prior to determination with the aim of agreeing mutually acceptable operating hours and scheme designs.

14.66 There are circumstances when, as a condition of planning permission, a terminal hour has been set for the use of premises for commercial purposes. Where these hours are different to the licensing hours, the applicant must observe the earlier closing time. Premises operating in breach of their planning permission would be liable to prosecution under planning law. Proper integration should be assured by licensing committees, where appropriate, providing regular reports to the planning committee.

14.67 Where there is an application for planning permission, the National Planning Policy Framework expects new development can be integrated effectively with existing businesses and community facilities (such as places of worship, pubs, music venues and sports clubs). Existing businesses and facilities should not have unreasonable restrictions placed on them as a result of development permitted after they were established. Where the operation of an existing business or community facility could have a significant adverse effect on new development (including changes of use) in its vicinity, the applicant (or 'agent of change') should be required by the local planning authority to provide suitable mitigation before the development has been completed.

2.5.10 Promotion of equality

The Guidance at paras.14.68 and 14.69 provides:

14.68 A statement of licensing policy should recognise that the Equality Act 2010 places a legal obligation on public authorities to have due regard to the need to eliminate unlawful discrimination, harassment and victimisation; to advance equality of opportunity; and to foster good relations, between persons with different protected characteristics. The protected characteristics are age, disability, gender reassignment, pregnancy and maternity, race, religion or belief, sex, and sexual orientation.

14.69 Public authorities are required to publish information at least annually to demonstrate their compliance with the Equality Duty. The statement of licensing policy should refer to this legislation, and explain how the Equality Duty has been complied with. Further guidance is available from Government Equalities Office and the Equality and Human Rights Commission.

2.5.11 Administration, exercise and delegation of functions

Paragraphs 14.70, 14.71 and 14.72 of the Guidance provide:

14.70 The 2003 Act provides that the functions of the licensing authority (including its determinations) are to be taken or carried out by its licensing committee (except those relating to the making of a statement of licensing policy or where another of its committees has the matter referred to it). The licensing committee may delegate these functions to sub-committees consisting of three members of the committee, or in appropriate cases to officials supporting the licensing authority. Where licensing functions are not automatically transferred to licensing committees, the functions must be carried out by the licensing authority as a whole and not by its executive. Statements of licensing policy should indicate how the licensing authority intends to approach its various functions. Many of the decisions and functions will be purely administrative in nature and statements of licensing policy should underline the principle of delegation in the interests of speed, efficiency and cost-effectiveness.

14.71 The 2003 Act does not prevent the development by a licensing authority of collective working practices with other parts of the local authority or other licensing authorities for work of a purely administrative nature, e.g. mail-outs. In addition, such administrative tasks may be contracted out to private businesses. But any matters regarding licensing decisions must be carried out by the licensing committee, its sub-committees or officers.

14.72 Where, under the provisions of the 2003 Act, there are no relevant representations on an application for the grant of a premises licence or club premises certificate or police objection to an application for a personal licence or to an activity taking place under the authority of a temporary event notice, these matters should be dealt with by officers in order to speed matters through the system. Licensing committees should receive regular reports on decisions made by officers so that they maintain an overview of the general situation.

The Guidance at para.14.72 contains a 'Recommended delegation of functions' as shown in **Table 2.1**.

Table 2.1: Recommended delegation of functions (Guidance, para.14.72)

Matter to be dealt with	Sub Committee	Officers
Application for personal licence	If a police or immigration enforcement objection	If no objection made
Application for personal licence with unspent convictions	If a police objection	If no objection made
Application for premises licence/club premises certificate	If a relevant representation made	If no relevant representation made
Application for provisional statement	If a relevant representation made	If no relevant representation made
Application to vary premises licence/club premises certificate	If a relevant representation made	If no relevant representation made
Application to vary designated premises supervisor	If a police objection	All other cases
Request to be removed as designated premises supervisor		All cases
Application for transfer of premises licence	If a police objection	All other cases
Applications for interim authorities	If a police objection	All other cases
Application to review premises licence/club premises certificate	All cases	
Decision on whether a representation is irrelevant frivolous vexatious etc		All cases
Decision to object when local authority is a consultee and not the relevant authority considering the application	All cases	
Determination of an objection to a temporary event notice	All cases	
Determination of application to vary premises licence at community premises to include alternative licence condition	If a police objection	All other cases
Decision whether to consult other responsible authorities on minor variation application		All cases
Determination of minor variation application		All cases

29

2.6 CHALLENGING A STATEMENT OF LICENSING POLICY

A licensing policy may be challenged by judicial review on the ground that it is unlawful. Circumstances where this could be appropriate might be where the licensing authority has not consulted properly under s.5(3) before determining its statement of licensing policy or where the policy contains material which does not relate to the licensing objectives. A successful challenge to a licensing policy was brought in *British Beer & Pub Association* v. *Canterbury City Council* [2005] EWHC 1318 (Admin); (2005) 169 JP 521, where the licensing policy was found to be unlawful as it purported to dictate the contents of an application for a premises licence and impose conditions beyond those which were consistent with the Act. Relief was not, however, granted as the licensing authority proposed an addendum to the policy to mitigate the problems.

It may be possible to challenge a licensing policy under the Human Rights Act 1998, for example if the policy infringes the protection of property under art.1 of the First Protocol. It is unlikely that a challenge could be brought under art.6(1) (the right to a fair trial) as the preparation of a licensing policy is not the 'determination of civil rights and obligations' (see *R. (on the application of Aggregate Industries UK Ltd)* v. *English Nature* [2002] EWHC 908 (Admin); [2003] Env LR 3 where this was decided in relation to a development plan and its statements of policy and it is submitted that a licensing policy could be treated in the same way).

2.7 LICENSING COMMITTEES

Section 6 provides that each licensing authority, except the Sub-Treasurer of the Inner Temple or the Under-Treasurer of the Middle Temple, must establish a licensing committee consisting of at least 10, but not more than 15, members of the authority. The Inner Temple and the Middle Temple will discharge all the licensing functions themselves.

Each licensing committee discharges all the licensing authority's licensing functions, except for the determination and publication of the licensing policy and the making, and varying or revoking, of an EMRO (s.7(1)). The licensing authority may decide that its licensing committee must also discharge additional functions of the authority that are related to its licensing functions, and if it decides to do so it must consider any relevant report prepared by the licensing committee before acting in any such matter, unless it is urgent. This ensures that the licensing committee will have an input into any matter relating to the authority's licensing functions.

Where a matter concerns other functions in addition to licensing functions, a licensing authority may choose to refer the matter either to its licensing committee, having first consulted it, or to another of its committees. If it decides to refer the matter to another committee, then when that committee considers the matter it must, unless the matter is urgent, consider any report prepared by the licensing committee. Alternatively, if it decides to refer the matter to the licensing committee, this committee must, in its considerations, consider any report about the matter prepared by any of the authority's other committees, unless the matter is urgent.

If a licensing committee is unable to discharge any of its functions because some of its members are prevented from considering or voting on a matter, for example where they are disqualified under the licensing authority's standing orders because they have a financial interest in the matter, then the matter must be referred back to the licensing authority for it to discharge its functions in relation to the matter (s.7(9)). In *R. (on the application of Port Regis School Ltd)* v. *North Dorset DC* [2006] EWHC 742 (Admin); [2007] 1 P & CR 29, it was held that a freemason was not to be regarded, by reason of his being a freemason, as restrained from participating in local government decision making whenever another freemason or branch of freemasonry had an interest in the outcome of the decision.

2.8 THE LICENSING REGISTER

Section 8 requires every licensing authority to keep a register containing:

- a record of each premises licence, club premises certificate and personal licence which it has issued;
- a record of each temporary event notice it has received;
- a record of the following matters:

    - an application for the grant of a premises licence;
    - an application relating to the theft, loss or destruction of or damage to a premises licence or summary;
    - a notice of surrender of a premises licence;
    - an application by way of a provisional notice in respect of premises;
    - a notice of a change of name or address of a holder of a premises licence;
    - an application for a variation of a premises licence;
    - an application for a variation of the designated premises supervisor;
    - a request from a designated premises supervisor for removal from a premises licence;
    - an application for the transfer of a premises licence;
    - an interim authority notice;
    - an application for the review of a premises licence;
    - an application for a club premises certificate;
    - an application relating to the theft, loss or destruction of or damage to a club premises certificate or summary;
    - a notice of surrender of a club premises certificate;

- a notice of a change of name of a club or alteration of its rules;
- an application to vary a club premises certificate;
- an application for the review of a club premises certificate;
- a notice of the withdrawal of a temporary event notice;
- a counter notice following a police objection to a temporary event notice;
- a copy of a temporary event notice given following the making of modifications to a temporary event notice with police consent;
- an application relating to the theft, loss or destruction of or damage to a temporary event notice;
- a notice of the surrender of a personal licence;
- an application for the grant of a personal licence;
- an application relating to the theft, loss or destruction of or damage to a personal licence;
- a notice of the change of name or address of a personal licence holder;
- a notice given to it by a magistrates' court to notify its determination made after closure order;
- an application for the conversion of an old licence into a premises licence; and
- an application for the conversion of a club certificate into a club premises certificate; and

- such other information as may be prescribed. The Licensing Act 2003 (Licensing Authority's Register) (Other Information) Regulations 2005, SI 2005/43 has prescribed that each licensing authority must record in its register:
  - the operating schedule which accompanies an application for a premises licence, provided that the name and address of the premises supervisor, if any, shall be removed from the schedule before it is recorded, and the plan of the premises to which the application relates;
  - the schedule of works and plans of the work being or about to be done at the premises which accompany an application for a provisional statement;
  - the revised operating schedule which accompanies an application to vary a premises licence, provided that the name and address of the premises supervisor, if any, shall be removed from the schedule before it is recorded;
  - the club operating schedule and plan of the premises to which the application relates which accompany an application for a club premises certificate;
  - the revised club operating schedule which accompanies an application to vary a club premises certificate;

- the details of the proposed variation or variations as given in an application for minor variation of a premises licence or an application for a minor variation of a club premises certificate;
- the ground or grounds for reviews set out in applications for a review of a premises licence or club premises certificate and the determination of the magistrates' court on its consideration of a closure order;
- the fact that an application for a summary review on the application of a senior police officer has been made and that it has been made on the basis of the opinion of a senior police officer that the premises are associated with serious crime or serious disorder or both; and
- the existing licensable activities and existing qualifying club activities and plans of the premises which accompany applications for the conversion of existing licences and existing club certificates.

Regulations may require a register to be in a prescribed form and kept in a prescribed manner. No such regulations have been made.

A licensing authority must provide facilities for making the information contained in the entries in its register available for inspection in a legible form by any person during office hours and without payment (s.8(3)). It must on request supply a person with a copy of the information contained in any entry in its register in legible form, and may charge such reasonable fee as it may determine (s.8(4) and (5)).

The Secretary of State may arrange for the duties conferred on licensing authorities to keep a register to be discharged by means of one or more central registers, and may require licensing authorities to participate in and contribute towards the cost of any such central registers (s.8(6) and (7)). No such arrangements have been made.

2.9 NOTIFICATION TO PERSONS WITH AN INTEREST IN THE PREMISES

Section 178 provides for a person with a 'property interest' in premises affected by licensing matters to be notified of any changes in the register kept under s.8.

A person has a property interest in premises if:

- he has a legal interest in the premises as freeholder or leaseholder;
- he is a legal mortgagee (within the meaning of the Law of Property Act 1925) in respect of the premises;
- he is in occupation of the premises; or
- he has a prescribed interest in the premises (at the time of writing, no interests have been prescribed).

In order to receive notification, a person with a property interest must give notice of his interest to the licensing authority. This notice must be in the prescribed form which is set out in the Licensing Act 2003 (Premises Licences and Club

Premises Certificates) Regulations 2005, SI 2005/42 ('Premises Licenses Regulations'), Sched.1 and be accompanied by the prescribed fee. The notice has effect for a period of 12 months beginning with the date it is received by the licensing authority. It must be renewed annually.

Once a notice has been given, and while it remains in effect, any changes relating to the premises to which the notice relates made in the register must be notified forthwith by the licensing authority to the person who gave the notice. The notification must also set out the right under s.8 to request a copy of the information contained in any entry in the register.

It is submitted that the requirement to 'forthwith' notify a change means that it may be notified as soon as is reasonably practicable rather than on the same day the change is made to the register. This would accord with the view taken by the Privy Council in *Sameen* v. *Abeyewickrema* [1963] AC 597; [1963] 2 WLR 1114 in relation to the meaning of 'forthwith' in the Civil Procedure Code of Ceylon.

2.10 PROCEEDINGS OF THE LICENSING COMMITTEE

Each licensing committee may establish one or more subcommittees consisting of three members of the licensing committee (s.9(1)). The procedure to be adopted by the licensing committee and its subcommittees is set out in the Hearings Regulations (see further **Chapter 25**). Subject to these regulations, each licensing committee may regulate its own procedure and that of its subcommittees.

2.11 DELEGATION OF FUNCTIONS BY A LICENSING COMMITTEE

A licensing committee may arrange for its functions to be discharged by a subcommittee or by an officer of the licensing authority (s.10(1)). A useful review of the delegation of powers by a licensing committee can be found in *R. (on the application of Raphael)* v. *Highbury Corner Magistrates' Court* [2011] EWCA Civ 462; [2012] PTSR 427, where a decision of a local authority's licensing subcommittee to reduce the amount of hours a night club could operate was valid as the licensing committee had properly delegated its powers under the Act to the subcommittee. As to delegation to an officer, see *Extreme Oyster and Star Oyster Ltd* v. *Guildford BC* [2013] EWHC 2174 (Admin); [2014] PTSR 325.

Where a function has been delegated to a subcommittee, the subcommittee may in turn arrange for an officer of the licensing authority to discharge that function; however, this power is subject to any direction given by the licensing committee to the subcommittee. More than one subcommittee or officer may discharge the same function concurrently.

The following functions may not, under s.10(4), be delegated to an officer:

- the determination of an application for a premises licence where representations have been made;
- the determination of an application for a provisional statement where representations have been made;
- the determination of an application for a variation of a premises licence where representations have been made;
- the determination of an application to vary the designated premises supervisor following an objection;
- the determination of an application for a transfer of a premises licence following a police objection;
- the consideration of an objection made to an interim authority notice;
- the determination of interim steps pending summary review;
- the determination of an application for a club premises certificate where representations have been made;
- the determination of an application to vary a club premises certificate where representations have been made;
- the decision to give a counter notice following a police objection to a temporary event notice;
- the determination of an application for the grant of a personal licence following an objection;
- the revocation of a licence where convictions come to light after its grant;
- the revocation or suspension of licence by local authority where it becomes aware of convictions or immigration penalties;
- the determination of interim steps pending summary off-sales review;
- the determination of an application for the review of a premises licence where relevant representations have been made;
- a review following a review notice in a case where relevant representations have been made;
- the determination of an application for the review of a club premises certificate where relevant representations have been made;
- a review following a closure order where relevant representations have been made; and
- an off-sales review following a review application where relevant representations have been made.

In due course, when the Police Reform and Social Responsibility Act 2011, s.121 comes into force, the making of regulations about fees will be added to this list.

2.12 MINISTERIAL GUIDANCE

The Secretary of State is required under s.182 to issue guidance to licensing authorities on how they are to discharge their functions under the Act. The current version of the Guidance is available at **www.gov.uk/government/ publications/explanatory-memorandum-revised-guidance-issued-under-s-182-of-licensing-act-2003**. Paragraphs 1.7 and 1.8 of the Guidance provide:

> 1.7   This Guidance is provided to licensing authorities in relation to the carrying out of their functions under the 2003 Act. It also provides information to magistrates' courts hearing appeals against licensing decisions and has been made widely available for the benefit of those who run licensed premises, their legal advisers and the general public. It is a key medium for promoting best practice, ensuring consistent application of licensing powers across England and Wales and for promoting fairness, equal treatment and proportionality.
>
> 1.8   The police remain key enforcers of licensing law. This Guidance does not bind police officers who, within the parameters of their force orders and the law, remain operationally independent. However, this Guidance is provided to support and assist police officers in interpreting and implementing the 2003 Act in the promotion of the four licensing objectives.

The Secretary of State may, from time to time, revise the Guidance. A revised version of the Guidance will not come into force until the Secretary of State lays it before Parliament. Where either House, before the end of the period of 40 days beginning with the day on which a revised version of the Guidance is laid before it, disapproves that version by resolution the Secretary of State must make such further revisions to the Guidance as appear to him to be required in the circumstances. Before the end of the period of 40 days beginning with the date on which the resolution is made, he must lay a further revised version of the Guidance before Parliament. In calculating the 40-day period, no account is to be taken of any time during which Parliament is dissolved or prorogued, or when both Houses are adjourned for more than four days.

The Secretary of State must arrange for the Guidance to be published in such manner as he considers appropriate, and for these purposes the Guidance is published on **www.gov.uk**. In addition, a local authority or other organisation is free to publish the Guidance on its own website or provide an appropriate link to either of these websites.

The legal status of the Guidance is set out in paras.1.9 and 1.10 as follows:

> 1.9   Section 4 of the 2003 Act provides that, in carrying out its functions, a licensing authority must 'have regard to' guidance issued by the Secretary of State under section 182. This Guidance is therefore binding on all licensing authorities to that extent. However, this Guidance cannot anticipate every possible scenario or set of circumstances that may arise and, as long as licensing authorities have properly understood this Guidance, they may depart from it if they have good reason to do so and can provide full reasons. Departure from this Guidance could give rise to an appeal or judicial review, and the reasons given will then be a key consideration for the courts when considering the lawfulness and merits of any decision taken.
>
> 1.10   Nothing in this Guidance should be taken as indicating that any requirement of licensing law or any other law may be overridden (including the obligations placed on any public authorities under human rights legislation). This Guidance does not in any way replace the statutory provisions of the 2003 Act or add to its scope and licensing authorities should note that interpretation of the 2003 Act is

a matter for the courts. Licensing authorities and others using this Guidance must take their own professional and legal advice about its implementation.

The Guidance will be considered in a licensing application or an appeal. In *R. (on the application of Daniel Thwaites Plc)* v. *Wirral Borough Magistrates' Court* [2008] EWHC 838 (Admin); [2008] 1 All ER 239, Black J said (at [38]):

> There is no doubt that regard must be had to the Guidance by the magistrates but that its force is less than that of a statute. That is common ground between the parties. The Guidance contains advice of varying degrees of specificity. At one end of the spectrum, it reinforces the general philosophy and approach of the Act. However, it also provides firm advice on particular issues, an example being what could almost be described as a prohibition on local authorities seeking to engineer staggered closing times by setting quotas for particular closing times. I accept that any individual licensing decision may give rise to a need to balance conflicting factors which are included in the Guidance and that in resolving this conflict, a licensing authority or magistrates' court may justifiably give less weight to some parts of the Guidance and more to others. As the Guidance itself says, it may also depart from the Guidance if particular features of the individual case require that. What a licensing authority or magistrates' court is not entitled to do is simply to ignore the Guidance or fail to give it any weight, whether because it does not agree with the Government's policy or its methods of regulating licensable activities or for any other reason. Furthermore, when a magistrates' court is entitled to depart from the Guidance and justifiably does so, it must, in my view, give proper reasons for so doing.

Extracts of the Guidance are included where appropriate throughout the text of this book.

2.13 INFORMATION

Information which is held by or on behalf of a licensing authority or a responsible authority is subject to strict controls. It may be supplied to a licensing authority, or to a responsible authority, in order to facilitate the exercise of the authority's functions under the Act, but cannot be otherwise disclosed (s.185).

2.14 PROCEDURES FOR GIVING NOTICES

Section 184 sets out the rules in relation to any document which is required by the Act to be given to any person.

Where a document has to be given to a licensing authority, it must be given by addressing it to the licensing authority and leaving it at or sending it by post to its principal office or any other office at which it will accept such documents.

In any other case, the document may be given to the person in question by delivering it to him, or by leaving it at his proper address, or by sending it by post to him at that address. In the case of a body corporate other than a licensing authority, a document may be given to the secretary or clerk of that body; in the case of a partnership, it may be given to a partner or a person having the control or management of the partnership business; and in the case of an unincorporated association other than a partnership, it may be given to an officer of the association.

A person's proper address will be his last known address except that:

- for a body corporate or its secretary or clerk, it will be the address of the registered office of that body or its principal office in the United Kingdom;
- for a partnership, a partner or a person having control or management of the partnership business, it will be the address of the principal office of the partnership in the United Kingdom; and
- for an unincorporated association other than a partnership or any officer of the association, it will be the address of its principal office in the United Kingdom.

Where a document is to be given to a person in his capacity as the holder of a premises licence, club premises certificate or personal licence or as the designated premises supervisor under a premises licence, his proper address will be the address recorded for him in the licensing register.

2.15 LATE NIGHT LEVY

A licensing authority has power under the Police Reform and Social Responsibility Act 2011, Part 2, Chapter 2 to introduce a late night levy ('the Levy'), as a means of raising a contribution towards the costs of policing the late night economy. The decision to introduce the Levy is an option available to all licensing authorities and may apply to the whole of the licensing authority's area or to a part of their area where the night time economy places demand on policing. A licensing authority may decide that different late night levy requirements are to apply in different parts of its area.

The Levy will be payable by the holders of any premises licence or club premises certificate which authorise the sale or supply of alcohol on any days during a period (the 'late night supply period') beginning at or after midnight and ending at or before 6 am. It will also be payable by the holders of a premises licence which authorises the provision of late night refreshment and does not also authorise the supply of alcohol during the late night supply period. The Levy will be payable regardless of whether the holder's premises are actually operating during the late night supply period, for example, a holder in relation to a supermarket with a 24-hour licence will be required to pay the Levy regardless of its actual opening hours.

The Home Office has published guidance on the Levy ('the Levy Guidance') that is available at **www.gov.uk**.

2.15.1 Procedure for introducing the Levy

When deciding whether to introduce, a licensing authority must consider the desirability of introducing the Levy in relation to the costs of policing and other arrangements for the reduction or prevention of crime and disorder, in connection with the supply of alcohol between midnight and 6 am. The decision to introduce, vary or end the requirement for the Levy should be made by the full council (Levy Guidance, para.1.14). If introduced, the Levy will apply to boats which are licensed at the place where they are usually moored or berthed, and to mobile bars, which are required to be licensed at the place where they are parked and carry on the licensable activity.

The licensing authority will decide the design of the Levy. Where it decides to introduce the Levy, it must also decide when the Levy is to start and the late night supply period, any exemptions or reductions that may apply and the proportion of revenue, after the licensing authority's costs are deducted, which will be paid to the Police and Crime Commissioner (PCC), with the remainder being retained by the licensing authority to fund other activities to tackle late night alcohol-related crime and disorder. The late night supply period must begin at or after midnight, end at or before 6 am and can be for any length of time within these parameters but must be the same every day.

The first step in introducing the Levy is to carry out a consultation. The Levy Guidance, para.1.12 suggests that before doing this the licensing authority should discuss the need for the Levy with the relevant PCC and the relevant chief officer of police. The relevant PCC also has the right to formally request that a licensing authority consult on implementing the Levy. The procedure for the consultation is contained in reg.9 of the Late Night Levy (Application and Administration) Regulations 2012, SI 2012/2730 ('the Late Night Levy Regulations'). The licensing authority must consult with the relevant PCC, relevant chief officer of police and the holders of 'relevant late night authorisations' by sending them notice of the proposal. The Late Night Levy Regulations do not contain a definition of 'relevant late night authorisations' and the definition of 'relevant late night authorisations' in the Police Reform and Social Responsibility Act 2011, s.126 has been replaced by separate definitions of 'relevant late night alcohol authorisation' and 'relevant late night refreshment authorisation'. However, the Levy Guidance at para.1.13 states:

> The consultation is intended to be targeted at those affected by the levy, particularly businesses, the police, residents and other interested parties. The consultation process, including the period, is expected to be proportionate and targeted, so that the type and scale of engagement is relative to the potential impacts of the proposal.

Notice of the proposal must also be placed on the licensing authority's website and published in a local newspaper or, if there is none, in a local newsletter, circular or similar document circulating in the licensing authority's area. The notice placed on the licensing authority's website must set out:

- the date on which the late night levy requirement is first to apply;
- the late night supply period;
- the permitted exemption categories (if any) which are to apply;
- the permitted reduction categories (if any) which are to apply; and
- the specified proportion.

The Levy Guidance, para.1.12 envisages the licensing authority producing a consultation document which will 'state its intention to introduce a levy, its proposed design (including the late night supply period and proposed exemption and/or reduction categories) and the services that the licensing authority intends to fund with its share of the levy revenue'.

Once the consultation has taken place the licensing authority will assess the responses and make a final decision about whether to introduce (or vary) the Levy and, if so, its design. The decision to introduce the Levy, and its design, will then be put to the full council to approve.

The licensing authority must notify the relevant chief officer of police, the PCC and all holders of 'relevant late night authorisations' of the start date for the Levy, the late night supply period, any exemptions and reductions, and how the revenue will be shared between the police force and licensing authority. Holders of relevant late night authorisations should also be notified of the date before which any applications for a minor variation must be made to the authority. The Levy Guidance, para.1.16 recommends that licensing authorities set the start date of the Levy no less than three months after those notifications to relevant persons of the introduction of the Levy have been sent.

Holders of relevant late night authorisations may make a free variation to their licence to reduce their licensed hours to avoid operating in the late night supply period. The Levy Guidance, para.1.17 recommends that licensing authorities may wish to allow holders no less than two months to make such applications. The cost of processing free variations will be a deductible expense from the Levy receipts in the first year in which the Levy is introduced by the licensing authority.

A licensing authority must publish on its website an estimate of the costs it will deduct from the Levy revenue each year. The Levy will apply indefinitely until the licensing authority decides that it will cease to apply in its area. A decision that the Levy should cease to apply can only be made at the end of a Levy year. The Levy Guidance, para.1.19 suggests that licensing authorities may wish to review the requirements for the Levy at appropriate intervals and that they may wish to notify holders of a relevant late night authorisation of any decision that the Levy is to cease.

2.15.2 Exemptions from the Levy

Regulations may prescribe categories of holders of relevant late night authorisations in relation to whom, if a licensing authority so decides, the requirement to pay the Levy is not to apply. Licensing authorities are not able to choose a category of premises for an exemption from the Levy, if it is not prescribed in regulations. Likewise, licensing authorities are not able to exempt specific premises from the requirement to pay the Levy. Licensing authorities can decide, when considering the Levy, if any of the following permitted categories of premises prescribed by the Late Night Levy (Expenses, Exemptions and Reductions) Regulations 2012, SI 2012/2550 should be exempt from the requirement to pay the Levy:

- a hotel or guest house, lodging house or hostel at which the supply of alcohol between midnight and 6 am on any day may only be made to a person who is staying at the premises for consumption on the premises;
- a theatre at which the supply of alcohol between midnight and 6 am on any day may only be made to a person for consumption on the premises who is:
    - a ticket holder in relation to a relevant production at the premises;
    - concerned in the performance, organisation or management of the relevant production; or
    - invited to the premises as a guest to attend an event to which the public do not have access;
- a cinema at which the supply of alcohol between midnight and 6 am on any day may only be made to a person for consumption on the premises who is:
    - a ticket holder in relation to the exhibition of a film at the premises; or
    - invited to the premises as a guest to attend an event to which the public do not have access;
- premises in respect of which:
    - the provision of facilities for the playing of bingo is authorised by a bingo premises licence granted in accordance with the Gambling Act 2005, s.163;
    - the holder of the bingo premises licence is authorised to provide facilities for the playing of bingo by virtue of a non-remote bingo operating licence granted in accordance with the Gambling Act 2005, s.74; and
    - the playing of bingo is the primary activity carried on at the premises;
- a club which is registered as a community amateur sports club by virtue of the Corporation Tax Act 2010, s.658;
- community premises in relation to which the premises licence contains the alternative licence condition;
- a public house which is a hereditament in respect of which the ratepayer is subject to a non-domestic rate calculated in accordance with the Local Gov-

ernment Finance Act 1988, s.43(6A), i.e. the sole pub situated within a designated rural settlement with a population of less than 3,000;

- a hereditament in respect of which:

    – the ratepayer is liable for a business improvement district (BID) levy in accordance with the Local Government Act 2003, s.46; and
    – the BID arrangements in relation to which a BID levy is imposed are established for purposes which include relevant purposes; or

- premises authorised to be used to supply alcohol for consumption on the premises between midnight and 6 am on 1 January in every year (but are not so authorised at those times on any other day in any year).

The Levy will not apply to temporary event notices. In addition, if the Levy relates to a late night refreshment authorisation, the holder of that authorisation is not liable to pay the Levy if only hot drinks are supplied (or held out for supply).

2.15.3 Reductions from the Levy

Regulations may prescribe categories of holders of relevant late night authorisations in relation to whom, if a licensing authority so decides, a reduced amount of the Levy is to apply. The Late Night Levy (Expenses, Exemptions and Reductions) Regulations 2012, SI 2012/2550 provide for certain categories of holders of relevant late night authorisations to be eligible for a reduction from the Levy. Licensing authorities can then consider if such holders should benefit from a reduction. The eligible categories are holders of relevant late night authorisations who are:

- members of a relevant arrangement; or
- in relation to premises at which the authorisation permits the supply of alcohol for consumption on the premises only, which are a hereditament in respect of which the ratepayer is subject to a non-domestic rate calculated in accordance with the Local Government Finance Act 1988, s.43(4A), and the rateable value is not more than £12,000.

A 'relevant arrangement' is one which:

- is established for purposes which include relevant purposes, i.e. purposes which result in, or are likely to result in, the reduction or prevention of crime and disorder in connection with the supply of alcohol between midnight and 6 am at premises in relation to which a relevant late night authorisation has effect;
- requires its members to take steps to promote the relevant purposes; and
- contains provision for the cessation of the membership of a holder of a relevant late night authorisation who has failed to take steps to promote the relevant purposes.

So, a licensing authority may use the Levy to promote and support participation by premises in business-led best practice schemes and can decide, when considering the Levy, if holders whose premises participate in such schemes should benefit from a reduction to the amount they are required to pay under the Levy. In relation to relevant arrangements, the Levy Guidance at para.1.36 provides:

> Licensing authorities have discretion as to how best practice schemes can demonstrate that they meet these benchmarks. We expect licensing authorities to use their existing partnerships with best practice schemes, and understanding of a scheme's operation in their area, to identify eligible schemes in their areas. Licensing officials could visit representatives from best practice schemes in their area, or request written details of the scheme's objectives, if they decide to consider this reduction category.

The second category of reduction applies to holders in relation to on-trade premises that are in receipt of small business rate relief and have a rateable value of £12,000 or less. This reduction is only available to holders in relation to premises that supply alcohol for consumption on the premises and late night refreshment premises.

Eligible premises will receive a 30 per cent reduction from the Levy. There is no cumulative discount available for holders in relation to premises that are eligible for more than one reduction category.

If a licensing authority decides to introduce or remove categories of exemption and/or reduction after the first year of the Levy, it will need to follow the same procedure for consultation as set out in **2.15.1**, although the consultation should only refer to the new proposal. The Levy Guidance, para.1.38 provides that if a licensing authority chooses to remove categories of exemption and/or reduction after the first year, it should consider that the opportunity for businesses to make a free variation to their licences is only available when the Levy is initially introduced.

2.15.4 Levy revenue

The net amount of the Levy revenue must be split between the licensing authority and the relevant PCC. A licensing authority must pay at least 70 per cent of the net Levy revenue to the police. This must be paid within 28 days of the end of the Levy year to which the revenue relates. The licensing authority can choose to amend the portion of the net Levy revenue that will be given to the PCC in future Levy years and this decision must be subject to consultation in the same way as a decision to introduce the Levy.

In calculating the net Levy amount the deductible costs may include (but are not necessarily limited to) the following (Levy Guidance at para.1.44):

- the preparation and publication of the consultation document, including publishing it online and sending details to the PCC, the relevant chief officer of police and all premises licence and club premises certificate holders whose authorisations permit the supply of alcohol after midnight on any day;
- the collection of levy payments;

- the enforcement of levy payments; and
- the cost of processing applications for a variation in relation to the introduction of the levy.

In relation to expenses the Levy Guidance at para.1.45 provides:

> There will be no specific restrictions on the amount of the expenses which licensing authorities can claim in expenses, however licensing authorities will have to account for their expenses following existing procedures. The government may specify a cap on the amount of expenses in further regulations if considered necessary.

The Levy Guidance at para.1.42 provides:

> ... the licensing authority is able to retain up to 30% of the net levy revenue to fund services it provides to tackle late night alcohol related crime and disorder and services connected to the management of the night time economy. Specifically, these activities must have regard to the connection with the supply of alcohol during the late night supply period and related to arrangements for:

- the reduction of crime and disorder;
- the promotion of public safety;
- the reduction or prevention of public nuisance; or
- the cleaning of any relevant highway or relevant land in the local authority area.

2.15.5 Levy charge and collection

The amount of the Levy is prescribed nationally by the Late Night Levy Regulations. The annual charges for the Levy are shown in **Table 2.2**.

Table 2.2: Levy charges

	A	B	C	D	E	D × 2	E × 3
Rateable Value Bands	No rateable value to £4,300	£4,301 to £33,000	£33,001 to £87,000	£87,001 to £125,000	£125,001 and above	Multiplier applies to premises in category D that primarily or exclusively sell alcohol	Multiplier applies to premises in category E that primarily or exclusively sell alcohol
Levy Charges	£299	£768	£1,259	£1,365	£1,493	£2,730	£4,440

A multiplier is applied to premises in Bands D and E that primarily or exclusively sell alcohol for consumption on the premises to ensure that larger clubs and bars make a higher contribution towards the Levy. Premises that do not have a rateable value will be in Band A and premises that are in the course of construction will be in Band C.

The Levy will be collected at the same time as the annual licence fee (except in relation to holders' premises who obtain a relevant late night authorisation during a Levy year). For holders whose licences exist at the time that the first Levy year begins, the payment year will be the same as the Levy year and they will make their first Levy payment when they pay their annual fee. For holders who are granted a licence in the first or subsequent Levy years, the payment year runs from the date of the grant of the licence and for each year thereafter. Their first payment will be made 14 days after the grant of the licence, and thereafter when they pay their annual fee.

In the following circumstances, licensing authorities should adjust a holder's liability to the Levy:

- a licence lapses if the holder of the licence dies, becomes mentally incapable, becomes insolvent, if the partnership holding the licence is dissolved or if it is a club, ceases to be a recognised club; or
- an EMRO is made which prohibits premises from serving alcohol at any time when the levy applies.

The amount of the levy reduction is the amount found by applying the formula: $R = (L/365) \times N$ (where R is the levy reduction, L is the amount of the Levy payable and N is the number of days in the payment year beginning on the day following the day on which the relevant event occurred).

A licensing authority also has discretion to adjust a holder's liability if the licence is surrendered.

Any payment of the Levy, which is owed to the licensing authority, can be recovered as a debt due to the authority. Non-payment of the Levy can result in suspension of a premises licence or suspension of a club premises certificate.

CHAPTER 3

Licensable activities

3.1 INTRODUCTION

The Act sets out in s.1 the types of licensable activity which require authorisation under the Act by means of a premises licence, a club premises certificate or a temporary event notice.

Section 1(1) provides that 'licensable activities' are:

- the sale by retail of alcohol;
- the supply of alcohol by or on behalf of a club to, or to the order of, a member of the club;
- the provision of regulated entertainment; and
- the provision of late night refreshment.

In addition, certain licensable activities are 'qualifying club activities' if they occur on club premises. In effect, they are the activities which qualify a club for the grant of a club premises certificate (see **Chapter 17**). Section 1(2) provides that 'qualifying club activities' are:

- the supply of alcohol by or on behalf of a club to, or to the order of, a member of the club;
- the sale by retail of alcohol by or on behalf of a club to a guest of a member of the club for consumption on the premises where the sale takes place; and
- the provision of regulated entertainment where that provision is by or on behalf of a club for members of the club or members of the club and their guests.

The provision of late night refreshment in a qualifying club is an exempt supply and does not require authorisation (Sched.2, para.3).

3.2 THE SALE BY RETAIL OF ALCOHOL

Section 1(1) provides that there are two types of licensable activity so far as alcohol is concerned: the sale by retail of alcohol and the supply of alcohol by or on behalf of a club to or to the order of a member of the club otherwise than by way of sale.

3.2.1 Sale by retail

The Act defines 'sale by retail' in s.192, in relation to any alcohol, as a sale of alcohol to any person, other than a sale of alcohol that is:

- to a trader for the purposes of his trade;
- to a club, which holds a club premises certificate, for the purposes of that club;
- to the holder of a personal licence for the purpose of making sales authorised by a premises licence;
- to the holder of a premises licence for the purpose of making sales authorised by that licence; or
- to the premises user in relation to a temporary event notice for the purpose of making sales authorised by that notice.

In addition, the sale must be made from premises owned by the person making the sale, or occupied by him under a lease to which the provisions of the Land-lord and Tenant Act 1954, Part 2 apply, and be made for consumption off the premises.

There is no exemption for large quantities and a wholesaler will therefore require a premises licence to sell alcohol in wholesale quantities to members of the public. Sales made to other traders for the purposes of their trade will not be a licensable activity. Similarly, sales made to holders of premises licences, club premises certificates or personal licences will not be a licensable activity if the sale is for the purposes authorised by the premises licence or for the purposes of the qualifying club. The wholesale sale of alcohol to premises users operating under a temporary event notice will also not be a licensable activity. In cases of doubt, it will be advisable to check with the local licensing authority to see whether the sale is a licensable activity.

Another effect of the definition is that a person may require a premises licence if he sells alcohol to his friends from his house. All sales of alcohol to members of the public, even in wholesale quantities, from any premises will require an authorisation and there will need to be a designated premises supervisor for the premises if the authorisation is in the form of a premises licence.

Businesses which sell alcohol must ensure that the UK wholesalers from which they buy alcohol have been approved by HM Revenue and Customs (HMRC) under the Alcohol Wholesaler Registration Scheme (AWRS). They will need to check their wholesalers Unique Registration Number (URN) against the HMRC online database. This is an ongoing obligation and if a business is found to have bought alcohol from an unapproved wholesaler, they may be liable to a penalty or could even face criminal prosecution and their alcohol stock may be seized. Any trader who buys alcohol from a wholesaler for onward sale to the general public, for example pubs, clubs, restaurants, cafes, retailers and hotels, does not need to register unless they sell alcohol to other businesses. However, they will need to check that the wholesaler they purchase alcohol from is registered with HMRC. Further information may be found at **www.gov.uk/guidance/ the-alcohol-wholesaler-registration-scheme-awrs**.

3.2.2 Alcohol

Not everything which contains alcohol will be treated as alcohol under the Act. Section 191 defines 'alcohol' as spirits, wine, beer, cider or any other fermented, distilled or spirituous liquor (in any state), but not including:

- alcohol which does not exceed a strength of 0.5 per cent at the time of the sale or supply;
- perfume;
- flavouring essences recognised by the Commissioners for HMRC as not being intended for consumption as or with dutiable alcoholic liquor;
- Angostura bitters;
- alcohol which is, or is included in, a medicinal product or a veterinary medicinal product;
- denatured alcohol, that is alcohol which has been made unfit for drinking by the addition of another substance but is still useful for other purposes (formerly called methylated spirits);
- methyl alcohol, that is methanol;
- naphtha, that is inflammable oil obtained by the distillation of organic substances; or
- alcohol contained in liqueur confectionery.

For these purposes:

- 'beer' is defined by s.193 to have the same meaning as in the Alcoholic Liquor Duties Act 1979, however this Act has been repealed by the Finance (No.2) Act 2023. The definition of 'beer' in the Finance (No.2) Act 2023 is found in Sched.6, para.3 and is that 'beer' means ale, porter, stout, any other type of beer, and any other product which is made or sold as beer or as a substitute for beer;
- 'cider' is defined by s.193 to have the same meaning as in the Alcoholic Liquor Duties Act 1979, however this Act has been repealed by the Finance (No.2) Act 2023. The definition of 'cider' in the Finance (No.2) Act 2023 is found in Sched.6, para.5 and is that 'cider' means a product which:

- – is obtained from the fermentation of apple juice or pear juice,
- – has been produced without the addition, at any time, of:

  - another alcoholic product, or
  - anything, other than a permitted substance, which communicates colour or flavour,

- – satisfies the juice content requirements, and
- – is of an alcoholic strength of less than 8.5 per cent.

- Paragraph 6–10 contain definitions of 'permitted substance', 'juice content requirements', 'sparkling cider' and 'still cider';
- 'denatured alcohol' is defined in s.191 to have the same meaning as in the Finance Act 1995, s.5, however this provision has been repealed by the Finance (No.2) Act 2023. The Finance (No.2) Act 2023, s.90 provides that 'denatured alcohol' means an alcoholic product which has been mixed with a substance, and in a manner, specified by or under regulations (currently the Denatured Alcohol Regulations 2005, SI 2005/1524);
- 'dutiable alcoholic liquor' is defined by s.191 as having the same meaning as in the Alcoholic Liquor Duties Act 1979; however, this Act has been repealed by the Finance (No.2) Act 2023. There is no definition of 'dutiable alcoholic liquor' in the Finance (No.2) Act 2023; however, s.44 provides that 'alcoholic product' means spirits, beer, cider, wine and any other fermented product (but none of these will be an alcoholic product if it is of an alcoholic strength of 1.2 per cent or less);
- 'liqueur confectionery' means confectionery which:

  - – contains alcohol in a proportion not greater than 0.2 litres of alcohol of a strength not exceeding 57 per cent per kilogram of the confectionery; and
  - – either consists of separate pieces weighing not more than 42 g or is designed to be broken into such pieces for the purpose of consumption (Licensing Act 2003, s.191(2));

- 'medicinal product' has the same meaning as in the Medicines Act 1968, s.130, that is, the meaning given by reg.2 of the Human Medicines Regulations 2012, SI 2012/1916 and means:

  - – any substance or combination of substances presented as having properties of preventing or treating disease in human beings; or
  - – any substance or combination of substances that may be used by or administered to human beings with a view to restoring, correcting or modifying a physiological function by exerting a pharmacological, immunological or metabolic action, or making a medical diagnosis;

- 'strength' is defined by s.191 as to be construed in accordance with the Alcoholic Liquor Duties Act 1979, s.2; however, this Act has been repealed by the

Finance (No.2) Act 2023. The Finance (No.2) Act 2023, s.45 contains a definition of 'alcoholic strength';

- 'veterinary medicinal product' is defined in s.191 as having the same meaning as in reg.2 of the Veterinary Medicines Regulations 2006, SI 2006/2407; however, these regulations have been repealed and the current definition can be found in the Veterinary Medicines Regulations 2013, SI 2013/2033 and that is:

  - any substance or combination of substances presented as having properties for treating or preventing disease in animals; or
  - any substance or combination of substances that may be used in, or administered to, animals with a view either to restoring, correcting or modifying physiological functions by exerting a pharmacological, immunological or metabolic action, or to making a medical diagnosis; or
  - any substance or combination of substances that may be used for the purposes of euthanising an animal;

- 'wine' is defined by s.193 to have the same meaning as in the Alcoholic Liquor Duties Act 1979; however, this Act has been repealed by the Finance (No.2) Act 2023. The definition of 'wine' in the Finance (No.2) Act 2023 is found in Sched.6, para.11 and is that 'wine' means any product obtained from the alcoholic fermentation of fresh grapes or of the must of fresh grapes (whether or not the product is fortified with spirits).

3.3 THE SUPPLY OF ALCOHOL BY OR ON BEHALF OF A CLUB TO, OR TO THE ORDER OF, A MEMBER OF THE CLUB

There are two types of club. A proprietary club is run as a business and the club assets are owned by the proprietor of the business. In the case of a proprietary club there is a retail sale when a member of the club purchases alcohol and a premises licence will be required. A members' club is a club where all the assets are owned by the members jointly, for example a working men's club. The alcohol in a members' club is treated as being owned equally by all the members and so when a member purchases alcohol in the club there is a release to that member of the proprietary rights of the other members. The Act makes the supply of alcohol by a club to its members a licensable activity.

3.4 THE PROVISION OF REGULATED ENTERTAINMENT

'Entertainment' is defined in Sched.1 as:

- a performance of a play;

- an exhibition of a film;
- an indoor sporting event;
- a boxing or wrestling entertainment;
- a performance of live music;
- any playing of recorded music;
- a performance of dance; or
- entertainment of a similar description to a performance of live music, any playing of recorded music or a performance of dance;

where the following conditions are satisfied, so far as relevant:

- The first condition is that the entertainment:

  - takes place in the presence of an audience; and
  - is provided for the purpose, or for purposes which include the purpose, of entertaining that audience.

- The second condition is relevant only to a performance of a play, and is that one or more of the following applies:

  - the audience consists of more than 500 persons;
  - the entertainment takes place before 8 am on any day;
  - the entertainment takes place after 11 pm on any day.

- The third condition is relevant only to an indoor sporting event, and is that one or more of the following applies:

  - the audience consists of more than 1,000 persons;
  - the entertainment takes place before 8 am on any day;
  - the entertainment takes place after 11 pm on any day.

- The fourth condition is relevant only to a performance of dance, and is that one or more of the following applies:

  - the audience consists of more than 500 persons;
  - the entertainment takes place before 8 am on any day;
  - the entertainment takes place after 11 pm on any day;
  - the entertainment is relevant entertainment within the meaning of the Local Government (Miscellaneous Provisions) Act 1982, Sched.3, para.2A (see **4.3.10**).

In order to be 'regulated entertainment' two conditions must be satisfied:

- the entertainment must be provided:

  - to any extent for the public or a section of the public;
  - exclusively for members and their guests of a club which is a qualifying club in relation to the provision of regulated entertainment; or
  - where neither of the above applies, for consideration and with a view to profit; and

51

- the premises on which the entertainment is provided are made available for the purpose, or for purposes which include the purpose, of enabling the entertainment to take place.

3.5 THE PROVISION OF LATE NIGHT REFRESHMENT

Under the Act authorisation is required for the provision of late night refreshment. Section 1(5) provides that:

> Schedule 2 makes provision about what constitutes the provision of late night refreshment for those purposes (including provision that certain activities carried on in relation to certain clubs or hotels etc, or certain employees, do not constitute provision of late night refreshment and are, accordingly, not licensable activities).

Late night refreshment is the supply of hot food or hot drink to the public, for consumption on or off the premises, between 11 pm and 5 am or the supply of hot food or hot drink to any persons between those hours on or from premises to which the public has access.

Food or drink is 'hot' for the purposes of the Act if it is heated on the premises or elsewhere before it is supplied for the purpose of enabling it to be consumed at above ambient air temperature, or if it may be heated on the premises for this purpose after it is supplied.

The Act provides that the provision of hot drinks by vending machines in certain circumstances, the supply free of charge of hot food or hot drink and the supply by a registered charity are exempt supplies which will not constitute the provision of late night refreshment.

3.6 AUTHORISATION FOR LICENSABLE ACTIVITIES AND QUALIFYING CLUB ACTIVITIES

Section 2 provides that a licensable activity may only be carried on in accordance with a premises licence (see **Chapter 7**), or a temporary event notice (see **Chapter 20**), and that a qualifying club activity may only be carried on in accordance with a club premises certificate (see **Chapter 17**).

Section 2(3) provides that there is nothing in the Act to prevent two or more authorisations having effect concurrently in respect of the whole or a part of the same premises or in respect of the same person. This would enable, for example, a qualifying club that wished to provide entertainment to members of the public on certain days to hold both a club premises certificate to cover its normal operation and a premises licence to authorise the provision of entertainment in respect of the same premises. Another example would be where premises have both a premises licence authorising the sale of alcohol in the bar area and another premises licence authorising a different licensable activity in the bar or in another part of the premises.

A club which is not a qualifying club will be able to carry out licensable activities under either a premises licence or a temporary event notice. A club which has a club premises certificate is not prevented from having a premises licence or a temporary event notice as well.

CHAPTER 4

Regulated entertainment

4.1 INTRODUCTION

The Act provides that the provision of regulated entertainment is a licensable activity.

4.1.1 Entertainment

The descriptions of entertainment for the purposes of the Act are:

- the performance of a play;
- an exhibition of a film;
- an indoor sporting event;
- boxing or wrestling entertainment;
- a performance of live music;
- any playing of recorded music;
- a performance of dance; or
- entertainment of a similar description to live music, recorded music or dance.

The entertainment must take place in the presence of an audience, and be provided for the purpose, or for purposes which include the purpose, of entertaining that audience.

In addition, in relation to a performance of a play, either the audience consists of more than 500 persons, the entertainment takes place before 8 am on any day, or the entertainment takes place after 11 pm on any day.

In relation to an indoor sporting event, either the audience consists of more than 1,000 persons, the entertainment takes place before 8 am on any day, or the entertainment takes place after 11 pm on any day.

Finally, in relation to a performance of dance, either the audience consists of more than 500 persons, the entertainment takes place before 8 am on any day, the entertainment takes place after 11 pm on any day, or the entertainment is relevant entertainment within the meaning of the Local Government (Miscellaneous Provisions) Act 1982, Sched.3, para.2A.

Audience

The Guidance at para.16.11 provides:

> For the purposes of regulated entertainment, the term 'audience' refers to any person for whose entertainment (at least in part) any licensable activities are provided. An audience member need not be, or want to be, entertained: what matters is that an audience is present and that the purpose of the licensable activity is (at least in part) intended to entertain any person present. The audience will not include performers, together with any person who contributes technical skills in substantial support of a performer (for example, a sound engineer or stage technician), during any associated activities. This includes setting up before the entertainment, reasonable breaks (including intervals) between activities and packing up thereafter. Similarly, security staff and bar workers will not form part of the audience while undertaking their duties.

In some circumstances, such as un-ticketed live music events, a degree of judgement may be required as to whether persons are part of an audience. Factors to consider could include whether a person is within the perimeter of the premises, the audible range of the performance and their visibility of the entertainment. In order to meet the definition of an entertainment activity in the Act, the activity must take place in the presence of an audience and be provided for the purpose, or for purposes which include the purpose of, entertaining that audience.

The Guidance at para.16.12 provides that:

> More than one entertainment activity (or for a single activity, more than one performance or event) can be held concurrently, provided that the audience for each such performance or event does not exceed the threshold at which such a performance or event becomes licensable. In some circumstances, there will be a clear distinction between performances or events; for example, their taking place in separate rooms or on separate floors. However, organisers will have to ensure that audiences do not grow or migrate, so that the audience exceeds the relevant limit for any one performance or event at any time. If there is the possibility of audience migration, it might be easier and more flexible to secure an appropriate authorisation.

Circumstances in which entertainment is not licensable

Activities which do not involve entertaining an audience are not licensable and the Guidance, para.16.5 provides that the following activities are examples of entertainment which are not licensable:

- education – teaching students to perform music or to dance;
- activities which involve participation as acts of worship in a religious context;
- activities that take place in places of public religious worship;
- the demonstration of a product – for example, a guitar – in a music shop;
- the rehearsal of a play or performance of music for a private audience where no charge is made with a view to making a profit;
- morris dancing (or similar);
- incidental music – the performance of live music or the playing of recorded music if it is incidental to some other activity;

- incidental film – an exhibition of moving pictures if it is incidental to some other activity;
- a spontaneous performance of music, singing or dancing;
- garden fetes – or similar if not being promoted or held for purposes of private gain;
- films for advertisement, information, education or in museums or art galleries;
- television or radio broadcasts – as long as the programme is live and simultaneous;
- vehicles in motion – at a time when the vehicle is not permanently or temporarily parked;
- games played in pubs, youth clubs, etc. (e.g. pool, darts, table tennis and billiards);
- stand-up comedy; and
- the provision of entertainment facilities (such as dance floors).

In addition, the following activities are not licensable to the extent that they take place between 8 am and 11 pm on any day:

- a performance of a play in the presence of any audience of no more than 500 people;
- an indoor sporting event in the presence of any audience of no more than 1,000 people;
- performances of dance in the presence of any audience of no more than 500 people (but see **4.3.10** in relation to dance that is adult entertainment and remains licensable);
- 'not-for-profit' film exhibitions held in community premises (see **7.11.3**) provided that the audience does not exceed 500 and the organiser gets consent to the screening from a person who is responsible for the premises; and ensures that each such screening abides by age classification ratings;
- a contest, exhibition or display of Greco-Roman wrestling or freestyle wrestling provided that the audience does not exceed 1,000;
- any playing of recorded music on premises authorised to sell alcohol for consumption on those premises, provided that the audience does not exceed 500;
- any playing of recorded music in a church hall, village hall, community hall or other similar community premises, that is not licensed by a premises licence to sell alcohol, provided that the audience does not exceed 500, and the organiser gets consent for the performance from a person who is responsible for the premises;
- any playing of recorded music at the non-residential premises of a local authority, a school or a hospital, provided that the audience does not exceed 500, and the organiser gets consent for the performance on the relevant premises from the local authority concerned, the school proprietor or the health care provider for the hospital;
- a performance of unamplified live music on any premises;

- a performance of amplified live music on premises authorised to sell alcohol for consumption on those premises provided that the audience does not exceed 500 and that a number of other conditions are satisfied (see **4.2.5**);
- a performance of amplified live music in a workplace that does not have a licence, provided that the audience does not exceed 500 (but note that if premises are licensed under the Act, they cannot also be treated as a workplace for the purpose of the Live Music Act 2012);
- a performance of amplified live music in a church hall, village hall, community hall or other similar community premises, that is not licensed by a premises licence to sell alcohol, provided that the audience does not exceed 500, and the organiser gets consent for the performance from a person who is responsible for the premises;
- a performance of amplified live music at the non-residential premises of a local authority, a school or a hospital, provided that the audience does not exceed 500, and the organiser gets consent for the performance on the relevant premises from the local authority concerned, the school proprietor or the health care provider for the hospital;
- any entertainment taking place on the premises of the local authority where the entertainment is provided by or on behalf of the local authority with no limit on audience size;
- any entertainment taking place on the hospital premises of the health care provider where the entertainment is provided by or on behalf of the health care provider with no limit on audience size;
- any entertainment taking place on the premises of the school where the entertainment is provided by or on behalf of the school proprietor with no limit on audience size; and
- any entertainment (excluding films and a boxing or wrestling entertainment) taking place at a travelling circus with no limit on audience size, provided that it takes place within a moveable structure that accommodates the audience, and that the travelling circus has not been located on the same site for more than 28 consecutive days.

So, for example, an indoor sporting event that takes place between 7 am and 11.30 pm on a particular day is licensable in respect of activities taking place between 7 am and 8 am and 11 pm and 11.30 pm. Similarly, where the audience for a performance of dance fluctuates, those activities are licensable if, and for so long as, the number of people in the audience exceeds 500. The Guidance at para.16.7 provides:

> If organisers are uncertain as to audience sizes or if audience migration is likely, it might be easier and more flexible to secure an appropriate authorisation. Examples of where a Temporary Event Notice (TEN) could still be required include if the activity is the playing of recorded music or the exhibition of a film that requires an authorisation; or if the entertainment is not authorised by an existing licence or certificate and its conditions.

The various effects of the changes made to entertainment licensing by deregulatory changes are described in greater detail in subsequent paragraphs.

4.1.2 Requirements for regulated entertainment

In order for the provision of entertainment to be regulated, Sched.1 provides that two conditions must be satisfied:

- the entertainment must be provided:

    - to any extent for the public or a section of the public;
    - exclusively for members and their guests of a club which is a qualifying club in relation to the provision of regulated entertainment; or
    - where neither of the above applies, for consideration and with a view to profit; and

- the premises on which the entertainment is provided are made available for the purpose, or for purposes which include the purpose, of enabling the entertainment to take place.

For the purposes of the first condition, the entertainment is to be regarded as provided for consideration only if any charge (which includes any charge for the provision of goods or services):

- is made by or on behalf of any person concerned in the organisation or management of that entertainment; and
- is paid by or on behalf of some or all of the persons for whom that entertainment is provided.

Where the entertainment consists of the performance of live music or the playing of recorded music, a person performing or playing the music is not concerned in the organisation or management of the entertainment by reason only that he chooses the music to be performed or played, or determines the manner in which he performs or plays it. So a disc jockey or musician who is not responsible for the organisation or management of the performance will not have to obtain a licence if he is paid to play at a private event.

The charge for the entertainment must be made by those involved in some way in the organisation or management of the entertainment and be paid by or on behalf of some or all of the persons for whom the entertainment is provided. In relation to private events, the Guidance at para.16.13 provides:

> Events held in private are not licensable unless those attending are charged for the entertainment with a view to making a profit (including raising money for charity). For example, where a party is held for friends in a private dwelling featuring amplified live music, if a charge or contribution is made solely to cover the costs of the entertainment, the activity is not regulated entertainment. Similarly, any charge made to the organiser of a private event by musicians, other performers, or their agents does not of itself make that entertainment licensable – it would only do so if the guests attending

were themselves charged by the organiser for that entertainment with a view to achieving a profit. The fact that this might inadvertently result in the organiser making a profit would be irrelevant, as long as there had not been an intention to make a profit.

4.2 TYPES OF ENTERTAINMENT

4.2.1 The performance of a play

The performance of a play is defined in Sched.1, para.14 as a performance of any dramatic piece, whether involving improvisation or not, which is given wholly or in part by one or more persons actually present and performing, and in which the whole or a major proportion of what is done by the person or persons performing, whether by way of speech, singing or action, involves the playing of a role. 'Performance' includes a rehearsal, though the rehearsal of a play for a private audience where no charge is made with a view to making a profit is not licensable.

4.2.2 An exhibition of a film

Schedule 1, para.15 provides that an 'exhibition of a film' means any exhibition of moving pictures. An exhibition of moving pictures is the showing of moving pictures to an audience as opposed to the display of moving objects on a screen (*British Amusement Catering Trades Association (BACTA)* v. *Westminster City Council* [1989] AC 147 (HL); [1988] 2 WLR 485).

By Sched.1, paras.5 and 6 the provision of entertainment consisting of the exhibition of a film will not amount to the provision of regulated entertainment if:

- its sole or main purpose is to demonstrate any product, advertise any goods or services, or provide information, education or instruction; or
- it consists of or forms part of an exhibit put on show for any purposes of a museum or art gallery.

4.2.3 An indoor sporting event

An 'indoor sporting event' is defined in Sched.1, para.16 as a sporting event which takes place wholly inside a building and at which the spectators present at the event are accommodated wholly inside the building. A 'sporting event' is defined as any contest, exhibition or display of any sport other than a boxing or wrestling entertainment, and 'sport' includes any game in which physical skill is the predominant factor, and any form of physical recreation which is also engaged in for purposes of competition or display. Thus it would include such events as darts tournaments, gymnastics and indoor athletic meetings. 'Building' is defined as any roofed structure, other than a structure with a roof which may be opened or closed, and includes a vehicle, vessel or moveable structure. This means that a structure with a moving roof, such as the Millennium Stadium in Cardiff and the Centre Court at Wimbledon, are excluded and are treated as outdoor premises.

4.2.4 Boxing or wrestling entertainment

A boxing or wrestling entertainment is any contest, exhibition or display of boxing or wrestling or which combines boxing or wrestling with one or more martial arts (Sched.1, para.17). It does not matter whether the entertainment takes place outside or inside.

4.2.5 A performance of live music

'Music' includes vocal or instrumental music or any combination of the two (Sched.1, para.18).

The Guidance at para.16.26 provides:

Live music is licensable:

- where a performance of live music – whether amplified or unamplified – takes place before 08.00 or after 23.00 on any day;
- where a performance of amplified live music does not take place either on relevant licensed premises, or at a workplace that is not licensed other than for the provision of late night refreshment;
- where a performance of amplified live music takes place at a time when the relevant licensed premises are not open for the purposes of being used for the sale or supply of alcohol for consumption on the premises;
- where a performance of amplified live music takes place at relevant licensed premises, or workplaces, in the presence of an audience of more than 500 people; or
- where a licensing authority intentionally removes the effect of the deregulation provided for by the 2003 Act when imposing a condition on a premises licence or club premises certificate as a result of a licence review.

The Guidance at para.16.30 provides:

... 'Live music' is a performance of live music in the presence of an audience which it is intended to entertain. While a performance of live music can include the playing of some recorded music, 'live' music requires that the performance does not consist entirely of the playing of recorded music without any additional (substantial and continual) creative contribution being made. So, for example, a drum machine or backing track being used to accompany a vocalist or a band would be part of the performance of amplified live music. The performance of a DJ who is merely playing tracks would not be classified as live music, but it might if he or she was performing a set which largely consisted of mixing recorded music in a live performance to create new sounds. There will inevitably be a degree of judgement as to whether a performance is live music (or recorded music) and organisers of events should check with their licensing authority if this consideration is relevant to whether the activity is authorised by a licence or certificate. In the event of a dispute about whether a performance is live music or not, it will be for the licensing authority initially and ultimately, for the courts to decide in the individual circumstances of any case.

For live music in small premises, see **11.10**.

4.2.6 Any playing of recorded music

This is not defined in the Act but is self-explanatory.

4.2.7 A performance of dance

This is not defined in the Act but is self-explanatory.

4.2.8 Entertainment of a similar description to live music, recorded music or dance

This is a sweeping up provision and covers entertainment of a similar kind to music or the performance of dance, for example a skating performance to music.

4.2.9 Modification of the definition

The Secretary of State may add to, vary or remove any of the descriptions of entertainment in the Act.

4.3 EXEMPTIONS

Part 2 of Sched.1 sets out exemptions where the provision of regulated entertainment does not amount to a licensable activity.

4.3.1 Film exhibitions for the purposes of advertisement, information, education, etc.

Entertainment which consists of the exhibition of a film is outside the definition of the provision of regulated entertainment if its sole or main purpose is to demonstrate any product, advertise any goods or services or provide information, education or instruction. Thus, educational films shown in schools or special advertisements shown at product display stands in shopping centres are exempt.

4.3.2 Film exhibitions in museums and art galleries

The exhibition of a film is not the provision of regulated entertainment if it consists of or forms part of an exhibit put on show for any purposes of a museum or art gallery.

4.3.3 Film exhibitions in community premises

The exhibition of a film at community premises is not the provision of regulated entertainment if:

- prior written consent for the entertainment to take place at the community premises has been obtained by or on behalf of a person concerned in the organisation or management of the entertainment from the management committee of the community premises, or where there is no management committee, from a person who has control of the community premises (as occupier or otherwise) in connection with the carrying on by that person of a trade, business or other undertaking (for profit or not), or where there is no such person, an owner of the community premises;
- the entertainment is not provided with a view to profit;
- the entertainment takes place in the presence of an audience of no more than 500 persons;
- the entertainment takes place between 8 am and 11 pm on the same day; and
- the film classification body or the relevant licensing authority has made a recommendation concerning the admission of children to an exhibition of the film and:

    - where a recommendation has been made only by the film classification body, the admission of children is subject to such restrictions, if any, as are necessary to comply with the recommendation of that body;
    - where a recommendation has been made only by the relevant licensing authority, the admission of children is subject to such restrictions, if any, as are necessary to comply with the recommendation of that authority; or
    - where recommendations have been made both by the film classification body and the relevant licensing authority, the admission of children is subject to such restrictions, if any, as are necessary to comply with the recommendation of the relevant licensing authority.

Community premises are defined in s.193 and are premises that are or form part of a church hall, chapel hall or other similar building, or a village hall, parish hall, community hall or other similar building.

4.3.4 Music and film incidental to certain other activities

The provision of entertainment which consists of the performance of live music, the playing of recorded music or the exhibition of a film is not the provision of regulated entertainment if it is incidental to some other activity which is not itself one of the entertainments described in the Act. So, a jukebox in a pub will not be required to be authorised unless say a dance floor is also provided or it is not incidental to some other activity.

The incidental music exemption can apply to an indoor sporting event or a performance of a play or dance for which no licence is required, as it takes place between 8 am and 11 pm on the same day and before an audience which does not exceed the relevant limit.

Whether or not music will be 'incidental' to another activity will depend on the facts of each case. The Guidance at para.16.49 provides that relevant factors to consider will include whether:

- against a background of the other activities already taking place, the addition of music will create the potential to undermine the promotion of one or more of the licensing objectives in the Act;
- the music is the main, or one of the main, reasons for people attending the premises and being charged;
- the music is advertised as the main attraction; and
- the volume of the music disrupts or predominates over other activities, or whether it could it be described as 'background' music.

Paragraph 16.50 of the Guidance provides that factors which would not normally be relevant in themselves will include:

- the number of musicians, e.g. an orchestra providing incidental music at a large exhibition;
- whether musicians are paid;
- whether the performance is pre-arranged; and
- whether a charge is made for admission to the premises.

In any disputed case, it will be for the licensing authority initially and, ultimately, for the courts to consider whether music is 'incidental' in the individual circumstances of any case.

4.3.5 Use of television or radio receivers

The provision of any entertainment is not the provision of regulated entertainment if it consists of the simultaneous reception and playing of a programme included in a programme service within the meaning of the Broadcasting Act 1990. Live broadcast entertainment is therefore exempt. However, showing pre-recorded entertainment, for example a video or a DVD, would require a licence.

4.3.6 Religious services, places of worship, etc.

The provision of any entertainment for the purposes of or for purposes incidental to a religious meeting or service, or at a place of public religious worship, is not the provision of regulated entertainment. This will exempt the singing of hymns during a church service.

4.3.7 Garden fêtes, etc.

The provision of any entertainment at a garden fête, or at a similar function or event, will not amount to the provision of regulated entertainment unless the fête, function or event is promoted with a view to applying the whole or part of its proceeds for purposes of private gain.

'Private gain' is construed in accordance with the Gambling Act 2005, s.19(3) and so the provision of a benefit to one or more individuals will not be a provision for private gain if it is made in the course of the activities of a society that is a non-commercial society by virtue of being established and conducted either for charitable purposes (i.e. purposes which are exclusively charitable) or for the purpose of enabling participation in, or of supporting, sport, athletics or a cultural activity.

4.3.8 Morris dancing, etc.

The provision of any entertainment is not the provision of regulated entertainment if it is the provision of a performance of morris dancing or any dancing of a similar nature or is the playing of live or recorded music that forms an integral part of such a performance.

4.3.9 Vehicles in motion

The provision of any entertainment on premises consisting of or forming part of a vehicle at a time when the vehicle is not permanently or temporarily parked is not to be regarded as the provision of regulated entertainment. This will exempt music or videos provided on coaches or other vehicles.

4.3.10 Sexual entertainment venues

The provision of relevant entertainment at premises for which a licence for a sexual entertainment venue is required (or the requirement has been waived) by virtue of the Local Government (Miscellaneous Provisions) Act 1982, Sched.3 and of a kind, and in a way, by virtue of which the premises qualify as such a venue, is not to be regarded as the provision of regulated entertainment.

A sexual entertainment venue and relevant entertainment are defined in the Local Government (Miscellaneous Provisions) Act 1982, Sched.3. Sexual entertainment venue means any premises at which relevant entertainment is provided before a live audience for the financial gain of the organiser or the entertainer. Relevant entertainment means any live performance or any live display of nudity which is of such a nature that, ignoring financial gain, it must reasonably be assumed to be provided solely or principally for the purpose of sexually stimulating any member of the audience (whether by verbal or other means). This will include the following forms of entertainment, as they are commonly understood:

- lap dancing;
- pole dancing;
- table dancing;
- strip shows;
- peep shows; and
- live sex shows.

So, dance that is sufficiently sexual in nature will be regulated.

In almost all cases where a performance of dance is potentially licensable as both the provision of relevant entertainment, under the Local Government (Miscellaneous Provisions) Act 1982, and regulated entertainment under the Act, the Local Government (Miscellaneous Provisions) Act 1982 disapplies the entertainment licensing regime in the Act in favour of its stricter regime for the control of sex establishments. However, an authorisation under the Act rather than the Local Government (Miscellaneous Provisions) Act 1982 will be required where:

- the premises are not licensed as a sex entertainment venue under the Local Government (Miscellaneous Provisions) Act 1982;
- there have not been more than 11 occasions on which relevant entertainment has been provided which fall (wholly or partly) within the period of 12 months ending with that time;
- no such occasion has lasted for more than 24 hours; and
- no such occasion has begun within the period of one month beginning with the end of any previous occasion on which relevant entertainment has been so provided (whether or not that previous occasion falls within the 12-month period).

The provision of entertainment consisting of the performance of live music or the playing of recorded music is not regarded as the provision of regulated entertainment for the purposes of the Act to the extent that it is an integral part of such provision of relevant entertainment.

4.3.11 Entertainment provided by healthcare providers, local authorities and school proprietors

The provision of any entertainment by or on behalf of a health care provider, local authority or school proprietor is not to be regarded as the provision of regulated entertainment if:

- the entertainment takes place:
    - if it is provided by or on behalf of a health care provider, on any premises forming part of a hospital in which that provider has a relevant property interest, or which are lawfully occupied by that provider;

- if it is provided by or on behalf of a local authority, on any premises in which that authority has a relevant property interest or which are lawfully occupied by that authority; and
- if it is provided by or on behalf of a school proprietor, on the premises of the school.

- the premises are not domestic premises;
- the entertainment takes place between 8 am and 11 pm on the same day (or, where an order under s.172 has effect in relation to that entertainment, during any times specified under that order (see **11.4.2**)); and
- the entertainment is not relevant entertainment within the meaning of the Local Government (Miscellaneous Provisions) Act 1982, Sched.3, para.2A(2).

For these purposes, a person has a relevant property interest in premises if that person is for the time being entitled to dispose of the fee simple in the premises, whether in possession or in reversion, or holds or is entitled to the rents and profits of the premises under a lease which, when granted, was for a term of not less than three years. 'Domestic premises' means premises occupied as a private dwelling, including any garden, yard, garage, outhouse or other appurtenance of such premises whether or not used in common by the occupants of more than one such dwelling. Other terms used in this exemption, such as 'local authority', 'health care', 'health care provider', 'hospital', 'school' and 'school premises' are also defined in Sched.1, paras.19, 20 and 21.

The Guidance at paras.16.17 and 16.18 provides:

16.17 This Guidance cannot give examples of every eventuality where entertainment is not licensable under this exemption through being provided 'by or on behalf of'. It will depend on the facts in each case. However, the following are examples of activities that are not usually considered to be licensable under this exemption:

- Any entertainment activity hosted by a local authority on their own premises, where there is a significant relationship between the local authority and the provider of the entertainment (e.g. principal and agent);
- Any entertainment activity organised on a local authority's behalf on that local authority's premises by a cultural trust in discharge of a local authority's discretionary power to arrange entertainment provision and support for the arts, including festivals and celebrations.
- Any entertainment activity organised by a healthcare provider on their own hospital premises in partnership with a hospital charity;
- Any entertainment event on school premises organised by the Parent Teacher Association (PTA) to benefit the school.

16.18 It is for the local authority, health care provider or school proprietor to determine whether, and on what basis, they can (or wish) to provide entertainment activity under this exemption, including consideration of issues around fundraising, profit making, governance or use of public funds. However a pure hire of premises by a third party does not constitute the provision of an entertainment event 'on behalf of' a local authority, healthcare provider, or school proprietor and nor does commercial entertainment which the local authority merely facilitates through providing a public space.

4.3.12 Music at community premises, etc.

The provision of entertainment consisting of one or both of a performance of live music or the playing of recorded music is not to be regarded as the provision of regulated entertainment if:

- the entertainment takes place at community premises that are not authorised, by a premises licence or club premises certificate, to be used for the supply of alcohol for consumption on the premises, the premises of a hospital, premises in which a local authority has a relevant property interest or which are lawfully occupied by a local authority, or the premises of a school;
- the premises are not domestic premises;
- the entertainment takes place in the presence of an audience of no more than 500 persons;
- the entertainment takes place between 8 am and 11 pm on the same day (or, where an order under s.172 has effect in relation to that entertainment, during any times specified under that order (see **11.4.2**)); and
- a person concerned in the organisation or management of the entertainment has obtained the prior written consent of a relevant person for the entertainment to take place.

See **7.11.3** for the definition of 'community premises' and see **4.3.11** for the definition of 'relevant property interest'. 'Relevant person' means:

- where the entertainment takes place at community premises the management committee of the premises, or if there is no management committee, a person who has control of the premises (as occupier or otherwise) in connection with the carrying on by that person of a trade, business or other undertaking (for profit or not) or (in the absence of such a person) a person with a relevant property interest in the premises;
- where the entertainment takes place at the premises of a hospital, a health care provider which has a relevant property interest in or lawfully occupies those premises;
- where the entertainment takes place at premises in which a local authority has a relevant property interest or which are lawfully occupied by a local authority, that authority; and
- where the entertainment takes place at the premises of a school, the school proprietor.

4.3.13 Music in licensed venues

The provision of entertainment consisting of one or both of a performance of live music or the playing of recorded music is not to be regarded as the provision of regulated entertainment if:

- the music takes place on premises which are authorised to be used for the supply of alcohol for consumption on the premises by a premises licence or club premises certificate;
- at the time of the music, the premises are open for the purpose of being used for the supply of alcohol for consumption on the premises;
- if the live music is amplified, it takes place in the presence of an audience of no more than 500 people;
- the music takes place between 8 am and 11 pm on the same day (or, where an order under s.172 has effect in relation to music, during any times specified under that order (see **11.4.2**)); and
- conditions have not been included in the licence or certificate by virtue of s.177A(3) or (4).

On a review of a premises licence or club premises certificate, s.177A(3) permits a licensing authority to alter the licence or certificate so as to include a statement that s.177A does not apply. Under s.177A(4), a licensing authority on a review of a premises licence or club premises certificate may add a condition relating to music as if music were regulated entertainment, and as if that premises licence or club premises certificate licensed the music.

4.3.14 Live music in workplaces

The provision of entertainment consisting of a performance of live music is not to be regarded as the provision of regulated entertainment, provided that:

- the place where the performance is provided is not licensed under the Act (or is so licensed only for the provision of late night refreshment) but is a workplace as defined in reg.2(1) of the Workplace (Health, Safety and Welfare) Regulations 1992, SI 1992/3004;
- the performance takes place in the presence of an audience of no more than 500 persons; and
- the performance takes place between 8 am and 11 pm on the same day.

A 'workplace' is anywhere that is made available to any person as a place of work. This is a very wide definition and can include outdoor spaces, as well as the means of entry and exit.

4.3.15 Live unamplified music

The provision of entertainment consisting of a performance of live music is not (subject to s.177A(3) and (4)) to be regarded as the provision of regulated entertainment provided that the music is unamplified and the performance takes place between 8 am and 11 pm on the same day.

4.3.16 Circuses

The provision of any entertainment that consists of or forms part of a performance by a travelling circus is not to be regarded as the provision of regulated entertainment if:

- the entertainment is not of an exhibition of a film or boxing or wrestling entertainment;
- the entertainment takes place between 8 am and 11 pm on the same day;
- the entertainment takes place wholly within a moveable structure and the audience present is accommodated wholly inside that moveable structure; and
- the travelling circus has not been located on the same site for more than 28 consecutive days.

A 'travelling circus' is a circus which travels from site to site for the purpose of giving performances.

4.3.17 Boxing or wrestling entertainment – certain forms of wrestling

The provision of entertainment consisting of a boxing or wrestling entertainment is not to be regarded as the provision of regulated entertainment if:

- it is a contest, exhibition or display of Greco-Roman wrestling or of freestyle wrestling, between two participants (regardless of their sex);
- it takes place in the presence of no more than 1,000 spectators;
- it takes place between 8 am and 11 pm on the same day;
- it takes place wholly inside a building; and
- the spectators present at that entertainment are accommodated wholly inside that building.

4.4 PARTICULAR PREMISES AND EVENTS

4.4.1 Beer gardens

The Guidance at paras.16.42 to 16.44 provides:

> 16.42 Beer gardens are often included as part of a premises licence or club premises certificate. Live amplified music that takes place in a beer garden is exempt from licensing requirements, provided the beer garden is included in the licence or

certificate applying to the relevant licensed premises, and the performance takes place between 08.00 and 23.00 on the same day before an audience of 500 people or fewer.

16.43 Where a beer garden does not form part of the relevant licensed premises and so is not included in plans attached to a premises licence or club premises certificate, it is nevertheless very likely that it will be a workplace. Paragraph 12B of Schedule 1 to the 2003 Act says that a performance of live music in a workplace that does not have a licence (except to provide late night refreshment) is not regulated entertainment if it takes place between 08.00 and 23.00 on the same day in front of an audience of no more than 500 people. Note that the exemption in paragraph 12B does not apply to the playing of recorded music.

16.44 However, a licensing authority may, where justified, impose a licence condition that relates to the performance of live music in an unlicensed beer garden being served by any associated premises licence or club premises certificate. Provided such a condition is lawfully imposed, it takes effect in accordance with its terms.

4.4.2 Busking

The Guidance at paras.16.62 to 16.64 provides:

16.62 Busking or street performance is the practice of performing in public spaces for money. Performances are not limited to music or singing and can take the form of a wide range of activities that people find entertaining.

16.63 Busking is generally *not* licensable under the 2003 Act as:

- it often occurs in a place that is not a premises made available (at least in part) for the purposes of providing entertainment;
- the entertainment is usually incidental to another activity, such as shopping or sightseeing, as there are few circumstances in which anyone would go out specifically to watch buskers; and
- any unamplified live music is not licensable between 08.00 and 23.00.

16.64 Local authorities may have policies on busking, including codes of conduct or permit regimes and occasionally byelaws and legislation specific to a local authority – although many localities have no policy or restrictions.

4.4.3 Entertainment activity provided as part of childcare

The Guidance at para.16.69 provides:

16.69 Entertainment activity that is provided as part of childcare will generally not be licensable. This includes entertainment activity in a nursery or private home. In addition, paragraph 5 of Schedule 1 to the 2003 Act includes a licensing exemption for an exhibition of a film where the main purpose is to provide education. Education will generally include all forms of pre-school child and day care. Furthermore, an exhibition of a film, or the playing of live or recorded music, will generally be incidental to the activity of childcare and so the incidental music and film exemption in paragraph 7 of Schedule 1 will also apply. This will generally be the case for any entertainment activity organised as part of wraparound childcare, including breakfast clubs, after school clubs or holiday clubs linked to the child's school or based in the local community.

4.4.4 Private events

The Guidance at paras.16.13 and 16.14 provides:

16.13 Events held in private are not licensable unless those attending are charged for the entertainment with a view to making a profit (including raising money for charity). For example, where a party is held for friends in a private dwelling featuring amplified live music, if a charge or contribution is made solely to cover the costs of the entertainment, the activity is not regulated entertainment. Similarly, any charge made to the organiser of a private event by musicians, other performers, or their agents does not of itself make that entertainment licensable – it would only do so if the guests attending were themselves charged by the organiser for that entertainment with a view to achieving a profit. The fact that this might inadvertently result in the organiser making a profit would be irrelevant, as long as there had not been an intention to make a profit.

16.14 Schedule 1 to the 2003 Act also makes it clear that before entertainment is regarded as being provided for consideration, a charge has to be:

- made by or on behalf of a person concerned with the organisation or management of the entertainment; and
- paid by or on behalf of some or all of the persons for whom the entertainment is provided.

CHAPTER 5

Late night refreshment

5.1 INTRODUCTION

The Act provides that the provision of late night refreshment is a licensable activity (s.1(1)). This means that a premises licence will be required by establishments such as takeaways, fish and chip shops, mobile catering vehicles and fast food outlets that wish to provide late night refreshment. It is possible for the supply of alcohol, the provision of regulated entertainment and the provision of late night refreshment to be carried on under one premises licence.

The effect of this is that if a business, such as a supermarket, a garage, a takeaway or a fast food outlet is heating food or drink for customers to consume on or off the premises between 11 pm and 5 am, or provides facilities for customers that enable the food or drink to be heated above the ambient temperature, a late night refreshment licence will be required. However, if a business is selling only cold food and drink and not providing facilities to enable the food or drink to be heated on the premises, then a licence authorising the provision of late night refreshment will not be required.

In relation to premises where the main licensable activity is not the provision of late night refreshment, the Guidance at para.3.16 provides that:

> It is not expected that the provision of late night refreshment as a secondary activity in licensed premises open for other purposes such as public houses, cinemas or nightclubs or casinos should give rise to a need for significant additional conditions.

5.2 WHAT IS LATE NIGHT REFRESHMENT?

Section 1(5) provides for Sched.2 to make provisions about what constitutes late night refreshment. A person provides late night refreshment if:

- at any time between the hours of 11 pm and 5 am, he supplies hot food or hot drink to members of the public, or a section of the public, on or from any premises, whether for consumption on or off the premises; or

- at any time between those hours when members of the public, or a section of the public, are admitted to any premises, he supplies, or holds himself out as willing to supply, hot food or hot drink to any persons, or to persons of a particular description, on or from those premises whether for consumption on or off the premises,

unless the supply is an exempt supply.

5.3 HOT FOOD OR HOT DRINK

Food or drink supplied on or from any premises is 'hot' if the food or drink, or any part of it:

- before it is supplied, is heated on the premises or elsewhere for the purpose of enabling it to be consumed at a temperature above the ambient air temperature and, at the time of supply, is above that temperature, for example fish and chips; or
- after it is supplied, may be heated on the premises for the purpose of enabling it to be consumed at a temperature above the ambient air temperature, for example in a microwave in the premises provided by the business for that purpose.

The second limb of this definition would appear to include shops and supermarkets which open late and provide a microwave in which customers can heat up food which they have bought. Whether this is the intention is not clear and the Guidance at para.3.13 provides:

> Shops, stores and supermarkets selling only cold food and cold drink, whether it is immediately consumable or not, from 23.00 are not licensable as providing late night refreshment. The 2003 Act affects premises such as night cafés and takeaway food outlets where people may gather at any time from 23.00 and until 05.00. In this case, supply takes place when the hot food or hot drink is given to the customer and not when payment is made. For example, supply takes place when a table meal is served in a restaurant or when a takeaway is handed to a customer over the counter.

In practice such premises are likely to have a premises licence for other licensable activities and the premises licence could also include authorisation for late night refreshment.

5.4 EXEMPT SUPPLIES

Certain supplies are exempt under Sched.2 from being late night refreshment and so do not require authorisation.

5.4.1 Designated areas, descriptions of premises and times

A licensing authority has the power to exempt premises, in certain circumstances, from the requirement to have a licence to provide late night refreshment. The Guidance at para.3.22 provides:

> Decisions to exempt supplies of late night refreshment are best made with local knowledge. The powers therefore allow licensing authorities to choose to apply an exemption specifically where they think it will be helpful to businesses and where there are no problems with anti-social behaviour, disorder associated with the night time economy, or illegal working in licensed premises. As well as freeing up the businesses in question from unnecessary costs, this can also provide greater flexibility for licensing authorities to target their resources more effectively.

The supply of hot food or hot drink is an exempt supply if it takes place:

- on or from premises which are wholly situated in an area designated by the licensing authority;
- on or from premises which are of a description designated by the licensing authority; or
- during a period (beginning no earlier than 11.00 pm and ending no later than 5.00 am) designated by the licensing authority.

When choosing to designate particular categories of premises as exempt under the second of these, a licensing authority can only exempt types of premises prescribed by regulations. The exempted premises designated by the Licensing Act 2003 (Late Night Refreshment) Regulations 2015, SI 2015/1781 are as follows:

- premises situated on land for the time being used for the provision of facilities to be used in connection with the use of a special road provided for the use of traffic of class I (with or without other classes) (motorway service area);
- premises used for the retailing of petrol or derv;
- premises in which a local authority has a relevant property interest or which are lawfully occupied by that authority, except:

  - any domestic premises within those premises; or
  - when an event is taking place at which more than 500 people are present;

- the premises of a school except:

  - any domestic premises within the school; or
  - when an event is taking place at which more than 500 people are present;

- premises used as a hospital, except any domestic premises within the hospital;
- community premises, except when an event is taking place at which more than 500 people are present;

- licensed premises authorised to sell by retail alcohol for consumption on the premises between the hours of 11 pm and 5 am.

For these purposes, 'domestic premises' has the meaning given by para.12ZA(7) of Sched.1 to the Act; 'premises used as a hospital' has the meaning given by para.19(3) of Sched.1 to the Act; 'local authority' has the meaning given by para.20 of Sched.1 to the Act; and 'school' has the meaning given by para.21 of Sched.1 to the Act. Furthermore, a local authority has a relevant property interest in premises if that local authority is for the time being entitled to dispose of the fee simple in the premises, whether in possession or in reversion, or holds or is entitled to the rents and profits of the premises under a lease which (when granted) was for a term of not less than three years.

When choosing to exempt the provision of late night refreshment at particular times, the licensing authority must determine the times between 11 pm and 5 am when the exemption applies. The exemption and any subsequent change to the time will apply to the whole licensing authority area.

A licensing authority may use more than one type of exemption at the same time, for example by changing the times across its area during which licensing requirements will apply and also exempting premises by type across the whole licensing authority area. However, it cannot use different forms of exemption in conjunction with one another, for example, it would not be permitted to change the times in one geographic area only.

The Guidance at paras.3.29, 3.31 and 3.32 provides:

3.29 Licensing authorities should consider deregulation where possible. However, they do not have to use the exemptions and can continue to require all late night refreshment providers to be licensed where this is appropriate for the promotion of the licensing objectives.

3.31 When deciding which exemption to use, if any, the relevant licensing authority should always first consider what the risks are in terms of the promotion of the licensing objectives, including the prevention of illegal working in those premises. The decision to make an exemption is a licensing function that licensing authorities should include within their statement of licensing policy. It would then therefore be subject to the statutory consultation process with other responsible authorities and relevant parties set out in section 5 of the 2003 Act. However, it is for the licensing authority to decide on the detail and extent of the consultation beyond the statutory minimum; for example, in areas where there are concerns about illegal working in licensed premises the licensing authority should consult Home Office Immigration Enforcement. The licensing authority may decide to only consult on the proposed exemption or, alternatively, it may form part of a wider review of other matters within its statement of licensing policy.

3.32 When applying any of the exemptions the relevant licensing authority must publicise the changes and should decide on the most appropriate way to do this, in addition to updating its statement of licensing policy as soon as is practical. There is no requirement for licensing authorities to tell premises individually, however they should publicise the exemption in a way that ensures that those who are likely to be affected may benefit from it. If any fees are paid prior to an exemption coming into effect, licensing authorities should consider whether a refund or partial refund is appropriate. It is for each individual licensing author-ity to develop its own refund policy and ensure that it is communicated appro-priately to all licence holders that are likely to be affected by an exemption.

A licensing authority can review the exemptions at any time, to change the times, locations, or types. However, unlike many other types of licensing decisions, these exemptions are not made on a case-by-case basis and there is no recourse to bring an individual premises back into the licensing regime if there is a pro-blem with that particular premises. In such cases, the licensing authority would have to take a decision about the entire exemption and apply it across the whole area. Alternatively, depending on the scale of the problem, other powers could be used such as closure powers under the Anti-social Behaviour, Crime and Policing Act 2014. Environmental health legislation around noise nuisance may also offer a solution.

5.4.2 Clubs, hotels, etc. and employees

The next exemption relates to the supply to members of certain clubs, supply to guests in hotels and similar premises, supply to employees of a particular employer, supply to persons in particular trades, professions or vocations and guests of any of the above.

The supply of hot food or hot drink on or from any premises at any time is an exempt supply if, at that time, a person will neither be admitted to the premises, nor be supplied with hot food or hot drink on or from the premises, unless:

- he is a member of a recognised club, that is a members' club which meets the general qualifying conditions for a club premises certificate;
- he is a person staying at a hotel, a guest house, lodging house or hostel, a caravan site, camping site or any other premises the main purpose of main-taining which is the provision of facilities for overnight accommodation, for the night in question;
- he is an employee of a particular employer, for example at a staff canteen;
- he is engaged in a particular trade, he is a member of a particular profession or he follows a particular vocation, for example a tradesman carrying out work at particular premises; or
- he is a guest of the above persons.

Where a club is not a recognised club, the supply of hot food or hot drink to a member or his guest will not be exempt and will require authorisation.

5.4.3 Premises licensed under other statutes

There are two exemptions here and both have effect only in London.

The supply of hot food or hot drink on or from any premises is an exempt supply if it takes place during a period for which the premises may be used for a public exhibition of a kind described in the Greater London Council (General

Powers) Act 1966, s.21(1) by virtue of a licence under that section. The premises concerned are Alexandra Palace, Wood Green, Haringey; Central Hall, Tothill Street, City of Westminster, SW1; Earls Court, Warwick Road, Kensington and Chelsea, SW5; Olympia, Blythe Road and Hammersmith Road, Kensington and Chelsea, W14; Royal Festival Hall, South Bank, Lambeth, SE1; The Royal Horticultural Halls, Vincent Square, City of Westminster, SW1; and Seymour Hall, Seymour Place, City of Westminster, W1.

The second exemption relates to premises which may be used as near beer premises within the meaning of the London Local Authorities Act 1995, s.14 by virtue of a licence under s.16 of that Act. A near beer premises means any premises (including a vehicle, vessel or stall) which:

- consists to a significant degree of:

  – the sale to customers of any drink for consumption on the premises which includes in its trade description any of the following words: beer, lager, pils, shandy, cider, wine, champagne, cocktail, sherry, gin, brandy, whisky, vodka or other words which imply that the drink contains or would reasonably be expected to contain alcohol; or
  – the sale to customers of any drink for consumption on the premises which would be expected to contain alcohol or calculated to represent any alcoholic drink; and

- offers, expressly or by implication, whether on payment of a fee or not, either or both of the following:

  – companions for customers; and/or
  – live entertainment on the premises

but does not include any premises which has a premises licence which permits the sale of alcohol, or regulated entertainment comprising either music, dancing, plays or film exhibitions during the hours permitted by that licence.

Near beer premises are common in London's Soho area.

5.4.4 Miscellaneous exempt supplies

The following supplies of hot food or hot drink are exempt supplies:

- the supply of hot drink which consists of or contains alcohol;
- the supply of hot drink by means of a vending machine where the payment for the hot drink is inserted into the machine by a member of the public, and the hot drink is supplied directly by the machine to a member of the public (but this exemption does not apply to hot food supplied by vending machine);
- the supply of hot food or hot drink free of charge, and these will not be regarded as supplied free of charge if, in order to obtain them, a charge must be paid for admission to the premises, or for some other item;

- the supply of hot food or hot drink by a charity which is registered under the Charities Act 2011, s.30, or by a charity which by virtue of the Charities Act 2011, s.30(2) is not required to be so registered, or a person authorised by such charities; and
- the supply of hot food or hot drink on a vehicle at a time when the vehicle is not permanently or temporarily parked.

The supply of hot drink which consists of or contains alcohol is exempt under the Act as late night refreshment because it is caught by the provisions relating to the sale or supply of alcohol (Guidance, para.3.17). The supply of hot food or hot drink free of charge is not a licensable activity. However, where any charge is made either for admission to the premises or for some other item in order to obtain the hot food or hot drink it will not be regarded as 'free of charge'. Supplies by a registered charity or anyone authorised by a registered charity are also exempt. Similarly supplies made on moving vehicles, for example boats, trains and coaches, are also exempt. However, supplies made from a vehicle which is permanently or temporarily parked, for example a mobile takeaway van, are not exempt (Guidance, para.3.19). The Guidance at para.3.34 provides:

> Under section 189 of the 2003 Act, a vehicle which is not permanently situated in the same place and is or is proposed to be used for one or more licensable activities while parked at a particular place, is to be treated as if it were premises situated at that place. Therefore, a mobile provider of late night refreshment, such as a kebab van, could be treated as exempt if it supplied hot food to the public late at night in an area which had been designated as exempt. If the mobile van drove to and began operating in a non-exempt area, a licence to carry on this activity would be required. Should the licensing authority introduce an exemption, and subsequently wish to revoke it if problems arise, it has the power to do so. Areas which are likely to be considered for exemption by licensing authorities (for example, an area outside a town centre) are unlikely to be areas in which mobile kebab vans would frequently operate. As such, mobile vehicles selling late night refreshment are likely to still require licences in the areas in which they are more commonly found.

CHAPTER 6

Personal licences

6.1 INTRODUCTION

Part 6 of the Act provides for a system of personal licences for controlling the sale or supply of alcohol. Any person who wants to sell alcohol by retail or to supply it by or on behalf of a club or to the order of a member of the club must possess a personal licence. A personal licence is separate from a premises licence and the rationale behind this separation is to make it easier for individuals to move between licensed premises without the need to have to apply for a transfer of licence, thus allowing greater flexibility. No matter which licensing authority issues the personal licence it will be valid for use anywhere in England and Wales. A personal licence is not required for the provision of regulated entertainment or late night refreshment. It is only required for the sale or supply of alcohol under a premises licence.

While the Act provides that all supplies of alcohol under a premises licence must be made by or under the authority of a personal licence holder, there is no requirement that every person employed in the licensed premises must hold a personal licence. It is sufficient that an employee working in licensed premises and who does not hold a personal licence is supplying alcohol under the authority of a personal licence holder (s.19(3)). Nor is it necessary for the personal licence holder to be on the premises at all times to physically authorise every sale of alcohol, and the Guidance at para.4.3 states:

> the requirement that every sale of alcohol must at least be authorised by a personal licence holder does not mean that the licence holder has to be present on the premises or oversee each sale; it is sufficient that such sales are authorised.

A personal licence holder may authorise members of staff to make sales of alcohol during the course of an evening, but may be absent at times from the premises when a transaction takes place. However, the personal licence holder will not be able to escape responsibility for the actions of those he authorises to make such sales.

A premises licence which specifies that the supply of alcohol is a licensable activity must also specify a person to be the designated premises supervisor (see **Chapter 9**). This is the person who is responsible for the day-to-day running of the premises. The designated premises supervisor must always hold a personal licence. There may be other individuals at the premises who hold a personal licence but only one of them can be the designated premises supervisor. There is an exception for community premises in respect of which there has been a successful application to remove the requirement for a designated premises supervisor.

6.2 DEFINITION OF PERSONAL LICENCE

A personal licence is defined in s.111 as a licence which is granted by a licensing authority to an individual authorising that person either to supply alcohol or to authorise its supply in accordance with a premises licence. The supply of alcohol includes selling alcohol by retail, or supplying it by or on behalf of a club or to the order of a member of the club. Where club premises operate under a club premises certificate a personal licence is not required in order to supply alcohol to members or their guests.

A personal licence does not authorise its holder to supply alcohol anywhere other than from premises which have a premises licence authorising the supply of alcohol, or from other premises under the authority of a temporary event notice.

6.3 WHO CAN APPLY FOR A PERSONAL LICENCE?

Section 117(2) provides that an application for a personal licence may only be made by an individual. It is not possible for an application to be made by a corporate body.

The requirements for the grant of a personal licence are laid down in s.120(2) and the effect of these is that an application for a personal licence can be made by any individual who:

- is at least 18 years old;
- is entitled to work in the United Kingdom;
- possesses an accredited licensing qualification or is a person of a description prescribed by regulation;
- has not had a personal licence forfeited within the five years immediately preceding the date when the application was made; and
- has not been convicted of any relevant offence or foreign offence or required to pay an immigration penalty.

There is no requirement that an applicant for a personal licence be employed in the licensing trade or have business interests associated with the use of the licence.

A person can only hold one personal licence at a time. A person who has applied for a personal licence cannot make an application for another personal licence until the first application has been withdrawn or determined by the licensing authority (s.118(1)). If the holder of a personal licence is subsequently granted another personal licence, then that second licence will be void (s.118(2)).

6.4 APPLICATION FOR A PERSONAL LICENCE

An application for a personal licence must be made either to the licensing authority for the area in which the applicant is ordinarily resident or, if the applicant is not ordinarily resident in the area of any particular licensing authority, to any licensing authority (s.117(2)). This is referred to in the Act as the 'relevant licensing authority' and it takes responsibility for the personal licence once it has been granted. The licensing authority which issues a personal licence remains the relevant licensing authority even if the holder moves out of its area.

The application form, the information it must contain and the documentation which must accompany it are prescribed by the Licensing Act 2003 (Personal Licences) Regulations 2005, SI 2005/41 ('the Personal Licences Regulations').

In order to apply for a personal licence, an applicant must submit to the relevant licensing authority:

- a completed application form;
- two photographs of the applicant which are:
    - taken against a light background so that the applicant's features are distinguishable and contrast against the background;
    - 45 mm by 35 mm;
    - with full face uncovered and without sunglasses and, unless the applicant wears a head covering because of the applicant's religious beliefs, without a head covering; and
    - on photographic paper;

    and one of the photographs must be endorsed with a statement verifying the likeness of the photograph to the applicant by a solicitor, notary, a person of standing in the community, such as a bank or building society official, a police officer, a civil servant or a minister of religion or any individual with a professional qualification;

- the applicant's licensing qualification;
- either a criminal conviction certificate issued under the Police Act 1997, s.112, a criminal record certificate issued under the Police Act 1997, s.113A or the results of a request made under Regulation (EU) 2016/679 on the protection of natural persons with regard to the processing of personal data and on the free movement of such data (United Kingdom General Data Protection Regulation) ('the UK GDPR'), art.15 or the Data Protection Act 2018, s.45

(rights of access by the data subject) to the National Identification Service for information contained in the Police National Computer. Whichever of these is produced, it must not have been issued more than one calendar month before the application for the personal licence is submitted to the licensing authority;

- a declaration by the applicant, in the prescribed form, that the applicant has not been convicted of a relevant offence or a foreign offence, has not been required to pay an immigration penalty or that the applicant has been convicted of a relevant offence or a foreign offence or required to pay an immigration penalty accompanied by details of the nature and date of the conviction and any sentence imposed on him in respect of such conviction; and

- the prescribed fee.

It is suggested that some form of seniority will be required for the person endorsing the photograph, for example a bank or building society manager rather than a junior employee. Individuals with professional qualifications would presumably include persons such as doctors, accountants, solicitors, barristers, legal executives and teachers.

6.5 ENTITLEMENT TO WORK IN THE UNITED KINGDOM

An applicant for a personal licence must be entitled to work in the United Kingdom and their application must be accompanied by one of the documents listed at Annex A of the Home Office's Employer right to work checks supporting guidance published at **www.gov.uk/government/publications/right-to-work-checks-employers-guide** to show that they have permission to be in the United Kingdom and are permitted to undertake work in a licensable activity. Alternatively, an applicant may demonstrate their right to work by allowing the licensing authority to carry out a check with the Home Office online right to work checking service. See the Guidance paras.4.8 to 4.48 for more information.

Section 192A provides that an individual is entitled to work in the United Kingdom if:

- the individual does not, under the Immigration Act 1971, require leave to enter or remain in the United Kingdom; or
- the individual has been granted such leave and the leave:

    – is not invalid;
    – has not ceased to have effect (whether by reason of curtailment, revocation, cancellation, passage of time or otherwise); and
    – is not subject to a condition preventing the individual from doing work relating to the carrying on of the sale by retail of alcohol or the provision of late night refreshment.

Where an individual is on immigration bail within the meaning of the Immigration Act 2016 Sched.10, Part 1, the individual is to be treated for the above purposes as if the individual had been granted leave to enter the United Kingdom, but any condition as to the individual's work in the United Kingdom to which the individual's immigration bail is subject is to be treated for those purposes as a condition of leave.

6.6 THE APPLICATION FORM

6.6.1 Obtaining an application form

A relevant licensing authority must provide a potential applicant with an application form on request. An electronic version may be provided on a licensing authority's website which a potential applicant can download, print off and complete (Personal Licences Regulations, reg.10). An application cannot be rejected purely because it has been made on a form which was not provided by the relevant licensing authority but which in all other respects complies with the requirements of the Personal Licences Regulations, reg.11.

6.6.2 Completing the application form

Guidance in completing the application form may be obtained from **www.gov.uk** or the relevant licensing authority. The form may be completed by being either typed or written legibly in block capitals. All answers must be inside the boxes and written or typed in black ink. Care must be taken when completing the application form as any mistakes will be built into the new licence.

The application form is divided into five parts, as follows.

Part 1 – personal details

This section asks for details of the applicant, such as their full name, any previous names, confirmation that the applicant is 18 years old or over, the address where the applicant is ordinarily resident (the licensing authority will use this address to correspond with the applicant unless the applicant specifies an alternative correspondence address, such as their business address), the applicant's daytime, evening and mobile telephone numbers and fax number and finally the applicant's email address if the applicant would prefer the licensing authority to correspond with them by email.

Part 2 – licensing qualification

This section asks the applicant to indicate their licensing qualification and to give details, such as the name of their qualification, the date it was issued and the name of the issuing body.

Part 3 – previous or outstanding applications for a personal licence

The applicant must indicate whether they currently hold a personal licence, has an outstanding application for a personal licence waiting to be dealt with or has had a personal licence forfeited within the previous five years.

Part 4 – checklist

This part is made up of a checklist of the enclosures which must be sent with the application so that the applicant can make sure that the application is complete before it is submitted.

Part 5 – declaration

By signing this part the applicant is making a declaration that the information in the application form is correct to the best of their knowledge and belief and that they are entitled to work in the United Kingdom and are not subject to a condition preventing them from doing work relating to the carrying on of a licensable activity. It is an offence to make a false statement in or in connection with the application. This is an offence which on conviction may incur a fine not exceeding level 5 on the standard scale.

6.6.3 Making an application

The Personal Licences Regulations, reg.9 provides that an application must be made in writing. However, notwithstanding this requirement, an application can also be made electronically, provided:

- the text of the application is transmitted by electronic means, is capable of being accessed by the recipient, is legible in all material respects, and is capable of being read and reproduced in written form and used for subsequent reference;
- the person to whom the application is to be given has agreed in advance that an application may be given by electronic means; and
- forthwith on sending the text of the application by electronic means, the application is given to the recipient in writing.

As the application must be accompanied by a fee and other documents, where the text of the application is transmitted by electronic means, the application will not be treated as being made until the fee and other documents have been received by the relevant licensing authority.

Table 6.1: Checklist for a personal licence application

	Original to relevant licensing authority
Completed application form	
Two photographs of the applicant, one of which is endorsed as a true likeness	
Completed disclosure of criminal convictions and declaration form	
Criminal conviction certificate or criminal record certificate or the results of a subject access search of the police national computer by the National Identification Service	
Proof of right to work in the United Kingdom or the applicant's share code issued by the Home Office online right to work checking service	
Licensing qualification	
Payment of the prescribed fee	

6.7 DETERMINATION OF AN APPLICATION

6.7.1 Mandatory grant

If an application has been made in accordance with the procedural requirements, s.120(2) provides that the application must be granted if the applicant:

- is at least 18 years old;
- is entitled to work in the United Kingdom;
- possesses an accredited licensing qualification or is a person of a prescribed description;
- has not had a personal licence forfeited in the five years immediately preceding the date when the application was made; and
- has not been convicted of any relevant offence or foreign offence or required to pay an immigration penalty.

The licensing authority has no discretion to refuse an application where these criteria are met.

There appears to be nothing to stop a person aged under 18 years old from applying for a personal licence provided that he is 18 years old when the licensing authority considers his application.

6.7.2 Mandatory refusal

An application must be rejected if the applicant is not at least 18 years old, is not entitled to work in the United Kingdom, does not possess an accredited licensing qualification or is not a person of a prescribed description, or has had a personal licence forfeited in the previous five years (s.120(3)).

6.7.3 Discretionary grant

If the applicant satisfies the first four conditions in s.120(2) but fails to satisfy the final condition, in other words the applicant has been convicted of a relevant offence or foreign offence or has been required to pay an immigration penalty, then the licensing authority must give notice of this to the chief officer of police for its area (s.120(4)). If the chief officer of police is then satisfied that granting the licence would undermine the crime prevention objective, the chief officer of police must, within 14 days beginning on the day they received the notice, give the licensing authority an objection notice stating the reasons why they are satisfied that granting the licence would undermine the crime prevention objective. The personal licence must be granted if the police do not give an objection notice within the 14-day period or if an objection notice is withdrawn.

If the applicant satisfies the first four conditions in s.120(2) but fails to satisfy the final condition by virtue of having been convicted of an immigration offence, convicted of a foreign offence that the licensing authority considers to be comparable to an immigration offence, or required to pay an immigration penalty, the licensing authority must give notice of this to the Secretary of State (through Home Office Immigration Enforcement). If the Secretary of State is then satisfied that granting the licence would be prejudicial to the prevention of illegal working in licensed premises, the Secretary of State must, within 14 days beginning on the day the Secretary of State received the notice, give the licensing authority an immigration objection notice stating the reasons why the Secretary of State is satisfied that granting the licence would be prejudicial to the prevention of illegal working in licensed premises. The personal licence must be granted if the Secretary of State does not give an immigration objection notice within the 14-day period or if an immigration objection notice is withdrawn. If an objection notice or an immigration objection notice is given within the 14-day period, the licensing authority must hold a hearing to consider it, unless the applicant, the person who gave the notice and the licensing authority all agree that a hearing is not necessary. The hearing must be held within 20 working days beginning with the day after the end of the 14-day period for the police to give an objection notice (Hearings Regulations, reg.5 and Sched.1, para.12). Notice of the hearing must be given to the applicant and the chief officer of police no later than 10 working days before the day or the first day on which the hearing is to be held (Hearings Regulations, reg.6(4) and Sched.2, para.12). The applicant must be given the notice of objection with the notice of hearing (Hearings Regulations, reg.7(2) and Sched.3, para.11). The Hearing Regulations do not make provision for a hearing where an immigration objection notice is given.

The licensing authority must reject the application for the personal licence if, having regard to the notice, where it is an objection notice, it considers it appropriate to do so for the promotion of the crime prevention objective, or where it is an immigration objection notice, it considers it appropriate to do so for the prevention of illegal working in licensed premises (s.120)7)(b)). Otherwise the personal licence must be granted (s.120(7A)). The issue of police objections to an application for a personal licence was considered in *R. (on the application of South Northamptonshire Council)* v. *Towcester Magistrates' Court* [2008] EWHC 381 (Admin) at [33], where the court said in relation to the test in s.120(7) that '... the Guidance does not purport to set out the test, impose a new or different test or to add a gloss to the test itself'. The Guidance at para.4.54 provides:

> A number of relevant offences never become spent. However, where an applicant is able to demonstrate that the offence in question took place so long ago and that the applicant no longer has a propensity to re-offend, a licensing authority may consider that it is appropriate to grant the application on the basis that doing so would not undermine the crime prevention objective.

6.8 NOTIFICATION OF THE GRANT OR REFUSAL OF A PERSONAL LICENCE

When a personal licence has been granted, the licensing authority must give notice of its decision to the applicant and the chief officer of police, and where either the chief officer of police or the Secretary of State (through Home Office Immigration Enforcement) objected to the grant and has not withdrawn their objection, the notice must set out the reasons why the licensing authority has granted the application (s.122(1)). If the personal licence is not granted, notice must be given to the applicant and the chief officer of police setting out the reasons for the refusal (s.122(2)). Where the Secretary of State gave an immigration objection notice, which was not withdrawn, notice must also be given to the Secretary of State (s.122(2A)).

Notice must be given by the licensing authority forthwith (see **2.9**) on making the determination, and must be accompanied by information regarding the right of a party to appeal against the determination.

6.9 ISSUING OF A PERSONAL LICENCE

Section 125 provides that a personal licence once granted must be issued forthwith (see **2.9**).

A personal licence must:

- specify the holder's name and address;

- identify the licensing authority which granted it;
- contain a record of:

    – each relevant offence and each foreign offence of which the holder has been convicted, the date of each conviction and the sentence imposed in respect of it; and
    – each immigration penalty that the holder has been required to pay and the date of each notice by which such a penalty was imposed; and

- be in the prescribed form.

The Personal Licences Regulations, reg.5 prescribes the form of a personal licence. A personal licence must take the form of a physical document in two separate parts. The first part must be produced in durable form, be of a size no larger than 70 mm by 100 mm and contain the holder's name and address, the licensing authority which granted it, a photograph of the holder, a number allocated by the licensing authority that is unique to the licence and an identifier for the licensing authority granting the licence. The second part must contain a record of each relevant offence and each foreign offence of which the holder has been convicted, the date of each conviction and the sentence imposed in respect of it and a record of each immigration penalty that the holder has been required to pay and the date of each notice by which such a penalty was imposed together with all the matters in the first part of the licence with the exception of the photograph of the holder.

6.10 ACCREDITED LICENSING QUALIFICATIONS

Section 120 defines a 'licensing qualification' as:

- a qualification which is both accredited by the Secretary of State and awarded by a body accredited by the Secretary of State;
- a qualification awarded before the coming into force of s.120 which the Secretary of State certifies is to be treated as if it were a qualification which is both accredited by the Secretary of State and awarded by a body accredited by the Secretary of State; or
- a qualification obtained in Scotland or Northern Ireland or in an EEA State which is equivalent to a qualification which is both accredited by the Secretary of State and awarded by a body accredited by the Secretary of State. For this purpose, 'EEA State' means a state which is a contracting party to the Agreement on the European Economic Area signed at Oporto on 2 May 1992, as adjusted by the protocol signed at Brussels on 17 March 1993.

Details of the licensing qualifications which have been accredited by the Secretary of State can be found at **www.gov.uk**. The following qualifications have been accredited, as from 1 December 2017:

BIIAB (QCF Recognition number RN5118)
BIIAB Level 2 Award for Personal Licence Holders
Qualification number: 603/2468/5
Qualification approval/designation number: C00/1212/8
BIIAB Level 2 Award for Personal Licence Holders (QCF)
Qualification number: 501/1494/3
Website: **www.biiab.co.uk**
Email: customersupport@biiab.co.uk

HABC
Highfield Level 2 Award for Personal Licence Holders (RQF)
Qualification number: 603/2597/5
Qualification approval/designation number: C00/1221/1
Website: **www.highfieldqualifications.com**
Email: info@highfieldabc.com

LASER (QCF Recognition number RN5326)
LASER Level 2 Award for Personal Licence Holders
Qualification number: 603/2603/7
Laser Level 2 Award for Personal Licence Holders
Qualification accreditation number 600/6446/8
Website: **https://laser-awards.org.uk**
Email: enquiries@laser-awards.org.uk

Pearson Education Ltd (QCF Recognition number RN5133)
Pearson BTEC Level 2 Award for Personal Licence Holders
Qualification number: 603/2538/0
Pearson BTEC Level 2 Award for Personal Licence Holders (QCF)
Qualification number: 601/3483/5
Website: **https://qualifications.pearson.com/en/home.html**
Email: wblcustomerservices@pearson.com

QNUK (RQF Recognition number RN5133)
QNUK Level 2 Award for Personal Licence Holders
Qualification number: 603/2619/0
QNUK Level 2 Award for Personal Licence Holders
Qualification number: 603/1021/2
Website: **https://qualifications-network.co.uk**

Qualsafe Awards (RQF Recognition number RN5291)
QA Level 2 Award for Personal Licence Holders (RQF)
Qualification number: 603/5343/0
Website: **www.qualsafe.org**
Email: info@qualsafeawards.org

SQA (QCF Recognition number RN5167)
SQA Level 2 Award for Personal Licence Holders
Qualification number: 603/2596/3
SQA Level 2 Award for Personal Licence Holders (QCF)
Qualification number: 600/1269/9
Email: customer@sqa.org.uk

Training Qualifications UK (Recognition number: RN5355)
TQUK Level 2 Award for Personal Licence Holders (RQF)
Qualification number: 603/2835/6
TQUK Level 2 Award for Personal Licence Holders (QCF)
Qualification number: 601/6508/X
Website: **www.tquk.org**
Email: account.managers@tquk.org

The following courses were formerly accredited:

BIIAB Level 2 National Certificate for Personal Licence Holders (QCA)
Accreditation number: 100/4866/2

CIEH Level 2 Award for Personal Licence Holders (QCF)
Accreditation number: 601/2104/X

EDI Level 2 National Certificate for Personal Licence Holders (QCA)
Accreditation number: 100/4865/0

EDI Level 2 Award for Personal Licence Holders (QCF)
Accreditation number 500/9146/3

GQAL Level 2 National Certificate for Personal Licence Holders (QCA)
Accreditation number: 100/5040/1

HABC Level 2 Award for Personal Licence Holders (QCA)
Accreditation number: 500/7383/7

HABC Level 2 Award for Personal Licence Holders (QCF)
Accreditation number 500/9974/7

IQ (QCF Recognition number: RN5330) IQ Level 2 Award for Personal Licence Holders
Qualification number: 603/2659/1

IQ Level 2 Award for Personal Licence Holders (QCF)
Qualification number: 601/4980/2

NCFE Level 2 National Certificate for Personal Licence Holders (QCA)
Accreditation number: 500/4228/2, 600/1323/0

SFJ Awards – Level 2 Award for Personal Licence Holders
Qualification number: 603/2659/1

SQA Level 2 Award for Personal Licence Holders (QCA)
Accreditation number: 500/8025/8

A person does not need to have a recognised licensing qualification if he is a person of prescribed description. The only persons who have been prescribed by the Personal Licences Regulations are:

- A member of the company of the Master, Wardens, Freeman and Commonalty of the Mistery of the Vintners of the City of London. The privileges of the Vintners originate by a Royal Charter granted in 1611 and they have been allowed to sell wine in the City of London and in other 'port' and 'thoroughfare' towns.
- A person operating under a licence granted by the University of Cambridge. Under a Charter of Richard II dated 1382, the Vice Chancellor of the University of Cambridge may grant licences to sell alcohol.
- A person operating premises under a licence granted by the Board of Green Cloth. The Board of the Green Cloth is an ancient committee of the Royal Household and is the last surviving court of the Royal Prerogative. It had responsibility for licensing inns 'within the verge of the Palace'.

However, as all these ancient privileges have been abolished by the Act, these prescribed descriptions have little relevance now.

6.11 CONVICTIONS FOR A RELEVANT OFFENCE OR FOREIGN OFFENCE

An applicant must disclose whether or not he has a conviction for a relevant offence or a foreign offence, unless it has become spent for the purposes of the Rehabilitation of Offenders Act 1974.

6.11.1 Relevant offence

Section 113(1) provides that an offence is a relevant offence if it is one of those listed in Sched.4 as follows:

- An offence under the Act.
- An offence under any of the following previous licensing legislation:

  - London Government Act 1963, Sched.12;
  - Licensing Act 1964;
  - Private Places of Entertainment (Licensing) Act 1967;
  - Theatres Act 1968, s.13;
  - Late Night Refreshment Houses Act 1969;
  - Local Government (Miscellaneous Provisions) Act 1982, s.6 or Sched.1;
  - Licensing (Occasional Permissions) Act 1983;
  - Cinemas Act 1985;
  - London Local Authorities Act 1990.

- An offence under the Public Health (Minimum Price for Alcohol) (Wales) Act 2018.
- An offence under the Firearms Act 1968.
- An offence under the Trade Descriptions Act 1968, s.1 of applying a false trade description of goods, or supplying or offering to supply goods to which a false trade description is applied, in circumstances where the goods in question are or include alcohol.
- The following offences under the Theft Act 1968:

  - theft (s.1);
  - robbery (s.8);
  - burglary (s.9);
  - aggravated burglary (s.10);
  - removal of articles from places open to the public (s.11);
  - aggravated vehicle-taking (s.12A), in circumstances where s.12(2)(b) applies and the accident caused the death of any person;
  - abstracting of electricity (s.13);
  - obtaining property by deception (s.15);
  - obtaining a money transfer by deception (s.15A);
  - obtaining pecuniary advantage by deception (s.16);
  - false accounting (s.17);
  - false statements by company directors, etc. (s.19);
  - suppression, etc. of documents (s.20);
  - blackmail (s.21);
  - handling stolen goods (s.22);
  - dishonestly retaining a wrongful credit (s.24A);
  - going equipped for stealing, etc. (s.25).

- An offence under the Gaming Act 1968, s.7(2) of allowing a child to take part in gaming on premises licensed for the sale of alcohol.
- The following offences under the Misuse of Drugs Act 1971:

    - production of a controlled drug (s.4(2));
    - supply of a controlled drug (s.4(3));
    - possession of a controlled drug with intent to supply (s.5(3));
    - permitting activities to take place on premises (s.8).

- An offence under any of the Immigration Acts.
- The following offences under the Theft Act 1978:

    - obtaining services by deception (s.1);
    - evasion of liability by deception (s.2).

- The following offences under the Customs and Excise Management Act 1979:

    - fraudulent evasion of duty (s.170 (disregarding subsection (1)(a)));
    - taking preparatory steps for evasion of duty (s.170B).

- The following offences under the Tobacco Products Duty Act 1979:

    - possession and sale of unmarked tobacco (s.8G);
    - use of premises for sale of unmarked tobacco (s.8H).

- An offence under the Forgery and Counterfeiting Act 1981 other than an offence under s.18 or s.19.
- The following offences under the Copyright, Designs and Patents Act 1988:

    - public exhibition in the course of a business of an article infringing copyright (s.107(1)(d)(iii));
    - infringement of copyright by public performance of work (s.107(3));
    - broadcast, etc. of recording of a performance made without sufficient consent (s.198(2));
    - fraudulent reception of transmission (s.297(1));
    - supply, etc. of unauthorised decoder (s.297A(1)).

- The following offences under the Road Traffic Act 1988:

    - causing death by careless driving while under the influence of drink or drugs (s.3A);
    - driving a vehicle when under the influence of drink or drugs (s.4);
    - driving a vehicle with alcohol concentration above the prescribed limit (s.5);
    - failing to co-operate with a preliminary test (s.6(6)).

- The following offences under the Food Safety Act 1990 in circumstances where the food in question is or includes alcohol:

- – selling food or drink not of the nature, substance or quality demanded (s.14);
- – falsely describing or presenting food or drink (s.15).

- An offence under the Trade Marks Act 1994, s.92(1) or (2) of unauthorised use of trade mark, etc. in relation to goods in circumstances where the goods in question are or include alcohol.
- An offence under the Firearms (Amendment) Act 1997.
- The following sexual offences:

  - – an offence listed in the Criminal Justice Act 2003, Sched.15, Part 2, other than the offence mentioned in para.95 of procuring others to commit homosexual acts (Sexual Offences Act 1967, s.4);
  - – an offence listed in the Sexual Offences Act 2003, Sched.3, being sexual offences for the purposes of notification and orders;
  - – intercourse with a defective (Sexual Offences Act 1956, s.8);
  - – fraudulent abduction of an heiress (Sexual Offences Act 1956, s.18).

- A specified violent offence listed in the Criminal Justice Act 2003, Sched.15, Part 1.
- A specified terrorism offence listed in the Criminal Justice Act 2003, Sched.15, Part 3.
- A violent offence, being any offence which leads, or is intended or likely to lead, to a person's death or to physical injury to a person, including an offence which is required to be charged as arson (whether or not it would otherwise fall within this definition).
- An offence under the Private Security Industry Act 2001, s.3 of engaging in certain activities relating to security without a licence.
- An offence under the Gambling Act 2005, s.46 if the child or young person was invited, caused or permitted to gamble on premises in respect of which a premises licence had effect.
- An offence under the Fraud Act 2006.
- The following offences under the Violent Crime Reduction Act 2006:

  - – using someone to mind a weapon (s.28);
  - – manufacturing, importing or selling realistic imitation firearms (s.36).

- An offence under the Business Protection from Misleading Marketing Regulations 2008, SI 2008/1276, reg.6 of misleading advertising in circumstances where the advertising in question relates to alcohol or to goods that include alcohol.
- An offence under the Consumer Protection from Unfair Trading Regulations 2008, SI 2008/1277, regs.8, 9, 10, 11 or 12 relating to unfair commercial practices in circumstances where the commercial practice in question is directly connected with the promotion, sale or supply of alcohol or of a product that includes alcohol.

- The following offences under the Psychoactive Substances Act 2016:
    - producing a psychoactive substance (s.4);
    - supplying, or offering to supply, a psychoactive substance (s.5);
    - possession of a psychoactive substance (s.7);
    - importing or exporting a psychoactive substance (s.8).
- A terrorism offence listed in the Counter-Terrorism Act 2008, s.41.
- An offence under the Criminal Attempts Act 1981, s.1 of attempting to commit an offence that is a relevant offence.
- An offence under the Criminal Law Act 1977, s.1 of conspiracy to commit an offence that is a relevant offence.
- The offence at common law of conspiracy to defraud.

6.11.2 Foreign offence

A foreign offence is an offence (other than a relevant offence) under the law of a country outside England and Wales (s.113(3)). This will include offences committed in Scotland and Northern Ireland. Offences under foreign laws which are equivalent to relevant offences will not necessarily exist in exactly the same form as relevant offences.

An applicant must disclose whether or not he has a conviction for a foreign offence unless it has been spent for the purposes of the Rehabilitation of Offenders Act 1974.

The Act does not prescribe how an applicant should disclose a foreign offence. However, the Personal Licences Regulations provide that in order to disclose whether or not an applicant has been convicted of a foreign offence, he must submit a declaration, in the prescribed form, that either he has not been convicted of a foreign offence or that he has been convicted of a foreign offence accompanied by details of the nature and date of the conviction and any sentence imposed on him in respect of it. This declaration also relates to relevant offences and civil immigration penalties. The form of declaration is set out in the Personal Licences Regulations, Sched.3.

It is not expected that an applicant will disclose all foreign offences, only those equivalent to a relevant offence. The Guidance, para.4.50 provides that 'All applicants are also required to make a clear statement as to whether or not they have been convicted outside England and Wales of a relevant offence or an equivalent foreign offence'. If a foreign offence which is not equivalent to a relevant offence is disclosed, the police will be notified by the relevant licensing authority but may not be able to object on the basis of that foreign offence as they can only object where the chief officer of police considers that the foreign offence is comparable to a relevant offence (s.120(5)).

6.11.3 Spent convictions

A conviction for a relevant offence or a foreign offence must be disregarded if it is spent for the purposes of the Rehabilitation of Offenders Act 1974 (s.114).

Under the Rehabilitation of Offenders Act 1974, s.1 all convictions (other than those excluded from rehabilitation, for example life imprisonment or certain custodial sentences imposed for offences specified in the Sentencing Code, Sched.18 (serious violent, sexual and terrorism offences)) are 'spent' and no longer need to be disclosed after a specified period of time which depends on the particular sentence. The length of the rehabilitation period is specified in the Rehabilitation of Offenders Act 1974, s.5. Since 10 March 2014, the rehabilitation periods for adult offenders are as set out in **Table 6.2**.

Table 6.2: Rehabilitation periods for adult offenders

Sentence	Rehabilitation period
Custodial sentences over four years	Seven years beginning with the day on which the sentence, including any period on licence, is completed
Custodial sentences over one year, up to four years	Four years beginning with the day on which the sentence, including any period on licence, is completed
Custodial sentences up to one year	One year beginning with the day on which the sentence, including any period on licence, is completed
Fines	One year beginning with the date of the conviction in respect of which the fine is imposed
Community or youth rehabilitation order	The last day on which the order has effect. But in relation to any community or youth rehabilitation order which has no specified end date, the rehabilitation period is two years from the date of conviction.
Absolute discharge	No rehabilitation period

In respect of unspent convictions the Guidance at para.4.54 provides:

A number of relevant offences never become spent. However, where an applicant is able to demonstrate that the offence in question took place so long ago and that the applicant no longer has a propensity to re-offend, a licensing authority may consider that it is appropriate to grant the application on the basis that doing so would not undermine the crime prevention objective.

The Rehabilitation of Offenders Act 1974, s.7(3) provides that at any stage in any proceedings before a judicial authority, the authority can admit spent convictions or require evidence as to spent convictions if it is satisfied that justice cannot otherwise be done. A licensing authority will be a judicial authority for these purposes (see *Adamson* v. *Waveney DC* [1997] 2 All ER 898 (QBD)). Thus, where justice cannot be done otherwise than by admitting a spent conviction, it may be admitted. This does not mean that the licensing authority has a discretion to admit a spent conviction (see *R.* v. *Hastings Justices ex p. McSpirit* (1998) 162 JP 44 (QBD); *Adamson* v. *Waveney DC*).

6.11.4 Establishing a conviction

The Act does not set out how an applicant should establish whether or not they have a conviction for a relevant offence or foreign offence; however, the Personal Licences Regulations provide that an applicant must submit a declaration in the prescribed form that either he has not been convicted of a relevant offence or foreign offence or he has been convicted of a relevant offence or foreign offence, accompanied by details of the nature and date of the conviction and any sentence imposed on him in respect of it. The form of declaration is set out in the Personal Licences Regulations, Sched.3.

In addition, an applicant must also submit with their application:

- a criminal conviction certificate issued under the Police Act 1997, s.112 ('a basic DBS certificate');
- a criminal record certificate issued under the Police Act 1997, s.113A ('a standard DBS certificate'); or
- the results of a request made under UK GDPR, art.15 or Data Protection Act 2018, s.45 (rights of access by the data subject) to the National Identification Service for information contained in the Police National Computer.

Only one of these needs to be submitted with the application, and whichever is submitted it must not have been issued more than one month before the application for the personal licence is submitted to the relevant licensing authority.

6.11.5 Basic DBS certificate

An individual aged 16 or over at the time they make the application is entitled to apply for a basic DBS certificate from the Disclosure and Barring Service under the Police Act 1997, s.112. A basic DBS certificate contains details of unspent criminal convictions, conditional and unconditional cautions, or a statement that the individual has no such convictions or cautions. An application to the DBS for a basic certificate must be made using their online application form (**www.gov. uk/request-copy-criminal-record**). A fee is payable.

6.11.6 Standard DBS certificate

Disclosure may also be made by a means of a standard DBS certificate issued under the Police Act 1997, s.113A.

An application for a standard DBS certificate can be made by an individual aged 16 or over at the time they make the application but the application must be countersigned, or submitted electronically, by a registered person confirming that the certificate is required for the purposes of an exempted question. A fee is payable. An 'exempted question' so far as it applies to convictions, is a question in relation to which the Rehabilitation of Offenders Act 1974, s.4(2)(a) or (b) has been excluded by an order of the Secretary of State under s.4(4) of that Act, and so far as it applies to cautions, is a question to which paras.3(3) or (4) of Sched. 2 to that Act has been excluded by an order of the Secretary of State under para.4 of that Schedule. A registered person is a person who is listed in a register maintained by the Disclosure and Barring Service.

A standard DBS certificate will contain details of the individual's convictions, both spent and unspent, cautions, both spent and unspent and police reprimands and warnings. In *R. (on the application of T)* v. *Chief Constable of Greater Manchester* [2014] UKSC 35; [2015] AC 49, the Supreme Court considered generally cases involving a failure to disclose spent convictions under the Rehabilitation of Offenders Act 1974 (Exceptions) Order 1975, SI 1975/1023 and the Police Act 1997, ss.113A and 113B. See also *Hussain* v. *Waltham Forest LBC* [2020] EWCA Civ 1539; [2021] 1 WLR 922, where the Court of Appeal considered the circumstances in which a decision-maker was entitled to take into account a person's spent convictions and/or the conduct underlying such convictions.

6.11.7 Subject access search

A subject access search will disclose to individuals under the Data Protection Act 2018 information held about them on the Police National Computer. This search makes no allowance for the Rehabilitation of Offenders Act 1974 and so everything is included in the result even though it is officially no longer relevant. The ACRO Criminal Records Office (ACRO) provides subject access disclosures from the Police National Computer on behalf of police forces in England and Wales (see further **www.acro.police.uk**).

The Data Protection Act 2018, s.45 provides that a 'data subject' (the person to whom the personal data refer) is entitled to be informed whether or not personal data concerning them is being processed. If such personal data is being processed, the 'data subject' is entitled to be given access to the personal data and the information set out in Data Protection Act 2018, s.45(2) which includes the reasons why the data is being processed.

An application for a subject access search should be made to ACRO using the application form which can be downloaded from **www.acro.police.uk**. The completed application form must be emailed to subjectaccessrequest@acro.police.uk and must be accompanied by proof of identity which shows the applicant's full name and date of birth, for example a passport or driving licence and valid e-mail address. There is no charge for a subject access search as it is a Subject Right under Data Protection Act 2018. A subject access search application must be processed by ACRO within one calendar month.

6.12 IMMIGRATION PENALTY

The Act does not set out how an applicant should establish whether or not they have been required to pay an immigration penalty; however, the Personal Licences Regulations provide that the declaration which an applicant must submit with their application for a personal licence must set out whether or not the applicant has been required to pay an immigration penalty, accompanied by details of the nature and date of any such penalty. The form of declaration is set out in the Personal Licences Regulations, Sched.3.

An immigration penalty is a penalty issued under the Immigration, Asylum and Nationality Act 2006, s.15 or the Immigration Act 2014, s.23. The former relates to a penalty given to an employer who employees an illegal worker, while the latter is a penalty given to a landlord who allows an adult to occupy premises under a residential tenancy agreement if the adult is disqualified as a result of their immigration status.

The Guidance at para.4.52 provides:

> Civil penalties received after 6 April 2017 for immigration matters are treated in the same way as relevant offences. Licensing authorities are required to notify the Secretary of State for the Home Department (through Home Office Immigration Enforcement) when an applicant declares that they have been issued with an immigration penalty or convicted of an immigration offence or a foreign offence comparable to an immigration offence. The Home Office may object to an application on grounds that granting the personal licence would be prejudicial to the prevention of illegal working in licensed premises. Civil penalties for immigration matters were added to the Licensing Act with effect from 6 April 2017, and penalties received before that date cannot be taken into account in respect of grant, revocation or suspension of a personal licence.

6.13 APPEALS

If a licensing authority rejects an application for the grant of a personal licence, the applicant may appeal against the decision (Sched.5, para.17(1)). Where a licensing authority grants an application for a personal licence after a chief officer of police has given notice that granting the licence would undermine the crime prevention objective, the chief officer of police may appeal against the decision (Sched.5, para.17(2)). Where a licensing authority grants an application for a personal licence after the Secretary of State (through Home Office Immigration Enforcement) has given notice that granting the licence would be prejudicial to the prevention of illegal working in licensed premises, the Secretary of State may appeal against the decision (Sched.5, para.17(2A).

The holder of a personal licence which is revoked because of convictions which have come to light after it was granted or renewed may also appeal against the revocation (Sched.5, para.17(4)).

A chief officer of police who gave notice to the relevant licensing authority that continuation of the licence would undermine the crime prevention objective may appeal against a decision of the authority not to revoke the licence, as long as the notice has not been withdrawn (Sched.5, para.17(5)). If the Secretary of State (through Home Office Immigration Enforcement) gave notice to the relevant licensing authority that continuation of the licence would be prejudicial to the prevention of illegal working in licensed premises, the Secretary of State may appeal against a decision of the authority not to revoke the licence, as long as the notice has not been withdrawn (Sched.5, para.17(5A)).Where a licensing authority revokes or suspends a personal licence, the holder of the licence may appeal against that decision (Sched.5, para.17(5B)).

Any appeal must be made to a magistrates' court (Sched.5, para.17(6)). The appeal must be commenced by the service of a notice on the designated officer for the magistrates' court within 21 days beginning with the date on which the appellant was notified by the licensing authority of its decision (Sched.5, para.17(7)). In the case of an appeal by a chief officer of police or the Secretary of State, the holder of the personal licence, as well as the licensing authority, is to be treated as a respondent (Sched.5, para.17(8)).

6.14 DURATION OF A PERSONAL LICENCE

A personal licence has effect indefinitely (s.115(1)). A personal licence will cease to have effect if the licence holder ceases to be entitled to work in the United Kingdom, or the licence is revoked or forfeited (s.115(2A), (3)). A personal licence does not have effect during any period when it is suspended (s.115(4)).

The Guidance at para.4.58 provides:

> Personal licences remain valid unless surrendered, suspended, revoked or declared forfeit by the courts. For applications made on or after 6 April 2017, a licence granted to someone subject to immigration control will lapse if the individual ceases to be entitled to work in the UK. The requirement to renew a personal licence was removed from the Licensing Act 2003 by the Deregulation Act 2015. While personal licences issued before the 2015 Act have expiry dates, these licences will remain valid and such dates no longer have an effect. Once granted, the licensing authority which issued the licence remains the 'relevant licensing authority' for it and its holder, even though the individual may move out of the area or take employment elsewhere. The personal licence itself will give details of the issuing licensing authority.

6.15 CONVICTIONS DURING THE APPLICATION PROCESS

Where an applicant for the grant of a personal licence is convicted of a relevant offence or a foreign offence or is required to pay an immigration penalty during the period following submission of their application and its determination, they must as soon as reasonably practicable notify the licensing authority of their conviction or the requirement to pay (s.123(1)). Failure to notify the licensing authority without having a reasonable excuse is an offence punishable on summary conviction by a fine not exceeding level 4 on the standard scale (s.123(2) and (3)).

Where a licensing authority has granted a personal licence and it subsequently discovers that the applicant was convicted during the application period of a relevant offence or a foreign offence or was required to pay an immigration penalty, it must give a notice of the conviction to the chief officer of police for its area (s.124(2)). If the chief officer of police is satisfied that continuation of the licence would undermine the crime prevention objective, having taken into account any conviction for a relevant offence or a foreign offence comparable to a relevant offence which occurred before the end of the application period or any immigration penalty which the applicant has been required to pay during such period, he must, within 14 days beginning with the day he received the notice from the licensing authority, give the authority an objection notice setting out the reasons why he is so satisfied (s.124(3)).

Where a licensing authority has granted a personal licence and it subsequently discovers that the applicant was convicted during the application period of an immigration offence or a foreign offence that the licensing authority considers to be comparable to an immigration offence or was required to pay an immigration penalty, it must give a notice to that effect to the Secretary of State (through Home Office Immigration Enforcement) (s.124(3A)). If the Secretary of State is satisfied that continuation of the licence would be prejudicial to the prevention of illegal working in licensed premises, having taken into account any conviction for an immigration offence or a foreign offence comparable to an immigration offence which occurred before the end of the application period or any immigration penalty which the applicant has been required to pay during such period, the Secretary of State must, within 14 days beginning with the day the Secretary of State received the notice from the licensing authority, give the authority an immigration objection notice setting out the reasons for being so satisfied (s.124(3B)).

Where an objection notice or an immigration objection notice is given within the 14-day period, and it is not withdrawn, the licensing authority must hold a hearing to consider the objection notice, unless the holder of the licence, the person who gave the notice and the authority agree it is unnecessary, and having regard to the notice, must where it is an objection notice revoke the licence if it considers it appropriate for the promotion of the crime prevention objective to do so or where it is an immigration objection notice, revoke the licence if it considers it appropriate for the prevention of illegal working in licensed premises to do so (s.124(4)). The hearing must be held within 20 working days beginning with the day after the end of the period within which the chief officer of police may give an objection notice (Hearings Regulations, reg.5 and Sched.1, para.14). Notice of the hearing must be given to the personal licence holder and the police no later than 10 working days before the day or the first day on which the hearing is to be held (Hearings Regulations, reg.6(4) and Sched.2, para.14). The personal licence holder must be given the notice of objection with the notice of hearing (Hearings Regulations, reg.7(2) and Sched.3, para.13). The Hearing Regulations do not make provision for a hearing where an immigration objection notice is given.

Whether the licensing authority revokes or decides not to revoke the personal licence it must notify the offender and the chief officer of police of the decision and its reasons for making it (s.124(5)). Where the authority revokes or decides not to revoke a licence as it considers it appropriate to do so for the prevention of illegal working in licensed premises it must also notify the Secretary of State of the decision and its reasons for making it (s.124(5A)). The notice must be given by the licensing authority forthwith (see **2.9**) on making the determination and it must be accompanied by information regarding the right of a party to appeal against the determination.

Any decision to revoke a personal licence does not have effect until the end of the period for appealing against the decision, or if the decision is appealed against, until the appeal is disposed of (s.124(6)).

The application period means the period that begins when the application for the grant of a personal licence is made and ends at the time of the grant (s.123(7)).

6.16 CONVICTIONS DURING THE CURRENCY OF A PERSONAL LICENCE

6.16.1 Notifying the court of the personal licence

If a personal licence holder is charged with a relevant offence, he must produce his personal licence to the magistrates' court no later than when he first appears before them in connection with the offence (s.128(1)). If he cannot produce his licence, he must explain to the court why it is not available and provide details of the licensing authority which issued the licence to him.

A person charged with a relevant offence who is subsequently granted a personal licence after his first appearance in a magistrates' court in connection with the offence must produce the licence or its details and an explanation for its absence at the next appearance in court in connection with the offence (s.128(3)).

Where a personal licence has been produced to the court or the court has been notified of its existence, a personal licence holder charged with a relevant offence must notify the court of any surrender or revocation of the licence at the next appearance in court in connection with the offence (s.128(4)).

Failure without reasonable excuse to provide a court with the relevant details concerning a personal licence is an offence punishable on summary conviction with a fine not exceeding level 2 on the standard scale (s.128(6) and (7)).

6.16.2 Forfeiture or suspension of a personal licence by a court

If a court in England or Wales convicts a personal licence holder of a relevant offence, it may order that the licence be forfeited or be suspended for a period up to six months (s.129(2)). When deciding whether to make an order for forfeiture or suspension, the court may consider any previous conviction of the licence holder for a relevant offence (s.129(3)). The court making an order forfeiting or suspending a personal licence may suspend the order pending an appeal against it (s.129(4)). In *R. v. Bell (Jennifer)* [2009] EWCA Crim 875, the Court of Appeal ordered the forfeiture of a personal licence where the holder had been convicted of handling stolen goods.

An appellate court can suspend an order forfeiting or suspending a personal licence (s.130). The power is exercisable on such terms as the court thinks fit by the court to which a person convicted of a relevant offence has appealed, applied for leave to appeal, stated a case or applied for a quashing order (s.130(7)). The appellate court must give notice of any suspension to the relevant licensing authority (s.130(8)). If the original order forfeited the licence and the appellate court suspends that order it will be reinstated for the period during which the order is suspended (s.130(9)).

6.16.3 The court's duty to notify the relevant licensing authority

Where a court convicts a personal licence holder of a relevant offence it must, as soon as is reasonably practicable, under s.131 send a notice to the relevant licensing authority a notice containing details of:

- the name and address of the convicted licence holder;
- the nature and date of the conviction; and
- the sentence passed including any order for forfeiture or suspension of the licence.

A copy of the notice must also be sent to the licence holder. The Guidance at paras.4.73 and 4.74 provides that:

> 4.73 Where a personal licence holder is convicted by a court for a relevant offence, the court is under a duty to notify the relevant licensing authority of the conviction and of any decision to order that the personal licence is suspended or declared forfeit. The sentence of the court has immediate effect despite the fact that an appeal may be lodged against conviction or sentence (although the court may suspend the forfeiture or suspension of the licence pending the outcome of any appeal).
>
> 4.74 When the licensing authority receives such a notification, it should contact the holder and request the licence so that the necessary action can be taken. The holder must then produce the relevant licence to the authority within 14 days. It is expected that the chief officer of police for the area in which the holder resides would be advised if they do not respond promptly. The licensing authority should record the details of the conviction, endorse them on the licence, together

with any period of suspension and then return the licence to the holder. If the licence is declared forfeit, it should be retained by the licensing authority.

If a personal licence holder appeals against the conviction or sentence imposed for a relevant offence the appeal court must, as soon as is reasonably practicable, notify the relevant licensing authority if the conviction is quashed or a new sentence substituted (s.131(3)). A copy of the notice given to the licensing authority must be sent to the licence holder. Where the Court of Appeal is asked to consider the leniency of a sentence imposed on a personal licence holder following conviction for a relevant offence, the court must notify the relevant licensing authority of any action taken, and a copy of the notice must also be sent to the licence holder (s.131(4)).

6.16.4 The licence holder's duty to notify the relevant licensing authority

Where a court dealing with a personal licence holder for a relevant offence is not aware of the existence of the licence or a personal licence holder is convicted of a foreign offence a duty is imposed on the personal licence holder, as soon as is reasonably practicable after conviction, to notify the relevant licensing authority of the nature and date of the conviction and any sentence imposed as a result (s.132(2)). Similar provisions apply where the existence of a personal licence is not known to a court hearing an appeal or the Court of Appeal to which a reference has been made concerning leniency of a sentence. As soon as reasonably practicable following determination of the appeal or referral, the personal licence holder must give notice of the determination to the relevant licensing authority. Where a personal licence holder is required to pay an immigration penalty, the personal licence holder must, as soon as is reasonably practicable after being required to pay the penalty, give the relevant licensing authority a notice containing details of the penalty, including the date of the notice by which the penalty was imposed (s.132(2B)). Any such notice given to the relevant licensing authority must be accompanied by the personal licence or an explanation for its omission (s.132(3)). A personal licence holder who fails, without reasonable excuse, to comply with the obligation to notify the licensing authority of a conviction or other relevant matter commits an offence punishable on summary conviction by a fine not exceeding level 2 on the standard scale (s.132(4) and (5)).

6.16.5 Suspension or revocation of a personal licence by a licensing authority

Where a personal licence holder has been, at any time before or after the grant of the licence convicted of any relevant offence or foreign offence, or required to pay an immigration penalty, the relevant licensing authority may suspend the licence for a period not exceeding six months or revoke the licence (s.132A(3)). The Guidance at para.4.75 provides that:

This is a discretionary power; licensing authorities are not obliged to give consideration to all personal licence holders subject to convictions for relevant offences, foreign offences or civil penalties for immigration matters.

If the relevant licensing authority is considering whether to suspend or revoke the licence, it must give notice to the licence holder inviting the licence holder to make representations regarding the relevant offence, foreign offence or immigration penalty that has caused the relevant licensing authority to issue the notice, any decision of a court to forfeit or suspend the licence or suspend any such forfeiture or suspension, and any other relevant information (including information regarding the licence holder's personal circumstances) (s.132A(4), (5)). The licence holder may make such representations to the relevant licensing authority within the period of 28 days beginning with the day the notice was issued (s.132A(6)).

Before deciding whether to suspend or revoke the licence, the relevant licensing authority must take into account any representations made by the licence holder, any decision of a court to forfeit or suspend the licence or suspend any such forfeiture or suspension of which the licensing authority is aware, and any other information which the authority considers relevant (s.132A(7)). Having taken into account these matters the relevant licensing authority may make a decision whether to suspend or revoke a licence or not (s.132A(8)). If the relevant licensing authority proposes not to revoke the licence, it must give notice to the chief officer of police for its area that it proposes not to revoke the licence, and invite the officer to make representations regarding the issue of whether the licence should be suspended or revoked having regard to the crime prevention objective (s.132A(10)). The chief officer of police may make such representations within the period of 14 days beginning with the day the notice was received (s.132A(11)). Where the relevant licensing authority has given notice to the chief officer of police, it must take into account any representations from the officer, and any representations made by the licence holder, any decision of a court to forfeit or suspend the licence or suspend any such forfeiture or suspension of which the licensing authority is aware, and any other information which the authority considers relevant and then make a decision whether to suspend or revoke the licence (s.132A(12)).

The relevant licensing authority must give notice of any decision to suspend or revoke the personal licence to the licence holder and the chief officer of police, including reasons for the decision (s.132A(13)).

A decision to suspend or revoke does not have effect until the end of the period given for appealing against the decision, or if the decision is appealed against, until the appeal is disposed of (s.132A(14)).

6.17 SURRENDER OF A PERSONAL LICENCE

A holder of a personal licence may decide that they wish to surrender their licence and can do so by giving notice that they wish to do so to the relevant licensing authority (s.116(1)). Such a notice must be accompanied by the personal licence or, if that is not practicable, by a statement setting out the reasons why the licence cannot be produced (s.116(2)). Once a notice of surrender is given the personal licence lapses on receipt of the notice by the relevant licensing authority (s.116(3)).

6.18 THEFT OR LOSS OF A PERSONAL LICENCE

A holder of a personal licence who has lost his licence, or had it stolen, damaged or destroyed, can apply to the relevant licensing authority for a copy of his licence (s.126(1)). There is a prescribed fee for issuing a copy of a licence. There is no prescribed application form and a letter will suffice.

A licensing authority can only issue a copy of a licence if it is satisfied that the licence has been lost, stolen, damaged or destroyed (s.126(3)). The copy which is issued must be certified by the authority to be a true copy, and must be a copy of the licence in the form in which it existed immediately before it was lost, stolen, damaged or destroyed.

A certified copy has the same effect under the Act as the original licence (s.126(5)).

6.19 DUTY TO NOTIFY CHANGES

The holder of a personal licence must, as soon as is reasonably practicable, notify the relevant licensing authority of any change in his name or address as stated in the personal licence (s.127(1)). The notification must be accompanied by the prescribed fee. There is no prescribed form of notification and a letter will suffice.

The notice must be accompanied by the personal licence or, if that is not practicable, by a statement setting out the reasons why the licence cannot be produced (s.127(3)).

A personal licensee who fails to give notice of any change in his name or address commits an offence and, on summary conviction, may be fined a sum not exceeding level 2 on the standard scale (s.127(4) and (5)).

6.20 UPDATING A PERSONAL LICENCE

Where a relevant licensing authority:

- revokes or decides not to revoke a personal licence where convictions come to light after the licence has been granted or renewed;

- receives a notice of convictions during the application period;
- receives notification of a change in the licence holder's name or address;
- receives notification from a court of convictions; or
- receives notification from a licence holder of convictions;

or an appeal against a decision made in respect of a personal licence is disposed of, then the licensing authority must make any appropriate amendments to the licence (s.134(1)).

Where notice is given of an order to forfeit or suspend a personal licence, the relevant licensing authority must endorse the licence with the terms of the order (s.134(2)). Any such endorsement must be cancelled if a notice is subsequently received that the order has been quashed (s.134(3)).

In order to allow the licence to be updated, a licensing authority which is not in possession of the personal licence may require the licensee to produce it to the authority within a period of 14 days beginning with the day on which he is notified that the authority requires the licence (s.134(4)). A personal licensee who then fails to produce his licence commits an offence and, on summary conviction, may be fined a sum not exceeding level 2 on the standard scale (s.134(5) and (6)).

6.21 DUTY TO PRODUCE A PERSONAL LICENCE

A constable or an officer of a licensing authority who has been authorised by the authority may require the holder of a personal licence who is on the premises in order make or authorise the supply of alcohol under a premises licence or a temporary event notice to produce his licence for inspection (s.135(2)). An authorised officer of a licensing authority must produce evidence of his authority if requested (s.135(3)). A personal licensee who fails to produce his licence, without a reasonable excuse, commits an offence and, on summary conviction, may be fined a sum not exceeding level 2 on the standard scale (s.135(5) and (6)).

CHAPTER 7

Premises licences

7.1 THE MEANING OF PREMISES LICENCES

A premises licence is defined by s.11 as a licence granted under Part 3 of the Act, in respect of any premises, which authorises the premises to be used for one or more licensable activity.

7.1.1 The definition of premises

The term 'premises' is defined in s.193 to mean any place and includes a vehicle, vessel or moveable structure. While this definition appears to be broad, s.176 prohibits the sale or supply of alcohol at certain places, and there are also places and activities specified in ss.173, 174 and 175 which are exempt from the requirement to have a premises licence.

'Any place'

A premises licence is required for licensable activities which occur at, on or in 'any place'. This means that not only do licensable activities which take place inside buildings, for example public houses, theatres, etc., require a premises licence but licensable activities which take place outside, for example open air concerts and plays, also require a premises licence. Outside activities often take place on land owned by a local authority and a Register of Licensed Public Spaces in England and Wales was published in 2007 to assist event organisers and touring entertainment providers plan events where licensable activities will be carried on (the register is available at **www.gov.uk**). Where a site may be licensed for a particular activity that does not mean that it can be used without the permission of the relevant local authority and the local authority should always be contacted for further information and permission to use the land. Where the licensable activity takes place at several places a separate premises licence is required for each place.

Where the place of sale of alcohol is different from the place of supply, s.190 treats the sale as having happened at the place from which the alcohol is appropriated to the contract. This will cover internet, mail order and telephone sales, and so the sale will be regarded as having taken place at the warehouse from which the alcohol is to be delivered and not the internet or the call centre receiving orders for the sale of alcohol. The requirement for a premises licence will therefore apply to the warehouse rather than the call centre. The Guidance at para.3.10 provides:

> Persons who run premises providing 'alcohol delivery services' should notify the relevant licensing authority that they are operating such a service in their operating schedule. This ensures that the licensing authority can properly consider what conditions are appropriate. Premises with an existing premises licence, which choose to operate such a service in addition to their existing licensable activities, may consider contacting their licensing authority for its view on whether this form of alcohol sale is already permitted or whether an application to vary the licence will be required.

'Vehicle, vessel or moveable structure'

A 'vehicle' is defined in s.193 to mean a vehicle intended or adapted for use on roads. This definition will include vehicles which are towed such as caravans or trailers. A 'vessel' is also defined in s.193 to include a ship, boat, raft or other apparatus constructed or adapted for floating on water. There is no definition of 'moveable structure' but it would presumably include a tent or inflatable building.

The situation where vehicles, vessels and moveable structures are not permanently located in one place is dealt with in s.189. Where a vessel is not permanently moored or berthed in a particular place, a premises licence will be required as the vessel will treated as though it were premises situated at the place where it is normally moored or berthed. A vehicle or moveable structure which is not permanently located in the same place will be treated as premises located at any place where it is parked or set. This means for example that a fast food van which provides late night refreshment in a number of locations will need a separate premises licence in respect of each location, as will a business which provides alcohol from a marquee at events such as fairs and village fêtes. Each application must be made to the relevant authority for that particular location and so applications may have to be made to several relevant authorities.

The provisions in the Act relating to provisional statements do not apply to vessels, vehicles or moveable structures (s.189(5)).

7.1.2 Premises excluded from premises licences

Certain premises are 'excluded premises' under s.176 which means that no sale by retail or supply of alcohol can take place on or from them. These fall into the following two categories:

- service areas on 'special roads', which has the same meaning as in the High-ways Act 1980 except that it also includes a trunk road; these will thus include service areas on motorways and trunk roads; and
- premises used primarily as a garage or which form part of premises which are primarily so used.

The Secretary of State may by order amend this definition of excluded premises so as to include or exclude any other premises of such description as may be specified in the order.

Garage premises

Premises which are used primarily as a garage or which form part of premises which are primarily used as a garage are excluded premises.

Premises are used as a garage if they are used for one or more of the following activities:

- the retailing of petrol;
- the retailing of derv;
- the sale of motor vehicles; or
- the maintenance of motor vehicles.

It will be for a licensing authority to decide in the light of the facts whether or not premises are used primarily as a garage. This will be relevant where for example the premises comprise a petrol filling station and a convenience store which sells items such as food, newspapers, etc. The test is not whether the premises are primarily used as a shop. For premises to be excluded there must be significantly more use as a garage than for any other use.

In order to determine the primary use, it will be necessary to look at the intensity of use of the premises by customers. It is accepted that this will usually be proved by evidence such as an analysis of till receipts over a recent period of time.

In *Green* v. *Inner London Justices* (1994) 19 LR 13, a case decided under the Licensing Act 1964, the gross turnover from fuel sales was compared to the net turnover from other sales, but this was held not to be an accurate method bearing in mind the taxes and duties on fuel. If figures for turnover are used, they must be net of taxes and duties. In *R.* v. *Liverpool Crown Court ex p. Goodwin* [2002] LLR 698, the court said that the test must be to consider the intensity of use by customers at the premises and that evidence such as customer lists might be highly material. Having regard to the appearance of the premises and how they were known in the locality was 'erroneous'. The Guidance at paras.5.23 and 5.24 provides:

> 5.23 It is for the licensing authority to decide, based on the licensing objectives, whether it is appropriate for that premises to be granted a licence, taking into

account the documents and information listed in section 17(3) and (4) which must accompany the application.

5.24   If a licence is granted in respect of a premises and the primary use of that premises subsequently changes (for example, the primary use becomes that of a garage rather than a shop) it would no longer be legal to sell alcohol on that premises. If a relevant representation is made, the licensing authority must decide whether or not the premises are used primarily as a garage. The licensing authority may ask the licence holder to provide further information to help establish what the primary use of the premises is.

It would therefore appear that in determining the primary use a consideration of the intensity of use of the premises by customers will be used and a comparison of the net turnovers for the different activities carried on at the premises may be taken into account. In *R. (on the application of Murco Petroleum Ltd)* v. *Bristol City Council* [2010] EWHC 1992 (Admin), a licensing sub-committee was entitled to adjourn an application for a premises licence to sell alcohol for a service station where insufficient information regarding its primary usage had been provided despite several requests for further trading information.

7.1.3 Exempt premises

Certain licensable activities will not require a premises licence if they are carried on at premises which are exempt. Section 173(1) provides that an activity is not a licensable activity if it is carried on:

- aboard an aircraft, hovercraft or railway vehicle engaged on a journey;
- aboard a vessel engaged on an international journey;
- at an approved wharf at a designated port or hoverport;
- at an examination station at a designated airport;
- at a royal palace;
- at premises which, at the time when the activity is carried on, are permanently or temporarily occupied for the purposes of the armed forces of the Crown;
- at premises in respect of which a certificate issued under s.174 (exemption for national security) has effect; or
- at such other place as may be prescribed.

Journeys

The period during which an aircraft, hovercraft, railway vehicle or vessel is engaged on a journey includes any period ending with its departure when preparations are being made for the journey, and any period after its arrival at its destination when it continues to be occupied by the passengers, or any of them, who made the journey or any part of it.

An international journey is either a journey from a place in the United Kingdom to an immediate destination outside the United Kingdom, or a journey from a place outside the United Kingdom to an immediate destination in the United Kingdom.

'Railway vehicle' has the meaning given by the Railways Act 1993, s.83 (see **21.5.2**).

Designated airports, ports and hoverports

Only certain parts of designated airports, ports and hoverports are exempt. In relation to airports, only the part of the airport which is an 'examination station' is exempt. This area has the meaning given by the Customs and Excise Management Act 1979, s.22A and is essentially that part of an airport beyond the security check in, i.e. 'airside'. In respect of ports and hoverports this area is an approved wharf which has the meaning given by the Customs and Excise Management Act 1979, s.20A, i.e. 'wharfside'. These are areas to which the non-travelling public do not have access and are subject to stringent by-laws. This exemption allows refreshment of all kinds to be provided to travellers at all times of the day and night. Other parts of designated ports, hoverports and airports are subject to the normal licensing controls.

The Secretary of State may by order designate a port, hoverport or airport in the future if it appears to him to be one at which there is a substantial amount of international passenger traffic. Alternatively, an order may be made to remove designation from any port, airport or hoverport.

The airports which have been designated are Birmingham, Bournemouth, Bristol, Cardiff, Coventry, Exeter, Humberside, Leeds Bradford, Liverpool John Lennon, London City, London Gatwick, London Heathrow, London Stansted, London Luton, Manchester, Manston, Newcastle, Norwich, Nottingham East Midlands, Sheffield City, Southampton, Southend, and Teesside (Airports Licensing (Liquor) Order 2005, SI 2005/1733).

Royal palaces

Royal palaces are exempt from the need to have a premises licence. Such palaces include Buckingham Palace, the Banqueting House, the Tower of London, Hampton Court Palace, Kensington Palace, Windsor Castle and St James' Palace.

Premises used by the armed forces

Premises used by the armed forces are exempt. These include premises which are permanently or temporarily occupied by the armed forces.

Premises exempt on national security grounds

A Minister of the Crown of Cabinet rank or the Attorney General may issue a certificate under s.174 in respect of any premises if he considers that it is appropriate to do so for the purposes of safeguarding national security. The effect of the certificate will be that any activities carried on at the premises will not be licensable activities. The certificate may identify the premises by means of a general description but there are no other requirements as to its contents. It is expected that this power will be used where the inspection of a particular premises for purposes of the licensing regime would give rise to a security risk.

A document purporting to be a certificate is to be received in evidence and treated as being a certificate unless the contrary is proved. A document which purports to be certified by or on behalf of a minister of the Crown as a true copy of a certificate given by a minister of the Crown is evidence of that certificate.

A minister of the Crown may cancel a certificate issued by him or any other minister of the Crown.

7.1.4 Exempt lotteries

A lottery where one or more of the prizes consists of or includes alcohol in a sealed container will be exempt under s.175 from requiring a premises licence where the lottery is an incidental non-commercial lottery within the meaning of the Gambling Act 2005, Sched.11, Part 1.

7.2 APPLICANTS FOR PREMISES LICENCES

Section 16 sets out a wide list of persons or bodies who can apply for a premises licence. It also provides that an individual may not apply for a premises licence unless they are aged 18 or over, and if they are resident in the United Kingdom they may not apply for a premises licence authorising premises to be used for the sale by retail of alcohol or the provision of late night refreshment unless they are entitled to work in the United Kingdom.

The full list of persons or bodies who can apply for a premises licence is as follows:

- a person who carries on, or proposes to carry on, a business which involves the use of the premises for the licensable activities to which the application relates;
- a person who makes the application pursuant to any statutory function discharged by that person which relates to those licensable activities, for example a local authority, a fire and rescue authority and the Prison Service;
- a person who makes the application pursuant to any function discharged by that person by virtue of His Majesty's prerogative;
- a recognised club, which is a club which satisfies the first three requirements in s.62 (see **17.3**);
- a charity;

- the proprietor of an educational institution (for these purposes 'educational institution' means either a school or an institution within the further education sector within the meaning of the Education Act 1996, s.4, an institution within the higher education sector within the meaning given by the Further and Higher Education Act 1992, s.91(5) or a college (including any institution in the nature of a college), school, hall or other institution of a university in circumstances where the university receives financial support under the Further and Higher Education Act 1992, s.65 or Higher Education and Research Act 2017, ss.39 or 97 and 'proprietor' in relation to a school within the meaning of the Education Act 1996, s.4 has the same meaning as in s.579(1) of that Act, and in relation to an educational institution other than such a school means the governing body of that institution within the meaning of the Further and Higher Education Act 1992, s.90(1));
- a health service body (for these purposes 'health service body' means either an NHS trust established by virtue of the National Health Service Act 2006, s.25 or National Health Service (Wales) Act 2006, s.18, or a local health board established by virtue of the National Health Service (Wales) Act 2006, s.11);
- a person who is registered under the Care Standards Act 2000, Part 2 in respect of an independent hospital in Wales (for these purposes 'independent hospital' has the same meaning as in the Care Standards Act 2000, s.2(2) which provides that a hospital which is not a health service hospital is an independent hospital);
- a person who is registered under the Health and Social Care Act 2008, Part 1, Ch.2 in respect of the carrying on of a regulated activity in an independent hospital in England, and for these purposes 'independent hospital' means a hospital (as defined by National Health Service Act 2006, s.275) that is not a health service hospital as defined by that section, or any other establishment in which any of the following services are provided and which is not a health service hospital as so defined:

  - medical treatment under anaesthesia or intravenously administered sedation;
  - dental treatment under general anaesthesia;
  - obstetric services and, in connection with childbirth, medical services;
  - termination of pregnancies;
  - cosmetic surgery, other than:

    - ear and body piercing;
    - tattooing;
    - the subcutaneous injection of a substance or substances into the skin for cosmetic purposes; or
    - the removal of hair roots or small blemishes on the skin by the application of heat using an electric current;

- the chief officer of police of a police force in England and Wales; and
- a person of such other description as may be prescribed.

7.2.1 Persons who carry on or propose to carry on a business involving licensable activities on the premises

The principal category of those who are eligible to apply for a premises licence will be those persons who carry on or propose to carry on a business involving licensable activities on the premises. If the applicant is an individual then he they must be aged 18 or over and if they are resident in the United Kingdom they may not apply for a premises licence authorising premises to be used for the sale by retail of alcohol or the provision of late night refreshment unless they are entitled to work in the United Kingdom. Additionally, for these purposes, a 'person' includes a business or partnership, and the Guidance at para.8.16 provides that:

> Licensing authorities should not require the nomination of an individual to hold the licence or determine the identity of the most appropriate person to hold the licence.

It is not for the licensing authority to decide who is the most appropriate person to hold the licence. For example, in respect of most leased public houses, a tenant may run or propose to run the business at the premises in agreement with a pub owning company. Both would be eligible to apply for the appropriate licence and it is for these businesses or individuals to agree contractually among themselves who should do so. It is not for the licensing authority to interfere in that decision. However, in the case of a managed public house, the pub operating company should apply for the licence as the manager (an employee) would not be entitled to do so. Similarly, with cinema chains, the normal holder of the premises licence would be the company owning the cinema and not the cinema manager (an employee of the main company).

There is no requirement that an applicant for a premises licence must have a legal or equitable interest in the premises or a contractual right to use them. So an application for a premises licence could be made by someone who was proposing to buy the premises and use them for licensable activities. While there is nothing to prevent an application being made before premises have been built, extended or altered, a developer could not make an application unless he proposed subsequently to use the premises for a licensable activity. A developer in such a situation should apply instead for a provisional statement (see **Chapter 13**).

7.2.2 Joint applications

It is possible for a joint application to be made for a premises licence, though this is likely to be rare as each applicant must be carrying on a business which involves the use of the premises for licensable activities at the premises. In the case of a tenanted public house, for example, it would be far easier for the tenant to show this than for a pub owning company which was not itself carrying on licensable activities.

Where a public house is owned, or a tenancy is held, jointly by a husband and wife, civil partners or other partnerships of a similar nature and both parties actively involve themselves in the business of carrying on licensable activities at the premises, then the husband and wife or the partners could make a joint application for the premises licence even if they were not formally partners in business terms. According to the Guidance this is unlikely to lead to the same issues of clouded accountability that could arise where two separate businesses applied jointly for the licence (para.8.18). If the application is then granted the premises licence would identify the holder as both people and any subsequent applications, for example for a variation of the licence, would have to be made jointly. Before making a joint application, consideration should be given as to whether it will provide sufficient flexibility for the business or whether a single application, given that it would be possible later to apply for transfer and interim authority, would be preferable.

7.2.3 Multiple licences

There is no bar on there being more than one premises licence in force at any given time in respect of the same premises. For example, a property could have a premises licence authorising the sale of alcohol which was held by one person and another person could hold a premises licence for those premises or part of those premises which authorised regulated entertainment. So, the fact that there is already a premises licence in force should not prevent another premises licence being applied for.

7.2.4 Shadow licences

A shadow licence is a term used to describe a second or subsequent licence for premises where a licence already exists. Although they are not explicitly referred to in the Act, the concept of shadow licences was approved in *Extreme Oyster and Star Oyster Ltd* v. *Guildford BC* [2013] EWHC 2174 (Admin); [2014] PTSR 325.

A common situation in which a shadow licence may be applied for is when a landlord's licensed premises are operated by a tenant and the licence is held in the name of the tenant. In these circumstances, there are several ways in which the tenant's actions could have a negative impact on the licence, for example they might become insolvent or bankrupt and the licence will lapse, or the licence might be reviewed due to poor management of the premises resulting in restrictive conditions being added, hours cut back or even revocation. A shadow licence can protect the landlord in such circumstances. A shadow licence will typically be granted on the same terms as the existing licence being operated by the tenant.

7.2.5 Entitlement to work and immigration status

A licence may not be issued to an individual, or an individual in a partnership which is not a limited liability partnership, who is resident in the United Kingdom and who does not have the right to live and work in the United Kingdom, or who is subject to a condition preventing them from doing work relating to the carrying on of a licensable activity. An applicant must demonstrate that they have the right to work in the United Kingdom and are not subject to a condition preventing them from doing work relating to the carrying on of a licensable activity. They can do this either:

- by providing with their application, copies or scanned copies of the relevant documents, which do not need to be certified, as set out on **www.gov.uk** which demonstrate their entitlement to work in the United Kingdom; or
- by providing their 'share code' to enable the licensing authority to carry out a check using the Home Office online right to work checking service (**www.gov.uk/prove-right-to-work**).

Section 192A provides that an individual is entitled to work in the United Kingdom if:

- the individual does not, under the Immigration Act 1971, require leave to enter or remain in the United Kingdom; or
- the individual has been granted such leave and the leave:
    - is not invalid;
    - has not ceased to have effect (whether by reason of curtailment, revocation, cancellation, passage of time or otherwise); and
    - is not subject to a condition preventing the individual from doing work relating to the carrying on of the sale by retail of alcohol or the provision of late night refreshment.

Where an individual is on immigration bail within the meaning of the Immigration Act 2016, Sched.10, Part 1, the individual is to be treated for the above purposes as if the individual had been granted leave to enter the United Kingdom, but any condition as to the individual's work in the United Kingdom to which the individual's immigration bail is subject is to be treated for those purposes as a condition of leave.

7.3 MAKING AN APPLICATION

An application for a premises licence must be made to the 'relevant licensing authority' (s.17(1)). In the majority of cases this will be the authority in whose area the premises are situated. Where part of the premises is situated in one authority area and another part of the premises is situated in the area of another authority, the relevant licensing authority will be the authority in whose area the greater or greatest part of the premises is situated (s.12(3)(a)). If the premises are split equally between neighbouring authorities, then the applicant must nominate which of the authorities is to be the relevant licensing authority (s.12(3)(b)).

An applicant must submit the following to the relevant licensing authority:

- a completed application form;
- an operating schedule;
- a plan of the premises in the prescribed form;
- if the application requests the authorisation to supply alcohol, the written consent of the proposed designated premises supervisor in the prescribed form; and
- the prescribed fee.

Notice of the application must be given to each of the responsible authorities (see **7.8**). The application must also be advertised (see **7.6–7.7**).

7.4 THE APPLICATION FORM

An application for a premises licence must be in the prescribed form which is set out in the Premises Licences Regulations, Sched.2.

7.4.1 Completing the application form

Guidance in completing the application form may be obtained from **www.gov.uk** or the relevant licensing authority. The form may be completed by being either typed or written legibly in block capitals. All answers must be inside the boxes and written in black ink. Care must be taken when completing the application form as any mistakes will be built into the new licence.

In the opening statement, the name of the applicant or applicants applying for the premises licence should be inserted.

The application form is then divided into four parts.

Part 1

The applicant must set out the following details of the premises:

- the postal address;
- the telephone number at the premises, if any; and
- the non-domestic rateable value of the premises.

If the premises have no postal address, the location of the premises should be described or the Ordnance Survey map reference should be given.

The trading name of the premises should also be included.

The non-domestic rateable value of the premises will determine the fee to be paid both for the initial application and annually. The non-domestic rateable value is based on the annual rent that the premises could have been let for on the open market at a particular date. It can be checked on the Valuation Office Agency website (**www.voa.gov.uk**).

Part 2

Part 2 deals with details of the applicant. The applicant must state in which capacity he is applying for a premises licence. If he is applying as an individual, a limited company, a partnership, an unincorporated association or a statutory corporation he must confirm that he is carrying on or proposing to carry on a business which involves the use of the premises for licensable activities, or that he is making the application pursuant to a statutory function or a function discharged by virtue of His Majesty's prerogative.

The applicant must then give further details such as his name and address, nationality, telephone number, email address (this is optional), confirmation, where relevant, that he is at least 18 years old, and, where applicable, if demonstrating a right to work via the Home Office online right to work checking service, the 'share code' provided to the applicant by that service.

Part 3

Part 3 contains the operating schedule (see **Chapter 8**). It starts by requiring the applicant to state when they want the premises licence to start and, if they want it only to be valid for a limited period of time, when they want it to end.

The applicant must then give a general description of the premises, for example the type of premises, their general situation and layout and any other information which could be relevant to the licensing objectives. Where the application includes off-supplies of alcohol and the applicant intends to provide a place for these to be consumed, for example a beer garden, he must include a description of where the place will be and its proximity to the premises.

If 5,000 or more people are expected to attend the premises at any one time, the applicant must state the number expected to attend. This question is asked in order to determine whether an additional fee is payable. The figure of 5,000 relates to the maximum number of people on the licensed premises at any one time. It does not relate to areas which do not form part of the licensed premises; for example more than 5,000 people may attend a country show but a beer tent at that show is unlikely to hold 5,000 people all at the same time and so would not trigger the additional fee.

The applicant must then specify which licensable activities they intend to carry on from the premises, and give further details of these in the appropriate boxes A–M using the 24-hour clock. Where it is intended that the supply of alcohol is to be carried on, the applicant must set out the full name, address and, if known, the personal licence number (and issuing authority) of the proposed designated premises supervisor (see further **Chapter 9**).

All applicants must complete boxes K, L and M. Box K requires an applicant to highlight any adult entertainment or services, activities, other entertainment or matters ancillary to the use of the premises which may give rise to concern in respect of children. When completing this box an applicant should give information about anything intended to occur at the premises or ancillary to the use of the premises which may give rise to concern in respect of children, regardless of whether it is intended that children have access to the premises (for example, nudity or semi-nudity, films for restricted age groups or the presence of gaming machines).

Details of the hours during which the premises will be open to the public must be stated in box L, together with any seasonal variation or non-standard timings. A difference is therefore drawn between the hours during which the licensable activities will take place and the hours during which the public will be permitted to be on the premises. Reference should be made to the statement of licensing policy of the relevant licensing authority for any requirements as to how long customers should be allowed to remain on the premises after the cessation of licensable activities. Finally box M requires an applicant to list the steps which he will take to promote the four licensing objectives (see **2.3**).

Further guidance on completing the operating schedule can be found in **Chapter 8**.

There is then a checklist, together with warnings that it is an offence, liable on summary conviction to a fine not exceeding level 5 on the standard scale, under s.158 to make a false statement in or in connection with the application and that it is an offence under the Immigration Act 1971, s.24b for a person to work when they know, or have reasonable cause to believe, that they are disqualified from doing so by reason of their immigration status. Those who employ an adult without leave or who is subject to conditions as to employment will be liable to a civil penalty under the Immigration, Asylum and Nationality Act 2006, s.15 and pursuant to s.21 of the same Act, will be committing an offence where they do so in the knowledge, or with reasonable cause to believe, that the employee is disqualified.

Part 4

The application form must be signed by the applicant. It can also be signed by the applicant's solicitor or other duly authorised agent; anyone signing on behalf of the applicant must state in what capacity they sign. Where there are joint applicants, both applicants or their respective agents must sign the application form. If the application is made by a limited company, partnership or unincorporated association, someone who has the capacity to bind the applicant should sign.

7.4.2 Obtaining an application form

The Provision of Services Regulations 2009, SI 2009/2999 require local authorities to ensure that all procedures relating to access to, or the exercise of, a service activity may be easily completed, at a distance and by electronic means. Electronic application facilities for premises licences may be found either on **www.gov. uk** or the licensing authority's own website. It remains acceptable to make an application in writing and a licensing authority must provide an applicant on request with a printed application form, although usually these will be made available via its website for an applicant to download, print and complete.

7.4.3 Making an application

The Premises Licences Regulations, reg.21 provides that an application must be made in writing. However, notwithstanding this requirement, an application can also be made electronically (Premises Licences Regulations, reg.21A(1)). Where the application is transmitted by electronic means, the application will not be treated as being given until the information, and any accompanying plan or document, becomes accessible to the relevant licensing authority by means of that facility (Premises Licences Regulations, reg.21A(3)). In addition, as a fee must accompany the application, the application will not be taken as given until the fee has been received by the relevant licensing authority (Premises Licences Regulations, reg.21A(4)).

An applicant may apply using the licence application forms available on **www. gov.uk**, or will be re-directed from **www.gov.uk** to the licensing authority's own electronic facility if one is available. Applicants may also apply directly to the licensing authority's facility without going through **www.gov.uk**.

If an electronic application is made via **www.gov.uk**, a notification will be sent by **www.gov.uk** to the licensing authority that a completed application form is available for it to download from **www.gov.uk**. This is the day that the application is taken to be 'given' even if the application is downloaded at a later stage. Where an application is made via the licensing authority's own electronic facility, the application will be taken to be 'given' when the applicant has submitted a complete application form and paid the fee. The application is given at the point at which it becomes accessible to the authority by means of the facility.

The Guidance at paras.8.26 to 8.29 deals with 'holding' and 'deferring' electronic applications:

> 8.26 The Government recommends (as for written applications) that electronic applications should not be returned if they contain obvious and minor errors such as typing mistakes, or small errors that can be rectified with information already in the authority's possession. However, if this is not the case and required information is missing or incorrect, the licensing authority may 'hold' the application until the applicant has supplied all the required information. This effectively resets the 28 day period for determining an application and may be done any number of times until the application form is complete. Licensing authorities

must ensure that they notify the applicant as quickly as possible of any missing (or incorrect) information, and explain how this will affect the statutory time-scale and advertising requirements.

8.27 If an application has been given at the weekend, the notice advertising the application (where applicable) may already be displayed outside the premises by the time that the licensing authority downloads the application. It is therefore recommended that, if a licensing authority holds an application, it should inform the applicant that the original (or if necessary, amended) notice must be displayed until the end of the revised period. The licensing authority should also advise the applicant that they should not advertise the application in a local newspaper until they have received confirmation from the licensing authority that the application includes all the required information. To ensure clarity for applicants, the Government recommends that licensing authorities include similar advice on their electronic application facilities (where these exist) to ensure that applicants do not incur any unnecessary costs.

8.28 If an applicant persistently fails to supply the required information, the licensing authority may refuse the application and the applicant must submit a new application.

8.29 Licensing authorities may also 'defer' electronic applications once if the application is particularly complicated, for example if representations are received and a hearing is required. This allows the licensing authority to extend the statutory time period for the determination of the application by such time as is necessary, including, if required, arranging and holding a hearing. Licensing authorities must ensure that applicants are informed as quickly as possible of a decision to defer, and the reasons for the deferral, before the original 28 days has expired.

Table 7.1: Checklist for a premises licence application

	Original to relevant licensing authority	Copy to the police, where notice must be given by applicant	Copy to responsible authorities, where notice must be given by applicant
Completed application form	·		
Form of consent from the proposed designated premises supervisor where sale of alcohol is to take place at the premises			
Plan of the premises			
Payment of the fee			
Confirmation that the application has been advertised on the premises and that this will be maintained for 28 days			
Has the application been advertised in a local newspaper?	Name of newspaper:		Date:

7.5 THE PLAN

The Premises Licences Regulations, reg.23 provides that an application for a premises licence must be accompanied by a plan of the premises and that the information contained in the plan must be clear and legible in all material respects. This means that the plan must be accessible and provide sufficient detail for the licensing authority to be able to determine the application, including the relative size of any features relevant to the application (Guidance, para.8.34). There is no requirement that the plan be to any particular scale.

The plan must show:

- the extent of the boundary of the building, if relevant, and any external and internal walls of the building and, if different, the perimeter of the premises;
- the location of points of access to and egress from the premises and, if different, the location of escape routes from the premises;
- if the premises are to be used for more than one licensable activity, the area within the premises used for each activity;
- fixed structures (including furniture) or similar objects temporarily in a fixed location (but not furniture) which may affect the ability of individuals on the premises to use exits or escape routes without impediment;
- if the premises include a stage or raised area, the location and height of each stage or area relative to the floor;
- if the premises include any steps, stairs, elevators or lifts, the location of the steps, stairs, elevators or lifts;
- if the premises include any room or rooms containing public conveniences, the location of the room or rooms;
- the location and type of any fire safety and any other safety equipment including, if applicable, marine safety equipment; and
- the location of a kitchen, if any, on the premises.

The plan may also include a legend so that the above can be sufficiently illustrated by using symbols on the plan. There is no requirement to have a plan professionally drawn provided it meets the above requirements. The plan does not need to show any areas which are not part of the premises where the licensable activities will take place, for example a beer garden where alcohol is consumed. Such areas must, however, be described as part of the general description of the premises which must be given in Part 3 of the application form.

Providing facilities for the public to dance is a licensable activity. It is not necessary to show the precise location of any dance floor in the premises on the plan. It will be sufficient to clearly mark the relevant part of the premises or room where the dancing will take place.

The plan will form part of the licence (s.24). The licensing authority will need to make a copy of the plan to attach to the premises licence. Alternatively, a licensing authority may request an applicant to provide an additional copy of the plan with their application. There is, however, no legal requirement for an applicant to submit an additional plan.

7.6 ADVERTISING THE APPLICATION BY THE APPLICANT

An applicant must advertise his application for a premises licence in the prescribed form and in the manner which is prescribed and is likely to bring the application to the attention of the persons who live, or are involved in a business, in the relevant licensing authority's area and who are likely to be affected by it (s.17(5)(a)). The Premises Licences Regulations, reg.25 provides that a notice must be displayed at or on the premises and be published in a local newspaper. The Premises Licences Regulations, reg.26 sets out the prescribed information which both notices must contain (see **7.6.3**).

A licensing authority may provide a specimen form of notice for an applicant to use. A suggested form of notice can be found at **Box 7.1**.

7.6.1 Notice to be displayed at or on the premises

An applicant must advertise his application for a premises licence by prominently displaying a notice containing prescribed information at or on the premises to which the application relates for a period of not less than 28 consecutive days starting on the day after the day on which the application was given to the relevant licensing authority.

The notice must be:

- of a size equal to or larger than A4;
- of a pale blue colour; and
- printed legibly in black ink or typed in black in a font of a size equal to or larger than 16 points.

It must be displayed prominently at or on the premises to which the application relates where it can be conveniently read from the exterior of the premises. Where the premises cover an area of more than 50 metres square, further notices in the same form and subject to the same requirements must be displayed every 50 metres along the external perimeter of the premises abutting any highway (50 metres square is not the same as 50 square metres and a common mistake is to interpret this requirement as applying to premises exceeding 50 square metres in area, which is not correct).

7.6.2 Notice published in a local newspaper

An applicant must also publish a notice containing prescribed information in a local newspaper or, if there is none, in a local newsletter, circular or similar document, circulating in the vicinity of the premises on at least one occasion during the 10 working days starting on the day after the day on which the application was given to the relevant licensing authority.

It is important that the notice is published in a local newspaper and an applicant should check with the relevant licensing authority to find out which newspapers are acceptable. An advertising paper may only be used if there is no local newspaper.

7.6.3 Contents of the notice

The notices to be displayed at or on the premises and to be published in a local newspaper must:

- contain a statement of the relevant licensable activities which it is proposed will be carried out on or from the premises;
- state the name of the applicant;
- state the postal address of the premises, if any, or if there is no postal address for the premises a description of those premises sufficient to enable the location and extent of the premises to be identified;
- state the postal address and, where applicable, the worldwide web address where the register of the relevant licensing authority is kept and where and when the record of the application may be inspected;
- state the date by which a responsible authority or any other person may make representations to the relevant licensing authority;
- state that representations shall be made in writing; and
- state that it is an offence knowingly or recklessly to make a false statement in connection with an application and the maximum fine for which a person is liable on summary conviction for the offence.

An applicant should check with the relevant licensing authority to see whether it provides a specimen form of notice to use. If not, a suggested form of notice is given in **Box 7.1**.

BOX 7.1: SUGGESTED FORM OF NOTICE OF AN APPLICATION FOR A PREMISES LICENCE

Licensing Act 2003

Notice of application for the grant of a premises licence

Notice is hereby given that [*insert the full name of the applicant*] has applied to the [*insert the full name of the licensing authority*] on [*insert the date of application to the licensing authority*] for the grant of a new premises licence for [*insert name of premises and full postal address of the premises*].

The proposed application is to permit [*insert details of each licensable activity including days and hours*].

The public register where applications are available to be viewed by members of the public can be accessed online by visiting at [*insert details*].

Any person who wishes to make a representation in relation to this application must give notice in writing of his/her representation to [*insert name and address of the licensing authority*], giving in detail the grounds of objection by [*insert the date by which all relevant representations must be received by the licensing authority, i.e. 28 consecutive days starting on the day after the day on which the application is given to the licensing authority*]. The Licensing Authority must receive representations by the date given above. The Licensing Authority will have regard to any such representation in considering the application.

It is an offence liable on conviction under section 158 of the Licensing Act 2003 to knowingly or recklessly make a false statement in connection with this application.

7.7 ADVERTISING THE APPLICATION BY THE LICENSING AUTHORITY

In addition to the application being advertised by the applicant, the relevant licensing authority must also advertise an application for a premises licence in the prescribed form and in a manner which is prescribed and is likely to bring the application to the attention of the persons who are likely to be affected by it (s.17(5)(aa)).

The Premises Licences Regulations, reg.26B provides that the relevant licensing authority must advertise the application for a period of not less than 28 consecutive days starting on the day after the day on which the application was given to the relevant licensing authority by the publication of a notice on its website containing the information prescribed in reg.26C.

The following information must be contained in the notice:

- a statement of the relevant licensable activities which it is proposed will be carried on on or from the premises;
- the name of the applicant;
- the postal address of the premises, if any, or if there is no postal address for the premises a description of those premises sufficient to enable the location and extent of the premises to be identified;
- the postal address and, where applicable, the worldwide web address where the register of the relevant licensing authority is kept and where and when the record of the application may be inspected;
- the date by which a responsible authority or any other person may make representations to the relevant licensing authority;
- that representations must be made in writing; and
- that it is an offence knowingly or recklessly to make a false statement in connection with the application and the maximum fine for which a person is liable on summary conviction for the offence.

7.8 NOTICE TO RESPONSIBLE AUTHORITIES

An applicant must give notice of his application for a premises licence to each responsible authority by giving each such authority a copy of the application together with its accompanying plan, document or other information (s.17(6)(a) and Premises Licence Regulations, reg.27A). Notice is to be given on the same day as the day on which the application is given to the relevant licensing authority.

Where the application is made electronically, the relevant licensing authority must give a copy of the application together with any accompanying plan or document to each responsible authority (s.17(6)(b); Premises Licence Regulations, reg.27). Notice must be given no later than the first working day after the application was given to the relevant licensing authority. The applicant is not required to send copies of the application to the responsible authorities if the application is made electronically.

A responsible authority may then make representations to the relevant licensing authority about the application within 28 consecutive days starting on the day after the day on which the application to which the representation relates was given to the responsible authority by the applicant (Premises Licence Regulations, reg.22).

Responsible authorities are listed in s.13(4) as being:

- the relevant licensing authority and any other licensing authority in whose area part of the premises is situated;
- the chief officer of police for any police area in which the premises are situated;
- the fire and rescue authority for any area in which the premises are situated;
- the Local Health Board for any area in which the premises are situated;
- the local authority in England whose public health functions within the meaning of the National Health Service Act 2006 are exercisable in respect of any area in which the premises are situated;
- the enforcing authority within the meaning given by the Health and Safety at Work etc. Act 1974, s.18 for any area in which the premises are situated;
- the local planning authority within the meaning of the Town and Country Planning Act 1990 for any area in which the premises are situated;
- the local authority which exercises the statutory functions in any area in which the premises are situated in relation to minimising or preventing the risk of pollution of the environment or of harm to human health;
- a body which represents those who, in relation to any such area, are responsible for or interested in matters relating to the protection of children from harm, and is recognised by the licensing authority for that area for the purposes of this section as being competent to advise it on such matters;
- in relation to a vessel, a navigation authority (within the meaning of the Water Resources Act 1991, s.221(1)) having functions in relation to the waters

where the vessel is usually moored or berthed or any waters where it is, or is proposed to be, navigated at a time when it is used for licensable activities, the Environment Agency, the Canal & River Trust or the Secretary of State;

- where the premises, not being a vessel, are being, or are proposed to be, used for the sale by retail of alcohol or the provision of late night refreshment, the Secretary of State; and
- a person prescribed for these purposes.

In relation to the Secretary of State acting as a responsible authority, the Guidance at para.9.25 provides:

> The Immigration Act 2016 made the Secretary of State a responsible authority in respect of premises licensed to sell alcohol or late night refreshment with effect from 6 April 2017. In effect this conveys the role of responsible authority to Home Office Immigration Enforcement who exercises the powers on the Secretary of State's behalf. When Immigration Enforcement exercises its powers as a responsible authority it will do so in respect of the prevention of crime and disorder licensing objective because it is concerned with the prevention of illegal working or immigration offences more broadly.

The Premises Licences Regulations, reg.7 prescribes that the local weights and measures authority within the meaning of the Weights and Measures Act 1985, s.69 for any area in which the premises are situated is a responsible authority. This will be the local authority trading standards department.

A licensing authority may have drawn up a list of the relevant responsible authorities for its area and their contact details. An applicant should therefore contact the relevant licensing authority to obtain such a list.

Guidance for responsible authorities has been published and is available at **www.gov.uk/government/publications/alcohol-licensing-making-representations/a-practical-approach-to-making-representations-to-a-licensing-authority**. Additional guidance for health bodies on acting as a responsible authority has also been published and is available at **www.gov.uk/government/publications/additional-guidance-for-health-bodies-on-exercising-functions**.

7.9 INSPECTION OF PREMISES

A constable or an authorised person may, at any reasonable time before the determination of an application for a premises licence, enter the premises to which the application relates to assess the likely effect of the grant of the application on the promotion of the licensing objectives (s.59).

The following are designated by s.13(2) as authorised persons:

- an officer of a licensing authority in whose area the premises are situated who is authorised by that authority for the purposes of the Act;
- an inspector appointed by the fire and rescue authority for the area in which the premises are situated;

- an inspector appointed under the Health and Safety at Work etc. Act 1974, s.19;
- an officer of a local authority in whose area the premises are situated, who is authorised by that authority for the purposes of exercising one or more of its statutory functions in relation to minimising or preventing the risk of pollution of the environment or of harm to human health;
- in relation to a vessel, an inspector, or a surveyor of ships, appointed under the Merchant Shipping Act 1995, s.256; and
- a person prescribed for these purposes.

An authorised person who is exercising the power to enter the premises must, if so requested, produce evidence of his authority to exercise the power (s.59(3)). Anyone who intentionally obstructs an authorised person exercising the power of entry commits an offence, and is liable on summary conviction to a fine not exceeding level 2 on the standard scale (s.59(5) and (6)). Obstruction of a constable will constitute an offence of obstructing a constable in the execution of his duty under the Police Act 1996, s.89(2), and a person will be liable on summary conviction to imprisonment for a term not exceeding one month (this will increase to 51 weeks when the Criminal Justice Act 2003 takes effect) or to a fine not exceeding level 3 on the standard scale, or to both.

7.10 DETERMINATION OF THE APPLICATION

7.10.1 Preliminary determination

When a licensing authority receives an application for a premises licence, it must initially determine whether the application has been made properly in accordance with s.17 and with the Premises Licences Regulations. The Guidance at para.8.26 gives recommendations for licensing authorities where applications contain errors (see **7.4.3**). Any failure to observe the notice requirements will render the application invalid.

7.10.2 Unopposed applications

Where no relevant representations have been made, and the applicant has complied with all statutory requirements, s.18 provides that the licensing authority must grant the licence in the terms sought, subject only to such conditions as are consistent with the operating schedule and any conditions which must be imposed under the Act (*British Beer and Pub Association* v. *Canterbury City Council* [2005] EWHC 1318 (Admin); (2005) 169 JP 521). There is no requirement that the premises licence be granted in accordance with the operating schedule, nor for the operating schedule to be incorporated; neither is there a legal obligation to impose a condition, in order to promote the licensing objectives, to give effect to anything contained in the operating schedule where the licensing authority considers that compliance with other legislation will be sufficient for that purpose (*R. (on the application of Bristol Council)* v. *Bristol Magistrates Court* [2009] EWHC 625 (Admin)).

In discharging its duty, a licensing authority may grant a licence subject to different conditions in respect of either different parts of the premises, or different licensable activities (s.18(10)).

The Guidance at para.9.2 provides:

> A hearing is not required where an application has been properly made and no responsible authority or other person has made a relevant representation or where representations are made and subsequently withdrawn. In these cases, the licensing authority must grant the application in the terms sought, subject only to conditions which are consistent with the operating schedule and relevant mandatory conditions under the 2003 Act. This should be undertaken as a simple administrative process by the licensing authority's officials who may replicate some of the proposals contained in the operating schedule to promote the licensing objectives in the form of clear and enforceable licence conditions. Licensing authorities should not hold hearings for uncontested applications, for example in situations where representations have been made and conditions have subsequently been agreed.

7.10.3 Applications where representations have been made

If relevant representations have been made by a responsible authority or other person, s.18(3)(a) provides that the licensing authority must hold a hearing to consider them. Relevant representations are considered further in **Chapter 10**. The Hearings Regulations regulate hearings under the Act (see **Chapter 25**).

The hearing must be held within a period of 20 working days beginning with the day after the end of the period during which representations may be made (Hearings Regulations, reg.5 and Sched.5, para.1). The period during which representations may be made is 28 consecutive days after the day on which the application is given to the authority. Notice of the hearing must be given to the applicant and persons who made relevant representations no later than 10 working days before the day or the first day on which the hearing is to be held (Hearings Regulations, reg.6(4) and Sched.2, para.1). The applicant must be given the relevant representations with the notice of the hearing (Hearings Regulations, reg.7(2) and Sched.3, para.1).

A hearing may be dispensed with if the licensing authority, the applicant and each person who made representations agree that it is unnecessary. This may be because they have reached agreement following mediation or negotiation.

Following the hearing, the licensing authority must, having regard to the representations, then take such of the following steps, if any, as it considers appropriate to promote the licensing objectives:

- grant the licence subject to conditions that are consistent with the applicant's operating schedule modified to the extent the licensing authority considers appropriate for the promotion of the licensing objectives, and any mandatory condition which must be included in the licence under the Act. For these purposes, conditions are modified if any of them is altered or omitted or any new condition is added;

- exclude from the scope of the licence any of the licensable activities to which the application relates; for example, a licensing authority might decide to remove the playing of amplified recorded music after 11 pm from the scope of the licence applied for by a tenant of a pub in the middle of a quiet residential area, or it might prohibit the admittance of under-18s to premises where adult entertainment is provided;
- refuse to specify a person in the licence as the premises supervisor, for example following a police objection where the proposed premises supervisor has been removed as premises supervisor for other premises following review; or
- reject the application. The licensing authority can only reject an application where it considers that taking any of the other steps mentioned above will not be sufficient to promote the licensing objectives. In practice, a rejection is likely to be rare.

The licensing authority must 'have regard' to the representations before taking any of the above steps. There is nothing to indicate that it may not take into account other matters not included in the representations.

A licensing authority may refuse a premises licence where evidence suggests that an increased licensed capacity would have a negative effect on crime and disorder in areas beyond the premises licence holder's control (*Luminar Leisure Ltd* v. *Wakefield Magistrates Court* [2008] EWHC 1002 (Admin); (2008) 172 JP 345).

There is no requirement for a licensing authority to notify the applicant and anyone who made representations of its reasons for any decision it makes as to whether or not to take any of the above steps. In practice, reasons will usually be given as the licensing authority will need to comply with the ECHR, art.6(1) providing the right to a fair trial, which includes giving reasons. These reasons need not be elaborate or lengthy but should tell the parties in broad terms the reason for the decision.

A licensing authority does not have to take any of the above steps. If it does not consider any of them appropriate for the promotion of the licensing objectives, it can grant the licence in the terms sought by the applicant, subject only to such conditions as are consistent with the operating schedule and any conditions which must be imposed under the Act.

In discharging its duty a licensing authority may grant a licence subject to different conditions in respect of either different parts of the premises or different licensable activities (s.18(10)).

Representations must be made within 28 consecutive days after the day on which the application is given to the authority. In *R. (on the application of Albert Court Residents' Association)* v. *Westminster City Council* [2011] EWCA Civ

430; [2012] PTSR 604, the court held that there is no power for a licensing authority to consider late representations.

7.11 CONDITIONS

7.11.1 Introduction

When a licensing authority grants a premises licence it may impose conditions on the licence where they are appropriate for the promotion of one or more of the licensing objectives. The types of conditions which may be imposed are considered further in **Chapter 11**.

In addition, certain conditions must be attached to a premises licence which authorises the supply of alcohol, a premises licence which authorises the exhibition of films and a premises licence which contains a condition that door supervisors must be at the premises.

7.11.2 Mandatory conditions – premises licensed to supply alcohol

Where a premises licence authorises the supply of alcohol, s.19 provides that the licence must include the following conditions:

- that no supply of alcohol may be made under the premises licence at a time when there is no designated premises supervisor in respect of the premises licence or at a time when the designated premises supervisor does not hold a personal licence or his personal licence is suspended;
- that every supply of alcohol under the premises licence must be made or authorised by a person who holds a personal licence; and
- any conditions specified in an order made under s.19A and applicable to the premises licence.

The first two conditions do not require that either the designated premises supervisor or a personal licence holder be physically present when there is a sale of alcohol. The Guidance at para.10.28 provides:

> The 2003 Act does not require a designated premises supervisor or any other personal licence holder to be present on the premises at all times when alcohol is sold. However, the designated premises supervisor and the premises licence holder remain responsible for the premises at all times including compliance with the terms of the 2003 Act and conditions attached to the premises licence to promote the licensing objectives.

It must be demonstrated that a sale has been sanctioned by either the designated premises supervisor or a personal licence holder and this will ultimately come down to a question of fact – was the sale sanctioned directly or by way of written or oral authority? The Guidance at paras.10.31 to 10.34 provides:

> 10.31 'Authorisation' does not imply direct supervision by a personal licence holder of each sale of alcohol. The question arises as to how sales can be authorised.

Ultimately, whether an authorisation has been given is a question of fact that would have to be decided by the courts on the evidence before it in the course of a criminal prosecution.

10.32 The following factors should be relevant in considering whether or not an authorisation has been given:

- the person(s) authorised to sell alcohol at any particular premises should be clearly identified;
- the authorisation should have specified the acts which may be carried out by the person who is authorised to supply alcohol;
- there should be an overt act of authorisation, for example, a specific written statement given to the individual who is authorised to supply alcohol; and
- there should be in place sensible arrangements for the personal licence holder to monitor the activity that they have authorised on a reasonably regular basis.

10.33 It is strongly recommended that personal licence holders give specific written authorisations to individuals whom they are authorising to retail alcohol. A single written authorisation would be sufficient to cover multiple sales over an unlimited period. This would assist personal licence holders in demonstrating due diligence should issues arise with enforcement authorities; and would protect employees if they themselves are challenged in respect of their authority to sell alcohol.

10.34 Written authorisation is not a requirement of the 2003 Act and its absence alone could not give rise to enforcement action.

Section 19A allows the Secretary of State to specify conditions relating to the supply of alcohol which will apply to premises licences. The number of such conditions must not at any time exceed nine. The following conditions have been prescribed by the Licensing Act 2003 (Mandatory Licensing Conditions) Order 2010, SI 2010/860:

1. (1) The responsible person must ensure that staff on relevant premises do not carry out, arrange or participate in any irresponsible promotions in relation to the premises.

    (2) In this paragraph, an irresponsible promotion means any one or more of the following activities, or substantially similar activities, carried on for the purpose of encouraging the sale or supply of alcohol for consumption on the premises –

        (a) games or other activities which require or encourage, or are designed to require or encourage, individuals to –

            (i) drink a quantity of alcohol within a time limit (other than to drink alcohol sold or supplied on the premises before the cessation of the period in which the responsible person is authorised to sell or supply alcohol), or

            (ii) drink as much alcohol as possible (whether within a time limit or otherwise);

        (b) provision of unlimited or unspecified quantities of alcohol free or for a fixed or discounted fee to the public or to a group defined by a particular characteristic in a manner which carries a significant risk of undermining a licensing objective;

(c)   provision of free or discounted alcohol or any other thing as a prize to encourage or reward the purchase and consumption of alcohol over a period of 24 hours or less in a manner which carries a significant risk of undermining a licensing objective;

(d)   selling or supplying alcohol in association with promotional posters or flyers on, or in the vicinity of, the premises which can reasonably be considered to condone, encourage or glamorise anti-social behaviour or to refer to the effects of drunkenness in any favourable manner;

(e)   dispensing alcohol directly by one person into the mouth of another (other than where that other person is unable to drink without assistance by reason of disability).

2.   The responsible person must ensure that free potable water is provided on request to customers where it is reasonably available.

3.   (1)   The premises licence holder or club premises certificate holder must ensure that an age verification policy is adopted in respect of the premises in relation to the sale or supply of alcohol.

    (2)   The designated premises supervisor in relation to the premises licence must ensure that the supply of alcohol at the premises is carried on in accordance with the age verification policy.

    (3)   The policy must require individuals who appear to the responsible person to be under 18 years of age (or such older age as may be specified in the policy) to produce on request, before being served alcohol, identification bearing their photograph, date of birth and either –

        (a)   a holographic mark, or
        (b)   an ultraviolet feature.

4.   The responsible person must ensure that –

(a)   where any of the following alcoholic drinks is sold or supplied for consumption on the premises (other than alcoholic drinks sold or supplied having been made up in advance ready for sale or supply in a securely closed container) it is available to customers in the following measures –

    (i)   beer or cider: $\frac{1}{2}$ pint;
    (ii)   gin, rum, vodka or whisky: 25 ml or 35 ml; and
    (iii)   still wine in a glass: 125 ml;

(b)   these measures are displayed in a menu, price list or other printed material which is available to customers on the premises; and

(c)   where a customer does not in relation to a sale of alcohol specify the quantity of alcohol to be sold, the customer is made aware that these measures are available.

The conditions in paras.1, 2 and 4 do not apply where the premises licence authorises the sale by retail or supply of alcohol only for consumption off the premises.

In addition, the following mandatory condition has been prescribed by the Licensing Act 2003 (Mandatory Conditions) Order 2014, SI 2014/1252:

1. A relevant person shall ensure that no alcohol is sold or supplied for consumption on or off the premises for a price which is less than the permitted price.

2. For the purposes of the condition set out in paragraph 1 –

    (a) 'duty' is to be construed in accordance with the Alcoholic Liquor Duties Act 1979;

    (b) 'permitted price' is the price found by applying the formula –

    $$P = D + (D \times V)$$
    Where –

        (i) P is the permitted price,

        (ii) D is the amount of duty chargeable in relation to the alcohol as if the duty were charged on the date of the sale or supply of the alcohol, and

        (iii) V is the rate of value added tax chargeable in relation to the alcohol as if the value added tax were charged on the date of the sale or supply of the alcohol;

    (c) 'relevant person' means, in relation to premises in respect of which there is in force a premises licence –

        (i) the holder of the premises licence,

        (ii) the designated premises supervisor (if any) in respect of such a licence, or

        (iii) the personal licence holder who makes or authorises a supply of alcohol under such a licence;

    (d) 'relevant person' means, in relation to premises in respect of which there is in force a club premises certificate, any member or officer of the club present on the premises in a capacity which enables the member or officer to prevent the supply in question; and

    (e) 'value added tax' means value added tax charged in accordance with the Value Added Tax Act 1994.

3. Where the permitted price given by Paragraph (b) of paragraph 2 would (apart from this paragraph) not be a whole number of pennies, the price given by that sub-paragraph shall be taken to be the price actually given by that sub-paragraph rounded up to the nearest penny.

4. (1) Sub-paragraph (2) applies where the permitted price given by Paragraph (b) of paragraph 2 on a day ('the first day') would be different from the permitted price on the next day ('the second day') as a result of a change to the rate of duty or value added tax.

    (2) The permitted price which would apply on the first day applies to sales or supplies of alcohol which take place before the expiry of the period of 14 days beginning on the second day.

The mandatory conditions do not have to be physically included in the premises licence but nonetheless will apply to every premises licence authorising the sale and supply of alcohol for consumption on the premises.

Irresponsible promotions

The Guidance at para.10.39 provides:

> Under this condition, the 'responsible person' (defined in the 2003 Act as the holder of a premises licence, designated premises supervisor, a person aged 18 or over who is authorised to allow the sale or supply of alcohol by an under 18 or a member or officer of a club present on the club premises who can oversee the supply of alcohol) should be able to demonstrate that they have ensured that staff do not carry out, arrange or participate in any irresponsible promotions. An irresponsible promotion is one that fits one of the descriptions below (or is substantially similar), is carried on for the purpose of encouraging the sale or supply of alcohol for consumption on the premises. The aim of the condition is to prohibit or restrict promotions which encourage people to drink more than they might ordinarily do and in a manner which undermines the licensing objectives.

Drinking games

The Guidance at para.10.40 provides:

> Drinking games which require or encourage individuals to drink a quantity of alcohol within a time limit, or drink as much alcohol as possible within a time limit or otherwise, are prohibited. For example, this may include organised 'drink downing' competitions. This would not prevent the responsible person from requiring all drinks to be consumed or abandoned at, or before, the closing time of the premises. Nor does it necessarily prohibit 'happy hours' as long as these are not designed to encourage individuals to drink excessively or rapidly.

Large quantities of alcohol for free or for a fixed price

The Guidance at para.10.41 provides:

> Irresponsible promotions can include the provision of unlimited or unspecified quantities of alcohol free or for a fixed or discounted price, where there is a significant risk that such a promotion would undermine one or more of the licensing objectives. This includes alcohol provided to the public or to a group defined by a particular characteristic, for example, a promotion which offers women free drinks before a certain time or 'all you can drink for £10'. Promotions can be designed with a particular group in mind (for example, over 65s). A common sense approach is encouraged, which may include specifying the quantity of alcohol included in it or not targeting a group which could become more vulnerable or present a greater risk of crime and disorder as a result of excessive alcohol consumption.

Prizes and rewards

The Guidance at para.10.42 provides:

> The sale, supply or provision of free or discounted alcohol or any other item as a prize to encourage or reward the purchase and consumption of alcohol can be within the definition of an irresponsible promotion, where there is a significant risk that such a promotion would undermine one or more of the licensing objectives. This may include

promotions under which free or discounted alcohol is offered as a part of the sale of alcohol, for example, 'Buy one and get two free' and 'Buy one cocktail and get a second cocktail for 25p'. This includes promotions which involve the provision of free or discounted alcohol within the same 24 hour period.

Posters and flyers

The Guidance at para.10.43 provides:

Irresponsible promotions can also include the sale or supply of alcohol in association with promotional materials on display in or around the premises, which can either be reasonably considered to condone, encourage or glamorise anti social behaviour or refer to the effects of drunkenness in any favourable manner.

Dispensing alcohol directly into the mouth

The Guidance at para.10.44 provides:

The responsible person (see paragraph 10.39) must ensure that no alcohol is dispensed directly into the mouth of a customer. For example, this may include drinking games such as the 'dentist's chair' where a drink is poured continuously into the mouth of another individual and may also prevent a premises from allowing another body to promote its products by employing someone to dispense alcohol directly into customers' mouths. An exception to this condition would be when an individual is unable to drink without assistance due to a disability.

Free potable water

The Guidance at para.10.45 provides:

The responsible person (see paragraph 10.39) must ensure that free potable tap water is provided on request to customers where it is reasonably available on the premises. What is meant by reasonably available is a question of fact; for example, it would not be reasonable to expect free tap water to be available in premises for which the water supply had temporarily been lost because of a broken mains water supply. However, it may be reasonable to expect bottled water to be provided in such circumstances.

Age verification

The Guidance at paras.10.46 to 10.50 provides:

10.46 The premises licence holder or club premises certificate holder must ensure that an age verification policy applies to the premises in relation to the sale or supply of alcohol. This must as a minimum require individuals who appear to the responsible person (see paragraph 10.39) to be under the age of 18 years of age to produce on request, before being served alcohol, identification bearing their photograph, date of birth, and either a holographic mark or ultraviolet feature. The Home Office encourages licensed premises to accept cards bearing the Proof of Age Standards Scheme (PASS) hologram as their preferred proof of age, while acknowledging that many other forms of identification meet the requirements of the mandatory condition.

10.47 The premises licence holder or club premises certificate holder must ensure that staff (in particular, staff who are involved in the supply of alcohol) are made aware of the existence and content of the age verification policy which applies to the premises.

10.48 The designated premises supervisor (where there is one) must ensure that the supply of alcohol at the premises is carried on in accordance with the age verification policy. This means that the DPS has personal responsibility for ensuring that staff are not only aware of, but are also applying, the age verification policy.

10.49 It is acceptable, and indeed encouraged, for premises to have an age verification policy which requires individuals who appear to the responsible person to be under an age greater than 18 to produce such identification on request. For example, if premises have a policy that requires any individual that appears to be under the age of 21 to produce identification that meets the criteria listed above, this is perfectly acceptable under the mandatory code.

10.50 Licence holders should consider carefully what steps they are required to take to comply with the age verification requirements under the 2003 Act in relation to sales of alcohol made remotely. These include sales made online, by telephone and mail order sales, and alcohol delivery services. Each of these sales must comply with the requirements of the 2003 Act. The mandatory condition requires that age verification takes place before a person is served alcohol. Where alcohol is sold remotely (for example, online) or through a telephone transaction, the sale is made at this point but the alcohol is not actually served until it is delivered to the customer. Age verification measures (for example, online age verification) should be used to ensure that alcohol is not sold to any person under the age of 18. However, licence holders should also consider carefully what steps are appropriate to ensure that age verification takes place before the alcohol is served (i.e. physically delivered) to the customer to be satisfied that the customer is aged 18 or over. It is, therefore, the responsibility of the person serving or delivering the alcohol to ensure that age verification has taken place and that photo ID has been checked if the person appears to be less than 18 years of age.

Smaller measures

The Guidance at paras.10.51 to 10.54 provides:

10.51 The responsible person (see paragraph 10.39) shall ensure that the following drinks, if sold or supplied on the premises, are available in the following measures:

- Beer or cider: $\frac{1}{2}$ pint
- Gin, rum, vodka or whisky: 25ml or 35ml
- Still wine in a glass: 125ml

10.52 As well as making the drinks available in the above measures, the responsible person must also make customers aware of the availability of these measures by displaying them on printed materials available to customers on the premises. This can include making their availability clear on menus and price lists, and ensuring that these are displayed in a prominent and conspicuous place in the relevant premises (for example, at the bar). Moreover, staff must make customers aware of the availability of small measures when customers do not request that they be sold alcohol in a particular measure.

10.53 This condition does not apply if the drinks in question are sold or supplied having been made up in advance ready for sale or supply in a securely closed container. For example, if beer is only available in pre-sealed bottles the requirement to make it available in $\frac{1}{2}$ pints does not apply.

10.54 The premises licence holder or club premises certificate holder must ensure that staff are made aware of the application of this condition.

The Weights and Measures (Intoxicating Liquor) Order 1988, SI 1988/2039 permits retail sales of 2/3 pint of draught beer or cider, wines (other than fortified wines) to be sold in a quantity of less than 75 ml without quantity indications and fortified wines to be sold only in specified quantities of 50 ml or 70 ml with quantity indications.

Ban on sales of alcohol below the permitted price

The Guidance at paras.10.55 to 10.58 provides:

10.55 The relevant person (the holder of the premises licence, the designated premises supervisor (if any) in respect of such a licence, the personal licence holder who makes or authorises a supply of alcohol under such a licence, or any member or officer of a club present on the premises in a capacity which enables the member or officer to prevent the supply in question) shall ensure that no alcohol is sold or supplied for consumption on or off the premises for a price which is less than the permitted price.

10.56 The permitted price is defined as the aggregate of the duty chargeable in relation to the alcohol on the date of its sale or supply and the amount of that duty multiplied by a percentage which represents the rate of VAT chargeable in relation to the alcohol on the date of its sale or supply. Detailed guidance on how to make this calculation and a calculator to determine permitted prices for each product are available on the GOV.UK website.

10.57 Where there is a change to the rate of duty or VAT applying to alcohol (for instance, following a Budget), the relevant person should ensure that the permitted price reflects the new rates within fourteen days of the introduction of the new rate.

10.58 It is still permitted to sell alcohol using promotions (as long as they are compatible with any other licensing condition that may be in force), and the relevant person should ensure that the price of the alcohol is not less than the permitted price. Detailed guidance on the use of promotions is given in the guidance document available on the GOV.UK website.

7.11.3 Supply of alcohol from community premises

Where a management committee of community premises applies for a premises licence authorising the sale of alcohol, s.25A provides that the application may include an application for a condition that every supply of alcohol under the premises licence must be made or authorised by the management committee (known as the alternative licence condition) to be included in the licence instead of the mandatory conditions that no supply of alcohol may be made under the premises licence at a time when there is no designated premises supervisor in respect of the premises licence or at a time when the designated premises supervisor does not hold a personal licence or his personal licence is suspended and that every supply of alcohol under the premises licence must be made or authorised by a person who holds a personal licence.

The effect of this provision is that the management committee will be responsible for the supervision and authorisation of all alcohol sales authorised by the licence. There will be no requirement for a designated premises supervisor or for alcohol sales to be authorised by a personal licence holder.

Community premises are defined in s.193 as premises that are or form part of a church hall, chapel hall or other similar building; or a village hall, parish hall or community hall or other similar building. In most cases, it should be self-evident whether particular premises fall within the definition of community premises. But if it is not, the Guidance at paras.4.91 to 4.93 provides:

> 4.91 Where it is not clear whether premises are 'community premises', licensing authorities will need to approach the matter on a case-by-case basis. The main consideration in most cases will be how the premises are predominately used. If they are genuinely made available for community benefit most of the time, and accessible by a broad range of persons and sectors of the local community for purposes which include purposes beneficial to the community as a whole, the premises will be likely to meet the definition.
>
> 4.92 Many community premises such as school and private halls are available for private hire by the general public. This fact alone would not be sufficient for such halls to qualify as 'community premises'. The statutory test is directed at the nature of the premises themselves, as reflected in their predominant use, and not only at the usefulness of the premises for members of the community for private purposes.
>
> 4.93 If the general use of the premises is contingent upon membership of a particular organisation or organisations, this would strongly suggest that the premises in question are not a 'community premises' within the definition. However, the hire of the premises to individual organisations and users who restrict their activities to their own members and guests would not necessarily conflict with the status of the premises as a 'community premises', provided the premises are generally available for use by the community in the sense described above. It is not the intention that qualifying clubs, which are able to apply for a club premises certificate, should instead seek a premises licence with the removal of the usual mandatory conditions in sections 19(2) and 19(3) of the 2003 Act relating to the supply of alcohol.

'Management committee' is defined in s.193 as a committee or board of individuals with responsibility for the management of the premises. This will cover any formally constituted, transparent and accountable management committee or structure, and will include management committees, executive committees and boards of trustees. The Guidance at paras.4.96 to 4.98 provides:

> 4.96 The application form requires applicants to set out how the premises is managed, its committee structure and how the supervision of alcohol sales is to be ensured in different situations (e.g. when the hall is hired to private parties) and how responsibility for this is to be determined in individual cases and discussed within the committee procedure in the event of any issues arising. The applica-

tion form requires that the community premises submit copies of any constitution or other management documents with their applications and that they provide the names of their key officers. Where the management arrangements are less clear, licensing authorities may wish to ask for further details to confirm that the management board or committee is properly constituted and accountable before taking a decision on whether to grant the application (subject to the views of the police). Community premises may wish to check with the licensing authority before making an application. The management committee is strongly encouraged to notify the licensing authority if there are key changes in the committee's composition and to submit a copy to the chief officer of police. A failure to do so may form the basis of an application to review the premises licence, or be taken into account as part of the consideration of such an application.

4.97   As the premise licence holder, the management committee will collectively be responsible for ensuring compliance with licence conditions and the law (and may remain liable to prosecution for one of the offences in the 2003 Act) although there would not necessarily be any individual member always present at the premises. While overall responsibility will lie with the management committee, where the premises are hired out the hirer may be clearly identified as having responsibility for matters falling within his or her control (e.g. under the contract for hire offered by the licence holder), much in the same way that the event organiser may be responsible for an event held under a Temporary Event Notice. Where hirers are provided with a written summary of their responsibilities under the 2003 Act in relation to the sale of alcohol, the management committee is likely to be treated as having taken adequate steps to avoid liability to prosecution if a licensing offence is committed.

4.98   As indicated above, sections 25A(6) and 41D(5) of the 2003 Act require the licensing authority to consider whether the arrangements for the management of the premises by the committee are sufficient to ensure adequate supervision of the supply of alcohol on the premises. Where private hire for events which include the sale of alcohol is permitted by the licence, it would be necessary to have an effective hiring agreement. Licensing authorities may wish to consider model hiring agreements that have been made available by organisations such as ACRE and Community Matters. Such model agreements can be revised to cater for the circumstances surrounding each hire arrangement; for example to state that the hirer is aware of the licensing objectives and offences in the 2003 Act and will ensure that it will take all appropriate steps to ensure that no offences are committed during the period of the hire.

An application for the alternative licence condition to be included in the premises licence must be made using the prescribed form which is contained in the Premises Licence Regulations, Sched.4A. Where the management committee of a community premises is applying for authorisation for the sale of alcohol for the first time, it should include the form with the new premises licence application or the premises licence variation application. No extra payment is required beyond the existing fee for a new application or a variation. Where a community premises already has a premises licence to sell alcohol, but the management committee wishes to include the alternative licence condition in place of the usual mandatory conditions in s.19(2) and (3), it should submit the form on its own together with the appropriate fee.

In exceptional circumstances, the chief officer of police for the area in which the community premises is situated can object to a request for inclusion of the alternative licence condition on the grounds of crime and disorder, and any responsible authority or other person can seek reinstatement of the mandatory conditions through a review of the licence (as provided in s.52A). The police will want to consider any history of incidents at an establishment in light of the actual or proposed management arrangements, including the use of appropriate hire agreements. If the chief officer of police issues a notice seeking the refusal of the application to include the alternative licence condition, the licensing authority must hold a hearing in order to reach a decision on whether to grant the application.

Where the chief officer of police has made relevant representations against the inclusion of the alternative licence condition on the grant of a licence, or on an application by the management committee to vary the premises licence to include the alternative licence condition, that including the alternative licence condition would undermine the crime prevention objective, which was not withdrawn, the chief officer of police can appeal the decision of the licensing authority to allow the inclusion of the alternative licence condition. Similarly, the management committee of a community premises can appeal a decision by the licensing authority to refuse to include the alternative licence condition following a hearing triggered by relevant representations or by a notice given under s.41D(6). Following a review of the licence in which the mandatory conditions are reinstated, the licence holder may appeal against the decision. If the alternative licence condition is retained on review, the applicant for the review or any person who made relevant representations may appeal against the decision.

7.11.4 Mandatory condition – exhibition of films

Where a premises licence authorises the exhibition of films, s.20 provides that the licence must include a condition requiring the admission of children to the exhibition of any film to be restricted as follows:

- where the film classification body is specified in the licence, then unless the provision below applies, admission of children must be restricted in accordance with any recommendation made by that body; or
- where the film classification body is not specified in the licence, or the relevant licensing authority has notified the holder of the licence that subs.(3) applies to the film in question, admission of children must be restricted in accordance with any recommendation made by that licensing authority.

For these purposes, 'children' means persons aged under 18, and 'film classification body' means the person or persons designated as the authority under the Video Recordings Act 1984, s.4 which will be either the British Board of Film Classification or the licensing authority if it operates its own classification system.

7.11.5 Mandatory condition – door supervision

Where a premises licence includes a condition that at specified times one or more individuals must be at the premises to carry out a security activity, i.e. door supervisors, s.21 provides that the licence must include a condition that each such individual must be authorised to carry out that activity by a licence granted under the Private Security Industry Act 2001 or be entitled to carry out that activity by virtue of s.4 of that Act.

The requirement that individuals must be authorised or be entitled does not however apply to:

- premises within the Private Security Industry Act 2001, Sched.2, para.8(3)(a), i.e. premises with a premises licence authorising plays or films;
- premises on any occasion mentioned in the Private Security Industry Act 2001, Sched.2, para.8(3)(b) or (c), i.e. premises being used exclusively by a club with a club premises certificate, under a temporary event notice authorising plays or films, or under a gaming licence; or
- premises on any occasion within the Private Security Industry Act 2001, Sched.2, para.8(3)(d), i.e. occasions prescribed by regulations under that Act.

The licensing of door supervisors is carried out by the Security Industry Authority (SIA). Unless an exemption has been given under the Private Security Industry Act 2001, s.4(4), it is a criminal offence to work as a door supervisor without a licence from the SIA. A person guilty of this offence is liable on conviction to imprisonment for a term not exceeding six months or to a fine not exceeding level 5 on the standard scale or both.

A 'security activity' means an activity to which the Private Security Industry Act 2001, Sched.2, para.2(1)(a) applies and which is licensable conduct for the purposes of that Act (see Private Security Industry Act 2001, s.3(2)), that is, guarding premises against unauthorised access or occupation, against outbreaks of disorder, or against damage: in other words door supervision.

7.11.6 Prohibited conditions – plays

In relation to a premises licence which authorises the performance of plays, s.22 provides that a licensing authority cannot attach a condition to the licence as to the nature of the plays which may be performed, or the manner of performing plays, under the licence. However, this does not prevent a licensing authority imposing any condition which it considers appropriate on the grounds of public safety.

7.11.7 Discretionary conditions

A licensing authority may attach conditions to a licence other than the mandatory ones, but these must be appropriate for the promotion of the licensing objectives (these are discussed further in **Chapter 11**). Conditions cannot be imposed for any other reason. The conditions that are appropriate for the promotion of the licensing objectives should initially emerge from the applicant's risk assessment undertaken before the application for a premises licence was made.

Where no relevant representations are made about an application for a premises licence, the licensing authority must grant the licence subject only to conditions that are consistent with the operating schedule and any mandatory conditions prescribed in the Act. The licensing authority may not therefore impose any conditions unless its discretion has been engaged following the making of relevant representations and it has been satisfied at a hearing of the necessity to impose conditions due to the representations raised. It may then only impose such conditions as are appropriate to promote the licensing objectives arising out of the consideration of the representations. It is suggested that it might be sensible for an applicant to consult with the responsible authorities when preparing his operating schedule so that there can be proper liaison before representations prove necessary. It is clear that the conditions should not duplicate areas covered by other legislation, for example, employers and self-employed persons are required by the Management of Health and Safety at Work Regulations 1999, SI 1999/3242 to assess the risks to their workers and any others (for example, members of the public visiting the premises) who may be affected by their business so as to identify what measures are needed to avoid or control risks.

The Act provides that where an operating schedule has been submitted with an application and no relevant representations made, the licence must be granted subject only to such conditions as are consistent with the schedule accompanying the application and any mandatory conditions required by the Act itself. This means that the effect of any condition which is imposed should be substantially the same as that intended by the terms of the operating schedule. The Guidance recommends that it is not acceptable for a licensing authority to simply replicate the wording from an applicant's operating schedule and a condition should be interpreted in accordance with the applicant's intention and be appropriate and proportionate for the promotion of the licensing objectives (para.10.5). Conditions must be clear to the licence holder, to enforcement officers and to the courts.

By providing that only appropriate conditions may be imposed, the Act requires that licensing conditions should be tailored to the size, style, characteristics and activities taking place at the premises concerned. This effectively rules out standardised conditions which ignore these individual matters.

Many licensing authorities have produced pools of model conditions in respect of each of the licensing objectives which may be used where appropriate.

7.12 NOTIFICATION OF THE GRANT OR REFUSAL OF AN APPLICATION

Where an application for a premises licence is granted, s.23 provides that the relevant licensing authority must forthwith (see **2.9**) give a notice to that effect to:

- the applicant;
- any person who made relevant representations in respect of the application; and
- the chief officer of police for the police area (or each police area) in which the premises are situated.

It must also issue the applicant with the licence and a summary of it.

If relevant representations were made in respect of the application, the notice must state the authority's reasons for its decision as to the steps, if any, which must be taken for the promotion of the licensing objectives.

Where an application is rejected, the relevant licensing authority must forthwith give a notice to that effect, stating its reasons for the decision, to:

- the applicant;
- any person who made relevant representations in respect of the application; and
- the chief officer of police for the police area (or each police area) in which the premises are situated.

7.13 FORM OF LICENCE AND SUMMARY

Section 24 provides that a premises licence and the summary of a premises licence must be in the prescribed form, and that regulations must, in particular, provide for the licence to:

- specify the name and address of the holder;
- include a plan of the premises to which the licence relates;
- if the licence has effect for a limited period, specify that period;
- specify the licensable activities for which the premises may be used;
- if the licensable activities include the supply of alcohol, specify the name and address of the individual (if any) who is the premises supervisor in respect of the licence; and
- specify the conditions subject to which the licence is issued.

The form of both a premises licence and its summary are prescribed by the Premises Licences Regulations, reg.33. A premises licence must be in the form set out in the Premises Licences Regulations, Sched.12, Part A (see Welsh Language (Gambling and Licensing Forms) Regulations 2010, SI 2010/2440 for the Welsh version). It must identify the relevant licensing authority, include the premises licence number and contain the information required by the prescribed form.

This information includes the information required by s.24 together with additional details such as the designated premises supervisor's telephone number, personal licence number and the name of the issuing authority, the times at which licensable activities may take place and whether alcohol is supplied for consumption on and off or just on the premises.

The Premises Licences Regulations, reg.34 provides that a summary of a premises licence must be in the form and contain the information set out in the Premises Licences Regulations, Sched.12, Part B and must identify the relevant licensing authority, include the premises licence number, and be printed on paper of a size equal to or larger than A4.

7.14 THEFT OR LOSS OF A LICENCE

Where a premises licence or summary is lost, stolen, damaged or destroyed, s.25 provides that the licence holder may apply to the relevant licensing authority for a copy of the licence or summary. The appropriate fee must accompany the application. There is no prescribed form of application. Where such an application is made, the relevant licensing authority must issue the licence holder with a certified copy of the licence or summary provided it is satisfied that the licence or summary has been lost, stolen, damaged or destroyed. A copy issued by the licensing authority must be a copy of the premises licence or summary in the form in which it existed immediately before it was lost, stolen, damaged or destroyed. The Act applies in relation to a copy as it applies in relation to an original licence or summary.

Should the lost or stolen licence or summary be returned to the licence holder, there is no requirement that he must return either the original document or the copy to the licensing authority.

7.15 DURATION OF A PREMISES LICENCE

Section 26 provides that a premises licence does not need to be renewed and once granted will continue in effect until it is revoked, is suspended by a licensing authority when it determines an application for review, or lapses either due to the incapacity of the licence holder or because it is surrendered. If it was originally granted for a limited period, it will cease to have effect once that period has expired. A premises licence will not have effect during any period during which it is suspended following a review under s.52 or it is suspended under s.55A where the annual fee has not been paid.

7.16 LAPSE OF A LICENCE

A premises licence will lapse under s.27 if the holder of the licence:

- dies;
- becomes a person who lacks capacity within the meaning of the Mental Capacity Act 2005 to hold the licence, i.e. he is unable to make a decision for himself because of an impairment of, or a disturbance in the functioning of, the mind or brain;
- becomes insolvent;
- is dissolved; or
- if it is a club, ceases to be a recognised club.

A premises licence that authorises premises to be used for the sale by retail of alcohol or the provision of late night refreshment also lapses if the holder of the licence ceases to be entitled to work in the United Kingdom at a time when the holder of the licence is resident in the United Kingdom (or becomes so resident without being entitled to work in the United Kingdom).

An individual becomes insolvent on:

- the approval of a voluntary arrangement proposed by him;
- being made bankrupt or having his estate sequestrated; or
- entering into a trust deed for his creditors.

A company becomes insolvent on:

- the approval of a voluntary arrangement proposed by its directors;
- the appointment of an administrator in respect of the company;
- the appointment of an administrative receiver in respect of the company; or
- going into liquidation.

A company which is dissolved and then administratively restored to the register, by virtue of the Companies Act 2006, s.1028 is deemed not to have been dissolved and its premises licence will therefore be deemed not to have lapsed as a result of that dissolution (*Beauchamp Pizza Ltd* v. *Coventry City Council* [2010] EWHC 926 (Ch); [2020] LLR 1).

It may be possible to reinstate a licence which has lapsed (see **12.6**).

7.17 SURRENDER

The holder of a premises licence may surrender his licence under s.28 by giving notice to the relevant licensing authority together with the premises licence or, if that is not practicable, for example where it has been lost, by a statement of the reasons for the failure to provide the licence. The premises licence will then lapse when the licensing authority receives the notice. In certain circumstances a licence which has been surrendered can be reinstated (see **Chapter 12**).

There is no requirement to give notice to the designated premises supervisor or the owner of the premises.

7.18 UPDATING A PREMISES LICENCE

7.18.1 Notification of change of name or address

Following the grant of a premises licence, s.33 puts the licence holder under a duty, as soon as is reasonably practicable, to notify the relevant licensing authority of any change in his name or address, and the name or address of the designated premises supervisor, unless the supervisor has already notified the authority. The notice must be accompanied by the appropriate fee and the premises licence, or the appropriate part of the licence or, if that is not practicable, by a statement of the reasons for the failure to produce the licence, or part.

Where the designated premises supervisor under a premises licence is not the holder of the licence, he may notify the relevant licensing authority of any change in his name or address. If he does so, he must, as soon as is reasonably practicable, give the holder of the premises licence a copy of his notice.

A person commits an offence if he fails, without reasonable excuse, to comply with these requirements, and a person guilty of such an offence is liable on summary conviction to a fine not exceeding level 2 on the standard scale.

7.18.2 A licensing authority's duty to update a premises licence

Where a premises licence is modified, lapses or an appeal is determined, the relevant licensing authority must under s.56 make any appropriate amendments to the licence and, if necessary, issue a new summary of it.

Where the licensing authority is not in possession of the licence or the appropriate part of it, it may require the licence holder to produce the licence or the appropriate part within 14 days from the date on which he was notified of the requirement. A person commits an offence if he fails, without reasonable excuse, to comply with such a requirement and a person guilty of such an offence is liable on summary conviction to a fine not exceeding level 2 on the standard scale.

7.19 DUTY TO KEEP AND PRODUCE A PREMISES LICENCE

Section 57 provides that a licence holder is under a duty to keep the premises licence or a certified copy of it and a list of any relevant mandatory conditions applicable to the licence at the premises. It must be kept in the custody or under the control of either the licence holder, or a person who works at the premises and whom the licence holder has nominated in writing. A summary of the licence or a certified copy of that summary, and a notice specifying the position held at the premises by any person nominated by the licence holder, must be prominently displayed at the premises. A licence holder will commit an offence if he fails, without reasonable excuse, to comply with these requirements, and a person guilty of such an offence is liable on summary conviction to a fine not exceeding level 2 on the standard scale.

A constable or an authorised person may require the person who has custody or control of the premises licence, or a certified copy of it or a list of relevant mandatory conditions (i.e. the conditions applicable to the licence by virtue of s.19(4) or s.19A) to produce the licence or such a copy or the list for examination. An authorised person exercising this power must, if so requested, produce evidence of his authority to exercise the power. Any certified copy which is produced must be a copy of the document in the form in which it exists at the time. A person will commit an offence if he fails, without reasonable excuse, to produce a premises licence or a certified copy of a premises licence or a list of mandatory conditions. A person guilty of such an offence is liable on summary conviction to a fine not exceeding level 2 on the standard scale.

References to a certified copy of any document are (under s.58) references to a copy of that document which is certified to be a true copy by the relevant licensing authority, a solicitor or notary, or a person of a prescribed description. A document which purports to be a certified copy of a document is to be taken to be such a copy and to be a copy of the document in the form in which it exists at the time unless the contrary is shown. For these purposes, 'notary' means a person (other than a solicitor) who, for the purposes of the Legal Services Act 2007, is an authorised person in relation to any activity which constitutes a notarial activity.

7.20 SUSPENSION OF A PREMISES LICENCE

A licensing authority must suspend a premises licence under s.55A if the licence holder fails to pay the annual fee for the renewal of the licence. Where a licence is suspended, the licensing authority must give notice of the suspension to the licence holder specifying the day the suspension takes effect, which must be at least two working days after the day the notice is given. If the licence holder pays the annual fee, the licensing authority must give the licence holder a written receipt which specifies the day the licensing authority received the fee ('the receipt day'). The receipt must be given to the licence holder as soon as reasonably practicable but in any event if the receipt day was a working day, before the end of the first working day after the receipt day, but otherwise, before the end of the second working day after the receipt day. A suspension ceases to have effect on the receipt day.

A premises licence will not be suspended if either the licence holder failed to pay the fee due to an administrative error or before or at the time the fee became due, the licence holder notified the licensing authority in writing that it disputed liability for, or the amount of, the fee, and in both cases the grace period for payment of the fee has not expired. The grace period is the period of 21 days, beginning on the day after the day the fee became due.

CHAPTER 8

The operating schedule

8.1 INTRODUCTION

An application for a premises licence must be accompanied by an operating schedule (s.17(3)). An application for a club premises certificate must be accompanied by a club operating schedule (s.71(4)). An operating schedule details how the applicant proposes to operate the premises when carrying out the relevant licensable activities or qualifying club activities and needs to set out all the relevant information which will be needed in order to assess whether the steps which the applicant proposes to take in order to promote the licensing objectives are satisfactory. In this way it is the applicant who initially determines the nature and extent of the activities and the conditions relating to carrying them out.

In practice, the operating schedule forms part of the prescribed application form and, if the application is successful, it will be incorporated into the licence or certificate itself so that it is clear which activities are permitted on the licensed premises and any limitations on them.

8.2 CONTENTS OF THE OPERATING SCHEDULE

Section 17(4) provides that an operating schedule must state:

- the relevant licensable activities;
- the times during which it is proposed that the relevant licensable activities are to take place;
- any other times during which it is proposed that the premises are to be open to the public;
- where the applicant wishes the licence to have effect for a limited period, that period;
- where the relevant licensable activities include the supply of alcohol, prescribed information in respect of the individual whom the applicant wishes to have specified in the premises licence as the premises supervisor;

- where the relevant licensable activities include the supply of alcohol, whether the supplies are proposed to be for consumption on the premises or off the premises or both;
- the steps which it is proposed to take to promote the licensing objectives; and
- such other matters as may be prescribed.

Section 71(5) provides that a club operating schedule must state:

- the qualifying club activities to which the application relates;
- the times during which it is proposed that the relevant qualifying club activities are to take place;
- any other times during which it is proposed that the premises are to be open to members and their guests;
- where the relevant qualifying club activities include the supply of alcohol, whether the supplies are proposed to be for consumption on the premises or both on or off the premises;
- the steps which it is proposed to take to promote the licensing objectives; and
- such other matters as may be prescribed.

The Guidance includes advice on completing the operating schedule as follows:

8.41 In completing an operating schedule, applicants are expected to have regard to the statement of licensing policy for their area. They must also be aware of the expectations of the licensing authority and the responsible authorities as to the steps that are appropriate for the promotion of the licensing objectives, and to demonstrate knowledge of their local area when describing the steps they propose to take to promote the licensing objectives. Licensing authorities and responsible authorities are expected to publish information about what is meant by the promotion of the licensing objectives and to ensure that applicants can readily access advice about these matters. However, applicants are also expected to undertake their own enquiries about the area in which the premises are situated to inform the content of the application.

8.42 Applicants are, in particular, expected to obtain sufficient information to enable them to demonstrate, when setting out the steps they propose to take to promote the licensing objectives, that they understand:

- the layout of the local area and physical environment including crime and disorder hotspots, proximity to residential premises and proximity to areas where children may congregate;
- any risk posed to the local area by the applicants' proposed licensable activities; and
- any local initiatives (for example, local crime reduction initiatives or voluntary schemes including local taxi-marshalling schemes, street pastors and other schemes) which may help to mitigate potential risks.

8.43 Applicants are expected to include positive proposals in their application on how they will manage any potential risks. Where specific policies apply in the area (for example, a cumulative impact assessment), applicants are also expected to demonstrate an understanding of how the policy impacts on their application; any measures they will take to mitigate the impact; and why they consider the application should be an exception to the policy.

8.44 It is expected that enquiries about the locality will assist applicants when determining the steps that are appropriate for the promotion of the licensing objectives. For example, premises with close proximity to residential premises should consider what effect this will have on their smoking, noise management and dispersal policies to ensure the promotion of the public nuisance objective. Applicants must consider all factors which may be relevant to the promotion of the licensing objectives, and where there are no known concerns, acknowledge this in their application.

8.45 The majority of information which applicants will require should be available in the licensing policy statement in the area. Other publicly available sources which may be of use to applicants include:

- the Crime Mapping website;
- Neighbourhood Statistics websites;
- websites or publications by local responsible authorities;
- websites or publications by local voluntary schemes and initiatives; and
- on-line mapping tools.

8.46 While applicants are not required to seek the views of responsible authorities before formally submitting their application, they may find them to be a useful source of expert advice on local issues that should be taken into consideration when making an application. Licensing authorities may wish to encourage co-operation between applicants, responsible authorities and, where relevant, local residents and businesses before applications are submitted in order to minimise the scope for disputes to arise.

8.47 Applicants are expected to provide licensing authorities with sufficient information in this section to determine the extent to which their proposed steps are appropriate to promote the licensing objectives in the local area. Applications must not be based on providing a set of standard conditions to promote the licensing objectives and applicants are expected to make it clear why the steps they are proposing are appropriate for the premises.

8.48 All parties are expected to work together in partnership to ensure that the licensing objectives are promoted collectively. Where there are no disputes, the steps that applicants propose to take to promote the licensing objectives, as set out in the operating schedule, will very often translate directly into conditions that will be attached to premises licences with the minimum of fuss.

8.49 For some premises, it is possible that no measures will be appropriate to promote one or more of the licensing objectives, for example, because they are adequately covered by other existing legislation. It is however important that all operating schedules should be precise and clear about the consideration given to the licensing objectives and any measures that are proposed to promote them.

8.3 COMPLETING THE STANDARD FORM OF OPERATING SCHEDULE

8.3.1 Licensed activities and opening times

An applicant must tick what licensable activities he intends to provide and complete the relevant boxes. Times must be given in the 24-hour clock format.

8.3.2 Indoors or outdoors

If licensed activities will take place in a building or similar structure, an applicant will need to tick 'indoors'. If activities are to take place in the open air then he will tick 'outdoors'. If for example the premises are a pub with a garden and the applicant would like activities to take place in the garden, he would tick the 'both' box.

8.3.3 Further details

An applicant should state the type of activity to be authorised and the frequency of these activities. Examples are as follows.

Plays

If the premises licence is for a one-off event, an applicant should give the play title. Otherwise an applicant should state, for example, whether the plays are for children only, a mixed audience, for an amateur dramatics association, etc. An applicant should also set out how often he is likely to use the licence, e.g. 'Plays will only be held once a month for no more than three days at a time'.

Film exhibitions

If the premises are a cinema, an applicant should say here how many screens there are, and describe the type of films it is intended to show, e.g. art films, mixed films for all age ranges, etc.

Indoor sporting events

An applicant should describe the type of sports he intends to provide.

Boxing and wrestling entertainments

The category of fights an applicant may wish to provide should be described, how often he is likely to use the licence, and whether the events will be professional or amateur.

Live music

An applicant should state how many musicians he intends to have performing, what type of music they will play and whether the music will be amplified.

Recorded music

An applicant should describe what sort of recorded music will be played. Will it be a DJ or a sound system? What is the power output of any sound system to be used? Will he be providing karaoke?

Performances of dance

An applicant should describe what type of dancing will be performed. Will there be a stage or will it be roaming dancers? Will it involve strippers?

Anything of a similar description to that falling within live music, recorded music or performance of dance

The type of entertainment should be described, e.g. comedy shows, hypnotism performances, etc.

Late night refreshment

An applicant should set out what he intends to do, e.g. selling food for takeaway purposes only, selling food for consumption on the premises, the type of food he will sell, etc.

Supply of alcohol

An applicant should state whether the supply of alcohol would be for consumption on the premises, off the premises, or both.

8.3.4 Seasonal variations

This would allow an applicant to open later on Christmas Eve for example or during the summer months (specifying which months). An applicant would also need to state when he wanted to open and for how long.

8.3.5 Non-standard timings

This relates to such occasions as special events or bank holidays. For example, premises may normally open until 11 pm on a Monday but on the first Monday of every month the applicant may wish to have a disco and would like to provide alcohol and regulated entertainment until midnight.

8.3.6 Activities that may give rise to concern regarding children

This would include activities which involve nudity or semi-nudity, films for restricted age groups or the presence of gaming machines. This should be completed whether or not it is intended for children to have access to the premises.

8.3.7 Hours premises are open to the public

An applicant should state the earliest the premises or club would be open to members of the public and the latest time they will leave (i.e. drinking up time).

8.3.8 Licensing objectives

This section will need to be completed carefully as it is here that an applicant will need to demonstrate that he can run the premises in accordance with the licensing objectives. The more information which can be provided in demonstrating how these licensing objectives will be met will mean that there will be less chance of an objection being made to the application. An applicant is not expected to address issues already covered by existing legislation. Anything which is put in this section will become a condition on the licence and an applicant should not therefore volunteer to do anything that he is not able or not prepared to do if the application is granted. Examples of conditions which an applicant may wish to consider are discussed in **Chapter 11**.

8.4 OPENING HOURS

When completing the operating schedule the applicant must specify the times on each day of the week when he intends to use the premises for each licensable activity. These times may not be the same as the hours when the premises are open to the public. This may well be the case in relation to the sale or supply of alcohol for consumption on the premises.

While there is no provision in the operating schedule to specify 'drinking up time', an applicant should take into account any 'drinking up time' he wishes to allow his customers when specifying the hours during which the premises will be open to the public.

8.5 PREPARING AN OPERATING SCHEDULE

When preparing an operating schedule an applicant needs to be aware of the expectations of the licensing authority and the responsible authorities about the steps that are necessary in order to promote the licensing objectives (Guidance, para.8.41). This will involve carrying out a risk assessment and liaising with the responsible authorities. Where an operating schedule meets the requirements of a responsible authority it is unlikely that the authority will make a representation about the application and so the need for a hearing will be avoided.

An applicant does not have to check his operating schedule with the responsible authorities before submitting it, but when an applicant is uncertain about something the responsible authorities can provide expert advice on matters relating to the licensing objectives. For example, advice on crime prevention should be sought from the local police. An applicant will find it useful to discuss his operating schedule with the responsible authorities prior to submitting his application. The contact details of the responsible authorities can usually be obtained from the relevant licensing authority.

The operating schedule will allow the responsible authorities to evaluate the application and to decide whether they should make a representation about it or not. If no representations are made about an application, the licensing authority will grant the licence and attach to it only conditions relating to the operating schedule and any mandatory conditions required by the Act. For example, if the operating schedule were to state that windows of the premises would be kept closed when live music was being played, this could be made a condition of the licence. However, unless there was a representation from a responsible authority, a condition could not be made that the windows should be double-glazed. If a representation were to be made by a responsible authority, unless it was subsequently withdrawn a hearing would be held to consider the representation. After the licensing authority had listened to both the applicant and the responsible authority that made the representation, the licensing authority would decide whether to grant the licence or not and what if any conditions it should apply.

In preparing an operating schedule, the Guidance at para.8.41 recommends that an applicant should have regard to statements of licensing policy published by the relevant licensing authority, and all parties are expected to work together in partnership to ensure that the licensing objectives are promoted collectively. In straightforward cases, it is expected that the steps that an applicant proposes to take to promote the licensing objectives that he has set out in the operating schedule will very often translate directly into conditions that will be attached to the premises licence.

A guide to preparing an operating schedule may be available from the relevant licensing authority, and this should be obtained early in the process. This will assist an applicant in becoming aware of the likely requirements of the responsible authorities. These can be further clarified by consultation on individual applications. With this knowledge, an applicant will be able to decide whether it is possible for him to meet the requirements of the responsible authorities and so avoid a hearing. As a licensing authority will keep such a guide under review it is important for an applicant to make sure that he has the most up-to-date version of the guide.

8.6 RISK ASSESSMENT

Before preparing an operating schedule, an applicant should carry out a risk assessment in order to identify actual or potential risks associated with the proposed use and design of the premises. He can then identify measures which will either eliminate or minimise those risks. These measures should then be included in the operating schedule and may subsequently be converted into conditions on the premises licence. The relevant licensing authority may be able to provide an applicant with guidance on how to meet its policy requirements and promoting the licensing objectives. A number of licensing authorities have produced a 'tool-kit' which an applicant can use to identify the measures he will need to include in his operating schedule (see **Appendix A** for an example of such a 'tool-kit').

Once carried out, the risk assessment should be dated and a note made of the details of the person who carried it out. An applicant may wish to submit a copy of the risk assessment with his application.

8.7 PREVENTION OF CRIME AND DISORDER

The prevention of crime and disorder will be a central feature of a licensing authority's policy. An applicant will need to set out in his operating schedule the steps which he intends to take to promote this objective. An applicant should obtain details of the issues which the relevant licensing authority expects an applicant to consider. Enquiry should also be made with the police to obtain any guidance which they have issued; for example some police forces have a code of practice which they expect licensees to adhere to.

While each licensing authority will have its own issues which it will expect an applicant to consider, the following should be considered as useful when preparing an operating schedule:

- membership of a local pubwatch scheme where a communication link is set up between the police and other members of the scheme to alert them to the fact that there are potential trouble makers or individuals suspected of criminal behaviour in a particular area;
- the provision of door supervisors registered by the SIA. The number of door supervisors required would depend on the type of clientele, the capacity of the venue and the type of activity taking place;
- the provision of staff training in crime prevention measures appropriate to the premises;
- implementing effective customer search policies for drugs and weapons;
- development of clear procedures to deal with violence and antisocial behaviour on the premises including instances relating to drunken customers and those under the influence of illegal drugs;
- operation of a responsible drinks promotion practice;

- devising procedures for risk assessing promotions such as 'happy hours' which may contribute to the impact on crime and disorder, and plans for minimising such risks;
- raising awareness of safer drinking, date-rape drug issues, safe travel at night including the display of telephone numbers for certified licensed taxi and minicab companies, etc.;
- the use of plastic bottles and glasses or toughened glass to prevent glass bottles and drinking glasses being used as weapons;
- the installation of CCTV cameras;
- restriction on the areas where alcohol may be consumed after it has been purchased at the bar, e.g. in areas such as the terracing of sports grounds during sporting events;
- setting a capacity limit to prevent overcrowding;
- having a policy to prevent under-age sales, e.g. the production of 'proof of age' cards;
- displaying notices to warn customers of pickpockets or bag snatchers; and
- providing an appropriate ratio of tables and chairs to customers based on the capacity of the premises in order to prevent high volume vertical drinking and reduce over-consumption of alcohol and aggressive behaviour.

An applicant should ascertain whether the premises are in an area which has been designated as a saturation area. Details of areas which have been designated as saturated with licensed premises may be obtained from the relevant licensing authority. An applicant should be prepared for the police to object to a new application in any area that has been so declared.

8.8 PUBLIC SAFETY

The public safety objective is primarily focused on physical safety rather than public health matters. A licensing authority will therefore expect licensed premises to be constructed, maintained and managed so that people can work in and visit the premises safely. An applicant will be expected to detail in his operating schedule the measures identified to promote this objective and how they will be implemented and maintained to ensure public safety.

A fire risk assessment of the premises should be carried out, and an applicant should contact the local fire and rescue authority for advice. The relevant licensing authority will be able to provide the contact details. Licensed premises are covered by the Regulatory Reform (Fire Safety) Order 2005, SI 2005/1541 which requires 'the responsible person' to carry out a fire risk assessment of the premises. The fire risk assessment should consider the adequacy of the means of escape, fire safety signs and notices, emergency lighting, fire warning systems, fire-fighting equipment and training. The significant outcomes of this risk assessment, including occupancy figures, designated escape routes, evacuation procedures, etc. should be included in the operating schedule accompanying the application to facilitate an evaluation as to their suitability. Further guidance can be found at **www.gov.uk**.

For certain premises, the Health and Safety Executive may also be a responsible authority for public safety.

The type of measures which a licensing authority might expect to see in an operating schedule, where relevant, to promote this objective would include:

- describing arrangements in place for the safe evacuation of disabled people and ensuring that the disabled people on the premises are aware of those arrangements;
- specifying the measures in place to maintain escape routes and exits; this may include ensuring that:

    - all exit doors are easily openable without the use of a key, card, code or similar means;
    - doors at such exits are regularly checked to ensure that they function satisfactorily and that a record of the check is kept;
    - any removable security fastenings are removed whenever the premises are open to members of the public or staff;
    - all fire doors are maintained effectively self-closing and are not held open other than by approved devices (e.g. electromagnetic releases operated by smoke detectors);
    - fire resisting doors to ducts, service shafts and cupboards are kept locked shut;
    - the edges of the treads of steps and stairways are maintained so as to be conspicuous; and
    - all customers, especially those that may not be able to hear or see the fire alarm or may be unable to move easily when evacuating a building, are aware of the evacuation procedures;

- safety checks are carried out and recorded prior to the admission of the public;
- hangings, curtains and temporary decorations are maintained in a flame retardant condition;
- a capacity limit is set and controlled;
- notices are displayed detailing the action to be taken in the event of a fire or an emergency;
- access for emergency vehicles is kept clear and free from obstruction;
- an adequate supply of first aid material is available on site and, where appropriate, a suitably trained first aider;
- the provision of adequate lighting, including fire safety signs and emergency lighting;
- the safety of the electrical installation is maintained;

- if an indoor sporting event is included, extra provisions are made, e.g. for a qualified medical practitioner to be present, for distances to be maintained between the ring and the audience, etc.;
- the detailing of special effects that may be used in the premises such as dry ice machines and cryogenic fog; smoke machines and fog generators; pyrotechnics, including fireworks; real flame; firearms; motor vehicles; strobe lighting; lasers; explosives and highly flammable substances. In certain circumstances, it may be necessary to require that certain special effects are only used with the prior notification of the licensing authority;
- the provision of attendants for closely seated audiences, such as in theatres or cinemas; and
- the measures employed to ensure that the scenery, safety curtain, ceilings and seating are safe are recorded.

8.9 THE PREVENTION OF PUBLIC NUISANCE

The types of steps which a licensing authority might expect to see in an operating schedule, where applicable, to promote the objective of preventing public nuisance might include:

- the control of the level of music and other entertainments so that it is contained within the structure of the premises and does not give rise to a nuisance to neighbours;
- doors and windows being kept closed to ensure that noise from music and other entertainments does not break out and disturb neighbours;
- noisy activities being restricted to areas of the premises that are best able to contain noise, with outside areas such as forecourts and beer gardens not being used for music and entertainment;
- any noise limiter device fitted within the premises being set at an agreed level and access to the controls restricted to prevent it being tampered with;
- noise levels being reduced before doors are opened and customers leaving in numbers;
- liaison meetings with residents to discuss any problems they may be experiencing as a result of noise or other nuisances arising from activities at the premises;
- stewarding or supervising of customers queuing to enter the premises;
- stewarding or supervising customers as they leave the premises, especially at the end of the evening when the premises close;
- signs displayed requesting customers to respect the neighbourhood when leaving the premises;
- appropriate security and advertising lighting installed so as to ensure that light overspill does not adversely affect neighbours;

- litter caused by customers being considered and addressed through the provision of bins and litter patrols as necessary;
- the timing of deliveries, refuse and in particular bottle collections being arranged so as to cause the minimum disturbance to neighbours; and
- all plant and equipment utilised at the premises being correctly installed and maintained to ensure that it operates without causing nuisance to neighbours from odours or noise.

All licensed premises that have the potential to generate noise from within the premises or from their customers in the immediate vicinity of the premises must take steps to prevent public nuisance. These steps should be determined by carrying out a noise impact assessment from which a strategy for noise management can be developed, and this should then be included in the operating schedule. The first step is for an applicant to carry out a noise impact assessment, as follows:

1. A list of the sources of noise likely to be generated by the premises should be drawn up. Examples include:

    (a)   amplified music (pre-recorded or live);
    (b)   amplified voices (karaoke, DJ or announcements);
    (c)   noise from patrons using the premises (pub gardens, play areas);
    (d)   plant noise (refrigeration units, air conditioning units, etc.);
    (e)   noise from patrons leaving the premises.

2. The applicant should then determine how, and from where, each of these noises could be emitted from the premises. For all internal noises the doors, windows and ventilation openings through which they could escape should be determined, and for external noises, the areas of the premises where they will be created should be determined.

3. The nature of the surrounding community and where the nearest persons who will be affected by noise from the premises live should then be established.

4. The whereabouts of other local premises that may encourage street activity should be established, in particular fast food outlets, for these may encourage customers leaving a licensed premises to remain in the area longer than would otherwise be the case.

5. The likelihood that most customers leaving the premises at closing time will pass through a residential area, and how the effects on the community could be minimised, should be considered. Any other local licensed premises which will also contribute to this should also be identified.

All of this information should then be used to establish what local properties are at greatest risk of being affected by noise from the premises. If the answer is that there are no local residential properties likely to be affected, then there is no need for the applicant to develop a noise management strategy. It is important that the reasons for this decision are justified in the operating schedule.

Once an applicant has identified potential problems by carrying out a noise impact assessment, consideration should then be given to the possible solutions to these potential problems. Measures to protect immediate neighbours will differ from those protecting residents living further away. The method of controlling noise is a matter for the licensee, but his goal should be for noise from the premises not to exceed the background noise at the boundary of the nearest residential property. The following steps should be considered as part of developing a noise management strategy:

1. If the volume of music needs to be controlled, a noise-limiting device should be used. Once set this should be inaccessible to the licensee or his staff. Access to the device should only be available to an appropriate 'noise engineer'.
2. 'Zoning' within licensed premises may be appropriate, e.g. noisy areas, such as dance floors should if possible be away from external walls, windows or doors where noise breakout may occur.
3. Where there is a residential building close to the premises all windows should be closed after a specified time, particularly for 'concertina' style windows or 'patio doors' that allow a large opening in an external wall. Licensees and managers should ensure that ventilation and air conditioning is sufficiently adequate to discourage customers from opening windows or doors in warm weather.
4. Other than for special events there should be no outside speakers.
5. Sound trap lobbies or automatic door closers should be installed to prevent noise escaping through external doors.
6. Emergency exits should be fitted with acoustic doors to prevent noise breaking through.
7. Windows in rooms where noise could be problematic should be either double-glazed or acoustically sealed as appropriate.
8. Openings in the wall for ventilation should be acoustically protected. Better still, ventilation openings can be sealed if air conditioning is installed.
9. The type, position and orientation of loud speakers should be such as to focus music where it is wanted and avoid it escaping to where it is not wanted.
10. The bass content of the music should be controlled to ensure it does not cause nuisance.
11. Noise from beer gardens (or other outdoor areas) of licensed premises is a common, if sometimes seasonal, problem in residential areas. Music should not be audible from a garden in such circumstances. Even if music is inaudible outside the garden boundary, music audible within the boundary will cause higher noise levels from customers talking over the music.
12. Rowdy behaviour of patrons in beer gardens and outdoor areas should be controlled by premises managers.

13. The use of any beer garden or other outside area located near to noise sensitive premises should be limited to daytime and early evening, with serious consideration being given to limiting access to these areas after a specified time (perhaps 9.30 pm or 10.00 pm) where practical.

14. Children's play equipment must be located away from boundaries shared with noise sensitive premises, with hours limited as for beer gardens and other outdoor areas.

15. As a general rule fireworks should not be used.

16. Consider the possibility of restricting times of use of the car park (by locking an entrance gate at a specified time).

17. Zone larger car parks so that areas adjacent to residential premises are restricted to use by staff, who are more likely to leave quietly.

18. Appropriate lighting of car parks will discourage noisy behaviour, as well as improving security.

19. Notices or announcements requesting that patrons are respectful of local residents as they leave should be used at all exit points.

20. CCTV can monitor activity in the immediate vicinity of licensed premises and often discourages antisocial street activity.

21. Use acoustic screens or acoustic enclosures to prevent the spread of noise from equipment.

22. Proper maintenance of external plant can prevent mechanical deterioration, which often leads to more noise.

23. When commissioning new equipment, look for quieter models. Any extra expense that may be involved initially may be beneficial in the long term.

24. External storage areas should be sited to prevent disruption or danger. Deliveries and collections, particularly bottle and waste collections, should be carried out during the hours 7.30 am and 6 pm Monday to Friday and 8.30 am and 6 pm on weekends and recognised bank holidays.

8.10 THE PROTECTION OF CHILDREN FROM HARM

The type of steps which a licensing authority might expect to see in an operating schedule, where applicable, to promote the objective of the protection of children from harm might include:

- age restrictions all or part of the time that the premises are open; this might include times at which there was adult entertainment, events for young age groups, drink promotion nights such as happy hours, etc.;
- limitations on the hours when children may be present;
- mandatory 'proof of age' scheme;
- limitations on, or exclusions of, children being provided access to the premises when certain activities are taking place;
- requirements for an accompanying adult;

- making adequate arrangements for the appropriate supervision of unaccompanied children at events;
- films being classified by the British Board of Film Classification;
- notices being displayed both inside and outside the premises so that persons entering can readily be made aware of the classification of a film;
- a minimum number of attendants with seated audiences or door supervisors registered with the SIA;
- risk assessment of any particular risks to children taking part in performances where particular attention is paid to the venue, fire safety, special effects and the general care of the child, etc.; and
- compliance with the Portman Group's Code of Practice on the Naming, Packaging and Promotion of Alcoholic Drinks (see **www.portmangroup. org.uk**).

8.11 BEST PRACTICE GUIDANCE PUBLICATIONS

In addition to the relevant licensing authority's statement of licensing policy, there are other sources of information which an applicant might find useful.

8.11.1 Crime and disorder

- Safer Clubbing Guide (The Home Office);
- Licensed Property: Security in Design (**www.beerandpub.com**);
- Drugs and Pubs: A Guide to Keeping a Drug Free Pub (**www.beerandpub. com**);
- Keeping the Peace: A Guide to the Prevention of Alcohol Related Disorder (**www.portmangroup.org.uk**);
- Code of Practice on the Naming, Packaging and Promotion of Alcoholic Drinks (**www.portmangroup.org.uk**);
- National Pubwatch Good Practice Guide (**www.nationalpubwatch.org.uk**).

8.11.2 Public safety

- The Purple Guide to Health, Safety and Welfare at Outdoor Events (**www.thepurpleguide.co.uk**);
- Fire safety risk assessment: Open air events and venues (**www.gov.uk**);
- Managing Crowds Safely (**www.hse.gov.uk**);
- The Safety of Laser Lighting Displays (**www.hse.gov.uk**);
- Organising Firework Displays (**www.hse.gov.uk**);
- The Guide to Safety at Sports Grounds (**https://sgsa.org.uk**);
- Technical Standards for Places of Entertainment (**www.technical-standards-for-places-of-entertainment.co.uk**);
- Managing Safety in Bars, Clubs and Pubs (**www.beerandpub.com**);

- Approved Document M – Access to and Use of Buildings (**www.gov.uk**);
- Noise Council code of practice on environmental noise control at concerts (**www.cieh.org**);
- Guide to Fire Precautions in Existing Places of Entertainment and Like Premises (ISBN 0-11-340907-9).

8.11.3 Public nuisance

- Good Practice Guide on the Control of Noise from Pubs and Clubs (**www.ioa.org.uk**);
- Sound Advice – noise at work in music and entertainment (**www.hse. gov.uk**);
- BS 8233:1999 Sound insulation and noise reduction for buildings (**www.bsigroup.com**);
- BS 4142:1997 Method for rating industrial noise affecting mixed residential and industrial areas (**www.bsigroup.com**).

8.11.4 Children

- BBFC Classification Guidelines (**www.bbfc.co.uk**);
- National Proof of Age Standards Scheme (PASS) (**www.pass-scheme. org.uk**);
- Code of Practice of the Naming, Packaging and Promotion of Alcoholic Drinks (**www.portmangroup.org.uk**).

CHAPTER 9

Designated premises supervisor

9.1 INTRODUCTION

Where a premises licence authorises the supply of alcohol, the licence must include a condition that alcohol cannot be supplied at any time when there is no designated premises supervisor in respect of the premises licence, or at a time when the designated premises supervisor does not hold a personal licence or his personal licence is suspended.

This means that there must always be a designated premises supervisor in respect of all premises licensed to supply alcohol and that that person must hold a valid personal licence. The only exception is for community premises in respect of which there has been a successful application to remove the usual mandatory conditions (see **7.11.3**).

The main purpose of having a designated premises supervisor is to ensure that there is always one specified individual who can be readily identified for the premises where a premises licence is in force. If the designated premises supervisor is not also the premises licence holder he will usually be given day-to-day responsibility for running the premises by the premises licence holder.

9.2 WHO IS THE DESIGNATED PREMISES SUPERVISOR?

A designated premises supervisor is the individual for the time being specified in the licence as the premises supervisor (s.15(1)). Only an individual can be a designated premises supervisor. It is not possible for a corporate body to be one. There is nothing to prevent the person who holds the premises licence being the designated premises supervisor (s.15(2)). Only one person at any point in time can be the designated premises supervisor in relation to a particular premises but there is no prohibition on a person being the designated premises supervisor for more than one premises. The Guidance at para.4.67 states that:

Only one DPS may be specified in a single premises licence, but a DPS may supervise two or more premises as long as the DPS is able to ensure that the licensing objectives are properly promoted and that each premises complies with the 2003 Act and conditions on the premises licence. The DPS is not required to be present at all times when licensed premises are used for the sale of alcohol.

The main purpose of the designated premises supervisor is to ensure that there is always one specified individual who can be readily identified for the premises where a premises licence is in force. The Guidance at para.4.62 provides:

> The Government considers it essential that police officers, fire officers or officers of the licensing authority can identify immediately the DPS so that any problems can be dealt with swiftly. For this reason, the name of the DPS and contact details must be specified on the premises licence and this must be held at the premises and displayed in summary form. The DPS' personal address should not be included in the summary form in order to protect their privacy.

9.3 INITIAL APPOINTMENT OF A DESIGNATED PREMISES SUPERVISOR

Where the relevant licensable activities include the supply of alcohol, the operating schedule accompanying an application for a premises licence must specify the name and address of the individual whom the applicant wishes to have specified in the premises licence as the designated supervisor, together with that person's personal licence number, if known, and the name of the licensing authority which issued the personal licence, if known.

The application must also be accompanied by the written consent of the proposed designated premises supervisor in the prescribed form, which is found in the Premises Licences Regulations, Sched.11.

9.4 CHANGE OF DESIGNATED PREMISES SUPERVISOR

9.4.1 Introduction

The holder of a premises licence which authorises the supply of alcohol may apply under s.37 to change the person named in the licence as the designated premises supervisor.

An applicant must submit the following to the relevant licensing authority:

- a completed application form. The application form is prescribed and is set out in the Premises Licences Regulations, Sched.5;
- the consent of the person proposed as the designated premises supervisor. The consent form is prescribed and is set out in the Premises Licences Regulations, Sched.11;

- the premises licence (or the appropriate part of it), or if that is not practicable, a statement of the reasons why it cannot be provided; and
- the prescribed fee.

9.4.2 The application form

Guidance in completing the application form may be obtained from **www.gov.uk** or the relevant licensing authority. The form may be completed by being either typed or written legibly in block capitals. All answers must be inside the boxes and written in black ink.

In the opening statement, the name of the applicant or applicants applying to vary the premises licence to specify a new premises supervisor should be inserted, together with the premises licence number.

The application form is then divided into three parts.

Part 1

The applicant must set out the following details of the premises:

- the postal address; and
- the telephone number at the premises, if any.

If the premises have no postal address, the location of the premises should be described or the Ordnance Survey map reference should be given. A description of the premises must also be given, for example the type of premises and the trading name.

Part 2

Part 2 of the form asks for the full name, nationality, place of birth, date of birth and personal licence number of the proposed designated premises supervisor together with its issuing authority. The full name of the existing designated premises supervisor must also be given.

The applicant must indicate whether he would like the application to have immediate effect. He must confirm that he has enclosed the premises licence or relevant part of it. If the premises licence, or relevant part, cannot be enclosed with the application, an explanation must be given. There is a checklist for the applicant to complete so that nothing is overlooked. Finally there are warnings that it is an offence, liable on conviction to an unlimited fine, under s.158 to make a false statement in or in connection with the application, that it is an offence under the Immigration Act 1971, s.24b for a person to work when they know, or have reasonable cause to believe, that they are disqualified from doing so by reason of their immigration status, and that those who employ an adult without a valid leave to enter or remain in the United Kingdom or an adult who is subject to conditions which would prevent that person from taking up employment will be liable to a civil penalty under the Immigration, Asylum and Nationality Act 2006, s.15 and, pursuant to s.21 of the same Act, will be committing an offence where they do so in the knowledge, or with reasonable cause to believe, that the employee is disqualified by virtue of their immigration status.

Part 3

Part 3 provides for the applicant to sign the form. The form can also be signed by the applicant's solicitor or other duly authorised agent, and someone signing on behalf of the applicant must state in what capacity they sign. Where there are joint applicants, both applicants or their respective agents must sign the application form.

9.4.3 Obtaining an application form

For details on obtaining a form see **7.4.2**.

9.4.4 Making an application

The Premises Licences Regulations, reg.21 provides that an application must be made in writing. However, notwithstanding this requirement, an application can also be made electronically (Premises Licences Regulations, reg.21A(1)). See further **7.4.3**.

9.4.5 Notice to other persons

Notice of the application must be given to the chief officer of police for the police area (or each police area) in which the premises are situated and to the designated premises supervisor, if there is one, and the notice must state whether the application is for the variation to be given immediate effect (s.37(4)). Notice to the chief officer of police is to be given by the relevant licensing authority where the application has been made electronically, and by the holder of the premises licence in any other case (s.37(4A)). Notice to the designated premises supervisor is to be given by the holder of the premises licence whichever means of application is used (s.37(4B)).

9.4.6 Objections

The chief officer of police can object to the designation of a new premises supervisor in exceptional circumstances (see **9.5**). The existing designated premises supervisor cannot object. He is only notified of the application so that he knows that he will no longer be responsible for the premises.

9.4.7 Immediate effect

Where an application includes a request under s.38(1) that the variation applied for should have immediate effect, the premises licence has effect during the application period as if it had been varied in the manner set out in the application. This will allow for a situation where emergency cover is required, for example where the designated premises supervisor has died or is unable to work.

'The application period' is the period which begins when the application is received by the relevant licensing authority, and ends:

- if the application is granted, when the variation takes effect;
- if the application is rejected, at the time the rejection is notified to the applicant; or
- if the application is withdrawn before it is determined, at the time of the withdrawal.

9.4.8 Determination of the application

Section 39 provides that the application must be granted if it has been made in accordance with the statutory requirements, and the chief officer of police has not objected or has objected but has withdrawn the objection.

If the chief officer of police has given a notice objecting, and has not withdrawn it, the licensing authority must hold a hearing to consider it, unless the authority, the applicant and the chief officer of police who gave the notice agree that a hearing is unnecessary. A hearing must be held within 20 working days beginning with the day after the end of the period within which a chief officer of police may object (Hearings Regulations, reg.5 and Sched.1, para.4). Notice of the hearing must be given to the applicant, the chief officer of police and the person who is proposed as the new designated premises supervisor no later than 10 working days before the day or the first day on which the hearing is to be held (Hearings Regulations, reg.6(4) and Sched.2, para.4). The applicant must be given the notice of objection with the notice of the hearing (Hearings Regulations, reg.7(2) and Sched.3, para.4).

The licensing authority must reject the application if, having regard to the notice of objection, it considers that it is appropriate for the promotion of the crime prevention objective.

9.4.9 Notification of the decision

Whether an application is granted or rejected, the relevant licensing authority must forthwith (see **2.9**) give a notice of the decision to:

- the applicant;
- the individual who is proposed as the new designated premises supervisor; and

- the chief officer of police for the police area (or each police area) in which the premises are situated.

The notice must be accompanied by information regarding the right of a party to appeal against the decision.

This notice must, if the chief officer of police gave a notice of objection and did not withdraw it, state the reasons why the licensing authority has granted or rejected the application. In addition, where the application is granted, the notice must specify the time when the variation takes effect. This will either be the time specified in the application or, if the applicant is given the notice after that time, such later time as the relevant licensing authority specifies in the notice.

Section 40 deals with the duty of an applicant following the determination of an application. When the holder of a premises licence is notified by the licensing authority that his application has been granted, he must forthwith (see **2.9**) notify the person, if any, who has been replaced as the designated premises supervisor. If his application has been rejected, he must forthwith (see **2.9**) give the designated premises supervisor, if any, notice to that effect. An offence will be committed by the licence holder if he fails, without reasonable excuse, to give the appropriate notice and he will be liable on summary conviction to a fine not exceeding level 3 on the standard scale.

9.5 POLICE OBJECTIONS

The chief officer of police can object to the designation of a new premises supervisor under s.37(5) where, in exceptional circumstances, he believes that the appointment would undermine the crime prevention objective. The police might object where the presence of a particular designated premises supervisor would give rise to exceptional concerns, for example, where a personal licence holder has been allowed by the courts to retain his licence despite convictions for selling alcohol to minors and he then moves to premises which suffer from some degree of notoriety for under-age drinking. Where the police object, the licensing authority must arrange for a hearing at which the issue can be considered and both parties can put their arguments (see **9.4.8**). If the chief officer of police is satisfied that the exceptional circumstances of the case are such that if the application was granted it would undermine the crime prevention objective, he must give the relevant licensing authority a notice of the reasons why he is so satisfied within 14 days beginning with the day on which he is notified of the application (s.37(6)).

In respect of police objections, the Guidance provides at paras.4.71 and 4.72:

> 4.71 The portability of personal licences between premises is an important concept under the 2003 Act. It is expected that police objections would arise in only genuinely exceptional circumstances. If a licensing authority believes that the police are routinely objecting to the designation of new premises supervisors on

grounds which are not exceptional, they should raise the matter with the chief officer of police as a matter of urgency.

4.72 The 2003 Act also provides for the suspension and forfeiture of personal licences by the courts and licensing authorities following convictions for relevant offences, including breaches of licensing law. The police can at any stage after the appointment of a DPS seek a review of a premises licence on any grounds relating to the licensing objectives if problems arise relating to the performance of a DPS. The portability of personal licences is also important to industry because of the frequency with which some businesses move managers from premises to premises. It is not expected that licensing authorities or the police should seek to use the power of intervention as a routine mechanism for hindering the portability of a licence or use hearings of this kind as a fishing expedition to test out the individual's background and character. It is expected that such hearings should be rare and genuinely exceptional.

9.6 REQUEST TO BE REMOVED AS DESIGNATED PREMISES SUPERVISOR

Section 41 provides that where a designated premises supervisor decides that he no longer wishes to carry on in that role, he may give the relevant licensing authority a notice to that effect. The section is subject to s.54 which empowers the Secretary of State to prescribe forms of notices to be used for various applications under the Act, but, at the time of writing, no form has been prescribed. Presumably the notice must be in writing and may be given electronically (see the Premises Licences Regulations, regs.21 and 21A). A licensing authority may provide a form on its website.

Where the designated premises supervisor is also the holder of the premises licence, the notice must be accompanied by the premises licence, or the appropriate part of the licence or, if that is not practicable, by a statement of the reasons for the failure to provide the licence, or that part.

In all other situations, the designated premises supervisor must within 48 hours after giving the notice to the relevant licensing authority give the holder of the premises licence a copy of the notice, and a notice directing the licence holder to send to the relevant licensing authority within 14 days of receiving the notice either the premises licence, or the appropriate part of the licence, or if that is not practicable, a statement of the reasons for the failure to provide the licence, or that part. A licence holder will commit an offence if he fails, without reasonable excuse, to comply with such a direction given to him and he will be liable on summary conviction to a fine not exceeding level 3 on the standard scale.

Where a designated premises supervisor has complied with these provisions, he is treated as if, from the relevant time, he were not the designated premises supervisor. For this purpose, 'the relevant time' means either the time the designated premises supervisor's notice is received by the relevant licensing authority or, if later, the time specified in the notice.

CHAPTER 10

Relevant representations

10.1 INTRODUCTION

Following the making of certain applications under the Act, objections in the form of representations may be made by a responsible authority or other person. If these amount to 'relevant representations' they can lead to a hearing to consider them. Where a representation is made, the licensing authority must initially decide whether it is relevant which will involve deciding:

- that it relates to a licensing objective;
- that it has been made by a responsible authority or other person; and
- where it has been made by a person who is not a responsible authority, that it is not, in the opinion of the relevant licensing authority frivolous or vexatious.

10.2 RELEVANT REPRESENTATIONS – GENERAL

10.2.1 A representation must be made by a responsible authority or other person

A representation must be made by a responsible authority or other person.

Responsible authority

Responsible authorities are listed in s.13(4) as being:

- the relevant licensing authority and any other licensing authority in whose area part of the premises is situated;
- the chief officer of police for any police area in which the premises are situated;
- the fire and rescue authority for any area in which the premises are situated;
- the Local Health Board for any area in which the premises are situated;

- the local authority in England whose public health functions within the meaning of the National Health Service Act 2006 are exercisable in respect of any area in which the premises are situated;
- the enforcing authority within the meaning given by the Health and Safety at Work etc. Act 1974, s.18 for any area in which the premises are situated;
- the local planning authority within the meaning of the Town and Country Planning Act 1990 for any area in which the premises are situated;
- the local authority which exercises the statutory functions in any area in which the premises are situated in relation to minimising or preventing the risk of pollution of the environment or of harm to human health;
- a body which represents those who, in relation to any such area, are responsible for, or interested in, matters relating to the protection of children from harm, and is recognised by the licensing authority for that area for the purposes of this section as being competent to advise it on such matters;
- in relation to a vessel, a navigation authority (within the meaning of the Water Resources Act 1991, s.221(1)) having functions in relation to the waters where the vessel is usually moored or berthed or any waters where it is, or is proposed to be, navigated at a time when it is used for licensable activities, the Environment Agency, the Canal & River Trust, or the Secretary of State;
- where the premises, not being a vessel, are being, or are proposed to be, used for the sale by retail of alcohol or the provision of late night entertainment, the Secretary of State;
- a person prescribed for these purposes.

The Premises Licences Regulations, reg.7 prescribes that the local weights and measures authority within the meaning of the Weights and Measures Act 1985, s.69 for any area in which the premises are situated is a responsible authority. This will be the local authority trading standards department.

While all responsible authorities may make representations regarding applications for licences and club premises certificates and full variation applications, it is the responsibility of each responsible authority to determine when they have appropriate grounds to do so (Guidance, para.9.11).

Representations from the police

In relation to representations from the police, the Guidance at para.9.12 provides:

Each responsible authority will be an expert in their respective field, and in some cases it is likely that a particular responsible authority will be the licensing authority's main source of advice in relation to a particular licensing objective. For example, the police have a key role in managing the night-time economy and should have good working relationships with those operating in their local area. The police should usually therefore be the licensing authority's main source of advice on matters relating to the promotion of the crime and disorder licensing objective. However, any responsible authority under the 2003 Act may make representations with regard to any of the licensing objectives if they have evidence to support such representations. Licensing authorities must therefore consider all relevant representations from responsible authorities carefully, even where the reason for a particular responsible authority's interest or expertise in the promotion of a particular objective may not be immediately apparent. However, it remains incumbent on all responsible authorities to ensure that their representations can withstand the scrutiny to which they would be subject at a hearing.

Home Office Immigration Enforcement acting as a responsible authority

The Guidance at para.9.25 provides:

> The Immigration Act 2016 made the Secretary of State a responsible authority in respect of premises licensed to sell alcohol or late night refreshment with effect from 6 April 2017. In effect this conveys the role of responsible authority to Home Office Immigration Enforcement who exercises the powers on the Secretary of State's behalf. When Immigration Enforcement exercises its powers as a responsible authority it will do so in respect of the prevention of crime and disorder licensing objective because it is concerned with the prevention of illegal working or immigration offences more broadly.

Licensing authorities acting as responsible authorities

Licensing authorities are included in the list of responsible authorities and so a licensing authority must decide when it considers it appropriate to act in its capacity as a responsible authority. Such a decision should be made in accordance with the duties of a licensing authority under s.4.

The Guidance at paras.9.14 to 9.19 provides:

> 9.14 Licensing authorities are not expected to act as responsible authorities on behalf of other parties (for example, local residents, local councillors or community groups) although there are occasions where the authority may decide to do so. Such parties can make relevant representations to the licensing authority in their own right, and it is reasonable for the licensing authority to expect them to make representations themselves where they are reasonably able to do so. However, if these parties have failed to take action and the licensing authority is aware of relevant grounds to make a representation, it may choose to act in its capacity as responsible authority.
>
> 9.15 It is also reasonable for licensing authorities to expect that other responsible authorities should intervene where the basis for the intervention falls within the remit of that other responsible authority. For example, the police should make representations where the representations are based on concerns about crime and disorder. Likewise, it is reasonable to expect the local authority exercising environmental health functions to make representations where there are concerns about noise nuisance. Each responsible authority has equal standing under the 2003 Act and may act independently without waiting for representations from any other responsible authority.
>
> 9.16 The 2003 Act enables licensing authorities to act as responsible authorities as a means of early intervention; they may do so where they consider it appropriate without having to wait for representations from other responsible authorities. For example, the licensing authority may (in a case where it has published a cumulative impact assessment) consider that granting a new licence application will add to the cumulative impact of licensed premises in its area and therefore

decide to make representations to that effect, without waiting for any other person to do so.

9.17 In cases where a licensing authority is also acting as responsible authority in relation to the same process, it is important to achieve a separation of responsibilities within the authority to ensure procedural fairness and eliminate conflicts of interest. In such cases licensing determinations will be made by the licensing committee or sub committee comprising elected members of the authority (although they are advised by a licensing officer). Therefore, a separation is achieved by allocating distinct functions (i.e. those of licensing authority and responsible authority) to different officials within the authority.

9.18 In these cases, licensing authorities should allocate the different responsibilities to different licensing officers or other officers within the local authority to ensure a proper separation of responsibilities. The officer advising the licensing committee (i.e. the authority acting in its capacity as the licensing authority) must be a different person from the officer who is acting for the responsible authority. The officer acting for the responsible authority should not be involved in the licensing decision process and should not discuss the merits of the case with those involved in making the determination by the licensing authority. For example, discussion should not take place between the officer acting as responsible authority and the officer handling the licence application regarding the merits of the case. Communication between these officers in relation to the case should remain professional and consistent with communication with other responsible authorities. Representations, subject to limited exceptions, must be made in writing. It is for the licensing authority to determine how the separate roles are divided to ensure an appropriate separation of responsibilities. This approach may not be appropriate for all licensing authorities and many authorities may already have processes in place to effectively achieve the same outcome.

9.19 Smaller licensing authorities, where such a separation of responsibilities is more difficult, may wish to involve officials from outside the licensing department to ensure a separation of responsibilities. However, these officials should still be officials employed by the authority.

Health bodies acting as responsible authorities

The Guidance at paras.9.20 to 9.24 provides:

9.20 Where a local authority's Director of Public Health in England (DPH) or Local Health Board (LHB) (in Wales) exercises its functions as a responsible authority, it should have sufficient knowledge of the licensing policy and health issues to ensure it is able to fulfil those functions. If the authority wishes to make representations, the DPH or LHB will need to decide how best to gather and coordinate evidence from other bodies which exercise health functions in the area, such as emergency departments and ambulance services.

9.21 Health bodies may hold information which other responsible authorities do not, but which would assist a licensing authority in exercising its functions. This information may be used by the health body to make representations in its own right or to support representations by other responsible authorities, such as the police. Such representations can potentially be made on the grounds of all four licensing objectives. Perhaps the most obvious example is where drunkenness leads to accidents and injuries from violence, resulting in attendances at emergency departments and the use of ambulance services. Some of these incidents will be reported to the police, but many will not. Such information will often be relevant to the public safety and crime and disorder objectives.

9.22 However, health bodies are encouraged to make representations in respect of any of the four licensing objectives without necessarily seeking views from other responsible authorities where they have appropriate evidence to do so. There is also potential for health bodies to participate in the licensing process in relation to the protection of children from harm. This objective not only concerns the physical safety of children, but also their moral and psychological well being.

9.23 Evidence relating to under 18s alcohol-related emergency department attendance, hospital admissions and underage sales of alcohol, could potentially have implications for both the protection of children from harm and the crime and disorder objectives. Health bodies can provide evidence to lead or support representations in relation to this objective. In relation to proxy purchases, data collected by health bodies could be used to inform other responsible authorities, including the police and licensing authorities, about a prevalence of proxy purchasing in a particular area. For example, the police could use this data to tackle instances of 'shoulder tapping' (where under 18s approach adults to buy alcohol on their behalf) and to suggest measures which retailers might be able to take to ensure, as far as possible, that they are not knowingly selling alcohol to an adult who is buying on behalf of a person aged under 18. Although less obvious, health bodies may also have a role to play in the prevention of public nuisance where its effect is prejudicial to health and where they hold relevant data.

9.24 DPHs and LHBs will need to consider how to collect anonymised information about incidents that relate to specific premises or premises in a particular area (for example, an area which is the subject of a cumulative impact assessment). Many areas have already developed procedures for local information sharing to tackle violence, which could provide useful evidence to support representations. The College of Emergency Medicine has issued guidelines for information sharing to reduce community violence which recommends that data about assault victims should be collected upon admission to emergency departments, including the date, time and location of the assault – i.e. the name of the pub, club or street where the incident occurred. Sometimes, it may be possible to link ambulance callouts or attendances at emergency departments to irresponsible practices at specific premises, such as serving alcohol to people who are intoxicated or targeting promotions involving unlimited or unspecified quantities of alcohol at particular groups.

Other person

There is no requirement that there must be a relationship to the vicinity of the premises for a representation to be made by any person. The test of 'vicinity' has been removed from the Act so that any person may make representations in relation to applications for the grant or variation (including a minor variation) of a premises licence or club premises certificate, the grant of a provisional statement and to make applications for the review of such authorisations, and to make representations in relation to other discrete processes. However, all representations will need to relate to the licensing objectives and must not be frivolous or vexatious.

10.2.2 A representation must be made within the prescribed period

The Act provides that the Secretary of State must by regulations prescribe the period during which representation may be made. The Premises Licences Regulations, reg.22 provides that a responsible authority or any other person may make representations (other than representations in relation to an application for a minor variation) at any time during the period of 28 consecutive days starting on the day after the day on which the application to which it relates was given to the authority by the applicant. There is an exception in relation to review of a premises licence following a closure order where representations may be made at any time up to and including seven days starting on the day after the day on which the authority received notice in relation to the closure order and any extension to it.

In *R. (on the application of Albert Court Residents' Association)* v. *Westminster City Council* [2011] EWCA Civ 430; [2012] PTSR 604 the court held that there is no power for a licensing authority to consider late representations. This will still be the case where the licensing authority fails to carry out a proper consultation process and in such a case the only remedy available to those who have not been properly consulted will be to apply for a review of the licence.

10.2.3 A representation must not be withdrawn

A representation must not have been withdrawn (s.18(7)(b)). The Hearings Regulations, reg.10 provides that a party who wishes to withdraw any representations they have made may do so by giving notice to the authority no later than 24 hours before the day or the first day on which the hearing is to be held, or orally at the hearing.

10.2.4 Relevant, vexatious and frivolous representations

A representation is only relevant if it relates to the likely effect of the application on the promotion of at least one of the four licensing objectives. A representation which does not do this is not relevant. The Guidance at para.9.4 provides that:

> A representation is 'relevant' if it relates to the likely effect of the grant of the licence on the promotion of at least one of the licensing objectives. For example, a representation from a local businessperson about the commercial damage caused by competition from new licensed premises would not be relevant. On the other hand, a representation by a businessperson that nuisance caused by new premises would deter customers from entering the local area, and the steps proposed by the applicant to prevent that nuisance were inadequate, would be relevant. In other words, representations should relate to the impact of licensable activities carried on from premises on the objectives. For representations in relation to variations to be relevant, they should be confined to the subject matter of the variation. There is no requirement for a responsible authority or other person to produce a recorded history of problems at premises to support their representations, and in fact this would not be possible for new premises.

A licensing authority must decide whether any representation (other than a representation from a responsible authority) is frivolous or vexatious and it must reach its decision on the basis of what might ordinarily be considered to be vexatious or frivolous. In relation to 'vexatious', the Guidance at para.9.5 provides:

> A representation may be considered to be vexatious if it appears to be intended to cause aggravation or annoyance, whether to a competitor or other person, without reasonable cause or justification. Vexatious circumstances may arise because of disputes between rival businesses and local knowledge will therefore be invaluable in considering such matters. Licensing authorities can consider the main effect of the representation, and whether any inconvenience or expense caused by it could reasonably be considered to be proportionate.

In relation to 'frivolous', the Guidance at para.9.6 provides:

> Frivolous representations would be essentially categorised by a lack of seriousness. Frivolous representations would concern issues which, at most, are minor and in relation to which no remedial steps would be warranted or proportionate.

The Guidance recommends that the decision on whether a representation is frivolous or vexatious should be delegated to an officer and para.9.8 provides:

> Licensing authorities should not take decisions about whether representations are frivolous, vexatious or relevant to the licensing objectives on the basis of any political judgement. This may be difficult for councillors who receive complaints from residents within their own wards. If consideration is not to be delegated, contrary to the recommendation in this Guidance, an assessment should be prepared by officials for consideration by the sub-committee before any decision is taken that necessitates a hearing. Any councillor who considers that their own interests are such that they are unable to consider the matter independently should disqualify themselves.

The Guidance at para.9.9 also recommends that in borderline cases, the benefit of the doubt about any aspect of a representation should be given to the person making the representation. The subsequent hearing would then provide an opportunity for the person or body making the representation to amplify and clarify it.

Where a licensing authority decides that a representation is frivolous or vexatious, it must notify the person who made it of the reasons for the decision. This notification must be given in writing and as soon as is reasonably practicable and in any event before the determination of the application to which the representation relates (Premises Licences Regulations, reg.31). There is no right of appeal but it may be possible to resubmit an amended representation if there is time. The Guidance at para.9.7 provides as well that:

> Any person who is aggrieved by a rejection of their representations on either of these grounds may lodge a complaint through the local authority's corporate complaints procedure. A person may also challenge the authority's decision by way of judicial review.

10.3 RELEVANT REPRESENTATIONS – SPECIFIC APPLICATIONS UNDER THE ACT

10.3.1 Application for a premises licence

In respect of an application for a premises licence, s.18(6) and (7) provides that a representation is a 'relevant representation' if it:

- is about the likely effect of the grant of the premises licence on the promotion of the licensing objectives;
- has been made by a responsible authority or other person within the prescribed time limit of 28 days starting on the day after the day on which the application for a premises licence was given to the licensing authority by the applicant;
- has not been withdrawn;
- in the case of a representation made by a person who is not a responsible authority, is not, in the opinion of the relevant licensing authority, frivolous or vexatious;
- relates to the identity of the person named in the application as the proposed premises supervisor, has been made by a chief officer of police for a police area in which the premises are situated, and includes a statement that, due to the exceptional circumstances of the case, he is satisfied that the designation of the person concerned as the premises supervisor under the premises licence would undermine the crime prevention objective; and
- is not an excluded representation by virtue of s.32 which restricts the making of representations following the issue of a provisional statement.

10.3.2 Application for a provisional statement

In respect of an application for a provisional statement, s.31(5) and (6) provides that a representation is a 'relevant representation' if it:

- is about the likely effect on the licensing objectives of the grant of a premises licence in the form described in the provisional statement application, if the work at the premises was satisfactorily completed;
- has been made by a responsible authority or other person at any time during a period of 28 days starting on the day after the day on which the application for a provisional statement was given to the licensing authority by the applicant;
- has not been withdrawn; and
- in the case of a representation made by a person who is not also a responsible authority, is not, in the opinion of the relevant licensing authority, frivolous or vexatious.

Section 32 contains restrictions on making representations following the issue of a provisional statement.

10.3.3 Application for a variation of a premises licence

In respect of an application for a variation of a premises licence, s.35(5) and (6) provides that a representation is a 'relevant representation' if it:

- is about the likely effect of the grant of the application on the promotion of the licensing objectives;
- has been made by a responsible authority or other person at any time during a period of 28 days starting on the day after the day on which the application for a variation was given to the licensing authority by the applicant;
- has not been withdrawn; and
- in the case of a representation made by a person who is not a responsible authority, is not, in the opinion of the relevant licensing authority, frivolous or vexatious.

10.3.4 Application for a minor variation of a premises licence

In respect of an application for a minor variation of a premises licence, s.41B(2) and (10) provide that a representation is a 'relevant representation' if it:

- is about the likely effect of the grant of the application on the promotion of the licensing objectives; and
- has been made by any of the responsible authorities which the relevant licensing authority considered appropriate to consult or any other person and received by the authority within 10 working days beginning on the first working day after the day on which the authority received the application.

10.3.5 Application for a review of a premises licence

In respect of an application for a review of a premises licence, s.52(7) and (8) provides that a representation is a 'relevant representation' if it:

- is relevant to one or more of the licensing objectives;
- has been made by the holder of the premises licence, a responsible authority or any other person at any time during a period of 28 days starting on the day after the day on which the application for a review was given to the licensing authority by the applicant;
- has not been withdrawn; and
- in the case of a representation made by a person who is not a responsible authority, is not, in the opinion of the relevant licensing authority, frivolous or vexatious.

10.3.6 Application for a review of a premises licence following a closure order

In respect of an application for a review of a premises licence following a closure order, s.167(9) and (10) provides that a representation is a 'relevant representation' if it:

- is relevant to one or more of the licensing objectives;
- has been made by the holder of the premises licence, a responsible authority or any other person at any time up to and including seven days starting on the day after the day on which the licensing authority received the notice of the magistrates' court determination and extension to it;
- has not been withdrawn; and
- in the case of a representation made by a person who is not a responsible authority, is not, in the opinion of the relevant licensing authority, frivolous or vexatious.

10.3.7 Application for a club premises certificate

In respect of an application for a club premises certificate, s.72(7) and (8) provides that a representation is a 'relevant representation' if it:

- is about the likely effect of the grant of the club premises certificate on the promotion of the licensing objectives;
- has been made by a responsible authority or other person at any time during a period of 28 days starting on the day after the day on which the application for a club premises certificate was given to the licensing authority by the applicant;
- has not been withdrawn; and
- in the case of a representation made by a person who is not a responsible authority, is not, in the opinion of the relevant licensing authority, frivolous or vexatious.

10.3.8 Application for a variation of a club premises certificate

In respect of an application for a variation of a club premises certificate, s.85(5) and (6) provides that a representation is a 'relevant representation' if it:

- is about the likely effect of the grant of the application on the promotion of the licensing objectives;
- has been made by a responsible authority or other person at any time during a period of 28 days starting on the day after the day on which the application for a variation was given to the licensing authority by the applicant;
- has not been withdrawn; and

- in the case of a representation made by a person who is not also a responsible authority, is not, in the opinion of the relevant licensing authority, frivolous or vexatious.

10.3.9 Application for a minor variation of a club premises certificate

In respect of an application for a minor variation of a club premises certificate, s.86B(2) and (10) provide that a representation is a 'relevant representation' if it:

- is about the likely effect of the grant of the application on the promotion of the licensing objectives; and
- has been made any of the responsible authorities which the relevant licensing authority considered appropriate to consult or any other person and received by the authority within 10 working days beginning on the first working day after the day on which the authority received the application.

10.3.10 Application for a review of a club premises certificate

In respect of an application for a review of a club premises certificate, s.88(7) and (8) provides that a representation is a 'relevant representation' if it:

- is relevant to one or more of the licensing objectives;
- has been made by the club, a responsible authority or any other person at any time during a period of 28 days starting on the day after the day on which the application for a review was given to the licensing authority by the applicant;
- has not been withdrawn; and
- in the case of a representation made by a person who is not a responsible authority, is not, in the opinion of the relevant licensing authority, frivolous or vexatious.

10.4 MAKING A REPRESENTATION

A representation must relate to one or more of the four licensing objectives. It should not relate to other matters such as planning permission, trade competition or the effect on house prices.

10.4.1 How does someone know that an application has been made?

Applications can be viewed at the licensing authority offices. In addition, a person will know if an application has been made if he sees:

- a notice displayed on the premises;
- an official notice in the notices section of a local newspaper; or
- a statement on the licensing authority's website.

10.4.2 Representations to be in writing

The Premises Licences Regulations, reg.21 provides that a representation (other than those made by a responsible authority in relation to an application for a minor variation) must be made in writing. However, notwithstanding this requirement, a representation can also be made electronically provided:

- the information comprising the representation is transmitted by electronic means (other than a relevant electronic facility), is capable of being accessed by the recipient, is clear and legible in all material respects (i.e. the information contained in the representation is available to the recipient to no lesser extent than it would be if given by means of a written document), and is capable of being read and reproduced in written form and used for subsequent reference;
- the person to whom the representation is to be given has agreed in advance that a representation may be given by electronic means; and
- forthwith (see **2.9**) on sending the text of the representation by electronic means, the representation is given to the recipient in writing (unless the recipient has agreed in advance that the representation need not be given in writing).

Where the text of the representation is transmitted by electronic means, the representation is taken as given at the time the first two sets of above requirements are satisfied with respect to the information and any accompanying plan or document.

10.4.3 Advice and standard forms of representation

A person wishing to make a representation should first consult the relevant licensing authority to see what advice it can provide. The Guidance, para.9.10 states: 'Licensing authorities should consider providing advice on their websites about how any person can make representations to them.' A licensing authority may provide a standard form for use when making a representation. Some may even provide an online form which can be used to submit a representation. **Appendix B** contains a suggested form for use when making a representation.

The representation must include the name and address of the person making the representation. The licensing authority is required under the Hearings Regulations to provide the applicant with copies of the relevant representations that have been made. In exceptional circumstances, persons making representations to the licensing authority may be reluctant to do so because of fears of intimidation or violence if their personal details, such as name and address, are divulged to the applicant. The Guidance at paras.9.28 to 9.30 provides:

> 9.28 Where licensing authorities consider that the person has a genuine and well-founded fear of intimidation and may be deterred from making a representation on this basis, they may wish to consider alternative approaches.

9.29 For instance, they could advise the persons to provide the relevant responsible authority with details of how they consider that the licensing objectives are being undermined so that the responsible authority can make representations if appropriate and justified.

9.30 The licensing authority may also decide to withhold some or all of the person's personal details from the applicant, giving only minimal details (such as street name or general location within a street). However, withholding such details should only be considered where the circumstances justify such action.

10.4.4 Evidence in support of a representation

A person making a representation should provide evidence to support the representation. Possible ways of doing this include using:

- a diary/record of events or incidents;
- photographs;
- video evidence;
- sound recordings;
- a record of complaints made to appropriate authorities; and
- supporting statements from neighbours/witnesses.

It will be essential that a written note or a diary is kept so that the date, the time and a brief description of any incidents that take place can be recorded. In addition, this should be supplemented with photographs, a video recording or a sound recording. It will also help if other people can also make notes about what happened (or keeps happening). If an incident prompted an official response, for example a noise complaint is logged or the police arrive, then details of this should be kept.

Where noise is a problem, a noise diary should be kept. The local environmental health authority may be able to provide a standard form of noise diary. Otherwise, a noise diary should set out:

- the date the noise happens;
- the time the noise started and finished;
- where the person completing the diary was when he heard the noise;
- the address of the premises where the noise is coming from;
- a description of the noise, e.g. loud music, people shouting, etc.;
- the level of the noise and the disturbance it caused;
- the name of the person causing the noise, if known; and
- the name and address of any witnesses (who should also keep their own noise diary).

Records should be kept over a period of time so as to prevent a licensee from arguing that something was just a one-off problem. It may also be useful to check whether:

- council records confirm that the premises have the right planning consent for what is going on;
- there are records of any other complaints;
- the local crime and disorder reduction partnership can assist;
- there have been articles in the local press about nuisance or trouble on the premises; and
- any of the relevant authorities support the representation.

A petition may be used to support a representation.

Difficulties may arise in the preparation of a case against an application for a proposed variation or provisional statement as this will have to include the fears of what may happen in the event that the application is granted. It may be easy for the applicant to deny that any problems will arise. It is important to include points that suggest whether:

- there has been a previous licence;
- there have been problems in the past;
- if the premises are part of a chain, there have been similar problems at other branches;
- similar premises in the area have shown similar problems; and
- the applicant has thought through how the premises will be operated in order to avoid problems.

CHAPTER 11

Conditions

11.1 INTRODUCTION

A licensing authority may impose conditions when granting a premises licence or a club premises certificate. These may be imposed because it is mandatory to do so or they may be imposed at the discretion of the licensing authority. Where no relevant representations have been made in respect of an application for a premises licence, no conditions can be imposed beyond those consistent with the operating schedule and any mandatory conditions (*British Beer and Pub Association* v. *Canterbury City Council* [2005] EWHC 1318 (Admin); (2005) 169 JP 521).

Conditions cannot be attached to a personal licence and may only be attached to a temporary event notice where the licensable activities include the supply of alcohol when a condition must be attached under s.100(6) that all supplies of alcohol must be made or authorised by the premises user (see **20.6**).

In certain circumstances, mandatory conditions must be attached to a premises licence or a club premises certificate (see **7.11** and **17.11**). There are also certain conditions which are prohibited from being included (see **7.11.6**, **17.11.3** and **17.11.4**). A licensing authority may also impose conditions at its discretion. Where no relevant representations have been made, a licensing authority may only attach such conditions as are consistent with the operating schedule (ss.18(2)(a) and 72(2)(a)). Where relevant representations have been made, a licensing authority can impose such conditions as are consistent with the operating schedule modified to the extent it considers appropriate for the promotion of the licensing objectives (ss.18(4)(a)(i) and 72(4)(a)(i)).

11.2 GENERAL REQUIREMENTS FOR CONDITIONS

Conditions may only be imposed on a premises licence or a club premises certificate where they are appropriate for the promotion of one or more of the four licensing objectives. Conditions may not be imposed for other purposes. Conditions must only apply while the licensable activities are taking place and so, for example conditions relating to night café and takeaway outlets operating from 11 pm must relate to the night-time operation of the premises and must not be used to impose conditions which relate to day-time operation. A condition must not duplicate something which is already imposed by the existing law.

Conditions are essentially the steps or actions that the holder of a premises licence or club premises certificate will be required to take or not take in relation to the carrying on of licensable activities at the premises. There are three types of conditions that may be attached to a licence or certificate – proposed, imposed and mandatory (Guidance, para.10.3).

11.2.1 Proposed conditions

The Guidance at paras.10.4 and 10.5 provides:

> 10.4 The conditions that are appropriate for the promotion of the licensing objectives should emerge initially from the risk assessment carried out by a prospective licence or certificate holder, which they should carry out before making their application for a premises licence or club premises certificate. This would be translated into the steps recorded in the operating schedule or club operating schedule, which must also set out the proposed hours during which licensable activities will be conducted and any other hours during which the premises will be open to the public.
>
> 10.5 It is not acceptable for licensing authorities to simply replicate the wording from an applicant's operating schedule. A condition should be interpreted in accordance with the applicant's intention and be appropriate and proportionate for the promotion of the licensing objectives.

Where an operating schedule or club operating schedule has been submitted with an application and there have been no relevant representations made by responsible authorities or any other person, the licence or certificate must be granted subject only to such conditions as are consistent with the schedule accompanying the application and any mandatory conditions required under the Act. The Guidance at para.10.7 provides:

> Consistency means that the effect of the condition should be substantially the same as that intended by the terms of the operating schedule. If conditions are broken, this may lead to a criminal prosecution or an application for a review and it is extremely important therefore that they should be expressed on the licence or certificate in unequivocal and unambiguous terms. The duty imposed by conditions on the licence holder or club must be clear to the licence holder, club, enforcement officers and the courts.

11.2.2 Imposed conditions

A licensing authority may not impose any conditions unless its discretion has been engaged following receipt of relevant representations and it is satisfied as a result of a hearing (unless all parties agree a hearing is not necessary) that it is appropriate to impose conditions to promote one or more of the four licensing objectives (Guidance, para.10.8). It is possible that in some cases no additional conditions will be appropriate to promote the licensing objectives (Guidance, para.10.9).

Standard conditions are effectively ruled out as the Guidance at para.10.10 provides:

> The 2003 Act requires that licensing conditions should be tailored to the size, type, location and characteristics and activities taking place at the premises concerned. Conditions should be determined on a case-by-case basis and standardised conditions which ignore these individual aspects should be avoided. For example, conditions should not be used to implement a general policy in a given area such as the use of CCTV, polycarbonate drinking vessels or identity scanners where they would not be appropriate to the specific premises. Conditions that are considered appropriate for the prevention of illegal working in premises licensed to sell alcohol or late night refreshment might include requiring a premises licence holder to undertake right to work checks on all staff employed at the licensed premises or requiring that evidence of a right to work check, either physical or digital (e.g. copy of any document checked or a clear copy of the online right to work check) is retained at the licensed premises. Licensing authorities may also wish to consider placing additional conditions on licences to safeguard patrons against spiking, if deemed appropriate and proportionate for a specific venue where there is evidence to justify such action (a definition of spiking can be found in para 2.7). Licensing authorities and other responsible authorities should be alive to the indirect costs that can arise because of conditions. These could be a deterrent to holding events that are valuable to the community or for the funding of good and important causes. Licensing authorities should therefore ensure that any conditions they impose are only those which are appropriate for the promotion of the licensing objectives.

There are, however, certain conditions which will be attached to most licences. In order that these should be formulated consistently, a pool of such conditions has been published for licensing authorities and applicants (available at **www.gov.uk**).

11.3 NAMING, PACKING AND PROMOTION IN RETAIL PREMISES

The Guidance at paras.10.11 and 10.12 provides:

> 10.11 The Government acknowledges that the irresponsible naming, packing or promotion of alcoholic drinks may contribute to alcohol related harms. Where there is direct evidence of specific incidents of irresponsible naming, packing or promotion of alcoholic drinks linked to the undermining of one of the licensing objectives, licensing authorities should, in the exercise of their licensing functions (in particular, in relation to an application for the grant, variation or review of a premises licence), consider whether it is appropriate to impose conditions on licences that require the licence holder to comply with the Portman Group's Retailer Alert Bulletins. This condition should be considered on a case by case basis and in the context of the promotion of the licensing objectives.
>
> 10.12 The Portman Group operates, on behalf of the alcohol industry, a Code of Practice on the Naming, Packaging and Promotion of Alcoholic Drinks. The Code seeks to ensure that drinks are packaged and promoted in a socially responsible manner and only to those who are 18 years old or older. Complaints about pro-

ducts under the Code are considered by an Independent Complaints Panel and the Panel's decisions are published on the Portman Group's website, in the trade press and in an annual report. If a product's packaging or point-of-sale advertising is found to be in breach of the Code, the Portman Group may issue a Retailer Alert Bulletin to notify retailers of the decision and ask them not to replenish stocks of any such product or to display such point-of-sale material, until there has been compliance with the decision.

11.4 HOURS OF TRADING

The hours during which licensable activities can take place can be regulated by conditions on a premises licence or club premises certificate. Clearly such conditions can only be imposed if they are appropriate for the promotion of the licensing objectives, particularly the prevention of crime and disorder and the prevention of public nuisance. The Guidance promotes flexibility in closing hours.

Where premises supply alcohol for consumption off the premises, for example shops, stores and supermarkets, it is recommended that they should generally be permitted to match the hours during which they may sell alcohol with their normal trading hours during which other sales take place, unless there are exceptional reasons relating to the licensing objectives, in particular the prevention of crime and disorder and public nuisance (Guidance, para.10.15). This means that a shop with 24-hour opening should be allowed to sell alcohol during those hours unless there are very good reasons as to why it is necessary for it not to do so.

11.4.1 Drinking up time

It is important to note that 'opening hours', the times when premises are open to the public, are not necessarily identical to the hours during which licensable activities may take place. In the case of the sale by retail of alcohol (or supply of alcohol by or on behalf of a club to, or to the order of, a member of a club) for consumption on the premises, it must also be noted that 'consumption' of alcohol is not a licensable activity. Accordingly, the authorised period specified in the premises licence, club premises certificate or temporary event notice relates to the period during which alcohol may be sold or supplied. It is therefore permissible for premises to allow the consumption of previously purchased alcohol, within the authorisation, outside the hours authorised for the sale or supply of alcohol. A licensing authority might therefore impose a condition that alcohol must be consumed within a reasonable time after the hours authorised for the sale or supply of alcohol have ended.

11.4.2 Relaxation of opening hours for local, national and international occasions

Section 172(1) provides that where the Secretary of State considers that there is an occasion of exceptional international, national or local significance, he may relax the opening hours by making a licensing hours order. Such a period is referred to as a 'celebration period'. Before making an order, the Secretary of State must consult such persons as he considers appropriate (s.172(4)). If an order is made it will provide that during the specified relaxation period, which may be up to four days, premises licences and club premises certificates will have effect as if the times specified in the order were included in their opening hours.

A licensing hours order may relax the hours generally throughout the country or may just apply to premises in specified areas. It may also make different provision in respect of different days during the specified relaxation period, and may make different provision in respect of different licensable activities.

11.5 THE PERFORMANCE OF PLAYS

The Act provides that other than for the purposes of public safety, conditions must not be attached to premises licences or club premises certificates authorising the performance of a play which attempt to censor or modify the content of plays in any way and any such condition would be *ultra vires* (Guidance, para.10.16).

11.6 CENSORSHIP

The Guidance at para.10.17 provides:

> In general, other than in the context of film classification for film exhibitions, licensing authorities should not use their powers under the 2003 Act to seek to impose conditions which censor the content of any form of regulated entertainment. This is not a proper function of licensing law and cannot be properly related to the licensing objectives. The content of regulated entertainment is a matter which is addressed by existing laws governing indecency and obscenity. Where the concern is about protecting children, their access should be restricted where appropriate. But no other limitation should normally be imposed.

11.7 MAJOR FESTIVALS AND CARNIVALS

The Guidance at paras.10.18 to 10.20 provides:

> 10.18 Licensing authorities should publicise the need for the organisers of major festivals and carnivals to approach them at the earliest opportunity to discuss arrangements for licensing activities falling under the 2003 Act. For some events, the organisers may seek a single premises licence to cover a wide range

of activities at varied locations within the premises. This would involve the preparation of a substantial operating schedule, and licensing authorities should offer advice and assistance about its preparation.

10.19 For other events, applications for many connected premises licences may be made which in combination will represent a single festival. It is important that licensing authorities should publicise the need for proper co-ordination of such arrangements and will need to ensure that responsible authorities are aware of the connected nature of the individual applications.

10.20 Local authorities should bear in mind their ability to seek premises licences from the licensing authority for land or buildings under public ownership within the community in their own name. This could include, for example, village greens, market squares, promenades, community halls, local authority owned art centres and similar public areas where festivals and carnivals might take place. Performers and entertainers would then have no need to obtain a licence or give a temporary event notice themselves to enable them to give performances in these places, although they would need the permission of the local authority to put on the event.

11.8 FIXED PRICES

In relation to fixed prices for alcohol, the Guidance at paras.10.21 and 10.22 provides:

10.21 Licensing authorities should not attach standardised blanket conditions relating to fixed prices for alcoholic drinks to premises licences or club licences or club premises certificates in an area. This may be unlawful under current law. However, it is important to note that the mandatory conditions made under sections 19A and 73B of the 2003 Act prohibit a number of types of drinks promotions including where they give rise to a significant risk to any one of the four licensing objectives; the mandatory conditions also prohibit the sale of alcohol below the permitted price, as defined in paragraph 10.56.

10.22 Where licensing authorities are asked by the police, other responsible authorities or other persons to impose restrictions on promotions in addition to those restricted by the mandatory conditions, they should consider each application on its individual merits, tailoring any conditions carefully to cover only irresponsible promotions in the particular and individual circumstances of any premises where these are appropriate for the promotion of the licensing objectives. In addition, when considering any relevant representations which demonstrate a clear causal link between sales promotions or price discounting and levels of crime and disorder on or near the premises, it would be appropriate for the licensing authority to consider the imposition of a new condition prohibiting irresponsible sales promotions or the discounting of prices of alcoholic beverages at those premises. However, before pursuing any form of restrictions at all, licensing authorities should take their own legal advice.

11.9 LARGE CAPACITY VENUES USED EXCLUSIVELY OR PRIMARILY FOR THE 'VERTICAL' CONSUMPTION OF ALCOHOL

Large capacity 'vertical drinking' premises, sometimes called high volume vertical drinking establishments (HVVDs), are premises with exceptionally high capacities, which are used primarily or exclusively for the sale and consumption of alcohol, and have little or no seating for patrons.

The Guidance at para.10.24 provides:

> Where appropriate, conditions can be attached to premises licences for the promotion of the prevention of crime and disorder at such premises that require the premises to observe:
>
> - a prescribed capacity;
> - an appropriate ratio of tables and chairs to customers based on the capacity; and
> - a requirement that security staff holding the appropriate SIA licence or exemption are present to control entry for the purpose of compliance with the capacity limit and to deny entry to individuals who appear drunk or disorderly or both.

11.10 DANCING IN CERTAIN SMALL PREMISES

There are special provisions in s.177 for dancing in small premises which have a premises licence authorising the supply of alcohol for consumption on the premises, and dancing, and the premises are used primarily for the supply of alcohol for consumption on the premises and have a permitted capacity of not more than 200 persons.

The provisions in s.177 allow a licensing authority to put conditions on a premises licence which relate to dancing.

'Dancing' is defined in s.177(8) by reference to Sched.1, para.2(1)(g).

Section 177 only applies where the permitted capacity is not more than 200 people. 'Permitted capacity', in relation to any premises, is determined by reference to any recommendation made by the fire and rescue authority. Section 177(8) provides that 'permitted capacity' means the limit on the number of persons who may be on the premises at any one time in accordance with a recommendation made by, or on behalf of, the fire and rescue authority for the area in which the premises are situated, or, if the premises are situated in the area of more than one fire and rescue authority, those authorities.

Where an applicant wishes to take advantage of the special provisions set out in s.177 he should conduct his own risk assessment as to the appropriate capacity of the premises, and then send this to the fire and rescue authority who will consider it and then decide what the 'permitted capacity' of those premises should be.

The general principle is that at any time when the premises are open for the purposes of being used for the supply of alcohol for consumption on the premises, and are being used for dancing, any licensing authority imposed condition of the premises licence which relates to dancing does not have effect, unless it relates to the prevention of crime and disorder or public safety. This means that any licensing authority imposed conditions will not have effect if they relate to prevention of public nuisance or the protection of children from harm.

A licensing authority imposed condition will also apply to small premises if, on a review of the premises licence, it is altered so as to include a statement that s.177 does not apply to it, or it is added to the licence and includes such a statement.

A 'licensing authority imposed condition' is a condition imposed by a licensing authority for the promotion of the licensing objectives, or a mandatory condition relating to door supervision under s.21. It does not include a condition volunteered by the applicant in the operating schedule.

For the purposes of s.177 'supply of alcohol' means the sale by retail of alcohol, or the supply of alcohol by or on behalf of a club to, or to the order of, a member of the club.

11.11 LICENCE REVIEW FOR LIVE AND RECORDED MUSIC

Section 177A deals with live and recorded music taking place in premises authorised to be used for the supply of alcohol for consumption on the premises. It provides that any condition of the premises licence or club premises certificate which relates to live music, recorded music or both does not have effect in relation to the music unless, on a review of the premises licence or club premises certificate the condition is altered so as to include a statement that s.177A does not apply to it, or the condition is added to the licence on a review of a premises licence or club premises certificate as if the music were regulated entertainment, and the licence or certificate licensed the music.

Section 177A applies where:

- music takes place on premises which are authorised by a premises licence or club premises certificate to be used for the supply of alcohol for consumption on the premises;
- at the time of the music, the premises are open for the purposes of being used for the supply of alcohol for consumption on the premises;
- if the music is amplified, it takes place in the presence of an audience of no more than 500 persons; and
- the music takes place between 8 am and 11 pm on the same day (or, where an order under s.172 has effect in relation to music, during any times specified under that order).

Section 177A does not apply to music which, by virtue of a provision other than Sched.1, para.12A or 12C, is not regarded as the provision of regulated entertainment for the purposes of the Act.

CHAPTER 12

Interim authorities

12.1 INTRODUCTION

A premises licence will lapse under s.27 where the licensee dies, becomes mentally incapable, becomes bankrupt or changes their immigration status so they are no longer entitled to work in the United Kingdom. While it is possible to apply for a transfer of the licence by reinstatement (see **12.6**) this may take some time, for example due to the length of time before a deceased licensee's estate can be dealt with or an administrative receiver appointed. So, the Act makes provision for the licence to be reinstated in such circumstances for up to three months by allowing an interim authority notice to be given. Without this, the carrying on of licensable activities would be an offence as an unauthorised licensable activity under s.136(1)(a) (see **21.2.1**). There is a 'defence of due diligence' in s.139 which may be relevant where, for example, the manager of particular premises is wholly unaware for a period of time that the premises licence holder has died. As soon as an interim authority notice is properly given, the business may continue to carry on any licensable activities permitted by the premises licence.

The Guidance at para.8.103 states:

> The 2003 Act provides special arrangements for the continuation of permissions under a premises licence when the holder of a licence dies suddenly, becomes bankrupt, mentally incapable or ceases to be entitled to work in the UK. In the normal course of events, the licence would lapse in such circumstances. However, there may also be some time before, for example, the deceased person's estate can be dealt with or an administrative receiver appointed. This could have a damaging effect on those with interests in the premises, such as an owner, lessor or employees working at the premises in question; and could bring unnecessary disruption to customers' plans. The 2003 Act therefore provides for the licence to be capable of being reinstated in a discrete period of time in certain circumstances.

12.2 GIVING AN INTERIM AUTHORITY

An interim authority notice can be given under s.47 where:

- the premises licence has lapsed due to the death, incapacity, insolvency or change of immigration status of the holder; and
- no application has been made for the reinstatement of the licence on transfer following the death, incapacity, insolvency or change of immigration status.

An interim authority notice can be given either by a person who has a prescribed interest in the premises, or by a person who is connected to the person who held the premises licence immediately before it lapsed. In respect of the first category, a person who has a legal interest in the premises as freeholder or leaseholder has been prescribed for these purposes (Premises Licences Regulations, reg.8). In respect of the second category, under s.47(5), a person is connected to the former holder of the premises licence if, and only if:

- the former holder has died and that person is his personal representative;
- the former holder lacks capacity (within the meaning of the Mental Capacity Act 2005) to hold the licence and that person acts for him under an enduring power of attorney or lasting power of attorney registered under the Act; or
- the former holder has become insolvent and that person is his insolvency practitioner.

Where the premises licence authorises the premises to be used for the sale by retail of alcohol or the provision of late night refreshment, a person who is an individual who is resident in the United Kingdom may give an interim authority notice only if they are entitled to work in the United Kingdom (s.47(3A)).

An interim authority notice must be given to the relevant licensing authority within the period of 28 days beginning with the day after the day the licence lapses. This is referred to in the Act as 'the initial 28 day period'. In addition, the appropriate fee must accompany the notice. Only one interim authority notice may be given (s.47(4)).

Where an application is made in writing, the person who gave the interim authority notice must also give a copy of the notice to the chief officer of police for the police area (or each police area) in which the premises are situated within the initial 28 day period. Failure to do so will mean that the premises licence lapses (s.47(7)(a)). Where an application is made in writing and the premises licence authorises the premises to be used for the sale by retail of alcohol or the provision of late night refreshment, the person who gave the interim authority notice must also give a copy of the notice to the Secretary of State within the initial 28 day period. Failure to do so will mean that the premises licence lapses (s.47(7)(aa)). Where the interim authority notice is given electronically (via **www.gov.uk** or the relevant licensing authority's electronic facility), the relevant licensing authority must forthwith (see **2.9**) give a copy of the notice to the chief officer of police for the police area (or each police area) in which the premises are situated and where the premises licence authorises the premises to be used for the sale by retail of alcohol or the provision of late night refreshment, the relevant licensing authority must also forthwith give a copy of the notice to the Secretary of State (s.47(7A)). However, para.8.104 of the Guidance states that the licensing authority must notify the police and the Secretary of State no later than the first working day after the notice is given.

Where a person becomes the holder of a premises licence by virtue of an interim authority notice, he must, unless he is the designated premises supervisor under the licence, forthwith (see **2.9**) notify the designated premises supervisor, if there is one, of the interim authority notice (s.49(4)). Failure to so notify the designated premises supervisor, without reasonable excuse, is an offence and a person guilty of such an offence is liable on summary conviction to a fine not exceeding level 3 on the standard scale (s.49(5), (6)).

There is nothing to prevent a person who gives an interim authority notice from making a relevant transfer application (s.47(8)).

12.3 FORM OF INTERIM NOTICE

The form of an interim notice is prescribed in the Premises Licences Regulations, Sched.7.

12.3.1 Completing the notice

Guidance in completing the application form may be obtained from **www.gov.uk** or the relevant licensing authority. The form may be completed by being either typed or written legibly in block capitals. All answers must be inside the boxes and written in black ink.

In the opening statement, the name of the person or persons who are giving the interim authority notice and the premises licence number, if known, should be inserted.

The notice is then divided into four parts.

Part 1

The person giving the interim authority notice must set out the postal address of the premises, and the telephone number at the premises, if any. If the premises have no postal address, the location of the premises should be described or the Ordnance Survey map reference should be given.

Part 2

Part 2 deals with details of the person giving the interim authority notice. He must state in which capacity he is giving the interim authority notice and give details of when and how the licence lapsed, for example the date on which the premises licence holder died or became insolvent. He must then give details of his name and address, telephone number, nationality, email address (this is optional), and confirmation, where relevant, that he is at least 18 years old, and, where applicable, if demonstrating a right to work via the Home Office online right to work checking service, the 'share code' provided to the applicant by that service.

Part 3

Part 3 asks whether an interim authority notice has been given previously in relation to the premises and the former premises licence holder. If an interim authority notice has not been given previously then the date from which the variation is to take effect must be stated. It also asks whether or not there has been an application to transfer the premises licence under s.50 (see **12.6**). There is a checklist for the person giving the interim authority notice so that nothing is overlooked. There are then three warnings. The first is a warning that the notice will lapse at the end of the initial 28-day period after the lapsing of the premises licence unless a copy of the notice has been given to the chief officer of police for the police area or each police area in which the premises are situated, and, if relevant, to the Secretary of State. There is also a warning that it is an offence under s.158, liable on conviction to a fine up to level 5 on the standard scale, to make a false statement in or in connection with the application. Finally, there is a warning that it is an offence under the Immigration Act 1971, s.24b for a person to work when they know, or have reasonable cause to believe, that they are disqualified from doing so by reason of their immigration status. Those who employ an adult without leave or who is subject to conditions as to employment, will be liable for a civil penalty under the Immigration, Asylum and Nationality Act 2006, s.15 and, pursuant to s.21 of the same Act, will be committing an offence where they do so in the knowledge, or with reasonable cause to believe, that the employee is disqualified.

Part 4

The final part of the form makes provision for the person giving the interim authority notice to sign the form. The application form must be signed. The form can also be signed by a solicitor or other duly authorised agent, and someone signing on behalf of the person giving the interim authority notice must state in what capacity he signs. Where there are joint persons giving the interim authority notice, both of them or their respective agents must sign the application form.

12.3.2 Obtaining an interim authority notice

For details on obtaining a form see **7.4.2**.

12.3.3 Giving a notice

The Premises Licences Regulations, reg.21 provides that an application must be made in writing. However, notwithstanding this requirement, an application can also be made electronically (Premises Licences Regulations, reg.21A(1)). Where the application is transmitted by electronic means, the application will not be treated as being given until the information becomes accessible to the relevant licensing authority by means of that facility (Premises Licences Regulations, reg.21A(3)). In addition, as a fee must accompany the application, the application will not be taken as given until the fee has been received by the relevant licensing authority (Premises Licences Regulations, reg.21A(4)).

On receipt of an interim authority notice, s.49(1) provides that the relevant licensing authority must issue to the person who gave the interim authority notice a copy of the licence and a copy of the summary of it. Each of these must be certified by the authority to be a true copy. The copies issued must be copies of the premises licence and summary in the form in which they existed immediately before the licence lapsed, except that they must specify the person who gave the interim authority notice as the person who is the holder (s.49(2)). The Act then applies in relation to the certified copies as it applies in relation to the original licence or summary (s.49(3)).

12.4 THE EFFECT OF AN INTERIM AUTHORITY NOTICE

The effect of an interim authority notice is that it reinstates the premises licence from the time the notice is received by the relevant licensing authority, and the person who gave the notice is from that time the holder of the premises licence (s.47(6)). The premises licence is reinstated for a period of up to three months ('the interim authority period'), and during this period an application for a transfer of the premises licence must be made. In this context, 'months' means calendar months (Interpretation Act 1978, s.5, Sched.1). There is no requirement that the transfer application must be made by the person who gave the interim authority notice and so it could be made by someone else. During the interim authority period the person who gave the notice can notify the relevant licensing authority that he is terminating the interim authority period and it will then come to an end (s.47(10)). Where application is made to transfer a premises licence within the interim authority period, the words of s.47(10) exclude from the calculation of the time period the day on which the interim authority notice was received (*R. (on the application of Bednash)* v. *Westminster City Council* [2014] EWHC 2160 (Admin)).

The premises licence will lapse at the end of the initial 28-day period if the person who gave the interim authority notice has not given a copy of the interim authority notice to the chief officer of police for the police area, or each police area, in which the premises are situated (s.47(7)(a)). Where the premises licence authorises the premises to be used for the sale by retail of alcohol or the provision of late night refreshment, the premises licence will also lapse at the end of the initial 28-day period if the person who gave the interim authority notice has not given a copy of the interim authority notice to the Secretary of State (s.47(7)(aa)). Neither of s.47(7)(a) nor s.47(7)(aa) will apply if where the interim authority notice was given to the relevant licensing authority electronically. The premises licence will also lapse at the end of the interim authority period unless a relevant transfer application is made during that time (s.47(7)(b)). If such an application is made and it is either rejected or withdrawn then the licence will lapse at the time of the rejection or the withdrawal (s.47(9)).

12.5 CANCELLATION OF AN INTERIM AUTHORITY FOLLOWING OBJECTIONS

Where an interim authority notice has been given to the chief officer of police for the police area, or each police area in which the premises are situated before the end of the initial 28-day period, and he is satisfied that the exceptional circumstances of the case are such that a failure to cancel the interim authority notice would undermine the crime prevention objective, then he must before the end of the second working day following the day on which after he receives the copy of the interim authority notice give the relevant licensing authority a notice stating why he is so satisfied (s.48(1), (2)).

Where an interim authority notice has been given to the Secretary of State (through Home Office Immigration Enforcement), and the Secretary of State is satisfied that the exceptional circumstances of the case are such that a failure to cancel the interim authority notice would be prejudicial to the prevention of illegal working in licensed premises, then the Secretary of State must before the end of the second working day following the day on which after he receives the copy of the interim authority notice give the relevant licensing authority a notice stating why the Secretary of State is so satisfied (s.48(2A), (2B)).

Where such a notice is given and not withdrawn, the relevant licensing authority must then hold a hearing to consider it, unless the licensing authority, the person who gave the interim authority notice and the person who gave the notice agree that a hearing is unnecessary. A hearing must be held within five working days beginning with the day after the end of the period within which the chief officer of police may give a notice (Hearings Regulations, reg.5 and Sched.1, para.6). Notice of the hearing must be given to the person who gave the interim authority notice and the chief officer of police no later than two working days before the day or the first day on which the hearing is to be held (Hearings Regulations, reg.6(2) and Sched.2, para.6). The person who gave the interim authority notice must be given the police notice of objection with the notice of hearing (Hearings Regulations, reg.7(2) and Sched.3, para.6). The Hearing Regulations do not provide for a hearing where the Secretary of State gives a notice but it is assumed that the requirements that apply to a notice given by a chief officer of police will be followed.

The Guidance states that a licensing authority should be alert to the need to consider the objection quickly (para.8.108).

If, on hearing a police objection, the licensing authority considers it appropriate for the promotion of the crime prevention objective, it must cancel the interim authority notice by giving the person who gave the interim authority notice a notice of cancellation together with the reasons for its decision. The licensing authority must also give a copy of the notice of cancellation to the chief officer of police for the police area or each police area in which the premises are situated.

If, on hearing an objection from the Secretary of State, the licensing authority considers it appropriate for the prevention of illegal working in licensed premises, it must cancel the interim authority notice by giving the person who gave the interim authority notice a notice of cancellation together with the reasons for its decision. The licensing authority must also give a copy of the notice of cancellation to the Secretary of State.

The premises licence will lapse when a notice cancelling it is given; however, there is a right of appeal against the cancellation. Where an appeal is lodged, the premises licence is reinstated pending the determination of the appeal by the magistrates' court. A person who gave the interim authority notice may appeal against a decision to cancel the interim authority notice, and a chief officer of police or the Secretary of State may appeal against a decision not to cancel the notice. Where an appeal is made, the magistrates' court may, on such terms as it thinks fit, order the reinstatement of the interim authority notice pending the disposal of the appeal, or the expiry of the interim authority period, whichever occurs first.

The relevant licensing authority must not cancel an interim authority notice after an application to transfer the premises licence with a request for this to have immediate effect has been made.

12.6 REINSTATEMENT OF A LAPSED LICENCE

Where a premises licence lapses either:

• due to the death, incapacity, insolvency or change in immigration status of the holder, and no interim authority notice has been given, or one has been given but has been cancelled or withdrawn; or
• by surrender,

s.50 provides that any person who is entitled to apply for a premises licence may apply for the licence to be transferred to him, even though the licence has lapsed. If the applicant is an individual, he must be aged 18 or over. Only one application for the transfer of the premises licence may be made in these circumstances. The procedure for a transfer can be found in **Chapter 16**.

An application for transfer must be made no later than 28 days after the day on which the licence lapsed and it must include a request that the transfer has immediate effect. Where such an application is made, the premises licence is reinstated from the time the application is received by the relevant licensing authority, and the requirements of s.43 are disregarded. These requirements include obtaining, or taking reasonable steps to obtain, the consent of the holder of the premises licence. This may be difficult where the licence has lapsed and will be impossible where this is due to the death of the licence holder.

The premises licence will lapse again if and when the applicant is notified of the rejection of the application, or the application is withdrawn.

In *Beauchamp Pizza Ltd* v. *Coventry City Council* [2010] EWHC 926 (Ch); [2020] LLR 1, it was decided that following the administrative restoration of a company to the register, by virtue of the Companies Act 2006, s.1028, the company was deemed not to have been dissolved and its premises licence was therefore deemed not to have lapsed as a result of that dissolution.

CHAPTER 13

Provisional statements

13.1 INTRODUCTION

Where premises are being or are about to be constructed, or are being or about to be extended or otherwise altered in order to be used for one or more of the licensable activities, the person proposing to carry out the work may not be able or prepared to proceed until not only is he assured that the project has appropriate planning permission but also he has some degree of assurance that a premises licence would be granted for the premises when the works are completed.

A provisional statement provides no guarantee that a premises licence will be granted once the works have been completed. All it does is describe the likely effect of the intended licensable activities and indicate what the prospects of any subsequent application for a premises licence will be. Instead of applying for a provisional statement, an applicant may decide to apply for a premises licence, and there is nothing to prevent him from doing so. However, the applicant would need to have clear plans of the proposed structure and would also need to prepare an operating schedule and it might not be possible to prepare these at this early stage. If the application is then granted, the licence would not have immediate effect but the licensing authority would include in the licence the date upon which it would have effect.

A provisional statement will normally only be required when an applicant is not able to provide the plan and operating schedule required to apply for a premises licence. The Guidance provides:

> 8.91 Any person falling within section 16 of the 2003 Act can apply for a premises licence before new premises are constructed, extended or changed. This would be possible where clear plans of the proposed structure exist and the applicant is in a position to complete an operating schedule including details of:
>
> - the activities to take place there;
> - the time at which such activities will take place;
> - the proposed hours of opening;
> - where the applicant wishes the licence to have effect for a limited period, that period;

- the steps to be taken to promote the licensing objectives; and
- where the sale of alcohol is involved, whether supplies are proposed to be for consumption on or off the premises (or both) and the name of the designated premises supervisor the applicant wishes to specify.

8.92 In such cases, the licensing authority would include in the licence the date upon which it would come into effect. A provisional statement will normally only be required when the information described above is not available.

13.2 PREMISES IN RESPECT OF WHICH AN APPLICATION CAN BE MADE

A provisional statement may be applied for in respect of premises which are being or are about to be constructed, extended or otherwise altered in order to be used for one or more licensable activities (s.29(1)).

The Act does not define what is meant by 'otherwise altered'; however, the Guidance at para.8.90 states that:

the alteration must relate to the purpose of being used for one or more licensable activities.

For example, if the building has a premises licence and is to be altered to allow a previously unlicensed area to be used for a licensable activity, a provisional statement may be sought in respect of the additional area.

'Premises' include a vessel, vehicle or structure. Section 189(5) provides that the provisions in the Act relating to provisional statements do not apply in relation to a vessel, vehicle or structure to which s.189 applies. Section 189 applies to vessels, vehicles or moveable structures which are not permanently located in one place. A provisional statement cannot therefore be applied for in respect of such premises. However, if the vessel, vehicle or structure is in a permanent location it would be possible to apply for a provisional statement in respect of it.

13.3 APPLICANTS FOR PROVISIONAL STATEMENTS

Any person who is interested in the premises and who, if he is an individual, is aged 18 or over, may apply to the relevant licensing authority for a provisional statement (s.29(2)).

A 'person' in this context can be either an individual or a company. The applicant could therefore be a firm of architects or a construction company or a financier. The class of potential applicants for a provisional statement is therefore wider than those who may apply for a premises licence.

An applicant must be 'interested' in the premises. There is nothing in the Act or the Guidance to indicate what is meant by this. It is suggested that some sort of proprietary interest in the premises, for example where the applicant is the owner or tenant of the premises, would suffice but there is nothing to confine the provision to such interests. Under the previous legislation (Licensing Act 1964, s.6(1)), the phrase 'interested in the premises' was construed broadly in the circumstances of each case. A person who occupied premises but who had no interest in the land and no contract with the owner was thus able to apply for a provisional grant (see *R. v. Dudley Crown Court ex p. Pask* (1983) 143 JP 417 where Taylor J said: 'I see no reason why one should import automatically any requirement of an interest in property legal or equitable nor any requirement of any actual contractual right to operate on the premises').

13.4 APPLYING FOR A PROVISIONAL STATEMENT

In order to apply for a provisional statement, an applicant must submit the following to the relevant licensing authority:

- a completed application form;
- a schedule of works in the prescribed form (in practice this forms part of the application form) which includes:

    – a statement made by or on behalf of the applicant setting out particulars of the premises to which the application relates and of the licensable activities for which the premises are to be used;
    – plans of the work being or about to be done at the premises; and
    – such other information as may be prescribed. The prescribed form requests written details of the work being done or about to be done at the premises; and

- the prescribed fee.

13.5 THE APPLICATION FORM

An application for a provisional statement must be in the prescribed form which is set out in the Premises Licences Regulations, Sched.3.

13.5.1 Completing the application form

Guidance in completing the application form may be obtained from **www.gov.uk** or the relevant licensing authority. The form may be completed by being either typed or written legibly in block capitals. All answers must be inside the boxes and written in black ink.

In the opening statement, the name of the applicant or applicants who are applying for the provisional statement should be inserted.

The application form is then divided into five parts, as follows.

Part 1

The applicant must set out the following details of the premises:

- the postal address;
- the telephone number at the premises, if any; and
- the non-domestic rateable value of the premises.

If the premises have no postal address, the location of the premises should be described or the Ordnance Survey map reference should be given.

Part 2

Part 2 deals with details of the applicant. The applicant must state in which capacity he is applying for a premises licence, and if he is applying as an individual, a limited company, a partnership, an unincorporated association or a statutory corporation, he must confirm that he is carrying on or proposing to carry on a business which involves the use of the premises for licensable activities, or that he is making the application pursuant to a statutory function or a function discharged by virtue of Her Majesty's prerogative.

The applicant, if an individual, must then give further details such as his name and address, telephone number, email address (this is optional) and confirmation, where relevant, that he is at least 18 years old. Other applicants must give their name, address, registered number (where applicable), a description of themselves, for example partnership, company, unincorporated association, telephone number and email address (this is optional). The applicant must then state the nature of their interest in the premises.

Part 3

Part 3 contains the schedule of works. The applicant must indicate whether the premises are about to be constructed or are being extended or altered. Details must then be provided of the work and there is a reminder that a plan or plans must be attached showing the work being done or about to be done at the premises. There do not appear to be any prescribed requirements for the plans and the requirements which apply to the plan to accompany an application for a premises licence do not apply. Particulars must also be given of the premises to which the application relates, though it may be in practice that this is a repetition of the information already given in Part 1. These particulars should include the type of premises, their general situation and layout and any other information which could be relevant to the licensing objectives. Where Part 4 is also being completed and the application includes off-supplies of alcohol and the applicant intends to provide a place for these to be consumed, a description of where the place will be and its proximity to the premises must be included. Finally, the licensable activities which the premises will be used for must be specified.

Part 4

Part 4 sets out an optional operating schedule which an applicant may choose to complete if he wishes. At this early stage, it may be too soon for these details to have been finalised. See **Chapter 8** as to operating schedules. Finally there is a checklist for the applicant to complete so that nothing is overlooked, together with a warning that it is an offence, liable on conviction to a fine up to level 5 on the standard scale, under s.158 to make a false statement in or in connection with the application.

Part 5

Part 5 provides for the applicant to sign the form. The form can also be signed by the applicant's solicitor or other duly authorised agent, and someone signing on behalf of the applicant must state in what capacity they sign. Where there are joint applicants both applicants or their respective agents must sign the application form.

13.5.2 Obtaining an application form

For details on obtaining a form see **7.4.2**.

13.5.3 Making an application

The Premises Licences Regulations, reg.21 provides that an application must be made in writing. For details on how to apply electronically see **7.4.3**.

Table 13.1: Checklist for a provisional statement application

	Original to relevant licensing authority	Copy to the police	Copy to responsible authorities
Completed application form			
Plan of the premises			
Payment of the fee			
Confirmation that the application has been advertised on the premises and that this will be maintained for 28 days			
Has the application been advertised in a local newspaper?	Name of newspaper:	Date:	

13.6 ADVERTISING

The applicant must advertise his application for a provisional statement in the same way as an application for the grant of a premises licence (s.30). Thus he must display a notice at or on the premises and publish a notice in a local newspaper (see **7.6** for the specific requirements). In addition:

- the notice must state that representations are restricted after the provisional statement has been issued (see below); and
- the notice may, where they are known, contain a statement of the relevant licensable activities which it is proposed will be carried out on or from the premises (Premises Licences Regulations, reg.26(2)).

An applicant should check with the relevant licensing authority to see whether it provides a specimen form of notice to use. If not, a suggested form of notice is given in **Box 13.1**.

BOX 13.1: SUGGESTED FORM OF NOTICE OF AN APPLICATION FOR A PROVISIONAL STATEMENT

Licensing Act 2003

Notice of application for a provisional statement

Notice is hereby given that [*insert the full name of the applicant*] has applied to the [*insert the full name of the licensing authority*] on [*insert the date of application to the licensing authority*] under the Licensing Act 2003 for a provisional statement for the premises at [*insert the name and full postal address of the premises, or if no address, a description of the site*]. The proposed relevant licensable activities (where these are known) are: the provision of regulated entertainment/provision of late night refreshment/the sale by retail of alcohol [*delete the inappropriate words*]. Any person who wishes to make a representation in relation to this application must give notice in writing of his/her representation by [*insert the date by which all relevant representations must be received by the licensing authority, i.e. 28 consecutive days starting on the day after the day on which the application is given to the licensing authority*] stating the grounds for making a representation to [*insert contact details for the licensing authority*]. The public register where applications are available to be viewed by members of the public can be viewed during normal office hours at [*insert details*]. The Licensing Authority must receive representations by the date given above. The Licensing Authority will have regard to any such representation in considering the application.

Representations are restricted after the issue of a provisional statement and cannot be made to the subsequent licence application if they could have been made to the application for the provisional statement (for details see section 32 of the Licensing Act 2003).

It is an offence liable on conviction to a fine under section 158 of the Licensing Act 2003 to knowingly or recklessly make a false statement in or in connection with an application for a provisional statement.

The notice to be displayed on or at the premises must also fulfil the requirements mentioned at **7.6**.

The relevant licensing authority must also advertise the application on its website in the same way as an application for the grant of a premises licence (see **7.7**). In addition:

- the notice must state that representations are restricted after the provisional statement has been issued (see below); and
- the notice may, where they are known, contain a statement of the relevant licensable activities which it is proposed will be carried on on or from the premises (Premises Licences Regulations, reg.26C(2)).

13.7 NOTICE TO RESPONSIBLE AUTHORITIES

Where an application is made electronically and any plan or document required to accompany the application is also given electronically, the relevant licensing authority must, no later than the first working day after the application was given to it, give notice of the application to each responsible authority (see **7.8**) by giving each authority a copy of the application together with any accompanying plan or document (Premises Licences Regulations, reg.27). In all other cases, an applicant must give notice of his application for a provisional statement to each responsible authority by giving each responsible authority a copy of his application together with its accompanying documents on the same day as the day on which the application is given to the relevant licensing authority (Premises Licences Regulations, reg.27A). A responsible authority may then make representations to the relevant licensing authority about the application.

13.8 DETERMINATION OF THE APPLICATION

13.8.1 Preliminary determination

When a licensing authority receives an application for a provisional statement, it must initially determine whether the application has been made properly in accordance with the Act and with the Premises Licences Regulations. An incomplete application is invalid and will be returned to the applicant. Any failure to observe the notice requirements will also render the application invalid.

13.8.2 Unopposed applications

Where no relevant representations have been made, the licensing authority must, provided the applicant has complied with the statutory requirements as to advertising and giving notice to each responsible authority, issue a statement confirming that no relevant representations have been made (s.31(2)). This statement will be the provisional statement (s.29(3)).

13.8.3 Applications where representations have been made

Where relevant representations have been made, the licensing authority must hold a hearing, unless it is satisfied that the applicant and each person making a representation agree that a hearing is unnecessary. The hearing must be held within 20 working days beginning with the day after the end of the period during which representations may be made (Hearings Regulations, reg.5 and Sched.1, para.2). Notice of the hearing must be given to the applicant and any person who has made a relevant representation not less than 10 working days before the day or the first day on which the hearing is to be held (Hearings Regulations, reg.6(4) and Sched.2, para.2). The notice to the applicant must include a copy of the relevant representations (Hearings Regulations, reg.7(2) and Sched.3, para.2).

Following the hearing, the licensing authority must determine whether, on the basis of the representations and the application for a provisional statement, it would consider it appropriate to take any of the following steps to promote the licensing objectives if, on the work being satisfactorily completed, it had to decide whether to grant a premises licence in the form described in the application for the provisional statement:

- to grant the premises licence subject to:

  - conditions that were consistent with the applicant's operating schedule modified to such extent as the licensing authority considered appropriate for the promotion of the licensing objectives; and
  - any mandatory condition which had to be included in the premises licence;

- to exclude from the scope of the licence any of the licensable activities to which the application related;
- to refuse to specify a person in the licence as the premises supervisor; or
- to reject the application.

Work is 'satisfactorily completed' when it has been completed in a manner which substantially complies with the schedule of work accompanying the application for the provisional statement (s.29(7)).

Once it has determined the application the licensing authority must issue the applicant with a provisional statement which gives details of the determination and sets out its reasons for its decision as to the steps, if any, that it would be appropriate to take in order to promote the licensing objectives (s.31(3)(c)). The Guidance, para.8.95 states that the licensing authority should give full and comprehensive reasons for its decision as this is important in anticipation of an appeal by any aggrieved party. The licensing authority must send the provisional statement to the applicant forthwith (see **2.9**) on making its decision (Hearings Regulations, reg.28(1)). The licensing authority must also give a copy of this provisional statement to anyone who made relevant representations and the chief officer of police for each police area in which the premises are situated.

For the purposes of these provisions, 'relevant representations' means representations which:

- are about the likely effect on the licensing objectives of the grant of a premises licence in the form described in the application for the provisional statement, if the work was satisfactorily completed; and
- meet the following requirements:

    – that they were made by a responsible authority or other person at any time during the period of 28 consecutive days starting on the day after the day on which the applicant gave the application to the licensing authority;
    – that they have not been withdrawn; and
    – in the case of representations made by a person who is not a responsible authority, that they are not, in the opinion of the relevant licensing authority, frivolous or vexatious (s.31(5), (6)).

If a licensing authority decides that a representation is frivolous or vexatious, it must notify the person who made the representation of both its decision and its reasons for reaching it (s.31(7)).

The applicant for a provisional statement or anyone who has made a relevant representation may appeal against the terms of the provisional statement.

13.9 SUBSEQUENT ACTION AND RESTRICTIONS ON REPRESENTATIONS

Once a provisional statement has been issued, the works may be carried out. Once the works have been completed an application can then be made for a premises licence. Section 32 imposes restrictions on the representations which can be made in respect of this application for a premises licence.

The application for a premises licence must be for the premises or a part of them, or for premises that are substantially the same as the premises or a part of them. This allows an application to be made for a premises licence in respect of only part of the premises for which the provisional statement was issued and the restrictions will apply. The restrictions will also apply if the application is for premises that are substantially the same as the premises for which the provisional statement was issued. There is nothing in the Act or the Guidance as to the meaning of 'substantially the same'.

The restrictions on representations will apply provided:

- the application for the premises licence is in the same form as the licence described in the provisional statement;
- the work described in the schedule of works accompanying the application for that statement has been satisfactorily completed;
- given the information provided in the application for the provisional statement, the person seeking to make a representation could have made the

same, or substantially the same, representations about that application but failed, without reasonable excuse, to do so; and

- there has been no material change in circumstances relating either to the premises or to the area in the vicinity of those premises since the provisional statement was made.

It is assumed that if the application relates to different licensable activities, then it will not be in the same form as the licence described in the provisional statement. But it is not clear what the effect of a change in the details of the specified licensable activities, for example by changing the hours for the licensable activities, would be.

These provisions therefore give some comfort to the applicant as representations to the grant of a premises licence for the same or similar premises may be excluded if he can show that the objector could have made the same, or substantially the same, representations about the application for the provisional statement but failed to do so without reasonable excuse. It will be a matter for the licensing authority to determine what would be a 'reasonable excuse' in the circumstances of each case. A person may have been in hospital during the period for making representations and therefore unable to make them, for example because he was unconscious or critically ill.

In addition, an applicant will have to show that there has been no material change in circumstances relating either to the premises or to the area in the vicinity of those premises since the provisional statement was made. So if the objector could not have raised such representations at the time of the original application or if there has been a material change to the premises or the area since the provisional statement, then the representations may be made. Whether or not there has been a material change will be a question of fact for the licensing authority to decide on the facts of each case.

A provisional statement does not have a time limit on it but the longer the delay before a premises licence is applied for the greater the potential for representations not to be excluded.

13.10 POWER TO INSPECT THE PREMISES

Section 59 provides that a constable or an authorised person may, at any reasonable time before the determination of an application for a provisional statement, enter the premises to which the application relates to assess the likely effect of the grant of the application on the promotion of the licensing objectives. Anyone who intentionally obstructs an authorised person exercising the power of entry commits an offence, and is liable on summary conviction to a fine not exceeding level 2 on the standard scale.

In addition, obstructing a constable exercising the right of entry will be an offence of obstructing a constable in the execution of his duties under the Police

Act 1996, s.89(2). A person guilty of such an offence is liable on summary conviction to imprisonment for a term not exceeding one month (this will increase to 51 weeks when the Criminal Justice Act 2003 takes effect) or to a fine not exceeding level 3 on the standard scale, or to both.

CHAPTER 14

Variation of a premises licence

14.1 INTRODUCTION

It is possible for the holder of a premises licence to apply to vary their licence, for example to alter the hours of operation or the authorised licensable activities. The process to be followed will depend on the nature of the variation and its potential impact on the licensing objectives.

There are simplified processes for making application in the following cases:

- a change of the name or address of a person named in a premises licence (s.33) (see **14.4**);
- an application to vary a premises licence to specify a new individual as the designated premises supervisor (s.37) (see **9.4**);
- a request to be removed as the designated premises supervisor (s.41) (see **9.6**);
- an application in relation to a premises licence in respect of community premises that authorises the sale of alcohol to disapply the mandatory conditions concerning the supervision of alcohol sales by a personal licence holder and the need for a designated premises supervisor who holds a personal licence (ss.25A and 41D) (see **7.11.3**); and
- an application for a minor variation of a premises licence (ss.41A to 41C).

All other changes to a premises licence require an application to vary under s.34. A premises licence cannot be varied under s.34 so as to extend the period for which the licence has effect, to transfer the licence from one holder to another or to transfer the licence from one premises to another. If such changes are required, an application must be made for a new premises licence under s.17 or an application to transfer the licence to another holder under s.42.

A licensing authority may also vary a premises licence so that it has effect subject to different conditions in respect of different parts of the premises or different licensable activities.

14.2 APPLYING FOR A MINOR VARIATION

The holder of a premises licence may at any time apply to the relevant licensing authority under s.41A for a minor variation to the premises licence. A minor variation is one which could not impact adversely on the licensing objectives.

The Guidance at para.8.61 provides that:

> Minor variations will generally fall into four categories: minor changes to the structure or layout of premises; small adjustments to licensing hours; the removal of out of date, irrelevant or unenforceable conditions or addition of volunteered conditions; and the addition of certain licensable activities. In all cases the overall test is whether the proposed variation could impact adversely on any of the four licensing objectives.

An application may not be made under s.41A to vary a premises licence so as to:

- extend the period for which the premises licence has effect;
- vary substantially the premises to which the premises licence relates (whether an intended variation will 'substantially' vary will be a question of fact in each case);
- specify an individual as the designated premises supervisor;
- add the supply of alcohol as an activity authorised by the premises licence;
- authorise the supply of alcohol at any time between 11 pm and 7 am;
- authorise an increase in the amount of time on any day during which alcohol may be sold by retail or supplied; or
- include in a premises licence in respect of community premises that authorises the sale of alcohol a condition that every supply of alcohol must be made or authorised by the management committee.

An applicant for a minor variation must submit the following to the relevant licensing authority:

- a completed application form;
- a plan, if appropriate, of the premises in scale (1 mm to 100 mm), unless otherwise agreed with the licensing authority;
- the premises licence, or the appropriate part of it, or if that is not practicable, a statement of the reasons why it cannot be provided; and
- the prescribed fee.

14.2.1 Application form

An application for a minor variation must be made in the prescribed form which is set out in the Premises Licences Regulations, Sched.4B.

14.2.2 Completing the application form

Guidance on completing the application form may be obtained from **www.gov.uk** or the relevant licensing authority. The form may be completed by being either typed or written legibly in block capitals. All answers must be inside the boxes and written in black ink.

In the opening statement, the name of the applicant or applicants who are applying for the variation should be inserted.

The application form is then divided into five parts, as follows.

Part 1

The applicant must set out the following details of the premises:

- the postal address, including the post town and the postcode;
- the telephone number at the premises, if any;
- a premises licence number; and
- a brief description of the premises.

If the premises have no postal address, the location of the premises should be described or the Ordnance Survey map reference should be given.

The brief description of the premises should include the type of premises, their general situation and layout and any other information which could be relevant to the licensing objectives. This should include any activities in or associated with the use of the premises which may give rise to concern in respect of children regardless of whether it is intended that children have access to the premises, for example (but not exclusively) nudity or semi-nudity, films for restricted age groups, the presence of gaming machines, etc.

Part 2

Part 2 deals with the details of the applicant. The applicant must give such details as his address, if this is not the same as the premises address, a contact telephone number during working hours, and an email address (this is optional).

Part 3

Part 3 deals with the proposed variation. The applicant must indicate whether he wants the proposed variation to have effect as soon as possible, or if not, from when he wants it to take effect. The applicant must also indicate whether the proposed variation is to have effect in relation to the introduction of the late night levy (no fee is payable if the only purpose of the variation is to avoid becoming liable to the late night levy). The applicant must then describe the nature of the proposed variation(s) and explain why he considers that the proposed variation(s) could not have an adverse effect on the promotion of any of the licensing objectives. This should include whether new or increased levels of licensable activities will be taking place indoors or outdoors (indoors may include a tent). Failure to provide sufficient information may lead to the application being refused. The applicant should cover each of the licensing objectives and state why he thinks there could be no adverse impact on that objective.

Relevant information to include in relation to variations to the licensable activities and the licensing activities will include:

- whether new or increased levels of licensable activities will be taking place indoors or outdoors (indoors may include a tent);
- relevant further details, for example whether music will be amplified or unamplified;
- standard days and timing when the activity will take place, including start and finish times;
- any seasonal variations in timings, e.g. additional days during the summer; and
- non-standard timings, e.g. where the applicant wishes the activity to go on longer on a particular day such as Christmas Eve.

The Guidance provides:

> 8.64 An application to remove a licensable activity should normally be approved as a minor variation. Variations to add the sale by retail or supply of alcohol to a licence are excluded from the minor variations process and must be treated as full variations in all cases.
>
> 8.65 For other licensable activities, licensing authorities will need to consider each application on a case by case basis and in light of any licence conditions put forward by the applicant.

Where the application is to vary the layout of the premises, a revised plan must be included.

The Guidance provides:

> 8.62 Many small variations to layout will have no adverse impact on the licensing objectives. However, changes to layout should be referred to the full variation process if they could potentially have an adverse impact on the promotion of the licensing objectives, for example by:
>
> - increasing the capacity for drinking on the premises;
> - affecting access between the public part of the premises and the rest of the premises or the street or public way, for instance, block emergency exits or routes to emergency exits; or
> - impeding the effective operation of a noise reduction measure such as an acoustic lobby.
>
> 8.63 Licensing authorities will also need to consider the combined effect of a series of applications for successive small layout changes (for example, as part of a rolling refurbishment of premises) which in themselves may not be significant, but which cumulatively may impact adversely on the licensing objectives. This emphasises the importance of having an up-to-date copy of the premises plan available.

The minor variation process may be used to remove conditions which are out of date or invalid and to revise conditions which are unclear (as long as the intention and effect remain the same), for example there may be no need for door supervision if a bar has been converted into a restaurant. It can also be used to add a new condition volunteered by the applicant or mutually agreed between the applicant and a responsible authority, such as the police or the environmental health authority (subject to impact on the licensing objectives). A licensing authority cannot impose its own conditions and if it considers that the proposed variation would impact adversely on the licensing objectives unless conditions are imposed, the application should be refused.

In relation to volunteered conditions, the Guidance at para.8.71 provides:

> For instance, there may be circumstances when the licence holder and a responsible authority such as the police or environmental health authority, agree that a new condition should be added to the licence (for example, that a nightclub adds the provision of door staff to its licence). Such a change would not normally impact adversely on the licensing objectives and could be expected to promote them by preventing crime and disorder or public nuisance. In these circumstances, the minor variation process may provide a less costly and onerous means of amending the licence than a review, with no risk to the licensing objectives. However, this route should only be used where the agreed variations are minor and the licence holder and the responsible authority have come to a genuine agreement. The licensing authority should be alive to any attempts to pressure licence or certificate holders into agreeing to new conditions where there is no evidence of a problem at the premises and, if there is any doubt, should discuss this with the relevant parties.

Changes in legislation may invalidate certain conditions and the Guidance at para.8.73 provides:

> Although the conditions do not have to be removed from the licence, licence holders and licensing authorities may agree that this is desirable to clarify the licence holder's legal obligations. There may also be cases where it is appropriate to revise the wording of a condition that is unclear or unenforceable. This would be acceptable as a minor variation as long as the purpose of the condition and its intended effect remain unchanged. Such a change could be expected to promote the licensing objectives by making it easier for the licence holder to understand and comply with the condition and easier for the licensing authority to enforce it.

Where the variation is to the opening hours, details of any changes to the hours when the premises are open to the public should be included. The Guidance provides:

8.66 Variations to the following are excluded from the minor variations process and must be treated as full variations in all cases:

- to extend licensing hours for the sale or supply of alcohol for consumption on or off the premises between the hours of 23.00 and 07.00; or
- to increase the amount of time on any day during which alcohol may be sold or supplied for consumption on or off the premises.

8.67 Applications to reduce licensing hours for the sale or supply of alcohol or, in some cases, to move (without increasing) the licensed hours between 07.00 and 23.00 will normally be processed as minor variations.

8.68   Applications to vary the time during which other licensable activities take place should be considered on a case-by-case basis with reference to the likely impact on the licensing objectives.

Part 4

Part 4 deals with the operating schedule and an applicant must tick those parts which would be subject to change if the application is successful. The applicant must confirm that the premises licence or relevant part and a copy of the plan (where the proposed variation will affect the layout) have been enclosed. If the premises licence, relevant part or plan cannot be enclosed with the application, an explanation must be given. There is space for the applicant to provide any further information to support the claim that the proposed variation is minor and could not have an adverse impact on the promotion of the licensing objectives. Finally, there is a checklist for the applicant to complete so that nothing is overlooked, together with a warning that it is an offence, liable on conviction to a fine up to level 5 on the standard scale, under s.158 to make a false statement in or in connection with the application.

Part 5

Part 5 provides for the applicant to sign the form. The form can also be signed by the applicant's solicitor or other duly authorised agent and someone signing on behalf of the applicant must state in what capacity they sign. Where there are joint applicants, both applicants or their respective agents must sign the application form.

14.2.3   Obtaining an application form

For details on obtaining a form, see **7.4.2**.

14.2.4   Making an application

The Premises Licences Regulations, reg.21 provides that an application must be made in writing. For information on submitting the form electronically, see **7.4.3**.

14.2.5   Advertising an application for a minor variation

The application must be advertised in accordance with the Premises Licences Regulations, reg.26A by displaying a notice at or on the premises for a continuous period beginning on the first working day after the application was given to the relevant licensing authority and ending at the expiry of the ninth consecutive working day after that day.

The notice must be:

- white;
- of a size equal to or larger than A4;
- printed legibly in black ink or typed in black.

The notice must include the following information:

- at or near the top of the notice the heading 'Licensing Act 2003: Minor Variation of Premises Licence';
- a brief description of the proposed variation or variations;
- the name of the applicant;
- the postal address of the premises, if any, or if there is no postal address for the premises a description of those premises sufficient to enable the location and extent of the premises to be identified;
- the postal address and, where applicable, the worldwide web address where the register of the relevant licensing authority is kept and where and when the record of the application may be inspected;
- the date by which a person may make representations to the relevant licensing authority; and
- that it is an offence knowingly or recklessly to make a false statement in connection with an application and the maximum fine for which a person is liable on summary conviction for the offence.

The information referred to in the first bullet point above must be printed or typed in a font of a size equal to or larger than 32 points. The remainder of the notice must be printed or typed in a font of a size equal to or larger than 16 points.

The notice must be displayed prominently at or on the premises to which the application relates so that it can be conveniently read from the exterior of the premises. Where any part of the external perimeter of the premises is 100 or more metres in length and abuts a public highway or other place accessible by the public, a notice must be displayed every 50 metres along that part of the perimeter.

An applicant should check with the relevant licensing authority to see whether it provides a specimen form of notice to use. If not, a suggested form of notice is as shown in **Box 14.1**.

BOX 14.1: SUGGESTED FORM OF NOTICE OF APPLICATION FOR A MINOR VARIATION TO A PREMISES LICENCE

Licensing Act 2003

Notice of application to vary a premises licence

PREMISES: [insert name and address of premises]

Notice is hereby given that [*insert the full name of the applicant*] has applied to the [*insert the full name of the licensing authority*] on [*insert the date of application to the licensing authority*] for a minor variation to a premises licence under the Licensing Act 2003.

The proposed variation is: [*set out details of the proposed variation*].

Anyone who wishes to make representations in relation to this application for a minor variation must give notice in writing by [*insert the date by which all relevant representations must be received by the licensing authority, i.e. 10 working days after the day on which the application is received by the licensing authority*] to [*insert contact details for the licensing authority*].

The public register where applications are available to be viewed by members of the public can be viewed during normal office hours at [*insert details*].

It is an offence liable on conviction to a fine under section 158 of the Licensing Act 2003 to knowingly or recklessly make a false statement in or in connection with this application.

14.2.6 Notice to responsible authorities of a minor variation

Where an application is made electronically and any plan or document required to accompany the application is also given electronically, the relevant licensing authority must, no later than the first working day after the application was given to it, give notice of the application to each responsible authority by giving each authority a copy of the application together with any accompanying plan or document (Premises Licences Regulations, reg.27).

Where an application is not made electronically, the applicant must give notice of his application to each responsible authority by giving each authority a copy of the application together with its accompanying plan, document or other information on the same day as the day on which the application is given to the relevant licensing authority (Premises Licences Regulations, reg.27A).

14.2.7 Determination of an application for a minor variation

Where a licensing authority is determining an application for a minor variation, it must consult such of the responsible authorities as it considers appropriate, and take into account any relevant representations made by those authorities or made by any other person and received by the licensing authority within 10 working days beginning on the first working day after the day on which the licensing authority received the application for the minor variation (s.41B(2)). In this context, relevant representations are those which are about the likely effect of the grant of the application on the promotion of the licensing objectives (s.41B(10)). There is no right to a hearing, but the licensing authority must take any representations into account in arriving at a decision.

If the licensing authority considers that the variation proposed in the application could not have an adverse effect on the promotion of any of the licensing objectives, or if more than one variation is proposed, none of them, whether considered separately or together could have such an effect, it must grant the application (s.41B(3)). In any other case, the licensing authority must reject the application (s.41B(4)). The test as to whether or not the application could have an adverse effect on the promotion of any of the licensing objectives is a strict one and where there is any doubt the licensing authority must reject the application.

The Guidance at para.8.55 provides that:

> On receipt of an application for a minor variation, the licensing authority must consider whether the variation could impact adversely on the licensing objectives. It is recommended that decisions on minor variations should be delegated to licensing officers.

A licensing authority must make a decision on an application for a minor variation within a period of 15 working days beginning on the first working day after the day on which the licensing authority received the application for the minor variation (s.41B(5)). As other persons have 10 working days from the day after the application is received by the licensing authority to submit representations, the licensing authority must wait until this period has elapsed before determining the application, but must do so at the latest within 15 working days, beginning on the first working day after the authority received the application.

If the licensing authority does not make a determination within the 15 working day period, the application is rejected and the licensing authority must forthwith return the fee that accompanied the application (s.41B(6)). Any fee may be recovered as a debt due to the applicant (s.41B(9)). Notwithstanding this, a licensing authority, with the agreement of the applicant, can treat a rejected application as a new application and treat the appropriate fee originally submitted as a fee for the new application (s.41B(7)). Such a new application will be treated as having been made on the date of the agreement, or on such other date as is specified in the agreement (s.41B(8)).

14.2.8 Notification of a decision relating to a minor variation

Where an application for a minor variation is granted, the licensing authority must forthwith (see **2.9**) give notice of this to the applicant (s.41C(1)).

The notice must specify any variation of the premises licence which is to have effect as a result of the grant of the application, and the time at which that variation takes effect (s.41C(2)). The time specified is the time specified in the application or, if that time is before the applicant is given notice of the decision, such later time as the licensing authority specifies in the notice (s.41C(3)).

Where an application for a minor variation is rejected, the licensing authority must forthwith (see **2.9**) give notice of this to the applicant and such notice must include a statement of the reasons for the licensing authority's decision (s.41C(4), (5)).

14.2.9 Appeal

There is no right of appeal against a decision in relation to a minor variation. However, where an application is refused, it may be resubmitted through the full variation process.

14.3 APPLYING FOR A FULL VARIATION

The holder of a premises licence may at any time apply to the relevant licensing authority to vary the premises licence. Section 34 provides that an applicant for a variation must submit the following to the relevant licensing authority:

- a completed application form;
- the premises licence, or the appropriate part of it, or if that is not practicable, a statement of the reasons why it cannot be provided; and
- the prescribed fee.

14.3.1 The application form

An application for a variation must be in the prescribed form which is set out in the Premises Licences Regulations, Sched.4.

14.3.2 Completing the application form

Guidance in completing the application form may be obtained from **www.gov.uk** or the relevant licensing authority. The form may be completed by being either typed or written legibly in block capitals. All answers must be inside the boxes and written in black ink.

In the opening statement, the name of the applicant or applicants who are applying for the variation and the premises licence number should be inserted.

The application form is then divided into five parts, as follows.

Part 1

The applicant must set out the following details of the premises:

- the postal address;
- the telephone number at the premises, if any; and
- the non-domestic rateable value of the premises.

If the premises have no postal address, the location of the premises should be described or the Ordnance Survey map reference should be given.

The non-domestic rateable value of the premises will determine the fee to be paid for the variation. The non-domestic rateable value is based on the annual rent that the premises could have been let for on the open market at a particular date. It can be checked on the Valuation Office Agency website (**www.voa.gov.uk**).

Part 2

Part 2 deals with the details of the applicant. The applicant must give such details as his address, if this is not the same as the premises address, a daytime contact telephone number and an email address (this is optional).

Part 3

Part 3 deals with the proposed variation. The applicant must indicate whether he wants the proposed variation to have effect as soon as possible, or if not, from when he wants it to take effect. The applicant must indicate whether the proposed variation is to have effect in relation to the introduction of the late night levy (no fee is payable if the only purpose of the variation is to avoid becoming liable to the late night levy). The applicant must then briefly describe the nature of the proposed variation. This description should include a description of the premises, for example the type of premises, its general situation and layout and any other information which could be relevant to the licensing objectives. Where the application includes off-supplies of alcohol and the applicant intends to provide a place for consumption of these off-supplies he must include a description of where the place will be and its proximity to the premises. If the variation would result in 5,000 or more people attending the premises at any one time, the applicant must state the number expected to attend.

Part 4

Part 4 is the operating schedule and an applicant must complete those parts which would be subject to change if the application is successful. The applicant must also identify any existing conditions which he believes could be removed if the variation is approved. If the premises licence, or relevant part, cannot be enclosed with the application, an explanation must be given. The applicant must then describe any additional steps he intends to take to promote the four licensing objectives as a result of the proposed variation. Finally there is a checklist for the applicant to complete so that nothing is overlooked, together with a warning that it is an offence, liable on conviction to a fine up to level 5 on the standard scale, under s.158 to make a false statement in or in connection with the application.

Part 5

Part 5 provides for the applicant to sign the form. The form can also be signed by the applicant's solicitor or other duly authorised agent and, someone signing on behalf of the applicant must state in what capacity they sign. Where there are joint applicants, both applicants or their respective agents must sign the application form.

14.3.3 Obtaining an application form

For details of obtaining a form, see **7.4.2**.

14.3.4 Making an application

The Premises Licences Regulations, reg.21 provides that an application must be made in writing. For information on submitting the form electronically, see **7.4.3**.

14.3.5 Advertising of the application by the applicant

The application (except where the only variation sought is the inclusion of the condition that every supply of alcohol under the licence must be made or authorised by the management committee) must be advertised in accordance with the Premises Licences Regulations, reg.25 (s.17(5)) by displaying a notice at or on the premises and by publishing a notice in a local newspaper.

An applicant must advertise his application by displaying a notice containing prescribed information on the premises for a period of not less than 28 consecutive days starting on the day after the day on which the application was given to the relevant licensing authority.

The notice must be:

- of a size equal to or larger than A4;
- of a pale blue colour; and
- printed legibly in black ink or typed in black in a font of a size equal to or larger than 16 points.

The notice must be displayed prominently at or on the premises to which the application relates where it can be conveniently read from the exterior of the premises. Where the premises cover an area of more than 50 metres square, a further notice in the same form and subject to the same requirements must be displayed every 50 metres along the external perimeter of the premises abutting any highway.

An applicant must publish a notice containing prescribed information in a local newspaper or, if there is none, in a local newsletter, circular or similar document, circulating in the vicinity of the premises on at least one occasion during the 10 working days starting on the day after the day on which the application was given to the relevant licensing authority.

The contents of the notices to be displayed at or on the premises and to be published in a local newspaper are specified in the Premises Licences Regulations, reg.26. The notices must:

- briefly describe the proposed variation;
- state the name of the applicant;

- state the postal address of the premises, if any, or if there is no postal address for the premises a description of those premises sufficient to enable the location and extent of the premises to be identified;
- state the postal address and, where applicable, the worldwide web address where the register of the relevant licensing authority is kept and where and when the record of the application may be inspected;
- state the date by which a responsible authority or any other person may make representations to the relevant licensing authority;
- state that representations shall be made in writing; and
- state that it is an offence knowingly or recklessly to make a false statement in connection with an application and the maximum fine for which a person is liable on summary conviction for the offence.

An applicant should check with the relevant licensing authority to see whether it provides a specimen form of notice to use. If not, a suggested form of notice is shown in **Box 14.2**.

BOX 14.2: SUGGESTED FORM OF NOTICE OF APPLICATION TO VARY A PREMISES LICENCE

Licensing Act 2003

Notice of application to vary a premises licence

PREMISES: [*insert name and address of premises*]

Notice is hereby given that [*insert the full name of the applicant*] has applied to the [*insert the full name of the licensing authority*] on [*insert the date of application to the licensing authority*] to vary a premises licence under the Licensing Act 2003.

The proposed variation is: [*set out details of the proposed variation*].

Anyone who wishes to make representations in relation to this application must give notice in writing by [*insert the date the by which all relevant representations must be received by the licensing authority, i.e. 28 consecutive days starting on the day after the day on which the application is given to the licensing authority*] to [*insert contact details for the licensing authority*].

The public register where applications are available to be viewed by members of the public can be viewed during normal office hours at [*insert details*].

The Licensing Authority must receive representations by the date given above. The Licensing Authority will have regard to any such representation in considering the application.

It is an offence liable on conviction under section 158 of the Licensing Act 2003 to knowingly or recklessly make a false statement in or in connection with this application.

14.3.6 Advertising of the application by the licensing authority

The application (except where the only variation sought is the inclusion of the condition that every supply of alcohol under the licence must be made or authorised by the management committee) must be advertised by the relevant licensing authority in accordance with of the Premises Licences Regulations, reg.26B for a period of no less than 28 consecutive days starting on the day after the day on which the application was given to the relevant licensing authority by publishing a notice on its website.

The contents of the notice are specified in the Premises Licences Regulations, reg.26C. The notice must:

- briefly describe the proposed variation;
- state the name of the applicant;
- state the postal address of the premises, if any, or if there is no postal address for the premises a description of those premises sufficient to enable the location and extent of the premises to be identified;
- state the postal address and, where applicable, the worldwide web address where the register of the relevant licensing authority is kept and where and when the record of the application may be inspected;
- state the date by which a responsible authority or any other person may make representations to the relevant licensing authority;
- state that representations shall be made in writing; and
- state that it is an offence knowingly or recklessly to make a false statement in connection with an application and the maximum fine for which a person is liable on summary conviction for the offence.

14.3.7 Notice to responsible authorities

Where an application is made electronically and any plan or document required to accompany the application is also given electronically, the relevant licensing authority must, no later than the first working day after the application was given to it, give notice of the application to each responsible authority by giving each authority a copy of the application together with any accompanying plan or document (Premises Licences Regulations, reg.27).

Where an application is not made electronically, the applicant must give notice of his application to each responsible authority by giving each authority a copy of the application together with its accompanying plan, document or other information on the same day as the day on which the application is given to the relevant licensing authority (Premises Licences Regulations, reg.27A).

14.3.8 Determination of the application

Preliminary determination

When a licensing authority receives an application for a variation, it must initially determine whether the application has been made properly in accordance with the Act and the Premises Licences Regulations. The Guidance at para.8.26 gives recommendations for licensing authorities where applications contain errors (see **7.4.3**). Any failure to observe the notice requirements will also render the application invalid.

Unopposed applications

Where a licensing authority has received an application to vary a premises licence and is satisfied that the applicant has complied with all the procedural requirements, and no relevant representations have been received there is no need for a hearing and it must grant the application (s.35(2)).

Applications where representations have been made

Where relevant representations are made, the licensing authority must hold a hearing to consider them, unless the licensing authority, the applicant and each person who has made such representations agree that a hearing is unnecessary (s.35(3)(a)). A hearing must be held within 20 working days beginning with the day after the end of the period during which representations may be made (Hearings Regulations, reg.5 and Sched.1, para.3). Notice of the hearing must be given to the applicant and persons who have made relevant representations no later than 10 working days before the day or the first day on which the hearing is to be held (Hearings Regulations, reg.6(4) and Sched.2, para.3). The applicant must be sent the relevant representations with the notice of hearing (Hearings Regulations, reg.7(2) and Sched.3, para.3).

If relevant representations are not received by the due date, the application must be granted, even if the licensing authority has failed to carry out a proper notification process (*R. (on the application of Albert Court Residents' Association)* v. *Westminster City Council* [2011] EWCA Civ 430; [2012] PTSR 604). The only remedy available to those who have not been properly consulted will be to apply for a review of the licence under s.51.

The hearing should focus only on the steps needed to promote the particular licensing objective which has given rise to the representation. Following the hearing the licensing authority may, having regard to the representations, modify the conditions of the licence, or reject the whole or part of the application, as it considers appropriate for the promotion of the licensing objectives (s.35(3)(b), (4)). The conditions are treated as being modified if any of them is altered or omitted or any new condition is added. The premises licence may be varied in such a way so that it has effect subject to different conditions in respect of different parts of the premises or different licensable activities (s.36(7)). If the licensing authority does not consider that any steps are necessary, it can grant the variation in accordance with the application.

Where relevant representations are received the licensing authority can liaise with the applicant and persons who have made relevant representations to see whether a compromise can be reached (*Taylor* v. *Manchester City Council* [2012] EWHC 3467 (Admin); [2013] 2 All ER 490).

For these purposes, 'relevant representations' means representations which:

- are about the likely effect of the grant of the application on the promotion of the licensing objectives;
- are made by a responsible authority or other person within the prescribed period for making them;
- have not been withdrawn; and
- in the case of representations made by a person who is not a responsible authority, are not, in the opinion of the relevant licensing authority, frivolous or vexatious.

When considering an application, the licensing authority must take into account the mandatory conditions which must be attached to a premises licence (s.35(7)).

Section 36(6) prevents a licensing authority from varying a premises licence so as to extend the period of its duration or from making a substantial variation in respect of the premises to which the licence relates.

14.3.9 Notification of a decision

When an application is granted either in whole or in part, the licensing authority must forthwith (see **2.9**) give notice of this to:

- the applicant:
- any person who made relevant representations in respect of the application; and
- the chief officer of police for the police area, or each police area, in which the premises are situated (s.36(1)).

If relevant representations were made in respect of the application, the notice must state the licensing authority's reasons for its decision as to any steps to be taken for the promotion of the licensing objectives.

The notice must also specify the time when the variation is to take effect (s.36(3)). This will be the time specified in the application if this is after the date when the applicant is given the notice, otherwise it will be such later time as the relevant licensing authority specifies in the notice.

Where an application, or any part of it, is rejected, the licensing authority must forthwith (see **2.9**) give a notice stating its reasons for rejecting the application to:

- the applicant;
- any person who made relevant representations in respect of the application; and
- the chief officer of police for the police area, or each police area, in which the premises are situated (s.36(4)).

Where the licensing authority decides that any representations are frivolous or vexatious, it must notify the person who made them of the reasons for its decision (s.36(5)).

14.3.10 Appeals

An applicant for a variation may appeal against a decision to reject either the whole or part of his application, or against a decision to modify the conditions of the premises licence. A person who made relevant representations may appeal on the ground that a variation should not have been made or that the licensing authority ought not to have modified the conditions of the premises licence or should have modified them differently. Any appeal must be brought within 21 days beginning with the day on which the appellant was notified of the licensing authority of its decision.

14.4 CHANGE OF NAME OR ADDRESS

Section 33 provides that the holder of a premises licence must, as soon as is reasonably practicable, notify the relevant licensing authority of any change in either his name or address. He must also, as soon as is reasonably practicable, notify the relevant licensing authority of any change in the name or address of the designated premises supervisor unless the designated premises supervisor has already notified the authority. Where the designated premises supervisor under a premises licence is not the holder of the licence, he may notify the relevant licensing authority of any change in his name or address and, if he does, he must, as soon as is reasonably practicable, give the holder of the premises licence a copy of that notice.

In all cases the notification to the relevant licensing authority must be accompanied by the prescribed fee and the premises licence, or the appropriate part of the licence, or, if that is not practicable, by a statement of the reasons for the failure to produce the licence or part.

A person commits an offence if he fails, without reasonable excuse, to comply with these requirements, and a person guilty of this offence is liable on summary conviction to a fine not exceeding level 2 on the standard scale.

CHAPTER 15

Review of a premises licence

15.1 INTRODUCTION

The Act provides a procedure whereby a premises licence can be reviewed at any time on the application of a responsible authority or any other person because of a matter arising at the premises in connection with any of the licensing objectives. This is necessary as otherwise there would be no other opportunity to deal with problems which might arise during the currency of the licence. The Guidance at para.11.1 provides that:

> The proceedings set out in the 2003 Act for reviewing premises licences and club premises certificates represent a key protection for the community where problems associated with the licensing objectives occur after the grant or variation of a premises licence or club premises certificate.

A review of a premises licence will also take place following a closure order or an illegal working compliance order (see **24.3**).

There is also an additional power of summary review which was introduced by the Violent Crime Reduction Act 2006 (see **15.12**). This allows the police to seek an expedited review of a premises licence which authorises the sale of alcohol where the premises are associated with serious crime and disorder. The licensing authority has the power to take interim steps, such as the imposition of additional conditions, pending the determination of the review.

15.2 WHO CAN APPLY FOR A REVIEW?

At any time a responsible authority or any other person may apply to the relevant licensing authority for a review of the licence (s.51). An application for review must relate to the licensing objectives in respect of specific premises rather than general problems in a locality. However, an application for a review need not be the first step where problems arise and it is suggested that it would be good practice for licence holders to be given early warning of any concerns about problems identified at the premises concerned and of the need for improvement. Failure to respond to such warnings would then lead to a decision to request a review.

A licensing authority cannot initiate a review. However, where a local authority is both the relevant licensing authority and a responsible authority, it may, in its capacity as a responsible authority, apply for a review of a premises licence and, in its capacity as licensing authority, determine the application (s.53). For example, an environmental health officer may request a review on a matter which relates to the promotion of one or more of the licensing objectives. In *Khan* v. *Coventry Magistrates' Court* [2011] EWCA Civ 751; (2011) 175 JP 429, where the application for a review was made by the city council, as a responsible authority, to its own licensing committee, as the local licensing authority, Moore-Bick LJ said (at [10]): 'Although such a procedure may seem strange, it is expressly provided for by section 53 of the Act.' Notwithstanding this it may be possible to challenge an application for review by a local authority under the Human Rights Act 1998, Sched.1, art.6 (entitlement to a fair hearing before an independent and partial tribunal) though it is suggested that the licensee's right of appeal to the magistrates' court would rectify a possible breach of art.6.

15.3 WHEN CAN AN APPLICATION BE MADE?

An application for a review may be made at any time where a premises licence has effect (s.51(1)). It is clear that an application can be made at any time as the Guidance at para.11.2 states:

> At any stage, following the grant of a premises licence or club premises certificate, a responsible authority, or any other person, may ask the licensing authority to review the licence or certificate because of a matter arising at the premises in connection with any of the four licensing objectives.

15.4 MAKING AN APPLICATION

An application for a review of a premises licence must be made to the relevant licensing authority (s.51(1)). There is no fee payable for a review.

A copy of the application must also be sent to the holder of the premises licence and each of the responsible authorities (see **15.5.4**). The application must also be advertised (see **15.6**).

15.5 THE APPLICATION FORM

An application for a review must be in the prescribed form which is set out in the Premises Licences Regulations, Sched.8.

15.5.1 Completing the application form

Guidance in completing the application form may be obtained from **www.gov.uk** or the relevant licensing authority. The form may be completed by being either typed or written legibly in block capitals. All answers must be inside the boxes and written in black ink.

In the opening statement, the name of the applicant or applicants who are applying for the review should be inserted.

The application form is then divided into three parts.

Part 1

The applicant must set out the postal address of the premises. If the premises have no postal address, the location of the premises should be described or the Ordnance Survey map reference should be given. The name of the premises licence holder and the number of the premises licence should then be given, if these are known.

Part 2

Part 2 deals with the details of the applicant and the reason for the review. The applicant must state whether he is an individual, body or business which is not a responsible authority, or a responsible authority. An individual applicant must then give such details as his name and address, telephone number, email address (optional) and confirmation that he is at least 18 years old. Other applicants must give their name and address, telephone number and email address (optional). A responsible authority must give its name and address, telephone number and email address (optional).

The applicant must then state which of the licensing objectives the application relates to, state the grounds for review and provide as much information as possible to support the application, such as details of problems which have occurred.

The form also asks whether the applicant has applied for a review in relation to the premises before and, if so, the date of that application.

If the applicant has made representations before in relation to the premises he must set them out and when they were made.

Part 2 also includes a checklist for the applicant so that nothing is overlooked, together with a warning that it is an offence, liable on conviction to a fine up to level 5 on the standard scale, under s.158 to make a false statement in or in connection with the application.

Part 3

Part 3 provides for the applicant to sign the form. The form can also be signed by the applicant's solicitor or other duly authorised agent, and someone signing on behalf of the applicant must state in what capacity they sign. Where there are joint applicants, both applicants or their respective agents must sign the application form.

15.5.2 Obtaining an application form

A relevant licensing authority must provide an applicant on request with a printed application form; however, an electronic version may be provided by a licensing authority on its website which a prospective applicant can download, print off and complete. An electronic copy is also provided on **www.gov.uk**.

15.5.3 Making an application

The Premises Licences Regulations, reg.21 provides that an application must be made in writing. However, notwithstanding this requirement, reg.21B provides that an application can also be made electronically provided:

- the text of the application is transmitted by electronic means, is capable of being accessed by the recipient, is clear and legible in all material respects and is capable of being read and reproduced in written form and used for subsequent reference by the recipient;
- the person to whom the application is to be given has agreed in advance that an application may be given by electronic means; and
- forthwith on sending the text of the application by electronic means, the application is given to the recipient in writing (but the recipient may agree in advance that the application need not be given in writing).

Where the text of the application is transmitted by electronic means, the giving of the application shall be effected at the time the first two sets of the above requirements are satisfied, provided that where any application is required to be accompanied by a plan or other document or information that application shall not be treated as given until the plan or other document or information has been received by the recipient. This means that where additional documentation is required the electronic transmission is not effective until that additional documentation is received by the recipient.

An application for review is outside the formal electronic application process and may not be submitted via **www.gov.uk** or a licensing authority's electronic facility.

15.5.4 Notice to responsible authorities and licence holder

The applicant must give a copy of the application form together with any accompanying documents to each responsible authority and to the holder of the premises licence on the same day as it is given to the licensing authority (Premises Licences Regulations, regs.27A and 29). It must also be advertised (see **15.6**). A responsible authority or any other person may then make a representation to the licensing authority within the period of 28 days starting on the day after the day on which the application for review was given to the licensing authority (Premises Licences Regulations, reg.22(1)(b)).

15.6 ADVERTISING THE APPLICATION

The Premises Licences Regulations, regs.38 and 39 set out the requirements for advertising the application. Once a licensing authority has received an application for review, it must advertise the application by displaying prominently for a period of no less than 28 consecutive days starting on the day after the day on which the application was given to the licensing authority a notice which is:

- of a size equal to or larger than A4;
- of a pale blue colour; and
- printed legibly in black ink or typed in black in a font of a size equal to or larger than 16 points.

The notice must be displayed:

- at, on or near the site of the premises to which the application relates where it can conveniently be read from the exterior of the premises by the public and in the case of a premises covering an area of more than 50 metres square, one further notice in the same form and subject to the same requirements shall be displayed every 50 metres along the external perimeter of the premises abutting any highway; and
- at the offices, or the main offices, of the licensing authority in a central and conspicuous place.

If the licensing authority has a website which it uses to advertise applications it receives, then a notice of the application for review must also be published on that website.

The notices displayed on the premises and on the website must state:

- the address of the premises about which an application for a review has been made;
- the dates between which responsible authorities and any other persons may make representations to the relevant licensing authority;
- the grounds of the application for review;
- the postal address and, where relevant, the worldwide web address where the register of the relevant licensing authority is kept and where and when the grounds for the review may be inspected; and
- that it is an offence knowingly or recklessly to make a false statement in connection with an application and the maximum fine for which a person is liable on summary conviction for the offence.

15.7 REJECTION OF THE APPLICATION

A licensing authority which receives an application for a review must initially consider whether the grounds for review stated in the application are relevant to the licensing objectives. Any ground for review specified in the application may, at any time, be rejected by the licensing authority if it is satisfied that the ground is not relevant to one or more of the licensing objectives, or, in the case of an application made by a person other than a responsible party, that the ground is frivolous or vexatious, or is a repetition (s.51(4)).

A ground will not be relevant if it does not relate to one or more of the licensing objectives. Rejection of a ground because it is frivolous or vexatious will be similar to a rejection of a relevant representation on an application for a premises licence.

A ground for review will be a repetition if:

- it is identical or substantially similar to:

    - a ground for review specified in an earlier application for review made in respect of the same premises licence which has been determined; or
    - representations considered by the relevant licensing authority before it originally granted the premises licence; or
    - representations which would have been so considered but for the fact that they were excluded as irrelevant, vexatious or frivolous; and

- a reasonable interval has not elapsed since that earlier application for review or the grant of the licence (s.51(5)).

'Substantially similar' has not been interpreted in the Act or the Guidance. It is suggested that in order to be 'substantially similar' a ground will have to relate not only to the same licensing objective but also to the same facet of the objective, for example a public nuisance caused by noise from music played in the licensed premises. The onus is on the licensing authority to demonstrate that the ground is substantially similar.

If a ground is found to be identical or substantially similar, this does not mean that it will automatically be ruled invalid. This will only occur where a reasonable interval has not elapsed since the ground was previously considered. The Guidance indicates that there should usually be an interval of 12 months. The Guidance at para.11.13 provides:

> Licensing authorities are expected to be aware of the need to prevent attempts to review licences merely as a further means of challenging the grant of the licence following the failure of representations to persuade the licensing authority on an earlier occasion. It is for licensing authorities themselves to judge what should be regarded as a reasonable interval in these circumstances. However, it is recommended that more than one review originating from a person other than a responsible authority in relation to a particular premises should not be permitted within a 12 month period on similar grounds save in

compelling circumstances or where it arises following a closure order or illegal working compliance order.

However, this does not apply to responsible authorities and the Guidance at para.11.14 states:

> The exclusion of a complaint on the grounds that it is repetitious does not apply to responsible authorities which may make more than one application for a review of a licence or certificate within a 12 month period.

If a licensing authority rejects a ground for review on the grounds that it is frivolous or vexatious or is a repetition, it must notify the applicant of its decision and if the ground was rejected because it was frivolous or vexatious it must also notify the applicant of its reasons for making that decision (s.51(6)). The notification in both cases must be given in writing as soon as reasonably practicable (Premises Licences Regulations, reg.32).

If an applicant has raised more than one ground for review in his application, and not all of them are rejected, then the application will be treated as only being rejected in respect of the ground which has been rejected. The application will still be valid in relation to any grounds which have not been rejected. Even though one of the grounds stated in the application may have been rejected the obligation to give notice still applies. By way of example, if a licensing authority receives an application which sets out two grounds for review and it decides that one of the grounds is frivolous it must give notice of this to the applicant together with the reasons for its decision, and then proceed to determine the application on the basis of the remaining ground.

15.8 DETERMINATION OF THE APPLICATION FOR REVIEW

Section 52 of the Act deals with the determination of an application for review.

Once the 28-day period in which representations can be made has come to an end, the licensing authority must hold a hearing within 20 working days beginning with the day after the end of that 28-day period to consider the application and any relevant representations (Hearings Regulations, reg.5 and Sched.1, para.7). See **15.10** for when a representation will be a relevant representation. Notice of the hearing must be given to the premises licence holder, anyone who has made a relevant representation and the person who has applied for the review no later than 10 working days before the day or the first day on which the hearing is to be held (Hearings Regulations, reg.6(4) and Sched.2, para.7). There is no provision for dispensing with the hearing if all the parties consider it unnecessary. A licensing authority does not have an implied power to refuse to consider an application for a review of a premises licence on the grounds that the application has been brought in an alleged breach of process (*R. (on the application of Harpers Leisure International Ltd)* v. *Chief Constable of Surrey* [2009] EWHC 2160 (Admin); [2010] PTSR 231).

The premises licence holder must be given the relevant representations with the notice of hearing (Hearings Regulations, reg.7(2) and Sched.3, para.7). The Guidance at para.11.15 reinforces this by stating that:

> It is particularly important that the premises licence holder is made fully aware of any representations made in respect of the premises, any evidence supporting the representations and that the holder or the holder's legal representative has therefore been able to prepare a response.

When determining the application, the licensing authority must have regard to the application and any relevant representations. It may decide that no action is required in order to promote the licensing objectives, or that informal action should be taken, for example by giving the holder of the premises licence an informal warning or a recommendation to improve matters within a specified period of time. The Guidance provides that:

> 11.17 The licensing authority may decide that the review does not require it to take any further steps appropriate to promoting the licensing objectives. In addition, there is nothing to prevent a licensing authority issuing an informal warning to the licence holder and/or to recommend improvement within a particular period of time. It is expected that licensing authorities will regard such informal warnings as an important mechanism for ensuring that the licensing objectives are effectively promoted and that warnings should be issued in writing to the licence holder.
>
> 11.18 However, where responsible authorities such as the police or environmental health officers have already issued warnings requiring improvement – either orally or in writing – that have failed as part of their own stepped approach to address concerns, licensing authorities should not merely repeat that approach and should take this into account when considering what further action is appropriate. Similarly, licensing authorities may take into account any civil immigration penalties which a licence holder has been required to pay for employing an illegal worker.

If, following the hearing, the licensing authority considers that formal action is required, it may take such of the following steps, if any, which it considers appropriate for the promotion of the licensing objectives:

- to modify the conditions of the licence. This will involve any of the conditions of the licence being altered or omitted or the addition of a new condition, for example, by reducing the hours of opening or by requiring door supervisors at particular times;
- to exclude a licensable activity from the scope of the licence, for example, by excluding the playing of live music;
- to remove the designated premises supervisor, for example, because the licensing authority considers that the problems are due to poor management;
- to suspend the licence for a period not exceeding three months; or
- to revoke the licence.

When reaching its decision, the licensing authority must have regard to the requirements in the Act to include mandatory conditions in the licence.

When reviewing a licence to sell alcohol on the grounds of alleged criminal activity, it will be appropriate and necessary to consider the wider public interest and the furtherance of the licensing objectives, which include the prevention of crime (*R. (on the application of Bassetlaw DC)* v. *Worksop Magistrates' Court* [2008] EWHC 3530 (Admin); (2009) 173 JP 599).

If a licensing authority decides that none of these steps is appropriate, then it need take no action.

Where a licensing authority takes one of the above steps its decision will not take effect until the end of the period for appealing against the decision, or if the decision is appealed against, until the appeal is disposed of. An appeal may be made by the holder of the licence, the applicant or any person who made relevant representations within 21 days. In *Khan* v. *Coventry Magistrates' Court* [2011] EWCA Civ 751; (2011) 175 JP 429, the Court of Appeal was satisfied that the magistrates hearing an appeal were not limited to considering only those grounds which were raised in the application for review or any representation which was made before the hearing by the licensing authority; however the licence holder should have had adequate notice of any new matters so that he could deal with them.

In *Carmarthenshire CC* v. *Llanelli Magistrates* [2009] EWHC 3016 (Admin); [2010] All ER (D) 209 (Apr), it was decided that magistrates who had reversed the revocation of a premises licence after concluding that revocation was not necessary or proportionate had applied the wrong test. On an appeal from a local authority's decision relating to a review of a premises licence, magistrates should take such steps as they considered necessary for the promotion of the licensing objectives (presumably this would now be such steps as they consider appropriate for the promotion of the licensing objectives).

If a licensing authority decides to modify the conditions of the premises licence or to exclude a licensable activity from the scope of the licence, it may provide that the modification or exclusion is to have temporary effect for a period not exceeding three months, as it may specify. In this respect, the Guidance at para.11.23 provides:

> Licensing authorities should also note that modifications of conditions and exclusions of licensable activities may be imposed either permanently or for a temporary period of up to three months. Temporary changes or suspension of the licence for up to three months could impact on the business holding the licence financially and would only be expected to be pursued as an appropriate means of promoting the licensing objectives or preventing illegal working. So, for instance, a licence could be suspended for a weekend as a means of deterring the holder from allowing the problems that gave rise to the review to happen again. However, it will always be important that any detrimental financial impact that may result from a licensing authority's decision is appropriate and proportionate to the promotion of the licensing objectives and for the prevention of illegal working in licensed premises. But where premises are found to be trading irresponsibly, the licensing authority should not hesitate, where appropriate to do so, to take tough action to tackle the problems at the premises and, where other measures are deemed insufficient, to revoke the licence.

In deciding which of its powers to invoke, the Guidance states that:

11.20 In deciding which of these powers to invoke, it is expected that licensing authorities should so far as possible seek to establish the cause or causes of the concerns that the representations identify. The remedial action taken should generally be directed at these causes and should always be no more than an appropriate and proportionate response to address the causes of concern that instigated the review.

11.21 For example, licensing authorities should be alive to the possibility that the removal and replacement of the designated premises supervisor may be sufficient to remedy a problem where the cause of the identified problem directly relates to poor management decisions made by that individual.

11.22 Equally, it may emerge that poor management is a direct reflection of poor company practice or policy and the mere removal of the designated premises supervisor may be an inadequate response to the problems presented. Indeed, where subsequent review hearings are generated, it should be rare merely to remove a succession of designated premises supervisors as this would be a clear indication of deeper problems that impact upon the licensing objectives.

Where the licensing authority is conducting a review on the ground that the premises have been used for criminal purposes, for example, because of drugs problems at the premises, money laundering by criminal gangs, the sale of contraband or stolen goods, the sale of firearms or the sexual exploitation of children, the licensing authority does not have the power to judge the criminality or otherwise of any issue. This is a matter for the courts. The licensing authority's role when determining such a review is not therefore to establish the guilt or innocence of any individual but to ensure the promotion of the crime prevention objective. The Guidance at para.11.26 makes it clear that only steps necessary in connection with the premises licence for the promotion of the crime prevention objective should be taken. It goes on to state:

It is important to recognise that certain criminal activity or associated problems may be taking place or have taken place despite the best efforts of the licence holder and the staff working at the premises and despite full compliance with the conditions attached to the licence. In such circumstances, the licensing authority is still empowered to take any appropriate steps to remedy the problems. The licensing authority's duty is to take steps with a view to the promotion of the licensing objectives and the prevention of illegal working in the interests of the wider community and not those of the individual licence holder.

There are certain criminal activities that may arise in connection with licensed premises, which the Guidance considers should be treated particularly seriously. These are set out in para.11.27 and are where the licensed premises are used:

- for the sale and distribution of drugs controlled under the Misuse of Drugs Act 1971 and the laundering of the proceeds of drugs crime;
- for the sale and distribution of illegal firearms;
- for the evasion of copyright in respect of pirated or unlicensed films and music, which does considerable damage to the industries affected;

- for the illegal purchase and consumption of alcohol by minors which impacts on the health, educational attainment, employment prospects and propensity for crime of young people;
- for prostitution or the sale of unlawful pornography;
- by organised groups of paedophiles to groom children;
- as the base for the organisation of criminal activity, particularly by gangs;
- for the organisation of racist activity or the promotion of racist attacks;
- for employing a person who is disqualified from that work by reason of their immigration status in the UK;
- for unlawful gambling; and
- for the sale or storage of smuggled tobacco and alcohol.

Paragraph 11.28 goes on to state:

It is envisaged that licensing authorities, the police, the Home Office (Immigration Enforcement) and other law enforcement agencies, which are responsible authorities, will use the review procedures effectively to deter such activities and crime. Where reviews arise and the licensing authority determines that the crime prevention objective is being undermined through the premises being used to further crimes, it is expected that revocation of the licence – even in the first instance – should be seriously considered.

15.9 NOTIFICATION OF THE DECISION

Once an application for a review has been determined, the licensing authority must notify the following of its decision and its reasons:

- the premises licence holder;
- the applicant;
- any person who made relevant representations; and
- the chief officer of police for the police area (or each police area) in which the premises are situated (s.52(10)).

15.10 RELEVANT REPRESENTATIONS

For the purposes of a review, s.52(7) and (8) provide that representations are relevant if they:

- are relevant to one or more of the licensing objectives;
- are made by the holder of the premises licence, a responsible authority or any other person within the 28-day period prescribed for making representations;
- have not been withdrawn; and
- if they are made by a person who is not a responsible authority, are not, in the opinion of the relevant licensing authority, frivolous or vexatious.

Where the licensing authority decides that a representation is frivolous or vexatious, it must notify the person who made it of its reasons for its decision.

Thus, for the purposes of a review, a representation must be relevant to one or more of the licensing objectives. This is different from representations made in respect of the grant or variation of a premises licence. In those situations, a representation must be 'about the likely effect of the grant ... on the promotion of the licensing objectives'. Thus it would seem that the requirement on review is less onerous than those on a grant or variation.

15.11 INSPECTION OF PREMISES

Section 59 provides that a constable or an authorised person may, at any reasonable time before the determination of an application for review, enter the premises to which the application relates to assess the effect of the activities authorised by the premises licence on the promotion of the licensing objectives.

An authorised person who is exercising the power to enter the premises must, if so requested, produce evidence of his authority to exercise the power (s.59(3)). A constable or an authorised person exercising the power to enter the premises in relation to an application for a review may, if necessary, use reasonable force (s.59(4)). Anyone who intentionally obstructs an authorised person exercising the power of entry commits an offence, and is liable on summary conviction to a fine not exceeding level 2 on the standard scale (s.59(5) and (6)).

In addition, obstructing a constable exercising the right of entry will be an offence of obstructing a constable in the execution of his duties under the Police Act 1996, s.89(2). A person guilty of such an offence is liable on summary conviction to imprisonment for a term not exceeding one month (this will increase to 51 weeks when the Criminal Justice Act 2003 takes effect) or to a fine not exceeding level 3 on the standard scale, or to both.

15.12 SUMMARY REVIEWS IN SERIOUS CASES OF CRIME OR DISORDER

Summary reviews can be undertaken when the police consider that the premises concerned are associated with serious crime or serious disorder (or both). The summary review process, set out under ss.53A–53D of the Act, allows interim conditions to be quickly attached to a licence and a fast track licence review. The powers apply only where a premises licence authorises the sale of alcohol. They do not apply in respect of other premises licences, or to premises operating under a club premises certificate.

15.12.1 Application for a summary review

The chief officer of police for a police area may apply to the relevant licensing authority for a review of the premises licence for any premises wholly or partly in that area if the premises are licensed premises in relation to the sale of alcohol by retail and a senior police officer of or above the rank of superintendent has certified that in his opinion the premises are associated with serious crime or serious disorder or both. The certificate must accompany the application. The form of certificate is not prescribed but a sample form is attached to the Summary Review Guidance.

A serious crime occurs where a person's conduct is an offence for which a person who has attained 21 years of age and who has no previous convictions could reasonably be expected to be sentenced to imprisonment for a term of three years or more, or where that conduct involves the use of violence, results in substantial financial gain or is conduct by a large number of persons in pursuit of a common purpose (see the Regulation of Investigatory Powers Act 2000, s.81(2) and (3)).

In deciding whether to sign a certificate, the Guidance at para.12.7 provides that the senior police officer will want to consider the following (as applicable):

- The track record of the licensed premises concerned and whether the police have previously had cause to give advice about serious criminal or disorderly conduct (or the likelihood of such conduct) attributable to activities taking place on the premises. It is not expected that this power will be used as a first response to a problem and summary reviews triggered by a single incident are likely to be the exception.
- The nature of the likely crime and/or disorder – is the potential incident sufficiently serious to warrant using this power?
- Should an alternative power be deployed? Is the incident sufficiently serious to warrant use of the powers in Part 4, Chapter 3 of the Anti-social Behaviour, Crime and Policing Act 2014, or section 38 of and Schedule 6 to the Immigration Act 2016, to close the premises? Or could the police trigger a standard licence review to address the problem? Alternatively, could expedited reviews be used in conjunction with other powers (for example, modifying licence conditions following the use of a closure power)?
- What added value will use of the expedited process bring? How would any interim steps that the licensing authority might take effectively address the problem?

Paragraph 12.8 goes on to provide that:

It is recommended that these points are addressed in the chief officer's application to the licensing authority. In particular, it is important to explain why other powers or actions are not considered to be appropriate. It is up to the police to decide whether to include this information in the certificate or in section 4 of the application for summary review. The police will also have an opportunity later to make representations in relation to the full review. In appropriate circumstances the police might want to make representations to the licensing authority suggesting that they modify the conditions of the premises licence to require searches of customers for offensive weapons upon entry. Under the powers in sections 53A to 53D, this could be done on an interim basis pending a full hearing of the issues within the prescribed 28-day timeframe or for an appropriate period determined by the licensing authority.

When a relevant licensing authority receives an application, it must within 48 hours of the time of its receipt consider whether it is necessary to take any interim steps pending the determination of a review of the premises licence, and within 28 days after the day of its receipt review the licence and reach a determination.

In computing the period of 48 hours, time that is not on a working day is to be disregarded.

An application for a review must be in the prescribed form which is set out in the Premises Licences Regulations, Sched.8A.

The relevant licensing authority must, within 48 hours of the time of the receipt of the application, give notice of the review to the holder of the premises licence to which the application relates and each responsible authority (Premises Licences Regulations, reg.36A). Such notice is given by giving to the licence holder and each responsible authority a copy of the application and a copy of the senior police officer's certificate. In computing the period of 48 hours, time that is not on a working day is to be disregarded.

In addition, the relevant licensing authority must advertise an application for review for a period of no less than seven consecutive days starting on the day after the day on which it received the application (Premises Licences Regulations, reg.38(2)(a)). The notice must be:

- of a size equal to or larger than A4;
- of a pale blue colour; and
- printed legibly in black ink or typed in black in a font of a size equal to or larger than 16 points.

The notice must be displayed:

- at, on or near the site of the premises to which the application relates where it can conveniently be read from the exterior of the premises by the public and in the case of a premises covering an area of more than 50 metres square, one further notice in the same form and subject to the same requirements shall be displayed every 50 metres along the external perimeter of the premises abutting any highway; and
- at the offices, or the main offices, of the licensing authority in a central and conspicuous place.

If the licensing authority has a website which it uses to advertise applications it receives, then a notice of the application for review must also be published on that website.

The notices displayed on the premises and on the website must state:

- the address of the premises about which an application for a review has been made;
- the dates between which responsible authorities and any other persons may make representations to the relevant licensing authority which shall be the date of the first working day after the day on which the notice was published, and the date of the ninth subsequent working day;
- the grounds of the application for review which shall be that in the opinion of a senior police officer the premises are associated with serious crime or serious disorder or both;

- the postal address and, where relevant, the worldwide web address where the register of the relevant licensing authority is kept and where and when the grounds for the review may be inspected; and
- that it is an offence knowingly or recklessly to make a false statement in connection with an application and the maximum fine for which a person is liable on summary conviction for the offence.

Representations may be made by the holder of the premises licence, any responsible authority or any other person within the period beginning on the first working day after the publication of the notice and ending on the ninth subsequent working day.

15.12.2 Interim steps pending review

A licensing authority which has received an application for a review must within 48 hours of its receipt consider whether it is necessary to take any interim steps pending the determination of a review of the premises licence (s.53A(2)). This consideration may take place without the holder of the premises licence having been given an opportunity to make representations to the relevant licensing authority (s.53B(2)).

Paragraph 12.11 of the Guidance suggests that the licensing authority may want to consult the police about the interim steps that it thinks are necessary, pending the determination of the review, to address the immediate problems with the premises, in particular the likelihood of serious crime and/or serious disorder. Paragraph 12.12 provides:

> The determination of interim steps is not a matter that may be delegated to an officer of the licensing authority. The relevant decisions are likely to be taken by a licensing sub-committee rather than the full committee. It should also be noted that there is no requirement for a formal hearing in order to take interim steps. This means that the relevant sub committee members can communicate by telephone or other remote means in order to reach a decision. A written record should always be produced as soon as possible after a decision is reached.

The interim steps to be considered are:

- the modification of the conditions of the premises licence (i.e. the alteration, modification or addition of a new condition);
- the exclusion of the sale of alcohol by retail from the scope of the licence;
- the removal of the designated premises supervisor from the licence; or
- the suspension of the licence.

Modification of the conditions of the premises licence can include the alteration or modification of existing conditions or addition of any new conditions, including those that restrict the times at which licensable activities authorised by the licence can take place.

If the licensing authority decides to take one or more of the interim steps, its decision takes effect immediately or at such later time as the authority directs. Notice of the decision and the reasons for making it must be given immediately to the holder of the premises licence, and the chief officer of police for the police area in which the premises are situated (or for each police area in which they are partly situated). There is no requirement that this notice must be in writing and so where the decision is to have immediate effect a telephone call may be used to give the notice, although this should be followed up as soon as possible with a written notice (see the Guidance para.12.14).

The Guidance at paras.12.15 and 12.16 provide:

12.15 The licensing authority, in deciding when its decision on interim steps should take effect, should consider the practical implications of compliance in relation to the premises. For example to comply with a modification of the conditions of a licence that requires employment of door supervisors, those running the premises may need some time to recruit appropriately qualified and accredited staff.

12.16 In addition, very careful consideration needs to be given to interim steps which would require significant cost or permanent or semi-permanent adjustments to premises which would be difficult to remove if the outcome of the subsequent full review was to withdraw or modify those steps. For example, making structural changes, installing additional CCTV or replacing all glassware with safer alternatives may be valid steps, but might be disproportionate if they are not likely to be deemed necessary following the full review (or any subsequent appeal). The focus for interim steps should be on the immediate measures that are necessary to prevent serious crime or serious disorder occurring.

If the licence holder makes, and does not withdraw, representations against any interim steps taken by the relevant licensing authority, the authority must, within 48 hours of receiving these representations, hold a hearing to consider them. In computing this 48-hour period time that is not on a working day is disregarded.

Advance notice of the hearing must be given to the holder of the premises licence, and the chief officer of police for the police area in which the premises are situated (or for each police area in which they are partly situated). Given that these measures are designed to deal with serious crime and/or serious disorder on an interim basis only, the process is designed to avoid delay and, as such, significant portions of the Hearings Regulations do not apply in order to streamline the hearing process. One result of this is that the licensing authority cannot adjourn the hearing to a later date if the licence holder fails to attend at the scheduled time and the licence holder does not have to be present for the hearing to take place. In addition, there is no timescale for notifying the licence holder of the hearing, providing the notification takes place before the hearing is held. However, the licence holder should be given as much notice as is possible in the circumstances to afford them a maximum practicable opportunity to prepare for and attend the hearing. At the hearing, the relevant licensing authority must consider whether the interim steps are appropriate for the promotion of the licensing objectives, and decide whether they should be withdrawn or modified. In considering these matters, the relevant licensing authority must have regard to the certificate that accompanied the application, any representations made by the chief officer of police for the police area in which the premises are situated (or for each police area in which they are partly situated) and any representations made by the licence holder. Where the relevant licensing authority has determined whether to withdraw or modify the interim steps taken, the holder of the premises licence may only make further representations if there has been a material change in circumstances since the authority made its determination. There is no right of appeal to a magistrates' court against the licensing authority's decision at this stage.

15.12.3 Review of a premises licence following a review notice

A licensing authority must hold a hearing within 28 days after the receipt of the chief officer's application to review the premises licence and consider any relevant representations. There can be no adjournment of the hearing or delay in reaching a determination beyond the end of the 28 day period. In order for representations to be 'relevant' they must be relevant to one or more of the licensing objectives, have been made by the holder of the premises licence, a responsible authority or any other person, have not been withdrawn and if made by a person who is not a responsible authority the licensing authority does not consider them to be frivolous or vexatious. The representations must also have been made within the period beginning on the first working day after the publication of the notice and ending on the ninth subsequent working day.

If a licensing authority decides that any representations are frivolous or vexatious it must notify the person who made the representations of the reasons for its decision.

Notice of the hearing must be given to the premises licence holder, anyone who has made a relevant representation and the chief officer of police who has applied for the review no later than five working days before the day or the first day on which the hearing is to be held (Hearings Regulations, reg.6(3) and Sched.2, para.7A). The premises licence holder must be given the relevant representations with the notice of hearing (Hearings Regulations, reg.7(2) and Sched.3, para.7A).

The licensing authority must:

- advertise the review inviting representations from any persons for no less than seven consecutive days by notice as described in the Premises Regulations regs.38 and 39 and, if applicable, on the licensing authority's website (see **15.6**). The relevant notices should be published on the day after the day of receipt of the chief officer's application.
- advertise that any representations which the premises licence holder, responsible authority or any other person want the licensing authority to consider at the review hearing, should be submitted to the licensing authority within 10 working days of the advertisement of the review appearing.

- give formal notice of the hearing no later than five working days before the day or first day on which the hearing is to be held to the premises licence holder and to every responsible authority.

A party must give the licensing authority a notice no later than two working days before the day or the first day on which the hearing is to be held stating whether he intends to attend or be represented at the hearing, whether he considers a hearing to be unnecessary and whether he would like permission for any other person (other than the person he intends to represent him at the hearing) to appear at the hearing and, if so, explain on which points that person will be able to contribute (Hearings Regulations, reg.8).

As a result of this review the authority must, if it considers it appropriate for the promotion of the licensing objectives, either:

- modify the conditions of the licence;
- exclude a licensable activity which the premises licence covers;
- remove the designated premises supervisor from the licence;
- suspend the licence for a period not exceeding three months; or
- revoke the licence.

If the licensing authority does not consider any of the steps to be appropriate for the promotion of the licensing objectives, it will leave the licence untouched.

Where the authority decides to modify the conditions of the licence, or exclude a licensable activity which the premises licence covers, it may decide that the modification or exclusion is to have effect only for a specified period not exceeding three months.

The licensing authority must notify the outcome of a review and its reasons for so deciding to the licence holder, the applicant, the chief officer of police for the police area in which the premises are situated (or for each police area in which they are partly situated), and any person who has made relevant representations.

The determination of an application for review will not take effect until any appeal has been disposed of, or if there is no appeal at the end of the period within which an appeal may be brought. An appeal against the final review decision may be made to a magistrates' court within 21 days of the appellant being notified of the licensing authority's determination on the review. An appeal may be made by the premises licence holder, the chief officer of police and/or any other person who made relevant representations.

15.12.4 Review of the interim steps

The licensing authority's determination of an application for review does not have effect until the end of the 21 day period given for appealing the decision, or until the disposal of any appeal that is lodged. To ensure that there are appropriate and proportionate safeguards in place at all times, the licensing authority is required at the hearing to consider an application for a review under s.53A to review any interim steps that have been taken under s.53B that have effect on the date of the hearing (s.53D(1)).

In conducting the review of the interim steps, the licensing authority must consider whether the interim steps are appropriate for the promotion of the licensing objectives, consider any relevant representations and determine whether to withdraw or modify the interim steps taken.

In order for representations to be 'relevant', they must be relevant to one or more of the licensing objectives, have been made by the holder of the premises licence, a responsible authority or any other person, have not been withdrawn and if made by a person who is not a responsible authority the licensing authority does not consider them to be frivolous or vexatious. The representations must also have been made within the period beginning on the first working day after the publication of the notice and ending on the ninth subsequent working day. If a licensing authority decides that any representations are frivolous or vexatious it must notify the person who made the representations of the reasons for its decision.

The licensing authority on a review of the interim steps has the power to take any of the following interim steps:

(a)   the modification of the conditions of the premises licence;
(b)   the exclusion of the sale of alcohol by retail from the scope of the licence;
(c)   the removal of the designated premises supervisor from the licence; or
(d)   the suspension of the licence.

The review of the interim steps should take place immediately after the review of the premises licence. Any interim steps taken at the review hearing apply until:

(a)   the end of the period given for appealing against a decision made following a review of the premises licence (21 days);
(b)   if the decision made following a review of the premises licence is appealed against, the time the appeal is disposed of; or
(c)   the end of a period determined by the relevant licensing authority (which may not be longer than the period of time for which such interim steps could apply under (a) or (b) above).

The licence holder or the chief officer of police may appeal against the decision made by the licensing authority concerning its review of the interim steps to a magistrates' court. The appeal must be made within 21 days of the appellant being notified of the licensing authority's decision and must be heard in full by the magistrates' court within 28 days beginning with the day on which the appellant lodged the appeal. Where appeals are lodged both against the decision following the review of the interim steps and against the final determination, the court may decide to consider the appeal against the final determination within the 28 day period, allowing the interim steps appeal to be disposed of at the same time.

CHAPTER 16

Transfer of a premises licence

16.1 INTRODUCTION

Where a business involving licensable activities is sold, the new owner will need to apply to have the premises licence transferred to him. A transfer of the licence will only change the identity of the holder of the licence and will not alter the licence in any way, and it is expected that most applications will be dealt with by a very simple administrative process.

16.2 WHO CAN APPLY FOR A TRANSFER?

Under s.42 any person who is eligible to apply for a premises licence (see **7.2**) may apply to have the licence transferred to him. Where an applicant is an individual he must be aged 18 or over. Where the applicant is an individual who is resident in the United Kingdom and the premises licence authorises premises to be used for the sale by retail of alcohol or the provision of late night refreshment, he must also be entitled to work in the United Kingdom.

16.3 APPLYING FOR A TRANSFER

In order to apply for a transfer, an applicant must submit the following to the relevant licensing authority:

- a completed application form. The application form is prescribed and is set out in the Premises Licences Regulations, Sched.6;
- the premises licence, or if that is not practicable, a statement of the reasons why it cannot be provided;
- the consent of the current licence holder, or if not available, a statement of the reasons why it cannot be provided and of the steps taken to try and obtain it. The Premises Licences Regulations, reg.24(2) provides that the consent shall

be in the form set out in the Premises Licences Regulations, Sched.11, Part B, however, Sched.11 was substituted on 6 April 2017 by the Licensing Act 2003 (Miscellaneous Amendments) Regulations 2017, SI 2017/411, reg.4(1), (14), Sched.15 and there is no longer a Part B. However, a consent form in the original form is still available at **www.gov.uk/government/publications/ premises-licence-application-forms**; and

● the prescribed fee.

16.3.1 Completing the application form

Guidance in completing the application form may be obtained from **www.gov.uk** or the relevant licensing authority. The form may be completed by being either typed or written legibly in block capitals. All answers must be inside the boxes and written in black ink. Care must be taken when completing the application form as any mistakes will be built into the new licence.

In the opening statement, the name of the applicant or applicants who are applying to transfer the premises licence should be inserted together with the premises licence number.

The application form is then divided into four parts.

Part 1

The applicant must set out the postal address of the premises, the telephone number at the premises, if any, and a brief description of the premises. If the premises have no postal address, the location of the premises should be described or the Ordnance Survey map reference should be given. The name of the current premises licence holder must also be given.

Part 2

Part 2 deals with details of the applicant. The applicant must state in which capacity he is applying for the premises licence to be transferred to him, and if he is applying as an individual, a limited company, a partnership, an unincorporated association or a statutory corporation, he must confirm that he is carrying on or proposing to carry on a business which involves the use of the premises for licensable activities, or that he is making the application pursuant to a statutory function or a function discharged by virtue of His Majesty's prerogative.

The applicant must then give further details such as his name and address, telephone number, email address (this is optional) and confirmation, where relevant, that he is at least 18 years old. Where the applicant is not an individual it must give details of its name, address, registered number, telephone number, email address (this is optional) and a description of itself, for example whether it is a company, partnership or unincorporated association. Where applicable, if demonstrating a right to work via the Home Office online right to work checking service, the applicant must provide the 'share code' provided to the applicant by the service.

Part 3

Part 3 asks whether the applicant is the holder of the premises licence under an interim authority notice, whether the applicant wishes the transfer to have immediate effect and if not when he would like the transfer to take effect. It asks for the consent form signed by the existing premises licence holder, and if this is not available a statement of the reasons why it is not enclosed must be given together with details of the steps the applicant has taken to try and obtain the consent. The applicant must confirm that if the licence is transferred he would be in a position to use the premises during the application period for the licensable activities authorised by the licence. The applicant must enclose the premises licence and if he cannot do this must set out the reasons why it is not enclosed. The form also includes a checklist for the applicant to complete so that nothing is overlooked, together with warnings that it is an offence, liable on conviction to a fine up to level 5 on the standard scale, under s.158 to make a false statement in or in connection with the application and that it is an offence under the Immigration Act 1971, s.24b for a person to work when they know, or have reasonable cause to believe, that they are disqualified from doing so by reason of their immigration status. Those who employ an adult without leave or who is subject to conditions as to employment will be liable to a civil penalty under the Immigration, Asylum and Nationality Act 2006, s.15 and pursuant to s.21 of the same Act, will be committing an offence where they do so in the knowledge, or with reasonable cause to believe, that the employee is disqualified. The applicant must also confirm that they understand they are not entitled to be issued with a licence if they do not have the entitlement to live and work in the United Kingdom (or if they are subject to a condition preventing them from doing work relating to the carrying on of a licensable activity) and that their licence will become invalid if they cease to be entitled to live and work in the United Kingdom.

Part 4

The final part of the form makes provision for the applicant to sign the form. The application form must be signed. The form can also be signed by the applicant's solicitor or other duly authorised agent, and someone signing on behalf of the applicant must state in what capacity they sign. Where there are joint applicants, both applicants or their respective agents must sign the application form.

16.3.2 Obtaining an application form

For details on obtaining a form see **7.4.2**.

16.3.3 Making an application

For details on making the application electronically see **7.4.3**.

16.3.4 Notice to the police and the Secretary of State

Notice of the application must be given to the chief officer of police for the police area, or each police area, in which the premises are situated by giving the chief officer of police a copy of the application together with its accompanying documents, if any, on the same day as the day on which the application is given to the relevant licensing authority. Notice must be given by the relevant licensing authority where the application has been made electronically, and by the applicant in any other case.

Where the premises licence authorises the premises to be used for the sale by retail of alcohol or the provision of late night entertainment, notice of the application must also be given to the Secretary of State (through Home Office Immigration Enforcement). Notice must be given by the relevant licensing authority where the application has been made electronically, and by the applicant in any other case.

16.3.5 Objections

If the chief officer of police is satisfied that the exceptional circumstances of the case are such that granting the application would undermine the crime prevention objective, he must give notice of objection to the relevant licensing authority. This notice must set out the reasons why he has decided to object. It must be given within 14 days beginning with the day on which the chief officer of police is notified of the transfer application.

If the Secretary of State (through Home Office Immigration Enforcement) is satisfied that the exceptional circumstances of the case are such that granting the application would be prejudicial to the prevention of illegal working in licensed premises, the Secretary of State must give a notice of objection to the relevant licensing authority. This notice must set out the reasons why he has decided to object. It must be given within 14 days beginning with the day on which the Secretary of State is notified of the transfer application.

The Guidance anticipates that such objections are expected to be rare and arise because the police or the Home Office (Immigration Enforcement) have evidence that the business or individuals seeking to hold the licence, or businesses or individuals linked to such persons, are involved in crime (or disorder) or employing illegal workers (para.8.101).

Objections should not be used routinely to vet applicants and para.8.102 of the Guidance states:

> Such objections (and therefore such hearings) should only arise in truly exceptional circumstances. If the licensing authority believes that the police or the Home Office

(Immigration Enforcement) are using this mechanism to vet transfer applicants routinely and to seek hearings as a fishing expedition to inquire into applicants' backgrounds, it is expected that it would raise the matter immediately with the chief officer of police or the Home Office (Immigration Enforcement).

16.4 INTERIM EFFECT

It is possible under s.43 for an applicant to request that his application for a transfer is given immediate effect. This will then allow the business carried on at the premises to continue during the period beginning with when the application is received by the relevant licensing authority, and ending either when the licence is transferred following the grant of the application, or if the application is rejected when the applicant is notified of the rejection, or when the application is withdrawn. Licensable activities can thus be carried on pending the determination of the transfer application.

Where a request has been made for the transfer to have immediate effect the applicant must forthwith (see **2.9**) notify any designated premises supervisor of the application (unless the applicant is the designated premises supervisor). He must also notify the designated premises supervisor if the application for transfer is subsequently granted.

An application for a transfer to have immediate effect may usually be made only with the consent of the holder of the premises licence. The Premises Licences Regulations, reg.24(2) provides that the consent shall be in the form set out in the Premises Licences Regulations, Sched.11, Part B, however, Sched.11 was substituted on 6 April 2017 by the Licensing Act 2003 (Miscellaneous Amendments) Regulations 2017, SI 2017/411, reg.4(1), (14), Sched.15 and there is no longer a Part B. However, a consent form in the original form is still available at **www.gov.uk/government/publications/premises-licence-application-forms**. Consent is not required where the applicant is the holder of the premises licence by virtue of an interim authority notice. If the consent of the holder of the premises licence is not available then s.43(5) provides that the relevant licensing authority must exempt the applicant from the requirement to obtain the holder's consent if the applicant shows to the authority's satisfaction:

- that he has taken all reasonable steps to obtain that consent; and
- that, if the application were treated as though the transfer had interim effect, he would be in a position to use the premises during the application period for the licensable activity or activities authorised by the premises licence.

Where the relevant licensing authority refuses to exempt an applicant from having to obtain the consent of the holder of the premises licence, it must notify the applicant of its reasons for that decision. In this situation, the applicant ceases to be treated as the holder of the licence and the licence reverts to the person who held it before the application was made.

16.5 DETERMINATION OF THE APPLICATION

If an application has been made in accordance with the statutory provisions, it will be granted (s.44). The Guidance, para.8.100 states that 'In the vast majority of cases, it is expected that a transfer will be a very simple administrative process'.

However, if the application for transfer includes a request for it to be given immediate effect, the licensing authority must reject the application unless the holder of the premises licence gives his consent to the transfer or the relevant licensing authority has exempted the applicant from having to obtain the consent.

The licensing authority must exempt the applicant from the requirement to obtain the consent of the holder of the premises licence if the applicant shows to the authority's satisfaction:

● that he has taken all reasonable steps to obtain that consent; and
● that, if the application were granted, he would be in a position to use the premises during the application period for the licensable activity or activities authorised by the premises licence.

If the relevant licensing authority refuses to exempt an applicant, it must notify the applicant of its reasons for that decision.

Where a notice is given by the chief officer of police that the crime prevention objective would be undermined if the application were granted or by the Secretary of State that granting the application would be prejudicial to the prevention of illegal working in licensed premises, the licensing authority must hold a hearing to consider it, unless the authority, the applicant and the person who gave the notice agree that a hearing is unnecessary. The hearing must be held within 20 working days beginning with the day after the end of the 14-day period within which the chief officer of police may object (Hearings Regulations, reg.5 and Sched.1, para.5). Notice of the hearing must be given to the applicant for the transfer, the chief officer of police and the premises licence holder no later than 10 working days before the day or the first day on which the hearing is to be held (Hearings Regulations, reg.6(4) and Sched.2, para.5). Both the applicant and the holder of the premises licence must be given a copy of the police notice of objection with the notice of the hearing (Hearings Regulations, reg.7(2) and Sched.3, para.5). The Hearing Regulations do not make provision for a hearing where a notice is given by the Secretary of State.

At the hearing, if the notice was given by the chief officer of police, the licensing authority must reject the application if it considers it appropriate to do so for the promotion of the crime prevention objective, or, if the notice was given by the Secretary of State, the licensing authority must reject the application if it considers it appropriate to do so for the prevention of illegal working in licensed premises. An applicant may appeal against the rejection to the magistrates' court. The chief officer of police or the Secretary of State may also appeal if the transfer is granted despite their objection.

16.6 NOTIFICATION OF THE DETERMINATION

Once an application for a transfer has been determined by being either granted or rejected, the relevant licensing authority must forthwith (see **2.9**) notify the applicant, and the chief officer of police for the police area, or each police area, in which the premises are situated (s.45(1)). Where the Secretary of State gave notice of objection, this notification must also be given to the Secretary of State. The notice must be accompanied by information regarding the right of a party to appeal against the decision.

If the chief officer of police gave notice that the crime prevention objective would be undermined if the application were granted or the Secretary of State gave notice that granting the application would be prejudicial to the prevention of illegal working in licensed premises, and this notice has not been withdrawn, the notice given by the licensing authority must state the licensing authority's reasons for granting or rejecting the application.

If the application has been granted, the notice must specify the time when the transfer is to take effect, and this must be either the time specified in the application or, if that time is before the applicant is given that notice, such later time as the relevant licensing authority specifies in the notice. So by way of example, if the applicant states that the transfer is to take effect on 1 September and the notice is not given until 5 September, the licensing authority must specify the date on which the transfer is to become effective.

If the application is granted, the licensing authority must also give a copy of the notice:

- to the holder of the licence immediately before the application was granted; or
- if the application was one which has been given interim effect, to the holder of the licence immediately before the application was made (if any).

If the application is rejected, the licensing authority must also give a copy of the notice to the holder of the premises licence, if there is one.

In addition, s.46 imposes a duty to notify the designated premises supervisor. If the applicant is not the designated premises supervisor, the applicant must notify the designated premises supervisor of the application. If the application is granted, the applicant must notify the designated premises supervisor of the transfer. An applicant will commit an offence if he fails, without reasonable excuse, to comply with these requirements and a person guilty of such an offence will be liable on summary conviction to a fine not exceeding level 3 on the standard scale.

CHAPTER 17

Clubs

17.1 INTRODUCTION

Club premises to which the public have restricted access and where alcohol is supplied other than for profit are treated differently under the Act from other licensed premises. Clubs are organisations where members have joined together for particular social, sporting or political purposes and then combined to buy alcohol in bulk as members of the organisation for supply in that context. Examples include Labour, Conservative and Liberal Clubs, the Royal British Legion and other ex-services clubs, working men's clubs, miners' welfare institutes and social and sports clubs, such as rugby and cricket clubs.

There are technically no sales by retail of alcohol by the club at such premises except to a guest when he purchases alcohol. Where a member purchases alcohol, there can be no sale by retail as each member owns part of the alcohol stock, and so the money passing across the bar is merely a mechanism to preserve equity between members where one may consume more than another (*Graff* v. *Evans* (1882) 8 QBD 373).

Under the Act, members' clubs must satisfy certain conditions in order to be a qualifying club so that they can then apply to the licensing authority for a club premises certificate. A club premises certificate means that a qualifying club is entitled to benefits including:

- the authority to supply alcohol to members and to sell it to members' guests on the premises to which the certificate relates without the need for any member or employee to hold a personal licence;
- authority to provide late night refreshment to members without requiring additional authorisation;
- more limited rights of entry for the police and authorised persons as club premises are private and not generally open to the public; and
- not being subject to potential orders of the magistrates' court for the closure of all licensed premises in an area when disorder is happening or expected.

It is important to distinguish between a qualifying club and a proprietary club. The latter is a commercially run club and so will require a premises licence. The distinction was summarised in the *Report of the Departmental Committee on Liquor Licensing* (Cmnd 5154, 1972), para.1.30 as follows:

> Proprietary clubs are clubs in which the premises and stock belong to a proprietor or group of proprietors. If the stock of liquor belongs to the proprietor, a 'sale' takes place when a member orders and pays for a drink ... In the case of 'members' clubs, all the property, including the stock of liquor, belongs to the members jointly, and when a member obtains liquor, even on payment, the position is that a 'supply' rather than a sale takes place.

A qualifying club can always apply for a premises licence if it decides that it wishes to offer its facilities commercially to members of the general public, including the sale of alcohol to them. However, this would not be necessary if the club wished to sell alcohol on a temporary basis to the general public. An individual on behalf of a club may give temporary event notices in respect of the premises to cover a period of up to 168 hours on up to 15 occasions each calendar year so long as no more than 499 people attend the event and subject to an overall maximum duration in the year of 21 days. On such occasions, the club may then sell alcohol to the public or hire out its premises for use by the public.

17.2 CLUB PREMISES CERTIFICATE

A club premises certificate is defined in s.60 as a certificate granted by the relevant licensing authority under Part 4 of the Act in respect of premises occupied by, and habitually used for the purposes of, a club and which certifies:

- that the premises may be used by the club for one or more qualifying club activities specified in the certificate; and
- that the club is a qualifying club in relation to each of those activities.

The qualifying club activities are set out in s.1(2) as follows:

- the supply of alcohol by or on behalf of a club to, or to the order of, a member of the club;
- the sale by retail of alcohol by or on behalf of a club to a guest of a member of the club for consumption on the premises where the sale takes place; and
- the provision of regulated entertainment where that provision is by or on behalf of a club for members of the club or members of the club and their guests.

The certificate will specify which of these qualifying club activities can be carried out. These will also be specified in the club rules.

17.3 QUALIFYING CLUBS

Section 61 provides that a club will be a qualifying club in relation to the provision of regulated entertainment if it satisfies the conditions in s.62. A club that wishes to be a qualifying club in relation to the supply of alcohol to members or guests must also satisfy the conditions in s.64 in addition to those in s.62.

17.3.1 The general conditions for a qualifying club

Section 62 sets out five general conditions which a club must satisfy in order to be a qualifying club as follows:

- the club rules provide that persons may not be admitted to membership, or be admitted as candidates for membership to any of the privileges of membership, without an interval of at least two days between their nomination or application for membership and their admission;
- the club rules provide that persons becoming members without prior nomination or application may not be admitted to the privileges of membership without an interval of at least two days between their becoming members and their admission;
- the club is established and conducted in good faith as a club (see **17.5**);
- the club has at least 25 members; and
- alcohol is not supplied, or intended to be supplied, to members on the premises otherwise than by or on behalf of the club, i.e. the bar is operated by the club rather than by a third party under a franchise or similar arrangement.

17.3.2 Additional conditions for the supply of alcohol

Section 64 sets out the following additional conditions which need to be met by a club which intends to supply alcohol to its members and guests:

- so far as it is not managed by the club in a general meeting or otherwise by the general body of members, the purchase of alcohol for the club, and the supply of alcohol by the club, are managed by a committee whose members are members of the club who have attained the age of 18 years, and who are elected by the members of the club (this condition does not apply to registered societies, friendly societies, etc. – see **17.6**);
- no arrangements are, or are intended to be, made for any person to receive at the expense of the club any commission, percentage or similar payment on, or with reference to, purchases of alcohol by the club; and
- no arrangements are, or are intended to be, made for any person directly or indirectly to derive any pecuniary benefit from the supply of alcohol by or on behalf of the club to members or guests, apart from a benefit accruing to the club as a whole, or any benefit which a person derives indirectly by reason of

the supply giving rise or contributing to a general gain from the carrying on of the club.

17.4 ASSOCIATE MEMBERS

In addition to admitting its own members and their guests, a qualifying club can admit an associate member and his guests. This reflects the traditional arrangements whereby a club makes its facilities available to members of other clubs on a reciprocal basis, for example, where clubs are part of the Club and Institute Union. A person is an associate member of a club if in accordance with the club rules, he is admitted to its premises as being a member of another club which is a recognised club (s.67).

A recognised club is defined in s.193 as a club where:

- the club rules provide that persons may not be admitted to membership, or be admitted, as candidates for membership, to any of the privileges of membership, without an interval of at least two days between their nomination or application for membership and their admission;
- the club rules provide that persons becoming members without prior nomination or application may not be admitted to the privileges of membership without an interval of at least two days between their becoming members and their admission; and
- the club is established and conducted in good faith as a club (see **17.5**).

The supply and sale of alcohol under a club premises certificate can therefore be made to club members and guests, and to associate members and guests. It would seem that alcohol cannot be supplied to anyone else who might be 'visiting' the club, for example a member of the public paying a green fee to a golf club in order to play a round of golf who wishes to buy a drink at the bar after he has played his round. A solution might be to make such a person a 'temporary member' of the club but as at least two days must elapse between nomination and admission of members this would not be practical for the golfer who turned up on the day to play his round and enjoy a drink afterwards. The Guidance at paras.6.7 and 6.8 provides:

6.7 The 2003 Act does not prevent visitors to a qualifying club being supplied with alcohol as long as they are 'guests' of any member of the club, and nothing in the 2003 Act prevents the admission of such people as guests without prior notice. The 2003 Act does not define 'guest' and whether or not somebody is a genuine guest would in all cases be a question of fact.

6.8 There is no mandatory requirement under the 2003 Act for guests to be signed in by a member of the club. However, a point may be reached where a club is providing commercial services to the general public in a way that is contrary to its qualifying club status. It is at this point that the club would no longer be conducted in 'good faith' and would no longer meet 'general condition 3' for qualifying clubs in section 62 of the 2003 Act. Under the 2003 Act, the licensing authority must decide when a club has ceased to operate in 'good faith' and give the club a notice withdrawing the club premises certificate. The club is entitled to appeal against such a decision to a magistrates' court. Unless the appeal is successful, the club would need to apply for a premises licence to authorise licensable activities taking place there.

17.5 THE ESTABLISHMENT AND CONDUCT OF A CLUB IN GOOD FAITH

The third requirement for a qualifying club is that it is established and conducted in good faith as a club. In determining whether this is the case, a licensing authority must under s.63 take into account:

- any arrangements restricting the club's freedom of purchase of alcohol;
- any provision in the rules, or arrangements, under which money or property of the club, or any gain arising from the carrying on of the club, is or may be applied otherwise than for the benefit of the club as a whole or for charitable, benevolent or political purposes;
- the arrangements for giving members information about the finances of the club;
- the books of account and other records kept to ensure the accuracy of the financial information given to members; and
- the nature of the premises occupied by the club.

If a licensing authority decides that a club does not satisfy the requirement that it is established and conducted in good faith, the authority must give the club notice of its decision and its reasons for it (s.63(3)). There are no provisions about the form of this notice but presumably it must be in writing.

17.6 REGISTERED SOCIETIES, FRIENDLY SOCIETIES, ETC.

Special provision is made for clubs which are registered societies within the meaning of the Co-operative and Community Benefit Societies Act 2014, registered societies within the meaning of the Friendly Societies Act 1974 and registered friendly societies within the meaning of the Friendly Societies Act 1992. These clubs are mainly working men's clubs.

Such clubs will be taken to satisfy the condition in s.64 that the purchase and supply of alcohol are managed by a committee elected by the members of the club if the purchase and supply are under the control of the members or of a committee appointed by the members (s.65(2)). Thus, where the committee is appointed rather than elected such a club is eligible to apply for a club premises certificate.

The Act also applies to an incorporated friendly society as it applies to a club (s.65(4)). An 'incorporated friendly society' has the same meaning as in the

Friendly Societies Act 1992. A friendly society is a voluntary mutual organisation whose main purpose is to assist members, usually financially, during sickness, unemployment or retirement and to provide life assurance. This means that the premises of the society are treated as the premises of a club, the members of the society are treated as the members of the club and anything done by or on behalf of the society is treated as done by or on behalf of the club. When deciding whether an incorporated friendly society is a qualifying club in relation to a qualifying club activity, the society is to be taken to satisfy the conditions in s.62 that it is established and conducted in good faith, and that alcohol is not supplied, or intended to be supplied, to members on the premises otherwise than by or on behalf of the club, together with the additional conditions in s.64.

17.7 MINERS' WELFARE INSTITUTES

Special provision is made for miners' welfare institutes. The Act applies to a miners' welfare institute as it applies to a club. This means that the premises of the institute are treated as the premises of a club, the persons enrolled as members of the institute are treated as the members of the club, and anything done by or on behalf of the trustees or managers in carrying on the institute is treated as done by or on behalf of the club (s.66(1)). When deciding whether a miners' welfare institute is a qualifying club in relation to a qualifying club activity, the institute is to be taken to satisfy the conditions in s.62 that it is established and conducted in good faith, that it has at least 25 members and that alcohol is not supplied, or intended to be supplied, to members on the premises otherwise than by or on behalf of the club, together with the additional conditions in s.64 (s.66(2)).

For the purposes of these provisions, 'miners' welfare institute' means an association organised for the social well-being and recreation of persons employed in or about coal mines, or of such persons in particular, and the Act will apply to a miners' welfare institute if the institute satisfies one of the following conditions:

- the institute is managed by a committee or board, and at least two-thirds of the committee or board consists partly of persons appointed or nominated, or appointed or elected from among persons nominated, by one or more licensed operators within the meaning of the Coal Industry Act 1994, and partly of persons appointed or nominated, or appointed or elected from among persons nominated, by one or more organisations representing persons employed in or about coal mines;
- the institute is managed by a committee or board, but the appointment or nomination of board members as provided for in the previous condition is not practicable or would not be appropriate, and at least two-thirds of the committee or board consists partly of persons employed, or formerly employed, in or about coal mines, and partly of persons appointed by the Coal Industry Social Welfare Organisation or a body or person to which the

functions of that Organisation have been transferred under the Miners' Welfare Act 1952, s.12(3); or

- the premises of the institute are held on trusts to which the Recreational Charities Act 1958, s.2 applies (while this provision has been repealed by the Charities Act 2011, the repeal does not prevent any such trusts from still being charitable if they still constitute a charity in accordance with the Charities Act 2011).

17.8 APPLICATION FOR A CLUB PREMISES CERTIFICATE

A club may apply for a club premises certificate in respect of any premises which are occupied by, and habitually used for the purposes of, the club (s.71(1)).

An application for a club premises certificate must be made to the relevant licensing authority (s.71(2)). This will be the licensing authority within whose area the club premises are situated. In addition, a copy of the application must be sent to each of the appropriate responsible authorities (see **7.8**).

The procedure for applying for a club premises certificate is very similar to that for a premises licence, and the Guidance at para.6.11 states:

> The arrangements for applying for or seeking to vary club premises certificates are extremely similar to those for a premises licence. Clubs may also use the minor variation process to make small changes to their certificates as long as these could have no adverse impact on the licensing objectives. Licensing authorities should refer to Chapter 8 of this Guidance on the handling of such applications. Licensing authorities do not have to satisfy themselves that applicants for club premises certificates are entitled to work in the UK before issuing a club premises certificate. Consequently, Home Office Immigration Enforcement is not a responsible authority in relation to club premises certificates.

However, it is not possible to apply for a provisional statement in respect of club premises that are being or are about to be constructed, altered or extended.

A club applying for a club premises certificate must submit the following to the relevant licensing authority:

- a completed application form;
- a club operating schedule;
- a plan of the club premises in the prescribed form;
- a copy of the club rules; and
- the prescribed fee.

In addition, a declaration as to qualifying club status must be submitted to the licensing authority either on or before an application is made for a club premises certificate. In practice, this will usually be submitted at the same time as the application for the club premises certificate. The prescribed form of declaration is set out in the Premises Licences Regulations, Sched.9, Part A.

The application must also be advertised (see **17.8.5**).

17.8.1 The application form

An application for a club premises certificate must be made using the prescribed form. This is set out in the Premises Licences Regulations, Sched.9, Part B.

Guidance in completing the application form may be obtained from **www.gov. uk** or the relevant licensing authority. The form may be completed by being either typed or written legibly in block capitals. All answers must be inside the boxes and written in black ink. Care must be taken when completing the application form as any mistakes will be built into the new licence.

In the opening statement, the name of club which is applying for the club premises certificate should be inserted.

The application form is divided into three parts.

Part 1 – club premises details

Part 1 asks for the name of the club, its postal address, or if none, the Ordnance Survey map reference or description, and the telephone number, if any, at the premises. It also asks for the name and address of the club secretary, together with his daytime telephone number, if any.

It also asks for the non-domestic rateable value of the premises. The non-domestic rateable value of the premises will determine the fee to be paid both for the initial application and annually. The non-domestic rateable value is based on the annual rent that the premises could have been let for on the open market at a particular date. It can be checked on the website of the Valuation Office Agency (**www.voa.gov.uk**).

The applicant club must confirm whether or not the club premises are occupied and habitually used by the club.

Part 2 – club operating schedule

Part 2 sets out the club operating schedule (see **17.8.4**). It starts by asking the club to specify when it wants the club premises certificate to start and if it wishes the certificate to be valid for a limited period only, to specify a date when it is to end.

A general description of the club must then be given, for example the type of premises, its general situation, layout and any other information which could be relevant to the licensing objectives. Where the application includes off-supplies of alcohol and the club intends to provide a place where these can be consumed, it must include a description of where that place will be and its proximity to the club premises.

Where 5,000 or more people are expected to attend the premises at any one time, the number expected to attend must be stated. This figure relates to the maximum number of people on the club premises at any one time and must include employees.

The club must then specify which qualifying club activities it intends to conduct on the club premises, and give further details of these in the appropriate boxes A–L using the 24-hour clock. All applicants must complete boxes M, N and O. Box M requires an applicant to specify the hours that the club premises are open to the members and the guests. Box N requires an applicant to highlight any adult entertainment or services, activities, other entertainment or matters ancillary to the use of the club premises which may give rise to concern in respect of children. Finally, box O requires an applicant to list the steps which it will take to promote the four licensing objectives.

There is a checklist for the club to complete so that nothing is overlooked, together with a warning that it is an offence, liable on conviction to a fine up to level 5 on the standard scale, under s.158 to make a false statement in or in connection with the application.

Part 3

Part 3 provides for the form to be signed on behalf of the club. The signatory must confirm that he is making the application on behalf of the club and has authority to bind the club. He must indicate the capacity in which he signs the form, for example as club secretary. The form can also be signed by the applicant's solicitor or other duly authorised agent, and someone signing on behalf of the applicant must state in what capacity they sign. There is also space for an address to be given for all correspondence associated with this application.

17.8.2 Obtaining an application form

For details on obtaining a form see **7.4.2**.

17.8.3 Making an application

For details on making an electronic application see **7.4.3**.

17.8.4 The club operating schedule

An application for a club premises certificate must be accompanied by a club operating schedule (s.71(4)). This forms part of the prescribed application form and, if the application is successful, it will be incorporated into the club premises certificate itself so that it is clear which activities are permitted on the club premises and any limitations on them.

A club operating schedule must state:

● the qualifying club activities;
● the times during which it is proposed that the qualifying club activities are to take place;

- any other times during which it is proposed that the premises are to be open to the members and their guests;
- where the relevant qualifying club activities include the supply of alcohol, whether the supplies are proposed to be for consumption on the premises or off the premises, or both;
- the steps which it is proposed to take to promote the licensing objectives; and
- such other matters as may be prescribed (s.71(5)).

There is no requirement to specify a designated premises supervisor. The contents of an operating schedule are discussed further in **Chapter 8** and the conditions in **Chapter 11**.

17.8.5 Advertising and notification of applications

An applicant must advertise an application for a club premises certificate (s.71(6)(a)). The requirements are the same as those for advertising an application for a premises licence (see **7.6**). A licensing authority may provide a specimen form of notice for a club to use. A suggested form of notice is set out in **Box 17.1**. In addition, the relevant licensing authority must also advertise the application and again the requirements are the same as those for advertising an application for a premises licence (see **7.7**).

Notice of an application must be given by the applicant to each responsible authority by giving to each of them a copy of the application together with its accompanying documents on the same day as the day on which the application is given to the relevant licensing authority. Where the application is made electronically, the relevant licensing authority must give notice to each responsible authority no later than the first working day after the application is given to the relevant licensing authority by giving to each of them a copy of the application together with its accompanying documents (see **7.8**) (s.71(7)). The applicant is not required to send copies of the application to the responsible authorities if the application is made electronically.

An applicant should check with the relevant licensing authority to see whether it provides a specimen form of notice to use. If not, a suggested form of notice is set out in **Box 17.1**.

BOX 17.1: SUGGESTED FORM OF NOTICE OF AN APPLICATION FOR A CLUB PREMISES CERTIFICATE

Licensing Act 2003

Notice of application for the grant of a club premises certificate

Notice is hereby given that [*insert the full name of the applicant*] has applied to the [*insert the full name of the licensing authority*] on [*insert the date of application to the licensing authority*] for the grant of a club premises certificate to use the premises [*insert name of premises*] at [*insert the name and full postal address of the premises*] for the following licensable activities:

[*insert details of each licensable activity including days and hours*]

The register of licensing applications can be inspected at [*insert details*].

Any person who wishes to make a representation in relation to this application must give notice in writing to [*insert name and address of the licensing authority*], giving in detail the grounds of objection by [*insert the date by which all relevant representations must be received by the licensing authority, i.e. 28 consecutive days starting on the day after the day on which the application is given to the licensing authority*]. The Licensing Authority must receive representations by the date given above. The Licensing Authority will have regard to any such representation in considering the application.

It is an offence liable on conviction to a fine under section 158 of the Licensing Act 2003 to knowingly or recklessly make a false statement in connection with this application.

17.8.6 Inspection of premises

A constable or an authorised person may, at any reasonable time before the determination of an application for a club premises certificate, enter the club premises to which the application relates to inspect them (s.96).

The following are designated by s.13(2) as authorised persons:

- an officer of a licensing authority in whose area the premises are situated who is authorised by that authority for the purposes of the Act;
- an inspector appointed by the fire and rescue authority for the area in which the premises are situated;
- an inspector appointed under the Health and Safety at Work etc. Act 1974, s.19;
- an officer of a local authority, in whose area the premises are situated, who is authorised by that authority for the purposes of exercising one or more of its statutory functions in relation to minimising or preventing the risk of pollution of the environment or of harm to human health;
- in relation to a vessel, an inspector, or a surveyor of ships, appointed under the Merchant Shipping Act 1995, s.256; and
- a person prescribed for these purposes.

A constable or an authorised person who is exercising the power to enter the premises must, if so requested, produce evidence of his authority to exercise the power (s.96(2)). Before an authorised person or constable can enter and inspect any premises, at least 48 hours' notice must be given to the club (s.96(4)). The entry and inspection must take place at a reasonable time on a day which is not more than 14 days after the application for the club premises certificate was made, and the date of the inspection must be in the notice (s.96(3)). Anyone who intentionally obstructs an authorised person exercising the power of entry commits an offence, and is liable on summary conviction to a fine not exceeding level 2 on the standard scale (s.96(5) and (6)). Obstruction of a constable will constitute an offence of obstructing a constable in the execution of his duty under the Police Act 1996, s.89(2), and a person will be liable on summary conviction to imprisonment for a term not exceeding one month (this will increase to 51 weeks when the Criminal Justice Act 2003 takes effect) or to a fine not exceeding level 3 on the standard scale, or to both.

The relevant licensing authority may, on the application of a responsible authority, extend by not more than seven days the time allowed for carrying out an entry and inspection (s.96(7)). The relevant licensing authority may allow such an extension of time only if it appears that reasonable steps had been taken for an authorised person or constable authorised by the applicant to inspect the premises in good time, but it was not possible for the inspection to take place within the time allowed (s.96(8)).

Table 17.1: Checklist for a club premises certificate application

	Original to relevant licensing authority	Copy to the police where notice must be given by applicant	Copy to responsible authorities where notice must be given by applicant
Completed application form			
Completed declaration form			
Copy of the club rules			
Plan of the premises			
Payment of the fee			
Confirmation that the application has been advertised on the premises and that this will be maintained for 28 days			
Has the application been advertised in a local newspaper?	Name of newspaper:		Date:

17.9 DETERMINATION OF THE APPLICATION

17.9.1 Preliminary determination

When a licensing authority receives an application for a club premises certificate, it must initially determine whether the application has been made properly in accordance with s.71 and with the Premises Licences Regulations. The Guidance at para.8.26 gives recommendations for licensing authorities where applications they contain errors (see **7.4.3**). Any failure to observe the notice requirements will also render the application invalid.

17.9.2 Unopposed applications

When no relevant representations have been made and the relevant licensing authority is satisfied that the applicant has complied with all the application requirements, it must grant the club premises certificate in accordance with the application subject only to such conditions as are consistent with the club operating schedule accompanying the application, and any mandatory conditions (see **17.11**) which must be included in the certificate (s.72(2)).

17.9.3 Applications where representations have been made

If relevant representations have been made by a responsible authority or other persons, s.72(3)(a) provides that the licensing authority must hold a hearing to consider them (see **Chapter 10**).

The hearing must be held within a period of 20 working days beginning with the day after the end of the period during which representations may be made, which is 28 consecutive days starting on the day after the day on which the application is given to the relevant licensing authority (Hearings Regulations, reg.5 and Sched.1, para.8). Notice of the hearing must be given to the club and persons who made relevant representations no later than 10 working days before the day or the first day on which the hearing is to be held (Hearings Regulations, reg.6(4) and Sched.2, para.8). The club must be given the relevant representations with the notice of the hearing (Hearings Regulations, reg.7(2) and Sched.3, para.8). A hearing may be dispensed with if the licensing authority, the club and each person who made representations agree that a hearing is unnecessary.

Following the hearing and having regard to the representations, the licensing authority must then take such of the following steps, if any, as it considers appropriate for the promotion of the licensing objectives:

- to grant the certificate subject to such conditions as are consistent with the club operating schedule accompanying the application modified to such extent as the authority considers appropriate for the promotion of the licensing objectives, and any mandatory conditions which must be included in the certificate. For these purposes, conditions are modified if any of them is altered or omitted or any new condition is added (s.72(6));
- to exclude from the scope of the certificate any of the qualifying club activities to which the application relates; or
- to reject the application (s.72(4)).

The licensing authority must 'have regard' to the representations before taking any of the above steps. This would appear to imply that it can also take into account other matters not included in the representations. A licensing authority does not have to take any of the above steps. So if it does not consider any of them appropriate for the promotion of the licensing objectives, it can grant the certificate in the terms sought by the applicant subject only to such conditions as are consistent with the operating schedule and any conditions which must be imposed under the Act.

Any conditions which are included in a club premises certificate must take account of s.73(1) which provides that a certificate can only authorise off-supplies if it also authorises supplies for consumption on the premises (s.72(5)).

A licensing authority may grant a club premises certificate subject to different conditions in respect of different parts of the premises concerned, or different qualifying club activities (s.72(10)).

17.9.4 Relevant representations

The position regarding relevant representations is the same as in respect of premises licences (see **Chapter 10** as to representations generally).

'Relevant representations' are defined in s.72(7) and (8) and mean representations which:

- are about the likely effect of the grant of the certificate on the promotion of the licensing objectives;
- were made by a responsible authority or other person within the prescribed period;
- have not been withdrawn; and
- in the case of representations made by a person who is not a responsible authority are not, in the opinion of the relevant licensing authority, frivolous or vexatious.

The prescribed period for making representations is 28 consecutive days starting on the day after the day on which the application is given to the relevant licensing authority.

Where the licensing authority determines that any representations are frivolous or vexatious, it must notify the person who made them of the reasons for its determination (s.72(9)).

17.10 ACTION FOLLOWING THE GRANT OR REJECTION OF AN APPLICATION

17.10.1 The grant of an application

Once an application for a club premises certificate has been granted, the licensing authority must forthwith (see **2.9**) give notice that it has been granted to:

- the applicant;
- any person who made relevant representations in respect of the application; and
- the chief officer of police for the police area, or each police area, in which the premises are situated (s.77(1)).

In addition, if relevant representations were made, the notice must set out the authority's reasons for its decision to take any steps to promote the licensing objectives (s.77(2)).

The licensing authority must also issue the club with the club premises certificate and a summary of it (see **17.12**).

17.10.2 The rejection of an application

If an application is rejected, the licensing authority must forthwith (see **2.9**) give notice that it has been rejected, stating its reasons for that decision, to:

- the applicant;
- any person who made relevant representations in respect of the application; and
- the chief officer of police for the police area, or each police area, in which the premises are situated (s.77(3)).

17.11   MANDATORY AND PROHIBITED CONDITIONS

17.11.1   Supply of alcohol to members or guests

A club premises certificate which authorises the supply of alcohol to members or guests must include any conditions specified in an order made under s.73B (s.73A). Section 73B allows the Secretary of State to specify conditions relating to the supply of alcohol which will apply to club premises certificates. The number of such conditions must not exceed, at any time, nine and they apply to both new and existing club premises certificates. Conditions have been prescribed by the Licensing Act 2003 (Mandatory Licensing Conditions) Order 2010, SI 2010/860 and the Licensing Act 2003 (Mandatory Conditions) Order 2014, SI 2014/1252 (see **7.11.2**).

17.11.2   Exhibition of films

Section 74 provides that where a club premises certificate authorises the exhibition of films, the certificate must include a condition requiring the admission of children to the exhibition of any film to be restricted in accordance with film classification recommendations. Such recommendations can be made either by the British Board of Film Classification or the relevant licensing authority if it operates its own film classification certificate.

17.11.3   Prohibited conditions: associate members and their guests

A licensing authority is prohibited, where the rules of a club provide for the sale by retail of alcohol on any premises by or on behalf of the club to, or to a guest of, an associate member of the club, from attaching a condition to a club premises certificate in respect of the sale by retail of alcohol on those premises by or on behalf of the club which would prevent the sale by retail of alcohol to any such associate member or guest (s.75(1)). In addition, where the rules of a club provide for the provision of any regulated entertainment on any premises by or on behalf of the club to, or to a guest of, an associate member of the club, no condition may be attached to a club premises certificate in respect of the provision of any such regulated entertainment on those premises by or on behalf of the club so as to prevent its provision to any such associate member or guest (s.75(2)).

17.11.4 Prohibited conditions: plays

Where a club premises certificate authorises the performance of plays, no condition may be attached to the certificate as to the nature of the plays which may be performed, or the manner of performing plays, under the certificate (s.76). This prohibition does not, however, prevent a licensing authority imposing any condition which it considers appropriate on the grounds of public safety.

17.12 THE FORM OF THE CERTIFICATE AND SUMMARY

17.12.1 Club premises certificate

A club premises certificate must be in the prescribed form (s.78). This is set out in the Premises Licences Regulations, Sched.13, Part A.

A club premises certificate must:

- identify the relevant licensing authority;
- include the certificate number;
- specify the name of the club and the address which is to be its relevant registered address which is defined in s.184(7) as the address given for the holder of the certificate recorded in the licensing authority's register;
- specify the address of the premises to which the certificate relates;
- include a plan of those premises;
- specify the qualifying club activities for which the premises may be used; and
- specify the conditions subject to which the certificate is issued.

17.12.2 Summary of a club premises certificate

A summary of a club premises certificate must be in the prescribed form (s.78(1)). This is set out in the Premises Licences Regulations, Sched.13, Part B. A summary must:

- identify the relevant licensing authority;
- include the certificate number;

- specify all matters mentioned in the certificate, except for a plan; and
- be printed on paper of at least A4 size.

17.13 THEFT OR LOSS

If a club premises certificate or summary is lost, stolen, damaged or destroyed, the club may apply to the relevant licensing authority for a copy (s.79). Presumably an application will be made by the club secretary or some other club official. The prescribed fee must accompany the application.

Where an application for a copy is made, the relevant licensing authority must issue the club with a copy of the certificate or summary if it is satisfied that the certificate or summary has been lost, stolen, damaged or destroyed. The copy must be certified by the authority to be a true copy of the original. It must be a copy of the club premises certificate or summary in the form in which it existed immediately before it was lost, stolen, damaged or destroyed. Once a copy has been issued, the Act will apply to the copy as it applies to an original club premises certificate or summary.

17.14 PERIOD OF VALIDITY OF A CLUB PREMISES CERTIFICATE

Once granted, a club premises certificate does not need to be renewed. Section 80 provides that a club premises certificate has effect until either it is withdrawn by the licensing authority or it lapses by the club surrendering it. A club premises certificate does not have effect during any period when it is suspended pending review or for failure to pay the annual fee.

17.15 SURRENDER OF A CLUB PREMISES CERTIFICATE

A club which holds a club premises certificate may decide it no longer requires the certificate. Presumably the club committee would reach such a decision. It should therefore surrender it back to the relevant licensing authority (s.81). This is done by giving the relevant licensing authority a notice to that effect. The notice must be accompanied by the club premises certificate or, if that is not practicable, by a statement of the reasons for the failure to produce the certificate. No fee is payable, nor need notice be given to anyone other than the relevant licensing authority.

Where a certificate is surrendered, it will lapse when the notice surrendering it is received by the relevant licensing authority.

There is no provision for a certificate which has been surrendered to be reinstated.

17.16 CHANGE OF CLUB NAME OR ALTERATION OF CLUB RULES

If a club decides to change its name, or alter its rules, the club secretary must notify the relevant licensing authority of the change or alteration (s.82). This requirement applies to a club which holds a club premises certificate, and to a club which has made an application for a club premises certificate which has not yet been determined by the relevant licensing authority. The notification must be accompanied by the prescribed fee and the club premises certificate or, if that is not practicable, by a statement of the reasons for the failure to produce the certificate.

When a licensing authority receives notification of a change in the name, or alteration to the rules, of a club it must amend the club premises certificate accordingly. However, this obligation to amend the certificate does not apply to any amendment which would change the premises to which the certificate relates. A club that wishes to change its premises must make an application to vary its club premises certificate.

Notification to the licensing authority must be given within 28 days following the day on which the change of name or alteration to the rules is made, otherwise the secretary of the club commits an offence. A person guilty of such an offence is liable on summary conviction to a fine not exceeding level 2 on the standard scale.

17.17 CHANGE OF RELEVANT REGISTERED ADDRESS OF A CLUB

If a club changes its relevant registered address (i.e. the address in the record for the certificate in the register kept by the licensing authority which granted the certificate), the club may give the relevant licensing authority notice of the change so that it can be recorded in the licensing register (s.83(1)). If a club ceases to have authority to use the address which is its relevant registered address, it must as soon as reasonably practicable give notice of this to the relevant licensing authority together with details of the new address that is to be its relevant registered address (s.83(2)).

Both of these applications must be accompanied by the prescribed fee and the club premises certificate or, if that is not practicable, by a statement of the reasons for the failure to produce the certificate.

A licensing authority which is notified of a change to be made in the relevant registered address of a club must amend the club premises certificate accordingly.

If a club fails, without reasonable excuse, where it ceases to have authority to use the address which is its relevant registered address, to give notice of this to the relevant licensing authority together with details of the new address that is to be its relevant registered address, the secretary commits an offence. A person guilty of such an offence is liable on summary conviction to a fine not exceeding level 2 on the standard scale.

17.18 WITHDRAWAL OF A CLUB PREMISES CERTIFICATE

17.18.1 Withdrawal on review

A club premises certificate can be withdrawn under s.88 following an application for review.

17.18.2 Withdrawal by the licensing authority

A club premises certificate may be withdrawn under s.90 if the club ceases to be a qualifying club. If it appears to the relevant licensing authority that a club does not satisfy the conditions for being a qualifying club in relation to a qualifying club activity to which the certificate relates, the authority must give the club a notice withdrawing the certificate so far as it relates to that activity. It does not seem that a licensing authority must be satisfied that a club does not satisfy the qualifying conditions. It must just 'appear' that the club does not do so. Section 90 is silent on when the withdrawal takes place. It is assumed that this will be the date the notice of withdrawal is given, particularly in view of the three-month requirement in s.90(2).

Where the only reason that the club does not satisfy qualifying club conditions in relation to the activity in question is because it has fewer than the required 25 members, s.90(2) provides that the notice withdrawing the certificate must state that the withdrawal:

- does not take effect until immediately after the end of the period of three months following the date of the notice; and
- will not take effect if, at the end of that period, the club again has at least the required number of members.

A licensing authority can give a further notice of withdrawal at any time (s.90(4)). This would allow an authority which has given a notice under s.90(2) which then discovers during the three-month duration of the notice that the club does not satisfy another of the qualifying conditions to give a further notice which would then have immediate effect.

A club which wishes to challenge a notice withdrawing its club premises certificate may appeal to the magistrates' court against the decision to withdraw the certificate (Sched.5, para.14). There is no other way of challenging a notice.

17.18.3 Entry and search of club premises

In order to obtain evidence that a club no longer satisfies the qualifying club conditions, an application may be made for a warrant to enter and search the club premises (s.90(5) and (6)).

Where a justice of the peace is satisfied, on information on oath, that there are reasonable grounds for believing:

- that a club which holds a club premises certificate does not satisfy the conditions for being a qualifying club in relation to a qualifying club activity to which the certificate relates; and
- that evidence of that fact is to be obtained at the premises to which the certificate relates,

he may issue a warrant authorising a constable to enter the premises, if necessary by force, at any time within one month from the time of the issue of the warrant, and search them. A person who enters premises under the authority of such a warrant may seize and remove any documents relating to the club's business.

17.19 DUTIES IN RELATION TO A CLUB PREMISES CERTIFICATE

17.19.1 A licensing authority's duty to update a club premises certificate

If a licensing authority makes a determination or receives a notice under the Act in respect of a club, or an appeal against a decision is disposed of, it must make any appropriate amendments to the certificate and, if necessary, issue a new summary of the certificate (s.93(1)).

Where a licensing authority is not in possession of the club premises certificate, it may, in order to make any amendments, require the secretary of the club to produce the certificate within 14 days of being notified of this requirement (s.93(2)). A person commits an offence if he fails, without reasonable excuse, to comply with this requirement. A person guilty of such an offence is liable on summary conviction to a fine not exceeding level 2 on the standard scale.

17.19.2 Duty to keep and produce a club premises certificate, etc.

Where club premises are being used for one or more qualifying club activities authorised by the club premises certificate, s.94 provides that the club secretary must ensure that the certificate, or a certified copy of it, and a list of any relevant mandatory conditions applicable to the certificate, are kept at the premises in the custody or under the control of a nominated person who:

- is either the secretary of the club, a member of the club, or a person who works at the premises for the purposes of the club;
- has been nominated for the purpose by the secretary in writing; and
- has been identified to the relevant licensing authority in a notice given by the secretary.

The nominated person must make sure that the summary of the certificate or a certified copy of that summary, and a notice specifying the position which he holds at the premises, are prominently displayed at the premises. There is no requirement that the summary and notice be displayed in the same place in the premises, though obviously this would be desirable.

Both the club secretary and the nominated person will commit an offence if they fail, without reasonable excuse, to comply with their obligations. A person guilty of such an offence is liable on summary conviction to a fine not exceeding level 2 on the standard scale.

A constable or an authorised person may require the nominated person to produce the club premises certificate, or certified copy, or any list of relevant mandatory conditions for examination. An authorised person exercising this power must, if so requested, produce evidence of his authority to exercise the power. A person commits an offence if he fails, without reasonable excuse, to produce a club premises certificate or certified copy of a club premises certificate or a list of relevant mandatory conditions when required to do so, and a person guilty of such an offence is liable on summary conviction to a fine not exceeding level 2 on the standard scale.

For these purposes 'relevant mandatory conditions', in relation to a club premises certificate, means conditions applicable to the certificate by virtue of s.73A or s.73B.

Under s.95 the reference above to a certified copy is a reference to a copy of the document which is certified to be a true copy by:

- the relevant licensing authority:
- a solicitor or notary; or
- a person of a prescribed description.

'Notary' means a person (other than a solicitor) who, for the purposes of the Legal Services Act 2007, is an authorised person in relation to any activity which constitutes a notarial activity (within the meaning of that Act).

Any certified copy which is produced to a constable or an authorised person must be a copy of the document in the form in which it exists at the time. A document which purports to be a certified copy of a document is to be taken to be such a copy, and to comply with the above requirements, unless the contrary is shown.

17.20 POLICE POWERS TO ENTER AND SEARCH CLUB PREMISES

Section 97 provides that a constable may enter and search premises which have a club premises certificate if he has reasonable cause to believe:

- that an offence of supplying or offering to supply, or being concerned in supplying or making an offer to supply, a controlled drug under the Misuse of Drugs Act 1971, s.4(3)(a), (b) or (c) has been, is being, or is about to be, committed there;

- that an offence of supplying, or offering to supply, a psychoactive substance under the Psychoactive Substances Act 2016, s.5(1) or (2) has been, is being, or is about to be, committed there; or
- that there is likely to be a breach of the peace there.

A constable exercising this power may, if necessary, use reasonable force.

17.21 SUSPENSION OF A CLUB PREMISES CERTIFICATE

A licensing authority must suspend a club premises certificate under s.92A if the holder of the certificate fails to pay the annual fee. Where a certificate is suspended, the licensing authority must give notice of the suspension to the holder of the certificate specifying the day the suspension takes effect, which must be at least two working days after the day the notice is given. If the holder of the certificate pays the annual fee, the licensing authority must give the holder a written receipt which specifies the day the licensing authority received the fee ('the receipt day'). The receipt must be given to the holder as soon as reasonably practicable but in any event if the receipt day was a working day, before the end of the first working day after the receipt day, but otherwise, before the end of the second working day after the receipt day.

A club premises certificate will not be suspended if either the holder failed to pay the fee due to an administrative error or before or at the time the fee became due, the holder notified the licensing authority in writing that it disputed liability for, or the amount of, the fee, and in both cases the grace period for payment of the fee has not expired. The grace period is the period of 21 days, beginning on the day after the day the fee became due.

CHAPTER 18

Variation of a club premises certificate

18.1 INTRODUCTION

Section 84 provides that a club which holds a club premises certificate may apply to the relevant licensing authority to vary its certificate. The variation could relate to the conditions attached to the certificate or a change in the licensable activities. The arrangements are similar to those for premises licences. Clubs may also use the minor variation process to make small changes to their certificates provided these could have no adverse impact on the licensing objectives. A club premises certificate may not be varied so as to vary substantially the premises to which it relates.

18.2 APPLYING FOR A MINOR VARIATION

A club which holds a club premises certificate may apply to the relevant licensing authority under s.86A (instead of under s.84 – see **18.3**) for a minor variation of the certificate. A minor variation cannot impact adversely on the licensing objectives.

The Guidance at para.8.61 provides that:

> Minor variations will generally fall into four categories: minor changes to the structure or layout of premises; small adjustments to licensing hours; the removal of out of date, irrelevant or unenforceable conditions or addition of volunteered conditions; and the addition of certain licensable activities. In all cases the overall test is whether the proposed variation could impact adversely on any of the four licensing objectives.

An application may not be made under s.86A to vary a club premises certificate so as to:

• vary substantially the premises to which the club premises certificate relates (whether an intended variation will 'substantially' vary will be a question of fact in each case);

- add the supply of alcohol to members or guests as an activity authorised by the club premises certificate;
- authorise the supply of alcohol to members or guests at any time between 11 pm and 7 am; or
- authorise an increase in the amount of time on any day during which alcohol may be supplied to members or guests.

An applicant for a minor variation must submit the following to the relevant licensing authority:

- a completed application form;
- a plan, if appropriate, of the premises in scale (1 mm to 100 mm), unless otherwise agreed with the licensing authority;
- the club premises certificate, or the appropriate part of it, or if that is not practicable, a statement of the reasons why it cannot be provided; and
- the prescribed fee.

18.2.1 Application form

An application for a minor variation must be made in the prescribed form which is set out in the Premises Licences Regulations, Sched.4B. This is the same form as is used for a minor variation of a premises licence. See **14.2** for details of the application form and its completion.

18.2.2 Making an application

Regulation 21 of the Premises Licences Regulations, reg.21 provides that an application must be made in writing. However, notwithstanding this requirement, an application can also be made electronically (Premises Licences Regulations, reg.21A(1)). See further **7.4.3**.

18.2.3 Advertising an application for a minor variation

The application must be advertised in accordance with the Premises Licences Regulations, reg.26A by displaying a notice prominently at or on the premises for a continuous period beginning on the first working day after the application was given to the relevant licensing authority and ending at the expiry of the ninth consecutive working day after that day.

The notice must be:

- white;
- of a size equal to or larger than A4; and
- printed legibly in black ink or typed in black.

The notice must include the following information:

- at or near the top of the notice the heading 'Licensing Act 2003: Minor Variation of Club Premises Certificate';
- a brief description of the proposed variation or variations;
- the name of the club;
- the postal address of the club premises, if any, or if there is no postal address for the premises a description of those premises sufficient to enable the location and extent of the club premises to be identified;
- the postal address and, where applicable, the worldwide web address where the register of the relevant licensing authority is kept and where and when the record of the application may be inspected;
- the date by which a person may make representations to the relevant licensing authority; and
- that it is an offence knowingly or recklessly to make a false statement in connection with an application and the maximum fine for which a person is liable on summary conviction for the offence.

The information above must be printed or typed in a font of a size equal to or larger than 32 points. The remainder of the notice must be printed or typed in a font of a size equal to or larger than 16 points.

The notice must be displayed prominently at or on the premises to which the application relates so that it can be conveniently read from the exterior of the premises. Where any part of the external perimeter of the premises is 100 or more metres in length and abuts a public highway or other place accessible by the public, a notice must be displayed every 50 metres along that part of the perimeter.

An applicant should check with the relevant licensing authority to see whether it provides a specimen form of notice to use. If not, a suggested form of notice is set out in **Box 18.1**.

BOX 18.1: SUGGESTED FORM OF NOTICE OF AN APPLICATION FOR A MINOR VARIATION OF A CLUB PREMISES CERTIFICATE

Licensing Act 2003

Notice of application for a minor variation to a club premises certificate

PREMISES: [*insert name and address of the club premises*]

Notice is hereby given that [*insert the full name of the club*] has applied to the [*insert the full name of the licensing authority*] on [*insert the date of application to the licensing authority*] for a minor variation to a club premises certificate under the Licensing Act 2003.

The proposed variation is: [*set out details of the proposed variation*].

Anyone who wishes to make representations in relation to this application for a minor variation must give notice in writing by [*insert the date the by which all relevant representations must be received by the licensing authority, i.e. 10 working days after the day on which the application is received by the licensing authority*] to [*insert contact details for the licensing authority*].

The public register where applications are available to be viewed by members of the public can be viewed during normal office hours at [*insert details*].

It is an offence liable on conviction to a fine under section 158 of the Licensing Act 2003 to knowingly or recklessly make a false statement in or in connection with this application.

18.2.4 Notice to responsible authorities of a minor variation

Where an application is made electronically and any plan or document required to accompany the application is also given electronically, the relevant licensing authority must, no later than the first working day after the application was given to it, give notice of the application to each responsible authority by giving each authority a copy of the application together with any accompanying plan or document (Premises Licences Regulations, reg.27).

Where an application is not made electronically, the applicant must give notice of the application to each responsible authority by giving each authority a copy of the application together with its accompanying plan, document or other information on the same day as the day on which the application is given to the relevant licensing authority (Premises Licences Regulations, reg.27A).

18.2.5 Determination of an application for a minor variation

Where a licensing authority is determining an application for a minor variation, it must consult such of the responsible authorities as it considers appropriate, and take into account any relevant representations made by those authorities or made by any other person and received by the licensing authority within 10 working days beginning on the first working day after the day on which the licensing authority received the application for the minor variation (s.86B(2)). In this context, relevant representations are those which are about the likely effect of the grant of the application on the promotion of the licensing objectives (s.86B(10)). There is no right to a hearing, but the licensing authority must take any representations into account in arriving at a decision.

If the licensing authority considers that the variation proposed in the application could not have an adverse effect on the promotion of any of the licensing objectives, or if more than one variation is proposed, none of them, whether considered separately or together could have such an effect, it must grant the application (s.86B(3)). In any other case, the licensing authority must reject the application (s.86B(4)). The test as to whether or not the application could have an adverse effect on the promotion of any of the licensing objectives is a strict one and where there is any doubt the licensing authority must reject the application.

The Guidance at para.8.55 provides that:

On receipt of an application for a minor variation, the licensing authority must consider whether the variation could impact adversely on the licensing objectives. It is recommended that decisions on minor variations should be delegated to licensing officers.

A licensing authority must make a decision on an application for a minor variation within a period of 15 working days beginning on the first working day after the day on which the licensing authority received the application for the minor variation (s.86B(5)). As other persons have 10 working days from the day after the application is received by the licensing authority to submit representations, the licensing authority must wait until this period has elapsed before determining the application, but must do so at the latest within 15 working days, beginning on the first working day after the authority received the application.

If the licensing authority does not make a determination within the 15-working day period, the application is rejected and the licensing authority must forthwith return the fee that accompanied the application (s.86B(6)). Any fee may be recovered as a debt due to the applicant (s.86B(9)). Notwithstanding this, a licensing authority, with the agreement of the applicant, can treat a rejected application as a new application and treat the appropriate fee originally submitted as a fee for the new application (s.86B(7)). Such a new application will be treated as having been made on the date of the agreement, or on such other date as is specified in the agreement (s.86B(8)).

18.2.6 Notification of a decision relating to a minor variation

Where an application for a minor variation is granted, the licensing authority must forthwith (see **2.9**) give notice of this to the applicant (s.86C(1)).

The notice must specify any variation of the club premises certificate which is to have effect as a result of the grant of the application, and the time at which that variation takes effect (s.86C(2)). The time specified is the time specified in the application or, if that time is before the applicant is given notice of the decision, such later time as the licensing authority specifies in the notice (s.86C(3)).

Where an application for a minor variation is rejected, the licensing authority must forthwith (see **2.9**) give notice of this to the applicant and such notice must include a statement of the reasons for the licensing authority's decision (s.86C(4), (5)).

18.2.7 Appeal

There is no right of appeal against a decision in relation to a minor variation. However, where an application is refused, it may be resubmitted through the full variation process.

18.3 APPLYING FOR A VARIATION

Where the minor variations procedure cannot be used a club which holds a club premises certificate may at any time apply to the relevant licensing authority to vary the premises licence under s.84.

A club seeking a variation must submit the following to the relevant licensing authority:

- a completed application form;
- the club premises certificate or, if that is not practicable, a statement of the reasons for the failure to provide the certificate; and
- the prescribed fee.

18.4 THE APPLICATION FORM

An application for a variation must be in the prescribed form which is set out in the Premises Licences Regulations, Sched.10.

18.4.1 Completing the application form

Guidance in completing the application form may be obtained from **www.gov.uk** or the relevant licensing authority. The form may be completed by being either typed or written legibly in block capitals. All answers must be inside the boxes and written in black ink.

In the opening statement, the name of the club which is applying for the variation should be inserted together with the number of its club premises certificate.

The application form is then divided into five parts, as follows.

Part 1

The applicant must set out the name of the club, the postal address or, if none, the ordnance survey map reference or a description of the premises, and its telephone number, if any. An email address can also be given though this is optional. The following details of the club secretary must also be given:

- the name of the club secretary;
- the address of the club secretary;
- a daytime contact telephone number, if any; and
- an email address (optional).

Part 2

Part 2 deals with the details of the applicant. The applicant must give such information as his address, if this is not the same as the club premises and daytime telephone number. An email address can also be given though this is optional.

Part 3

Part 3 deals with the proposed variation. The applicant must indicate whether the proposed variation is to have effect as soon as possible, or if not, when it is to take effect from. If the variation would result in 5,000 or more people attending the premises at any one time, the number expected to attend must be stated.

The nature of the proposed variation must be briefly described. This description should include a description of the premises, for example the type of premises, their general situation and layout and any other information which could be relevant to the licensing objectives. Where the application includes off-supplies of alcohol and it is intended to provide a place for consumption of these off-supplies, a description of where the place will be and its proximity to the premises must be included.

Part 4

Part 4 is the club operating schedule. Those parts which would be subject to change if the application is successful must be completed. The club must indicate the qualifying activities which it is intended to conduct on the club premises that will be affected by the application. Any adult entertainment or services, activities, other entertainment or matters ancillary to the use of the premises that may give rise to concern in respect of children must be highlighted. It must also identify any existing conditions which it believes could be removed if the variation were approved. If the club premises certificate, or relevant part, cannot be enclosed with the application, an explanation must be given.

The club must then describe any additional steps it intends to take to promote the four licensing objectives as a result of the proposed variation.

Finally, there is a checklist for the applicant to complete so that nothing is overlooked, together with a warning that it is an offence, liable on conviction to an unlimited fine, under s.158 to make a false statement in or in connection with the application.

Part 5

Part 5 makes provision for the applicant to sign the form. The form must be signed by a person who has authority to bind the club.

18.4.2 Obtaining an application form

For details on obtaining a form see **7.4.2**.

18.4.3 Making an application

The Premises Licences Regulations, reg.21 provides that an application must be made in writing. However, notwithstanding this requirement, an application can also be made electronically (Premises Licences Regulations, reg.21A(1)). See further **7.4.3**.

18.5 ADVERTISING

18.5.1 Advertising of the application by the applicant

The application must be advertised in accordance with the Premises Licences Regulations, reg.25 (s.84(4)) by displaying a notice at or on the premises and by publishing a notice in a local newspaper.

An applicant must advertise his application by displaying a notice containing prescribed information on the premises for a period of not less than 28 consecutive days starting on the day after the day on which the application was given to the relevant licensing authority.

The notice must be:

- of a size equal to or larger than A4;
- of a pale blue colour; and
- printed legibly in black ink or typed in black in a font of a size equal to or larger than 16 points.

The notice must be displayed prominently at or on the premises to which the application relates where it can be conveniently read from the exterior of the premises. Where the premises cover an area of more than 50 metres square, a further notice in the same form and subject to the same requirements must be displayed every 50 metres along the external perimeter of the premises abutting any highway.

An applicant must publish a notice containing prescribed information in a local newspaper or, if there is none, in a local newsletter, circular or similar document, circulating in the vicinity of the premises on at least one occasion during the 10 working days starting on the day after the day on which the application was given to the relevant licensing authority.

The contents of the notices to be displayed at or on the premises and to be published in a local newspaper are specified in the Premises Licences Regulations, reg.26. The notices must:

- briefly describe the proposed variation;

- state the name of the club;
- state the postal address of the club premises, if any, or if there is no postal address for the premises a description of those premises sufficient to enable the location and extent of the premises to be identified;
- state the postal address and, where applicable, the worldwide web address where the register of the relevant licensing authority is kept and where and when the record of the application may be inspected;
- state the date by which a responsible authority or any other person may make representations to the relevant licensing authority;
- state that representations shall be made in writing; and
- state that it is an offence knowingly or recklessly to make a false statement in connection with an application and the maximum fine for which a person is liable on summary conviction for the offence.

An applicant should check with the relevant licensing authority to see whether it provides a specimen form of notice to use. If not, a suggested form of notice is given in **Box 18.2**.

18.5.2 Advertising of the application by the licensing authority

The application must be advertised by the relevant licensing authority in accordance with the Premises Licences Regulations, reg.26B for a period of no less than 28 consecutive days starting on the day after the day on which the application was given to the relevant licensing authority by publishing a notice on its website.

The contents of the notice are specified in the Premises Licences Regulations, reg.26C. The notice must:

- briefly describe the proposed variation;
- state the name of the club;
- state the postal address of the club premises, if any, or if there is no postal address for the premises a description of those premises sufficient to enable the location and extent of the club premises to be identified;
- state the postal address and, where applicable, the worldwide web address where the register of the relevant licensing authority is kept and where and when the record of the application may be inspected;
- state the date by which a responsible authority or any other person may make representations to the relevant licensing authority;
- state that representations shall be made in writing; and
- state that it is an offence knowingly or recklessly to make a false statement in connection with an application and the maximum fine for which a person is liable on summary conviction for the offence.

18.6 NOTICE TO RESPONSIBLE AUTHORITIES

Where an application is made electronically and any plan or document required to accompany the application is also given electronically, the relevant licensing authority must, no later than the first working day after the application was given to it, give notice of the application to each responsible authority by giving each authority a copy of the application together with any accompanying plan or document (Premises Licences Regulations, reg.27).

Where an application is not made electronically, the applicant must give notice of his application to each responsible authority by giving each authority a copy of the application together with its accompanying plan, document or other information on the same day as the day on which the application is given to the relevant licensing authority (Premises Licences Regulations, reg.27A).

BOX 18.2: SUGGESTED FORM OF NOTICE OF AN APPLICATION TO VARY A CLUB PREMISES CERTIFICATE

Licensing Act 2003

Notice of application to vary a club premises certificate

PREMISES: [*insert address of premises*]

Notice is hereby given that [*insert the full name of the club*] has applied to the [*insert the full name of the licensing authority*] on [*insert the date of application to the licensing authority*] to vary a club premises certificate under the Licensing Act 2003.

The proposed variation is: [*set out details of the proposed variation*].

Any person who wishes to make a representation in relation to this application must give notice in writing of his/her representation by [*insert the date by which all relevant representations must be received by the licensing authority, i.e. 28 consecutive days starting on the day after the day on which the application is given to the licensing authority*] stating the grounds for making said representation to [*insert contact details for the licensing authority*]. The public register where applications are available to be viewed by members of the public can be viewed at [*insert details*]. The Licensing Authority must receive representations by the date given above. The Licensing Authority will have regard to any such representation in considering the application.

It is an offence liable on conviction to a fine under section 158 of the Licensing Act 2003 to knowingly or recklessly make a false statement in or in connection with an application for a club premises certificate.

18.7 DETERMINATION OF THE APPLICATION

18.7.1 Preliminary determination

When a licensing authority receives an application for a variation, it must initially determine whether the application has been made properly in accordance with the

Act and with the Premises Licences Regulations. The Guidance at para.8.26 gives recommendations for licensing authorities where applications they contain errors (see **7.4.3**). Any failure to observe the notice requirements will also render the application invalid.

18.7.2 Unopposed applications

Where a licensing authority has received an application to vary a club premises certificate and is satisfied that the applicant has complied with all the procedural requirements, and no relevant representations have been received there is no need for a hearing and it must grant the application (s.85(2)).

18.7.3 Applications where representations have been made

Where relevant representations are made, the authority must hold a hearing to consider them, unless the authority, the applicant and each person who has made such representations agree that a hearing is unnecessary (s.85(3)(a)). A hearing must be held within 20 working days beginning with the day after the end of the period during which representations may be made (Hearings Regulations, reg.5 and Sched.1, para.9). Notice of the hearing must be given to the club and persons who have made relevant representations no later than 10 working days before the day or the first day on which the hearing is to be held (Hearings Regulations, reg.6(4) and Sched.2, para.9). The club must be sent the relevant representations with the notice of hearing (Hearings Regulations, reg.7(2) and Sched.3, para.9).

The hearing should focus only on the steps needed to promote the particular licensing objective which has given rise to the representation. Following the hearing the licensing authority may, having regard to the representations, and if it considers it appropriate for the promotion of the licensing objectives, modify the conditions of the certificate, or reject the whole or part of the application (s.85(4)). The conditions are treated as being modified if any of them are altered or omitted or any new condition is added. The club premises certificate may be varied in such a way so that it has effect subject to different conditions in respect of different parts of the premises or different licensable activities (s.86(7)). If the licensing authority does not consider that any steps are appropriate, it can grant the variation in accordance with the application.

'Relevant representations' are representations which:

- are about the likely effect of the grant of the application on the promotion of the licensing objectives;
- are made by a responsible authority or other person within the period of 28 consecutive days starting on the day after the day on which the applicant gave the application to the licensing authority;
- have not been withdrawn; and

- in the case of representations made by a person who is not also a responsible authority are not, in the opinion of the relevant licensing authority, frivolous or vexatious.

When granting an unopposed application or making its decision where relevant representations have been made, a licensing authority must consider its duties in relation to the mandatory conditions relating to alcohol and to exhibition of films (s.85(7)).

18.8 NOTIFICATION OF A DECISION

When an application is granted either in whole or in part, s.86(1) provides that the licensing authority must forthwith (see **2.9**) give notice of this to:

- the applicant;
- any person who made relevant representations in respect of the application; and
- the chief officer of police for the police area (or each police area) in which the premises are situated.

Where relevant representations were made, the notice must set out the authority's reasons for its decision as to any steps it considers appropriate to take to promote the licensing objectives. The notice must also specify the time when the variation in question takes effect. This will either be the time specified in the application or, if that time is before the applicant is given the notice, such later time as the relevant licensing authority specifies in the notice.

Where an application, or any part of an application, is rejected s.86(4) provides that the relevant licensing authority must forthwith (see **2.9**) give a notice to that effect stating its reasons for rejecting the application to:

- the applicant;
- any person who made relevant representations; and
- the chief officer of police for the police area (or each police area) in which the premises are situated.

The notice must be accompanied by information regarding the right of a party to appeal against the determination.

Where a relevant licensing authority determines that any representations are frivolous or vexatious, it must give the person who made them its reasons for that determination.

18.9 INSPECTION OF PREMISES

A constable or an authorised person may, at any reasonable time before the deter-mination of an application for the variation of a club premises certificate, enter the premises to which the application relates to inspect them.

A constable or an authorised person who is exercising the power to enter the premises must, if so requested, produce evidence of his authority to exercise the power (s.96(2)). Before an authorised person or a constable can enter and inspect any premises, at least 48 hours' notice must be given to the club (s.96(4)). The entry and inspection must take place at a reasonable time on a day which is not more than 14 days after the application for the variation was made, and the date of the inspection must be in the notice (s.96(3)). Anyone who intentionally obstructs an authorised person exercising the power of entry commits an offence, and is liable on summary conviction to a fine not exceeding level 2 on the stan-dard scale (s.96(5) and (6)).

In addition, obstructing a constable exercising the right of entry will be an offence of obstructing a constable in the execution of his duties under the Police Act 1996, s.89(2). A person guilty of such an offence is liable on summary con-viction to imprisonment for a term not exceeding one month (this will increase to 51 weeks when the Criminal Justice Act 2003 takes effect) or to a fine not exceeding level 3 on the standard scale, or to both.

The relevant licensing authority may, on the application of a responsible authority, extend by not more than seven days the time allowed for carrying out an entry and inspection. The relevant licensing authority may allow such an extension of time only if it appears that reasonable steps had been taken for an authorised person or constable authorised by the applicant to inspect the premises in good time, but it was not possible for the inspection to take place within the time allowed.

CHAPTER 19

Review of a club premises certificate

19.1 INTRODUCTION

The Act provides a procedure whereby a club premises certificate can be reviewed at any time on the application of a responsible authority, such as the police, because of a matter arising at the premises in connection with any of the licensing objectives, or any other person, such as a resident living nearby the club premises or a member of the club. This procedure is necessary as otherwise there would be no other opportunity to deal with problems which may arise during the currency of the club premises certificate. A review must be based on one of the licensing objectives.

A review of a club premises certificate is very similar to a review of a premises licence and reference should be made to **Chapter 15**.

19.2 WHO CAN APPLY FOR A REVIEW?

At any time, a responsible authority or any other person may apply to the relevant licensing authority for a review of the club premises certificate (s.87(1)). However, an application for a review need not be the first step where problems arise and the Guidance at para.11.10 provides that:

> Where authorised persons and responsible authorities have concerns about problems identified at premises, it is good practice for them to give licence holders early warning of their concerns and the need for improvement, and where possible they should advise the licence or certificate holder of the steps they need to take to address those concerns. A failure by the holder to respond to such warnings is expected to lead to a decision to apply for a review. Co-operation at a local level in promoting the licensing objectives should be encouraged and reviews should not be used to undermine this co-operation.

A licensing authority cannot initiate a review. However, where a local authority is both the relevant licensing authority and a responsible authority, it may, in its capacity as a responsible authority, apply for a review of a club premises certificate and, in its capacity as licensing authority, determine the application (s.89).

For example, an environmental health officer may request a review on a matter which relates to the promotion of one or more of the licensing objectives.

19.3 WHEN CAN AN APPLICATION BE MADE?

An application for a review may be made at any time where a club premises certificate has effect (s.87(1)). It is clear that an application can be made at any time as the Guidance at para.11.2 states:

> At any stage, following the grant of a premises licence or club premises certificate, a responsible authority, or any other person, may ask the licensing authority to review the licence or certificate because of a matter arising at the premises in connection with any of the four licensing objectives.

19.4 MAKING AN APPLICATION

An application for a review of a club premises certificate must be made to the relevant licensing authority (s.87(1)). There is no fee payable for a review.

A copy of the application must also be sent to the club and each of the responsible authorities. The application must also be advertised (see **19.6**).

19.5 THE APPLICATION FORM

An application for a review must be in the prescribed form which is set out in the Premises Licences Regulations, Sched.8.

19.5.1 Completing the application form

Guidance in completing the application form may be obtained from **www.gov.uk** or the relevant licensing authority. The form may be completed by being either typed or written legibly in block capitals. All answers must be inside the boxes and written in black ink.

In the opening statement, the name of the applicant or applicants who are applying for the review should be inserted.

The application form is then divided into three parts.

Part 1

The applicant must set out the postal address of the club premises. If the club premises have no postal address, the location of the club premises should be described or the Ordnance Survey map reference should be given. The name of the club holding the club premises certificate and the number of the club premises certificate should then be given, if these are known.

Part 2

Part 2 deals with the details of the applicant and the reason for the review. The applicant must state whether he is an individual, body or business which is not a responsible authority, or a responsible authority. An individual applicant must then give such details as his name and address, telephone number, email address (optional) and confirmation that he is at least 18 years old. Other applicants must give their name and address, telephone number and email address (optional). A responsible authority must give its name and address, telephone number and email address (optional).

The applicant must then state which of the licensing objectives the application relates to and the grounds for review and provide as much information as possible to support the application, such as details of problems which have occurred.

The form also asks whether the applicant has applied for a review in relation to the club premises before and, if so, the date of that application. If the applicant has made representations before in relation to the club premises he must set them out and indicate when they were made.

Part 2 also includes a checklist for the applicant so that nothing is overlooked, together with a warning that it is an offence, liable on conviction to a fine up to level 5 on the standard scale, under s.158 to make a false statement in or in connection with the application.

Part 3

Part 3 provides for the applicant to sign the form. The form can also be signed by the applicant's solicitor or other duly authorised agent, and someone signing on behalf of the applicant must state in what capacity they sign. Where there are joint applicants, both applicants or their respective agents must sign the application form.

19.5.2 Obtaining an application form

A relevant licensing authority must provide an applicant on request with a printed application form; however, an electronic version may be provided by a licensing authority on its website which a prospective applicant can download, print off and complete. An electronic copy is also provided on **www.gov.uk**.

19.5.3 Making an application

For details on how to make the application see **15.5.3**.

19.5.4 Notice to responsible authorities and club

The applicant must give a copy of the application form together with any accompanying documents to each responsible authority and to the club in whose name the club premises certificate is held and to which the application relates on the same day as it is given to the licensing authority (Premises Licences Regulations, regs.27A, 29). It must also be advertised (see **19.6**). A responsible authority or any other person may then make a representation to the licensing authority within the period of 28 days starting on the day after the day on which the application for review was given to the licensing authority (Premises Licences Regulations, reg.22(1)(b)).

19.6 ADVERTISING THE APPLICATION

The Premises Licences Regulations regs.38 and 39 set out the requirements for advertising the application. Once a licensing authority has received an application for review, it must advertise it by displaying prominently for a period of no less than 28 consecutive days starting on the day after the day on which the application was given to the licensing authority a notice which is:

- of a size equal to or larger than A4;
- of a pale blue colour; and
- printed legibly in black ink or typed in black in a font of a size equal to or larger than 16 points.

The notice must be displayed:

- at, on or near the site of the club premises to which the application relates where it can conveniently be read from the exterior of the premises by the public and in the case of a premises covering an area of more than 50 metres square, one further notice in the same form and subject to the same requirements shall be displayed every 50 metres along the external perimeter of the premises abutting any highway; and
- at the offices, or the main offices, of the licensing authority in a central and conspicuous place.

If the licensing authority has a website which it uses to advertise applications it receives, then a notice of the application for review must also be published on that website.

All the notices must state:

- the address of the premises about which an application for a review has been made;
- the dates between which responsible authorities and any other persons may make representations to the relevant licensing authority;
- the grounds of the application for review;

- the postal address and, where relevant, the worldwide web address where the register of the relevant licensing authority is kept and where and when the grounds for the review may be inspected; and
- that it is an offence knowingly or recklessly to make a false statement in connection with an application and the maximum fine for which a person is liable on summary conviction for the offence.

19.7 REJECTION OF THE APPLICATION

Once an application for review has been received by a licensing authority, it must initially consider whether the grounds for review stated in the application are relevant to the licensing objectives. Any ground for review specified in the application may, at any time, be rejected by the licensing authority if it is satisfied that the ground is not relevant to one or more of the licensing objectives, or, in the case of an application made by a person other than a responsible authority, that the ground is frivolous or vexatious or is a repetition (s.87(4)).

A ground will not be relevant if it does not relate to one or more of the licensing objectives. Rejection of a ground because it is frivolous or vexatious will be similar to a rejection of a relevant representation by a person other than a responsible authority on an application for a premises licence.

A ground for review is a repetition under s.87(5) if:

- it is identical or substantially similar to:

  - a ground for review specified in an earlier application for review made in respect of the same club premises certificate which has been determined; or
  - representations considered by the relevant licensing authority before it originally granted the club premises certificate; and

- a reasonable interval has not elapsed since that earlier application for review or the grant of the club premises certificate. The Guidance, para.11.13 recommends that more than one review originating from a person other than a responsible authority should not be permitted within a period of 12 months on similar grounds save in compelling circumstances or where it arises following a closure order.

Rejection on the ground of repetition is similar to that in relation to the review of premises licences.

If a licensing authority rejects a ground for review, it must notify the applicant in writing of its decision as soon as reasonably practicable and, if the ground was rejected because it was frivolous or vexatious, it must include a statement of its reasons for making that decision (s.87(6)).

If the applicant had raised more than one ground in his application and not all of them are rejected then the application is only treated as being rejected in respect of the ground which has been rejected and it will still be valid in relation to any ground which has not been rejected (s.87(7)). Even though one of the grounds stated in the application may have been rejected, the obligation to give notice still applies. By way of example, if a licensing authority receives an application which sets out two grounds for review and it decides that one of the grounds is frivolous it must give notice of this to the applicant together with the reasons for its decision, and then proceed to determine the application on the basis of the remaining ground.

19.8 DETERMINATION OF THE APPLICATION FOR REVIEW

The position is the same as for a review of a premises licence and the paragraphs in the Guidance on such reviews apply equally here. Once the 28-day period for making representations has ended, the licensing authority must hold a hearing within 20 working days beginning with the day after the end of the 28-day period to consider the application and any relevant representations (Hearings Regulations, reg.5 and Sched.1, para.10). Notice of the hearing must be given to the club, persons who have made relevant representations and the applicant for the review no later than 10 working days before the day or the first day on which the hearing is to be held (Hearings Regulations, reg.6(4) and Sched.2, para.10). There is no provision for dispensing with the hearing if all the parties consider it unnecessary. The club must be given the relevant representations with the notice of hearing (Hearings Regulations, reg.7(2) and Sched.3, para.10).

When determining the application, the licensing authority must have regard to the application and any relevant representations. It may decide that no action is required in order to promote the licensing objectives, or that informal action should be taken, for example by giving the club an informal warning or a recommendation to improve matters within a specified period of time.

If, however, the licensing authority considers that formal action is required, it may take such of the following steps, if any, which it considers appropriate for the promotion of the licensing objectives:

- modify the conditions of the certificate (this will involve any of the conditions of the licence being altered or omitted or the addition of a new condition);
- exclude a qualifying club activity from the scope of the certificate;
- suspend the certificate for a period not exceeding three months; or
- withdraw the certificate (s.88(3), (4)).

When making its determination, the licensing authority must have regard to the requirements in the Act to include mandatory conditions relating to alcohol and to the exhibition of films in the certificate.

If a licensing authority decides that none of these steps is appropriate, then it need take no action.

Where a licensing authority takes one of the above steps, it may provide that the modification or exclusion is to have effect for a specified period only, not exceeding three months, as it may specify.

19.9 NOTIFICATION OF THE DECISION

Once an application for a review has been determined, the licensing authority must notify the following of its decision and its reasons:

- the club;
- the applicant;
- any person who made relevant representations; and
- the chief officer of police for the police area (or each police area) in which the premises are situated (s.88(10)).

The decision will not, however, take effect until the end of the period for appealing against the decision, or if the decision is appealed against, until the appeal is disposed of. An appeal may be made by the club, the applicant or any person who made relevant representations within 21 days.

19.10 RELEVANT REPRESENTATIONS

For the purposes of a review, s.88(7) and (8) provides that representations are relevant if they:

- are relevant to one or more of the licensing objectives;
- are made by the club, a responsible authority or any other persons within the 28-day period prescribed for making representations;
- have not been withdrawn; and
- if they are made by a person who is not a responsible authority, are not, in the opinion of the relevant licensing authority, frivolous or vexatious.

Where the licensing authority decides that a representation is frivolous or vexatious, it must notify the person who made it of its reasons for its decision.

19.11 INSPECTION OF PREMISES

A constable or an authorised person may, at any reasonable time before the determination of an application for a review of a club premises certificate, enter the premises to which the application relates to inspect them (s.96(1)).

A constable or an authorised person who is exercising the power to enter the premises must, if so requested, produce evidence of his authority to exercise the power (s.96(2)). Before an authorised person or a constable can enter and inspect any premises, at least 48 hours' notice must be given to the club (s.96(4)). The entry and inspection must take place at a reasonable time on a day which is not more than 14 days after the application for the review was made, and the date of the inspection must be in the notice (s.96(3)). Anyone who intentionally obstructs an authorised person exercising the power of entry commits an offence, and is liable on summary conviction to a fine not exceeding level 2 on the standard scale (s.96(5) and (6)).

In addition, obstructing a constable exercising the right of entry will be an offence of obstructing a constable in the execution of his duties under the Police Act 1996, s.89(2). A person guilty of such an offence is liable on summary conviction to imprisonment for a term not exceeding one month (this will increase to 51 weeks when the Criminal Justice Act 2003 takes effect) or to a fine not exceeding level 3 on the standard scale, or to both.

The relevant licensing authority may, on the application of a responsible authority, extend by not more than seven days the time allowed for carrying out an entry and inspection. The relevant licensing authority may allow such an extension of time only if it appears that reasonable steps had been taken for an authorised person or constable authorised by the applicant to inspect the premises in good time, but it was not possible for the inspection to take place within the time allowed.

CHAPTER 20

Permitted temporary activities

20.1 INTRODUCTION

Part 5 of the Act contains arrangements for the temporary carrying out of licen-sable activities which are not authorised by a premises licence or club premises certificate. No authorisation is required for these temporary events from the rele-vant licensing authority. All that is required is that notice be given to the licensing authority, the police and the local authority exercising environmental health func-tions. In general, only the police and the local authority exercising environmental health functions may intervene to prevent such an event taking place or to agree a modification of the arrangements for such an event. This is possible because of the limitations directly imposed on the use of the system by the Act itself. These limitations apply to:

- the number of times a premises user may give a temporary event notice (TEN) (50 times per calendar year for a personal licence holder but no more than 10 of the 50 can be given as late temporary event notices and five times per calendar year for other people but no more than two of the five can be given as late temporary event notices);
- the number of times a temporary event notice may be given in respect of any particular premises (15 times in a calendar year);
- the length of time a temporary event may last for these purposes (168 hours);
- the maximum aggregate duration of the periods covered by temporary event notices at any individual premises (21 days per calendar year);
- the scale of the event in terms of the maximum number of people attending at any one time (fewer than 500); and
- the minimum period between events authorised under separate temporary event notices in relation to the same premises (not including withdrawn tem-porary event notices) given by the same premises user (24 hours).

Situations where a temporary event notice might be used would include the run-ning of a temporary bar at a wedding reception or at a fundraising event being held in an unlicensed venue, the provision of live music in premises which are not licensed for the provision of entertainment or the provision of late night refreshment, e.g. the supply of hot food, at the end of a quiz night.

A temporary event notice can be given by any individual, including holders of personal licences. Where it is given by a person who does not hold a personal licence, the Guidance at para.7.24 provides:

> The 2003 Act provides that any individual aged 18 or over may give a TEN to author-ise the carrying on of all licensable activities under the Licensing Act 2003, whether or not that individual holds a personal licence. Such an individual will not, therefore, have met the requirements that apply to a personal licence holder under Part 6 of the 2003 Act. Where alcohol is not intended to be sold, this should not matter. However, many events will involve a combination of licensable activities and the 2003 Act limits the number of notices that may be given by any non-personal licence holder to five occa-sions in a calendar year (inclusive of any late TENs – subject to a maximum of 2 – in the same year). In every other respect, the Guidance and information set out in the paragraphs above applies.

There are two types of temporary event notices – standard and late. These are subject to different processes. A standard temporary event notice is given no later than 10 working days before the event to which it relates. A late temporary event notice may be given up to five working days but no earlier than nine work-ing days before the event.

20.2 MEANING OF 'PERMITTED TEMPORARY ACTIVITY'

Section 98 provides that a licensable activity is a permitted temporary activity if:

- it is carried out in accordance with a temporary event notice which has been properly given and any conditions imposed on it;
- the statutory requirements as to acknowledgement of the notice are met in relation to the notice;
- the notice has not been withdrawn; and
- a counter notice has not been given.

20.3 THE RELEVANT LICENSING AUTHORITY

In relation to temporary event notices, s.99 provides that the 'relevant licensing authority' in relation to any premises is the licensing authority in whose area the premises are situated or, where the premises are situated in the areas of two or more licensing authorities, each of those authorities. This means that where pre-mises are situated in two or more licensing areas, a temporary event notice must be given to each of the licensing authorities.

20.4 RELEVANT PERSON

A relevant person, in relation to any premises, will be the chief officer of police for any police area in which the premises are situated and the local authority by which statutory functions are exercisable in any area in which the premises are situated in relation to minimising or preventing the risk of pollution of the environment or of harm to human health (s.99A).

20.5 PERSONS ENTITLED TO GIVE A TEMPORARY EVENT NOTICE

A temporary event notice may only be given by an individual aged 18 or over who proposes to use premises for one or more licensable activities during a period not exceeding 168 hours (s.100(1)–(3)). Such a person is referred to in the Act as the 'premises user'.

20.6 FORM AND CONTENT OF A TEMPORARY EVENT NOTICE

Section 100(4)–(6) provides that a temporary event notice must be in the prescribed form and contain:

- a statement of the following matters:

    - the licensable activities which are proposed ('the relevant licensable activities');
    - the period, not exceeding 168 hours, during which it is proposed to use the premises for those activities ('the event period');
    - the times during the event period when the premises user proposes that those licensable activities shall take place;
    - the maximum number of persons, being under 500, which the premises user proposes should, during those times, be allowed on the premises at the same time;
    - where the relevant licensable activities include the supply of alcohol, whether supplies are proposed to be for consumption on the premises or off the premises, or both; and
    - such other matters as may be prescribed.

- where the relevant licensable activities include the supply of alcohol, a statement that it is a condition of using the premises for such supplies that all such supplies are made by or under the authority of the premises user. The supply of alcohol means the sale by retail of alcohol, or the supply of alcohol by or on behalf of a club to, or to the order of, a member of the club (s.100(9)); and
- such other information as may be prescribed.

The prescribed form of temporary event notice is contained in the Licensing Act 2003 (Permitted Temporary Activities) (Notices) Regulations 2005, SI 2005/2918 ('Permitted Temporary Activities Regulations'), Sched.1.

The 'event period' is a period not exceeding 168 hours. This will allow licensable activities to take place on seven consecutive days. However, there is no express requirement that they must take place on consecutive days. It would appear that licensable activities can take place on non-consecutive days provided those activities do not exceed 168 hours in total. For example, for an event lasting a week there might be licensable activities on Monday and Tuesday, none on Wednesday, licensable activities on Thursday and Friday, none on Saturday and then licensable activities on Sunday, Monday and Tuesday. If the licensable activities do not exceed 168 hours the statutory requirements will be satisfied even though the licensable activities take place on non-consecutive days. Having said that it may well be that the provision will be interpreted to require the licensable activities to take place on consecutive days as this was the position with occasional permissions under the previous law (see *R. v. Bromley Licensing Justices ex p. Bromley Licensed Victuallers* [1984] 1 WLR 585; [1984] 1 All ER 794 where 'a period not exceeding twenty four hours' was taken to mean a continuous period of 24 hours).

The Secretary of State may by order alter the length of the event period and the maximum number of people attending at any one time during the event (s.100(8)).

20.6.1 Obtaining a form of temporary event notice

The Permitted Temporary Activities Regulations are silent on whether a relevant licensing authority must provide a potential applicant with a temporary event notice on request. The provisions to this effect in the Premises Licences Regulations only apply to forms listed in the schedules to those regulations and not to other forms. In practice, licensing authorities will make printed copies available and may also provide electronic versions on their websites or via the website **www.gov.uk** which a potential applicant can download, print off and complete as well as providing the facility to apply online.

20.6.2 Completing the temporary event notice

Guidance for completing the temporary event notice may be obtained from the website **www.gov.uk** or the relevant licensing authority. The form may be completed by being either typed or written legibly in block capitals. All answers must be inside the boxes and written in black ink. A copy should be kept by the applicant for his records.

The temporary event notice in the Permitted Temporary Activities Regulations is divided into 10 parts, as follows.

Part 1 – personal details

This section asks for details of the premises user, such as his full name, any previous names, date and place of birth, national insurance number, current address (the licensing authority will use this address to correspond with the premises user unless he specifies an alternative correspondence address, such as his business address), telephone number, and fax number and email address (both these are optional).

Part 2 – the premises

This section asks for details of the premises where the premises user intends to carry on the licensable activities. If the premises do not have an address, for example where they are an open space, a detailed description including the Ordnance Survey references should be given. 'Premises' means any place and so will not always be a building with a formal address and postcode. Premises can include, for example, public parks, recreation grounds and private land. If the premises (or any part of the premises) have a premises licence or a club premises certificate then the licence or certificate number must be provided. Where only part of the premises is to be used or the area to which the application relates is to be restricted, a clear description of the area to be used must be given. Any licensable activities carried on outside this area will be unauthorised so it is important that the description covers all the areas where the licensable activities are to be carried on.

The nature of the premises must be described, for example, a church or village hall, a restaurant, an open field, a beer tent or a public house. The nature of the event must also be described, for example, a wedding with a pay bar, the supply of beer at a fair, a discotheque, the performance of a string quartet, a folk group or a rock band, etc. These descriptions will help the police and the local authority exercising environmental health functions to decide whether any issues relating to the licensing objectives are likely to arise.

Part 3 – the licensable activities

The applicant must state which licensable activities he intends to carry on at the premises, whether he is giving a late temporary event notice, the dates on which he intends to use the premises for these licensable activities, the times it is proposed to carry on licensable activities and the maximum number of people at any one time that it is intended to allow to be present at the premises. If the licensable activities will include the supply of alcohol, the applicant must state whether the supplies will be for consumption on or off the premises or both.

Part 4 – personal licence holders

If the applicant holds a personal licence, he must give details of it, for example, the name of the licensing authority which issued the personal licence, the licence number and its dates of issue and expiry.

Part 5 – previous temporary event notices

An applicant must indicate whether he has previously given a temporary event notice in respect of any premises for events falling in the same calendar year as the event for which he is now giving this temporary event notice and, if he has, he must state the number of temporary event notices. He must also indicate whether he has already given a temporary event notice for the same premises in which the event period ends 24 hours or less before, or begins 24 hours or less after the event period proposed in this temporary event notice.

Part 6 – associates and business colleagues

An applicant must indicate whether any associate or any person with whom he is in business carrying on licensable activities has given a temporary event notice for an event in the same calendar year as the event for which he is now giving a temporary event notice (see **20.14.4**), and if he has, he must state the number of temporary event notices the associate or business colleague has given. He must also indicate whether any associate or any person with whom he is in business carrying on licensable activities has already given a temporary event notice for the same premises in which the event period ends 24 hours or less before, or begins 24 hours or less after the event period proposed in this temporary event notice.

An 'associate' of the applicant is:

- the spouse or civil partner of the applicant;
- a child, parent, grandchild, grandparent, brother or sister of the applicant;
- an agent or employee of the applicant; or
- the spouse or civil partner of a child, parent, grandchild, grandparent, brother, sister, agent or employee of the applicant.

For these purposes, a person living with another as that person's husband or wife is to be treated as that person's spouse and 'civil partner' has the same meaning as in the Civil Partnership Act 2004.

Part 7 – checklist

This part is made up of a checklist so that an applicant does not overlook anything.

Part 8 – condition

This section contains a declaration that it will be a condition of the temporary event notice that where the relevant licensable activities described in Part 3 include the supply of alcohol that all such supplies are made by or under the authority of the premises user.

Part 9 – declaration

By signing this part, the applicant is making a declaration that the information in the form is correct to the best of his knowledge and belief. The applicant confirms that he understands that it is an offence:

- to knowingly or recklessly make a false statement in or in connection with the temporary event notice and that a person is liable on summary conviction for such an offence to a fine not exceeding level 5 on the standard scale; and
- to permit an unauthorised licensable activity to be carried on at any place and that a person is liable on summary conviction for any such offence to a fine of any amount or to imprisonment for a term not exceeding six months or to both.

Part 10 – acknowledgement

An applicant must leave this blank as it is for the licensing authority to use in order to acknowledge receipt of the temporary event notice.

20.7 MAKING AN APPLICATION – STANDARD TEMPORARY EVENT NOTICE

A standard temporary event notice must be given in writing (including by electronic means via **www.gov.uk** or the licensing authority's own facility) to the relevant licensing authority no later than 10 working days before the day on which the event period begins (s.100A(2)(a)). Unless the application has been submitted electronically, the premises user must also give a copy of the notice to the chief officer of police for the area in which the premises are situated and the local authority exercising environmental health functions no later than 10 working days before the day on which the event period begins (s.100A(2)(b)).

The temporary event notice must be accompanied by the prescribed fee when it is given by the premises user to the relevant licensing authority (s.100(7)).

Where the temporary event notice is given to the relevant licensing authority electronically, the licensing authority must give a copy of the notice to the chief officer of police for the area in which the premises are situated and the local authority exercising environmental health functions no later than the end of the first working day after the day on which the original notice was given to the licensing authority and the copy is to be treated as if it were the original notice (s.100A(4)).

Section 193 defines 'working day' as any day other than a Saturday, a Sunday, Christmas Day, Good Friday or a day which is a bank holiday under the Banking and Financial Dealings Act 1971 in England and Wales. The period of '10 working days' excludes the day the notice is received and the first day of the event (Guidance, para.7.9).

While a licensing authority has no power to extend the 10-working day notice period, a licensing authority may encourage a longer period of notice to be given, as the Guidance at para.7.11 states:

> Although ten clear working days is the minimum possible notice that may be given, licensing authorities should publicise their preferences in terms of advance notice and encourage premises users to provide the earliest possible notice of events planned by them. Licensing authorities should also consider publicising a preferred maximum time in advance of an event by when TENs should ideally be given to them.

Where an individual wishes to hold more than one event, he can give notice of them all at the same time. The Guidance at para.7.22 provides:

> There is nothing in the 2003 Act to prevent notification of multiple events at the same time, provided the first event is at least ten working days away (or five working days away in the case of a late TEN). For example, an individual personal licence holder wishing to exhibit and sell beer at a series of farmers' markets may wish to give several notices simultaneously. However, this would only be possible where the limits are not exceeded in the case of each notice. Where the events are due to take place in different licensing authority (and police) areas, the respective licensing authorities and relevant persons would each need to be notified accordingly.

20.8 MAKING AN APPLICATION – LATE TEMPORARY EVENT NOTICE

Late temporary event notices are intended to assist premises users who are required for reasons outside their control to, for example, change the venue for an event at short notice (Guidance, para.7.12). However, there is nothing to prevent a late temporary event notice being given in any circumstances provided the relevant time limits are not exceeded.

A late temporary event notice must be given in writing (including by electronic means via **www.gov.uk** or the licensing authority's own facility) to the relevant licensing authority no later than five working days, but no earlier than nine working days, before the day on which the event period begins (s.100A(3)). Unless the application has been submitted electronically, the premises user must also give a copy of the notice to the chief officer of police for the area in which the premises are situated and the local authority exercising environmental health functions no later than five working days before the day on which the event period begins and notice must be given to at least one of either the relevant licensing authority, the chief officer of police or the local authority exercising environmental health functions no earlier than nine working days before the day on which the event period begins.

A late temporary event notice given less than five working days before the event to which it relates will be returned to the premises user as void and the activities to which it relates will not be authorised.

The temporary event notice must be accompanied by the prescribed fee when it is given by the premises user to the relevant licensing authority (s.100(7)).

Where the temporary event notice is given to the relevant licensing authority electronically, the licensing authority must give a copy of the notice to the chief officer of police for the area in which the premises are situated and the local authority exercising environmental health functions no later than the end of the first working day after the day on which the original notice was given to the licensing authority and the copy is to be treated as if it were the original notice (s.100A(4)).

Section 193 defines 'working day' as any day other than a Saturday, a Sunday, Christmas Day, Good Friday or a day which is a bank holiday under the Banking and Financial Dealings Act 1971 in England and Wales. The period of '10 working days' excludes the day the notice is received and the first day of the event (Guidance, para.7.18).

20.9 MINIMUM PERIOD BETWEEN EVENT PERIODS

There must be a minimum of 24 hours between events notified by a premises user in respect of the same premises. If this is not the case then the temporary event notice will be void. This is to prevent evasion of the 168-hour limit on such events and the need to obtain a full premises licence or club premises certificate for more major or permanent events (Guidance, para.7.25).

Section 101 provides that a temporary event notice given by a premises user will be void if the event period specified in it does not:

- end at least 24 hours before the event period specified in any other temporary event notice given by the relevant premises user in respect of the same premises before or at the same time as the notice; or
- begin at least 24 hours after the event period specified in any other such notice.

A temporary event notice in respect of which a counter notice has been given or which has been withdrawn is disregarded when calculating the minimum period of 24 hours.

Section 101 attempts to prevent a premises user circumventing the 24-hour minimum period by having consecutive notices given by others on his behalf. It provides that a temporary event notice which is given by an individual who is an associate of the relevant premises user is treated as a notice given by the relevant premises user. While the definition of an 'associate' is very wide it does not include a friend of the premises user which therefore provides a premises user with a possibility for circumventing the minimum period. Section 101(3) provides that an individual is an associate of another person if he is:

- the spouse or civil partner of that person:
- a child, parent, grandchild, grandparent, brother or sister of that person;
- an agent or employee of that person;
- the spouse or civil partner of a child, parent, grandchild, grandparent, brother or sister of that person; or
- the spouse or civil partner of an agent or employee of that person.

A person living with another as that person's husband or wife is to be treated as that person's spouse (s.101(4)).

A temporary event notice given by an individual who is in business with the premises user will be treated as a temporary event notice given by the premises user if that business relates to one or more licensable activities, and both notices relate to one or more licensable activities to which the business relates, although not necessarily the same activity or activities (s.101(2)(c)). There is no definition in the Act of when an individual will be in business with a premises user.

Where two temporary event notices are given in respect of different parts of the same premises, they will be regarded as given in respect of the same premises (s.101(2)(d)).

20.10 ACKNOWLEDGEMENT OF A TEMPORARY EVENT NOTICE BY A LICENSING AUTHORITY

A licensing authority which receives a temporary event notice must give written acknowledgement of the receipt of the notice to the premises user (s.102). This must be done before the end of the first working day following the day on which it was received, or if the day on which it was received was not a working day, before the end of the second working day following that day. If the licensing authority does not acknowledge receipt then it may be that the premises user cannot stage the temporary event, as one of the conditions for a permitted temporary activity is that the acknowledgement requirements in s.102 are met. There is no sanction available for a premises user to take against a licensing authority which does not acknowledge receipt.

There is no prescribed form for the licensing authority to use as an acknowledgement. It may acknowledge receipt of the temporary event notice on a copy of the notice returned to the premises user, by letter or electronically.

The requirement to give written acknowledgement does not apply where, before the time by which acknowledgement of the receipt of the notice must be given, a counter notice has been given to the premises user under either s.104A (see **20.12.2**) or s.107 (see **20.14.5**).

20.11 WITHDRAWAL OF A TEMPORARY EVENT NOTICE

Section 103 allows a premises user to withdraw a temporary event notice by giving the relevant licensing authority a notice to that effect no later than 24 hours before the beginning of the event period specified in the temporary event notice. A notice once withdrawn will not count towards an individual's limit on the number of temporary event notices he can submit during a calendar year.

20.12 OBJECTION TO A TEMPORARY EVENT NOTICE

Notice of a temporary event must be given to the relevant persons, i.e. the police and the environmental health authority who may then object on the basis that the use of the premises in accordance with the temporary event notice would undermine a licensing objective. It is not possible for anyone else, for example a local resident or a responsible authority to object.

20.12.1 Objection by a relevant person

Where a relevant person who is given a temporary event notice is satisfied that allowing the premises to be used in accordance with the notice would undermine a licensing objective, the relevant person must give an objection notice setting out the reasons for the decision. This notice must be given to the relevant licensing authority, the premises user and every other relevant person. The objection notice must be given before the end of the third working day following the day on which the relevant person was given the temporary event notice.

The Guidance at para.7.32 states that the system gives the police and environmental health authorities the opportunity to consider whether they should object to a TEN on the basis of any of the licensing objectives. Paragraphs 7.35 and 7.36 state:

> 7.35 Such cases might arise because of concerns about the scale, location, timing of the event or concerns about public nuisance – even where the statutory limits on numbers are being observed. The premises user who signs the form is legally responsible for ensuring that the numbers present do not exceed the permitted limit at any one time. In cases where there is reason to doubt that the numbers will remain within the permitted limit the premises user should make clear what the nature of the event(s) is and how they will ensure that the permitted persons limit will not be exceeded. For example, where notices are being given for TENs simultaneously on adjacent plots of land it may be appropriate for door staff to be employed with counters. In each case it is important that licensing authorities and relevant persons can consider whether they believe that the premises user intends to exceed the 499 person limit, or will be unable to control or know whether the limit will be exceeded. Where the planned activities are likely to breach the statutory limits or undermine the licensing objectives, it is likely to be appropriate for the police or EHA to raise objections.

7.36 However, in most cases, where for example, alcohol is supplied away from licensed premises at a temporary bar under the control of a personal licence holder, (such as at weddings with a cash bar or small social or sporting events) this should not usually give rise to the use of these powers.

A relevant person who has received a copy of a counter notice given by the licensing authority under s.107 cannot give an objection notice (see **20.14.5**).

20.12.2 Counter notice following an objection to a late temporary event notice

Where a relevant person gives an objection notice in relation to a late temporary event notice, the relevant licensing authority must give a counter notice to the premises user (s.104A(1)).

The counter notice must be in the prescribed form and given to the premises user in the prescribed manner. The prescribed form of counter notice is contained in the Permitted Temporary Activities Regulations, Sched.2. The manner of giving the counter notice is prescribed by the Permitted Temporary Activities Regulations, reg.7 which provides that a counter notice will be given in the prescribed manner if it is:

- delivered to the premises user;
- left at the appropriate address;
- sent to that address by ordinary post; or
- sent by email to an appropriate email address.

The 'appropriate address' is the postal address indicated in s.1(8) of the temporary event notice or if there is no such address the postal address indicated in s.1(6) of the notice and the 'appropriate email address' is an email address indicated in s.1(9) of the temporary event notice or, if ss.1(8) and 1(9) have not been completed, an email address indicated in s.1(7) (Permitted Temporary Activities Regulations, reg.2).

The relevant licensing authority must, no later than 24 hours before the beginning of the event period, give the counter notice to the premises user and give a copy to each relevant person (s.104A(3)).

Once a relevant person has given a counter notice, the event is immediately vetoed and there is no provision for a hearing or to appeal against the objection.

20.12.3 Counter notice following an objection to a standard temporary event notice

If a relevant person gives an objection notice to a standard temporary event notice, the relevant licensing authority must hold a hearing to consider the objection notice, unless the premises user, the relevant person who gave the objection notice and the authority agree that a hearing is unnecessary (s.105).

The hearing must be held within seven working days beginning with the day after the end of the period within which a chief officer of police may give an objection notice (Hearings Regulations, reg.5 and Sched.1, para.11). The end of the period during which the police may give an objection notice is three working days after the premises user has given a copy of the temporary event notice to the relevant person. Notice of the hearing must be given to the premises user and the chief officer of police who has given a counter notice no later than two working days before the day or the first day on which the hearing is to be held (Hearings Regulations, reg.6(2) and Sched.2, para.11). There is nothing in the Hearings Regulations specifying that notice of the hearing must be given to the environmental health authority.

Following the hearing, the licensing authority must, having regard to the objection notice, give the premises user a counter notice if it considers it appropriate for the promotion of a licensing objective to do so. Such a counter notice will prevent the event going ahead. The licensing authority may also decide to impose conditions where there is an existing premises licence or club premises certificate at the venue.

At the hearing, the police, environmental health authority and the premises user may make representations to the licensing authority. The licensing authority must make its determination at the conclusion of the hearing (Hearings Regulations, reg.26(1)).

If the licensing authority gives a counter notice to the premises user, it must give with it a notice setting out its reasons for giving the counter notice. There is no provision in either the Act or the Permitted Temporary Activities Regulations about the form that either notice should take. Copies of both notices must also be given to each relevant person. The licensing authority must give notice forthwith (see **2.9**) on making the decision and the notice must be accompanied by information setting out the right of a party to appeal against the decision. If the licensing authority decides not to give a counter notice, it must give the premises user and each relevant person notice of its decision. There is no requirement for it to give its reasons for not giving a counter notice.

A decision as to whether or not to give a counter notice must be made, and the appropriate notices given, at least 24 hours before the beginning of the event period specified in the temporary event notice (s.105(4)). The Act does not set out the effect of non-compliance with this provision but it seems clear that a failure to comply with it will mean that the premises user will not be able to proceed with his event.

Where the premises are situated in the area of more than one licensing authority, the authorities must act jointly and hold a joint hearing (s.105(5)). It is not clear whether each authority will need to give its own notices or whether notices can be given by one of them on behalf of them all.

The provisions as to counter notices do not apply if the objection notice has been withdrawn, or if the premises user has been given a counter notice by the licensing authority that the permitted limits for temporary event notices have been exceeded (see **20.14.5**).

20.13 MODIFICATION OF A STANDARD TEMPORARY EVENT NOTICE FOLLOWING AN OBJECTION

Where a relevant person has given an objection notice in respect of a standard temporary event notice, and the objection notice has not been withdrawn, the relevant person may, with the agreement of the premises user and each other relevant person, modify the temporary event notice, for example by changing the details of the parts of the premises that are to be used for the event, the description of the nature of the intended activities or their duration (s.106). The relevant person may do this at any time before a hearing to consider the objection notice is held or dispensed with, and provided the premises user has not been given a counter notice by the licensing authority that the permitted limits for temporary event notices have been exceeded (see **20.14.5**).

A modification is made by making changes to the temporary event notice. A copy of the modified temporary event notice must be sent or delivered by the relevant person to the relevant licensing authority before a hearing is held or dispensed with (s.106(4)).

Where a temporary event notice is modified, the objection notice is treated as having been withdrawn from the time the temporary event notice is modified, and from that time the modified temporary event notice has effect (s.106(3)).

20.13.1 Conditions on a standard temporary event notice following an objection

Where a relevant person has given an objection notice in respect of a standard temporary event notice, the objection notice has not been withdrawn and the relevant licensing authority has decided not to give a counter notice, it may impose one or more conditions on the standard temporary event notice (s.106A). The decision to impose conditions is one for the licensing authority alone, regardless of the premises user's views or willingness to accept conditions (Guidance, para.7.39).

Conditions may be imposed if the licensing authority considers it appropriate for the promotion of the licensing objectives to do so. The conditions are also imposed on a premises licence or a club premises certificate that has effect in respect of the same premises, or any part of the same premises, as the temporary event notice, and the conditions would not be inconsistent with the carrying out of the licensable activities under the temporary event notice.

Where a licensing authority decides to impose one or more conditions it must give notice of its decision to the premises user. A separate statement setting out the conditions that have been imposed must accompany the notice. A copy of the notice and statement of conditions must be given to each relevant party.

The notice and the statement of conditions must be in the prescribed form, be given to the premises user in the prescribed manner and be given no later than 24 hours before the beginning of the event period specified in the temporary event notice. The prescribed form of notice and statement of conditions is contained in the Permitted Temporary Activities Regulations, Sched.3. The manner of giving the counter notice is prescribed by the Permitted Temporary Activities Regulations, reg.7 which provides that a counter notice will be given in the prescribed manner if it is:

- delivered to the premises user;
- left at the appropriate address;
- sent to that address by ordinary post; or
- sent by email to an appropriate email address.

The 'appropriate address' is the postal address indicated in s.1(8) of the temporary event notice or if there is no such address the postal address indicated in s.1(6) of the notice and the 'appropriate email address' is an email address indicated in s.1(9) of the temporary event notice or if ss.1(8) and 1(9) have not been completed, an email address indicated in s.1(7) (Permitted Temporary Activities Regulations, reg.2).

Where the premises are situated in the area of more than one licensing authority, the function to impose conditions must be exercised jointly.

20.14 LIMITS ON TEMPORARY EVENT NOTICES

20.14.1 Permitted limits – personal licence holders

An individual who holds a personal licence may give a maximum of 50 temporary event notices or 10 late temporary event notices in a calendar year (s.107(2)).

The Secretary of State may, by order, change the maximum number of temporary event notices which can be given in a calendar year.

20.14.2 Permitted limits – non-personal licence holders

An individual who does not hold a personal licence may give a maximum of five temporary event notices or two late temporary event notices in a calendar year (s.107(3)).

The Secretary of State may, by order, change the maximum number of temporary event notices which can be given in a calendar year.

20.14.3 Permitted limits – individual premises

No more than 15 temporary event notices can be given in respect of the same premises in a calendar year and these cannot cover a period of more than 21 days (s.107(4) and (5)).

As s.193 defines 'premises' as meaning 'any place', it could be argued that temporary event notices could be given in respect of part of a building or open space. However, in calculating the permitted limit, s.107(13)(a) provides that 'a temporary event notice is in respect of the same premises ... if it is in respect of the whole or any part of the relevant premises or premises which include the whole or any part of those premises'.

The Secretary of State may, by order, change the maximum number of temporary event notices which can be given in a calendar year and/or the maximum number of days which they can cover in a calendar year.

20.14.4 Calculating the permitted limits

For calculation of the permitted limits, the number of events are calculated by reference to a calendar year. If an event straddles two calendar years, it counts towards the limits for each of those years (s.107(6)).

No account is taken of any temporary event notice in respect of which a counter notice has been given by the licensing authority following an objection to a standard temporary event notice or by the licensing authority that the permitted limits for temporary event notices have been exceeded (s.107(9)).

In determining the number of temporary event notices given by an individual, a temporary event notice given by his associate or by someone who is in business with him is treated as a notice given by him (s.107(10)). For these purposes, 'an associate' has the same meaning as in s.101 (see **20.6.2**). Where the notice is given by someone who is in business with the individual, it will be treated as a notice given by him if the business relates to one or more licensable activities, and the temporary event notices relate to one or more licensable activities to which the business relates, but not necessarily the same activity or activities.

20.14.5 Giving a counter notice

Where a licensing authority receives a temporary event notice in respect of any premises, and is satisfied that one of the permitted limits will be exceeded if the event proceeds, it must give the premises user a counter notice (s.107(1)).

A counter notice must be in the prescribed form and be given to the premises user in the prescribed manner. It must be given at least 24 hours before the beginning of the event period specified in the temporary event notice.

The prescribed form of counter notice is contained in the Permitted Temporary Activities Regulations, Sched.4. The manner of giving the counter notice is prescribed by the Permitted Temporary Activities Regulations, reg.7 which provides that a counter notice will be given in the prescribed manner if it is:

- delivered to the premises user;
- left at the appropriate address;
- sent to that address by ordinary post; or
- sent by email to an appropriate email address.

The 'appropriate address' is the postal address indicated in s.1(8) of the temporary event notice or if there is no such address the postal address indicated in s.1(6) of the notice and the 'appropriate email address' is an email address indicated in s.1(9) of the temporary event notice or if ss.1(8) and 1(9) have not been completed, an email address indicated in s.1(7) (Permitted Temporary Activities Regulations, reg.2).

A copy of the counter notice must, forthwith (see **2.9**) be sent by the licensing authority each relevant authority.

20.15 RIGHT OF ENTRY WHERE A TEMPORARY EVENT NOTICE HAS BEEN GIVEN

Section 108 gives a constable or an authorised officer the right, at any reasonable time, to enter the premises to which a temporary event notice relates in order to assess the likely effect of the notice on the promotion of the crime prevention objective. There is no right for the use of reasonable force when gaining entry. Nor is there any provision as to when entry can be made, so entry could take place either before or during the event to which the notice relates.

For these purposes, an 'authorised officer' is an officer of the licensing authority in whose area the premises are situated, or if the premises are situated in the area of more than one licensing authority, an officer of any of those authorities, authorised for the purposes of the Act (s.108(5)). An authorised officer who exercises the right of entry must, if so requested, produce evidence of his authority (s.108(2)).

Anyone who intentionally obstructs an authorised officer exercising his right of entry commits an offence. A person guilty of such an offence is liable on summary conviction to a fine not exceeding level 2 on the standard scale. Obstructing a constable exercising the right of entry will be an offence of obstructing a constable in the execution of his duties under the Police Act 1996, s.89(2). A person guilty of such an offence is liable on summary conviction to imprisonment for a term not exceeding one month (this will increase to 51 weeks when the Criminal Justice Act 2003 takes effect) or to a fine not exceeding level 3 on the standard scale, or to both.

20.16 DUTY TO KEEP AND PRODUCE A TEMPORARY EVENT NOTICE AND STATEMENT OF CONDITIONS

Whenever premises are being used for one or more licensable activities which are or are purported to be permitted temporary activities, the premises user must under s.109 make sure either:

- that a copy of the temporary event notice together with a copy of any statement of conditions is prominently displayed at the premises; or
- that the temporary event notice together with a copy of any statement of conditions is kept at the premises in his custody, or in the custody of a person who is present and working at the premises and whom he has nominated for this purpose, and where the temporary event notice and any statement of conditions are in the custody of a nominated person, ensure that a notice specifying that fact and the position held at the premises by that person is prominently displayed at the premises.

A premises user will commit an offence if he fails, without reasonable excuse, to comply with these requirements. A person guilty of such an offence is liable on summary conviction to a fine not exceeding level 2 on the standard scale.

Where the temporary event notice together with a copy of any statement of conditions is not displayed as required and no notice is displayed specifying that the temporary event notice and any statement of conditions are in the custody of a nominated person and the position held at the premises by that person, a constable or an authorised officer may require the premises user to produce the temporary event notice or statement of conditions for examination (s.109(5)). An authorised officer when exercising this power must, if so requested, produce evidence of his authority. A person commits an offence if he fails, without reasonable excuse, to produce a temporary event notice in accordance with this requirement. A person guilty of such an offence is liable on summary conviction to a fine not exceeding level 2 on the standard scale.

Where a notice is displayed specifying that the temporary event notice and any statement of conditions is in the custody of a nominated person and the position held at the premises by that person, a constable or an authorised officer may require the person specified in the notice to produce the temporary event notice for examination (s.109(6)). An authorised officer when exercising this power must, if so requested, produce evidence of his authority. A person commits an offence if he fails, without reasonable excuse, to produce a temporary event notice in accordance with this requirement. A person guilty of such an offence is liable on summary conviction to a fine not exceeding level 2 on the standard scale.

20.17 THEFT, LOSS, ETC. OF A TEMPORARY EVENT NOTICE OR STATEMENT OF CONDITIONS

If a temporary event notice which has been acknowledged is lost, stolen, damaged or destroyed, the premises user may apply to the licensing authority which acknowledged the notice, or, if there is more than one such authority, any of them, for a copy of the notice (s.110). Similarly, if a statement of conditions is lost, stolen, damaged or destroyed, the premises user may apply to the licensing authority which gave the statement for a copy of the statement. The licensing authority must then issue the premises user with a copy of the temporary event notice or statement of conditions if it is satisfied that the notice or statement has been lost, stolen, damaged or destroyed. The copy must be a copy of the notice or statement in the form it existed immediately before it was lost, stolen, damaged or destroyed, and must be certified by the licensing authority as a true copy. The Act then applies to the copy as it applies in relation to an original temporary event notice.

An application must be accompanied by the prescribed fee. An application cannot be made more than one month after the end of the event period specified in the temporary event notice or statement of conditions.

CHAPTER 21

Offences

21.1 INTRODUCTION

Part 7 of the Act contains the main offences in the Act. There are a number of other offences in the Act which cover failure to comply with procedural requirements, and these have been dealt with earlier in this text where appropriate.

The offences in Part 7 are divided into six categories as follows.

21.1.1 Unauthorised licensable activities

- Unauthorised licensable activities (s.136)
- Exposing alcohol for unauthorised sale (s.137)
- Keeping alcohol on premises for unauthorised sale etc. (s.138)

21.1.2 Drunkenness and disorderly conduct

- Allowing disorderly conduct on licensed premises etc. (s.140)
- Sale of alcohol to a person who is drunk (s.141)
- Obtaining alcohol for a person who is drunk (s.142)
- Failure to leave licensed premises etc. (s.143)

21.1.3 Smuggled goods

- Keeping of smuggled goods (s.144)

21.1.4 Children and alcohol

- Unaccompanied children prohibited from certain premises (s.145)
- Sale of alcohol to children (s.146)
- Allowing the sale of alcohol to children (s.147)
- Persistently selling alcohol to children (s.147A)
- Purchase of alcohol by or on behalf of children (s.149)

- Consumption of alcohol by children (s.150)
- Delivering alcohol to children (s.151)
- Sending a child to obtain alcohol (s.152)
- Prohibition of unsupervised sales by children (s.153)

21.1.5 Vehicles and trains

- Prohibition on sale of alcohol on moving vehicles (s.156)
- Power to prohibit sale of alcohol on trains (s.157)

21.1.6 False statement relating to licensing etc.

- False statements (s.158)

21.1.7 Other offences

There are also offences relating to licensing law in other statutes, dealing with the following:

- giving intoxicating liquor to children under five;
- confiscation of alcohol;
- alcohol consumption in breach of a prohibition in a public spaces protection order; and
- in Wales, the supply of alcohol at a selling price below the applicable minimum price.

21.2 UNAUTHORISED LICENSABLE ACTIVITIES

21.2.1 Unauthorised licensable activities

Section 136(1)(a) provides that it is an offence to carry on or attempt to carry on a licensable activity on or from any premises otherwise than under and in accordance with a premises licence, a club premises certificate or a temporary event notice. Section 136(1)(b) provides that it is an offence to knowingly allow a licensable activity to be carried on without such authorisation. Premises are defined in s.193 as meaning any place and includes a vehicle, vessel or moveable structure.

These offences are very wide in their scope. They will cover not only premises which have no authorisation for any licensable activities, for example, an unlicensed drinking den or unlicensed film exhibitions, but also premises that have authorisation but not for the particular licensable activity which is being carried on, for example, premises licensed for the sale of alcohol but not for the provision of regulated entertainment, and premises which have authorisation for the licensable activity in question but where a breach of conditions has occurred.

The offence in s.136(1)(a) is committed by a person who carries on or attempts to carry on an unauthorised licensable activity. Persons carrying on a licensable activity will clearly include persons who have some role in the organisation or management of the licensable activity, for example, the premises licence holder, the club secretary or club committee or a premises user. Whether any other persons will be liable will depend on the interpretation of 'carries on'. There is a due diligence defence to this offence (see **21.2.4**).

Section 136(1)(a) was considered in *Hall & Woodhouse Ltd* v. *Poole BC* [2009] EWHC 1587 (Admin); [2010] 1 All ER 425 where it was held that for the purposes of the provision, acts of third parties were not to be imputed to the premises licence holder. Richards LJ said (at [17]) that 'In my judgment, section 136(1)(a) is directed at persons who, *as a matter of fact*, actually carry on or attempt to carry on a licensable activity on or from premises. That is the natural meaning of the language used'. He went on (at [18]) to say:

> Section 136(1)(a) is not directed at holders of premises licences as such. An offence may be committed by carrying on a licensable activity when no premises licence exists at all. Where there is a premises licence but a licensable activity is carried on outside the scope of that licence or in breach of the conditions of the licence, it must, in my view, be a question of fact whether it is carried on by the holder of the licence. The mere fact that he is the holder of a licence does not make him automatically liable in respect of the carrying of a licensable activity on or from the premises to which the licence relates.

The court also considered whether the acts of third parties on the premises should be imputed to the premises licence holder, subject to the due diligence defence (see **21.2.4**), but held that no such imputation was permitted. Richards LJ (at [29]) said 'it is clear ... that no such imputation is permitted. Section 136(1)(a) is concerned with the actual conduct of a person charged. It is not a section that establishes some form of criminal vicarious liability or imputation of criminal conduct, and the holder of a premises licence is not liable under section 136(1)(a) as a matter of criminal law for the acts of third parties.'

The offence in s.136(1)(b) requires a person to 'knowingly' allow a licensable activity to be carried on without authorisation. This will require not only that they have a positive belief that the licensable activity is being carried on but also that they have a positive belief that there is no authorisation for it (see *Westminster City Council* v. *Croyalgrange Ltd* [1986] 1 WLR 674 HL, a case relating to a sex establishment, where it was held that knowledge was needed not only as to the use of the premises but also as to the entertainment being carried on without a licence). A person will allow a licensable activity to be carried on where he has positively acted in such a way as to allow the activity to go ahead and also where he has failed to exercise control to prevent it going ahead where he has power to do so (*Barking and Dagenham LBC* v. *Bass Taverns* [1993] COD 453 DC).

Where the licensable activity in question is the provision of regulated entertainment, s.136(2) provides that a person does not commit an offence if his only involvement in the provision of the entertainment is that he:

- performs in a play;
- participates as a sportsman in an indoor sporting event;
- boxes or wrestles in a boxing or wrestling entertainment;
- performs live music;
- plays recorded music;
- performs dance; or
- does something coming within para.2(1)(h) of Sched.1 (entertainment similar to music, dance, etc.).

Thus the offences do not apply to performers or participants in regulated entertainment. However, if the individual also organised or helped to organise the event, then subject to the defence of due diligence, he may commit an offence under s.136(1)(a).

A person guilty of an offence under s.136 is liable on summary conviction to imprisonment for a term not exceeding six months or to an unlimited fine, or to both (s.136(4)).

21.2.2 Exposing alcohol for unauthorised sale

Section 137(1) provides that it is an offence to expose for sale by retail on any premises any alcohol in circumstances where the sale by retail of that alcohol on those premises would not be authorised by a premises licence, a club premises certificate or a temporary event notice. It is not necessary that there is a sale or attempted sale of the alcohol as all that is required is that the alcohol is exposed in such a way that any sale would be unauthorised. The offence can be committed by anyone who exposes the alcohol for sale.

An offence under this provision may also be committed where the sale by retail of alcohol is permitted, but there is a breach of the conditions of that authorisation, for example exposing alcohol for sale outside authorised hours will be an offence.

A person guilty of this offence is liable on summary conviction to imprisonment for a term not exceeding six months or to an unlimited fine, or to both. In addition, a court which convicts a person of this offence may order that the alcohol in question and its containers are forfeited and either destroyed or dealt with in such other manner as the court may order.

There is a due diligence defence to this offence (see **21.2.4**).

21.2.3 Keeping alcohol on premises for unauthorised sale

Section 138(1) provides that a person commits an offence if he has in his possession or under his control alcohol which he intends to sell by retail or supply by or on behalf of a club to, or to the order of, a member of the club in circumstances where that activity would be an unauthorised licensable activity, i.e. it is not authorised by a premises licence, a club premises certificate or a temporary event notice. The offence is committed where a person has possession or control of the alcohol. There is no requirement that he must own it or have any other proprietary right in it.

A person guilty of this offence is liable on summary conviction to a fine not exceeding level 2 on the standard scale. In addition, a court which convicts a person of this offence may order that the alcohol in question, and its containers, be forfeited and either destroyed or dealt with in such other manner as the court may order.

There is a due diligence defence to this offence (see **21.2.4**).

21.2.4 Defence of due diligence

Section 139 provides a due diligence defence for a person who has been charged with:

- an offence of carrying on an unauthorised licensable activity (s.136(1)(a));
- exposing alcohol for unauthorised sale (s.137); or
- keeping alcohol on premises for unauthorised sale (s.138).

It will be a defence for a person charged with these offences if:

- his act was due to a mistake, or to reliance on information given to him, or to an act or omission by another person, or to some other cause beyond his control; and
- he took all reasonable precautions and exercised all due diligence to avoid committing the offence.

Both elements of the defence must be satisfied for the defence to be effective. Whether the defence is established will be a question of fact in each case. The burden of satisfying the court falls on the person raising this defence and the standard of proof is on the balance of probabilities. A licensee must show that he has done all that he could be reasonably expected to have done, for example he has displayed notices, given his staff proper instructions and training, and required proof of identity and age where there is doubt about a person's age (in relation to the defence see *Davies* v. *Carmarthenshire CC* [2005] EWHC 464 (Admin); [2005] LLR 276; *Cambridgeshire CC* v. *Kama* [2006] EWHC 3148 (Admin); (2007) 171 JP 194 where a small corner shop could not reasonably be expected to have in place all the systems that, for example, a supermarket would have in place; and *Croydon LBC* v. *Pinch a Pound (UK) Ltd* [2010] EWHC 3283 (Admin); [2011] 1 WLR 1189 which while not a licensing case gives useful guidance on the defence).

21.2.5 Right of entry to investigate licensable activities

Section 179 provides that where a constable or an authorised person has reason to believe that any premises are being, or are about to be, used for a licensable activity, he may enter the premises with a view to seeing whether the activity is being, or is to be, carried on under and in accordance with a premises licence, a club premises certificate or an temporary event notice. Where an immigration officer has reason to believe that any premises are being used for the sale by retail of alcohol or the provision of late night entertainment, the officer may enter the premises with a view to seeing whether an offence under any of the Immigration Acts is being committed in connection with the carrying on of the activity. An authorised person or an immigration officer exercising the above a power must, if so requested, produce evidence of his authority to exercise the power and may, if necessary, use reasonable force. A person commits an offence if he intentionally obstructs an authorised person or an immigration officer exercising this power. A person guilty of such an offence is liable on summary conviction to a fine not exceeding level 3 on the standard scale.

21.2.6 Right of entry to investigate offences

Section 180 provides that a constable may enter and search any premises in respect of which he has reason to believe that an offence under the Act has been, is being or is about to be committed. When exercising this power, a constable may, if necessary, use reasonable force.

21.3 DRUNKENNESS AND DISORDERLY CONDUCT

21.3.1 Allowing disorderly conduct on licensed premises

Section 140 makes it an offence to knowingly allow disorderly conduct on licensed premises, premises which have a club premises certificate or premises which may be used for a permitted temporary activity.

This offence may be committed by:

- any person who works at the premises, whether paid or unpaid, in a capacity which authorises him to prevent the conduct;
- in the case of licensed premises, the holder of the premises licence, and the designated premises supervisor;
- in the case of premises which have a club premises certificate, any member or officer of the club who at the time the conduct takes place is present on the premises in a capacity which enables him to prevent it; and
- in the case of premises used for a permitted temporary activity, the premises user in relation to the temporary event notice in question.

There is no definition in the Act of what will amount to 'disorderly conduct'. However, it is suggested that it will include such matters as allowing drunkenness or violent behaviour on licensed premises, allowing licensed premises to be used by prostitutes or as a brothel or permitting illegal gaming on licensed premises.

The offence requires a person to have knowledge of the disorderly conduct. Apart from in relation to premises where a club premises certificate has effect, there is no requirement that the appropriate person must be on the premises at the time the conduct takes place. In this situation, it may be argued that there is no liability as that person has no personal knowledge of the conduct (see *Vane* v. *Yiannopoulos* [1965] AC 486 HL; [1964] 3 WLR 1218) unless he has completely delegated his authority to someone else who is present.

A person guilty of this offence is liable on summary conviction to a fine not exceeding level 3 on the standard scale.

21.3.2 Sale of alcohol to a person who is drunk

Section 141 provides that it is an offence for a person on licensed premises, premises which have a club premises certificate or premises which may be used for a permitted temporary activity, to knowingly sell or attempt to sell alcohol to a person who is drunk, or to knowingly allow alcohol to be sold to such a person.

The offence may be committed by:

- any person who works at the premises, whether paid or unpaid, in a capacity which authorises him to sell the alcohol concerned;
- in the case of licensed premises, the holder of the premises licence and the designated premises supervisor;
- in the case of premises which have a club premises certificate, any member or officer of the club who at the time the sale or attempted sale takes place is present on the premises in a capacity which enables him to prevent it; and
- in the case of premises used for a permitted temporary activity, the premises user in relation to the temporary event notice in question.

The offence also covers a supply of alcohol by or on behalf of a club to or to the order of a member of the club (s.141(3)).

There must be a sale of alcohol to a person who is drunk or an attempt to sell alcohol to such a person. Thus, the offence would not be committed where there was a bona fide gift of alcohol to someone who was drunk (*Petherick* v. *Sargent* (1862) 26 JP 135).

The offence requires a person to have knowledge of both the sale and that the person is drunk. Apart from in relation to premises where a club premises certificate has effect, there is no requirement that the appropriate person must be on the premises at the time the sale takes place (see **21.3.1** as to delegation).

The Act is silent as to when a person is 'drunk'. It is suggested that 'drunk' should be given its ordinary meaning. In *Neale* v. *RMJE (A Minor)* (1985) 80 Cr App R 20, the case involved an offence of drunken disorderly behaviour in a public place. Robert Goff LJ when considering the meaning of 'drunk' said at p.23:

> The primary meaning set out in the Shorter Oxford Dictionary (1933) is as follows: 'That has drunk intoxicating liquor to an extent which affects steady self-control' ...

In my judgment, that is indeed the natural and ordinary meaning of the word 'drunk' in ordinary common speech in 1984.

A person guilty of the offence is liable on summary conviction to a fine not exceeding level 3 on the standard scale. A penalty notice for disorder (PND) can be issued for this offence and the tariff is £90. Further information and guidance on PNDs can be found at **www.gov.uk**.

21.3.3 Obtaining alcohol for a person who is drunk

Section 142 provides that it is an offence for a person, on licensed premises, premises which have a club premises certificate or premises which may be used for a permitted temporary activity, to knowingly obtain or attempt to obtain alcohol for consumption on those premises by a person who is drunk.

A person guilty of this offence is liable on summary conviction to a fine not exceeding level 3 on the standard scale.

21.3.4 Failure to leave licensed premises

A person who is drunk or disorderly commits an offence under s.143 if, without reasonable excuse, he fails to leave licensed premises, premises which have a club premises certificate or premises which may be used for a permitted temporary activity when requested to do so by a police constable or by a person specified below, or he enters or attempts to enter such premises after a police constable or a person specified below has requested him not to enter them.

The persons specified for these purposes are:

- any person who works at the premises, whether paid or unpaid, in a capacity which authorises him to make such a request;
- in the case of licensed premises, the holder of the premises licence and the designated premises supervisor;
- in the case of premises which have a club premises certificate, any member or officer of the club who is present on the premises in a capacity which gives him authority to make such a request; and
- in the case of premises used for a permitted temporary activity, the premises user in relation to the temporary event notice in question.

A person guilty of this offence is liable on summary conviction to a fine not exceeding level 1 on the standard scale. There is a defence of reasonable excuse available to a person charged with this offence. This would assist a person who was unable to leave because he was ill, disabled or injured.

If requested to do so by one of the persons specified above, a police constable must help to expel from relevant premises a person who is drunk or disorderly, or help to prevent such a person from entering relevant premises (s.143(4)). In *Semple v. DPP* [2009] EWHC 3241 (Admin); [2010] 2 All ER 353, it was held that in helping to expel a person who was drunk and disorderly from licensed premises pursuant to s.143(4), a police officer was entitled to use reasonable force.

21.4 SMUGGLED GOODS

A person will commit an offence under s.144 if he knowingly keeps or allows to be kept, on any licensed premises, premises which have a club premises certificate or premises which may be used for a permitted temporary activity, any goods which have been imported without payment of duty or which have otherwise been unlawfully imported. A court which convicts a person of this offence may order that the goods in question, and any container for them, are to be forfeited and either destroyed or dealt with in such other manner as the court may order.

The persons who can commit this offence are:

- any person who works at the premises, whether paid or unpaid, in a capacity which gives him the authority to prevent those goods from being kept on the premises;
- in the case of licensed premises, the holder of the premises licence and the designated premises supervisor;
- in the case of premises which have a club premises certificate, any member or officer of the club who is present on the premises at the time when the goods are kept on the premises, in a capacity which gives him authority to prevent them being so kept; and
- in the case of premises used for a permitted temporary activity, the premises user in relation to the temporary event notice in question.

The scope of the offence extends beyond items imported without payment of duty. It also covers any goods which have been unlawfully imported, such as obscene materials, tobacco and cigarettes.

A person guilty of this offence is liable on summary conviction to a fine not exceeding level 3 on the standard scale.

21.5 OFFENCES ON VEHICLES AND TRAINS

21.5.1 Prohibition on sale of alcohol on moving vehicles

It is an offence under s.156 for a person to sell by retail alcohol on or from a vehicle at a time when the vehicle is not permanently or temporarily parked.

This does not amount to a ban on the consumption of alcohol on coach trips: only the sale by retail of alcohol is prohibited on moving vehicles. A vehicle is defined in s.193 as 'a vehicle intended or adapted for use on roads'. This will include coaches and minibuses, as well as caravans and trailers.

A person guilty of this offence is liable on summary conviction to imprisonment for a term not exceeding three months or to an unlimited fine, or to both.

It is a defence under s.156(3) in relation to this offence if the defendant can prove that:

- his act was due to a mistake, or to reliance on information given to him, or to an act or omission by another person or to some other cause beyond his control; and
- he took all reasonable precautions and exercised all due diligence to avoid committing the offence.

An example of where this defence could be used would be where a person mistakenly believed that the drink he was serving was non-alcoholic.

21.5.2 Power to prohibit sale of alcohol on trains

A magistrates' court acting for a local justice area may make an order under s.157 prohibiting the sale of alcohol, during such period as it may decide, on any railway vehicle at such station or stations as may be specified, being stations in that area, or travelling between such stations as may be specified, at least one of which is in the court's area.

An order can only be made on the application of a senior police officer, i.e. a police officer of, or above, the rank of inspector. Before granting an order, the court must be satisfied that it is necessary to prevent disorder.

Once an order is made, the senior police officer who applied for the order, or if the chief officer of police of the force in question has designated another senior police officer for the purpose, that other officer, must, forthwith (see **2.9**), serve a copy of the order on the train operators affected by the order. Any person who then knowingly sells or attempts to sell alcohol in contravention of the order, or who allows the sale of alcohol in contravention of the order will commit an offence.

A person guilty of an offence under s.157 is liable on summary conviction to imprisonment for a term not exceeding three months or to an unlimited fine, or to both.

A 'railway vehicle' has the meaning given by the Railways Act 1993, s.83, that is, it includes anything which, whether or not it is constructed or adapted to carry any person or load, is constructed or adapted to run on flanged wheels over or along track, and 'station' has the meaning given by the Railways Act 1993, s.83, that is any land or other property which consists of premises used as or for the purposes of or otherwise in connection with a railway passenger station or railway passenger terminal, including any approaches, forecourt, cycle store or car park, whether or not the land or other property is, or the premises are, also used for other purposes. 'Train operator' means a person authorised by a licence under the Railways Act 1993, s.8 to operate railway assets within the meaning of s.6 of that Act.

21.6 FALSE STATEMENTS

Section 158 provides that a person commits an offence if he knowingly or recklessly makes a false statement in or in connection with:

- an application for the grant, variation, transfer or review of a premises licence or club premises certificate;
- an application for a provisional statement;
- a temporary event notice, an interim authority notice or any other notice under the Act;
- an application for the grant of a personal licence; or
- a notice by freeholder of his right to be notified of changes to the licensing register.

A person is treated as making a false statement if he produces, furnishes, signs or otherwise makes use of a document that contains a false statement.

A person must act knowingly or recklessly. A person will act recklessly if he is aware of the risk of the statement being false and it is, in the circumstances known to him, unreasonable to take that risk (see *R.* v. *G* [2003] UKHL 50; [2004] 1 AC 1034 where it was held that this is a subjective test).

A person guilty of making a false statement will be liable on summary conviction to an unlimited fine (Legal Aid, Sentencing and Punishment of Offenders Act 2012, s.85).

21.7 PROSECUTIONS

Section 186 provides that proceedings for an offence under the Act may be brought by a licensing authority (except in the case of an offence under s.147A), by the Director of Public Prosecutions, or in the case of sales of alcohol to children (offences under s.146, s.147 or s.147A, see **Chapter 22**), by a local weights and measures authority.

All offences under the Act are summary only offences. Prosecutions for such offences must normally be brought within six months of the commission of the offence. However, in relation to any offence under the Act, the provision in the Magistrates' Courts Act 1980, s.127(1) that an information must be laid within that six-month period is amended so that an information must be laid within 12 months of an offence (s.186(3)).

21.8 OFFENCES BY BODIES CORPORATE, PARTNERSHIPS AND UNINCORPORATED ASSOCIATIONS

21.8.1 Bodies corporate

If an offence committed by a body corporate, for example a limited company, is shown to have been committed with the consent or connivance of an officer of that body corporate, or to be attributable to any neglect on his part, then the officer as well as the body corporate is guilty of the offence and is liable to prosecution and punishment (s.187(1)).

An 'officer' in relation to a body corporate, means:

- a director, member of the committee of management, chief executive, manager, secretary or other similar officer of the body or a person purporting to act in any such capacity; or
- an individual who is a controller of the body.

Where the affairs of a body corporate are managed by its members, for example where it is a members' club, the acts and defaults of a member in connection with his functions of management will have the same effect as if he were a director of the body, and so he may be prosecuted and punished (s.187(2)).

21.8.2 Partnerships

If an offence committed by a partnership is shown to have been committed with the consent or connivance of a partner, or to be attributable to any neglect on his part, the partner as well as the partnership will be guilty of the offence and be liable to be prosecuted and punished accordingly (s.187(4)). 'Partner' includes a person purporting to act as a partner.

21.8.3 Unincorporated associations

Where an offence is committed by an unincorporated association, other than a partnership, and it is shown that it was committed with the consent or connivance of an officer of the association or a member of its governing body, or is attributable to any neglect on the part of such an officer or member, then that officer or member as well as the association is guilty of the offence and liable to be prosecuted and punished accordingly (s.187(6)).

21.8.4 Overseas bodies

The Secretary of State may make regulations providing for the application of any of the above provisions, with such modifications as the Secretary of State considers appropriate, to a body corporate or unincorporated association formed or recognised under the law of a territory outside the United Kingdom (s.187(7)). No regulations have been made to date.

21.8.5 Jurisdiction and procedure

Any fine imposed on an unincorporated association on its conviction for an offence is to be paid out of the funds of the association (s.188(1)).

Proceedings for an offence alleged to have been committed by an unincorporated association must be brought in the name of the association, and not in that of any of its members (s.188(2)). Rules of court relating to the service of documents have effect as if the association were a body corporate (s.188(3)).

In proceedings for an offence brought against an unincorporated association, the Criminal Justice Act 1925, s.33 and the Magistrates' Courts Act 1980, Sched.3, which lay down the procedure for prosecuting a corporation, apply as they do in relation to a body corporate (s.188(4)).

Proceedings for an offence may be taken against a body corporate or unincorporated association at any place at which it has a place of business and against an individual at any place where he is for the time being (s.188(5)).

21.9 MINIMUM PRICING FOR ALCOHOL IN WALES

The Public Health (Minimum Price for Alcohol) (Wales) Act 2018 came into force on 2 March 2020 and introduced a minimum price below which alcohol cannot be supplied by alcohol retailers from qualifying premises in Wales. The objective is to help tackle alcohol related harm through reducing alcohol consumption in harmful and hazardous drinkers.

Online sales and telephone sales will be caught by the minimum pricing. If the alcohol is purchased online or by telephone in Wales and despatched from outside Wales or to someone outside Wales, minimum pricing will not apply.

Wholesale sales are excluded, so wholesalers will not be subject to any minimum pricing on their trade-to-trade sales. Where a retailer trades as both a retail and wholesale business, they must implement a dual pricing system with one price regime for consumers and one for trade.

The Welsh Ministers must, as soon as practicable after the end of the five-year period starting on 2 March 2020, lay before the National Assembly for Wales a report on the operation and effect of minimum pricing during that period. This report must be published as soon as practicable after it has been laid before the Assembly. The minimum pricing provisions are repealed with effect from the expiry of the six-year period starting on 2 March 2020, unless regulations providing otherwise are made. Regulations may, after the end of the five-year period starting on 2 March 2020 but before the end of the six-year period starting on 2 March 2020, provide that the minimum pricing provisions are not repealed.

21.9.1 Minimum price for alcohol

The applicable minimum price for alcohol is calculated by applying the formula 'M × S × V', where:

- M is whatever price is specified in regulations as being the minimum unit price, expressed in pounds sterling;

- S is the percentage strength of the alcohol, expressed as a cardinal number; and
- V is the volume of the alcohol, expressed in litres.

The minimum unit price has been set at £0.50 (Public Health (Minimum Price for Alcohol) (Minimum Unit Price) (Wales) Regulations 2019, SI 2019/1472 (W.260)).

For example, in the case of a bottle of wine, S (percentage strength of the wine) is 12.5 per cent, and V (volume of the wine) is 75 centilitres, so taking M (specified minimum unit price) to be £0.50, the applicable minimum price for the wine would be calculated as £0.50 × 12.5 × 0.75 = £4.69.

For these purposes, 'alcohol' means spirits, wine, beer, cider or any other fermented, distilled or spirituous liquor, but does not include any of the following:

- alcohol which is of a strength not exceeding 1.2 per cent when supplied;
- perfume;
- flavouring essences recognised by HMRC as not being intended for consumption as or with dutiable alcoholic liquor;
- the aromatic flavouring essence commonly known as Angostura bitters;
- alcohol which is, or is included in, a medicinal product or a veterinary medicinal product;
- denatured alcohol;
- methyl alcohol;
- naphtha;
- alcohol contained in liqueur confectionery.

21.9.2 Offences

It is an offence for a person who is an alcohol retailer:

- to supply alcohol from qualifying premises in Wales; or
- to authorise the supply of alcohol from qualifying premises in Wales

at a selling price below the applicable minimum price for the alcohol.

Prosecutions may be brought by a local authority. A person guilty of an offence is liable on summary conviction to a fine not exceeding level 3 on the standard scale. If an alcohol retailer is found to be selling, or authorising the sale of, alcohol below the applicable minimum price, a fixed penalty notice can be issued. The amount of the penalty will be £200 if payment is made within 29 days or £150 is payment is made within 15 days. A fixed penalty notice may be given by an authorised officer of a local authority.

It is a defence for a person charged with an offence to show that he took reasonable steps and exercised due diligence to avoid committing it. If a person charged with an offence relies on this defence, and evidence is adduced that is sufficient to raise an issue with respect to that defence, the court must assume that the defence is satisfied unless the prosecution proves beyond reasonable doubt that it is not.

It is immaterial for the purposes of authorising the supply of alcohol from qualifying premises in Wales whether the authorisation takes place in Wales or elsewhere.

For these purposes 'selling price', in relation to alcohol, means its price including VAT and all other taxes.

The supply of alcohol means:

- the sale by retail of alcohol to a person in Wales; or
- the supply of alcohol by or on behalf of a club to a member of the club who is in Wales, or to a person in Wales to the order of a member of the club.

Premises are qualifying premises if:

- a premises licence authorises the premises to be used for the supply of alcohol;
- a club premises certificate certifies that the premises may be used for the supply of alcohol; or
- the supply of alcohol on or from the premises is a permitted temporary activity.

In relation to the supply of alcohol from premises that have a premises licence, each of the following is treated as an alcohol retailer:

- an individual to whom a personal licence has been granted that authorises the individual to supply alcohol, or to authorise the supply of alcohol, in accordance with the premises licence concerned;
- the individual who is the designated premises supervisor.

In relation to the supply of alcohol from premises that have club premises certificate, the person who is the holder of the club premises certificate is to be treated as an alcohol retailer.

In relation to the supply of alcohol from premises that have a temporary event notice, the individual who is the premises user is to be treated as an alcohol retailer.

21.9.3 Special offers

Where alcohol is supplied in a multi-buy alcohol transaction, the applicable minimum price is to be calculated by reference to all of the alcohol included in the transaction.

Alcohol is supplied in a multi-buy alcohol transaction if:

- it is supplied free of charge by reference to the supply of other alcohol; or
- other alcohol is supplied free of charge by reference to it,

and, in either case, both the free alcohol and the alcohol by reference to which the free alcohol is supplied are to be treated as being included in the same transaction.

Alcohol is also supplied in a multi-buy alcohol transaction if:

- it is supplied at a price fixed by reference to the supply of other alcohol; or
- other alcohol is supplied at a price fixed by reference to it,

and, in either case, both the fixed price alcohol and the alcohol by reference to which the fixed price alcohol is supplied are to be treated as being included in the same transaction.

Alcohol is also supplied in a multi-buy alcohol transaction if it is supplied, together with other alcohol, for a fixed price, in which case all of the alcohol supplied for that price is to be treated as being included in the same transaction. But alcohol is not to be treated as being supplied in a multi-buy alcohol transaction if anything except alcohol is supplied in the transaction.

So, for example in a special offer, four cans of lager and four cans of cider are supplied together for a fixed price: S (percentage strength) is 4 per cent in relation to the lager, and 6 per cent in relation to the cider, while V (volume) is 440 ml in each case, so taking M (specified minimum unit price) to be £0.50, the applicable minimum price for the transaction is £8.80, that sum being the aggregate of the following calculations:

£0.50 $\times$ 4 $\times$ 1.76 = £3.52 (the minimum price of the lager); and
£0.50 $\times$ 6 $\times$ 1.76 = £5.28 (the minimum price of the cider).

Where alcohol is supplied together with goods other than alcohol, or with services, for a single price, the alcohol is to be treated as being supplied at that single price for the purpose of determining whether the selling price of the alcohol is below the applicable minimum price.

So, for example, in a special offer, the cans of lager and cider mentioned above are supplied with a pizza for a single price. Taking M (specified minimum unit price) to be £0.50, the selling price of the alcohol is to be treated as being the total price of the cans and the pizza, and that price must not be lower than £8.80, being the applicable minimum price for the lager and cider.

Where alcohol is supplied for a price fixed by reference to the supply of goods other than alcohol, or of services (a 'special price'), the alcohol is to be treated as being supplied at a price equal to the aggregate of the special price and the price (if any) for which the other goods and services are supplied.

So, for example, in a special offer, the cans of lager and cider mentioned above are supplied for a special price if a pizza is purchased for £5.00. Taking M (specified minimum unit price) to be £0.50, the selling price of the alcohol is the aggregate of the price of the pizza and the special price, and that special price must not be lower than £3.80, being the applicable minimum price for the cans of lager and cider (which is £8.80) less the price for the pizza (which is £5.00).

335

21.9.4 Miscellaneous

The Public Health (Minimum Price for Alcohol) (Wales) Act 2018 also provides for test purchases, the issue of warrants to enter dwellings and other premises, powers of inspection, appeals against retained property and compensation for appropriated property.

21.10 EXCLUSION ORDERS

The Licensed Premises (Exclusion of Certain Persons) Act 1980 provides that where a court convicts a person of an offence which was committed on licensed premises (i.e. premises with a premises licence authorising the supply of alcohol for consumption on the premises) and it is satisfied that in committing that offence he resorted to violence or offered or threatened to resort to violence, the court may make an exclusion order which prohibits him from entering those premises or any other specified premises, without the express consent of the licensee of the premises or his servant or agent.

An exclusion order may only be made either in addition to any sentence which is imposed in respect of the offence of which the person is convicted, or in addition to an order discharging him absolutely or conditionally.

The duration of an exclusion order must be specified in it but it must be for at least three months and not more than two years.

A person who enters any premises in breach of an exclusion order is guilty of an offence and is liable on summary conviction to a fine not exceeding level 4 on the standard scale or to imprisonment for a term not exceeding one month (this will be increased to 51 weeks when the Criminal Justice Act 2003 comes into force) or both. The court which convicts a person of this offence must also consider whether or not the exclusion order should continue in force, and may, if it thinks fit, by order terminate the exclusion order or vary it by deleting the name of any specified premises.

The licensee of licensed premises or his servant or agent may expel from those premises any person who has entered or whom he reasonably suspects of having entered the premises in breach of an exclusion order; and a constable shall on the demand of the licensee or his servant or agent help to expel from licensed premises any person whom the constable reasonably suspects of having entered in breach of an exclusion order.

Where a court makes an exclusion order or an order terminating or varying an exclusion order, the proper officer of the court shall send a copy of the order to the licensee of the premises to which the order relates. In relation to a magistrates' court, the proper officer is the designated officer for the court, and in relation to the Crown Court the proper officer is the appropriate officer.

The Violent Crime Reduction Act 2006 repeals the Licensed Premises (Exclusion of Certain Persons) Act 1980 on a date to be appointed.

CHAPTER 22

Offences involving children

22.1 INTRODUCTION

A range of offences relating to children and alcohol are contained in ss.145 to 155. The broad effects of the offences relating to children are that:

1. Young persons who are aged over 16, but under 18, can go into licensed premises at the licence holder's discretion but cannot consume or buy alcohol there, except if they are accompanied by an adult at a table meal and an adult is purchasing beer, wine or cider for consumption with the table meal.
2. A child under 16 can go into licensed premises at the licence holder's discretion, but if the premises are licensed primarily or exclusively for the supply of alcohol for consumption on the premises, in other words the premises are a pub or a bar, then the child must be accompanied by an adult.
3. A child under 16 can enter licensed premises where the premises are licensed, but not primarily or exclusively for the supply of alcohol for consumption on the premises, for example a restaurant, and a child only needs to be accompanied by an adult if there is a supply of alcohol taking place and it is between 12 midnight and 5 am.
4. The prohibitions on children's access to licensed premises only apply while such premises are open for the purpose of being used for the supply of alcohol for consumption there.

There are also powers to confiscate alcohol from persons under the age of 18 in the Confiscation of Alcohol (Young Persons) Act 1997.

22.2 UNACCOMPANIED CHILDREN PROHIBITED FROM CERTAIN PREMISES

22.2.1 Premises used exclusively or primarily for supplies of alcohol for consumption on the premises

Section 145 provides that it is an offence for a person, knowing that premises are those to which this offence applies, to allow an unaccompanied child under the age of 16 to be on those premises at a time when they are open for the purposes of being used for the supply of alcohol for consumption there. A child is unaccompanied if he is not in the company of an individual aged 18 or over.

The premises to which this offence applies are licensed premises, premises which have a club premises certificate or premises which may be used for a permitted temporary activity which:

- are exclusively or primarily used for the supply of alcohol for consumption on the premises; or
- are open for the purposes of being used for the supply of alcohol for consumption on the premises by virtue of a temporary event notice and, at the time the temporary event notice has effect, they are exclusively or primarily used for such supplies.

The 'supply of alcohol' means the sale by retail of alcohol, or the supply of alcohol by or on behalf of a club to, or to the order of, a member of the club.

It will be a question of fact as to whether premises are exclusively or primarily used for the supply of alcohol for consumption on the premises, and reference to the use of the premises as a whole should be made. The expression should be given its ordinary and natural meaning in the context of the particular circumstances. It will normally be quite clear that the business being operated at the premises is predominantly the sale and consumption of alcohol.

This means that where the exclusive or primary use is the supply of alcohol for consumption on the premises, unaccompanied children under 16 will not be allowed to be on the premises at any time. But this does not mean that unaccompanied children between the ages of 16 and 18 will have access to licensed premises. Subject only to the provisions of the Act and any licence or certificate conditions, admission will always be at the discretion of those managing the premises.

No offence is committed if the unaccompanied child is just passing through the premises solely for the purpose of passing to or from some other place to or from which there is no other convenient means of access or egress (s.145(5)). As this is not a defence, it is suggested that the burden of proof would be on the prosecution.

A person guilty of this offence is liable on summary conviction to a fine not exceeding level 3 on the standard scale.

22.2.2 Premises open for the supply of alcohol for consumption on the premises

Section 145 also provides that it is an offence for a person to allow an unaccompanied child under the age of 16 to be on licensed premises, premises which have a club premises certificate or premises which may be used for a permitted temporary activity at a time between the hours of midnight and 5 am when the premises are open for the purposes of being used for the supply of alcohol for consumption there. A child is unaccompanied if he is not in the company of an individual aged 18 or over.

The 'supply of alcohol' means the sale by retail of alcohol, or the supply of alcohol by or on behalf of a club to, or to the order of, a member of the club.

Thus, where there is no exclusive or primary use it will only be an offence to allow unaccompanied children to be on the premises between midnight and 5 am.

No offence is committed if the unaccompanied child is just passing through the premises solely for the purpose of passing to or from some other place to or from which there is no other convenient means of access or egress (s.145(5)). As this is not a defence, it is suggested that the burden of proof would be on the prosecution.

A person guilty of this offence is liable on summary conviction to a fine not exceeding level 3 on the standard scale.

22.2.3 Persons who can commit these offences

The offences in s.145 can only be committed by:

- any person who works at the premises in a capacity, whether paid or unpaid, which authorises him to request the unaccompanied child to leave the premises;
- in the case of licensed premises, the holder of a premises licence in respect of the premises and the designated premises supervisor under the licence;
- in the case of premises in respect of which a club premises certificate has effect, any member or officer of the club who is present on the premises in a capacity which enables him to make such a request; and
- in the case of premises which may be used for a permitted temporary activity, the premises user.

22.2.4 Defences

A person charged with one of these offences by reason of his own conduct has a defence under s.145(6) if:

- he believed that the unaccompanied child was aged 16 or over or that an individual accompanying him was aged 18 or over; and
- either he had taken all reasonable steps to establish the individual's age, or nobody could reasonably have suspected from the individual's appearance that he was aged under 16 or, as the case may be, under 18.

A person will be treated as having taken all reasonable steps to establish an individual's age if he asked the individual for evidence of his age, and the evidence would have convinced a reasonable person (s.145(7)).

Where a person is charged with one of these offences by reason of the act or default of some other person, it is a defence that he exercised all due diligence to avoid committing it (s.145(8)).

22.3 SALE OF ALCOHOL TO CHILDREN

There are three offences relating to the sale of alcohol to children. The principal offence is in s.146(1) which provides that it is an offence for a person to sell alcohol to an individual aged under 18.

In addition, a club commits an offence under s.146(2) if alcohol is supplied by it or on its behalf to, or to the order of, a member of the club who is aged under 18, or to the order of a member of the club, to an individual who is aged under 18.

Finally, s.146(3) provides that a person commits an offence if he supplies alcohol on behalf of a club to, or to the order of, a member of the club who is aged under 18, or to the order of a member of the club, to an individual who is aged under 18.

These offences may be committed by a corporate body, partnership or unincorporated association. The Interpretation Act 1978 provides that, unless the contrary intention appears, a person includes a corporate body. There is nothing in the Act to indicate such a contrary intention. In addition, the Act specifically provides for a corporate body to be capable of committing offences under the Act.

The offence under s.146(1) can be committed anywhere and is not limited to sales on licensed premises. It is thought that most prosecutions will arise out of sales on licensed premises.

A PND can be issued for the offences in s.146(1) and (3) and the tariff is £90. Further information and guidance on PNDs can be found at **www.gov.uk**.

Liability for all three offences is strict and only arises where there is a sale or supply. Section 146(4) provides for a defence of 'reasonable belief'. A person charged with one of these offences by reason of his own conduct has a defence if he believed that the individual was aged 18 or over, and either he had taken all reasonable steps to establish the individual's age, or nobody could reasonably have suspected from the individual's appearance that he was aged under 18.

This defence applies where the person has been charged 'by reason of his own conduct'. This implies that the person must have made the sale or supply personally for the defence to apply.

The second limb of this defence, that nobody could reasonably have suspected from the individual's appearance that he was aged under 18, will cover the situation where the purchaser who was under 18 looked exceptionally old for his age.

Where a purchaser does not look 'exceptionally old', a person will have to take 'all reasonable steps' to establish his age. Section 146(5) provides that a person is treated as having taken all reasonable steps to establish an individual's age if he asked the individual for evidence of his age, and the evidence would have convinced a reasonable person. Such evidence could be provided by a proof of age card. However, if it is proved by the prosecution that the evidence of age was such that no reasonable person would have been convinced by it because for example the proof of age was either an obvious forgery or clearly belonged to another person, the defence will fail.

There are several proof of age schemes in existence. The Proof of Age Standards Scheme (PASS) (**www.pass-scheme.org.uk**) is the United Kingdom's national proof of age accreditation scheme, endorsed by the National Police Chiefs' Council (NPCC) and the Security Industry Authority (SIA). The PASS card scheme provides accreditation to suppliers of proof of age cards. National proof of age card suppliers include CITIZENCARD (**www.citizencard.com**), TOTUM (**https://totum.com/proof-of-age-id-card**) and Luciditi (**https://ageproof.luciditi.co.uk**). The Home Office has published 'False ID Guidance' which provides a guide to the legislation relevant to false ID, to the types of valid ID, and to what action should be taken when presented with false ID (the guidance is available at **www.gov.uk**).

Where a person is charged with one of these offences by reason of the act or default of some other person, it is a defence that he exercised all due diligence to avoid committing it (s.146(6)).

A person guilty of one of these offences is liable on summary conviction to a fine not exceeding level 5 on the standard scale (s.146(7)).

Every local weights and measures authority in England and Wales, i.e. a trading standards department, is under a duty to enforce within its area these provisions, so far as they apply to sales of alcohol made on or from premises to which the public have access (s.154). The 'test purchasing' of alcohol is allowed (see **22.6.1**), and so a weights and measures inspector may make, or authorise any person to make on his behalf, such purchases of goods as appear expedient for the purpose of determining whether these provisions are being complied with. Guidance on test purchasing is available at **www.gov.uk**.

22.4 ALLOWING THE SALE OF ALCOHOL TO CHILDREN

Section 147 provides that a person who works, whether paid or unpaid, at licensed premises, premises which have a club premises certificate or premises which may be used for a permitted temporary activity, in a capacity which authorises him to prevent the sale, will commit an offence if he knowingly allows the sale of alcohol on those premises to an individual aged under 18.

A person who works on the premises in a capacity, whether paid or unpaid, which authorises him to prevent the supply, and any member or officer of the club who at the time of the supply is present on the relevant premises in a capacity which enables him to prevent it commits an offence if he knowingly allows alcohol to be supplied on those premises by or on behalf of a club to or to the order of a member of the club who is aged under 18, or to the order of a member of the club, to an individual who is aged under 18.

There is no statutory defence and a person guilty of an offence is liable on summary conviction to a fine not exceeding level 5 on the standard scale.

These offences may be committed by a corporate body, partnership or unincorporated association.

Every local weights and measures authority in England and Wales is under a duty to enforce within its area these provisions, so far as they apply to sales of alcohol made on or from premises to which the public have access. A weights and measures inspector may make, or authorise any person to make on his behalf, such purchases of goods as appear expedient for the purpose of determining whether these provisions are being complied with.

22.5 PERSISTENTLY SELLING ALCOHOL TO CHILDREN

An offence is committed under s.147A by a person if on two or more different occasions within a period of three consecutive months alcohol is unlawfully sold on the same premises to an individual aged under 18, and at the time of each sale the premises were either licensed premises or premises authorised to be used for a permitted temporary activity, and that person was a responsible person in relation to the premises at each such time. The individual to whom the sales are made may, but need not be, the same in each case.

Alcohol sold to an individual aged under 18 is unlawfully sold to him if the person making the sale believed the individual to be aged under 18, or that person did not have reasonable grounds for believing the individual to be aged 18 or over.

A person has reasonable grounds for believing an individual to be aged 18 or over only if he asked the individual for evidence of his age and that individual produced evidence that would have convinced a reasonable person, or nobody could reasonably have suspected from the individual's appearance that he was aged under 18.

A person is, in relation to premises and a time, a responsible person if, at that time, he is the person or one of the persons holding a premises licence in respect of the premises, or the person or one of the persons who is the premises user in respect of a temporary event notice by reference to which the premises are authorised to be used for a permitted temporary activity.

The same sale may not be counted in respect of different offences for the purpose of enabling the same person to be convicted of more than one offence under s.147A, or of enabling the same person to be convicted of both an offence under s.147A and an offence under s.146 or s.147.

In determining whether this offence has been committed, the following are admissible as evidence that there has been an unlawful sale of alcohol to an individual aged under 18 on any premises on any occasion:

- the conviction of a person for an offence under s.146 in respect of a sale to that individual on those premises on that occasion;
- the giving to a person of a caution (within the meaning of the Police Act 1997, Part 5) in respect of such an offence; or
- the payment by a person of a fixed penalty after a PND has been issued under the Criminal Justice and Police Act 2001, Part 1 in respect of such a sale.

A person guilty of this offence is liable, on summary conviction, to an unlimited fine.

Where a premises licence holder has been convicted of this offence in respect of sales on the premises to which the licence relates, the court may under s.147B order that so much of the licence as authorises the sale by retail of alcohol on those premises is suspended for a period not exceeding three months. Such an order will come into force at the time specified by the court that makes it. Where a magistrates' court makes an order, it may suspend its coming into force pending an appeal.

22.6   PURCHASE OF ALCOHOL BY OR ON BEHALF OF CHILDREN

22.6.1   Purchase of alcohol by a child

Section 149(1) provides that it is an offence for an individual under 18 to buy or attempt to buy alcohol or, where he is a member of a club, to have alcohol supplied to him or to his order by or on behalf of the club, as a result of his act or default, or to attempt to have alcohol supplied to him or to his order by or on behalf of the club. A child guilty of such an offence is liable on summary conviction to a fine not exceeding level 3 on the standard scale.

Test purchases to find out whether under-age sales are taking place are allowed. No offence is committed where the individual buys or attempts to buy the alcohol at the request of a constable, or a weights and measures inspector appointed under the Weights and Measures Act 1985, s.72(1), who is acting in the course of his duty (s.149(2)). Guidance on test purchasing is available at **www.gov.uk**.

22.6.2   Purchase of alcohol for a child

As well as being an offence for children to buy alcohol, it is also an offence for a person to buy or attempt to buy alcohol on behalf of an individual aged under 18, or where he is a member of a club, on behalf of an individual aged under 18 to make arrangements whereby alcohol is supplied to him or to his order by or on behalf of the club, or to attempt to make such arrangements (s.149(3)). So an offence will be committed if a child gives money to an adult to buy alcohol in an off-licence for consumption by the child.

343

A person charged with this offence has a defence if he had no reason to suspect that the individual was aged under 18 (s.149(6)).

A person guilty of this offence is liable on summary conviction to a fine not exceeding level 5 on the standard scale. A PND can be issued for this offence and the tariff is £90. Further information and guidance on PNDs can be found at **www.gov.uk**.

22.6.3 Purchase of alcohol for consumption by a child

Section 149(4) provides that it is an offence for a person to buy or attempt to buy alcohol for consumption on licensed premises, premises which have a club premises certificate or premises which may be used for a permitted temporary activity by an individual aged under 18, or where he is a member of a club by some act or default of his, alcohol is supplied to him, or to his order, by or on behalf of the club for consumption on licensed premises, premises which have a club premises certificate or premises which may be used for a permitted temporary activity by an individual aged under 18, or he attempts to have alcohol so supplied for such consumption.

Under s.149(5) an offence is not committed where:

- the person buying or being supplied the alcohol, or attempting to do so, is aged 18 or over;
- the individual consuming the alcohol is aged 16 or 17;
- the alcohol is beer, wine or cider;
- its purchase or supply is for consumption at a table meal on licensed premises, premises which have a club premises certificate or premises which may be used for a permitted temporary activity; and
- the individual is accompanied at the meal by an individual aged 18 or over.

It is not necessary that the person who purchases the alcohol accompanies the 16- or 17-year-old at the meal. All that is required is that someone aged 18 or over accompanies the 16- or 17-year-old at the meal.

A 'table meal' is defined in s.159 as a meal eaten by a person seated at a table, or at a counter or other structure which serves the purpose of a table and is not used for the service of refreshments for consumption by persons not seated at a table or structure serving the purpose of a table. It is submitted that it would not be sufficient for a person to claim that bar snacks amounted to a table meal. It is clear that something more than a snack will be required. In *Solomon* v. *Green* (1955) 119 JP 289, it was held that sandwiches and sausages on sticks constituted a meal though it was said that this was a borderline decision. In *Timmis* v. *Millman* (1965) 109 Sol Jo 31, the court decided that a substantial sandwich accompanied by beetroot and pickles, eaten at a table, might be a table meal.

A person charged with this offence has a defence if he had no reason to suspect that the individual was aged under 18.

A person guilty of this offence is liable on summary conviction to a fine not exceeding level 5 on the standard scale. A PND can be issued for this offence and the tariff is £90. Further information and guidance on PNDs can be found at **www.gov.uk**.

22.7 CONSUMPTION OF ALCOHOL BY CHILDREN

22.7.1 Consumption of alcohol by children

Section 150(1) provides that an individual aged under 18 commits an offence if he knowingly consumes alcohol on licensed premises, premises which have a club premises certificate or premises which may be used for a permitted temporary activity.

This offence does not involve strict liability and requires there to be knowing consumption of alcohol for the offence to be proved.

So, no offence will be committed if a child inadvertently consumes alcohol, for example, if his drink is spiked.

Nor will an offence be committed if the individual is aged 16 or 17, the alcohol is beer, wine or cider, its consumption is at a table meal on licensed premises, premises which have a club premises certificate or premises which may be used for a permitted temporary activity, and the individual is accompanied at the meal by an individual aged 18 or over.

A child guilty of such an offence is liable on summary conviction to a fine not exceeding level 3 on the standard scale.

22.7.2 Allowing the consumption of alcohol by children

Section 150(2) provides that a person who works at licensed premises, premises which have a club premises certificate or premises which may be used for a permitted temporary activity in a capacity, whether paid or unpaid, which authorises him to prevent the consumption, and where the alcohol was supplied by a club to or to the order of a member of the club, any member or officer of the club who is present at the premises at the time of the consumption in a capacity which enables him to prevent it, commits an offence if he knowingly allows the consumption of alcohol on those premises by an individual aged under 18.

No offence will be committed if the individual is aged 16 or 17, the alcohol is beer, wine or cider, its consumption is at a table meal on licensed premises, premises which have a club premises certificate or premises which may be used for a permitted temporary activity, and the individual is accompanied at the meal by an individual aged 18 or over.

This offence does not involve strict liability and it requires there to be knowing consumption of alcohol for the offence to be proved.

A person guilty of this offence is liable on summary conviction to a fine not exceeding level 5 on the standard scale. A PND can be issued for this offence and the tariff is £60. Further information and guidance on PNDs can be found on the website **www.gov.uk**.

22.8   DELIVERING ALCOHOL TO CHILDREN

Section 151(1) provides that a person who works on licensed premises, premises which have a club premises certificate or premises which may be used for a permitted temporary activity, in any capacity, whether paid or unpaid, commits an offence if he knowingly delivers to an individual aged under 18 alcohol sold on the premises, or alcohol supplied on the premises by or on behalf of a club to or to the order of a member of the club. The offence will cover, for example, circumstances where a child takes delivery of a consignment of alcohol ordered by an adult by telephone, in a case where the exceptions mentioned below do not apply.

A person who works on the premises in a capacity, whether paid or unpaid, which authorises him to prevent the delivery of the alcohol commits an offence under s.151(2) if he knowingly allows anybody else to deliver to an individual aged under 18 alcohol sold on licensed premises, premises which have a club premises certificate or premises which may be used for a permitted temporary activity. This offence would cover, for example, a person who authorised a delivery of the sort mentioned above in the knowledge that the recipient would be a child.

In addition, s.151(4) provides that a person who works on the premises in a capacity, whether paid or unpaid, which authorises him to prevent the supply, for example the club steward, and any member or officer of the club who at the time of the supply in question is present on the premises in a capacity which enables him to prevent the supply, commits an offence if he knowingly allows anybody else to deliver to an individual aged under 18 alcohol supplied on licensed premises, premises which have a club premises certificate or premises which may be used for a permitted temporary activity by or on behalf of a club to or to the order of a member of the club.

There are a number of exceptions in s.151(6). None of these offences will be committed where:

- the alcohol is delivered at a place where the buyer or, as the case may be, person supplied lives or works, for example, where a child answers the door and signs for the delivery of his father's order at his house;
- the individual aged under 18 works on licensed premises, premises which have a club premises certificate or premises which may be used for a permitted temporary activity in a capacity, whether paid or unpaid, which involves the delivery of alcohol, for example, where a 16-year-old office worker is sent to collect a delivery for his employer; or

- the alcohol is sold or supplied for consumption on licensed premises, premises which have a club premises certificate or premises which may be used for a permitted temporary activity.

A person guilty of one of these offences is liable on summary conviction to a fine not exceeding level 5 on the standard scale. A PND can be issued for this offence and the tariff is £90. Further information and guidance on PNDs can be found on the website **www.gov.uk**.

22.9 SENDING A CHILD TO OBTAIN ALCOHOL

Section 152(1) provides that it is an offence for a person to knowingly send an individual aged under 18 into licensed premises, premises which have a club premises certificate or premises which may be used for a permitted temporary activity in order to obtain alcohol sold or to be sold on for consumption off the premises, or alcohol supplied or to be supplied by or on behalf of a club to or to the order of a member of the club for such consumption.

This offence would cover, for example, circumstances where a parent sends their child to an off-licence to collect some alcohol which had been bought over the telephone. The offence is committed regardless of whether the child is sent to the actual premises from where the alcohol is sold or supplied, or whether he is sent to other premises to which the alcohol has been sent.

It is immaterial whether the individual aged under 18 is sent to obtain the alcohol from the licensed premises, premises which have a club premises certificate or premises which may be used for a permitted temporary activity or from other premises from which it is delivered in pursuance of the sale or supply (s.152(2)).

An offence is not committed:

- where the individual aged under 18 works on the relevant premises in a capacity, whether paid or unpaid, which involves the delivery of alcohol; or
- where the individual aged under 18 is sent by a constable, or a weights and measures inspector, i.e. a trading standards officer, who is acting in the course of his duty to carry out a 'test purchase'.

A person guilty of this offence is liable on summary conviction to a fine not exceeding level 5 on the standard scale.

22.10 PROHIBITION OF UNSUPERVISED SALES BY CHILDREN

Section 153 provides that it is an offence for a 'responsible person' on any licensed premises, premises which have a club premises certificate or premises which may be used for a permitted temporary activity knowingly to allow an individual aged under 18 to make on the premises any sale of alcohol, or any supply of alcohol by or on behalf of a club to or to the order of a member of the club, unless the sale or supply has been specifically approved by that or another responsible person. An offence is therefore not committed where the sale or supply is specifically approved, and there is no minimum age for the individual making the sale or supply.

For these purposes, a 'responsible person' is:

- in relation to licensed premises the holder of the premises licence, the designated premises supervisor or any individual aged 18 or over who is authorised by them;
- in relation to premises in respect of which there is in force a club premises certificate, any member or officer of the club present on the premises in a capacity which enables him to prevent the supply in question; and
- in relation to premises which may be used for a permitted temporary activity the premises user, or any individual aged 18 or over who is authorised by him.

An offence will not be committed where the alcohol is sold or supplied for consumption with a table meal, it is sold or supplied in premises which are being used for the service of table meals, or in a part of any premises which is being so used, and the premises are, or the part is, not used for the sale or supply of alcohol otherwise than to persons having table meals there and for consumption by such a person ancillary to his meal. This means that someone under 18 who works as a waiter in a restaurant can serve alcohol in the restaurant, or in a public house in a part set aside for table meals.

A person guilty of this offence is liable on summary conviction to a fine not exceeding level 1 on the standard scale.

22.11 GIVING INTOXICATING LIQUOR TO CHILDREN UNDER FIVE

It is an offence under the Children and Young Persons Act 1933, s.5 for a person to give, or cause to be given, to any child under the age of five any alcohol except upon the order of a duly qualified medical practitioner, or in case of sickness, apprehended sickness or other urgent cause.

A person guilty of this offence is liable, on summary conviction, to a fine not exceeding level 1 on the standard scale.

The meaning of alcohol for the purposes of this provision is the same as that in the Licensing Act 2003 except that denatured alcohol, methyl alcohol, naphtha and alcohol contained in liqueur confectionery are to be disregarded.

22.12 CONFISCATION OF ALCOHOL

The Confiscation of Alcohol (Young Persons) Act 1997, s.1 provides that where a constable reasonably suspects that a person in a relevant place is in possession of alcohol and that either:

- he is under 18;
- he intends that any of the alcohol should be consumed by a person who is under 18 in that or any other relevant place; or
- a person under 18 who is, or has recently been, with him has recently consumed alcohol in that or any other relevant place,

the constable may require him to surrender anything in his possession which is, or which the constable reasonably believes to be, alcohol or a container for alcohol, and to give him his name and address. The constable must inform the person of his suspicion and that failing without reasonable excuse to comply is an offence. A constable who imposes a requirement as mentioned may, if he reasonably suspects that the person is under the age of 16, remove the person to the person's place of residence or a place of safety.

A 'relevant place' for these purposes means:

- any public place, other than licensed premises; or
- any place, other than a public place, to which the person has unlawfully gained access;

and for this purpose, a place is a public place if at the material time the public or any section of the public has access to it, on payment or otherwise, as of right or by virtue of express or implied permission.

Anything which is surrendered to a police officer may be disposed of in any manner he considers appropriate.

Anyone who fails without reasonable excuse to comply will commit an offence and is liable on summary conviction to a fine not exceeding level 2 on the standard scale.

349

CHAPTER 23

Early morning alcohol restriction orders

23.1 INTRODUCTION

An early morning alcohol restriction order (EMRO) is designed to address recurring problems such as high levels of alcohol-related crime and disorder in specific areas at specific times, serious public nuisance and other instances of alcohol-related antisocial behaviour which is not directly attributable to specific premises. The power conferred on licensing authorities to make, vary or revoke an EMRO is set out in ss.172A to 172E. An EMRO:

- applies to the supply of alcohol authorised by premises licences, club premises certificates and temporary event notices;
- applies for any period beginning at or after 12 am and ending at or before 6 am. It does not have to apply on every day of the week, and can apply for different time periods on different days of the week;
- applies for a limited or unlimited period;
- applies to the whole or any part of the licensing authority's area;
- will not apply to any premises on New Year's Eve (defined as 12 am to 6 am on 1 January each year);
- will not apply to the supply of alcohol by those who provide hotel or similar accommodation to their residents between 12 am and 6 am, provided the alcohol is sold at those times only through mini-bars and/or room service; and
- will not apply to a relaxation of licensing hours by virtue of an order made under s.172.

The Guidance at para.17.9 provides:

> An EMRO is a powerful tool which will prevent licensed premises in the area to which the EMRO relates from supplying alcohol during the times at which the EMRO applies. The licensing authority should consider whether other measures may address the problems that they have identified as the basis for introducing an EMRO. As set out in paragraphs 9.42–9.44 of this Guidance, when determining whether a step is appropriate to promote the licensing objectives, a licensing authority is not required to decide that no lesser step will achieve the aim. They should, however, consider whether taking

that step is reasonable, justified and proportionate. The introduction of an EMRO may have far-reaching, wider impacts on the socio-economic circumstances in an area. In considering whether the introduction of an EMRO is an appropriate step to promote the licensing objectives, based on whether this is reasonable, justified and proportionate, a licensing authority may hold informal discussions early in the process with a range of interested partners; these include, but are not limited to, premises that may be affected by the introduction of the EMRO. Other measures that could be taken instead of making an EMRO might include:

- working in partnership with licensed premises on voluntary measures and encouraging the creation of business-led best practice schemes in the area;
- reviewing licences of specific problem premises;
- introducing a CIA;
- use of the new closure power in the Anti-social Behaviour, Crime and Policing Act 2014 which replaces section 161 of the 2003 Licensing Act. This new closure power can be used to protect victims and communities by quickly closing premises that are causing nuisance or disorder. Further guidance on this power can be found on the gov.uk website, under the Anti-social Behaviour, Crime and Policing Act: anti-social behaviour guidance;
- use of other mechanisms such as those set out in paragraph 14.47 of this Guidance.

23.2 POWER TO MAKE AN EARLY MORNING ALCOHOL RESTRICTION ORDER

If a licensing authority considers it appropriate for the promotion of the licensing objectives, it may make an order for an EMRO under s.172A.

When establishing its evidence base, a licensing authority may wish to consider the approach set out in paras.14.29 to 14.33 of the Guidance which includes indicative types of evidence, although this should not be considered an exhaustive list of the types of evidence which may be relevant (Guidance, para.17.7).

An EMRO will provide that:

- premises licences and club premises certificates granted by the authority, and temporary event notices given to the authority, do not have effect to the extent that they authorise the sale of alcohol during the period specified in the order; and
- club premises certificates granted by the authority do not have effect to the extent that they authorise the supply of alcohol by or on behalf of a club to, or to the order of, a member of the club during the period specified in the order.

The period that may be specified in the order must begin no earlier than midnight, and end no later than 6 am.

An EMRO may provide that it is to apply:

- in relation to the same period of every day on which it is to apply, or in relation to different periods of different days;
- every day or only on particular days (for example, particular days of the week or year);
- in relation to the whole or part of a licensing authority's area; or
- for a limited or unlimited period.

351

The Guidance at para.17.4 provides:

> An EMRO can apply to the whole or part of the licensing authority's area. The area may, for example, comprise a single floor of a shopping complex or exclude premises which have clearly demonstrated to the licensing authority that the licensable activities carried on there do not contribute to the problems which form the basis for the proposed EMRO.

In addition, an EMRO must be in the prescribed form and have the prescribed content. It must specify the days on which it is to apply and the period of those days, the area in relation to which it is to apply, if it is to apply for a limited period, that period and the date from which it is to apply. The form of an EMRO is set out in the Licensing Act 2003 (Early Morning Alcohol Restriction Orders) Regulations 2012, SI 2012/2551 ('EMRO Regulations'), Sched.1.

If the licensing authority has already published a cumulative impact assessment (CIA), it should consider the relationship between the CIA and proposed EMRO area, and the potential overall impact on its local licensing policy (Guidance, para.17.5).

23.3 PROCEDURAL REQUIREMENTS FOR EARLY MORNING ALCOHOL RESTRICTION ORDERS

A licensing authority which proposes to make an EMRO must advertise the proposed order in the prescribed manner, and hold a hearing to consider any relevant representations, unless the authority and each person who has made such representations agree that a hearing is unnecessary (s.172B(1)).

The EMRO Regulations, reg.4 provides that the proposal must be advertised:

- for a period of no less than 42 days by publication of a notice of the proposal on the licensing authority's website, and by displaying a notice in the area in relation to which the proposed order is to be made in a manner which is likely to bring the proposal to the attention of persons who have an interest in it; and
- on at least one occasion during the period of 42 days starting on the day on which the proposal is first advertised by publication of a notice of the proposal in a local newspaper or, if there is none, in a local newsletter, circular or similar document, circulating in the licensing authority's area and by notice sent to all affected persons.

The Guidance at para.17.11 provides that the advertisement should include a short summary of the evidence and the manner in which representations can be made, as well as the details of the proposed EMRO.

Representations will be 'relevant representations' if they:

- are about the likely effect of the making of the proposed order on the promotion of the licensing objectives;

- are made to the licensing authority by an affected person, a responsible authority or any other person;
- are made in the prescribed form and manner and within the prescribed period;
- have not been withdrawn; and
- in the case of representations made by a person who is not a responsible authority, are not, in the opinion of the licensing authority, frivolous or vexatious.

Where a licensing authority determines that any representations are frivolous or vexatious, it must notify the person who made them of its reasons for its determination.

An 'affected person' is:

- the holder of the premises licence or club premises certificate in respect of affected premises;
- the premises user in relation to a temporary event notice in respect of affected premises;
- a person who has applied for a premises licence or club premises certificate in respect of affected premises (where the application has not been determined); and
- a person to whom a provisional statement has been issued in respect of affected premises.

'Affected premises', in relation to a proposed EMRO, means premises in respect of which it will apply from the date specified in it.

The following will be a 'responsible authority':

- the licensing authority and any other licensing authority in whose area part of any affected premises is situated;
- the chief officer of police for a police area any part of which is in the area specified in the order;
- the fire and rescue authority for an area any part of which is in the area specified in the order;
- the Local Health Board for an area any part of which is in the area specified in the order;
- the local authority in England whose public health functions within the meaning of the National Health Service Act 2006 are exercisable in respect of an area any part of which is in the area specified in the order;
- the local weights and measures authority for any such area;
- the enforcing authority within the meaning given by the Health and Safety at Work etc. Act 1974, s.18 for any such area;
- the local planning authority within the meaning given by the Town and Country Planning Act 1990 for any such area;
- the local authority by which statutory functions are exercisable in the area specified in the order in relation to minimising or preventing the risk of pollution of the environment or of harm to human health;

- a body which:

  - represents those who, in relation to the area specified in the order, are responsible for, or interested in, matters relating to the protection of children from harm; and
  - is recognised by the licensing authority for the purposes of s.172B as being competent to advise on such matters;

- where affected premises are a vessel:

  - a navigation authority (within the meaning given by the Water Resources Act 1991, s.221(1)) having functions in relation to the waters where the vessel is usually moored or berthed or any waters where it is navigated at a time when it is used for licensable activities to which the proposed order relates;
  - the Environment Agency;
  - the Canal & River Trust; and
  - the Secretary of State; and

- a prescribed person (no one has been prescribed to date).

A responsible authority or any other person making representations to a licensing authority may make those representations at any time during a period of 42 days starting on the day after the day on which the proposal to make an order is advertised. Any representations must be in writing, and be in the form and must contain the information set out in the EMRO Regulations, Sched.2.

23.4 MAKING AN EARLY MORNING ALCOHOL RESTRICTION ORDER

A licensing authority may not make an EMRO in relation to an area not specified in the proposed order advertised under s.172B, a day not specified in that proposed order, or a period other than the period specified in that proposed order of any day so specified (s.172C).

The Guidance at para.17.22 provides that:

> If the licensing authority determines that the proposed EMRO is appropriate for the promotion of the licensing objectives, its determination must be put to the full council for its final decision. There is no time specified in legislation by which the full council must make this decision. This is intended to reflect the fact that the licensing authority may only meet in full council infrequently.

After making an EMRO, a licensing authority must publish it or otherwise make it available in the prescribed form and manner, and within the prescribed period. The EMRO Regulations, reg.14 provides that a licensing authority must, no later than seven days after the day on which it makes an EMRO, make the order available:

- by notice sent to all affected persons; and

- for a period of no less than 28 days by publication on its website, and by displaying a notice in the area in relation to which the order has been made in a manner which is likely to bring the order to the attention of persons interested in it.

23.5 HEARING

Where relevant representations have been made, the licensing authority must hold a hearing, unless it and each person making a representation agree that a hearing is unnecessary. The hearing must be held within 30 working days beginning with the day after the end of the period during which representations may be made (Hearings Regulations, reg.5 and Sched.1, para.15A). The hearing can be arranged to take place other than on consecutive working days if an authority considers this to be necessary for its consideration of any representations made by a party, or in the public interest (Hearings Regulations, reg.5(2)). Notice of the hearing must be given to any person who has made a relevant representation not less than 10 working days before the day or the first day on which the hearing is to be held (Hearings Regulations, reg.6(4) and Sched.2, para.15A). The notice to an affected person who has made relevant representations must include a copy of the relevant representations (Hearings Regulations, reg.7(2) and Sched.3, para.15).

Following the hearing, the licensing authority must make its determination within the period of 10 working days beginning with the day or the last day on which the hearing was held (Hearings Regulations, reg.26(3)). The licensing authority is not required to notify a party of its determination in respect of a hearing (Hearings Regulations, reg.28(3)).

As a result of a hearing, the licensing authority has three options:

- to decide that the proposed EMRO is appropriate for promotion of the licensing objectives;
- to decide that the proposed EMRO is not appropriate for the promotion of the objectives and therefore that the process should be ended; or
- to decide that the proposed EMRO should be modified. In this case, if the licensing authority proposes that the modified EMRO should differ from the initial proposal in relation to the area specified, any day not in the initial proposal or the period of any day specified, the licensing authority should advertise what is in effect a new proposal to make an EMRO in the manner described above, so that further representations are capable of being made.

23.6 VARIATION AND REVOCATION OF AN EARLY MORNING ALCOHOL RESTRICTION ORDER

A licensing authority may vary or revoke an EMRO (s.172D). The Guidance at para.17.26 provides that:

The variation or revocation of an order requires the licensing authority to undertake the same process as that which applied on its introduction; that is after gathering the appropriate evidence, it advertises its new EMRO proposal, following the process set out above so that those affected and anyone else can make representations.

23.7 EXCEPTIONS

An EMRO does not apply in prescribed cases or circumstances (s.172E). For these purposes, the EMRO Regulations, reg.15 provides that prescribed cases or circumstances are:

- premises which are a hotel or comparable premises (premises are 'comparable premises' to a hotel if they are a guest house, lodging house or hostel) at which the supply of alcohol between midnight and 6 am on any day may only be made to a person:
    - who is staying at the premises; and
    - for consumption only in the room at which the person is staying on the premises; and

- premises which are authorised to supply alcohol for consumption on the premises between midnight and 6 am on 1 January in every year (but are not so authorised at those times on any other day in any year).

23.8 ENFORCEMENT OF AN EARLY MORNING ALCOHOL RESTRICTION ORDER

The supply of alcohol in contravention of an EMRO is an unauthorised licensable activity which is an offence under s.136 (see **21.2**). It may also result in a closure notice being served on the premises under the Anti-social Behaviour, Crime and Policing Act 2014, s.76 as a precursor to an application for a closure order under s.80 of that Act (which requires the constable or authority that issued the notice to apply to a magistrates' court not later than 48 hours after the service of the closure notice). This may alternatively result in the licence being reviewed on crime prevention grounds.

An EMRO overrides all authorisations to supply alcohol under the Act (including temporary event notices). It is immaterial whether an authorisation was granted before or after an EMRO was made as there are no authorisations that have the effect of authorising the sale of alcohol during the EMRO period, with the only exception being a licensing hours order made under s.172 (see **11.4.2**). An EMRO will not apply on New Year's Eve in recognition of its status as a national celebration.

CHAPTER 24

Closure of premises

24.1 INTRODUCTION

Part 8 of the Act contains powers for the police to seek a court order to close premises with a premises licence or a temporary event notice in a geographical area that is experiencing or is likely to experience disorder, and to close down instantly individual licensed premises that are disorderly.

The Anti-social Behaviour, Crime and Policing Act 2014 (ABCPA 2014) contains provision for the closure of premises with a premises licence, a temporary event notice or a club premises certificate where a public nuisance is being caused or is likely to be caused. The provisions in ABCPA 2014 came into force on 20 October 2014 and replaced the provisions in ss.161–166 of the Act. Sections 169A and 169B of the Act allow the police and trading standards officers to close premises for at least 48 hours but no more than 336 hours where there is evidence of persistent unlawful selling of alcohol to children.

In addition, premises may be closed under the Criminal Justice and Police Act 2001 for the unauthorised sale of alcohol. A closure notice must first be served requiring the breach of the premises licence to be remedied. If this is not done then the police can apply to the magistrates' court for a closure order.

In addition, premises may be closed under a Prohibition Notice served under the Regulatory Reform (Fire Safety) Order 2005, SI 2005/1541 (Regulatory Reform (Fire Safety) Order 2005, SI 2005/1541, reg.31) or under an Illegal Working Closure Notice (Immigration Act 2016, s.38 and Sched.6).

24.2 ORDERS TO CLOSE PREMISES IN AN AREA EXPERIENCING DISORDER

Section 160 provides that where there is or is expected to be disorder in any local justice area, a magistrates' court acting in the area may make an order requiring all premises which have a premises licence or are subject to a temporary event notice and are situated at or near the place of the disorder or expected disorder, to be closed for a period not exceeding 24 hours. An application for an order must be made by a police officer of the rank of superintendent or above. The period of closure must be specified in the order.

An order can only be made if the magistrates' court is satisfied that it is necessary to make an order to prevent disorder. The proceedings are civil and, while the Act is silent, it is suggested that the standard of proof will be on the balance of probabilities. This power is intended to be used in emergencies where there is disorder, or where there is expected to be disorder. An example of when such an order may be used would be where there is going be a local 'derby' football match and the police anticipate some public disorder. Evidence which might be used could include the fact that disorder has taken place when the event last took place, and that there is intelligence to suggest that disorder may re-occur.

The Government has issued guidance to police officers about the operation of this power, 'Police Powers to Close Premises under the Licensing Act 2003' (available at **www.gov.uk**). This guidance has no binding effect on police officers but is provided to support and assist them in interpreting and implementing Part 8 of the Act in the interests of public safety, the prevention of disorder and the reduction of antisocial behaviour.

In relation to orders under s.160, the Guidance provides in paras.11 to 13:

11. These orders should normally be sought where the police anticipate public order problems (very often fuelled by the ready availability of alcohol) as a result of intelligence or publicly available information, but may also be used in an emergency.

12. Events which might justify action under section 160 could include football fixtures with a history of public order problems; and demonstrations which are thought likely to be hijacked by extreme or violent groups. Where it is possible to anticipate disorder in this way, the courts should be involved and make the decision on the application of a police officer of the rank of superintendent or above as to whether widespread closure is justified.

13. When seeking an order under section 160 of the 2003 Act, the burden of proof will fall on the police to satisfy the court that their intelligence or evidence is sufficient to demonstrate that such action is necessary. Where serious disorder is anticipated, many holders of premises licences and premises users who have given temporary event notices will want to co-operate with the police, not least for the protection of their premises and customers. So far as possible, and where time is available, police officers should initially seek voluntary agreement to closure in an area for a particular period of time. The courts should therefore only be involved where other alternatives are not available.

Once a closure order has been made, s.160(4) and (5) provide that the following persons will commit an offence if they knowingly keep open any premises to which the order relates, or allow any such premises to be kept open, during the period of the order:

- any manager of the premises (this means a person who works at the premises in a capacity whether paid or unpaid which authorises him to close them (s.171(5));

- in the case of licensed premises, the holder of a premises licence in respect of the premises, and the designated premises supervisor under the licence;
- in the case of premises in respect of which a temporary event notice has effect, the premises user in relation to that notice.

In order to be guilty of an offence a person must have knowledge of the facts both that the premises are open and that they are subject to a closure order.

A person guilty of such an offence is liable on summary conviction to a fine not exceeding level 3 on the standard scale (s.160(6)).

Section 171 provides that premises are 'open' if a person who is not an appropriate person in relation to the premises, a person who usually lives at the premises, or a member of the family of an appropriate person or a person who usually lives at the premises enters the premises and buys or is otherwise supplied with food, drink or anything usually sold on the premises, or while he is on the premises, they are used for the provision of regulated entertainment. An appropriate person means any premises licence holder in respect of the premises, any designated premises supervisor under such a licence, the premises user in relation to any temporary event notice which has effect in respect of the premises, or a manager of the premises.

In deciding whether the premises are open the following are to be disregarded:

- where no premises licence has effect in respect of the premises, any use of the premises for activities (other than licensable activities) which do not take place during an event period specified in a temporary event notice having effect in respect of the premises;
- any use of the premises for a qualifying club activity under and in accordance with a club premises certificate; and
- any exempt supply of hot food and drink by clubs, hotels, etc. (see **5.4**) in circumstances where a person will neither be admitted to the premises nor be supplied with hot food and drink on or from the premises, except by virtue of being a member of a recognised club or a guest of such a member.

A constable may use such force as may be necessary for the purpose of closing premises which have been ordered to be closed (s.160(7)).

24.3 CLOSURE OF PREMISES ASSOCIATED WITH NUISANCE OR DISORDER

24.3.1 Closure notice

ABCPA 2014, s.76(1) provides that a police officer of at least the rank of inspector, or the local authority, may issue a closure notice if satisfied on reasonable grounds that the use of particular premises has resulted, or (if the notice is not issued) is likely soon to result, in nuisance to members of the public, or that there has been, or (if the notice is not issued) is likely soon to be, disorder near those premises associated with the use of those premises, and that the notice is necessary to prevent the nuisance or disorder from continuing, recurring or occurring. The Secretary of State may by regulation specify that premises or descriptions of premises that may not be subject to a closure notice (ABCPA 2014, s.76(8)).

Before issuing a closure notice, the police officer or local authority must ensure that any body or individual the officer or authority thinks appropriate has been consulted (ABCPA 2014, s.76(7)).

A closure notice is a notice prohibiting access to the premises for a period specified in the notice (ABCPA 2014, s.76(2)).

A closure notice may prohibit access by all persons except those specified, or by all persons except those of a specified description at all times, or at all times except those specified in all circumstances, or in all circumstances except those specified (ABCPA 2014, s.76(3).

A closure notice may not prohibit access by people who habitually live on the premises, or the owner of the premises. Such persons must therefore be specified in the notice (ABCPA 2014, s.76(4)).

ABCPA 2014, s.76(5) provides that a closure notice must:

- identify the premises;
- explain the effect of the notice;
- state that failure to comply with the notice is an offence;
- state that an application will be made under s.80 for a closure order;
- specify when and where the application will be heard;
- explain the effect of a closure order;
- give information about the names of, and means of contacting, persons and organisations in the area that provide advice about housing and legal matters.

A closure notice may be issued only if reasonable efforts have been made to inform people who live on the premises (whether habitually or not), and any person who has control of or responsibility for the premises or who has an interest in them, that the notice is going to be issued (ABCPA 2014, s.76(6)).

ABCPA 2014, s.92(1)) provides that:

- 'Local authority' means in relation to England, a district council, a county council for an area for which there is no district council, a London borough council, the Common Council of the City of London or the Council of the Isles of Scilly, and in relation to Wales, a county council or a county borough council.
- 'Owner', in relation to premises, means a person (other than a mortgagee not in possession) entitled to dispose of the fee simple of the premises, whether in possession or in reversion and a person who holds or is entitled to the rents and profits of the premises under a lease that (when granted) was for a term of not less than three years.
- 'Premises' includes any land or other place (whether enclosed or not) and any outbuildings that are, or are used as, part of premises.

24.3.2 Duration of a closure notice

The maximum period that may be specified in a closure notice is 24 hours unless, in the case of a notice issued by a police officer, the officer is of at least the rank of superintendent, or in the case of a notice issued by a local authority, the notice is signed by the chief executive officer of the authority or a person designated by him or her for the purposes of this subsection, in which case the maximum period is 48 hours (in calculating when the period of 48 hours ends, Christmas Day is to be disregarded) (ABCPA 2014, s.77(1)–(3)).

Where a 24-hour notice is issued, that period may be extended by up to 24 hours if, in the case of a notice issued by a police officer, an extension notice is issued by an officer of at least the rank of superintendent, or if, in the case of a notice issued by a local authority, the authority issues an extension notice signed by the chief executive officer of the authority or a person designated by the chief executive officer for the purposes of this subsection (ABCPA 2014, s.77(4)). An extension notice is a notice which identifies the closure notice to which it relates and specifies the period of the extension (ABCPA 2014, s.77(5)).

24.3.3 Cancellation or variation of a closure notice

Where a closure notice is in force and the relevant officer or authority is no longer satisfied that the use of particular premises has resulted in nuisance to members of the public, or that there has been disorder near those premises associated with the use of those premises, and that the notice is no longer necessary to prevent the nuisance or disorder from continuing, recurring or occurring, either as regards the premises as a whole, or as regards a particular part of the premises, then the relevant officer or authority must issue a cancellation notice or a variation notice, as appropriate (ABCPA 2014, s.78(1)–(3)).

A cancellation notice or a variation notice that relates to a closure notice which was issued or extended by a local authority must be signed by the person who signed the closure notice or its extension (or, if that person is not available, by another person who could have signed (i.e. a person designated by the chief executive officer of the authority for the purposes of ABCPA 2014, s.77(2)(b)).

In the case of a closure notice issued by a police officer and not extended, the notice must be signed by that officer (or, if that officer is not available, another officer of the same or higher rank). In the case of a closure notice issued by a police officer and extended, it will be the officer who issued the extension notice (or, if that officer is not available, another officer of the same or higher rank) (ABCPA 2014, s.78(6)).

24.3.4 Service of notices

ABCPA 2014, s.79 contains detailed provisions, which must be followed, for the service of closure, extension, cancellation and variation notices.

A notice must be served by a constable, in the case of a notice issued by a police officer or a representative of the authority that issued the notice, in the case of a notice issued by a local authority. In relation to a local authority, 'representative' means an employee of the authority, or a person, or employee or a person, acting on behalf of the authority.

The constable or local authority representative must if possible:

- fix a copy of the notice to at least one prominent place on the premises;
- fix a copy of the notice to each normal means of access to the premises;
- fix a copy of the notice to any outbuildings that appear to the constable or representative to be used with or as part of the premises;
- give a copy of the notice to at least one person who appears to the constable or representative to have control of or responsibility for the premises; and
- give a copy of the notice to the people who live on the premises and to any person who does not live there but was informed (under ABCPA 2014, s.76(6)) that the notice was going to be issued.

If the constable or local authority representative reasonably believes, at the time of serving the notice, that there are persons occupying another part of the building or other structure in which the premises are situated whose access to that part will be impeded if a closure order is made under ABCPA 2014, s.80, the constable or representative must also if possible serve the notice on those persons.

The constable or local authority representative may enter any premises, using reasonable force if necessary, for the purposes of complying with the requirements as to serving the notice.

24.3.5 Application to a magistrates' court and its powers

Whenever a closure notice is issued an application must be made to a magistrates' court for a closure order (unless the notice has been cancelled under ABCPA 2014, s.78) (ABCPA 2014, s.80(1)). A closure order is an order prohibiting access to the premises for a period specified in the order, not exceeding three months (ABCPA 2014, s.80(6)).

The application for a closure order must be made by a constable if the closure notice was issued by a police officer or by the authority that issued the closure notice if the notice was issued by a local authority (ABCPA 2014, s.80(2)).

An application must be heard by the magistrates' court not later than 48 hours after service of the closure notice and, in calculating this period, Christmas Day is disregarded (ABCPA 2014, s.80(3), (4)).

A magistrates' court may make a closure order if it is satisfied that a person has engaged, or (if the order is not made) is likely to engage, in disorderly, offensive or criminal behaviour on the premises, or that the use of the premises has resulted, or (if the order is not made) is likely to result, in serious nuisance to members of the public, or that there has been, or (if the order is not made) is likely to be, disorder near those premises associated with the use of those premises, and that the order is necessary to prevent the behaviour, nuisance or disorder from continuing, recurring or occurring (ABCPA 2014, s.80(5)). 'Offensive behaviour' means behaviour by a person that causes or is likely to cause harassment, alarm or distress to one or more other persons not of the same household as that person and 'criminal behaviour' means behaviour that constitutes a criminal offence (ABCPA 2014, s.92(1)).

A closure order may prohibit access by all persons, or by all persons except those specified, or by all persons except those of a specified description at all times, or at all times except those specified in all circumstances, or in all circumstances except those specified (ABCPA 2014, s.80(7)).

A closure order may be made in respect of the whole or any part of the premises and may include provision about access to a part of the building or structure of which the premises form part (ABCPA 2014, s.80(8)).

Where there is a premises licence is in force, the court must notify the relevant licensing authority if it makes a closure order in relation to those premises (ABCPA 2014, s.80(9)).

If where an application has been made to a magistrates' court for a closure order and the court does not make a closure order it may nevertheless order that the closure notice continues in force for a specified further period of not more than 48 hours, if satisfied that the use of particular premises has resulted, or (if the notice is not continued) is likely soon to result, in nuisance to members of the public, or that there has been, or (if the notice is not continued) is likely soon to be, disorder near those premises associated with the use of those premises, and that the continuation of the notice is necessary to prevent the nuisance or disorder from continuing, recurring or occurring (ABCPA 2014, s.81(2)). The court may adjourn the hearing of the application for a period of not more than 14 days to enable the occupier of the premises, the person with control of or responsibility for the premises, or any other person with an interest in the premises, to show why a closure order should not be made (ABCPA 2014, s.81(3)). If the court adjourns the hearing it may order that the closure notice continues in force until the end of the period of the adjournment (ABCPA 2014, s.81(4)).

24.3.6 Extension of closure orders

At any time before the expiry of a closure order, an application may be made to a justice of the peace, by complaint, for an extension (or further extension) of the period for which the order is in force (ABCPA 2014, s.82(1)).

An application for an extension is made:

- where the closure order was made on the application of a constable, a police officer of at least the rank of inspector; or
- where the closure order was made on the application of a local authority, that authority (ABCPA 2014, s.82(2)).

A police officer or local authority may make an application only if satisfied on reasonable grounds that it is necessary for the period of the order to be extended to prevent the occurrence, recurrence or continuance of:

- disorderly, offensive or criminal behaviour on the premises;
- serious nuisance to members of the public resulting from the use of the premises; or
- disorder near the premises associated with the use of the premises;

and also satisfied that the appropriate consultee has been consulted about the intention to make the application (ABCPA 2014, s.82(3)).

For these purposes, 'the appropriate consultee' is either the local authority, in the case of an application by a police officer or the chief officer of police for the area in which the premises are situated, in the case of an application by a local authority (ABCPA 2014, s.82(4)).

Where an application is made, the justice of the peace may issue a summons directed to any person on whom the closure notice was served under ABCPA 2014, s.79, or any other person who appears to the justice to have an interest in the premises but on whom the closure notice was not served, requiring the person to appear before the magistrates' court to respond to the application (ABCPA 2014, s.82(5)).

If a summons is issued, a notice stating the date, time and place of the hearing of the application must be served on the persons to whom the summons is directed (ABCPA 2014, s.82(6)).

If the magistrates' court is satisfied on reasonable grounds that it is necessary for the period of the order to be extended to prevent the occurrence, recurrence or continuance of:

- disorderly, offensive or criminal behaviour on the premises;
- serious nuisance to members of the public resulting from the use of the premises; or
- disorder near the premises associated with the use of the premises;

it may make an order extending (or further extending) the period of the closure order by a period not exceeding three months (ABCPA 2014, s.82(7)).

The period of a closure order may not be extended so that the order lasts for more than six months (ABCPA 2014, s.82(8)).

24.3.7 Discharge of closure orders

At any time before the expiry of a closure order, an application may be made to a justice of the peace, by complaint, for the order to be discharged (ABCPA 2014, s.83(1)). Such an application can be made by:

- a constable, where the closure order was made on the application of a constable;

- the authority that applied for the closure order, where the order was made on the application of a local authority;
- a person on whom the closure notice was served under ABCPA 2014, s.79;
- anyone else who has an interest in the premises but on whom the closure notice was not served (ABCPA 2014, s.83(2)).

Where a person other than a constable makes an application for the discharge of an order that was made on the application of a constable, the justice may issue a summons directed to a constable considered appropriate by the justice requiring him or her to appear before the magistrates' court to respond to the application (ABCPA 2014, s.83(3)). If such a summons is issued, a notice stating the date, time and place of the hearing of the application must be served on the constable to whom the summons is directed, a person on whom the closure notice was served under ABCPA 2014, s.79 and anyone else who has an interest in the premises but on whom the closure notice was not served (other than the complainant) (ABCPA 2014, s.83(4)).

Where the order was made on the application of a local authority, and a person other than that authority makes an application for the discharge of the order, the justice may issue a summons directed to that authority requiring it to appear before the magistrates' court to respond to the application (ABCPA 2014, s.83(5)). If such a summons is issued, a notice stating the date, time and place of the hearing of the application must be served on the authority, a person on whom the closure notice was served under ABCPA 2014, s.79 and anyone else who has an interest in the premises but on whom the closure notice was not served (other than the complainant) (ABCPA 2014, s.83(6)).

The magistrates' court may not make an order discharging the closure order unless satisfied that the closure order is no longer necessary to prevent the occurrence, recurrence or continuance of:

- disorderly, offensive or criminal behaviour on the premises;
- serious nuisance to members of the public resulting from the use of the premises; or
- disorder near the premises associated with the use of the premises (ABCPA 2014, s.83(7)).

24.3.8 Appeals from the magistrates' court

Appeals against a decision of a magistrates' court are dealt with by ABCPA 2014, s.84.

An appeal against a decision to make or extend a closure order may be made by a person on whom the closure notice was served under ABCPA 2014, s.79 or anyone else who has an interest in the premises but on whom the closure notice was not served. A constable may appeal against a decision not to make a closure order applied for by a constable, a decision not to extend a closure order made on the application of a constable, or a decision (under ABCPA 2014, s.81) not to order the continuation in force of a closure notice issued by a constable. A local authority may appeal against a decision not to make a closure order applied for by that authority, a decision not to extend a closure order made on the application of that authority or a decision (under ABCPA 2014, s.81) not to order the continuation in force of a closure notice issued by that authority.

An appeal is to the Crown Court and must be made within the period of 21 days beginning with the date of the decision to which it relates.

On an appeal the Crown Court may make whatever order it thinks appropriate and must notify the relevant licensing authority if it makes a closure order in relation to premises in respect of which a premises licence is in force.

24.3.9 Enforcement of closure orders

An authorised person may:

- enter premises in respect of which a closure order is in force;
- do anything necessary to secure the premises against entry (ABCPA 2014, s.85(1)).

For these purposes 'authorised person' means:

- in relation to a closure order made on the application of a constable, a constable or a person authorised by the chief officer of police for the area in which the premises are situated;
- in relation to a closure order made on the application of a local authority, a person authorised by that authority (ABCPA 2014, s.85(2)).

An authorised person may use reasonable force (ABCPA 2014, s.85(3)).

A person seeking to enter premises must, if required to do so by or on behalf of the owner, occupier or other person in charge of the premises, produce evidence of his or her identity and authority before entering the premises (ABCPA 2014, s.85(4)).

An authorised person may also enter premises in respect of which a closure order is in force to carry out essential maintenance or repairs to the premises (ABCPA 2014, s.85(5)).

24.3.10 Offences

A person who without reasonable excuse remains on or enters premises in contravention of a closure notice (including a notice continued in force under ABCPA 2014, s.81) commits an offence (ABCPA 2014, s.86(1)). A person guilty of such an offence is liable on summary conviction to imprisonment for a period not exceeding three months, or to a fine, or to both.

A person who without reasonable excuse remains on or enters premises in contravention of a closure order commits an offence (ABCPA 2014, s.86(2)). A person guilty of such an offence is liable on summary conviction to imprisonment for a period not exceeding 51 weeks, or to a fine, or to both. In relation to an offence committed before the Criminal Justice Act 2003, s.281(5) comes into force, the reference to 51 weeks is to be read as a reference to six months (ABCPA 2014, s.86(6)).

A person who without reasonable excuse obstructs a person acting under ABCPA 2014, s.79 or s.85(1) commits an offence (ABCPA 2014, s.86(3)). A person guilty of such an offence is liable on summary conviction to imprisonment for a period not exceeding three months, or to a fine, or to both.

24.3.11 Access to other premises

Where access to premises is prohibited or restricted by, or as a result of, an order under ABCPA 2014, ss.80, 81, 82 or 84, and those premises are part of a building or structure, and there is another part of that building or structure that is not subject to the prohibition or restriction, an occupier or owner of that other part may apply to the appropriate court for an order as the court thinks appropriate in relation to access to any part of the building or structure (ABCPA 2014, s.87(1), (4)).

The appropriate court is the magistrates' court, in the case of an order under ABCPA 2014, ss.80, 81 or 82 or the Crown Court, in the case of an order under ABCPA 2014, s.84.

Notice of an application under this section must be given to:

- whatever constable the court thinks appropriate;
- the local authority;
- a person on whom the closure notice was served; and
- anyone else who has an interest in the premises but on whom the closure notice was not served (ABCPA 2014, s.87(3)).

24.3.12 Reimbursement of costs

A local policing body or a local authority that incurs expenditure for the purpose of clearing, securing or maintaining premises in respect of which a closure order is in force may apply to the court that made the order for an order for the reimbursement (in full or in part) by the owner or occupier of the premises of such expenditure and the court may make such order it thinks appropriate (ABCPA 2014, s.88(1), (2)).

An application for an order may not be heard unless it is made before the end of the period of three months starting with the day on which the closure order ceases to have effect (ABCPA 2014, s.88(3)).

An order may be made only against a person who has been served with the application for the order (ABCPA 2014, s.88(4)).

An application must also be served on the local policing body for the area in which the premises are situated, if the application is made by a local authority or the local authority, if the application is made by a local policing body (ABCPA 2014, s.88(5)).

24.3.13 Exemption from liability

A police officer, or the chief officer of police under whose direction or control he or she acts, or a local authority, is not liable for damages in proceedings for judicial review, or the tort of negligence or misfeasance in public office, arising out of anything done or omitted to be done by the police officer or the authority in the exercise or purported exercise of a power in respect of a closure notice or closure order (ABCPA 2014, s.89(1), (2)). This does not apply to an act or omission shown to have been in bad faith, nor so as to prevent an award of damages made in respect of an act or omission on the ground that the act or omission was unlawful by virtue of the Human Rights Act 1998, s.6(1). This also does not affect any other exemption from liability (whether at common law or otherwise).

24.3.14 Compensation

A person who claims to have incurred financial loss in consequence of a closure notice or a closure order may apply to the magistrates' court that considered the application for a closure order or to the Crown Court, in the case of a closure order that was made or extended by an order of that Court on an appeal for compensation (ABCPA 2014, s.90(1), (2)).

An application for compensation may not be heard unless it is made before the end of the period of three months starting with whichever of the following is applicable:

- the day on which the closure notice was cancelled;
- the day on which a closure order was refused;
- the day on which the closure order ceased to have effect (ABCPA 2014, s.90(3)).

For these purposes, the day on which a closure order was refused is either the day on which the magistrates' court decided not to make a closure order, or the day on which the Crown Court dismissed an appeal against a decision not to make a closure order (ABCPA 2014, s.90(4)).

On an application for compensation, the court may order the payment of compensation out of central funds if it is satisfied:

- that the applicant is not associated with the use of the premises, or the behaviour on the premises, on the basis of which the closure notice was issued or the closure order made;
- if the applicant is the owner or occupier of the premises, that the applicant took reasonable steps to prevent that use or behaviour;

- that the applicant has incurred financial loss in consequence of the notice or order; and
- that having regard to all the circumstances, it is appropriate to order payment of compensation in respect of that loss (ABCPA 2014, s.90(5)).

24.3.15 Guidance

The Secretary of State may issue guidance to chief officers of police about the exercise, by officers under their direction or control, of those officers' functions and to local authorities about the exercise of their functions and those of their representatives (ABCPA 2014, s.91). The Government has issued statutory guidance, 'Anti-social Behaviour, Crime and Policing Act 2014: Anti-social behaviour powers Statutory guidance for frontline professionals' (available at **www. gov.uk**).

24.3.16 Review of a premises licence following a closure order

Where a licensing authority is notified by the magistrates' court that it has made a closure order or by the Crown Court where it has made a closure order on appeal, the licensing authority must review the premises licence no later than 28 days after the day on which it receives the notice from the magistrates' court or the Crown Court (s.167(1)–(3)). A review must also take place where a court has made an illegal working compliance order under the Immigration Act 2016, Sched.6 and the relevant licensing authority has accordingly received a notice under that Schedule (s.167(1A)).

Notice of the review must be given to the holder of the premises licence and each responsible authority together with details of the closure order and any extension and details of any Order made by the magistrates' court or the Crown Court. The licensing authority must also advertise the review inviting relevant representations from responsible authorities and other persons. Representations from the holder of the premises licence, responsible authority or any other person must be received within the prescribed period (s.167(4); Premises Licences Regulations, regs.37–39). Representations can only be considered if they relate to the promotion of the licensing objectives. Representations from interested parties must not be frivolous or vexatious. Where the licensing authority determines that any representations are vexatious or frivolous it must notify the person who made them of the reasons for its decision (s.167(9)–(11)).

At the hearing, the licensing authority must have regard to the promotion of the licensing objectives and, in the light of these, must take such of the following steps, if any, as it considers appropriate to promote the licensing objectives:

- modify the conditions of the premises licence;
- exclude a licensable activity from the licence;
- remove the designated premises supervisor;

- suspend the licence for a period not exceeding three months; or
- revoke the licence (s.167(5) and (6)).

Where the authority modifies the conditions of the premises licence or excludes a licensable activity from the scope of the licence, it may provide that the modification or exclusion is only to have effect for a specified period of up to three months (s.167(8)).

Once a licensing authority has determined a review of a closure order it must notify the determination and its reasons for making it to:

- the holder of the premises licence;
- any person who made relevant representations; and
- the chief officer of police for the police area, or each police area, in which the premises are situated.

24.3.17   When does a review determination take effect?

A decision in relation to a review of a closure order will usually not have effect until 'the relevant time', which will be either the end of the period given for appealing against the decision, or if the decision is appealed against, the time the appeal is disposed of (s.168). However, this will not be the case where the relevant licensing authority has decided to take one or more of the steps it can take to modify the conditions on the licence, exclude a licensable activity from the licence, remove the designated premises supervisor or suspend the licence, and the premises to which the licence relates have been closed, by virtue of an order of the magistrates' court, or the Crown Court, until the licensing authority's decision was made. In these circumstances, the decision takes effect when it is notified to the holder of the premises licence, though this is subject to the right of relevant licensing authority, on such terms as it thinks fit, to suspend the operation of its decision, in whole or in part, until the relevant time or to suspend it pending appeal.

The premises must remain closed, but the premises licence will continue in force until the relevant time where the relevant licensing authority has decided on a review to revoke the premises licence, and the premises to which the licence relates have been closed, by virtue of an order of the magistrates' court, or of the Crown Court, until that decision was made. There is a right of appeal to the magistrates' court in these circumstances to request that the premises be allowed to remain open on such conditions as the court thinks fit pending appeal of the licensing authority's decision to revoke (see **26.8**).

24.3.18   Opening premises in contravention of a closure following a review

A person commits an offence if, without reasonable excuse, they allow premises to be open during the relevant time in contravention of an order by a relevant licensing authority to revoke the premises licence. A person guilty of this offence is liable on summary conviction to imprisonment for a term not exceeding three months or to an unlimited fine, or to both.

There is no requirement in the Act for the licence holder or the police to clear the premises of customers following the service of a closure order, and the presence of customers in the premises does not give rise to an offence. A customer does not commit an offence if they are not asked to leave and remain on the premises. A person who is drunk or disorderly who refuses to leave after being asked commits an offence (see **21.3.4**).

24.4 CLOSURE NOTICES FOR PERSISTENTLY SELLING ALCOHOL TO CHILDREN

Sections 169A and 169B deal with closure notices for persistently selling alcohol to children and their effect. A closure notice is an alternative to prosecution under s.147A for persistently selling alcohol to children.

A police officer of the rank of superintendent or above, or an inspector of weights and measures may give a closure notice in relation to any premises if:

- there is evidence that a person has committed an offence of persistently selling alcohol to children under s.147A in relation to those premises;
- he considers that the evidence is such that if the offender were prosecuted there would be a realistic prospect of them being convicted; and
- the offender is still, at the time the notice is given, the premises licence holder in respect of the premises, or one of the premises licence holders.

When considering the 'realistic prospect' test, it may be helpful to consider the guidance contained in the Code for Crown Prosecutors (see **www.cps.gov.uk/ publication/code-crown-prosecutors**):

> The finding that there is a realistic prospect of conviction is based on the prosecutor's objective assessment of the evidence, including the impact of any defence and any other information that the suspect has put forward or on which they might rely. It means that an objective, impartial and reasonable jury or bench of magistrates or judge hearing a case alone, properly directed and acting in accordance with the law, is more likely than not to convict the defendant of the charge alleged. This is a different test from the one that the criminal courts themselves must apply. A court may only convict if it is sure that the defendant is guilty.

A closure notice is a notice which proposes a prohibition, for the period specified in the notice, on sales of alcohol on the premises in question, and which offers the opportunity to discharge all criminal liability in respect of the alleged offence by the acceptance of the prohibition proposed by the notice.

A closure notice must:

- be in the prescribed form;
- specify the premises to which it applies;

- give such particulars of the circumstances believed to constitute the alleged offence (including the sales to which it relates) as are necessary to provide reasonable information about it;
- specify the length of the period during which it is proposed that sales of alcohol should be prohibited on those premises;
- specify when that period would begin if the prohibition is accepted;
- explain what would be the effect of the proposed prohibition and the consequences under the Act (including the maximum penalties) of a sale of alcohol on the premises during the period for which it is in force;
- explain the right of every person who, at the time of the alleged offence, held or was one of the holders of a premises licence in respect of those premises to be tried for that offence; and
- explain how that right may be exercised and how (where it is not exercised) the proposed prohibition may be accepted.

The form of closure notice is prescribed by the Licensing Act 2003 (Persistent Selling of Alcohol to Children) (Prescribed Form of Closure Notice) Regulations 2012, SI 2012/963.

The period specified for the length of the period during which it is proposed that sales of alcohol should be prohibited must be at least 48 hours but not more than 336 hours, and the time specified as the time from which that period would begin must be not less than 14 days after the date of the service of the closure notice.

The provision included in the notice explaining how the right may be exercised and how (where it is not exercised) the proposed prohibition may be accepted must:

- provide a means of identifying a police officer or trading standards officer to whom notice exercising the option to accept the prohibition may be given;
- set out particulars of where and how that notice may be given to that police officer or trading standards officer;
- require that notice to be given within 14 days after the date of the service of the closure notice; and
- explain that the right to be tried for the alleged offence will be taken to have been exercised unless every person who, at the time of the notice, holds or is one of the holders of the premises licence for the premises in question accepts the proposed prohibition.

A closure notice must be served on the premises to which it applies. It may be served on the premises to which it applies:

- only by being handed by a constable or trading standards officer to a person on the premises who appears to the constable or trading standards officer to have control of or responsibility for the premises (whether on his own or with others); and

- only at a time when it appears to that constable or trading standards officer that licensable activities are being carried on there.

A copy of every closure notice must be sent to the holder of the premises licence for the premises to which it applies at whatever address for that person is for the time being set out in the licence.

A closure notice must not be given more than three months after the time of the last of the sales to which the alleged offence relates. No more than one closure notice may be given in respect of offences relating to the same sales, nor may such a notice be given in respect of an offence in respect of which a prosecution has already been brought.

Where a closure notice is given then no proceedings may be brought for the alleged offence or any related offence (that is an offence under s.146 or s.147 in respect of any of the sales to which the alleged offence relates) at any time before the time when the prohibition proposed by the notice would take effect. If before that time every person who, at the time of the notice, holds or is one of the holders of the premises licence for the premises in question accepts the proposed prohibition in the manner specified in the notice then that prohibition takes effect at the time so specified in relation to the premises in question and no proceedings may subsequently be brought against any such person for the alleged offence or any related offence.

If the prohibition contained in a closure notice takes effect then so much of the premises licence as authorises the sale by retail of alcohol on the premises is suspended for the period specified in the closure notice.

The effect of the closure notice is not affected by any failure to send a copy of the closure notice to the holder of the premises licence for the premises to which it applies at whatever address for that person is for the time being set out in the licence.

24.5 CLOSURE OF UNLICENSED PREMISES

The Criminal Justice and Police Act 2001, s.19 enables a police constable or a local authority to serve a closure notice where:

- any premises are being used, or have been used within the last 24 hours, for the sale of alcohol for consumption on or in the vicinity of the premises; and
- this activity is or was carried on without an authorisation or not in accordance with the conditions of an authorisation for the sale of alcohol.

A local authority is in relation to England:

- a county council;
- a district council;
- a London borough council;

- the Common Council of the City of London in its capacity as a local authority;
- the Council of the Isles of Scilly;

and in relation to Wales, is a county council or a county borough council.

24.5.1 Closure notices

Where either a constable or a local authority is satisfied that any premises are being, or within the last 24 hours have been, used for the unauthorised sale of alcohol for consumption on, or in the vicinity of, the premises, a closure notice may be served in respect of the premises.

The constable or local authority must serve the closure notice on a person having control of, or responsibility for, the activities carried on at the premises.

A person having control of, or responsibility for, the activities carried on at the premises includes a person who:

- derives or seeks to derive profit from the carrying on of the activities;
- manages the activities;
- employs any person to manage the activities; or
- is involved in the conduct of the activities.

A closure notice must also be served by the constable or local authority on any person occupying another part of any building or other structure of which the premises form part if the constable or local authority reasonably believes, at the time of serving the closure notice, that the person's access to the other part of the building or other structure would be impeded if an order providing for the closure of the premises were made.

A closure notice may also be served by a constable or local authority on any other person having control of, or responsibility for, the activities carried on at the premises and any person who has an interest in the premises.

A closure notice must:

- specify the alleged use of the premises and the grounds on which the constable or local authority is satisfied that the premises are being, or within the last 24 hours have been, used for the unauthorised sale of alcohol for consumption on, or in the vicinity of, the premises;
- state that if unauthorised alcohol sales continue, an application may be made to a court for an order to close the premises; and
- specify the steps which may be taken to ensure that the alleged use of the premises ceases or does not recur.

A constable or local authority may cancel a closure notice by serving a notice of cancellation. Any such notice of cancellation is effective as soon as it is served on at least one person on whom the closure notice was served. Notice of cancellation must also be served on any other person on whom the closure notice was served.

24.5.2 Application for a closure order

Where a closure notice has been served, a constable or local authority may make a complaint to a justice of the peace for a closure order. The complaint must be made not less than seven days and not more than six days after the service of the closure notice.

A complaint cannot be made if the constable or local authority is satisfied that the use of the premises for the unauthorised sale of alcohol for consumption on, or in the vicinity of, the premises has ceased and there is no reasonable likelihood that the premises will be so used in the future.

Where a complaint has been made, the justice of the peace may issue a summons to answer to the complaint. The summons shall be directed to the person on whom the closure notice was served and any other person on whom the closure notice was served. If a summons is served, then a notice stating the date, time and place at which the complaint will be heard must be served on everyone on whom the closure notice was served.

The procedure on a complaint for a closure order shall be in accordance with the Magistrates' Courts Act 1980.

24.5.3 Closure order

On hearing a complaint for a closure order, the court may make such order as it considers appropriate if it is satisfied that the closure notice was served on a person having control of, or responsibility for, the activities carried on at the premises and the premises continue to be used for the unauthorised sale of alcohol for consumption on, or in the vicinity of, the premises or there is a reasonable likelihood that the premises will be so used in the future.

A closure order may, in particular, require:

- the premises in respect of which the closure notice was served to be closed immediately to the public and to remain closed until a constable or local authority concerned makes a certificate to the effect that they are satisfied that the need for the order has ceased and the order may include such conditions as the court considers appropriate relating to the admission of persons on to the premises and the access by persons to another part of any building or other structure of which the premises form part;
- the use of the premises for the unauthorised sale of alcohol for consumption on, or in the vicinity of, the premises to be discontinued immediately; and
- any defendant to pay into court such sum as the court determines and that the sum will not be released by the court to that person until the other requirements of the order are met.

The complainant shall, as soon as practicable after the making of a closure order, give notice of the order by fixing a copy of it in a conspicuous position on the premises in respect of which it was made.

Any sum which has been ordered to be paid into court is to be paid to the designated officer for the court.

24.5.4 Termination of a closure order

Where a closure order has been made, a constable or local authority may make a certificate to the effect that the constable or local authority is satisfied that the need for the order has ceased. Where a certificate has been made, the closure order ceases to have effect and any sum paid into court by a defendant under the order must be released by the court. Subject to this, a closure order may include such provision as the court considers appropriate for dealing with any consequences which would arise if the order were to cease to have effect by virtue of the making of a certificate.

The constable or local authority must, as soon as practicable after the making of a certificate:

- serve a copy of it on the person against whom the closure order has been made and the designated officer for the court which made the order; and
- fix a copy of it in a conspicuous position on the premises in respect of which the order was made.

The constable or local authority must also serve a copy of the certificate on any person who requests a copy.

24.5.5 Discharge of a closure order by the court

Where a closure order has been made any person on whom the closure notice concerned was served or any person who has an interest in the premises in respect of which the closure order was made but on whom no closure notice was served, may make a complaint to a justice of the peace for an order that the closure order is discharged.

The court may not make an order discharging a closure order unless it is satisfied that the need for the closure order has come to an end.

Where a complaint has been made to a justice of the peace, the justice may issue a summons directed to such constable as he considers appropriate or the local authority requiring that person to appear before the magistrates' court to answer to the complaint. Where such a summons is served, a notice stating the date, time and place at which the complaint will be heard shall be served on all persons on whom the closure notice concerned was served (other than the complainant).

The procedure on a complaint for an order shall be in accordance with the Magistrates' Courts Act 1980.

24.5.6 Appeals

An appeal against a closure order, an order for the discharge of a closure order or a decision not to make an order for the discharge of a closure order may be brought to the Crown Court at any time before the end of the period of 21 days beginning with the day on which the order or (as the case may be) the decision was made. An appeal against a closure order may be brought by any person on whom the closure notice concerned was served or any person who has an interest in the premises in respect of which the closure order was made but on whom no closure notice was so served. On an appeal, the Crown Court may make such order as it considers appropriate.

24.5.7 Enforcement

Where a closure order has been made, a constable or an authorised person (that is a person authorised for these purposes by a local authority in respect of premises situated in the area of the authority) may, if necessary using reasonable force, at any reasonable time enter the premises concerned and, having entered, do anything reasonably necessary for the purpose of securing compliance with the order.

A constable or an authorised person seeking to enter any premises must, if required by or on behalf of the owner or occupier or person in charge of the premises, produce evidence of his identity, and of his authority, before entering the premises.

Anyone who intentionally obstructs a constable or an authorised person in the exercise of his powers shall be guilty of an offence and shall be liable on summary conviction where the offence was committed in respect of a constable, to imprisonment for a term not exceeding one month or to a fine not exceeding level 5 on the standard scale or to both or where the offence was committed in respect of an authorised person, to a fine not exceeding level 5 on the standard scale. The maximum term of imprisonment will eventually be increased to 51 weeks when the Criminal Justice Act 2003, s.280(2)–(3), and Sched.26, para.56(1) and (2)(a) come into force.

Anyone who, without reasonable excuse, permits premises to be open in contravention of a closure order shall be guilty of an offence and shall be liable on summary conviction to imprisonment for a term not exceeding three months or to an unlimited fine or to both. The maximum term of imprisonment will eventually be increased to 51 weeks when the Criminal Justice Act 2003, s.280(2)–(3) and Sched.26, para.56(1) and (2)(b) come into force.

Anyone who, without reasonable excuse, otherwise fails to comply with, or does an act in contravention of, a closure order shall be guilty of an offence and shall be liable on summary conviction to imprisonment for a term not exceeding three months or to a fine not exceeding level 5 on the standard scale or to both. The maximum term of imprisonment will eventually be increased to 51 weeks when the Criminal Justice Act 2003, s.280(2)–(3) and Sched.26, para.56(1) and (2)(b) come into force.

Where one of the above offences committed by a body corporate is proved to have been committed with the consent or connivance of, or to be attributable to any neglect on the part of, a director, manager, secretary or other similar officer of the body corporate, he as well as the body corporate commits the offence and shall be liable to be proceeded against and punished accordingly. Where the affairs of a body corporate are managed by its members, this also applies in relation to the acts and defaults of a member in connection with his functions of management as if he were a director of the body corporate.

24.5.8 Service of notices

Any document required or authorised to be served as specified above on any person may be served in accordance with the Criminal Procedure Rules.

24.6 POLICE IMMUNITY FROM LIABILITY FOR DAMAGES

Section 170 provides immunity for the police and trading standards officers from liability for damages. Neither a constable nor a trading standards officer is liable for damages in respect of any act or omission of his in the performance or purported performance of his functions in relation to a closure order or any extension of it or of his functions in relation to a closure notice. Nor is a chief officer of police or a local weights and measures authority liable for damages in respect of any act or omission of a person in the performance or purported performance, while under the direction or control of such chief officer or local weights and measures authority, of a function of that person in relation to a closure order or any extension of it. For these purposes, the damages are damages awarded in proceedings for judicial review, the tort of negligence or misfeasance in public office. This does not affect any other exemption from liability for damages, whether at common law or otherwise.

For these purposes, 'constable' includes a person exercising the powers of a constable by virtue of a designation under the Police Reform Act 2002, s.38 (community support officers, etc.) and, in relation to such a person exercising such powers by virtue of such a designation by the Commissioner of Police of the City of London, the reference to a chief officer of police has effect as a reference to the Common Council of the City of London.

These exemptions do not apply if the act or omission is shown to have been in bad faith, or so as to prevent an award of damages in respect of an act or omission on the grounds that the act or omission was unlawful as a result of the Human Rights Act 1998, s.6(1) which provides that it is unlawful for a public authority to act in a way which is incompatible with a Convention right.

CHAPTER 25

Hearings

25.1 INTRODUCTION

The procedure to be followed in respect of all hearings required to be held by a licensing authority under the Act is set out in the Hearings Regulations. Guidance on the role of elected members in relation to licensing committee hearings has also been issued by the Local Government Association (formerly the Local Authorities Coordinators of Regulatory Services (LACORS)).

A hearing might arise following a relevant representation being made in respect of the following applications:

- the grant, transfer, review or variation of a premises licence;
- the grant of a provisional statement;
- the grant, review or variation of a club premises certificate; and
- the grant of a personal licence.

A hearing could also arise from:

- the cancellation of an interim authority notice following a police objection;
- an objection notice following a police objection to a temporary event notice; and
- convictions coming to light following the grant of a personal licence.

Where it is not possible to resolve, in the first instance, a relevant representation the licensing authority should:

- arrange a public hearing within the prescribed timescales for the type of application as laid down by the Hearings Regulations;
- notify all the relevant parties of the forthcoming hearing within the prescribed timescales as laid down by the Hearings Regulations;
- provide the applicant with copies of the relevant representations that have been made;
- supply appropriate information at each hearing; and
- supply appropriate information to all parties to a hearing.

The Guidance at para.9.34 provides:

> Applicants should be encouraged to contact responsible authorities and others, such as local residents, who may be affected by the application before formulating their applications so that the mediation process may begin before the statutory time limits come into effect after submission of an application. The hearing process must meet the requirements of regulations made under the 2003 Act. Where matters arise which are not covered by the regulations, licensing authorities may make arrangements as they see fit as long as they are lawful.

25.2 WHEN MUST A HEARING BE HELD?

When required a licensing authority must arrange for a hearing to be held within the period prescribed by the Hearings Regulations. There is no requirement that the hearing must be completed within this period, it merely has to have started before the period ends. Where a hearing will take longer than a day, it must be arranged so that it takes place on consecutive working days, so it could be held on the last day of the prescribed period and continue on the following day or days as required.

Most hearings must take place within 20 working days from the last date on which representations can be made. The exceptions to this are that a hearing must take place within:

- 10 working days from the day after the day a licensing authority receives the notice for review of a premises licence following a closure order;
- seven working days from the day after the end of the period within which the police can object to a temporary event notice;
- five working days beginning with the day after the end of the last date for the police to object to an interim authority notice; and
- 30 working days beginning with the day after the end of the period during which representations may be made in relation to an EMRO.

25.3 NOTICE OF HEARING

A licensing authority must give notice of a hearing to those persons who have been prescribed by the Hearings Regulations as being required to receive a notice of the date on which and the time and place at which the hearing is to be held.

The general rule is that notice of the hearing must be given by the licensing authority no later than 10 working days before the day or the first day on which the hearing is to be held. There are the following exceptions to this:

1. Where the hearing is in respect of the cancellation of an interim authority notice following a police objection (s.48(3)(a)), or a counter notice which has been given following a police objection to a temporary event notice

(s.105(2)(a)), notice of the hearing must be given by the licensing authority no later than two working days before the day or the first day on which the hearing is to be held.

2.   Where the hearing is in respect of the review of a premises licence following a closure order (s.167(5)(a)), notice of the hearing must be given by the licensing authority no later than five working days before the day or the first day on which the hearing is to be held.

In all cases the notice of the hearing must be accompanied by information which explains:

- that a party has the right to attend the hearing and to be assisted or represented at the hearing by any person who may or may not be legally qualified;
- that a party is entitled to make representations at the hearing, to question any other party, if allowed to, and to address the licensing authority;
- the consequences if a party does not attend or is not represented at the hearing;
- the procedure to be followed at the hearing; and
- any particular points on which the licensing authority considers that it will want clarification at the hearing from a party.

In respect of certain hearings, the notice must also be accompanied by relevant documents, e.g. relevant representations.

A licensing authority in Wales must give a notice where the hearing is held through remote means only, which gives details of the time of the hearing and how to access it or, where the hearing is held partly through remote means or not through remote means, gives details of the time and place of the hearing and how to access it.

25.4 ACTION FOLLOWING RECEIPT OF A NOTICE OF A HEARING

Following the receipt of a notice that there is to be a hearing, a recipient must himself give notice to the licensing authority stating whether he intends to attend or be represented at the hearing, whether he intends to call any witnesses, or whether he considers a hearing to be unnecessary.

In most cases, this notice must be given no later than five working days before the day on which the hearing is to be held. The exceptions to this are as follows:

- in the case of a hearing in respect of the cancellation of an interim authority notice following a police objection, or a counter notice following a police objection to a temporary event notice, the notice must be given no later than one working day before the day or the first day on which the hearing is to be held; and
- in the case of a hearing in respect of a review of a premises licence following a closure order, the notice must be given no later than two working days before the day or the first day on which the hearing is to be held.

If a party wishes anyone else to appear at the hearing, other than the person he intends to represent him, for example a witness, the notice must include a request for permission for that person to appear at the hearing together with details of that person's name and a brief description of the point on which that person may be able to assist the licensing authority in relation to the application, representations or notice of the party making the request.

25.5 DISPENSING WITH A HEARING

A licensing authority may dispense with a hearing with the agreement of the applicant and all of the persons who made relevant representations. Each person must give notice to the licensing authority that he does not think there should be a hearing. The licensing authority, if it then agrees that a hearing is not necessary, must forthwith (see **2.9**) give notice to the parties that the hearing is not to take place.

25.6 WITHDRAWAL OF A REPRESENTATION

A party which has made a representation may withdraw it by giving notice to the licensing authority either no later than 24 hours before the day of the hearing, or orally at the hearing. The Guidance at para.9.33 provides:

> The 2005 Hearings Regulations require that representations must be withdrawn 24 hours before the first day of any hearing. If they are withdrawn after this time, the hearing must proceed and the representations may be withdrawn orally at that hearing. However, where discussions between an applicant and those making representations are taking place and it is likely that all parties are on the point of reaching agreement, the licensing authority may wish to use the power given within the hearings regulations to extend time limits, if it considers this to be in the public interest.

25.7 POWER TO EXTEND TIME

A licensing authority may extend a time limit for holding a hearing or for giving notice if it considers it to be necessary in the public interest. If a time limit is extended the licensing authority must forthwith give notice to the parties setting out the period of extension and the reasons why it has decided to extend the time limit.

A licensing authority may also adjourn a hearing to a specified date, or arrange for a hearing to be held on specified additional dates, if it considers that this is necessary for its consideration of any representations or notice made by a party. Where a hearing is adjourned to a specified date the licensing authority must forthwith notify the parties of the date, time and place to which the hearing has been adjourned. Where a hearing is to be held on a specified additional date the licensing authority must forthwith notify the parties of the additional date on which, and time and place at which, the hearing is to be held.

A licensing authority may not exercise its powers to extend time, adjourn a hearing to a specified date, or arrange for a hearing to be held on a specified additional date in such a way that the effect will be that it would fail to reach a determination on the review of a premises licence following a closure order within the specified period for reaching a determination, which is 28 days after the day on which the licensing authority receives notice of the magistrates' court's determination.

25.8 THE HEARING

The hearing must take place in public; however, the licensing authority may exclude the public (which includes a party to the hearing and any person assisting or representing a party) for all or a part of the hearing if it considers that the public interest in doing so outweighs the public interest in the hearing, or that part of it, taking place in public. The Openness of Local Government Bodies Regulations 2014, SI 2014/2095 allow members of the public to report and commentate on public meetings of local government bodies in England, and also require written records to be kept of certain decisions taken by officers of these bodies.

Each licensing authority has established a licensing committee of 15 members. The prime purpose of the committee is to exercise all the licensing authority's functions under the Act and review strategy and licensing policy and make appropriate recommendations to the licensing authority. Licensing applications will usually be dealt with in two ways:

- by a licensing subcommittee of three members of the licensing committee; and
- by licensing officers within the delegations of the licensing committee as set out in the licensing authority's licensing policy.

A licensing officer should not make any recommendations to a licensing subcommittee in terms of the outcome of the committee hearing.

Anyone who has been given notice of the hearing may attend the hearing and may be assisted or represented by someone who may be legally qualified or not. In relation to attendance by responsible authorities, the Guidance at para.9.35 provides:

> There is no requirement in the 2003 Act for responsible authorities that have made representations to attend, but it is generally good practice and assists committees in reaching more informed decisions. Where several responsible authorities within a local authority have made representations on an application, a single local authority officer may represent them at the hearing if the responsible authorities and the licensing authority agree. This local authority officer representing other responsible authorities

may be a licensing officer, but only if this licensing officer is acting as a responsible authority on behalf of the licensing authority and has had no role in the licensing determination process. This is to ensure that the responsible authorities are represented by an independent officer separate from the licensing determination process.

A party is entitled at the hearing:

- in response to a point in respect of which the licensing authority has given notice before the hearing to a party that it will want clarification, to give further information in support of their application, representations or notice (as applicable);
- if given permission by the licensing authority, to question any other party; and
- to address the licensing authority.

Members of the licensing authority may ask any question of any party or other person appearing at the hearing.

In considering any representations or notice made by a party, the licensing authority may take into account documentary or other information produced by a party in support of their application, representations or notice (as applicable) either before the hearing or, with the consent of all the other parties, at the hearing.

The licensing authority must disregard any information given by a party or any person to whom permission to appear at the hearing is given by the licensing authority which is not relevant to their application, representations or notice (as applicable) or in the case of another person, the application, representations or notice of the party requesting their appearance, and the promotion of the licensing objectives or, in relation to a hearing to consider a notice given by a chief officer of police, the crime prevention objective.

25.9 PROCEDURE AT THE HEARING

It is up to each individual licensing authority to decide the procedure to be followed at the hearings it holds; however, the Hearings Regulations specifically provide that:

1. At the beginning of a hearing, the licensing authority must explain to the parties the procedure which it proposes to follow at the hearing. It must also at this stage consider any requests for permission for another person to appear at the hearing, and such permission must not be unreasonably withheld.
2. The hearing must take the form of a discussion led by the licensing authority and cross-examination is only allowed if the licensing authority considers that it is required for it to consider the representations, application or notice as the case may require.

3.   The licensing authority must allow each of the parties an equal maximum period of time in which to exercise their rights of clarification, questioning and address.

4.   The licensing authority may require any person attending the hearing who, in its opinion, is behaving in a disruptive manner to leave the hearing and may refuse to permit that person to return, or permit him to return only on such conditions as the authority may specify, but such a person may, before the end of the hearing, make a written submission to the licensing authority of any information which he would have been entitled to give orally had he not been required to leave.

Enquiries should always be made with the licensing authority to obtain details of the procedures which will be adopted at a hearing. Each licensing authority should have such a procedure so that licensing applications are dealt with in accordance with the law, that probity is observed at all times, and that there is effective public participation in the process.

The Guidance at para.9.37 provides:

> As a matter of practice, licensing authorities should seek to focus the hearing on the steps considered appropriate to promote the particular licensing objective or objectives that have given rise to the specific representation and avoid straying into undisputed areas. A responsible authority or other person may choose to rely on their written representation. They may not add further representations to those disclosed to the applicant prior to the hearing, but they may expand on their existing representation and should be allowed sufficient time to do so, within reasonable and practicable limits.

25.10   FAILURE OF PARTIES TO ATTEND THE HEARING

If a party has told the licensing authority that he does not intend to attend or be represented at a hearing, the hearing may proceed in his absence. If a party does not inform the licensing authority that he is not going to attend, and he subsequently fails to attend or be represented at a hearing, the licensing authority may either where it considers it to be necessary in the public interest adjourn the hearing to a specified date, or hold the hearing in the party's absence, in which case the licensing authority must consider at the hearing the application, representations or notice made by the party who has failed to attend. If the licensing authority adjourns the hearing to a specified date it must forthwith notify the parties of the date, time and place to which the hearing has been adjourned.

25.11   DETERMINATION OF THE APPLICATION

A licensing authority must make its decision within five working days beginning with the day or the last day on which the hearing was held. The exceptions to this are for hearings dealing with a counter notice following an objection by the police to a temporary event notice; interim steps pending review; the review of a premises licence following a review notice and the review of a premises licence following a closure order when the licensing authority must make its determination at the conclusion of the hearing; and a hearing to consider the relevant representations in relation to an EMRO when the licensing authority must make its determination within 10 working days, beginning with the day or the last day on which the hearing was heard.

If all the parties agree that the hearing may be dispensed with, the licensing authority must make its determination within 10 working days beginning with the day on which the licensing authority gave notice to the parties that it agreed that a hearing is unnecessary and can be dispensed with.

Once a licensing authority has made a determination it must notify the parties. If the Act does not make provision for the period in which this notification must be given, the licensing authority must give it forthwith on making its determination. The notice must be accompanied by information setting out the right of a party to appeal. Where the Act provides for the chief officer of police to be notified of a determination and he was not a party to the hearing, the licensing authority must notify him of its determination forthwith on making it.

25.12 RECORD OF A HEARING

A licensing authority must make a record of a hearing in a permanent and intelligible form. This must be kept for six years from the date of the determination, or where an appeal has been made, the disposal of the appeal.

25.13 IRREGULARITIES

An irregularity due to a failure to comply with the Hearings Regulations before a licensing authority has made a determination will not of itself render the proceedings void. If the licensing authority considers that any person may have been prejudiced by an irregularity, it must take such steps as it thinks fit to cure the irregularity before it makes its determination. A licensing authority may correct clerical errors in documentation recording a determination or errors arising in such documentation because of an accidental slip or omission.

25.14 NOTICES

Any notices which are required to be given under the Hearings Regulations must be in writing. Notwithstanding this, the requirement shall be satisfied where:

* the text of the notice:

- is transmitted by electronic means;
- is capable of being accessed by the recipient;
- is legible in all material respects; and
- is capable of being reproduced in written form and used for subsequent reference;

- the person to whom the notice is to be given has agreed in advance that such a notice may be given to them by electronic means; and
- forthwith on sending the text of the notice by electronic means, the notice is given to the recipient in writing.

Where the text of the notice is transmitted by electronic means, the notice is given at the time it is transmitted.

25.15   THE IMPACT OF THE HUMAN RIGHTS ACT 1998

The Human Rights Act 1998 requires that a public body ensures that everything it does is compatible with Convention rights and makes it unlawful for a public authority to act incompatibly with those rights. ECHR, art.6 concerns the right to a fair trial, and the key elements of this include:

- the right to a fair hearing;
- the right to a public hearing;
- the right to a hearing before an independent and impartial tribunal; and
- the right to a hearing within a reasonable time.

A licensing authority is part of a public authority and therefore subject to the requirements of the Human Rights Act 1998. However, it does not automatically follow that art.6 will apply. When hearing an application, the proceedings of a licensing committee, being a non-judicial body as opposed to a judicial body, need not meet the full requirements of art.6 where there is a right of appeal from the licensing committee to a court that does meet the full art.6 standards and can consider all aspects of the case, even though that does not include a full rehearing of the facts.

So, while it is good practice to make a hearing before the licensing committee as art.6 compliant as possible, it will not be a breach of the Human Rights Act 1998 if it is not. In any event, the hearing of all applications will be subject to the principles of natural justice and the requirement for decisions to be 'Wednesbury reasonable' (*Associated Provincial Picture Houses Ltd* v. *Wednesbury Corp* [1948] 1 KB 223 CA).

CHAPTER 26

Appeals

26.1 INTRODUCTION

Section 181 and Sched.5 provide for appeals against decisions of a licensing authority. The procedures in relation to appeals are set out in Sched.5. An appeal is made to a magistrates' court. There is no requirement that this must be the magistrates' court for the area in which the premises are situated (Courts Act 2003 (Consequential Provisions) Order 2005, SI 2005/886) but it is expected that an appeal would be brought in a magistrates' court in the area in which the applicant or the premises are situated (Guidance, para.13.2).

An appeal is brought by the appellant giving a notice of appeal to the designated officer for the magistrates' court within a period of 21 days beginning with the day on which the appellant was notified by the licensing authority of the decision to be appealed against. There is no requirement that notice of an appeal be given to any other person, for example a person who made a relevant representation, and nor does there seem to be any requirement for the court to notify such persons of the appeal. It is therefore unclear how they will know that an appeal has been made.

The licensing authority will always be a respondent to the appeal. Where a favourable decision has been made for an applicant, licence holder, club or premises user against the representations of a responsible authority or any other person, or the objections of the chief officer of police, the Home Office (Immigration Enforcement), or local authority exercising environmental health functions, the holder of the premises licence, the holder of the personal licence, the holder of the club premises certificate, the person who gave an interim authority notice or the premises user will also be a respondent to the appeal and the person who made the relevant representation or gave the objection will be the appellant (Guidance, para.13.4). There is no right for a responsible authority to be joined in as a respondent (*R. (on the application of Chief Constable of Nottinghamshire) v. Nottingham Magistrates' Court* [2009] EWHC 3182 (Admin); [2010] 2 All ER 342).

The Guidance at para.13.5 provides:

> Where an appeal has been made against a decision of the licensing authority, the licensing authority will in all cases be the respondent to the appeal and may call as a witness a responsible authority or any other person who made representations against the application, if it chooses to do so. For this reason, the licensing authority should consider keeping responsible authorities and others informed of developments in relation to appeals to allow them to consider their position. Provided the court considers it appropriate, the licensing authority may also call as witnesses any individual or body that they feel might assist their response to an appeal.

When dealing with an appeal against a decision of a licensing authority, s.181(2) provides that a magistrates' court may:

- dismiss the appeal;
- substitute for the decision appealed against any other decision which could have been made by the licensing authority; or
- remit the case to the licensing authority to dispose of it in accordance with the direction of the court (see *R. (on the application of Hammersmith and Fulham LBC)* v. *Food City Express Ltd* [2008] EWHC 3520 (Admin); [2008] All ER (D) 120 (Oct) as to the extent of the power to remit for alleged procedural failings)

and make such order as to costs as it thinks fit.

The usual procedure will be for the magistrates' court to hold an initial hearing to decide whether it will hear the appeal itself or remit it back to the licensing authority. Where the court decides to hear the matter it will normally then adjourn to a separate contested hearing date. A pre-trial review may be conducted either at the initial hearing or on a separate date before the contested hearing in order to establish the length of time which the case will take.

There is nothing in the Act as to the format the appeal hearing will take. The Guidance, para.13.6 provides that the court on hearing an appeal 'may review the merits of the decision on the facts and consider points of law or address both'. In *R. (on the application of Hope & Glory Public House Ltd)* v. *City of Westminster Magistrates' Court* [2009] EWIIC 1996 (Admin); [2009] LLR 742, it was held that the appeal will be by way of a rehearing rather than by way of a review of the decision of the licensing authority. Burton J held that he was bound by *Sagnata Investments Ltd* v. *Norwich Corp* [1971] 2 QB 614 CA; [1971] 3 WLR 133 where the court held that the proceedings were by way of a complete rehearing. Edmund Davies LJ in that case said that the proper approach was established in *Stepney BC* v. *Joffe* [1949] 1 KB 599 DC and quoted Lord Goddard CJ in that case at pp.602, 603:

> That does not mean to say that the court of appeal ... ought not to pay great attention to the fact that the duly constituted and elected local authority have come to an opinion on the matter, and it ought not lightly, of course, to reverse their opinion. It is constantly said ... that the function of a court of appeal is to exercise its powers when it

is satisfied that the judgment below is wrong, not merely because it is not satisfied that the judgment was right.

On this basis, Burton J decided that it is for the appellant to satisfy the court on appeal that the initial decision was wrong and that this could be done, if necessary, by calling different evidence.

The Court of Appeal dismissed an appeal against this decision in *R. (on the application of Hope & Glory Public House Ltd)* v. *City of Westminster Magistrates' Court* [2011] EWCA Civ 31; [2011] 3 All ER 579, where it held that it is for the appellant to present his case first. It was accepted that the evidence that could be called on the appeal could be different from the evidence that was called at the initial hearing. The court concluded (at [45]) that:

> It is right in all cases that the magistrates' court should pay careful attention to the reasons given by the licensing authority for arriving at the decision under appeal, bearing in mind that Parliament has chosen to place responsibility for making such decisions on local authorities. The weight which the magistrates should ultimately attach to those reasons must be a matter for their judgment in all the circumstances, taking into account the fullness and clarity of the reasons, the nature of the issues and the evidence given on the appeal.

This decision was applied in *R. (on the application of Developing Retail Ltd)* v. *East Hampshire Magistrates' Court* [2011] EWHC 618 (Admin), where Clare Montgomery QC sitting as a deputy High Court Judge explained the practical consequences of the decision (at [29]):

> In deciding whether the decision of the licensing committee is wrong the magistrates' court is not considering any question of *Wednesbury* unreasonableness since it is not a process of judicial review, it is instead a fresh evidential hearing. This means that the task of the magistrates' court, having heard the evidence and specifically addressed the decision of the authority below, is to give a decision whether, because they disagree with the decision below in the light of the evidence, it is wrong. The magistrates therefore have power not merely to review the decision on the grounds of an error of law but also on its merits. It is however for the appellant before the magistrates court to persuade the court that it should reverse the order under appeal, and in cases where a statutory discretion to attach conditions has been exercised, the magistrates' court should normally consider whether the exercise of discretion was wrong in the light of the reasons given for that exercise and the form of the conditions, rather than considering the discretion afresh in the hearing of the appeal.

In *R. (on the application of Townlink Ltd)* v. *Thames Magistrates' Court* [2011] EWHC 898 (Admin), Lindblom J said (at [36]) that:

> What the District Judge had to do was to consider the evidence before him with the relevant principles in mind. Those principles included the necessity that the licensing objectives be promoted, and proportionality. Bearing in mind the decision of the Council's licensing sub-committee and the significance of that decision as the result of the democratically elected members having applied their minds to the issue, the District Judge nevertheless had to adopt the approach approved by the court in *Joffe, Sagnata* and *Hope and Glory*. He had to do this by considering 'whether, because he [disagreed] with the decision below in the light of the evidence before him, it [was] therefore

wrong' (see per Burton J in paragraph 45 of his judgment at first instance in *Hope and Glory*).

In *Portsmouth City Council* v. *3D Entertainment Group (CRC) Ltd* [2011] EWHC 507 (Admin); [2011] ACD 52 it was held that when considering an appeal against a refusal to amend a premises licence, the magistrates were bound to follow the approach in *Sagnata Investments Ltd* v. *Norwich Corp* [1971] 2 QB 614.

In *Marathon Restaurant* v. *Camden LBC* [2011] EWHC 1339 (QB); [2011] All ER (D) 261 (May), Rafferty J set out a summary of the proper approach to appeals in the magistrates' court:

5. The approach of the magistrates' court to appeals under the Licensing Act 2003 has been canvassed by the Court of Appeal in *R (Hope and Glory Public House Ltd)* v *(1) City of Westminster Magistrates' Court (2) The Lord Mayor and Citizens of the City of Westminster* [2011] EWCA Civ 31 [*'Hope and Glory'*], and in *Daniel Thwaites Plc* v *Wirral Borough Magistrates' Court* [2008] EWHC 838 (Admin) [*'Thwaites'*]. *Hope and Glory*, in which Toulson LJ reviewed the history of the Act, which reflects the recognised importance to the licensing process of local residents, is authority for the following propositions:

    (a) deciding what (if any) conditions should be attached to a licence as necessary and proportionate to the promotion of the statutory licensing objectives is essentially a matter of judgment rather than a matter of pure fact;
    (b) Careful attention is to be paid by the magistrates' court to the reasons given by the licensing authority for reaching its decision;
    (c) The appellant bears the responsibility of persuading the court that the licensing authority's decision should be reversed;
    (d) The appellant must persuade the magistrates' court that the licensing authority should not have exercised its discretion in the way that it did.

6. Hearsay evidence is admissible on licensing appeals, an issue explored most recently in *Leeds City Council* v *Hussain* [2002] EWHC 1145 (Admin) where it was recognised that:

    'Some evidence such as gossip, speculation and unsubstantiated innuendo would be rightly disregarded. Other evidence, even if hearsay, might by its source, nature and inherent probability carry a greater degree of credibility. All would depend on the particular facts and circumstances.'

7. The evidential approach for the decision maker is rehearsed in *Thwaites*, authority for the following propositions:

    (i)   Regulation under the Act must be necessary and proportionate
    (ii)   Events between initial hearing and appeal are relevant
    (iii) Magistrates must give reasons for any departure from the Guidance issued by the Secretary of State pursuant to section 182 LA 2003 ('the Guidance').

In *R. (on the application of A3D2 Ltd (t/a Novus Leisure))* v. *Westminster Magistrates' Court* [2011] EWHC 1045 (Admin); [2011] LLR 303, the court held that when hearing an appeal a district judge was perfectly entitled to address and answer a preliminary issue raised by a party before hearing evidence in the case.

In *R. (on the application of the Chief Constable of Nottinghamshire Police)* v. *Nottingham Magistrates' Court* [2009] EWHC 3182 (Admin); [2010] 2 All E.R. 342, the court decided that a party who made representations at the hearing before the committee can be a party to an appeal.

The Court of Appeal in *Khan* v. *Coventry Magistrates' Court* [2011] EWCA Civ 751; (2011) 175 JP 429 was satisfied that a magistrates' court hearing an appeal against a decision by a licensing authority to revoke a licence to sell alcohol for consumption off the premises was not limited to considering only those grounds of complaint that were raised in the notice of application or in the representations, and it could consider the matter afresh. The licence holder should have adequate notice so that he can deal with any new matters especially if they raised a different area of complaint.

The magistrates may make such order as to costs as they think fit (s.181(2)). A costs order does not need to be made at the same time as the judgment although an order for payment will not be effective until the judgment is made (*Blustarling Ltd* v. *Westminster City Council* (unreported, QBD, *The Times*, 24 July 1996). In *R. (on the application of Cambridge City Council)* v. *Alex Nestling Ltd* [2006] EWHC 1374 (Admin); (2006) 170 JP 539 it was inequitable for a magistrates' court to order a licensing authority to pay half an appellant's costs of an appeal brought under s.181 where the appellant had been only partially successful and the licensing authority had acted correctly and in good faith. In *Crawley BC* v. *Attenborough* [2006] EWHC 1278 (Admin); (2006) 170 JP 593, it was held that it was clear from s.181 that the magistrates' court had a very wide discretion on what costs order it saw fit to make. In *Prasannan* v. *Kensington and Chelsea RLBC* [2010] EWHC 319 (Admin); [2011] 1 Costs LR 14, where the holder of premises licences had brought proceedings to revoke those licences entirely upon herself by her conduct, despite her success on appeal, it was held that the magistrates' court had been entitled to award costs against her in the sum of £20,000.

The position in relation to costs and non-parties was considered in *Aldemir* v. *Cornwall Council* [2019] EWHC 2407 (Admin). Magistrates acting under s.181 had the power to make a non-party costs order. It is good practice for the grounds for such an application to be reduced to writing; to be provided to the respondent before the application was made; and for the application to be heard and determined only after the non-party had had the chance to consider the grounds and respond to them. The matter was further considered in *McCarthy* v. *Jones* [2023] EWCA Civ 589, where an appeal against a decision that an unsuccessful party pay the costs involved in applications against a non-party was refused. The court held that the trial judge had a discretion to make such an order.

When considering an appeal, a magistrates' court is not entitled to entertain any question as to whether:

- an individual should be, or should have been, granted leave to enter or remain in the United Kingdom; or

- an individual has, after the date of the decision being appealed against, been granted leave to enter or remain in the United Kingdom.

26.2 PROCEDURE FOR AN APPEAL

The procedure for an appeal against the decision of a local authority is governed by the Magistrates' Courts Rules 1981, SI 1981/552, rule 34. This provides that 'Where under any enactment an appeal or application lies to a magistrates' court against or in respect of the decision, order, act or omission of a local authority or other authority, or other body or person, the appeal or application shall be by way of complaint for an order.'

Rule 14 governs the order of speeches and the calling of evidence as follows:

1. On the hearing of a complaint, except where the court determines under the Magistrates' Courts Act 1980, s.53(3) to make the order with the consent of the defendant without hearing evidence, the complainant shall call his evidence, and before doing so may address the court.
2. At the conclusion of the evidence for the complainant, the defendant may address the court, whether or not he afterwards calls evidence.
3. At the conclusion of the evidence, if any, for the defence, the complainant may call evidence to rebut that evidence.
4. At the conclusion of the evidence for the defence and the evidence, if any, in rebuttal, the defendant may address the court if he has not already done so.
5. Either party may, with the leave of the court, address the court a second time, but where the court grants leave to one party it shall not refuse leave to the other.
6. Where the defendant obtains leave to address the court for a second time his second address shall be made before the second address, if any, of the complainant.

In practice, it may be more rational for the licensing authority to present its evidence first.

In *R. (on the application of A3D2 Ltd (t/a Novus Leisure))* v. *Westminster Magistrates' Court* [2011] EWHC 1045 (Admin), the court held that a district judge was entitled on hearing an appeal to address and answer a preliminary issue raised by a party before hearing the evidence in the appeal.

Evidence will be admitted on the same basis as at the original hearing before the licensing authority. The court will not be bound by the rules of evidence and so will be able to take into account everything which the licensing authority heard, including hearsay evidence (*Kavanagh* v. *Chief Constable of Devon and Cornwall* [1974] QB 624 CA; [1974] 2 WLR 762; *Westminster City Council* v. *Zestfair* (1989) 153 JP 613 DC). The court can also take into account any local knowledge which the justices might have (*R.* v. *Howard (Licensing)* [1902] 2 KB

363 CA). In addition, the court can hear new evidence, for example, evidence which relates to events that have taken place since the licensing authority's decision.

26.3 LICENSING POLICY STATEMENTS AND THE SECRETARY OF STATE'S GUIDANCE

There is nothing in the Act requiring a magistrates' court to have regard to the relevant licensing authority's statement of licensing policy and the Guidance when reaching its decision. In relation to whether a magistrates' court dealing with an appeal must have regard to the relevant licensing authority's statement of licensing policy and the Guidance, the Guidance provides:

13.8 In hearing an appeal against any decision made by a licensing authority, the magistrates' court will have regard to that licensing authority's statement of licensing policy and this Guidance. However, the court would be entitled to depart from either the statement of licensing policy or this Guidance if it considered it was justified to do so because of the individual circumstances of any case. In other words, while the court will normally consider the matter as if it were 'standing in the shoes' of the licensing authority, it would be entitled to find that the licensing authority should have departed from its own policy or the Guidance because the particular circumstances would have justified such a decision.

13.9 In addition, the court is entitled to disregard any part of a licensing policy statement or this Guidance that it holds to be ultra vires the 2003 Act and therefore unlawful. The normal course for challenging a statement of licensing policy or this Guidance should be by way of judicial review, but where it is submitted to an appellate court that a statement of policy is itself ultra vires the 2003 Act and this has a direct bearing on the case before it, it would be inappropriate for the court, on accepting such a submission, to compound the original error by relying on that part of the statement of licensing policy affected.

26.4 PREMISES LICENCES

An appeal may be made:

- where an application for a premises licence is rejected;
- where there is a grant, variation, transfer or review of a premises licence;
- where an interim authority notice seeking reinstatement of a licence following lapse is given; or
- where a provisional statement is issued.

26.4.1 Appeal against the rejection of an application relating to a premises licence

An applicant may appeal against a decision of a licensing authority to:

- reject an application for a premises licence;
- reject, in whole or in part, an application to vary a premises licence;
- reject an application to vary a premises licence to specify an individual as the premises supervisor; or
- reject an application to transfer a premises licence.

26.4.2 Appeal against a decision to grant a premises licence or to impose conditions

Where a licensing authority grants a premises licence, the licence holder may appeal against any decision to impose conditions on the licence, to exclude a licensable activity, or to refuse to specify a person as the designated premises supervisor.

A person who made relevant representations in relation to the application may also appeal if he desires to contend:

- that the licence ought not to have been granted; or
- that, on granting the licence, the licensing authority ought to have imposed different or additional conditions, excluded a licensable activity, or refused to specify a person as the designated premises supervisor.

Where a licence has been granted, there is nothing in the Act to prevent the licence holder from operating the premises in accordance with the licence pending the determination of the appeal.

26.4.3 Variation of a premises licence

Where an application to vary a premises licence is granted, in whole or in part, the applicant may appeal against any decision to modify the conditions of the licence. There is a separate provision relating to variations by changing the designated premises supervisor.

A person who made relevant representations may also appeal against the decision if he desires to contend:

- that any variation made ought not to have been made; or
- that, when varying the licence, the licensing authority ought not to have modified the conditions of the licence, or ought to have modified them in a different way.

26.4.4 Variation of a premises licence to specify an individual as premises supervisor

The chief officer of police who gave a notice that was not withdrawn that granting an application to vary a premises licence to change the designated premises supervisor would undermine the crime prevention objective may appeal against the decision to vary the licence.

26.4.5 Transfer of a premises licence

The chief officer of police who gave a notice that was not withdrawn that granting an application to transfer a licence would undermine the crime prevention objective or the Secretary of State (through Home Office Immigration Enforcement) who gave a notice that was not withdrawn that granting an application to transfer would be prejudicial to the prevention of illegal working in licensed premises may appeal against the decision to transfer the premises licence.

26.4.6 Review of a premises licence

Where a licensing authority has made a decision in relation to an application for a review of a premises licence, an appeal may be made against that decision by:

- the applicant for the review;
- the holder of the premises licence; or
- any other person who made relevant representations in relation to the application.

26.4.7 Summary review of a premises licence

Where a licensing authority has made a decision in relation to an application for a summary review following the application of a senior police officer, an appeal may be made against that decision by:

- the chief officer of police for the police area (or each police area) in which the premises are situated;
- the holder of the premises licence; or
- any other person who made relevant representations in relation to the application.

26.4.8 Interim authority notice

Where a relevant licensing authority has decided to cancel an interim authority notice, the person who gave the interim authority notice may appeal against the decision.

Where the relevant licensing authority has decided not to cancel an interim authority notice after the giving of a notice by a chief officer of police that he is satisfied that the exceptional circumstances of the case are such that a failure to cancel the interim authority notice would undermine the crime prevention objective, the chief officer of police may appeal against that decision.

Where the relevant licensing authority has decided not to cancel an interim authority notice after the giving of a notice by the Secretary of State (through Home Office Immigration Enforcement) that the Secretary of State is satisfied that the exceptional circumstances of the case are such that a failure to cancel the interim authority notice would be prejudicial to the prevention of illegal working in licensed premises, the Secretary of State may appeal against that decision.

Where an appeal is brought, the court to which it is brought may, on such terms as it thinks fit, order the reinstatement of the interim authority notice pending the disposal of the appeal, or the expiry of the interim authority period, whichever occurs first.

Where the court makes an order for reinstatement, the premises licence is reinstated from the time the order is made.

Where a licence is reinstated after it has been suspended because of the death, incapacity or insolvency of the licence holder, the reinstatement will cease to have effect on the date when the appeal which gave rise to the reinstatement is abandoned or dismissed.

26.4.9 Issue of provisional statement

An appeal against the issue of a provisional statement may be made by the applicant, or any person who made relevant representations in relation to the application.

The Guidance at para.13.13 provides:

> To avoid confusion, it should be noted that a right of appeal only exists in respect of the terms of a provisional statement that is issued rather than one that is refused. This is because the 2003 Act does not empower a licensing authority to refuse to issue a provisional statement. After receiving and considering relevant representations, the licensing authority may only indicate, as part of the statement, that it would consider certain steps to be appropriate for the promotion of the licensing objectives when, and if, an application were made for a premises licence following the issuing of the provisional statement. Accordingly, the applicant or any person who has made relevant representations may appeal against the terms of the statement issued.

26.4.10 Review of interim steps

Where a review of any interim steps is decided at a hearing to consider an application for a summary review of a premises licence, the chief officer of police for the police area (or each police area) in which the premises are situated, or the holder of the premises licence may appeal against the decision. Such an appeal must be heard by the magistrates' court within 28 days beginning with the day on which the appellant commenced the appeal.

26.4.11 General provision about appeals in relation to applications regarding premises licences

Any of the appeals outlined above must be made to a magistrates' court. Such an appeal is brought by the appellant giving notice of appeal to the designated officer for the magistrates' court within the period of 21 days beginning with the day on which the appellant was notified by the licensing authority of the decision which is being appealed against.

The decision of the licensing authority will have effect during the 21-day period for appeals. If an appeal is made, the decision will also have effect until the appeal is disposed of. Where the appeal is against a review of a premises licence, the licensing authority's decision will not have effect until the end of the appeal period or the disposal of the appeal (s.52(11)).

In respect of the following appeals, the holder of the premises licence is to be the respondent in addition to the licensing authority:

- an appeal by a person who made relevant representations in relation to an application for the grant of a premises licence;
- an appeal by a person who made relevant representations in relation to the issue of a provisional statement;
- an appeal by a person who made relevant representations in relation to an application for the variation of a premises licence;
- an appeal by a chief officer of police in relation to an application to vary the designated premises supervisor;
- an appeal by a chief officer of police in relation to the transfer of a premises licence; and
- an appeal by an applicant for the review of a premises licence or any person who made relevant representations in respect of such an application.

On an appeal by a chief officer of police or the Secretary of State against a decision not to cancel an interim authority notice, the person who gave the interim authority notice is to be the respondent in addition to the licensing authority.

26.5 CLUB PREMISES CERTIFICATES

An appeal may be made:

- where an application for a club premises certificate is rejected; or
- where there is a grant, variation, review or withdrawal of a club premises certificate.

26.5.1 Rejection of an application to grant or vary a club premises certificate

Where a licensing authority rejects an application for a club premises certificate, or rejects, in whole or in part, an application to vary a club premises certificate, the club that made the application may appeal against the decision.

26.5.2 Decision to grant a club premises certificate or to impose conditions

Where a licensing authority grants a club premises certificate, the club which made the application may appeal against a decision to impose conditions on the certificate, or to exclude a qualifying club activity.

A person who made relevant representations may also appeal against the decision if he desires to contend:

- that the certificate ought not to have been granted; or
- that, on granting the certificate, the licensing authority ought to have imposed different or additional conditions, or excluded a qualifying club activity.

26.5.3 Variation of a club premises certificate

A club which has applied for a variation of its club premises certificate may appeal against any decision to modify the conditions of the certificate.

A person who made relevant representations may also appeal against the decision if he desires to contend:

- that any variation made ought not to have been made; or
- that, when varying the club premises certificate, the licensing authority ought not to have modified the conditions of the certificate, or ought to have modified them in a different way.

26.5.4 Review of a club premises certificate

Where an application for a review of a club premises certificate is decided by a licensing authority, an appeal may be made against that decision by:

- the applicant for the review;
- the club that holds or held the club premises certificate; or
- any other person who made relevant representations in relation to the application.

26.5.5 Withdrawal of a club premises certificate

Where a relevant licensing authority has given notice withdrawing a club premises certificate, the club which holds or held the certificate may appeal against the decision to withdraw it.

26.5.6 General provision about appeals in relation to applications regarding a club premises certificate

Any of the appeals outlined above must be made to a magistrates' court. Such an appeal is brought by the appellant giving notice of appeal to the designated officer for the magistrates' court within the period of 21 days beginning with the day on which the appellant was notified by the licensing authority of the decision which is being appealed against.

The decision of the licensing authority will have effect during the 21-day period for appeals. If an appeal is made, the decision will also have effect until the appeal is disposed of. Where the appeal is against a review of a club premises certificate, the licensing authority's decision will not have effect until the end of the appeal period or the disposal of the appeal (s.88(11)).

In respect of the following appeals, the club which holds or held the certificate is to be the respondent in addition to the licensing authority:

- an appeal by a person who made relevant representations in relation to the grant of a club premises certificate, or the imposition of conditions;
- an appeal by a person who made relevant representations in relation to an application for the variation of a club premises certificate;
- an appeal by an applicant for the review of a club premises certificate or any person who made relevant representations in respect of such an application.

26.6 TEMPORARY EVENT NOTICES

When a standard temporary event notice is given, and a relevant person gives an objection notice:

- the premises user may appeal against a decision by the relevant licensing authority to give a counter notice; and
- the relevant person may appeal against a decision by the relevant licensing authority not to give a counter notice.

A 'relevant person' is either the chief officer of police for any police area in which the premises are situated, or the local authority by which statutory functions are exercisable in any area in which the premises are situated in relation to minimising or preventing the risk of pollution of the environment or of harm to human health.

An appeal must be made to a magistrates' court. Such an appeal is brought by the appellant giving notice of appeal to the designated officer for the magistrates' court within the period of 21 days beginning with the day on which the appellant was notified by the licensing authority of the decision which is being appealed against. However, an appeal cannot be made later than five working days before the day on which the event period specified in the temporary event notice begins.

The premises user must be the respondent to the appeal together with the relevant licensing authority.

26.7 PERSONAL LICENCES

An appeal may be made:

- where an application for the grant of a personal licence is rejected;
- where there is a grant of a personal licence following objection by the police or Secretary of State;
- where a personal licence is revoked following objection by the police or the Secretary of State; or
- where there is a decision not to revoke a personal licence following objection by the police or Secretary of State.

26.7.1 Rejection of a grant

An applicant may appeal against a decision by the relevant licensing authority to reject an application for the grant of a personal licence.

26.7.2 Grant or renewal following objection

Where a licensing authority grants an application for a personal licence, either the chief officer of police or the Secretary of State who gave an objection notice may appeal against that decision.

26.7.3 Revocation following objection by the police or Secretary of State

A personal licence holder can appeal against a decision to revoke the personal licence under s.124.

26.7.4 Decision not to revoke following objection by the police or Secretary of State

Where convictions come to light after the grant of a personal licence, the chief officer of police for the licensing authority's area who gave a notice that continuation of the licence would undermine the crime prevention objective, and does not later withdraw it, may appeal against a decision of the licensing authority not to revoke the licence. Where the Secretary of State (through Home Office Immigration Enforcement) gave a notice that continuation of the licence would be prejudicial to the prevention of illegal working in licensed premises, and does not later withdraw it, the Secretary of State may appeal against a decision of the licensing authority not to revoke the licence.

26.7.5 General provision about appeals in relation to applications regarding personal licences

Any of the above appeals must be made to a magistrates' court. Such an appeal is brought by the appellant giving notice of appeal to the designated officer for the magistrates' court within the period of 21 days beginning with the day on which the appellant was notified by the licensing authority of the decision which is being appealed against. The personal licence holder must be the respondent to the appeal together with the relevant licensing authority.

Where objections have been raised by the chief officer of police, the personal licence holder must be the respondent to the appeal together with the relevant licensing authority.

26.8 CLOSURE ORDERS

If, on a review of a premises licence following a closure order, the relevant licensing authority decides:

- to modify the conditions of the premises licence;
- to exclude a licensable activity from the scope of the licence;
- to remove a designated premises supervisor from the licence;
- to suspend the licence for not more than three months;
- to revoke the licence; or
- not to do anything;

an appeal may be made against that decision by the holder of the premises licence, or anyone else who made relevant representations in relation to the review.

Where an appeal is made against a decision to:

- modify the conditions of the premises licence;
- exclude a licensable activity from the scope of the licence;
- remove a designated premises supervisor from the licence; or
- suspend the licence for not more than three months;

the magistrates' court may, if the premises were closed when the decision was taken:

- suspend, on such terms as it thinks fit, the operation of the decision in whole or part, if the relevant licensing authority did not make an order suspending the operation of the decision in whole or part; or
- if the relevant licensing authority has made such an order, cancel it or substitute for it any order suspending the operation of the decision in whole or part which could have been made by the relevant licensing authority.

Where an appeal is made in respect of premises in respect of which the relevant licensing authority has decided to revoke the premises licence and the premises have been closed until that decision was made, the magistrates' court may, on such conditions as it thinks fit, order that the requirement that the premises must remain closed pending the appeal is not to apply to the premises.

An appeal must be made to a magistrates' court. Such an appeal is brought by the appellant giving notice of appeal to the designated officer for the magistrates' court within the period of 21 days beginning with the day on which the appellant was notified by the licensing authority of the decision which is being appealed against.

The holder of the premises licence must be the respondent to the appeal together with the relevant licensing authority where an appeal is brought by a person other than the holder of the premises licence.

26.9 GIVING REASONS

The Guidance provides:

13.10 It is important that a licensing authority gives comprehensive reasons for its decisions in anticipation of any appeals. Failure to give adequate reasons could itself give rise to grounds for an appeal. It is particularly important that reasons should also address the extent to which the decision has been made with regard to the licensing authority's statement of policy and this Guidance. Reasons should be promulgated to all the parties of any process which might give rise to an appeal under the terms of the 2003 Act.

13.11 It is important that licensing authorities also provide all parties who were party to the original hearing, but not involved directly in the appeal, with clear reasons for any subsequent decisions where appeals are settled out of court. Local residents in particular, who have attended a hearing where the decision was subject to an appeal, are likely to expect the final determination to be made by a court.

26.10 IMPLEMENTING THE DETERMINATION OF THE MAGISTRATES' COURTS

Once a magistrates' court has reached a decision on an appeal, the relevant licensing authority should not delay its implementation. The Guidance at para.13.12 provides that:

As soon as the decision of the magistrates' court has been promulgated, licensing authorities should implement it without delay. Any attempt to delay implementation will only bring the appeal system into disrepute. Standing orders should therefore be in place that on receipt of the decision, appropriate action should be taken immediately unless ordered by the magistrates' court or a higher court to suspend such action (for example, as a result of an on-going judicial review). Except in the case of closure orders, the 2003 Act does not provide for a further appeal against the decision of the magistrates' courts and normal rules of challenging decisions of magistrates' courts will apply.

26.11 APPEALS TO THE HIGH COURT

26.11.1 By case stated

The Magistrates' Court Act 1980, s.111(1) provides that any person who is a party to any proceedings before a magistrates' court or is aggrieved by the court's order or determination may question the proceedings on the ground that the proceedings were wrong in law or were in excess of jurisdiction by applying to the magistrates to state a case for the opinion of the High Court on the question of law or jurisdiction involved. This right does not apply in respect of a decision against which there is a right of appeal to the High Court or which by virtue of the Licensing Act 2003 is final.

So an applicant for a licence, a licence holder, licensing authorities and persons who have made relevant representations will have a right of appeal by way of case stated. The magistrates must have finished dealing with the case before a case can be stated (*Streames* v. *Copping* [1985] QB 920 DC; [1985] 2 WLR 993).

An application for a case stated must be made within 21 days after the day on which the decision of the magistrates' court was made (Magistrates' Court Act 1980, s.111(2)). If the magistrates decide that an application is frivolous, they may refuse to state a case (Magistrates' Court Act 1980, s.111(5)). In such a case, if the applicant requires, the court must give him a certificate stating that the application has been refused. Where the magistrates refuse to state a case, the High Court may, on the application of the person who applied for the case to be stated, make a mandatory order requiring the justices to state a case (Magistrates' Court Act 1980, s.111(6)).

The requirements for making an application for a case stated are set out in the Magistrates' Courts Rules 1981, SI 1981/552, rules 76, 77 and 78. An application must be made in writing and signed by or on behalf of the applicant and shall identify the question or questions of law or jurisdiction on which the opinion of the High Court is sought. An application must be sent to the designated officer for the magistrates' court whose decision is questioned. Where one of the questions on which the opinion of the High Court is sought is whether there was evidence on which the magistrates' court could come to its decision, the particular finding of fact made by the magistrates' court which it is claimed cannot be supported by the evidence before the magistrates' court shall be specified in such application.

Within 21 days after the receipt of an application the designated officer must, unless the magistrates refuse to state a case, send a draft case to the applicant or his solicitor and a copy to the respondent or his solicitor. Within 21 days after receipt of the draft case, each party may make representations. These must be in writing and signed by or on behalf of the party making them and sent to the designated officer. Within 21 days after the latest day on which representations may be made, the magistrates can make such adjustments, if any, to the draft case as they think fit, after considering any such representations, and shall state and sign the case. Forthwith after the case has been stated and signed the designated officer must send it to the applicant or his solicitor.

Rule 81 provides that a case stated must state the facts found by the court and the question or questions of law or jurisdiction on which the opinion of the High Court is sought. Where one of the questions on which the opinion of the High Court is sought is whether there was evidence on which the magistrates' court could come to its decision, the particular finding of fact which it is claimed cannot be supported by the evidence before the magistrates' court shall be specified in the case. Unless one of the questions on which the opinion of the High Court is sought is whether there was evidence on which the magistrates' court could come to its decision, the case shall not contain a statement of evidence.

The powers of the High Court are set out in the Senior Courts Act 1981, s.28A(3). The High Court must determine the question arising on the case and reverse, affirm or amend the determination in respect of which the case has been stated, or remit the matter to the magistrates' court, with the opinion of the High Court. It may make such other order in relation to the matter, including as to costs, as it thinks fit. The decision of the High Court is final.

26.11.2 Judicial review

An application may be made to judicially review the magistrates' decision. The Senior Courts Act 1981, s.31 provides that an application can be made, with the leave of the High Court, for judicial review of a magistrates' court decision. Leave will only be granted where the High Court considers that the applicant has sufficient interest in the matter to which the application relates. If leave is granted, the High Court may grant a mandatory, prohibiting or quashing order, or it may award a declaration or damages. A mandatory order will compel the magistrates' court to carry out its functions properly. A quashing order will be appropriate to quash a decision where there has been some unlawfulness in the process used to reach the decision, while a prohibiting order can be used to prevent some unlawful action in the future.

The High Court may refuse to grant relief if it considers that the more appropriate remedy would have been an appeal by way of case stated.

Where the premises licence holder and the licensing authority reach agreement on an application for judicial review then the appropriate course for the court is to quash the magistrates' court's decision and direct it to reach a decision in accordance with the High Court's view that the agreed terms were appropriate (*R. (on the application of Festiva Ltd)* v. *Highbury Corner Magistrates' Court* [2011] EWHC 3043 (Admin); (2012) 109(17) LSG 18, where the agreement between a premises licence holder and the local licensing authority was to the hours of permitted licensed activities).

An appeal in judicial review proceedings can be made to the Court of Appeal with leave of the Court of Appeal. A further appeal lies to the Supreme Court with leave of either the Court of Appeal or the Supreme Court.

CHAPTER 27

Pavement licences

27.1 INTRODUCTION

The Business and Planning Act 2020, Part 1 provides for the grant in England of pavement licences which allow businesses to use some of the space outside their premises to provide more seats for customers who wish to have a table meal or consume alcohol seated, subject to the business holding a premises licence or temporary event notice under the Licensing Act 2003. Planning permission is not required for a pavement licence.

The Government has published guidance on pavement licences which is available at **www.gov.uk/government/publications/pavement-licences-guidance/pavement-licences-guidance#applications**. In exercising its functions in relation to pavement licences, a local authority must have regard to any guidance issued by the Secretary of State.

27.2 PAVEMENT LICENCES

A person whose use or proposed use of any premises in England is or includes use as a public house, wine bar or other drinking establishment and/or other use for the sale of food or drink for consumption on or off the premises may apply to the local authority in whose area the premises are situated for a pavement licence in respect of those premises.

A pavement licence allows the licence-holder to put removable furniture on part of a relevant highway adjacent to the premises for either or both of the following purposes:

(a) use of the furniture by the licence-holder to sell or serve food or drink supplied from, or in connection with relevant use of, the premises;

(b) use of the furniture by other persons for the purpose of consuming food or drink supplied from, or in connection with relevant use of, the premises.

For these purposes:

- 'relevant highway' means a highway to which the Highways Act 1980, Part 7A applies, and which is not over Crown land or maintained by Network Rail; and
- 'furniture' means:

    – counters or stalls for selling or serving food or drink;
    – tables, counters or shelves on which food or drink can be placed;
    – chairs, benches or other forms of seating; and
    – umbrellas, barriers, heaters and other articles used in connection with the outdoor consumption of food or drink.

27.3 APPLICATION FOR A PAVEMENT LICENCE

An application for a pavement licence must be made to the local authority in whose area the premises are situated. The application must be made in writing and in such form as the local authority may specify. A local authority may have a standard application form which they require applicants to use. In addition, the application must be sent to the local authority using electronic communications in such manner as the local authority may specify and be accompanied by the relevant fee.

An application must:

- specify the premises and the part of the relevant highway to which the application relates;
- specify the purpose, or purposes, for which the furniture will be used which must be for use by the licence-holder to sell or serve food or drink, and/or for use by other people for the consumption of food or drink. In both cases, the food or drink must be supplied from, or in connection with the use of the premises as a public house, wine bar or other drinking establishment or other use for the sale of food or drink for consumption on or off the premises;
- specify the days of the week on which and the hours between which it is proposed to have furniture on the highway;
- describe the type of furniture to which the application relates;
- specify the date on which the application is made;
- contain or be accompanied by such evidence of public liability insurance in respect of anything to be done pursuant to the licence as the local authority may require; and
- contain or be accompanied by such other information or material as the local authority may require.

The above requirements do not apply to a renewal application but such an application must be accompanied by such information or material as the local authority may require. A renewal application is one made by a person who already holds a pavement licence, is in respect of the premises to which the existing licence relates and is for a licence to begin on the expiry of the existing licence and on the same terms.

Local authorities may require the applicant to provide other information or material, and this could be included in their standard application form. Examples of the information a local authority might require include:

- a plan showing the location of the premises shown by a red line, so the application site can be clearly identified;
- a plan clearly showing the proposed area covered by the licence in relation to the relevant highway, if not to scale, with measurements clearly shown;
- the proposed duration of the licence (for e.g. three months, six months, a year etc.);
- evidence of the right to occupy the premises (e.g. the lease);
- contact details of the applicant;
- photos or brochures showing the proposed type of furniture and information on potential siting of it within the area applied;
- evidence that the applicant has met the requirement to give notice of the application (e.g. photograph);
- (if applicable) reference number of the existing pavement licence currently under consideration by the local authority;
- any other evidence that shows how the furniture to be introduced is in accordance with national guidance regarding accessibility (such as use of good colour contrast, suitable physical barriers around chairs and tables and/or other appropriate measures); and
- any other evidence needed to demonstrate how any local and national conditions will be satisfied.

27.4 FEE FOR A PAVEMENT LICENCE

The fee for a pavement licence is £350 where an application is made by a person who already holds a pavement licence and the application is in respect of the premises to which that existing licence relates (whether or not it is a renewal application). The fee in any other case is £500. See **www.gov.uk/government/publications/pavement-licences-guidance/pavement-licences-guidance**.

27.5 CONDITIONS

A pavement licence may be granted by a local authority subject to such conditions as it considers reasonable and may publish conditions subject to which it proposes to grant pavement licences. If these do not include a no-obstruction condition and a smoke-free seating condition then the Business and Planning Act 2020 provides that the licence will be deemed to be granted subject to these two conditions. Where a local authority sets a local condition that covers the same matter as either of these two conditions, then the locally set condition would take precedence where there is reasonable justification to do so.

27.5.1 No-obstruction condition

A 'no-obstruction condition' is a condition that anything done by the licence-holder pursuant to the licence, or any activity of other persons which is enabled by the licence, must not have the effect of:

(a) preventing traffic, other than vehicular traffic, from:

    (i) entering the relevant highway at a place where such traffic could otherwise enter it (ignoring any pedestrian planning order or traffic order made in relation to the highway);

    (ii) passing along the relevant highway; or

    (iii) having normal access to premises adjoining the relevant highway;

(b) preventing any use of vehicles which is permitted by a pedestrian planning order or which is not prohibited by a traffic order;

(c) preventing statutory undertakers having access to any apparatus of theirs under, in, on or over the highway; or

(d) preventing the operator of an electronic communications code network having access to any electronic communications apparatus kept installed for the purposes of that network under, in, on or over the highway.

When determining whether furniture constitutes an unacceptable obstruction in the light of the no-obstruction condition, local authorities must consider the needs of disabled people. In order to do this, local authorities should consider the following matters when setting conditions, determining applications (in the absence of local conditions), and when considering whether enforcement action is required:

• the Inclusive Mobility A Guide to Best Practice on Access to Pedestrian and Transport Infrastructure, s.2 (available at **www.gov.uk/government/publications/inclusive-mobility-making-transport-accessible-for-passengers-and-pedestrians**) gives advice on the needs of particular pavement users and sets out a range of recommended widths which would be required, depending on the needs of particular pavement users. Section 4.2 sets out that footways and footpaths should be as wide as practicable, but under normal circumstances a width of 2000mm is the minimum that should be provided, as this allows enough space for two wheelchair users to pass, even if they are using larger electric mobility scooters. Local authorities should take a proportionate approach if this is not feasible due to physical constraints. A minimum width of 1500mm could be regarded as the minimum acceptable distance between two obstacles under most circumstances, as this should enable a wheelchair user and a walker to pass each other;

- any need for a barrier to separate furniture from the rest of the footway so that the visually impaired can navigate around the furniture, such as colour contrast and a tap rail for long cane users. In some cases, it may be appropriate to use one or more rigid, removable objects to demarcate the area to which the licence applies, for example wooden tubs of flowers. However, as these are not necessary for the consumption of food, this will need to be balanced to ensure any barriers do not inhibit other street users, such as the mobility impaired, as such barriers may create a further obstacle in the highway. Advertising boards are not included in the definition of furniture within the pavement licensing regime, therefore, should not be used as a barrier;
- any conflict of street furniture with the principal lines of pedestrian movement particularly for disabled people, older people and those with mobility needs. The positioning of furniture should not discourage pedestrians from using the footway or force pedestrians into the highway. The available route must be entirely clear for pedestrians to use and not be impeded with tables and chairs;
- the cumulative impact of multiple pavement licences in close proximity to each other and if there is specific evidence that this may create a build-up furniture in a particular area and potentially cause obstruction on the footway for certain pavement users, such as disabled people;
- so that where possible, furniture is non-reflective and of reasonable substance such that it cannot easily be pushed or blown over by the wind, and thereby cause obstruction, for example, the local authority could refuse the use of plastic patio furniture, unless measures have been taken to ensure it is kept in place.

The Equality Act 2010, s.149 places duties on local authorities, to have due regard to the need to eliminate unlawful discrimination, advance equality of opportunity between people who share a protected characteristic and those who do not and foster or encourage good relations between people who share a protected characteristic and those who do not.

27.5.2 Smoke-free seating condition

A 'smoke-free seating condition' is a condition that, where the furniture to be put on the relevant highway consists of seating for use by persons for the purpose of consuming food or drink, the licence-holder must make reasonable provision for seating where smoking is not permitted.

Ways of meeting this condition could include:

- clear 'smoking' and 'non-smoking' areas, with 'no smoking' signage displayed in designated 'smoke-free' zones in accordance with Smoke-free (Signs) Regulations 2012, SI 2012/1536;
- no ash trays or similar receptacles to be provided or permitted to be left on furniture where smoke-free seating is identified; and

- licence holders should provide a minimum 2m distance between non-smoking and smoking areas, wherever possible.

Furthermore, businesses must continue to have regard to smoke-free legislation under the Health Act 2006, and the Smoke-free (Premises and Enforcement) Regulations 2006, SI 2006/ 3368.

27.6 ADVERTISING AN APPLICATION

A local authority to which an application for a pavement licence is made must in such manner as it considers appropriate:

- publish the application and any information or material required by the local authority; and
- publicise the fact that representations relating to the application may be made to the authority during the public consultation period (and indicate when that period comes to an end).

The 'public consultation period' is the period of 14 days beginning with the day after that on which the application is made.

An applicant for a pavement licence must:

- on the day the application is made, fix a notice of the application to the premises so that the notice is readily visible to, and can be read easily by, members of the public who are not on the premises; and
- secure that the notice remains in place until the end of the public consultation period.

The notice which is fixed to the premises must:

- be in such form as the local authority to which the application is made may require;
- state that the application has been made and the date on which it was made;
- indicate that representations relating to the application may be made to the local authority during the public consultation period (and indicate when that period comes to an end); and
- contain such other information or material as the local authority may require.

An application for a pavement licence is made on the day it is sent to the local authority.

27.7 DETERMINATION OF AN APPLICATION

Before making a determination in respect of an application for a pavement licence, a local authority must:

411

- take into account any representations made to it during the public consultation period;
- consult the highway authority for the relevant highway to which the application relates, where the local authority is not that authority; and
- consult such other persons as the local authority considers appropriate.

After the end of the 14 day public consultation period, the local authority may either grant a pavement licence to the applicant or reject the application.

A local authority may grant a pavement licence to the applicant in respect of any or all of the purposes in relation to which the application is made and some or all of the part of the relevant highway specified in the application.

A local authority may only grant a pavement licence if it considers that, taking into account any conditions subject to which it proposes to grant the licence, nothing done by the licence-holder pursuant to the licence would have the effect of:

- preventing traffic, other than vehicular traffic, from:
    - entering the relevant highway at a place where such traffic could otherwise enter it (ignoring any pedestrian planning order or traffic order made in relation to the highway);
    - passing along the relevant highway; or
    - having normal access to premises adjoining the relevant highway;
- preventing any use of vehicles which is permitted by a pedestrian planning order or which is not prohibited by a traffic order;
- preventing statutory undertakers having access to any apparatus of theirs under, in, on or over the highway; or
- preventing the operator of an electronic communications code network having access to any electronic communications apparatus kept installed for the purposes of that network under, in, on or over the highway.

Where a local authority is considering whether furniture put on a relevant highway by a licence-holder pursuant to a pavement licence has or would have the effect of preventing traffic, other than vehicular traffic, from:

- entering the relevant highway at a place where such traffic could otherwise enter it (ignoring any pedestrian planning order or traffic order made in relation to the highway);
- passing along the relevant highway; or
- having normal access to premises adjoining the relevant highway;

the local authority must have regard in particular to the needs of disabled people, and the recommended distances required for access by disabled people as set out in guidance issued by the Secretary of State.

If the local authority does not make a decision to either grant or reject the application within the period of 14 days beginning with the first day after the public consultation period then the licence is deemed to be granted ('the determination period').

27.8 DURATION OF A LICENCE

A pavement licence may be granted for such period as the local authority may specify provided that this does not exceed two years.

Where a licence is deemed to have been granted, it is granted for two years starting with the first day after the determination period.

A licence-holder may surrender a pavement licence at any time by giving notice to the local authority by which it is granted or deemed to be granted. Notice must be made in writing and sent using electronic communications in such manner as the local authority may specify.

27.9 ENFORCEMENT AND REVOCATION

If a local authority considers that the licence-holder has breached any condition of the licence, it may either revoke the licence, or serve a notice on the licence-holder requiring the taking of such steps to remedy the breach as are specified in the notice within such time as is so specified.

If a licence-holder on whom such a notice is served fails to comply with the notice, the local authority may revoke the notice, or take the steps itself and recover the costs of doing so from the licence-holder.

A local authority may also revoke the licence if it considers that:

- some or all of the part of the relevant highway to which the licence relates has become unsuitable for any purpose in relation to which the licence was granted or deemed to be granted;
- as a result of the licence:
    - there is a risk to public health or safety;
    - anti-social behaviour or public nuisance is being caused or risks being caused; or
    - the highway is being obstructed (other than by anything done by the licence-holder pursuant to the licence);
- anything material stated by the licence-holder in their application was false or misleading; or
- the licence-holder did not comply with the requirements on the day the application was made to fix a notice of the application to the premises so that the notice is readily visible to, and can be read easily by, members of the public who are not on the premises, and secure that the notice remains in place until the end of the public consultation period.

A local authority may, with the consent of the licence-holder, amend the licence if it considers that:

- some or all of the part of the relevant highway to which the licence relates has become unsuitable for any purpose in relation to which the licence was granted or deemed to be granted;
- as a result of the licence:
    - there is a risk to public health or safety;
    - anti-social behaviour or public nuisance is being caused or risks being caused; or
    - the highway is being obstructed (other than by anything done by the licence-holder pursuant to the licence); or
- a no-obstruction condition of the licence is not being complied with.

27.10 REMOVAL OF FURNITURE

Where a person who is not authorised to do so puts removable furniture on a relevant highway for a specified purpose, the local authority may by notice require the person to remove the furniture before a date specified in the notice, and to refrain from putting furniture on the highway unless authorised to do so.

The specified purposes are:

- use of the furniture by the person to sell or serve food or drink supplied from, or in connection with relevant use of, premises which are adjacent to the highway and are used or proposed to be used by the person; and
- use of the furniture by other persons for the purpose of consuming food or drink supplied from, or in connection with relevant use of, such premises.

If the person leaves or puts removable furniture on the relevant highway in contravention of the notice, the local authority may:

- remove the furniture and store it;
- require the person to pay the authority's reasonable costs in removing and storing the furniture; and
- refuse to return the furniture until those reasonable costs are paid.

If within the period of three months beginning with the day on which the notice is given the person does not pay the reasonable costs, or does not recover the furniture, the local authority may dispose of the furniture by sale or in any other way it thinks fit and retain any proceeds of sale for any purpose it thinks fit.

Operating schedule toolkit – risk assessment

1 THE PREVENTION OF CRIME AND DISORDER

1.1 Management of the premises

1.1.1 Is there an effective door control policy in place to prevent overcrowding and to ensure that potential troublemakers are excluded from the premises? If yes, give details.

1.1.2 How do you monitor the number of people on the premises at any one time?

1.1.3 How many security staff do you employ?

1.1.4 Are all door staff registered with the Security Industry Authority (SIA) scheme and have they all obtained the appropriate SIA qualifications?

1.1.5 Do you hold regular security reviews and, if you do, what happens as a result of these?

1.1.6 How did you assess the number of door supervisors on the premises needed to cope with the numbers of customers?

1.1.7 Do you have a search policy? If you do, give details.

1.1.8 Do you carry out risk assessments prior to holding specific events? If so, what issues do you consider?

1.1.9 Do you have an incident log of crime and disorder occurrences? If so, is this used, maintained and available for inspection as part of a risk assessment and intelligence gathering process?

1.1.10 Do you employ procedures to deal with customers under the influence of alcohol and/or illegal drugs? If so, what are they?

1.1.11 Do you have procedures to deal with violence and antisocial behaviour in the premises? If so, what are they?

1.1.12 Are you involved in any relevant community radio schemes?

1.1.13 What procedures do you have to deal with handbag theft when it occurs as this can be prevalent in busy pubs and clubs?

1.1.14 How do you discourage customers from removing glass, bottles or cans from the premises?

1.1.15 Do you use only safety/toughened glass in your premises to reduce the potential injury from any assaults?

1.1.16 Is up-to-date information made available to customers detailing late night public transport to enable them to travel home safely?

1.1.17 Do you ensure that only telephone numbers for registered taxi firms are displayed?

1.1.18 Do you provide local police with details of events involving outside promoters (i.e. give one month's notice)?

1.1.19 Do you have contractual agreements with outside promoters and if so are police contacted before agreements are signed?

1.2 Implementing appropriate policies for the management of patron behaviour

1.2.1 Do you use practices outlined in the British Beer and Pub Association Drugs and Pubs: A Guide to Keeping a Drug Free Pub (**www.beerandpub.com**)?

1.2.2 Do you have policies to search customers for drugs and/or weapons? If so, what are they?

1.2.3 How do you discourage the use or dealing of illicit substances in or around the premises?

1.2.4 Do you display materials that include the Frank National Drugs Helpline number (0800 776600)?

1.2.5 Do you actively promote drugs awareness among staff? If so, how do you do this?

1.2.6 What procedures do you have with regard to the retention or disposal of any controlled drugs found on the premises and any persons found in possession of them?

1.2.7 What measures do you take to ensure the safety of your customers in relation to drunkenness on the premises?

1.3 Drinks promotions

1.3.1 Are you a member of your local pubwatch scheme, if there is one?

1.3.2 Do you use only responsible drinks promotions practices, for example, those outlined in the British Beer and Pub Association Point of Sale Promotions: A Good Practice Guide for Pub Owners and Licensees?

1.3.3 Do you actively promote sensible drinking policies, giving careful consideration to the use of happy hours and drink promotions that may encourage binge drinking?

1.3.4 Do you encourage promotions for non-alcoholic drinks?

1.3.5 Do you promote safe drink and drive practices?

1.4 Responsible management of the local environment around the premises

1.4.1 What procedures do you use to deal with violence and antisocial behaviour outside the premises?

1.4.2 Do you have a queuing policy to encourage good behaviour outside the premises? If so, give details.

1.4.3 Do you have procedures to promptly remove or repair hazardous or damaged objects, materials or property from the premises and the immediate area? If so, give details.

1.4.4 Are regular routine checks of the premises and the immediate areas carried out, including the prompt removal of glass, antisocial deposits and graffiti? If so, give details.

1.4.5 Do you have procedures to remove graffiti and antisocial deposits from in and around the premises? If so, give details.

1.5 Entry and exit points

1.5.1 How many entry/exit points do the premises have?

1.5.2 Have the points of entry been reduced to a minimum?

1.5.3 Is there a separate point of entry for staff?

1.5.4   How are entry/exit points monitored?

1.5.5   Are emergency exit points alarmed so that staff are immediately notified of any unauthorised opening or tampering?

1.5.6   Are the doors signed as such?

1.6   Interior design

1.6.1   Is the burglar alarm linked to a system that will automatically contact the police if it is activated?

1.6.2   Are personal attack buttons incorporated in the burglar alarm system for use by staff in appropriate areas such as behind the bar or in the cash office?

1.6.3   Are all staff trained in their correct usage so that police are called to attend urgently when necessary?

1.6.4   Is the bar counter raised and widened for the better protection of staff?

1.6.5   Is the floor on the staff side raised to enable staff to monitor areas beyond the bar and to provide an added appearance of authority?

1.6.6   Are tills positioned so that staff face customers and are they protected from 'till snatch' by transparent screens or an under counter location?

1.6.7   Do staff have direct access to a place of safety behind the bar/counter area to retreat to if threatened with violence?

1.6.8   Are there reasonable means in place for the safe handling of cash both within and to and from the premises?

1.6.9   Have alcoves and blind spots been removed from the layout of the premises to improve natural surveillance? If not, has this lack of natural surveillance been compensated with CCTV coverage or other measures?

1.6.10 Have any wide-open areas been broken up into manageable, visible areas?

1.6.11 Is a cloakroom available to store coats and bags and is it clearly advertised?

1.6.12 Is the cloakroom queue managed at busy times and if so how?

1.6.13 Is furniture equipped with the facility for customers to secure their property?

1.7   Sanitary facilities

1.7.1   Are the entrances to the toilets easily visible from the bar?

1.7.2   Are toilet entrances located away from the main entrance/exit point?

1.7.3   Are toilet entrances located away from other at risk areas such as accommodation or kitchen entrances?

1.7.4   Are any cupboards or drawers located within the toilets kept locked?

1.7.5   Are the cisterns boxed in and secure to deter drug concealment?

1.7.6   Have all possible flat surfaces in the toilets been removed as otherwise these could facilitate drug use?

1.7.7   Do the cubicle doors have gaps at the top and bottom?

1.7.8   Is key access to the cubicles available to staff?

1.7.9   Are the toilets managed at peak times and kept in good order at other times? If so, what is the itinerary for management?

1.7.10 Are there sufficient toilets to meet peak demand?

1.8   Closed circuit television

1.8.1   Have the premises been assessed to see whether CCTV is necessary?

1.8.2   Are the premises equipped with CCTV?

1.8.3   Do high-resolution cameras monitor all entry and exit points?

1.8.4   Does the CCTV monitor the cash office door?

1.8.5   Is the CCTV system registered with the Information Commissioner, if required?
1.8.6   Is there a written operational requirement for the CCTV system?
1.8.7   Is the recording equipment stored in a secure area with access restricted to authorised staff only?
1.8.8   Does the CCTV system record clear images which can be used as valid evidence in a court of law?
1.8.9   Describe your tape management system in detail (including storage of tapes).

2   PUBLIC SAFETY

2.1   Capacity

2.1.1   What is the maximum capacity of the premises?
2.1.2   If appropriate, what is the maximum capacity for separate areas within the premises?
2.1.3   How was this capacity arrived at?

2.2   Disabled persons

2.2.1   What facilities are available for the access and egress for disabled persons?
2.2.2   How does the evacuation procedure for the premises allow for the evacuation of disabled persons?

2.3   Emergency access

2.3.1   Does your site allow for access by emergency vehicles?

2.4   Fire escapes

2.4.1   Has a fire risk assessment of the premises been carried out?
2.4.2   If so, what are the results of this risk assessment?
2.4.3   Do the premises have sufficient exits and are these exits readily available at all times?
2.4.4   Do all the exit routes lead to a place of safety?
2.4.5   If the premises include an auditorium, has the layout of the seating been designed to facilitate easy means of escape from fire?
2.4.6   Are all staircases which form part of an escape route suitable?

2.5   Fire safety

2.5.1   Is the licensed area of the premises or are the premises themselves separated by fire resisting construction from any adjoining building or any unlicensed part of a building?
2.5.2   Do all finishes, furniture and soft furnishings comply with the relevant standards?
2.5.3   Are the ventilation system and duct work fire rated and provided with dampers to provide fire separation of at least 30 minutes between the licensed part of the premises and unlicensed areas, and between the premises and escape routes?
2.5.4   If the premises have a stage, is there a safety curtain?
2.5.5   Do the premises have a sprinkler system, controls and arrangements for smoke ventilation, foam inlets, wet/dry risers, refuges for persons with impaired mobility, evacuation/fire fighting lifts, fire fighting staircases, gas cut off valves and other

emergency cut offs, fire fighters switches, or main electrical intakes and if so, are these indicated with signs? Please indicate which of these are present.

2.6 Fire and emergency warning systems

2.6.1 Do the premises have an automatic fire detection and a warning system?
2.6.2 Are there fire extinguishers, fire blankets, hose reels or sprinklers in the premises?
2.6.3 Do the premises have a secondary supply of electricity (generator)?

2.7 Structure

2.7.1 Is the building structurally safe and can it support any extra loads imposed by the proposed use?
2.7.2 Are all changes in level and balconies within the premises protected by barriers or guard rails?
2.7.3 Are all barriers and guard rails of sufficient structural strength?

2.8 Building services

2.8.1 Is the electrical system mechanically and electrically safe?
2.8.2 When was the electrical system last assessed?
2.8.3 Are all electrical sockets for use by performers provided with RCD protection?
2.8.4 Are the premises provided with adequate levels of illumination?
2.8.5 Is there an emergency lighting system?
2.8.6 Do the premises have a mechanical ventilation system?
2.8.7 Do the premises have a heating system and is this arranged so as not to cause a safety or fire hazard?
2.8.8 Do the premises have a permanent water supply and adequate drainage?

2.9 Hygiene

2.9.1 Is free drinking water provided for customers?

2.10 Communication systems

2.10.1 What systems are in place within the premises to provide adequate facilities for communication with staff and the public?
2.10.2 What safety signs and notices are there within the premises?

2.11 Special installations and lifts

2.11.1 What special installations are there within the premises, e.g. lifts, stair lifts, escalators, moveable seating?
2.11.2 Are there any specific risks associated with such special installations?
2.11.3 What special effects are used such as real flame, lasers, pyrotechnics, smoke, fog, foam or firearms? Has a risk assessment been carried out with regard to these?

2.12 Commissioning and inspection test certificates

2.12.1 Do you have current up-to-date certificates for the following if appropriate:

- the electrical installation;
- emergency lighting batteries;

- fire alarm warning system;
- fire-fighting equipment;
- gas installation and gas appliances;
- boilers or clarifiers;
- passenger lifts and escalators;
- emergency telephones;
- public address systems and refuge alarms;
- safety curtains;
- mechanical installation and suspended or lifting equipment.

Please state which are on the premises.

2.13 Staff training

2.13.1 Have all staff been trained in public safety issues such as evacuation procedures, first aid, dealing with conflict, spotting persons under the influence of alcohol or drugs, etc.?

2.13.2 If so, what training have they received and is this documented?

2.14 Drink and drugs

2.14.1 What procedures are in place when dealing with persons who are believed to be suffering adversely from the effect of either drink or drugs?

3 PREVENTION OF PUBLIC NUISANCE

3.1 Noise

3.1.1 Are the premises located in close proximity to residential accommodation? If they are, what and where?

3.1.2 Are the premises attached to any residential premises?

3.1.3 Is it intended to hold live music events at the premises (acoustic or amplified)?

3.1.4 Has an acoustic report being carried out with regard to the premises?

3.1.5 If so, what recommended works have been carried out?

3.1.6 If amplified music is provided, do the premises have a sound-limiting device?

3.1.7 If so, is it located in a lockable cupboard to which only the licensee has access?

3.1.8 Are all socket outlets used to supply the music connected to the sound-limiting device?

3.1.9 Is there a policy of keeping all doors and windows closed while amplified music is being played within the premises?

3.1.10 Do the external doors have acoustic lobbies?

3.1.11 Do the door supervisors ensure that doors are not left open when amplified music is being played?

3.1.12 Is the ventilation/air conditioning system adequate for the number of customers?

3.1.13 Are there air-handling units external to the premises?

3.1.14 If so, are they sound insulated to avoid late night nuisance?

3.1.15 Are the air-handling units serviced on a regular basis?

3.2 People arriving, departing and in the vicinity of the premises

3.2.1 How is it ensured that customers queuing outside the premises do so in a quiet and orderly manner?

3.2.2 Are customers encouraged to leave the premises quietly?

3.2.3 Is information provided on local public transport provision?

3.2.4 What measures are taken to lessen the impact of noise and nuisance generated from cars and taxis attending the premises?

3.2.5 Do the premises have a beer garden or patio area?

3.2.6 Do the premises have tables and chairs outside?

3.2.7 If so, how is noise from the external areas controlled and is there a restricted hours of use policy?

3.3 Deliveries and collections

3.3.1 What measures are taken to control any possible noise nuisance arising from deliveries or collections?

3.4 Odours

3.4.1 If food is provided at the premises, what is done to avoid cooking odours becoming a nuisance?

3.4.2 How is waste stored and how often is it collected?

3.5 Litter and fly posting

3.5.1 What measures are employed to discourage customers from creating litter on the streets in the vicinity of the premises, e.g. food wrappings or promotional material?

3.5.2 What is done to ensure that there is no fly posting associated with the premises?

3.6 Light

3.6.1 Do the premises have external lighting?

3.6.2 If so, what is done to ensure that excess light is not causing a nuisance to neighbours?

4 PROTECTION OF CHILDREN FROM HARM

4.1 Prevention of alcohol sales to under 18s

4.1.1 How is it intended to prevent under-age drinking in the premises?

4.1.2 Are all the staff trained in the 'under-age' policy?

4.2 Restricting access for children to licensed premises

4.2.1 Is access to be restricted for under 18s?

4.2.2 If so how, why and when?

4.3 Other measures to prevent harm to children

4.3.1 What is the procedure for dealing with the safety of lost and found children?

4.3.2 Is it expected that unaccompanied children will be present in the premises and if so, what ratios of staff to children are there expected to be?

4.3.3 Is it anticipated that children will be performing at the premises? If so, what facilities are there for them?

4.4 Children, cinemas and television

4.4.1 If films, television programmes or videos are to be shown in the premises, how is it proposed to prevent children being exposed to strong language, violence and sexual content?

4.4.2 If the premises are a cinema, how is it proposed to control entry in accordance with the BBFC classification system and to prevent films being viewed by under-age children?

Licensing Act 2003 representation form

FORM

Your name	
Postal and email address	
Contact telephone number	
Name of the premises you are making a representation about	
Address of the premises you are making a representation about	
Which of the four licensing objectives does your representation relate to?	Please detail the evidence supporting your representation, or the reason for your representation. Please use separate sheets if necessary.
To prevent crime and disorder	
Public safety	
To prevent public nuisance	
To protect children from harm	

Signed: Date:

Scale of fines

STANDARD SCALE OF FINES FOR SUMMARY OFFENCES

Level on scale	Amount of fine
1	£200
2	£500
3	£1,000
4	£2,500
5	Unlimited

Useful websites

Alcohol Education Research Council	**https://aerc.org.uk**
Arts Council	**www.artscouncil.org.uk**
Association of Convenience Stores	**www.acs.org.uk**
British Beer and Pub Association	**https://beerandpub.com**
British Board of Film Classification	**www.bbfc.co.uk**
British Institute of Innkeeping	**www.bii.org**
British Retail Consortium	**www.brc.org.uk**
British Standards Institution	**www.bsigroup.com**
BECTU	**https://bectu.org.uk**
Canal & River Trust	**https://canalrivertrust.org.uk**
Chartered Institute of Environmental Health	**www.cieh.org**
CitizenCard	**www.citizencard.com**
Department for Culture, Media and Sport	**www.gov.uk**
Disclosure and Barring Service	**www.gov.uk/government/organisations/disclosure-and-barring-service**
Entertainment Technology Press	**www.etbooks.co.uk**
Federation of Licensed Victuallers Associations	**https://flva.co.uk**
Health and Safety Executive	**www.hse.gov.uk**
Home Office	**www.gov.uk**
Institute of Acoustics	**www.ioa.org.uk**
Local Government Association	**www.local.gov.uk**
Magistrates' Association	**www.magistrates-association.org.uk**
Maritime and Coastguard Agency	**www.gov.uk/government/organisations/maritime-and-coastguard-agency**
Musician's Union	**https://musiciansunion.org.uk**
National Pubwatch	**https://nationalpubwatch.org.uk**
Security Industry Authority	**www.gov.uk/government/organisations/security-industry-authority**
Portman Group	**www.portmangroup.org.uk**
The Stationery Office	**www.tso.co.uk**
Transport for London	**www.tfl.gov.uk**
UK Hospitality	**www.ukhospitality.org.uk**
Valuation Office Agency	**www.gov.uk/government/organisations/valuation-office-agency**
Wine and Spirit Trade Association	**https://wsta.co.uk**

Index

ABCPA *see* Anti-social Behaviour, Crime
and Policing Act 2014
Advertising
alcohol promotions 7.11.2
Age verification 7.11.2, 8.10, 22.2.4, 22.3
Aircraft
premises licences 7.1.1, 7.1.3
Airports
premises licences 7.1.3
Alcohol
alcohol delivery services 7.1.1
confiscation 21.1.8, 22.1, 22.12
definition 3.2.2
dispensing directly into mouth 7.11.2
drinking games 7.11.2
exposure for unauthorised sale
21.1.1, 21.2.2
fixed prices 11.8
high volume vertical drinking
establishments (HVVDs) 11.9
irresponsible activities involving
7.11.2
keeping on premises for unauthorised
sale 21.1.1, 21.2.3
licensable activities 3.2
liqueur confectionery 3.2.2, 21.9.1,
22.11
minimum prices 7.11.2, 21.9
calculation 21.9.1
prohibition of sale below 21.1.8,
21.9.2
special offers 21.9.3
Wales 21.9
naming and packaging 11.3
online/telephone sales 21.9
operating schedule 8.3.3
promotions and discounts 7.11.2,
11.3, 11.8, 21.9.3
sale by retail 3.2
sale on vehicles in motion 21.1.5,
21.5

statutory measures 7.11.2
supply from community premises
7.11.3
supply to club members 3.3, 17.1
test purchasing 22.3, 22.6.1
weights and measures inspections
22.3, 22.4
wholesale pricing 21.9
**Anti-social Behaviour, Crime and
Policing Act 2014**
closure of premises 23.1, 23.8, 24.1
public spaces protection orders
(PSPOs) 2.5.5
statutory guidance 24.3.15
summary review of premises licence
15.12.1
Appeals 26.1
closure orders 24.3.8, 24.5.6, 26.8
club premises certificates 26.5
conditions, imposition of 26.5.2
general provisions 26.5.6
grant of licence 26.5.2
rejection of application 26.5.1
review application 26.5.4
variation application 18.2.7, 18.8,
26.5.3
withdrawal 26.5.5
costs orders 26.1
court powers 26.1
determination, implementation of
26.10
evidence 26.1, 26.2
giving reasons 26.9
hearings 26.1
High Court
by case stated 26.11.1
judicial review 26.11.2
judicial review 2.6, 26.3
High Court decisions 26.11.2
personal licences 6.13, 26.7

decision not to revoke following objection 26.7.4
general provisions 26.7.5
grant or renewal following objection 26.7.2
rejection of grant 26.7.1
revocation following objection 26.7.3
premises licences 26.4
conditions, imposition of 26.4.2
general provisions 26.4.11
grant of licence 26.4.2
interim authority notice 26.4.8
provisional statements 26.4.9
rejection of application 26.4.1
review 15.8, 15.12.3, 26.4.6
review of interim steps 26.4.10
summary review 26.4.7
transfer of licence 16.5, 16.6, 26.4.5
variation application 14.2.9, 14.3.10, 26.4.3
variation to specify individual as premises supervisor 26.4.4
procedure 26.1, 26.2
provisional statements 13.8.3
respondents 26.1, 26.4.11, 26.7.5
right of appeal 1.5.3
Secretary of State guidance 26.3
statements of licensing policy 26.3
temporary event notices 26.6
time limits 26.4.11, 26.5.6, 26.6, 26.7.5
Armed forces
premises licences 7.1.3
Audiences
private 4.1.1
regulated entertainment 3.4, 4.1.1

Beer gardens
noise from 8.9
regulated entertainment 4.4.1
Best practice guidelines 8.11
Boats 7.1.1
Boxing and wrestling entertainment
operating schedule 8.3.3
regulated entertainment 3.4, 4.2.4
exemptions 4.1.1, 4.3.17
Broadcasting
live broadcasts 4.1.1, 4.3.5
regulated entertainment 4.1.1, 4.3.5
Busking 4.4.2

Car parks 8.9
Carnivals 11.7
CCTV 8.9
Celebrations
relaxation of trading hours for 11.4.2
Charitable events
exempt entertainment 4.3.7
private gain 4.3.7
Charities
premises licences 7.2
Children
age verification 22.2.4, 22.3
reasonable belief defence 22.2.4, 22.3
best practice guidelines 8.11.4
childcare activities 4.4.3
film exhibitions 2.5.7, 4.3.3, 8.10, 11.6
offences involving see Offences involving children
operating schedule 8.3.6, 8.10
protection of 2.5.7, 8.3.6, 8.10, 8.11.4
regulated entertainment 4.4.3
statement of licensing policy 2.5.7
Church halls
premises licences 7.11.3
regulated entertainment 4.1.1
Churches
exempt entertainment 4.3.6
Circuses
regulated entertainment 4.1.1, 4.3.16
Closure of premises 24.1
ABCPA 2014, closure under 23.1, 23.8, 24.1
appeals 26.8
areas experiencing disorder 24.2
cancellation of closure order 24.3.3
closure notices
application to magistrates' court for closure order 24.3.5
cancellation 24.3.3
criteria for issue 24.3.1
duration 24.3.2
opening premises in contravention of 24.3.18
persistent selling of alcohol to children 22.5, 24.1, 24.4
review determination, date of effect 24.3.17
review of premises licence following 24.3.16

Closure of premises – *continued*
    scope of prohibition 24.3.1, 24.3.5
    service 24.3.4, 24.5.8
    unlicensed premises 24.5.1
    variation 24.3.3
  closure orders
    access to other premises, and
      24.3.11
    appeals 24.3.8, 24.5.6
    application to magistrates' court for
      24.3.5, 24.5.2
    cancellation 24.3.3
    costs, reimbursement 24.3.12
    discharge 24.3.7, 24.5.5
    enforcement 24.3.9, 24.5.7
    extension 24.3.6
    opening premises in contravention
      of 24.3.18
    review of premises licence
      following 24.3.16
    scope of 24.3.5
    unlicensed premises 24.5.2,
      24.5.3, 24.5.4, 24.5.5
  compensation 24.3.14
  disorder or nuisance
    closure notices 24.3.1
    premises associated with 24.3
    premises in area experiencing
      disorder 24.2
  magistrates' court powers 24.3.5
  offences
    entering or remaining on premises
      in contravention of closure notice
      24.3.10
    keeping premises open 24.2
    obstruction under ABCPA 2014
      24.3.10
  police immunity from liability for
    damages 24.3.13, 24.6
  premises associated with nuisance or
    disorder 24.3
  premises in area experiencing disorder
    24.2
  review of premises licence following
    closure order 24.3.16
    opening premises in contravention
      of closure following review
      24.3.18
    time of effect of determination
      24.3.17
  statutory guidance 24.3.15
  unlicensed premises 24.5

  appeals 24.5.6
  application for closure order
    24.5.2
  closure notices 24.5.1
  closure orders 24.5.2, 24.5.3,
    24.5.4
  discharge of closure order 24.5.5
  enforcement 24.5.7
  service of notices 24.5.8
  termination of closure orders
    24.5.4
Club premises certificates 1.4.4, 17.2
  appeals 26.5
    conditions, imposition of 26.5.2
    general provisions 26.5.6
    grant of licence 26.5.2
    rejection of application 26.5.1
    review application 26.5.4
    variation applications 18.2.7, 18.8,
      26.5.3
    withdrawal 26.5.5
  applications 17.8
    actions following grant or rejection
      17.10
    advertising 17.8.5
    determination 17.9
    form 17.8.1
    grant 17.10.1
    inspection of premises 17.8.6
    notice of 17.8.5
    process 17.8
    rejection 17.10.2
  associate members
    prohibited conditions 17.11.3
    supply of alcohol 17.4
  benefits 17.1
  change of club name 17.16
  change of registered address 17.17
  club rules, alteration of 17.16
  conditions 1.4.6, 11.1, 17.11
    censorship 11.6
    drinking up time 11.4.1
    film exhibitions 17.11.2
    fixed prices 11.8
    general requirements 11.2
    mandatory conditions 11.1,
      17.11.1, 17.11.2
    plays, performance of 11.5,
      17.11.4
    prohibited conditions 11.1,
      17.11.3, 17.11.4
    proposed conditions 11.2.1

relaxation of trading hours for
special occasions 11.4.2
supply of alcohol 17.11.1
trading hours 11.4
definition 17.2
determination of application 17.9
preliminary determination 17.9.1
relevant representations, and
17.9.3, 17.9.4
unopposed applications 17.9.2
drinking up time 11.4.1
duration 17.14
duty to keep and produce 17.19.2
duty to update 17.19.1
enforcement 1.4.6
entry and search of premises
pending withdrawal of certificate
17.18.3
police powers 17.20
film exhibitions 17.11.2
form 17.12.1
grant of application 17.10.1
inspection of premises 17.8.6, 18.9,
19.11
lapse 17.15
loss 17.13
notification of grant 17.10.1
notification of rejection 17.10.2
opening hours, relaxation of 11.4.2
operating schedule 17.8.1, 17.8.4
personal licences, and 6.2
plays, performance conditions 11.5,
17.11.4
police powers of entry and search
17.20
premises licences, differences from
17.1, 17.8
prohibited conditions 17.11.3,
17.11.4
qualifying clubs
activities 17.2
conditions 17.1, 17.3.1
proprietary clubs, distinguished
from 17.1
supply of alcohol 17.3.2
withdrawal of certificate 17.18.2
regulated entertainment 17.2, 17.3,
17.11.3
rejection of application 17.10.2
relevant representations
applications 10.3.7, 17.9.3, 17.9.4
review 10.3.10

variation applications 10.3.8,
10.3.9, 18.7.3
renewal 17.14
review see Review of club premises
certificates
revocation 1.4.6
summary 17.12.2
supply of alcohol
to associate members 17.4
conditions 17.1, 17.3.2, 17.11.1
to guests 17.1, 17.4
surrender 17.15
suspension 1.4.6, 17.21
theft 17.13
trading hours
conditions 11.4
drinking up time 11.4.1
relaxation for special occasions
11.4.2
updating 17.19.1
validity, period of 17.14
variation see Variation of club
premises certificates
withdrawal 17.14, 17.18
entry and search of premises
17.18.3
following review 17.18.1
licensing authority, by 17.18.2
Clubs 17.1
alcohol, supply to members 3.3, 17.1
associate members 17.4
authorisation of licensable activities
3.6
change of club name 17.16
change of registered address 17.17
club rules, alteration 17.16
definition 17.1
drinking up time 11.4.1
entry and search of premises 17.18.3
police powers 17.20
establishment and conduct in good
faith 17.5
examples 17.1
friendly societies 17.6
guests and visitors 17.1, 17.4
inspection of premises 17.8.6, 18.9,
19.11
late night refreshment, exempt
supplies 5.4.2, 17.1
licensable activities 3.1, 3.3, 3.6
members' clubs 3.3
membership conditions 17.3.1, 17.4

Clubs – *continued*
  miners' welfare institutes 17.7
  proprietary clubs 3.3, 17.1
  qualifying clubs 17.1, 17.3
    activities 3.1, 17.2
    conditions 17.1, 17.3.1
    proprietary clubs, distinguished
      from 17.1
    supply of alcohol 17.1, 17.3.2
  recognised clubs 17.4
  registered societies 17.6
  regulated entertainment 17.2, 17.3,
    17.11.3
  rights of entry 17.1
  supply of alcohol
    to associate members 17.4
    to guests 17.1, 17.4
    to members 17.1, 17.3.2
  temporary membership 17.4
  types 3.3
  working men's clubs 17.6
Coach trips
  sale of alcohol 21.1.5.1
Colleges
  exempt entertainment 4.3.11
  premises licences 7.2
  regulated entertainment 4.3.11
Community premises
  definition 7.11.3
  designated premises supervisor 9.1
  management committees 7.11.3
  premises licences 7.11.3
  regulated entertainment 4.1.1
  supply of alcohol 7.11.3
  variation of licence 14.1
Companies/bodies corporate
  offences by 21.8.1, 22.3, 22.4
Conditions 7.11, 11.1
  alcohol promotions in retail premises
    11.3
  appeals 26.4.2, 26.5.2
  carnivals 11.7
  censorship 11.6
  club premises certificates *see* Club
    premises certificates
  dancing in small premises 11.10
  designated premises supervisors
    7.11.2, 9.1
  discretionary conditions 7.11.7
  excluded activities 7.10.3
  festivals 11.7
  fixed prices 11.8

  general requirements 11.2
  high volume vertical drinking
    establishments (HVVDs) 11.9
  imposed conditions 11.2.2
  large capacity venues 11.9
  licence reviews for music 11.11
  mandatory conditions
    door supervision 7.11.5
    film exhibitions 7.11.4
    premises licensed to sell alcohol
      7.11.2
    supply of alcohol from community
      premises 7.11.3
  modification 15.8
  music, live/recorded 11.11
  operating schedule 11.1
  pavement licences
    no-obstruction 27.5.1
    smoke-free seating 27.5.2
  plays, performance 7.11.6, 11.5
  premises licences *see* Premises
    licences
  prohibited conditions 7.11.6
  proposed conditions 11.2.1
  restrictions on 11.2
  statement of licensing policy 2.5.1
  temporary event notices 11.1
  trading hours 11.4
    drinking up time 11.4.1
    relaxation for celebratory occasions
      11.4.2
Convention rights 1.5.1, 1.5.2
  discrimination, prohibition of 1.5.6
  protection of property 1.5.4
  right to fair trial 1.5.3, 25.15
    applicants for authorisation 1.5.3
    objectors 1.5.3
    reasons for refusal of licence
      7.10.3
    tribunal independence and
      impartiality 1.5.3
  right to respect for private and family
    life 1.5.5
  see also Human Rights Act 1998
Crime
  best practice guidelines 8.11.1
  licensing objections on grounds of
    crime and disorder 7.11.3
  see also Offences; Offences involving
    children
Crown premises
  premises licences 7.1.3

Cumulative impact policies 2.4, 2.5.4

Dance performance
audiences 3.4, 4.1.1
entertainment similar to 4.2.8
incidental to other activities 4.3.4
morris dancing 4.3.8
operating schedule 8.3.3
regulated entertainment 3.4, 4.2.7,
4.3.4, 4.3.10
sexual entertainment venue, in 4.3.10
spontaneous performance 4.1.1
Dancing
small premises 11.10
Designated premises supervisors 9.1
appeals 26.4.4
appointment 9.3
change of 9.4, 14.1
appeals 26.4.4
application 9.4
determination 9.4.8
effect of 9.4.7
notice of application 9.4.5
notification of decision 9.4.9
objections 9.4.6
conditions 9.1
eligible persons 9.2
exception 9.1
personal licences 6.1
police objections 9.4.6, 9.5
premises licences 7.11.2
purpose 9.1, 9.2
removal of, request for 9.6
transfer of premises licence 16.4,
16.6
Disclosure and Barring Service (DBS)
basic DBS certificate 6.11.4, 6.11.5
standard DBS certificate 6.11.4,
6.11.6
Discrimination
disability access, pavement licences
27.5.1, 27.7
equality, promotion of
statement of licensing policy
2.5.10
prohibition of 1.5.6
Door supervision
door supervisor licensing 7.11.5
premises licences, mandatory
conditions 7.11.5
Drinking games 7.11.2
Drinking up time 8.4, 11.4.1

Drunkenness and disorderly conduct *see*
Offences

**Early morning alcohol restriction orders
(EMROs)** 23.1
advertising 23.3
affected persons/premises 23.3
alternative measures 23.1
cumulative impact policies, and 2.5.4
determination 23.5
effect on other authorisations 23.8
enforcement 23.8
exceptions 23.7
hearings 23.5
local authority powers 23.2
notification of 23.4
procedural requirements 23.3
process 23.4
purpose 23.1
relevant representations 23.3
revocation 23.6
variation 23.6
Educational establishments
premises licences 7.2
regulated entertainment 4.1.1, 4.2.2,
4.3.1
childcare activities 4.4.3
exemptions 4.3.11, 4.4.3
Enforcement
closure orders 24.3.9, 24.5.7
early morning alcohol restriction
orders 23.8
test purchases 22.3
weights and measures inspections
22.3, 22.4
see also Closure of premises;
Offences; Offences involving
children
Entertainment *see* Regulated
entertainment
Entitlement to work in United Kingdom
immigration penalty 6.12
immigration objection notices 6.15
record on licence 6.9
personal licences 6.5, 6.9, 6.12, 6.15
premises licences 7.2.1, 7.2.5
relevant representations, secretary of
State for Home Office 10.2.1
Equality, promotion of
disability access, pavement licences
27.5.1, 27.7
statement of licensing policy 2.5.10

European Convention on Human Rights
  see Convention rights
Exclusion orders 21.10

Fair trial *see* Convention rights
False statements
  offence of making 21.1.6, 21.6
Family life
  right to respect for 1.5.5
Fast food vans
  premises licences 7.1.1
Festivals
  conditions 11.7
Fights *see* Boxing and wrestling
  entertainment
Film exhibitions 3.4
  advertisement purposes 4.1.1, 4.3.1
  censorship 11.6
  children, and 2.5.7, 4.3.3, 8.10, 11.6,
    17.11.2
  club premises certificates 17.11.2
  community premises 4.3.3
  definition 4.2.2
  educational purposes 4.1.1, 4.3.1
  film classification 7.11.4
  incidental to other activities 4.1.1,
    4.3.4
  informational purposes 4.1.1, 4.3.1
  museums and art galleries 4.1.1,
    4.2.2, 4.3.2
  operating schedule 8.3.3
  premises licences, mandatory
    conditions 7.11.4
  regulated entertainment 4.2.2
    exemptions 4.1.1, 4.2.2, 4.3.1,
      4.3.3, 4.3.4
  statement of licensing policy 2.5.7
Fines, scale of App.C
Fire safety
  risk assessments 8.8
Friendly societies 17.6

Garages
  premises licences 7.1.2
Garden fêtes
  exempt entertainment 4.1.1, 4.3.7

Happy hours 7.11.2
Health and Safety Executive
  public safety responsibility 8.8
Health bodies
  relevant representations 10.2.1

Hearings 25.1
  action following receipt of notice
    25.4
  appeals 26.1
  attendance and participation 25.8,
    25.10
  decision-making 25.11
  dispensing with 25.5
  EMROs 23.5
  failure of parties to attend 25.10
  Human Rights Act 1998, impact of
    25.15
  irregularities 25.13
  notice of 25.3
  notices 25.14
  procedure 25.9
  reasons for 25.1
  record-keeping 25.12
  requirements 25.1, 25.2
  time limits and extensions 25.7
  timing 25.2
  withdrawal of representation 25.6
High Court
  appeals to 26.11
**High volume vertical drinking
  establishments (HVVDs)** 11.9
Hospitals and healthcare premises
  premises licences 7.2
  regulated entertainment 4.1.1, 4.3.11
Hotels
  late night refreshment 5.4.2
Hours of trading *see* Trading hours
Hovercraft
  premises licences 7.1.1, 7.1.3
Hoverports
  premises licences 7.1.3
Human Rights Act 1998 1.5.1
  hearings 25.15
  licensing policy, challenging 2.6
  public authorities 1.5.1
  see also Convention rights

Immigration *see* Entitlement to work in
  United Kingdom
Indoor sporting events
  audiences 3.4, 4.1.1
  incidental music 4.3.4
  'indoor,' definition 4.2.3
  operating schedule 8.3.3
  regulated entertainment 3.4, 4.1.1,
    4.2.3

Inspection of premises
  club premises certificates 17.8.6
    review 19.11
    variation 18.9
  premises licences 7.9, 13.10
    review of premises licences 15.11
Interim authorities 12.1
  appeals 26.4.8
  cancellation following objections
    12.5
  due diligence defence 12.1
  eligibility criteria for obtaining 12.2
  interim notice
    applications 12.3
    effect of 12.4
    form 12.3.1
    lapse 12.4
  notification of police 12.2
  reinstatement of lapsed licence 12.1,
    12.6
  time limits 12.2

Judicial review
  licensing policy 2.6, 26.3
    High Court decisions 26.11.2
  statement of licensing policy 2.6

Late night levy 2.15
  charge and collection 2.15.4
  consultation 2.15.1
  exemptions 2.15.2
  introduction procedures 2.15.1
  reductions 2.15.3
  revenue 2.15.4
Late night refreshment 5.1
  clubs 5.4.2, 17.1
  designated areas, premises and times
    5.4.1
  employees, for 5.4.2
  exempt supplies 3.1, 5.4, 5.4.4
  hot food or drink 5.3
  hotels 5.4.2
  licensable activities 3.1, 3.5, 5.1
  meaning 3.5, 5.2
  operating schedule 8.3.3
  premises licensed under other statutes
    5.4.3
Licensable activities 3.1
  authorisation 3.6
  civil rights of persons involved in
    1.5.3
  definition 3.1

  late night refreshment 3.5
  permitted temporary activities 20.2
  regulated entertainment 3.4, 4.1–4.4
  retail sale of alcohol 3.2
  supply of alcohol to clubs/club
    members 3.3
  types 3.1
  see also Unauthorised licensable
    activities
Licensing Act 2003
  background 1.1, 1.2
  club premises certificates 1.4.4
  divisions 1.3
  enforcement 1.4.6
  licensable activities 3.1–3.6
  Licensing authorities 1.4.1
  licensing objectives 1.3
  offences 1.4.7
  overview 1.1, 1.3, 1.4
  personal licences 1.4.2
  premises licences 1.4.3
  representation form App.B
  temporary event notices 1.4.5
Licensing authorities 1.4.1
  administration, exercise and
    delegation of functions 2.5.11
  areas 2.2
  committees *see* Licensing committees
  cumulative impact policies 2.4, 2.5.4
  definition 2.2
  enforcement powers 1.4.6
  general duties 2.3
  information control and disclosure
    2.13
  late night levy *see* Late night levy
  licensing policy *see* Statement of
    licensing policy
  licensing register 2.8
  Ministerial guidance 2.12
  notices procedures 2.14
  notification to persons with interest in
    premises 2.9
  prejudicial interest 1.5.3
  relevant representations 10.2.1
  responsibilities, reasons for 2.1
  temporary event notices (TENs) 20.3
  withdrawal of club premises
    certificates 17.18.2
Licensing committees 2.7
  delegation of functions 2.5.11
  prejudicial interest 1.5.3
  proceedings 2.5.10

Licensing committees – *continued*
Statement of licensing policy 2.5.11
Licensing hours
statement of licensing policy 2.5.6
Licensing hours orders 11.4.2
Licensing register 2.8
notification to persons with interest in premises 2.9
Licensing statement *see* Statement of licensing policy
Local authority premises
regulated entertainment 4.3.11
Lotteries 7.1.4

Market squares 11.7
Marquees
premises licences 7.1.1
Miners' welfare institutes 17.7
Morris dancing 4.3.8
Moveable structures
premises licences 7.1.1
Museums and art galleries
film exhibitions 4.1.1, 4.2.2, 4.3.2
regulated entertainment 4.1.1, 4.2.2, 4.3.1
Music
incidental to other activities 4.1.1, 4.3.4
live performance 3.4, 4.2.5
audiences 4.1.1
beer gardens 4.4.1
busking 4.4.2
entertainment similar to 4.2.8
exemptions 4.3.13
licence condition reviews 11.1
licensed venues 4.3.13
operating schedule 8.3.3
private homes and gardens 4.1.2
unamplified music 4.3.15
workplaces 4.3.14
operating schedule 8.3.3
pop festivals 11.7
recorded music 3.4, 4.2.6
entertainment similar to 4.2.8
licence condition reviews 11.1
operating schedule 8.3.3
private homes and gardens 4.1.2
regulated entertainment exemption 4.1.1
regulated entertainment 3.4, 4.1.1, 4.1.2, 4.2.5, 4.2.6, 4.2.8
community premises 4.3.12

exemptions 4.1.1, 4.3.6, 4.3.14, 4.3.15
vehicles in motion 4.3.9
religious services 4.3.6
small premises 11.10
spontaneous performance 4.1.1

National security
premises licences 7.1.3
Noise
best practice guidelines 8.11.3
impact assessments 8.8
operating schedule 8.8, 8.9
prevention 8.9

Offences 1.4.7, 21.1
certificates
criminal conviction certificate (basic DBS) 6.11.4, 6.11.5
criminal record certificate (standard DBS) 6.11.4, 6.11.6
children, involving *see* Offences involving children
closure of premises
entering or remaining on premises 24.3.10
keeping premises open 24.2
obstruction under ABCPA 2014 24.3.10
companies/bodies corporate 21.8.1, 22.3
confiscation of alcohol 21.1.8
continuation of licensable activities following death of licensee 12.1
drunkenness and disorderly conduct 21.1.2, 21.3
allowing on licensed premises 21.1.2, 21.3.1
drunk, meaning 21.3.2
failure to leave licensed premises 21.1.2, 21.3.4
knowledge requirement 21.3.1, 21.3.2
obtaining alcohol for person who is drunk 21.1.2, 21.3.3
sale of alcohol to person who is drunk 21.1.2, 21.3.2
due diligence defence 21.2.4, 21.9.2
exclusion orders 21.10
false statements 21.1.6, 21.6
fines, scale of App.C
jurisdiction 21.8.5

keeping open premises subject to closure order 24.2

obstruction of authorised officer 20.15

overseas bodies 21.8.4

partnerships 21.8.2, 22.3

prosecutions
jurisdiction and proceedings 21.8.5
procedure 21.7

right of entry to investigate
licensable activities 21.2.5
offences 21.2.6

sale of alcohol, and
to children *see* Offences involving children
exposing for unauthorised sale 21.1.1, 21.2.2
keeping on premises for unauthorised sale 21.1.1, 21.2.3
minimum pricing 21.1.8, 21.9
obtaining for person who is drunk 21.1.2, 21.3.3
to person who is drunk 21.1.2, 21.3.2
on vehicles in motion 21.1.5, 21.5

smuggled goods 21.1.3, 21.4

unauthorised licensable activities 21.1.1, 21.2
due diligence defence 21.2.4
exposing alcohol for unauthorised sale 21.1.1, 21.2.2
keeping alcohol on premises for unauthorised sale 21.1.1, 21.2.3
knowledge requirement 21.2.1
regulated entertainment 21.2.1
right of entry to investigate 21.2.5, 21.2.6
scope of offences 21.2.1

unincorporated associations 21.8.3, 21.8.5, 22.3

vehicles and trains, on 21.1.5, 21.5

Offences involving children 21.1.4, 22.1
age verification, reasonable steps 22.2.4, 22.3
confiscation of alcohol 22.1, 22.12
consumption of alcohol by children 21.1.4, 22.7.1
allowing 22.7.2
children under five years 21.1.8
liqueur confectionery 22.11
purchase for 22.6.3

delivering alcohol to children 21.1.4, 22.8

giving intoxicating liquor to children under five 21.1.8, 22.11

persons who can commit offences 22.3, 22.4, 22.8, 22.10

purchase of alcohol
by a child 21.1.4, 22.6.1
for a child 21.1.4, 22.6.2, 22.6.3
for consumption by a child 22.6.3
test purchasing 22.6.1

reasonable belief defence 22.2.4, 22.3

'responsible person,' definition 22.10

sale of alcohol to children 21.1.4, 22.3
allowing 21.1.4, 22.4
persistent selling 21.1.4, 22.5, 24.1, 24.4
persons who can commit offence 22.3, 22.4
reasonable belief defence 22.2.4, 22.3, 22.5
test purchasing 22.3
unsupervised sales to children, prohibition 21.1.4, 22.10

sending child to obtain alcohol 21.1.4, 22.9

unaccompanied children, prohibition from certain premises 21.1.4, 22.2
persons who can commit offence 22.2.3
prohibited premises 22.2.1, 22.2.2

unsupervised sales to children, prohibition 21.1.4, 22.10

Operating schedule 8.1
alcohol, supply of 8.3.3
best practice guidelines 8.11
boxing and wrestling 8.3.3
children, protection of 8.3.6, 8.10
club premises certificates 17.8.1, 17.8.4
conditions 11.1
contents 8.2
crime and disorder prevention 8.7
dance performance 8.3.3
film exhibitions 8.3.3
hours open to public 8.3.7, 8.4
indoor or outdoor activities 8.3.2
indoor sporting events 8.3.3
late night refreshment 8.3.3
licensing objectives 8.3.8, 8.5

Operating schedule – *continued*
   music, live/recorded 8.3.3
   non-standard timings 8.3.4
   opening hours 8.3.5, 8.3.7, 8.4
   play performance 8.3.3
   preparation 8.5
   public nuisance prevention 8.9
   public safety 8.8
   purpose 8.1
   risk assessment 8.5, 8.6
     toolkit App.A
   seasonal variations 8.3.4
   standard form
     completion 8.3
     indoor or outdoor activities 8.3.2
     licensed activities 8.3.1
     opening hours 8.3.1
     type and frequency of activities
       8.3.3
Overseas bodies
   offences by 21.8.4

Partnerships
   offences by 21.8.2, 22.3, 22.4
Pavement licences 27.1, 27.2
   amendment 27.9
   applications 27.3
     advertising 27.6
     determination 27.7
     public consultation 27.6
   conditions 27.5
     no-obstruction 27.5.1
     smoke-free seating 27.5.2
   disability access, non-discrimination
     27.5.1, 27.7
   duration 27.8
   enforcement 27.9
   fees 27.4
   furniture
     definition 27.2
     no-obstruction requirement 27.5.1
     removal 27.10
   notices, display 27.6
   planning permission 27.1
   plans 27.3
   relevant highway 27.2
   renewal 27.3
   revocation 27.9
   surrender 27.8
Permitted temporary activities 20.1
   meaning 20.2

   see also Temporary event notices
     (TENs)
Personal licences 1.4.2
   accredited licensing qualifications
     6.10
   appeals 6.13, 26.7
     decision not to revoke following
       objection 26.7.4
     general provisions 26.7.5
     grant or renewal following
       objection 26.7.2
     rejection of grant 26.7.1
     revocation following objection
       26.7.3
   applications
     appeals 6.13
     applicants 6.3, 6.5
     convictions during applications
       process 6.15
     determination 6.7
     entitlement to work in United
       Kingdom 6.5
     form 6.6
     grant 6.7.1, 6.7.3
     immigration objection notices 6.15
     notification of grant or refusal 6.8
     objection notices 6.15
     procedure 6.4, 6.6
     refusal 6.7.2
     relevant licensing authority 6.4
   changes, duty to notify 6.19
   convictions during application process
     6.15
   convictions during currency of licence
     6.16
     forfeiture of licence 6.16.2
     notification of court 6.16.1
     notification of relevant licensing
       authority 6.16.3, 6.16.4
     revocation of licence 6.16.5
     suspension of licence 6.16.2,
       6.16.5
   convictions for relevant offence/
     foreign offence 6.11
     criminal conviction certificate
       (basic DBS certificate) 6.11.4,
       6.11.5
     criminal record certificate (standard
       DBS certificate) 6.11.5, 6.11.6
     establishing a conviction 6.11.4
     foreign offence 6.11.2
     record on licence 6.9

relevant offence 6.11.1
spent convictions 6.11.3
subject access searches 6.11.7
definition 6.2
designated premises supervisors 6.1
determination of application 6.7
discretionary grant 6.7.3
duration 6.14
duty to produce licence 6.21
entitlement to work in United
    Kingdom 6.5
forfeiture 6.16.2
immigration penalty 6.12
    immigration objection notices 6.15
    record on licence 6.9
issuing of 6.9
licensing qualifications 6.10
loss 6.18
mandatory grant 6.7.1
mandatory refusal 6.7.2
notification of grant or refusal 6.8
refusal 6.7.2
renewal 6.14
requirement for 6.1
revocation 6.14, 6.15, 6.16.5
surrender 6.17
suspension 6.14, 6.16.2, 6.16.5
theft 6.18
updating 6.20
validity 6.1
Petrol filling stations
premises licences 7.1.2
Places of worship
exempt entertainment 4.3.6
Play performance
audiences 3.4, 4.1.1
censorship 11.5
club premises certificates 17.11.4
conditions 11.5, 17.11.4
operating schedule 8.3.3
prohibited conditions 7.11.6, 17.11.4
regulated entertainment 3.4, 4.1.1,
    4.2.1
Police
objections by 9.4.6, 9.5
relevant representations 10.2.1
right of entry to investigate
    unauthorised licensable activities/
    offences 21.2.5
Pop festivals
conditions 11.7

**Portman Group Code of Practice on
Naming, Packaging and Promotion of
Alcoholic Drinks** 11.3
Ports
premises licences 7.1.3
Posters and flyers 7.11.2
Premises licences 1.4.3
advertising of application, by
    applicant 7.6
    display at/on premises 7.6.1
    notice contents 7.6.3
    publication in local newspaper
        7.6.2
advertising of application, by
    licensing authority 7.7
age verification 7.11.2
airports and aircraft 7.1.3
alcohol delivery services 7.1.1
alcohol promotions and discounts
    7.11.2
'any place,' definition 7.1.1
appeals 26.4
    conditions, imposition of 26.4.2
    general provisions 26.4.11
    grant of licence 26.4.2
    interim authority notice 26.4.8
    provisional statement 26.4.9
    provisional statements 13.8.3
    rejection of application 26.4.1
    review 15.8, 15.12.3, 26.4.6
    review of interim steps 26.4.10
    summary review 26.4.7
    transfer of licence 16.5, 16.6,
        26.4.5
    variation application 26.4.3
    variation applications 14.2.9,
        14.3.10
    variation to specify individual as
        premises supervisor 26.4.4
applications
    advertising, by applicant 7.6
    advertising, by licensing authority
        7.7
    applicants 7.2
    business involving licensable
        activities 7.2.1
    conditions 1.4.3
    determination 7.10
    electronic applications 7.4.2, 7.4.3,
        7.8
    entitlement to work in United
        Kingdom 7.2.1, 7.2.5

Premises licences – *continued*
forms 7.4
inspection of premises 7.9, 13.10
joint applications 7.2.2
multiple licences 7.2.3
notice to responsible authorities
7.8
notification of grant or refusal 7.12
operating schedule 7.4.1
plan of premises 7.5
procedure 7.3, 7.4.2, 7.4.3
relevant representations 7.10.3,
10.3.1
revocation 1.4.6
shadow licences 7.2.4
suspension 1.4.6
unopposed applications 7.10.2
armed forces premises 7.1.3
authorisation of licensable activities
3.6
change of name or address 7.18.1,
14.4
conditions 1.4.3, 7.11, 11.1
alcohol promotions in retail
premises 11.3
carnivals 11.7
censorship 11.6
dancing in small premises 11.10
designated premises supervisors
9.1
discretionary conditions 7.11.7
drinking up time 11.4.1
excluded activities 7.10.3
festivals 11.7
fixed prices 11.8
general requirements 11.2
high volume vertical drinking
establishments (HVVDs) 11.9
imposed conditions 11.2.2
large capacity venues 11.9
licence reviews for music 11.11
mandatory conditions 7.11.2,
7.11.4, 7.11.5, 11.1
modification during review 15.8
music, live/recorded 11.11
operating schedule 11.1
plays, performance of 11.5
prohibited conditions 7.11.6, 11.1
proposed conditions 11.2.1
relaxation of trading hours, special
occasions 11.4.2
restrictions on 11.2

supply of alcohol from community
premises 7.11.3
trading hours 11.4
Crown premises 7.1.3
designated premises supervisors
7.11.2, 9.1
determination of licence
applications with relevant
representations 7.10.3
conditions 7.10.3
hearings 7.10.3
notification of reasons 7.10.3
preliminary determination 7.10.1
unopposed applications 7.10.2
door supervision 7.11.5
duration 7.15
duty to keep/produce 7.19
enforcement 1.4.6
excluded premises 7.1.2
exempt premises 7.1.1, 7.1.3
form of licence 7.13
garages 7.1.2
grant 7.10.3, 7.12
inspection of premises 7.9, 13.10
review of premises licences 15.11
interim authorities *see* Interim
authorities
journeys 7.1.3
lapse 7.16, 12.1
lapsed licences 12.1, 12.6
licensable activities 7.1.1
loss 7.14
lotteries exemption 7.1.4
mandatory conditions
door supervision 7.11.5
film exhibitions 7.11.4
premises licensed to sell alcohol
7.11.2
supply of alcohol from community
premises 7.11.3
meaning 7.1
moveable structures 7.1.1
national security exemption 7.1.3
notice of licence
contents 7.6.3
display at/on premises 7.6.1
publication in local newspaper
7.6.2
notification of grant or refusal 7.12
operating schedule *see* Operating
schedule
outside activities 7.1.1

petrol filling stations 7.1.2
ports, hoverports and wharves 7.1.3
'premises,' definition 7.1.1, 13.2
primary use considerations 7.1.2
prohibited conditions 7.11.6, 11.1
refusal 7.10.3, 7.12
reinstatement of lapsed licence 12.1,
 12.6
rejection 7.10.3
relevant representations 15.12.3
 applications 10.3.1
 provisional statements 10.3.2
 review after closure order 10.3.6
 review applications 10.3.5, 10.3.6,
  15.8, 15.10
 summary reviews in cases of crime
  or disorder 15.12.3
 variation applications 10.3.3,
  10.3.4, 14.3.8
review of see Review of premises
 licences
roads 7.1.2
Royal palaces 7.1.3
shops 7.1.2
summary of licence 7.13
summary reviews in cases of crime or
 disorder 15.12.3
surrender 7.17
suspension 1.4.6, 7.20
theft 7.14
transfer see Transfer of premises
 licences
updating 7.18
vehicles and vessels 7.1.1, 7.1.3
vehicles in motion 7.1.3
village fêtes 7.1.1
warehouses 7.1.1
Private gain
 definition 4.3.7
Private homes and gardens
 'domestic premises', definition
  4.3.11
 live music performances 4.1.1, 4.1.2
Private life
 right to respect for 1.5.5
Prizes and rewards 7.11.2
Promotional offers, alcohol 7.11.2
Property, protection of
 Convention rights 1.5.4
Prosecutions
 alcohol related offences, for 21.7

Provisional statements 13.1
 advertising 13.6
 appeals 13.8.3, 26.4.9
 applicants 13.3
 applications
  form 13.5.1
  premises relevant 13.2
  process 13.4, 13.5
  schedule of works 13.5.1
 determination of application 13.8
  applications involving
   representations 13.8.3
  preliminary determinations 13.8.1
  unopposed applications 13.8.2
 notice to responsible authorities 13.7
 power to inspect premises 13.10
 preliminary determination 13.8.1
 relevant premises 13.2
 relevant representations 10.3.2,
  13.8.3
 requirement for 13.1
 restrictions on representations 13.9
 subsequent actions 13.9
 unopposed applications 13.8.2
Public authorities
 Convention rights, and 1.5.1
 Human Rights Act 1998, and 1.5.1
 meaning 1.5.1
Public nuisance
 best practice guidelines 8.11.3
 noise see Noise
 operating schedule 8.9
Public safety
 best practice guidelines 8.11.2
 operating schedule 8.8
Public spaces protection orders (PSPOs)
 2.5.5

Radio receivers
 exempt entertainment 4.3.5
Railway vehicles
 definition 21.5.2
 premises licences 7.1.1, 7.1.3
 sale of alcohol on 21.1.5, 21.5.2
Registered societies
 clubs 17.6
Regulated entertainment
 audiences 3.4, 4.1.1
 beer gardens 4.4.1
 boxing and wrestling 3.4, 4.1.1,
  4.2.4, 4.3.17
 busking 4.4.2

Regulated entertainment – *continued*
  childcare activities 4.4.3
  circuses 4.3.16
  club premises certificates 17.2, 17.3,
    17.11.3
  clubs 17.2
  community premises 4.3.12
  conditions 3.4
  dance *see* Dance performance
  educational facilities 4.3.11
  'entertainment,' definition 3.4, 4.1.1,
    4.2.9
  entertainment facilities 4.1
  exemptions 4.1.1, 4.3
  film exhibitions 4.1.1, 4.2.2, 4.3.1,
    4.3.2, 4.3.3
  hospitals and healthcare premises
    4.3.11
  indoor sporting events 3.4, 4.1.1,
    4.2.3
  licensable activities 3.1, 3.4, 4.1–4.4
  live television broadcasts 4.3.5
  museums and art galleries 4.1.1,
    4.2.2, 4.3.2
  music *see* Music
  particular premises/events 4.4
  play performance 3.4, 4.1.1, 4.2.1
  pre-recorded television broadcasts
    4.3.5
  private events 4.1.1, 4.1.2, 4.4.4
  provision 3.4, 4.1–4.4
  rehearsal halls 4.1.1
  requirements 4.1.2
  schools and colleges 4.3.11
  sexual entertainment venue 4.3.10
  street performance 4.4.2
  types of entertainment 4.2
  unauthorised licensable activities
    21.2.1
Rehearsal halls
  regulated entertainment 4.1.1
Relevant representations 10.1
  advice 10.4.3
  club premises certificates
    applications 10.3.7, 17.9.3, 17.9.4
    review 10.3.10, 19.10
    variation applications 10.3.8,
      10.3.9, 18.7.3
  EMROs 23.3
  evidence supporting 10.4.4
  form of 10.4.2, 10.4.3

  frivolous representations 10.2.1,
    10.2.4
  health bodies 10.2.1
  knowledge of application 10.4.1
  licensing authorities 10.2.1
  other persons 10.2.1
  police representations 10.2.1
  premises licences
    applications 10.3.1
    provisional statements 10.3.2
    review after closure order 10.3.6
    review applications 10.3.5, 10.3.6,
      15.8, 15.10
    summary reviews in cases of crime
      or disorder 15.12.3
    variation applications 10.3.3,
      10.3.4, 14.3.8
  prescribed period, within 10.2.2
  procedure for making 10.4
  provisional statement applications
    10.3.2
  relevance 10.2.4
  requirement not to be withdrawn
    10.2.3
  responsible authorities 10.2.1
  review of premises licences 15.8,
    15.10
  Secretary of State for Home Office
    10.2.1
  variation of club premises certificate
    18.7.3
  vexatious representations 10.2.1,
    10.2.4
  in writing 10.4.2
Religious services
  exempt entertainment 4.3.6
Responsible authorities
  notification of
    premises licences 7.8
    provisional statements 13.7
    review of club premises certificates
      19.5.4
    variation of club premises
      certificate 18.2.4, 18.6
    variation of premises licence
      14.2.6, 14.3.7
  relevant representations 10.2.1
Review of club premises certificates
19.1
  appeals 26.5.4
  applicants 19.2
  applications

advertising 19.6
determination 19.8
form 19.5
inspection of premises 19.11
notice to responsible authorities
19.5.4
process 19.4
rejection 19.7
relevant representations 19.10
timing 19.3
inspection of premises 19.11
notification of decision 19.9
withdrawal of certificate 17.18.1
Review of premises licences 15.1
appeals 15.8, 15.12.3, 26.4.10
applicants 15.2
applications
advertising 15.5.4, 15.6
determination 15.8
form 15.5
notice to licence holder 15.5.4
notice to responsible authorities
15.5.4
notification 15.9
process 15.4
rejection 15.7
timing 15.3
closure order, following 15.1
crime or disorder, following 15.1,
15.12
criteria for 15.1
following closure order 24.3.16
opening premises in contravention
of closure following review
24.3.18
time of effect of determination
24.3.17
frivolous grounds 15.7
identical or substantially similar
grounds 15.7
illegal working compliance order,
following 15.1
inspection of premises 15.11
modification of licence conditions
15.8
notification of decision 15.9
proportionality 15.9
relevant representations 15.8, 15.10,
15.12.3
summary reviews in cases of crime or
disorder 15.1, 15.12
applications 15.12.1

hearing following review notice
15.12.3
interim steps pending review
15.12.2
relevant representations 15.12.3
review of interim steps 15.12.4
vexatious grounds 15.7
Risk assessments
fire safety 8.8
operating schedule 8.6
toolkit App.A
Roads
premises licences 7.1.2
Royal palaces
premises licences 7.1.3

Schools
premises licences 7.2
regulated entertainment 4.3.11
Seaside promenades 11.7
Secretary of State for the Home Office
appeals guidance 26.3
notification of transfer of premises
licence 16.3.4
relevant representations 10.2.1
Security activity, meaning 7.11.5
Sexual entertainment venue
exempt entertainment 4.3.10
Shops
premises licences 7.1.2
Smoking/non-smoking areas 27.5.2
Sporting activities
irresponsible promotions 7.11.2
Sporting events
boxing and wrestling entertainment
3.4, 4.1.1, 4.2.4, 4.3.17, 8.3.3
indoor sporting events *see* Indoor
sporting events
operating schedule 8.3.3
regulated entertainment 3.4, 4.1.1,
4.2.4, 4.3.17
Stand-up comedy
exempt entertainment 4.1.1
Statement of licensing policy 1.4.1, 2.4
administration, exercise and
delegation of functions 2.5.11
challenging 2.6
children 2.5.7
consultation 2.4
content 2.5
cumulative impact policy 2.4, 2.5.4
enforcement 2.5.2

Statement of licensing policy – *continued*
  entertainment provision 2.5.3
  equality, promotion of 2.5.10
  film exhibitions 2.5.7
  five year period 2.4
  integration with other policies 2.5.8
  judicial review 2.6
  licence conditions 2.5.1
  licensing hours 2.5.6
  planning and building control 2.5.9
  public spaces protection orders
    (PSPOs) 2.5.5
  statutory obligations 1.4.1, 2.4
Street performances 4.4.2

Television
  live broadcasts 4.1.1, 4.3.5
  regulated entertainment 4.1.1, 4.3.5
Temporary event notices (TENs) 1.4.5
  acknowledgment by licensing
    authority 20.10
  appeals 26.6
  applications
    late temporary event notice 20.8
    limitations on number of 20.1
    notice periods 20.7
    process 20.6, 20.8
    standard temporary event notice
      20.7
  associates, notice given by 20.9
  authorised officers, rights of entry
    20.15
  conditions 11.1
    imposed following objection 20.13.1
    statement of 20.13.1, 20.16, 20.17
  counter notices 20.10, 20.14.5
  duty to keep and produce 20.16
  entry, right of 20.15
  event periods
    definition 20.6
    duration 20.1, 20.6
    minimum period between 20.1,
      20.9
  form and content 20.6
  intervention rights 20.1
  late notice
    applications 20.8
    objections and counter notices
      20.12.2
  loss 20.17
  notice periods 2.08, 20.7
  notifications

  to local authority 20.7, 20.8
  to police 20.7, 20.8
  objections 20.12
    conditions imposed following
      20.13.1
    counter notices 20.12.2, 20.12.3
    late notice 20.12.2
    modification following 20.13
    by relevant person 20.12.1
    standard notice 20.12.3, 20.13
  permitted limits 20.14
    calculation 20.14.4
    counter notices 20.14.5
    individual premises 20.14.3
    non-personal licence holders
      20.14.2
    personal licence holders 20.14.1
  'permitted temporary activities,'
    definition 20.2
  persons entitled to grant 20.1, 20.5
  relevant licensing authority 20.3
  relevant person 20.4
  scale of event 20.1
  standard notice
    applications 20.7
    conditions imposed following
      objection 20.13.1
    modification following objection
      20.13
    objections and counter notices
      20.12.3
    statement of conditions 20.13.1
    duty to keep and produce 20.16
    loss or theft 20.17
    theft 20.17
  withdrawal 20.11
Tents and marquees
  premises licences 7.1.1
Trading hours
  conditions 11.4
  drinking up time 8.4, 11.4.1
  operating schedule 8.3.1
  relaxation for special occasions
    11.4.2
Trains
  premises licences 7.1.1, 7.1.3
  prohibition of sale of alcohol on
    21.1.5, 21.5.2
  'railway vehicle,' definition 21.5.2
Transfer of premises licences 16.1
  appeals 16.5, 16.6, 26.4.5
  applicants 16.2

applications
  consent of current licence holder
    16.4
  determination 16.5, 16.6
  notification of relevant authorities
    16.3.4
  objections 16.3.5
  process 16.3
date of effect of transfer 16.6
determination 16.5
  crime prevention hearings 16.5
  notification 16.6
interim effect 16.4
notifications
  to designated premises supervisor
    16.4, 16.6
  to police 16.3.4
  to Secretary of State 16.3.4
police objections 16.3.5
rejection 16.6

Unauthorised licensable activities
21.1.1, 21.2
  due diligence defence 21.2.4
  exposing alcohol for unauthorised sale
    21.1.1, 21.2.2
  keeping alcohol on premises for
    unauthorised sale 21.1.1, 21.2.3
  knowledge requirement 21.2.1
  regulated entertainment 21.2.1
  right of entry
    to investigate licensable activities
      21.2.5
    to investigate offences 21.2.6
  scope of offences 21.2.1
Unincorporated associations
  offences by 21.8.3, 21.8.5, 22.3, 22.4
Universities
  premises licences 7.2
Unlicensed premises
  closure 24.5

Variation of club premises certificate
18.1
  advertising 18.5
    by applicant 18.5.1
    by licensing authority 18.5.2
    minor variations 18.2.3
  appeals 18.8
    minor variations 18.2.7
  applications
    advertising 18.5

    determination 18.7
    form 18.4
    minor variations 18.2
    process 18.3, 18.4
  determination of application 18.7
    preliminary determination 18.7.1
    relevant representations 18.7.3
    unopposed applications 18.7.2
  inspection of premises 18.9
  minor variations
    advertising an application 18.2.3
    appeals 18.2.7
    determination of application
      18.2.5
    form 18.2.1
    notification of decision 18.2.6
    notification of responsible
      authorities 18.2.4
    process 18.2
  notifications
    of decision 18.8
    to responsible authorities 18.6
  relevant representations 18.7.3
Variation of premises licences 14.1
  appeals 14.2.9, 14.3.10, 26.4.3
  change of designated premises
    supervisor 9.4, 14.1
  change of name or address 14.4
  full variation 14.3
    advertising an application 14.3.5,
      14.3.6
    appeals 14.3.10
    determination 14.3.8
    form and content 14.3.1–14.3.4
    notice to responsible authorities
      14.3.7
    notification of decision 14.3.9
    relevant representations 14.3.8
  minor variations 14.2
    advertising an application 14.2.5
    appeals 14.2.9
    determination 14.2.7
    form and content 14.2.2–14.2.4
    notice to responsible authorities
      14.2.6
    notification of decision 14.2.8
  preliminary determination 14.3.8
  relevant representations 10.3.3,
    10.3.4, 14.3.8
  unopposed applications 14.3.8
Vehicles
  definition 7.1.1, 21.5.1, 21.5.2

Vehicles – *continued*
  premises licences 7.1.1
Vehicles in motion
  premises licences 7.1.1, 7.1.3
  prohibition of sale of alcohol 21.1.5,
  21.5.1
    coach trips 21.5.1
    defences 21.5.1
    trains 21.1.5.2
  regulated entertainment 4.1.1, 4.3.9
Vessels
  premises licences 7.1.1, 7.1.3
Village fêtes 7.1.1
Village greens 11.7
Village halls
  premises licences 7.11.3

regulated entertainment 4.1.1

Wales
  alcohol, minimum pricing 21.9
    calculation 21.9.1, 21.9.2
    offence of sale below 21.9.2
    special offers 21.9.3
Water, free provision 7.11.2
Websites App.D
**White Paper: *Time for Reform: Proposals
  for the Modernisation of Our Licensing
  Laws*** 1.2, 2.1
Working men's clubs 17.6
Workplaces
  exempt entertainment 4.3.14